P9-EDP-783

LAW AND
MENTAL HEALTH

Pergamon Titles of Related Interest

Apter/Goldstein YOUTH VIOLENCE: Programs and Prospects
Brassard/Germain/Hart PSYCHOLOGICAL MALTREATMENT OF
CHILDREN AND YOUTH
Nietzel/Dillehay PSYCHOLOGICAL CONSULTATION IN THE COURTROOM
Weisstub LAW AND MENTAL HEALTH: International Perspectives, Volume 1
Weisstub LAW AND PSYCHIATRY IN THE CANADIAN CONTEXT:
Cases, Notes and Materials

Related Journals
(Free sample copies available upon request.)

INTERNATIONAL JOURNAL OF LAW AND PSYCHIATRY
JOURNAL OF CRIMINAL JUSTICE

Law and Mental Health: International Perspectives, Volume 2

Advisory Board of Editors

Lionel Beliveau   Bruce Sales
Frank Beyaert   Saleem Shah
Yvon Gautheir   David B. Wexler
Loren H. Roth

LAW AND MENTAL HEALTH

International Perspectives
Volume 2

Edited by
David N. Weisstub

Institut Philip Pinel, Université de Montréal
Osgoode Hall Law School, Toronto

PERGAMON PRESS
New York • Oxford • Toronto • Sydney • Frankfurt

Pergamon Press Offices:

U.S.A.	Pergamon Press, Maxwell House, Fairview Park, Elmsford, New York 10523, U.S.A.
U.K.	Pergamon Press, Headington Hill Hall, Oxford OX3 0BW, England
PEOPLE'S REPUBLIC OF CHINA	Pergamon Press, Qianmen Hotel, Beijing, People's Republic of China
FEDERAL REPUBLIC OF GERMANY	Pergamon Press, Hammerweg 6, D-6242 Kronberg-Taunus, Federal Republic of Germany
BRAZIL	Pergamon Editora, Rua Eça de Queiros, 346, CEP 04011, São Paulo, Brazil
AUSTRALIA	Pergamon Press (Aust.) Pty., P.O. Box 544, Potts Point, NSW 2011, Australia
JAPAN	Pergamon Press, 8th Floor, Matsuoka Central Building, 1-7-1 Nishishinjuku, Shinjuku, Tokyo 160, Japan
CANADA	Pergamon Press Canada, Suite 104, 150 Consumers Road, Willowdale, Ontario M2J 1P9, Canada

Copyright © 1986 Pergamon Press Inc.

All rights reserved. No part of this publication may be reproduced, stored in a retrieval system or transmitted in any form or by any means: electronic, electrostatic, magnetic tape, mechanical, photocopying, recording or otherwise, without permission in writing from the publishers.

First printing 1986

Library of Congress Cataloging in Publication Data
(Revised for vol. 2)
Main entry under title:

Law and mental health : international perspectives

 Preface and summaries in English and French.
 Includes bibliographies and indexes.
 1. Mental health laws. 2. Mental health--Legislation.
3. Forensic psychiatry. I. Weisstub, David N.,
1944- . [DNLM: WM 33.1 L416]
K3608.I38 1984   344'.044 84-2926
ISBN 0-08-032781-8   342.444

V.2

49,398

Printed in the United States of America

Law and Mental Health, Volume 2, has been published under the generous sponsorship of the Institut Philippe Pinel, Montreal.

Law and Mental Health, Volume 2, a été publié grâce à l'aide généreuse de l'Institut Philippe Pinel de Montréal.

CAMROSE LUTHERAN COLLEGE
LIBRARY

CONTENTS

Preface

The second volume of *Law and Mental Health: International Perspectives* attempts to follow the pattern and general philosophy established in volume 1, which was to offer the highly diversified readership in this multidisciplinary area an appraisal of recent trends and conditions in the spheres of law and scientific research. Because the field is ever expanding and is in the process of even undergoing rapid transformations, in the second volume we have tried to focus on topics and legal jurisdictions that are most in tune with broadly felt international concerns and needs.

In the first chapter, which is devoted to covering current legislative changes and court decisions throughout the British Commonwealth, we have realized a much awaited opportunity to be able to put the Commonwealth countries in perspective against American developments that have foreshadowed and even to some extent pre-empted the evolution of legal doctrine and practices elsewhere, particularly in Anglo-Saxon jurisdictions. Gordon and Verdun-Jones isolate some general tendencies in the Commonwealth to fashion what is called a New Legalism, which on reflection may have some distinctive qualities that differentiate it from a more confrontative legalistic platform that has dominated the American constitutional adjudicative instruments since the mid-1960s. The authors caution however that, not unlike the experience of the United States, in the Commonwealth the new emergent reality or, put in another way, consequence of legalistic intervention, has been a denial of access to services for the most needy, a side effect that certainly invites further commentary.

Chapter 2 treats the issue of malpractice in the American legal system. Although at first glance, one might assume that malpractice recoveries have been quiescent with a more conservative political climate and accompanying downturn in fiscal conditions, the authors point out that there has been a rather sudden escalation of malprac-tice decisions in the mental health sector with attendant damages of substantial proportions. Because of the unpredictable outcome that has typified many of the decisions that have showed up in the tort system under the penumbra of negligence, the authors have probed the underlying models that the tort system has been using to approach the psychotherapist–patient relationship. This investigation into the theory of the relationship is then finally connected to a search for the most integrated theoretical and practical model to regulate claims made against psycho-therapists and physicians in the mental health system. The challenge to legal systems everywhere in the industrial world is to balance the concept of justified fault against outcomes that are economically sound and efficient. From this perspective, it is hoped that the Tancredi–Weiss-tub chapter will assist planners in sorting out which are the most beneficial social policy options in regulating the practices of mental health professionals.

The third and fourth chapters are dedicated to two topics that are often seen in the popular press and have far-reaching implications for the role and function of legal intervention and associated ethical prescriptions. There are strong sentiments in society about whether or not we can legitimate bio-criminal research if it serves to isolate a small part of the population as a target group for genetic predisposition. For some decades, Sarnoff Mednick and his associates, in this case his co-authors Terrie Moffitt and Jan Velavka, have consistently struggled to demystify what is called bio-criminality by providing data that can identify certain genetic variables; the authors argue that these data can sensitize a democratic and liberal society to the need for socially responsible prevention that is not only in society's best interest but even more directed to the end of protecting a vulnerable group of criminal actors who have potentially destructive inherited characteristics. This kind of research will remain the subject of heated controversy among legalists and ethical philosophers. What we have attempted to do in the prospect of furthering that debate is to set the record down so that a scientific database is neutrally available for our discipline to respond to. The authors themselves point out that it is crucial to delimit the importance of the findings presented in their work. Their argument is however that because the data do illuminate a small but highly intense concentration of criminal activity in the hands of relatively few serious offenders, it behooves us to study the correlates. In addition to investigating twin and adoption studies that cast up evidence of genetically influenced disorders, the authors canvas heritable characteristics with regard to autonomic nervous system responsiveness and neurophysiological status.

Pedophilia and societal responses to it represent the most intense example of public polarization about sexual deviancy; thus it is a welcomed addition to the general literature to have available to us the painstaking and exhaustive account of Vernon L. Quinsey. He explores what we do and do not know with respect to the anthropological and sociohistorical sources of pedophiliac practice and, moreover, with regard to subgroups within the pedophiliac population that represent those who use recidivistic and physically threatening acts against young children. Quinsey separates out historical and cultural considerations from what might be called the hardcore practices of child molesters and gives a scientific account of their profiles to the extent that they can properly be described in the scientific literature. Despite this comprehensive exegesis, Vernon Quinsey insists that substantial research has yet to be done before a theoretical structure can be provided to explain inappropriate sexual age preferences. He concludes that in fact we need to know more about the development of normal sexual age preferences in order to clarify how and when inappropriate sexual behavior occurs. In the world of child molestation itself, the author believes that many comparative studies are yet to be done to contrast sadistic and nonsadistic molestation with the discreet practices of homosexual, bisexual, and heterosexual molestation.

The last chapter, written by Michael J. Churgin, deals with the psychotherapist–patient privilege, which has a long history in the legal literature, both in common and civil law jurisdictions. This is surely no accident because the question of a privilege to withhold giving testimony about information obtained in the privacy of psychotherapeutic treatment becomes intertwined with questions about the rules of evidence and truth-finding that are natural to the judicial process. In the international legal literature, there is a tendency to compartmentalize the issue of a psychotherapeutic privilege such that the United States is designated as having such a privilege, the continental countries as having a strict one applying to physicians, and the British Commonwealth countries as lacking it. Churgin's chapter systematically goes through the history of the debate about a federal privilege in the United States and thereafter meticulously looks at each U.S. state to see what kind of privileges are in fact the reality and with which sorts of exceptions. About 45 U.S. states have some form of special statutes, but because the statutes are by no means strict in practice, Churgin's review of statutory exceptions and judicial interpretations is extremely helpful. Looking at the courts, Churgin differentiates civil from criminal functions, which is essential if we are to be able to qualitatively assess what these privileges represent in applied legal realities. Although Churgin's treatment of nonAmerican jurisdictions is done in a more summary form, the international section is in general terms complete and reveals that some of our assumptions about privilege when looked at in the light of legislative refinements and court reviews would suggest less of a categorical differentiation among the jurisdictions than might have been supposed.

In such a large project as this series, it has been a sustaining force behind the research to have had the intellectual and financial support of the Institut Philippe Pinel de Montréal, under the able leadership of its Directeur général, Docteur Lionel Béliveau, who is also Secretary General of the International Academy of Law and Mental Health. Within the institute, the project has enjoyed the on-going feedback of the clinical staff and of the research department. One of the special contributions from the Institut Philippe Pinel during the past year has come from Dr. Vernon Quinsey, who in his capacity as visiting senior scholar has given valuable insight and scientific critiques throughout.

The general reception of the project has also been enhanced during the past year by the creation of the International Academy of Law and Mental Health, which was initiated in June 1984 in Banff, Alberta. Its first President is Dr. Abraham Halpern, former President of the American Academy of Psychiatry and Law and current

President of the American Board of Forensic Psychiatric Examiners. The XIth International Congress on Law and Psychiatry was held in March of 1985 in Florence, Italy, in collaboration with the International Academy of Law and Mental Health. It attracted approximately 550 participants, many of whom expressed an interest in seeing that there should be an increasing attention paid to making available international trends in mental health legislation to a wide international readership. It was also stressed that it is critical that the International Academy should support the dissemination of research, as it is often the case that foreign language research is inaccessible to researchers. It is the aim of this five-volume series to address these needs in this and upcoming volumes. In fact, in volumes 3 and 4, there will be chapters summarizing an array of topics that have been researched for the past decades in such places as Holland, Germany, and France, and which have not entered the English literature.

This volume of course reflects not only the significant abilities of the respective authors but also the spirit of a team effort from the Pinel Institute and the individual members of the editorial committee. I would also like to personally record my indebtedness to my research associates, Dr. Eli Bernard Weisstub of the Stanford University Department of Psychiatry and Ms. Nicole Fernbach.

David N. Weisstub

Préface

Le deuxième volume de la série on *Law and Mental Health: International Perspectives* épouse le modèle et la philosophie générale établis dans le premier volume, à savoir offrir au public très varié de ce domaine multidisciplinaire une évaluation des tendances récentes, tant dans le droit que dans la recherche scientifique. Comme le domaine est en pleine expansion et connaît des transformations rapides, nous avons essayé de nous concentrer, dans le deuxième volume, sur des sujets et sur des pays qui soient le plus en rapport avec les préoccupations et les besoins qui se font sentir en général.

Dans le premier chapitre qui est consacré à l'évolution actuelle de la législation et des décisions judiciaires dans l'ensemble du Commonwealth britannique, nous avons enfin pu placer les pays du Commonwealth dans la perspective des changements survenus aux États-Unis, mouvement qui laissait prévoir et même, dans une certaine mesure, précédait l'évolution de la doctrine et de la pratique juridique dans les autres pays, en particulier dans les pays anglo-saxons. Gordon et Verdun-Jones mettent en évidence certaines tendances générales dans le Commonwealth pour en arriver à un concept de néo-légalisme qui, à la réflexion, présente des qualités distinctes de la tendance plus légaliste que reflètent les textes législatifs et judiciaires américains depuis le milieu des années soixante. Cependant, les auteurs font valoir qu'à l'instar de l'expérience aux États-Unis, les nouvelles réalités, ou encore, l'intervention légaliste avec les conséquences qui l'accompagnent, ont abouti à sacrifier l'accès aux services pour les plus nécessiteux; il s'agit là d'un phénomène qui invite d'autres commentaires.

Le deuxième chapitre traite des actions en responsabilité civile dans le système juridique américain. Bien que l'on puisse supposer, de prime abord, que le nombre des actions ait diminué avec le climat politique plus conservateur et la détérioration des conditions économiques, les auteurs montrent qu'il y a eu une augmentation plutôt brutale du nombre des actions judiciaires dans le secteur de la santé mentale avec des indemnisations aux proportions substantielles. Du fait de la nature imprévisible des décisions judiciaires en responsabilité civile pour faute professionnelle, les auteurs ont étudié les modèles sous-jacents utilisés en responsabilité civile pour comprendre la relation entre le psychothérapeute et son patient. Cette étude sur la théorie de la relation mène enfin à rechercher le modèle théorique et pratique le plus intégré pour contrôler les actions en responsabilité contre les psychothérapeutes et les médecins dans le régime de la santé mentale. Dans tous les pays industriels, le défi pour les systèmes juridiques consiste à trouver un équilibre entre le concept de la faute justifiée, d'une part, et celui de l'efficacité sur le plan économique, d'autre part. Dans cette perspective, il est à souhaiter que le chapitre de Tancredi et Weisstub aidera les planificateurs à trancher sur les options de politique sociale les plus bénéfiques pour contrôler les pratiques des professionnels de la santé mentale.

Les troisième et quatrième chapitres portent sur des sujets souvent traités dans la presse qui ont des répercussions importantes sur le rôle et la fonction de l'intervention juridique et les prescriptions éthiques connexes. La société s'interroge de façon très marquée sur le caractère légitime ou non de la recherche biocriminelle, vu qu'elle vise à isoler une petite partie de la population comme groupe-cible pour les prédispositions génétiques. Pendant quelques décennies, Sarnoff-Mednick et ses confrères, en l'espèce les co-auteurs Terrie Moffitt et Jan Volavka, ont constamment cherché à démystifier la prétendue biocriminalité en mettant à jour des données pour l'identification de variables génétiques; les auteurs soutiennent que ces données peuvent sensibiliser une société démocratique et libérale à la nécessité d'une prévention responsable sur le plan social qui soit non seulement dans l'intérêt de la société mais qui vise encore plus à protéger un groupe vulnérable d'agents criminels dont les caractéristiques héréditaires sont potentiellement destructrices. Ce type de recherche fera toujours l'objet d'une controverse brûlante entre les légalistes et les philosophes de l'éthique. Pour faire avancer le débat, on a cherché à dégager une base de données scientifiques neutres pour notre discipline. Les auteurs eux-mêmes font remarquer qu'il est crucial de cerner l'importance des conclusions présentées dans leurs travaux. Ils soutiennent cependant que, du fait que les données mettent à jour une concentration réduite mais très intense d'activités criminelles chez quelques auteurs de délits graves, il est nécessaire de faire une étude des correlaires. Ils présentent des études menées sur les jumeaux et les enfants adoptifs qui conduisent à l'évidence de troubles d'origine génétique, et ils se livrent au recensement des caractéristiques héréditaires touchant à la réponse du système nerveux autonome et à l'état neurophysiologique.

La pédophilie et les réactions qu'elle engendre dans la société constituent l'exemple le plus manifeste de la polarisation de l'opinion publique en matière de déviance sexuelle; l'étude minutieuse et exhaustive réalisée par Vernon L. Quinsey est une heureuse contribution qui complète la recherche générale. Celui-ci explore les connaissances actuelles, et aussi les lacunes, en ce qui concerne les sources anthropologiques et socio-historiques de la pratique pédophile et aussi les sous-groupes au sein de cette population qui commet des actes de récidive et des agressions à l'encontre de jeunes enfants. Quinsey fait une distinction entre les considérations historiques et culturelles et les pratiques fondamentales des agresseurs d'enfants. Il fait un compte rendu scientifique sur leur profil dans la mesure où il peut correctement être décrit dans les ouvrages scientifiques. Au-delà de cette exégèse complète, Quinsey ajoute qu'il est encore nécessaire de faire des recherches plus poussées si l'on veut parvenir à un modèle théorique permettant d'expliquer les préférences sexuelles inappropriées par rapport à l'âge avant de conclure qu'en réalité, ce sont les connaissances sur le développement des préférences sexuelles normales à cet égard qu'il faudrait approfondir. Cela permettrait ainsi de mieux savoir comment et quand un comportement sexuel inapproprié se manifeste. Dans le monde de l'agression sexuelle à l'égard des enfants, l'auteur estime que de nombreuses études comparatives doivent encore être faites pour opposer les agressions sadiques et non sadiques aux pratiques discrètes de nature homosexuelle, bisexuelle et hétérosexuelle.

Le dernier chapitre, écrit par Michael J. Churgin, traite du privilège de la communication entre le psychothérapeute et son patient, question étudiée depuis longtemps dans les ouvrages juridiques, tant des pays du common law que de ceux de droit civil. C'est un phénomène inévitable parce qu'au droit de refuser de témoigner sur des renseignements obtenus dans l'intimité du traitement psychothérapeutique viennent se greffer les problèmes des règles de preuve et de la recherche de la vérité qui sont inhérents au processus judiciaire. On a souvent tendance dans les ouvrages de droit à établir des distinctions sur le privilège du psychothérapeute, à savoir que si l'Amérique reconnaît ce droit, les pays européens ont, eux, un régime qui s'applique strictement aux médecins alors que ce privilège est inexistant dans les pays du Commonwealth britannique. Dans ce chapitre, Churgin fait systématiquement l'historique du débat sur le privilège fédéral aux États-Unis avant d'analyser, de façon méticuleuse, le cas des États américains pour voir quels droits existent dans la réalité et de quelles exceptions ils sont assortis. Aux États-Unis, 45 États environ sont dotés d'une certaine forme de législation, mais du fait qu'elle n'est en aucune façon d'application stricte, le compte rendu des exceptions législatives et des interprétations judiciaires s'avère extrêmement utile. Dans son étude des tribunaux, il distingue les fonctions civiles des fonctions criminelles, ce qui constitue un aspect essentiel pour pouvoir évaluer, sur le plan qualitatif, ce que ces privilèges représentent dans la réalité juridique concrète. Bien que l'étude des juridictions non américaines soit beaucoup plus sommaire, la section à caractère international est tout à fait complète, et l'on peut voir que d'après certaines suppositions en matière de communication privilégiée, à la lumière des raffinements législatifs et des examens judiciaires, il existe une différence bien moindre que celle que l'on pouvait supposer, d'une juridiction à l'autre.

Le vaste projet que représente cette série a été réalisé grâce au soutien intellectuel et financier de l'Institut Philippe Pinel de Montréal, sous la direction du docteur Lionel Béliveau qui est aussi secrétaire général de l'Académie de droit et de santé mentale. Il a bénéficié des consultations permanentes avec le personnel clinique et le service de la recherche de l'Institut. L'une des contributions particulières de l'Institut Philippe Pinel au cours de l'année écoulée a été celle de Vernon Quinsey qui, en sa qualité de chercheur invité, a offert ses conseils utiles et commentaires critiques pendant la durée du projet.

La création de l'Académie internationale de droit et de santé mentale, en juin 1984 à Banff en Alberta, a contribué à renforcer l'intérêt manifesté pour le projet. Son premier Président est le Dr Abraham Halpern, ancien président de l'American Academy of Psychiatry and Law et actuel président de l'American Board of Forensic Psychiatric Examiners. Le XIème Congrès de droit et de psychiatrie a eu lieu en mars 1985 à Florence (Italie) en collaboration avec l'Académie internationale de droit et de santé mentale. Il a réuni environ cinq cent cinquante participants dont bon nombre avaient fait valoir qu'il était souhaitable de faire connaître au plus grand nombre de lecteurs dans le monde entier l'évolution internationale et les tendances de la législation sur la santé mentale. Il a été souligné qu'il était important pour l'Académie internationale de favoriser la diffusion de la recherche parce que, très souvent, les chercheurs n'ont pas accès aux travaux faits en langue étrangère. La série de cinq volumes vise à répondre à ces besoins par le présent volume et par ceux qui suivront. En fait, les troisième et quatrième volumes renfermeront des chapitres résumant un éventail de sujets ayant fait l'objet de recherches au cours des dernières décennies dans des pays comme la Hollande, l'Allemagne et la France et qui ne figurent pas dans les ouvrages en langue anglaise.

Le présent volume reflète, bien entendu, non seulement les compétences des différents auteurs, mais il est aussi le fruit d'un effort de groupe de la part des membres de l'Institut Pinel et du comité de rédaction. Je voudrais aussi exprimer ma gratitude à mes collaborateurs de recherche, le Dr. Eli Bernard Weisstub du département de Psychiatrie de l'Université Stanford et à madame Nicole Fernbach.

David N. Weisstub

1.
Mental Health Law and Law Reform in the Commonwealth: The Rise of the "New Legalism"?

Robert M. Gordon
Simon N. Verdun-Jones

ABSTRACT. *The winds of reform are beginning to blow through the halls of Commonwealth mental health jurisprudence. The present chapter examines the nature and score of recent developments in the mental health law of the British Commonwealth countries of Australia, Canada, Great Britain, and New Zealand. This undertaking involves a comparative analysis of the legislation and jurisprudence of more than 20 separate jurisdictions within these countries.*

The analysis is necessarily limited to a selected number of areas of mental health law. In the context of civil procedures, the focus is upon changes in the statutory definition of "mental illness" or "mental disorder," the establishment of criteria for involuntary commitment, the issue of the right to refuse treatment and the prohibition of certain treatment modalities, the emergence of mental health review tribunals, and the provision of legal services to mental health patients. In the criminal justice context, the analysis is confined to the issues of determining criminal responsibility, fitness to stand trial, and the use of medical dispositions (such as hospital orders) in the sentencing process.

In analyzing recent developments in Commonwealth mental health law, the authors examine the thesis that a "new legalism" is emerging as a dominant characteristic of law reform in this area. The "new legalism" concept has been identified by Gostin (1983b, 1983c) and encompasses such matters as the introduction of a "right" to effective mental health services, protection against unjustifiable deprivation of liberty, and the prevention of discrimination by maintaining the civil and social status of patients. In sharp contrast to the concept of "new legalism," Gostin counterposes the concept of "professional discretion" as a means of characterizing the essential nature of the mental health legislation that has held sway since the 1950s. The salient feature of the "professional discretion" concept is the application of a policy that renders access to treatment and the administration of care as matters that fall entirely within the discretionary decision-making powers of mental health professionals. The authors survey recent Commonwealth developments in light of the proposition that mental health law may be characterized as moving from a model based on "professional discretion," to a model that is founded upon the "new legalism."

The authors conclude that the majority of Commonwealth jurisdictions surveyed lie somewhere in the middle of the "new legalism"/"professional discretion" spectrum. The situation

The authors gratefully wish to acknowledge that their research has been partially supported by grants from the Law Foundations of British Columbia and Saskatchewan, Simon Fraser University (Canada), and Macquarie University (Australia).

in these jurisdictions may best be described as "quasi-legalistic," in that legal requirements are clearly imposed in relation to such issues as the civil commitment of patients and the periodic review of the status of detained patients; however, the actual application and interpretation of these legislative requirements is left firmly in the hands of mental health professionals. In the civil sphere, developments in a number of jurisdictions have moved legislation toward the "new legalism" pole of the spectrum. However, with few exceptions, these developments have not significantly altered the basic structure of the dominant "quasi-legalistic" approach. With the notable exception of New South Wales and Ontario, professional control over the commitment and treatment processes has been left largely unchallenged and the hegemony of mental health professionals continues. In the criminal justice sphere, there have been numerous developments that have collectively operated to free the mentally disordered offender from a situation in which his or her release was totally dependent upon the exercise of discretion by the executive branch of government. Such developments, to some extent, bear the imprints of the "new legalism."

Despite their cautionary notes, the authors contend that it is possible to identify a distinct and significant period of reform that is occurring throughout the Commonwealth jurisdictions surveyed. They observe that the reforms, encompassed by the terms "new legalism" and "quasi-legalism," do not limit the powers of mental health professionals per se. However, the reforms do seem to embody an attempt to limit access to public mental health services and therefore might be aligned with a policy of constriction in such services. In this sense, an explanation for the current reform movement may rest in the economics of mental health systems as they are affected by wider economic changes besetting the welfare state.

SOMMAIRE. La jurisprudence en matière de santé mentale est actuellement l'objet d'une vague de réformes dans tout le Commonwealth. Le présent article porte sur la nature et les résultats de l'évolution récente du droit de la santé mentale dans les pays du Commonwealth britannique, plus précisément en Australie, au Canada, en Grande-Bretagne et en Nouvelle-Zélande. Il s'agit là d'une analyse comparative de la législation et de la jurisprudence de plus de 20 jurisdictions distinctes dans ces pays.

L'étude est nécessairement restreinte à un certain nombre de domaines du droit de la santé mentale. Dans le contexte de la procédure civile, elle porte avant tout sur les changements de la définition législative de la maladie mentale ou des troubles mentaux, l'établissement des critères de l'internement, le droit au refus du traitement et l'interdiction de certaines modalités de traitement, la naissance des tribunaux de révision en matière de santé mentale et l'offre de services juridiques aux handicapés mentaux. Dans le contexte de la justice criminelle, l'analyse est restreinte aux questions de la détermination de la responsabilité criminelle, de l'aptitude à subir le procès et de l'utilisation des dispositions médicales (comme les ordonnances des hôpitaux) dans le processus sentenciel.

Tout en examinant l'évolution récente du droit de la santé mentale dans le Commonwealth, les auteurs se demandent si un néo-légalisme fait son apparition et deviendra peut-être un élément prépondérant dans la réforme du droit de la santé mentale. Le concept de néo-légalisme mis en évidence par Gostin embrasse des questions comme l'introduction d'un droit à des services efficaces en matière de santé mentale, la protection contre la privation de liberté injustifiée et la prévention de toute discrimination grâce au maintien du statut civil et social des patients. En contraste très net avec ce concept de néo-légalisme, Gostin avance le principe du pouvoir discrétionnaire professionnel qui, selon lui, caractériserait essentiellement la législation de la santé mentale depuis les années 1950. Ce dernier concept aurait conduit à une politique selon laquelle l'accès au traitement et l'administration des questions de soins seraient entièrement laissés au pouvoir de décision discrétionnaire des professionnels de la santé mentale. Dans leur étude de l'évolution récente dans le Commonwealth, les auteurs prennent comme hypothèse que le droit de la santé mentale abandonne progressivement une conception fondée sur la discrétion professionnelle pour aller vers un néo-légalisme.

Ils concluent que la majorité des juridictions du Commonwealth étudiées se situent à peu près à mi-chemin entre un néo-légalisme et le pouvoir discrétionnaire professionnel. Cette situation correspond plus exactement à une conception quasi-légaliste, vu que les exigences juridiques sont clairement imposées dans des cas comme l'internement civil des patients et la révision périodique du statut des patients détenus; cependant, l'application et l'interprétation effective de ces prescriptions législatives demeurent très nettement entre les mains des professionnels de la santé mentale. Au civil, l'évolution dans un certain nombre de juridictions s'est faite en direction d'un néo-légalisme. Cependant, à de rares exceptions près, l'approche quasi-légaliste dominante n'a presque pas été modifiée. À l'exception de la New South Wales et de l'Ontario, le contrôle professionnel sur les processus d'internement et de traitement est pratiquement resté le même partout ailleurs, et l'hégémonie des professionnels de la santé mentale n'a pas été menacée. Dans la justice criminelle, de nombreux développements se sont produits de façon conjointe pour libérer le délinquant handicapé mental d'une situation où sa libération était absolument soumise au pouvoir discrétionnaire de l'État. Une telle évolution traduit en quelque sorte l'apparition d'un néo-légalisme.

Après des remarques de prudence, les auteurs prétendent qu'une vague distincte et importante de réformes s'est manifestée en même temps dans toutes les juridictions du Commonwealth étudiées. Ils expliquent que la réforme visée par les termes "néo-légalisme" et "quasi-légalisme" ne limitait pas les pouvoirs des professionnels de la santé mentale. Elle semblait cependant viser à restreindre l'accès aux services publics de santé mentale et pouvait, par conséquent, correspondre à une politique de restriction de ces services. C'est ainsi que le mouvement de réforme actuel peut être relié à l'économie de la santé mentale puisque ce domaine est touché par les changements économiques plus larges qui bouleversent actuellement l'État-Providence.

Although developments in the United States have tended to dominate academic analyses of the changes affecting mental health law over the last decade, it should not be overlooked that significant progress has also been made in many Commonwealth jurisdictions. In Britain, the proclamation of the England and Wales Mental Health Act (1983) marks the culmination of several years of intense lobbying and discussion, and, in Canada, significant reforms have occurred in relation to the mental health legislation of the provinces of Ontario, Alberta, and Nova Scotia. In Australia, new mental health acts have been introduced in the states of South Australia, Western Australia, New South Wales, and the Northern Territory, and further major reforms are pending in the state of Victoria. The Northern Ireland legislation is also reported to have been under review (Carson, 1983). In many jurisdictions, changes have been made to, or are being proposed for, legislation directly connected to mental health issues; notably, that which is concerned with guardianship of the person and estate. In addition, significant changes have been made to, or are proposed for, the legislation and procedures relating to mentally disordered persons involved with criminal law.

This widespread activity, which is increasing rather than diminishing in pace, may at first glance appear to be confusing. The objectives of this essay are not only to review and describe some of the key developments, but also to attempt to delineate and interpret the patterns of change. For example, although developments in the United

Kingdom have, in the past, been a barometer for reform throughout the Commonwealth (Gostin, 1979a), the current atmosphere affecting these jurisdictions can best be described as one in which various United States' developments have been combined with specific localized initiatives. Indeed, some of these developments and initiatives appear to have been incorporated within the recent mental health legislation of England and Wales, and, therefore, in most respects, the "mother country" can no longer be seen as a leader in this particular area of law.

At the outset, however, it is necessary to clarify several issues. First, the term "mental health law" has now entered the lexicon of Commonwealth jurisprudence and legal discourse. As such, it suggests the presence of a distinct area of legal practice and specialization. Although such an area of specialization may have emerged in the United States, the same cannot be said of Commonwealth jurisdictions. Certainly, in the latter, there are many organizations and agencies that concentrate all — or a major part — of their efforts on mental health law issues. Key examples are the National Association for Mental Health (MIND) in Britain, the Committee on Mental Health Advocacy (COMHA) in Australia, and the National Institute on Mental Retardation (NIMR) in Canada. There is, however, no single, over-arching body, and therefore no coordination of reform efforts or synthesis of legal developments.

Second, "mental health law" in Commonwealth jurisdictions is an avowed conglomerate. In theory and in practice it involves an amalgamation of several areas of legal specialization. At its core lies an emerging focus on the legislation and jurisprudence connected with the regulation of the mental health system: the establishment of hospitals and other facilities, the specification of the duties and powers of facility directors, the rights of patients, the procedures for voluntary and involuntary commitment, and so on. Associated with this body of law are other areas of specialization: administrative law, contract law, torts, wills and estates, civil rights and liberties, family law, medical law, social welfare law, guardianship law, and criminal law (including the law affecting juvenile justice systems). Mental health law is thus a complex body of law and legal activity that still awaits a meaningful and practical synthesis.

Third, it is necessary to establish what is meant by "Commonwealth jurisdictions." In this chapter we are concerned only with a select group of Commonwealth countries, namely, Canada, Britain, New Zealand, and Australia. Many other Commonwealth nations are excluded, primarily on the basis of the impracticality of surveying a vast number of jurisdictions. In Britain, three separate jurisdictions coexist: Northern Ireland, Scotland, and England and Wales. Our focus is principally on England and Wales. New Zealand is a unitary jurisdiction. Canada and Australia have federal politico-legal systems, the provinces (Canada) and the states (Australia) each having autonomy with regard to (inter alia) the enactment of mental health and related legislation as well as to the operation of mental health systems. The provinces and states thus form separate jurisdictions although they are constitutionally bonded and, in the case of Canada, affected by constitutional instruments such as the Charter of Rights and Freedoms (Constitution Act of 1982, Part I: en. by the Canada Act of 1982 (U.K.), C.11, Sched. B). Canada also has a single Criminal Code (R.S.C. 1970, C-34) affecting all provincial jurisdictions, unlike Australia, where the individual states as well as the Commonwealth of Australia have separate (albeit similar) bodies of legislation dealing with criminal law matters. All of these Commonwealth jurisdictions (with the exception of Quebec) share the English Common Law tradition. Consequently, legal doctrines and principles established in any one jurisdiction may be effectively transported to another, although this process is governed by the complicated rules of precedent and judicial interpretation.

The common bond with the English Common Law was forged during Britain's colonial expansion of the 18th and 19th centuries. For the mental health law context, this expansion led, in particular, to a transportation of British legislative initiatives relating to the management and treatment of mentally disordered persons. An awareness of this history is critical to the development of an understanding of current trends in mental health law. As many contemporary analysts of the evolution of mental health law and services have indicated, the England and Wales Lunacy Act of 1890 is, in many respects, an important starting point in that the statute placed great emphasis on establishing procedures designed to ensure that the sane were not improperly incarcerated (Bean, 1980; Jones, 1960, 1972; Noble, 1981; O'Sullivan, 1981; Unsworth, 1979). These procedures followed a "legal" model and involved a number of safeguards for the protection of the liberty of the subject. Significantly, the statute represented the culmination of nearly a century of reform efforts and was opposed by the medical and administrative components of the established "lunacy system" on the basis that excessive judicial involvement in the process of commitment would adversely affect the possibility of "cure" (Unsworth, 1979). The "legal needs vs. health needs" conflict affecting law and psychiatry at the present time is thus by no means a modern debate; indeed, as Noble (1981) indicates, the conflict traces back nearly 200 years.

In most Commonwealth jurisdictions, the Lunacy Act "model" was introduced shortly after its enactment in Britain and remained the principal guiding statute until the next major period of reform, following World War II (Kirby, 1981). Certainly, there were intervening moments of reform which reflected the rise of (and changes within) psychiatry as it evolved into a respectable branch of medicine. In England and Wales, for example, the Mental Treatment Act of 1930 introduced changes that switched the legislative focus from legal safeguards to medical care. The extent to which this development was followed in Commonwealth jurisdictions remains to be explored in detail. What is clear is that most jurisdictions (e.g., Northern Ireland and Tasmania) engaged in a significant revision of mental health legislation during the late 1950s and the 1960s, apparently following a yardstick provided by the England and Wales Mental Health Act of 1959. Such legislation reflected an integration of social work and psychiatric medicine. The procedures— which were established with regard to commitment, detention and treatment—clearly reflected the dominance of a concern with the "health needs" of mentally disordered persons (Kirby, 1981; Unsworth, 1979). Legal safeguards were accorded a low priority; however, an attempt was made to preserve an acceptable degree of legal protection by the introduction of mental health review tribunals. A minority of jurisdictions (e.g., New South Wales, New Zealand, and Scotland) adopted a different strategy as exemplified by the Mental Health (Scotland) Act of 1960. The Scottish legislation seemed to adopt a different approach. Although the same social work and medical concerns dominated the procedures and underlying philosophy, legal safeguards were preserved by retaining a central role for the sheriff in the processes of, *inter alia*, involuntary commitment and continued detention (Hoggett, 1976; Whitehead, 1982). Likewise, the mental health acts of New South Wales and New Zealand retained a central role for their equivalent of a sheriff—the magistrate.

As Unsworth (1979) has effectively demonstrated, the reasons for this period of reform have received a number of interpretations. Whereas Jones (1960), for example, attributes the reform to changes in the relative power of professional interest groups, Unsworth locates the change in the formation and development of an effective welfare state. Whatever the causes, the changes wrought during the 1950s and 1960s tend to dominate the mental health legislation of most Commonwealth jurisdictions at the present time. However, as many writers have observed, the situation is far from stable and there is evidence that an era of "new legalism" is dawning (Carson, 1983; Gostin, 1983b, 1983c; Toews, Prabhu, & El-Guebaly, 1980).

For Gostin, the principal advocate of the "new legalism" thesis, the dawn of a new era is reflected in key changes to the England and Wales Mental Health Act of 1959, enacted through the England and Wales Mental Health (Amendment) Act of 1982 and now consolidated in the England and Wales Mental Health Act of 1983. These changes are perceived as encompassing the introduction of a "right" to effective services, protection against unjustified deprivation of liberty, and the prevention of discrimination by maintaining the civil and social status of patients. However, as Shapland and Williams (1983) indicate, these developments may not reflect the *major* switch in emphasis, suggested by Gostin. Indeed, they contend that the new legislation is merely an exercise in "tinkering"

and that the psychiatric perspective continues to dominate the procedures related to the delivery of mental health services. This view is shared by Carson (1983), who argues that the new statute is merely "symbolic" and is unlikely to have any real effect on the management of mentally disordered people.

The counterarguments have some validity, particularly in light of the evidence available regarding, for example, the conduct of mental health review tribunals (Peay, 1981), and the limitations pertaining to the so-called "right to refuse treatment" (Gordon & Verdun-Jones, 1983). However, when viewed as a whole, Commonwealth legislative developments clearly manifest the growth of a significant reform movement that, at first glance, *appears* to be resulting in the *reestablishment* of legal controls over the activities of mental health professionals. The word *reestablishment* is chosen because in many respects the reforms that are being introduced seem to constitute a reformulation of the principles (but not the procedures) underpinning the old England and Wales Lunacy Act of 1890; notably, the construction of safeguards to protect the individual from the potential excesses of mental health professionals. The word *appears* is selected because, on closer examination, the actual content of the particular reforms does not necessarily support the idea that we are witnessing the emergence of a "new legalism," the specific effect of which will be to impose controls on the exercise of professional or clinical discretion. This issue is of critical importance and serves as a conceptual anchor that will rest at the base of this review.

Because the terms will be used throughout this chapter, what is meant by the words *new legalism* and *professional discretion*? For Gostin (1983c), the former is a state of affairs similar to, but not entirely embodying, the traditional legal formalism found in the lunacy laws of the late 19th and early 20th centuries. This legislation, he argues, encompassed "a set of principles whereby the use of compulsory powers in mental health should be carefully limited by clear criteria and legal procedures" (p. 47). However, it was, in essence, both "negative" and "reactive" to be more concerned with regulation than positive "activism" in the interests of those using mental health services. The "new legalism" does not involve the construction of a "cumbersome legal framework or (the introduction of) technical legal procedures (p. 48). Instead, the term is meant to reflect an approach that embodies a central role for law in providing effective health services for patients (e.g., by articulating a right to effective treatment), effective facilities and resources for mental health professionals, and protections for patients by "setting limits on established psychiatric measures relating, for example, to compulsory admission and treatment" (p. 49) as well as the restoration of their civil status (e.g., through enfranchisement). Gostin (1983c) contends:

It is important to remain vigilant to any attempt by the legal profession to erect a superstructure of technical procedures or cumbersome legal regulations; nor should the discretion of lawyers and courts be substituted for that of mental health professionals on matters of treatment. The modern function of law . . . does not usurp the function of caring professionals. It seeks to alter social perceptions of the mental health services, which should place an emphasis on the person distressed and not on the concerns of society or the profession. (pp. 66–67)

This, it seems, is the central principle of the "new legalism," and for Gostin its emergence is heralded by, and reflected in, the recent England and Wales Mental Health Act of 1983.

In defining the "new legalism," Gostin is evidently responding to the charge that greater legal involvement in mental health systems is counterproductive to the task of providing services for patients. Although there is not, as yet, a specific debate between the two, he is apparently tackling Jones' (1980) position that mental health systems need more resources, not more law, and that current efforts by the modern "Diceyists" (advocates who are obsessed with the concept of the rule of law) of the patients' rights movement are reproducing legal formalism rather than providing sound social policy. As Jones (1980) argues, in a critique of the perspective advanced by Gostin and MIND prior to the passage of the England and Wales Mental Health (Amendment) Act of 1982, the difficulty with their ideas for reform was, "that most of these proposals, though comparatively easy to make the subject of regulation, are very difficult to ensure in practice; for this is just where the Law fails. It is essentially regulative and remedial, not creative or inspiring" (p. 11). Rather than concentrating on more "legal prescription," which creates an atmosphere of "fear, secrecy and deception," the "Diceyists" should be concentrating on the construction of

social policy that will create, "professional attitudes and a working climate in which . . . abuses are unthinkable" (p. 12) and in which the provision of effective services is a paramount concern. This is not to say that Jones is supportive of full "professional discretion." As she points out, this was a key feature of the England and Wales Mental Health Act of 1959, and it did not appear to result in effective mental health services, just as the old legal formula embodied in the England and Wales Lunacy Act of 1890 was found to be a defective strategy. However, for Jones, a discretionary approach did not work because resources were not made available to mental health professionals, particularly in the area of community care. Had resources been available, the situation would have been different. This, however, is a social policy rather than a legal issue. In light of this argument, it is possible to see why Gostin envisages his approach to reform as a *new* type of legalism; it is not reproducing the old legal formalism condemned by Jones but, rather, is active in creating new social policy. Where the use of the political process fails to result in effective services, legal activism becomes a viable alternative.

For Gostin, "professional discretion" appears to be the antithesis of the "new legalism" and is an approach that was clearly reflected in the old England and Wales Mental Health Act of 1959. On this point he clearly agrees with Jones. Unfortunately, although he presents the phenomenon as something that has been replaced by the "new legalism," he does not provide a clear statement of all that would be encompassed by the term. It is possible, though, to deduce the following characteristics: When matters regarding access to treatment and care are entirely subject to the decisions of mental health professionals, and when review procedures are limited to a specific and small class of patients, practice is *de facto* in nature, and is "exercised by an administrative tribunal with a medical component" (Gostin, 1983c, p. 47). As its central principle, the approach envisages the mental health professions as the only legitimate source of knowledge and guidance vis-à-vis the needs and interests of the patients. They can only provide effective services to patients (individually and collectively) if they are left alone, especially by the legal profession, which does not have "the experience or expertise in areas of health and social services to enable them to identify needs and to propose workable solutions" (p. 49).

As Gostin (1983b, 1983c) and Jones (1980) both

point out, the clash between "legalism" and "professional discretion" is probably the main source of disagreement at the interface of psychiatry and law. In many respects, however, the "new legalism" may be interpreted as an attempt to effect a reconciliation or, perhaps, an armistice between conflicting professional interests. Such an attempt surely would be most timely, following, as it does, at least a decade of internecine conflict that has continued with little regard for the "best interests" of mental health patients. Although the accomplishment of a reconciliation or an armistice is, without doubt, a noble goal, there are a number of questions that must immediately spring to mind:

1. Does the "new legalism" represent a trend that can be considered to be emerging throughout the various Commonwealth jurisdictions?
2. Has the "new legalism" exerted an influence in both the civil and criminal spheres?
3. Does the "new legalism" represent a genuine armistice (i.e., a mutually acceptable and workable truce) between rival professional groups or merely a euphemistic facade concealing a further entrenchment of "professional discretion"?

The intention here is to explore these questions in light of recent developments in Commonwealth mental health law.

Undertaking such a review is a potentially Herculean task, because it involves a comparative analysis of the legislation and jurisprudence of over 20 jurisdictions. It has, therefore, been necessary to confine the analysis to a limited number of areas. In the context of civil procedures, the focus is on changes in the statutory definition of "mental illness" or "mental disorder," the establishment of criteria for involuntary commitment, the issue of the right to refuse treatment and the exclusion of certain treatment modalities, the emergence of mental health review tribunals, and the provision of legal services for mental health patients. In the criminal context, analysis is confined to the issues of determining criminal responsibility, fitness to stand trial, and the use of medical dispositions through such devices as "hospital orders." Any selection necessarily involves a certain degree of arbitrariness. In this regard, a number of possible areas of analysis have regrettably been excluded; notably, they are procedures for continued, involuntary hospitalization following commitment, the presence or absence of penal clauses in mental health legisla-

tion designed to "protect" patients from abuse or neglect, the establishment of a miscellany of patients' "rights" (e.g., the rights to visitation and communication and the right to vote), and the issue of guardianship.

STATUTORY DEFINITIONS OF MENTAL ILLNESS/DISORDER AND THE CRITERIA FOR INVOLUNTARY CIVIL COMMITMENT

For Gostin (1983c), one indicator of the decline of "professional discretion" is the appearance of legislative reform that reduces the power of psychiatrists to admit people compulsorily to hospitals. The various dimensions of this issue are well illustrated by a brief examination of the England and Wales Mental Health Act of 1983.

Although the new legislation does not significantly reconstruct the preexisting legal definition of "mental disorder," it does adopt a significant innovation by excluding certain specific forms of behavior from the scope of the term. A person may no longer be "classified as mentally disordered by reason *only* of promiscuity or other immoral conduct, sexual deviancy or dependence on alcohol or drugs" (Gostin, 1983c, p. 56). The Act leaves in place a relatively broad definition of "mental disorder," namely, "mental illness (this is not defined further), arrested or incomplete development of mind, psychopathic disorder, and any other disorder or disability of mind" (Sec. 1(2) of Mental Health Act, 1983, as discussed by Carson, 1983; Gostin, 1983c; Gunn, 1983). At the same time, however, limitations have been placed on the extent to which "arrested or incomplete development of mind" and "psychopathic disorder" can constitute a "mental disorder"; in order to do so, they must be associated with "abnormally aggressive or seriously irresponsible behaviour" (Gostin, 1983c, p. 56). As Gostin (1982a) has indicated, this new provision will limit the extent to which mentally handicapped people will be liable for compulsory admission for treatment. However, reform in this area does not seem to have affected significantly the situation pertaining to the "mentally ill" (Carson, 1983).

Inasmuch as changes in the statutory definition of mental disorder can reflect a trend toward limiting professional discretion, so too can refinements of the criteria for involuntary civil commitment. Gostin's (1983a, 1983b, 1983c) analyses of the recently enacted England and Wales Mental

Health Act of 1983 clearly illustrate the considerable importance of this issue. As he points out, the new Act "changed the requirements relating to the application and recommendations needed for an emergency admission for assessment; the purpose of the changes are to provide greater assurance that the provisions will be used only in genuine emergencies" (Gostin, 1982a, p. 1128). Basically, these changes involve a drastic shortening of the time allowed between the examination of a patient and the application for his or her admission (from 3 days to 24 hours). In addition, new provisions have been introduced to cover admissions for "assessment" (formerly "observation") under nonemergency situations. An application may only be made on the grounds that a person is suffering from a mental disorder of a nature or degree which warrants detention for assessment, *and* that the person should be detained for his or her own health or safety or with a view to protecting others (Gostin, 1982a, 1983a). Similarly, in the context of admissions for treatment, such an application may only be made on the grounds that (a) a person is suffering from a mental disorder of a nature or degree that makes treatment appropriate; (b) where a person has a psychopathic disorder or mental impairment, these conditions are "treatable"; and (c) admission is necessary for the patient's health or safety or for the protection of others and compulsory admission is the only way in which he or she will receive such treatment. Although the "treatability" criterion does not apply to those with a "mental illness" or "severe impairment" at the time of admission, a modified "treatability" requirement does apply when renewal of detention becomes necessary (i.e., after 6 months).

In addition to these new criteria, applications for the admission of a patient must be accompanied by two medical recommendations (one of which should be "independent"). In the case of admissions for treatment, the recommendations must specify the grounds for the practitioner's opinion and the reasons that alternatives to commitment are inappropriate (Gostin, 1982a).

This very brief overview of the new situation in England and Wales suggests that although some restrictions have been placed on the exercise of professional discretion, they are far from sweeping and, as Carson (1983) argues, can be considered largely symbolic in nature. In the context of defining those who will fall involuntarily within the reach of the mental health system, the recent changes seem to affect only the mentally handicapped and those deemed to be suffering from "psychopathic disorders." "Mental illness" is still undefined, and, therefore, determination of what constitutes such a condition is a decision that remains squarely in the hands of mental health professionals. The criteria for the involuntary civil commitment of the mentally ill are, likewise, still some way from being specific. Although the new provisions may have introduced a requirement that involuntary detention only occur where it is necessary for the protection of the person or others, the criteria for actually determining *when* a condition of this type exists are left unspecified. Presumably, this remains a matter for medical opinion, and it is, therefore, open to the exercise of professional discretion. If all of this is indicative of a "new legalism," the effect of this development would merely appear to be a specification of the areas where discretion is to be applied, rather than the creation of constraints on its exercise. This does not appear to be consistent with Gostin's own definition and vision of "new legalism." If this is the case, what form would a statute embracing the "new legalism" take?

To clarify the issue, it is useful to consider three possible models of mental health legislation. In the first such model, a statute could contain definitions of mental disorder and the associated procedures for involuntary commitment that are so specific that they narrow both the population that might be eligible for commitment and the circumstances under which involuntary commitment can be exercised. For example, a definition of mental disorder might be constructed in a way that narrows the eligible population to include only those diagnosed as suffering from certain types of psychosis as defined in a particular nosology (e.g., DSM-III). Having defined the relevant population, the statute might then articulate the types of circumstances under which the involuntary commitment of members of this group may proceed. For example, the statute might provide that commitment is only possible where an individual is actually exhibiting certain (specifically stated) forms of behavior, such as self-mutilation or self-starvation. Specificity might be enhanced by the use of detailed exclusionary clauses; for example, the legislation might provide that commitment is invalid where, all other criteria being met, an individual (during lucid moments) expresses a clear wish to continue with self-starvation as a political gesture.

It will be apparent that this model of legislation is an "ideal-type" one. However, it does represent the type of legislation that might epitomize a "new legalism." Professional discretion still exists, and, in this respect, the statute is markedly different from the "old legalism" because decision-making with regard to commitment is not passed into the hands of the judiciary. Constraints exist in that, too, for although professional discretion is exercised in relation to the categorization of patients as being "mentally disordered," it is conditioned by the canons of a specific nosology. The commitment decision is unequivocally *medical* in nature; however, it is controlled by the requirement that objectively determinable conditions exist. It is submitted that the extent to which legislation, in a particular jurisdiction, approaches this "model" is a measure of the extent to which a "new legalism" can be said to exist.

A second model of legislation might involve a detailed specification both of the relevant population and the criteria for involuntary commitment; however, it would do so without necessarily narrowing or constraining the exercise of professional discretion. For example, rather than using a broad and perhaps circular definition of mental disorder or illness (e.g., "a mental disorder is a disease or disability of the mind"), such legislation might instead define behaviors in a manner that appears, at first glance, to be specific but that nevertheless accords a broad discretionary power to professionals. Such a statute might provide a general definition of "mental disorder," which includes a number of subcategories or terms that are then further defined. A "mental disorder" may be defined as mental illness, mental retardation, psychopathic disorder, or any other disorder or disability of the mind, these terms then being "clarified" in a way that is either circular or very broad. "Mental illness" may be seen as a disorder of the mind resulting in a behavioral disturbance or disturbance of feelings, thoughts, and conversation, resulting in distress or impairment or an inability to associate with others or to react appropriately to the environment. Such a definition gives the impression of specificity but, in effect, permits discretionary decisions at a number of points and is, in any case, built upon the exercise of "opinion" rather than upon a requirement that there be reference to some objectively determinable events. Similarly, although the criteria for involuntary commitment might appear to be narrow or constraining, they nevertheless might have little impact on the exercise of discretion. For example, a statute might require that one or two physicians examine a person to determine whether he or she is suffering from a mental disorder, and might only permit involuntary commitment where the physicians find that a mental disorder is present and where, in their *opinion*, the subject is in a condition that presents a danger to the subject or to other persons. No specific test of "dangerousness" is required, and specific definitions of the situations that are the only permissible grounds for commitment are not provided. This type of legislation might give the appearance that a set of new "legal" controls has emerged; however, on closer examination, it is clear that it leaves professional discretion relatively intact. Indeed, it may simply be an expression of policies and procedures that have been informally adopted by psychiatrists for some time and thus have no impact on their future behavior, vis-à-vis the involuntary commitment of patients.

The third, and final, model of legislation is one that enshrines professional discretion by providing definitions of mental disorder that are vague or circular and by specifying that involuntary commitment may occur whenever a physician feels it is appropriate. For example, mental disorder might be defined as a "lack of reason or lack of control of behavior," or as "any disease or disability of the mind." The criteria for commitment might require an examination by one or two physicians, during which they need be concerned only with whether or not a person suffers from a mental disorder and whether or not the person should be admitted because he or she requires the services available in a hospital. A statute of this type is, clearly, the epitome of professional discretion and places virtually no legal controls on the process of defining a relevant population or on the circumstances that must exist before involuntary commitment can occur.

Although these three "models" are artificial constructions, they nevertheless serve as useful heuristic devices with which to review the relevant provisions of mental health legislation in Commonwealth jurisdictions, develop a picture of the current situation and trends, and assess the validity of Gostin's "new legalism" thesis. At the outset, however, it is important to stress two points. First, in practice, mental health legislation manifests a mixture of legal controls and professional discretion. Although in some places a loose definition of mental disorder might exist, this may be "balanced" by very specific criteria for involuntary commitment. Similarly, loose criteria for commitment may be counterbalanced by a specific and narrow definition of mental disorder. Second, although legislation might lay out certain formal requirements, there is no guarantee that physicians and mental health professionals will comply with them in practice.

Taken as a whole, the relevant provisions of Commonwealth mental health legislation correspond to many of the elements contained in the second model outlined above; however, they also reflect some of the elements of the professional discretion model. In only one jurisdiction (New South Wales) does the mental health legislation reflect elements of the "new legalism." The situation in England and Wales has already been briefly outlined, and it will be clear from the relevant discussion that, although some important reforms have been made, these have really only moved the jurisdiction from one where close to full discretion was allowed, to one where some new but limited controls have been introduced. In this respect, the changes merely indicate a tentative move toward, rather than a full acceptance of, the "new legalism" model. However, what is the situation in other Commonwealth jurisdictions?

In Canada, circumstances similar to those in England and Wales appear to exist. However, in some jurisdictions, this is by no means the product of recent reform. First, in the context of definitions of mental disorder, 8 of the 10 provinces use a broad and nonspecific definition;[1] for example, in Alberta (Mental Health Act, R.S.A. 1980, Sec. 1), a mental disorder is defined as "a lack of reason or lack of control of behaviour," whereas the other jurisdictions generally rely on a definition commonly used throughout the Commonwealth: namely, "a mental disorder is any disease or disability of mind." In this respect, 3 of the provinces (Ontario, Alberta, and Nova Scotia) have changed their mental health legislation in the last decade and are generally recognized as leaders in mental health law reform. These reforms, however, did not extend to narrowing the eligible population or controlling professional discretion in this area. On the other hand, Ontario has made progress by tightening the commitment criteria in such a way that it effectively restricts the definition of mental disorder (discussed further later in the chapter).

In the remaining two jurisdictions (Manitoba and Saskatchewan), specific (but nevertheless broad) definitions exist (see MacKinnon, 1979). Mental disorder is defined by reference to a series of conditions (mental illness, mental retardation, psychoneurosis, psychopathic disorder, and so on), and these conditions are then further defined. For example, mental illness, in Saskatchewan, is a "disorder of the mind . . . that results in a disturbance in a person's behaviour or feelings or thoughts and conversation and that results in mental distress or impaired ability to associate with others or results in a person's inability to react appropriately or efficiently to his environment and in respect of which medical treatment is advisable" (Mental Health Act, R.S.S. 1978, C. M.-13, Sec. 2). This definition may be specific, but it is as broad as it is bulky and clearly invites the exercise of professional judgment at numerous points. The same can be said of the other conditions contained within the definition of "mental disorder."

Second, in the context of involuntary commitment, 9 of the 10 provinces have a specific but, in most cases, broad set of criteria in place. The exception is Ontario, which is the only jurisdiction that has attempted to narrow the specific criteria for civil commitment through recent legislative reform (Mental Health Act, S.O. 1978, c.50, now R.S.O. 1980, c.262). Involuntary commitment may only occur if there are reasonable grounds to believe that a person has threatened or attempted to inflict harm upon him or herself, or has engaged in violence toward another, or has led another to fear violence, or has demonstrated a lack of competence to care for him or herself, and (of course) is suffering from a mental disorder as defined in the Act. The mental disorder, however, must be of a nature or quality that will likely result in serious bodily harm to the person, or to another person, or imminent and serious physical impairment of the person (Mental Health Act, R.S.O. 1980, c.262, Secs. 9–14). Thus the broad definition that is articulated in the Act (i.e., a mental disorder is any disease or disability of the mind) is conditioned, in the context of its application in the process of involuntary commitment, by the requirement that the disorder be of a certain nature or quality — namely, that the person be, in part, "dangerously" mentally disordered. The combined effects of these definitions of men-

---

[1]Alberta, Ontario, Nova Scotia, New Brunswick, Prince Edward Island, Newfoundland, Quebec, and British Columbia.

tal disorder and the criteria for civil commitments are to limit professional discretion; however, the impact of the limitation is reduced by leaving decision-making in the hands of physicians, who are only required to express an "opinion." As long as a physician has "reasonable cause to believe" that the criteria apply to a particular person and sets out the facts that led to the formation of his or her opinion, then involuntary commitment can occur. On the other hand, there is a requirement that *some* objectively determinable conditions be employed by decision-makers when arriving at their opinions.

In the other provinces, the criteria follow a similar format except that the statutory definitions of mental disorder are not further narrowed by the criteria for civil commitment. Typically, a general "health, welfare, and safety" clause is employed as the only condition limiting the exercise of discretion. This can be illustrated by reference to the relevant provisions of the British Columbia legislation (Mental Health Act, R.S.B.C. 1979, c.256), section 1 of which defines a "mentally ill" person as

a person suffering from a disorder of the mind: a) that seriously impairs his ability to react appropriately to his environment or to associate with others; and b) that requires medical treatment *or* makes care, supervision and control of the person necessary for his protection or welfare or for the protection of others.

A person may be involuntarily committed provided that an application for admission is supported by two medical certificates completed by independent physicians. In these certificates, the physicians must, *inter alia*, state that *in their opinion* an individual is disordered (giving the reasons for the opinion) and that, *in their opinion*, the person requires treatment and care, supervision, and control for his or her own protection or welfare or for the protection of others (Sec. 20). The manifest concern of the legislation is to protect patients from themselves and to protect others; however, decision-making rests on *opinion*, the exercise of which is directed toward very broadly defined sets of circumstances. The exercise of such discretion is certainly not constrained by a requirement that specific and objectively determinable conditions exist before commitment can proceed.

"Health, welfare, and safety" clauses vary slightly from jurisdiction to jurisdiction. In Quebec (Mental Patient Protection Act, R.S.Q. 1977,

c.P-41, Sec. 11), the concern is with people who suffer from a "mental disorder" that might "endanger" their "health or security" or the "health or security" of others. As Hill (1977) notes, this provision was introduced in 1972 as part of a general overhaul of the province's mental health legislation. The main thrust of the reform was to give psychiatrists a *more* significant role in the process of admitting patients to hospital. Although it appears to introduce a test of "dangerousness" (and thereby appears to place some limitation on the exercise of psychiatric discretion), the effect is quite the opposite. The use of such vague terms as "health" and "security" leaves the field open to broad interpretation and, in any case, it is now axiomatic that "dangerousness" is difficult to establish and predict in an objective fashion (Monahan, 1981; Pfohl, 1978). Nevertheless, "dangerousness" is specifically mentioned in the Nova Scotia legislation (Hospitals Act, R.S.N.S. 1967, c.249 (consld. 1979, c.H-19), Sec. 26). If a physician has "reasonable and probable grounds" for believing that a patient suffers from a "psychiatric disorder" (any disease or disability of mind) and should be admitted both because he or she needs services and care and because the patient is a danger to him or herself (i.e., his or her "own safety") or is a danger to the "safety" of others, then involuntary commitment may occur. Similarly, in Alberta, "dangerousness" to oneself or others is a major factor to be considered in the commitment process (Mental Health Act, R.S.A. 1980, c.M-13, Secs. 14, 18). In Manitoba and Saskatchewan, the "protection or welfare" of the person or others are the main limiting criteria (Mental Health Act, R.S.M. 1970, c.M-110, Sec. 2; Mental Health Act, R.S.S. 1978, c.M-13, Sec. 16), while in New Brunswick and Prince Edward Island the concern is with the person's "safety" or the "safety" of others (Mental Health Act, R.S.N.B. 1973, c.M-10, Sec. 8; Mental Health Act, R.S.P.E.I. 1974, c.M-9, Sec. 10). Newfoundland is also concerned with the safety of the individual and others (Mental Health Act, S.N. 1971, No. 80, Sec. 6) but, in addition, is eager to protect *property* from mentally disordered persons.

Overall, the situation in Canada is one that suggests a move away from a purely discretionary model and toward a situation where some controls are placed on mental health professionals involved in the commitment process. Ontario has probably traveled the farthest toward a "new legalism" model by employing a specific definition of mental disorder in the case of involuntary commitments and by laying out three sets of circumstances where commitment may occur. Each of these embodies a notion of *physical* "dangerousness" but overcomes the vagueness associated with the term by articulating the circumstances that must be present to constitute "dangerousness." Nevertheless, decision-making is still in the hands of physicians who are only required to form an *opinion* that commitment is justifiable on "reasonable grounds." As is the case with "tests" of "dangerousness," the question of "reasonableness" is highly problematic. Close on the heels of Ontario in this respect are the Provinces of Alberta, Quebec, and Nova Scotia, where "dangerousness" is clearly identified as a *relevant* factor in decision-making concerning involuntary commitment. However, there is no attempt in the respective statutes to define the term or to specify the concrete circumstances in which commitment may take place on the basis of "dangerousness." Furthermore, in Quebec and Nova Scotia, the applicable statutory provisions raise the issue of dangerousness within the somewhat vague context of the question of whether a patient's condition "endangers" the safety, health, or security of him or herself or others. Significantly, somewhat broad definitions of mental disorder are in place in Alberta, Quebec, and Nova Scotia, thus granting a wide discretionary power to mental health professionals in the context of initially locating the population eligible for involuntary commitment. The remaining Canadian provinces may, in some cases, attempt to be specific in the context of defining "mental disorder," but they then prescribe criteria for involuntary commitment that refer only to a very general concern for the "health, welfare, and safety" of the person or others. Thus, in all of these jurisdictions, decision-making is effectively based on the *opinions* of medical practitioners.

By comparison, the situation in the Australian states tends, overall, to indicate a greater concern with the consolidation of professional discretion. The single exception is New South Wales where the Mental Health Act of 1983 appears to present a set of statutory provisions that closely correspond to the "new legalism" model. Before examining the situation in this state, however, a general review of legislation in the *other* six jurisdictions is necessary and will begin with the issue of defining "mental disorder."

In his review of Australian legislation, O'Sullivan (1981) notes that although one might expect the concept of mental disorder to be carefully defined, this is not the case. In some jurisdictions,

there is "no attempt at a definition while some others simply replace the expression by the words 'psychiatric illness'" (O'Sullivan, 1981, p. 1). In Queensland and the Northern Territory, the relevant statutes are bereft of any definitions (Mental Health Act of 1974 (Queensland); Mental Health Act of 1979 (Northern Territory)). As O'Sullivan notes (relying on the judgment of Lawton, L. J. in *W. v. L.* (1974)), "in the absence of a statutory definition the words 'mental illness' would evidently have to be construed in the way ordinary, sensible people would construe them" (p. 8). This is the epitome of vagueness and leaves interpretation wide open to the exercise of professional discretion. In this regard, it is interesting to note that, when the Queensland government introduced the statute in 1974, the expressed intention was to grant a maximum amount of discretion to physicians (O'Sullivan, 1981). The Queensland statute does specify that drug dependence and mental retardation are forms of mental illness and the Northern Territory Act contains a provision specifying that the "biochemical or psychological effect of a drug or psychotropic substance may be an indication of mental illness." Otherwise, the statutes are silent on what is to be *included* within the realm of behavior of interest to a mental health system. On the other hand, the Northern Territory Act (which is one of the most recently enacted mental health statutes in Australia) does contain an important *exclusionary* provision. Section 4(2) states that individuals may not be deemed mentally ill merely because they express or refuse to acknowledge a particular opinion or they engage in (or do not engage in) a particular activity. The wording of the section suggests that the intention is to prevent the labeling and commitment of those who deviate from mainstream social and political conventions. In this regard, it is interesting to note that a similar provision has been in place in Tasmania for over 20 years. In this state, where a "mental disorder" is broadly defined, the Mental Health Act specifies that "promiscuity or other immoral conduct is not, without more, sufficient to justify categorization as mentally ill" (Mental Health Act of 1963; Sec. 4(5)).

Elsewhere, mental illness or disorder is defined in circular terms, that are reminiscent of some Canadian mental health statutes. In South Australia (Mental Health Act of 1976–1977, Sec. 5), where the mental health statute is relatively recent, a mental illness is defined as "any illness or disorder of the mind." Similarly, in Western

Australia, another state with recently "reformed" legislation, mental illness is "a psychiatric or other illness or condition that substantially impairs mental health" (Mental Health Act of 1981, Sec. 5). Similar definitions hold sway in the states of Victoria and Tasmania. Clearly, such legislation grants a wide discretion to the relevant mental health personnel. As will be seen, this trend is reinforced when the criteria for involuntary commitment are considered.

The state that comes closest to granting full discretion to the medical profession is Victoria. Any person may be involuntarily committed to a psychiatric facility on request, provided they are "mentally ill" and the request is supported by the recommendations of a medical practitioner based upon a recent examination (Mental Health Act of 1959, no. 6605, Sec. 42). No other criteria are prescribed. The same type of broad power existed in Western Australia prior to the passage of the Mental Health Act of 1981; however, a "health, welfare and safety" clause has been introduced. The recent reforms to the mental health legislation provide that, in order for civil commitment to take place, the person's illness must be of a nature or degree which warrants detention for treatment in the interest of the patient's welfare or for the protection of others (Mental Health Act of 1981, Sec. 28 & 48). It has recently been recommended that the state of Victoria should follow this approach (Myers, Fitzgerald, & Ball, 1981). If such reforms are introduced, it will bring the jurisdiction in line with the provisions in most other states.

Queensland, South Australia, and Tasmania each require that before an individual is involuntarily committed, there must be some indication that it is necessary for his or her own welfare (health or safety) or for the protection of others.[2] In the Northern Territory, the general "health, welfare and safety" theme applies except that the statute appears to be more specific and more concerned with "dangerousness." Commitment may occur if there is "reasonable cause" to believe that a mentally ill person (undefined) requires "care, treatment or control," is incapable of managing him or herself or his or her affairs; is not being cared for or controlled adequately; and is likely, as a consequence, to cause death or serious bodily harm to him or herself or to another and should

be detained in his or her own interests or in the public interest (Northern Territory Mental Health Act of 1979, Sec. 9). The state thus employs a "test" of *physical* dangerousness that, in a manner similar to that adopted in Ontario, attempts to articulate the specific circumstances that constitute such a condition. To a significant degree, this approach counter-balances the lack of a definition specifying the meaning of "mental disorder." As is the case in Ontario, the Northern Territory appears to be a jurisdiction that has moved away from full discretion and toward a "new legalism." On the other hand, the majority of the Australian states still appear to enshrine professional discretion in their civil commitment legislation (albeit modified by a general "health, welfare and safety" provision). The exception is New South Wales, a state where the "new legalism" model now appears to be firmly in harness.

The New South Wales Mental Health Act of 1983 is a product of nearly a decade of controversy, sometimes fierce, in which the clash between the health and legal needs of patients has been most evident. One indication of this lies in the preamble to the Act, where the essence of the conflict is expressed with remarkable economy. It is recognized that community-based and hospital care facilities are needed and that the latter should be provided on both an "informal and voluntary basis"; however, it is also acknowledged that, in a limited number of situations, mental health services may have to be administered on an involuntary basis. Furthermore, "the civil rights of persons should be protected and, at the same time, . . . opportunity should be given for persons with mental illness to have access to appropriate care" (New South Wales Mental Health Act of 1983: Preamble). The extent to which the legislators have attempted to balance these competing needs is most significant.

Further reference to the provisions of the Act will be made in subsequent sections of this review. At this point, however, the intention is to consider the twin issues of the definition of mental disorder or a "mentally ill person" and the articulation of the criteria for involuntary commitment. First, in the context of statutory definitions, the Act provides the most comprehensive, detailed, and specific statement to be found in any Commonwealth jurisdiction. Briefly, a "mentally ill person" is a

---

[2]Mental Health Act of 1974, section 6 (Queensland); Mental Health Act of 1976–1977, section 14 (South Australia); Mental Health Act of 1963, sections 14–17 (Tasmania).

person who requires care, treatment, *or* control for their own protection *or* for the protection of others. In each case, however, specific sets of circumstances are laid out in detail, the main theme of which is the delineation of a series of "dangerous" situations. According to the Act, a person requires care, treatment, or control for his or her *own* protection where, because of mental illness, (a) he or she has attempted to kill, or cause serious bodily harm to, him or herself; (b) there are reasonable grounds for believing that he or she will attempt to kill or cause bodily harm to him or herself; (c) there are reasonable grounds for believing that he or she will suffer serious bodily harm due to neglect; (d) he or she has "recently performed an act, engaged in a course of activity or constructed or set up a device or arrangement which will probably result in the infliction of serious bodily harm" upon him or herself; *or* (e) he or she is in the "manic phase of a manic-depressive illness and there are reasonable grounds for believing that it is probable that the person will thereby suffer serious financial harm or harm to his or her reputation or standing in the community" (Sec. 5(1)(a)(i)-(v)).

A person requires care, treatment, or control for the protection of *others* where, because of mental illness, (a) the person has inflicted, attempted to inflict, or made a recent and "credible" threat to inflict serious bodily harm on another; (b) the person has performed or attempted to perform an act of violence against another or against property that indicates the person will inflict serious bodily harm on another; (c) the person has "recently performed an act, engaged in a course of activity or constructed or set up a device or arrangement which will probably result in the infliction of serious bodily harm upon another person"; or (d) the person has been harassing or has been a nuisance to others, where the behavior might lead to violence and is "so far beyond the limits of normal social behaviour that a reasonable person would consider it intolerable" (Sec. 5(1)(b)(i)-(iv)). Thus, the forms of behavior that are to constitute grounds for involuntary commitment are specifically delineated in the Act.

The statute also *excludes* certain forms of behavior from the scope of "mental illness." A person is not deemed mentally ill simply because he or she expresses a particular political or religious opinion, has a particular sexual preference or orientation or is (or has been) sexually promiscuous, engages in immoral or illegal conduct, has a developmental disability of the mind, and/or uses drugs or alcohol. However, in the last case, a person may be regarded as "mentally ill" if he or she is suffering from the "serious and permanent" effects of drug-taking (Secs. 5(2), 5(3)).

The definition has a specific application in a number of areas, one of which is the process of involuntary commitment. In this regard, the relevant procedures follow a convention established in many other Commonwealth jurisdictions: A person may be taken to (and detained in) a hospital upon the certificate of one medical practitioner who has examined or observed the person immediately before completing the certificate, is of the opinion that the person is mentally ill, is satisfied that commitment is necessary, and is not a "near relative" of the person (Sec. 72(1)). "As soon as practicable" after the patient's arrival, the patient must be examined by the medical superintendent of the hospital. If the examiner determines that the patient is, indeed, a "mentally ill" person, then the patient must be examined by another medical practitioner. If the superintendent is not a psychiatrist, then the second medical practitioner must be such a specialist. If the second practitioner confirms the classification of the patient as a "mentally ill" person, then the latter may continue in detention (Secs. 79, 82-84). However, the involuntarily commitment of a patient must swiftly be confirmed by a magistrate after a formal hearing (Secs. 86-92). The requirement of a judicial hearing (long a feature of New South Wales mental health legislation) represents an unequivocal element of "legalism."

The new legislation in New South Wales is clearly without precedent anywhere in the Commonwealth, and it represents a radical departure from the general tenor of the statutes in most other Australian states where, despite some recent reform efforts, professional discretion seems to be deeply entrenched. Certainly, the new Northern Territory statute appears to establish some constraints by delineating a set of specific circumstances that serve as indicators of "dangerousness"; however, elsewhere in Australia, vague "health, welfare, and safety" clauses are freely employed in the various mental health statutes. The state of Victoria exemplifies the full "professional discretion" model and, in the Commonwealth as a whole, shares this position with only one other jurisdiction so far neglected in this review — New Zealand. The New Zealand statute (Mental Health Act, 1969, Sec. 2) provides a circular definition of "mental disorder" (i.e., a mentally ill person is someone requiring care and treatment for a mental illness) and places few constraints on the exercise of discretion in relation to the imposition of involuntary commitment. Where it is "expedient" that a mentally disordered person be placed under care and treatment in a hospital, either in the interests of his or her "welfare" or in the public interest, and a request for commitment is supported by two medical certificates, a person may be admitted to and detained in a hospital (Sec. 19).

Viewed as a whole, legislative developments in the Commonwealth appear to have clarified, rather than constrained, the nature of professional discretion in the context of involuntary civil commitment. Broad or circular definitions of "mental disorder" remain intact despite recent overhauls of legislation. Likewise, the criteria for commitment have not been specifically articulated, the favorite "constraining" provision being nothing more than the requirement that commitment proceed only if it is necessary for the "health, welfare or safety" of the person or others. Determining whether or not such a condition exists is left to the physician contemplating the commitment of a person. Certainly, there are exceptions to this situation; New South Wales, Ontario, and the Northern Territory stand out as jurisdictions where new legislation has imposed varying degrees of constraint on the exercise of discretion. However, recent legislation in other jurisdictions (e.g., Western Australia, South Australia, Nova Scotia, and England and Wales) has not established new controls of the same magnitude. Indeed, by introducing "health, welfare or safety" clauses as alleged reforms, they are really doing no more than "re-inventing the wheel"; such provisions have been in place in other jurisdictions for some time.

Statutory provisions relating to the definition of mentally disordered persons and the criteria for involuntary commitment of such persons do not, therefore, appear to impose more effective controls on the exercise of professional discretion. In addition, the available empirical research into the practices of physicians who exercise such discretion suggests that, even where such controls are in place, they may be "honored in the breach." There is some evidence to suggest that, regardless of legal reforms, mental health professionals will continue to insist on the primacy of their view of what is in a patient's "best interests," exercise their discretion accordingly, and, if necessary, circumvent statutory provisions.

In Australia, for example, Briscoe's study (1968)

of 100 consecutive commitments to a Sydney hospital indicated that many physicians had completed the required certificates in a way that should have resulted in a refusal to admit the patient. He argued that only 34% of the admissions were appropriate within the meaning of the New South Wales statute (Mental Health Act of 1958). The majority of people who were admitted required control or assistance that should have been provided by criminal justice, social welfare, or other health service agencies. As Goodman (1977, p. 965) argues, this finding "raises fundamental questions about the proper use of involuntary admissions." Physicians were clearly taking insufficient care in the process of selecting those who were in need of mental health services.

A major problem in relation to citation of Briscoe's work rests in its vintage. As Flaherty and Hall (1981) have argued, there have been significant changes in the organization of New South Wales mental health services since Briscoe's (1968) study was undertaken, and therefore, these findings no longer reflect current admission practices. Indeed, their own recent study suggests that, although some applications and admissions may be unnecessary, the proportion is much smaller than that discovered in Briscoe's research. Unfortunately, there are no published data pertaining to the situation in other states although there is no reason to believe that problems in the commitment process are experienced only in New South Wales.

Canadian researchers have been examining this issue for over a decade, the principal focus being on determining the extent to which physicians, who complete commitment forms, comply with the relevant provincial statutes. Studies by Page and Firth (1979), Page and Yates (1973, 1974, 1975) and Reitsma (1973) have consistently shown that committing physicians do not follow the prescribed procedures. As Toews, Prabhu, and El-Guebaly (1980) point out, the various studies suggest that an estimated 80–90% of documents "did not meet legal requirements as represented by common rules of evidence, logic, and statutory certificate requirement" (p. 613). Unfortunately, research has not established the reason why this situation might exist or the extent to which the behavior is widespread; in the latter case, this is because most of the research has been conducted in Ontario. Some limited analysis by Draper (1976a) suggests that Alberta physicians follow the practices of their Ontario colleagues, and consequently, there is no reason to believe that Ontario is a special case. However, the situation has been rendered somewhat more complex in light of recent research by McCready and Merskey (1981, 1982), which suggests that there is now a considerably greater degree of compliance with statutory requirements in Ontario than was identified in earlier studies.

One of the most detailed, recent, and methodologically rigorous studies of admission procedures in England and Wales has been undertaken by Bean (1980). In a 2-year study of commitment practices followed at one hospital, Bean examined the activities of psychiatrists, physicians in general practice, and social workers. In the case of psychiatrists, he found that only 9% of patients were admitted and detained in circumstances that involved a specific contravention of the provisions of the England and Wales Mental Health Act of 1959. However, he found that psychiatrists also acted contrary to the "spirit of the Act"; that is, they acted in a way that involved a questionable interpretation of legislative provisions. For example, they would admit people for "treatment" when there were only grounds to admit for "observation." When these types of actions were added to the cases of specific "rule infraction," nearly 40% of patients were being involuntarily committed under questionable circumstances. General practitioners and social workers were also found to be involved in "rule infraction" and to be acting contrary to the "spirit of the Act," and when the three professional groups were combined, Bean found that over 50% of commitments were questionable and/or illegal. The reasons for such conduct are to be found in a number of areas. In the case of general practitioners and social workers, the problem appeared to lie in their poor understanding of legislative requirements. General practitioners also tended to defer to psychiatric opinion and did not seem to be fulfilling their role as a "second opinion" in the certification process. Social workers also simply "rubber-stamped" the decisions of psychiatrists. Indeed, Bean (1980) argued that "psychiatrists tended to run the 1959 Act as they wished. Whenever the psychiatrists were placed in positions where they

were not in control, unstable interaction occurred to the detriment of the patient" (p. 177).

In light of such findings, an important question might be raised; namely, why is it that the parties affected by the actions of committing physicians have not turned to the courts for protection and compensation when wrongful commitments have occurred? Part of the answer rests with the difficulties associated with obtaining access to legal services and the courts. Another part of the answer can be gleaned from a brief glance at developments in a pertinent area of the law of torts.

In a discussion of the Canadian situation, Yake (1976) has pointed out that generally the courts have been "charitable" to physicians who err and that in most instances, particularly where a mental illness is involved, they have been absolved of liability. This comment would seem to apply equally well to the situation in other Commonwealth jurisdictions. In the specific area of tort law which is seen to be most applicable to cases of inappropriate civil commitment — "false imprisonment" — Draper (1976b) has found more confusion than clear and consistent doctrine. Courts have done little more than express a general concern that wrongful, compulsory admission be avoided, possibly because so few cases are presented to them. However, even when such opportunities have arisen, little appears to have been accomplished. For example, a relatively recent case dealing with wrongful commitment found its way to the Supreme Court of Canada (*Coulombe v. Watier*, [1973] S.C.R.673) but did not result in a ruling that could be applied nationally; the judiciary was concerned, primarily, with procedures relating only to the province of Quebec.

On the other hand, in some cases the courts in Commonwealth jurisdictions have appeared willing to award appropriate damages for wrongful imprisonment where a doctor incorrectly certifies a person as mentally disordered and dangerous and where he or she has not acted in good faith or exercised reasonable care.[3] However, it is apparent that liability will be found, and damages awarded, only where the circumstances indicate

---

[3]*Schmidt v. Katz and Shrider* (1954), 13 W.W.R.654 (Sask. Q.B.); *X v. Y* (1970) Que. CA 795; *Gifford v. Kelson* (1943) 2 W.W.R.76 (Man. K.B.); *Marshall v. Watson* (1972), 124 C.L.R.640 (V.S.C.). This judicial doctrine is based on precedents that were established in England over 100 years ago and have since been followed by Australian, Canadian, and English Courts. (See *Hall v. Semple* (1862), 3 F&F337; 176 E.R.151 (Q.B.); *Williams v. Beaumont and Duke* (1894), 10 T.L.R.543 (CA); *Smith v. Ifla* (1881), 7 V.L.R.435; *Everett v. Griffiths* (1921) 1 A.C.631; 37 T.L.R.481 (HL); *Lumsden v. Glidden* (1920), 18 O.W.N.354 (Ont. H.C.); *Hartnett v. Fisher* (1927) A.C.573; *Mincham v. Beemer* (1929), 37 W.W.N.52 (Ont. H.C.).

an obvious and severe form of wrongdoing (Draper, 1976b). Indeed, the courts appear to be reluctant to become involved in the process of constraining and disciplining mental health professionals; this is a conclusion that is, in part, supported by the outcome of a recent Alberta case. In *Tanner v. Norys* (1979) substantial damages were awarded against a physician who wrongfully committed a patient. However, on appeal the judgment of the lower court was reversed (*Tanner v. Norys*, 1980). The general posture of the Court of Appeal suggests that, in Canada at least, a "charitable" attitude still prevails and that the courts are not eager to control the exercise of professional discretion through the medium of damages — even where a physician's actions are shown to be wrong and to have led to the unwarranted detention of an individual.

It is to be expected that this approach by the courts will continue although, as Heffey's (1983) recent work in this area suggests, the use of the tort of negligence, rather than false imprisonment, may be a preferable strategy to adopt for those acting for mental health patients. Practitioners are under a special duty of care and, if a wrongful commitment occurs as a consequence of a practitioner failing to comply with statutorily prescribed procedures, then he or she may be deemed negligent.

Having been committed to a mental health facility, an individual may then be subject to treatment. This is another area where developments in Commonwealth jurisdictions might be expected to reflect either a "new legalism" or the entrenchment of professional discretion.

THE RIGHT TO REFUSE TREATMENT

The extent to which the "new legalism" necessarily implies the imposition of legal controls upon the exercise of professional discretion is starkly illustrated within the context of the so-called right to refuse psychiatric treatment. As Gostin (1983b) points out:

> Legal concern for the welfare and rights of the psychiatric patient has traditionally ceased at the hospital door on the assumption that, while the law could reasonably set procedural and substantive standards in respect of compulsory admission, it could not interfere in the clinical relationship which must be established following admis-

sion. The traditional legal view resulted in the failure of mental health legislation to establish general principles protecting the position of detained psychiatric patients to decide what treatment they should receive. (p. 42)

In Gostin's view (1983b), the "new legalism" is predicated upon two basic principles that should be applied in this context. First, a psychiatric patient who withholds consent to treatment should be "entitled to protection under the law." Secondly, a treatment should not be administered to a patient unless the attending psychiatrist can demonstrate that it is "reasonably efficacious" and that "it acts without disproportionate risks of adverse effects" (p. 46). In recent years there have been a number of significant attempts to enshrine limited versions of these two principles in Commonwealth mental health legislation. In this respect, it appears that the "new legalism" is gradually beginning to permeate the patchwork fabric of Commonwealth mental health law (see also Gostin, 1983c). However, it must be recognized that reforms have been generally cautious and, by no means, uniform in the various jurisdictions (see Gordon & Verdun-Jones, 1983).

The issues to be examined are (a) whether a mental health patient, who has been involuntarily committed, retains the right to refuse treatment and (b) whether legal controls have been imposed that are perceived as being particularly hazardous in relation to the administration of treatments. Unfortunately, the debate concerning the emergence of a right to refuse psychiatric treatment has been clouded by an excess of rhetoric on the part of both lawyers and psychiatrists. Indeed, the reader who thumbs through the rapid burgeoning literature in this area cannot fail to be struck by the apocalyptic tone of such titles as "Limiting the Therapeutic Orgy" (Plotkin, 1977) and "Rotting with Your Rights On" (Gutheil, 1980). There is little doubt that the right to refuse treatment has become an issue that sharply highlights the fundamentally opposed views of many civil libertarians, on the one hand, and many mental health professionals, on the other (see generally Kaufman, Roth, Leidz, and Meisel, 1981). The former group tends to emphasize the absolute rights of competent mental health patients to autonomy and self-determination regardless of whether they have been civilly committed. For a considerable number of mental health professionals, however, the very diagnosis of a serious mental illness per se demonstrates the patient's incompetence to participate meaningfully in the making of decisions concerning treatment; they, therefore, assert their therapeutic privilege to make the ultimate treatment decisions in the "best interests" of their patients. It is against this background of interprofessional conflict that the emergence of a right to refuse treatment must be traced.

It has long been accepted, in common law jurisdictions, that a patient, outside of the mental health system, has a right to refuse medical treatment—even if the failure to accept such treatment will inexorably result in extreme suffering or, perhaps, death (see generally Castel, 1978; Law Reform Commission of Canada, 1979a, 1979b; Rozovsky, 1973). As Chief Justice Laskin put it, in the Supreme Court of Canada, every patient has the right "to decide what (if anything) should be done with his body" (*Hopp v. Lepp*, 1980, p. 70).

In Margaret Somerville's view, this "right of self-determination expresses the principle, or value choice, of autonomy of the person" (Law Reform Commission of Canada, 1979a, p. 3). If the right is intentionally infringed upon, then a medical practitioner may well render himself liable to a criminal charge of assault (see Law Reform Commission of Canada, 1980, pp. 62-74) or a civil action in tort (assault and battery). In recent years, courts have not only required that consent to medical treatment be given by a *competent* patient on a *voluntary* basis but have also insisted that the patient's choice be appropriately *informed* (see Castel, 1978, pp. 298-303 and Law Reform Commission of Canada, 1979a, pp. 11-66). However, the requirement of adequate information has been held to be relevant to a tort action in *negligence* rather than assault and battery (*Reibl v. Hughes*, 1980, *Freeman v. Home Office*, 1983).

The requirement that a medical practitioner obtain the consent of his patient to treatment has, of course, been modified in two exceptional circumstances: in emergencies, where it is not possible to obtain the consent of the patient or nearest relative (see Law Reform Commission of Canada, 1980, pp. 73-74; Rozovsky, 1973, p. 112; Skegg, 1974), and in the situation where the patient is not

competent (see Law Reform Commission of Canada, 1980, pp. 67-70). In the latter situation, substitute consent (of a relative or guardian) is normally required.[4]

Commonwealth jurisdictions have traditionally treated involuntarily committed mental health patients on an entirely different basis. Even if they are competent to make treatment decisions, such patients have generally been denied a right to refuse treatment in spite of what may be regarded as inherently reasonable claims to autonomy of both the body and the mind (see Morris, 1981). Specific reasons for the refusal of treatment may well be found in fear of the potential side-effects of certain mental health treatments. Over the past few decades, particular attention has been paid to the more "dramatic" psychiatric treatments, such as psychosurgery and electro-convulsive therapy (ECT), which may involve potentially hazardous and/or irreversible side effects (see, e.g., Clare, 1978; Earp, 1979; Gostin, 1982c; Plotkin, 1977). More recently, however, equal concern has been expressed in relation to the potential consequences flowing from long-term treatment with psychotropic drugs (Beyer, 1980; Rhoden, 1980).

In particular, it has become apparent that at least 10-20% of patients treated with antipsychotic drugs on a long-term basis will suffer from the potentially irreversible side effect of tardive dyskinesia (Munetz, Roth, and Cornes, 1981, p. 77). However, even the temporary side effects of anti-psychotic drug therapy may include such unpleasant conditions as akathisia, akinesia, dyskinesia and parkinsonism (see Beyer, 1980, pp. 511-513; Plotkin, 1977, pp. 474-479; Rhoden, 1980, pp. 380-382). Significantly, very little research has been undertaken to evaluate the impact of compulsory treatment on patients' attitudes. An Australian study (Shannon, 1976), however, suggests that many involuntary patients are angered by their lack of control over their lives and that such anger tends to militate against the forging of an ongoing therapeutic relationship with their medical practitioners. Although tentative in nature, this study suggests yet another valid reason for granting the competent mental health patient a general right to refuse treatment.

Despite a growing recognition of the unpleasant and, in certain cases, hazardous and/or irreversi-

---

[4]For the problems associated with obtaining substitute consent in relation to the sterilization of the intellectually handicapped, see Law Reform Commission of Canada, 1979c; *Re Eve* (1980, 1981), 115 D.L.R. (3d) 283 (P.E.I.S.C., *in banco*).

ble side effects of many mental health therapies, the majority of Commonwealth jurisdictions still maintains legislative provisions (see, e.g., Gordon and Verdun-Jones, 1983; Schiffer, 1982, pp. 180–181) that either explicitly or implicitly authorize the compulsory treatment of all involuntarily committed patients (the specific provisions of each jurisdiction are set out in Table 1.1). Significantly, these provisions do not include the requirement, applicable outside the mental health system, that a medical practitioner obtain the substitute consent of a relative or guardian prior to the administration of treatment to an incompetent patient. Of course, *voluntary* (or "informal") mental health patients retain a right to refuse treatment because, in the last resort, they may remove themselves from a hospital altogether; in this respect, they enjoy the same right to refuse treatment as patients outside the mental health system.

It is not entirely clear why, in most Commonwealth jurisdictions, the involuntarily committed patient has been denied the same right to refuse treatment that has been accorded to all other patients. There appears to be an underlying assumption that all involuntarily committed patients are incompetent to participate meaningfully in treatment decisions. However, an increasing number of psychiatrists have clearly rejected the validity of such an assumption (see, for example, Stone, 1981). For example, Loren Roth (1979) has emphasized that, in light of the currently existing criteria for civil commitment in most jurisdictions, there are many involuntary mental health patients who retain the competence to make treatment decisions. In his view, the apparent illogicality of this situation will continue as long as the civil commitment process fails to include a formal adjudication of the patient's competence to make treatment decisions. According to Roth (1979), the issue of competence[5] should be determined in light of the following questions:

1. Does the patient understand the generally agreed-upon consequences (the potential benefits and potential risks) both of being treated and of *not* being treated?

2. Does the patient understand why a particular form of treatment is being recommended?
3. Does the patient express a choice for or against treatment? (p. 1122)

Roth has suggested that an order for civil commitment should normally not be made unless it has first been established that the patient is incompetent to make treatment decisions; once ruled incompetent, the patient should be entitled to have a guardian appointed to make treatment decisions on his/her behalf. It is clear that psychiatrists have been increasingly willing to acknowledge that, given the presently applicable criteria for civil commitment in most Commonwealth jurisdictions, significant numbers of involuntary mental health patients retain their competence to participate in the making of decisions concerning their treatment. Indeed, the Canadian Psychiatric Association (Cahn, 1980, 1982) has recently taken the position that, in the absence of a "true" emergency,[6] it is unethical for a psychiatrist to impose treatment against the will of a competent patient — regardless of whether that patient has been civilly committed.

Although in the majority of Commonwealth jurisdictions legislation permits the routine imposition of treatment upon all involuntary mental health patients (whether competent or not),[7] there have been significant departures from this approach in a small, but gradually increasing, number of other Commonwealth jurisdictions. The state of Western Australia has chosen to tread the path advocated by Roth and has included lack of competence to make treatment decisions among the criteria for civil commitment (Mental Health Act of 1981; Sec. 38). However, whereas Roth (1979, pp. 1122–1123) contends that commitment should be a judicial decision, the Western Australia legislation leaves the issue to be determined by the exercise of psychiatric discretion. In this sense, the Western Australia approach represents a further entrenchment of the "professional discretion" model rather than an application of the "new legalism."

Only in the Canadian Provinces of Nova Sco-

---

[5]For discussion of the most commonly employed criteria for the determination of a mental health patient's competence to make treatment decisions, see Meisel, 1977; Roth et al., 1977.

[6]"True emergencies" are defined (Cahn, 1982, p. 71) as situations "where a patient's behaviour due to mental illness is obviously dangerous to himself or others."

[7]A stark illustration of the apparently routine imposition of E.C.T. upon competent patients (in the absence of any "emergency") is furnished by the case of *Barsy v. Government of Manitoba et al.* (1966), 57 W.W.R. 169 (Man. Q.B.).

Table 1.1. Power to Impose Treatment Without Consent of Involuntary Patient in Commonwealth Jurisdictions

Australia

1. New South Wales
(Mental Health Act, 1983,
Part X, Ss. 146–183)

No general, explicit power to impose treatment: such a power must be "implied." Certain treatments require informed consent: psychosurgery and E.C.T. (except in emergencies). Surgical operations (including sterilization) require informed consent or substitute consent (authorized officer or Mental Health Review Tribunal)

2. Queensland
(Mental Health Act, 1974–1978)

No general, explicit power to impose treatment; such a power must be "implied."

3. Northern Territory
(Mental Health Act, 1979, S. 14)

Chief medical officer is granted an explicit power to impose treatment:
    1. if it is authorized by a magistrate
    2. in an "emergency"
    3. if it is, in his/her opinion, "a recognized, standard medical treatment"
Note. A magistrate may not authorize sterilization "for the reason only that" the patient "is mentally ill"

4. South Australia
(Mental Health Act, 1976–1977,
S. 19)

No general, explicit power to impose treatment; such a power must be "implied."
Act legislates restrictions in relation to two categories of treatment: (a) includes psychosurgery; (b) includes E.C.T.
Category (a) requires the patient's informed consent ("where the patient has sufficient command of his mental faculties to make a rational judgment on the matter") or, if incompetent, the consent of a guardian/relative.
Category (b) requires informed consent of patient or a guardian/relative except in an emergency.

5. Tasmania
(Mental Health Act, 1963,as am.)

No general, explicit power to impose treatment; such a power must be "implied."

6. Victoria
(Mental Health Act, 1959,
as am., S. 102, Reg. 702)

Superintendent of institution may impose any treatment or surgical operation with the exception of leucotomy (which requires approval of authorized medical officer). This restriction has been expanded, by regulation, to include pallidectomy and any surgical operation involving the excision of any part of the brain.

7. Western Australia
(Mental Health Act, 1981, S. 28)

No general, explicit power to impose treatment, such a power must be "implied." However, one of the criteria for commitment is the patient's lack of competence to make treatment decisions: "He does not, by reason of his mental illness, appreciate that he needs treatment for it."

New Zealand

8. New Zealand
(Mental Health Act, 1969,
as am., S. 25)

The making of a reception order is "sufficient authority" for the superintendent of the hospital to give the patient "care and treatment."

England and Wales

9. England and Wales
(Mental Health Act, 1983,
Ss. 56–63)

The patient's consent is not necessary when he/she is being treated for a mental disorder provided the treatment is given by, or under the direction of, the responsible medical officer. Special restrictions apply to certain treatments. Psychosurgery and surgical implantation of hormones (for the reduction of male sex drive) require informed consent (except in emergencies). E.C.T. and the administration of drugs, for a continuous period of more than 3 months, require consent *or* a second medical opinion (except in emergencies).

Canada

10. Alberta
(Mental Health Act, R.S.A.
1980, Ss. 15, 19, 20)

Explicit power to impose treatment once the necessary certificates have been completed.

(continued)

Table 1.1. *(Continued)*

Canada (continued)

11. British Columbia (Mental Health Act, R.S.B.C. 1979, as am., Ss. 8, 25.2)	The director of a Provincial mental health facility "may sign consent to treatment forms" for an involuntary patient. "Treatment authorized by the director shall be deemed to be given with the consent of the [patient]."
12. Manitoba (Mental Health Act, R.S.M. 1965, as am., S. 4)	Treatment may be imposed where a patient is found to be "mentally disordered."
13. New Brunswick (Mental Health Act, R.S.N.B. 1973, as am., S. 4)	A prescribed medical certificate is "sufficient authority" for "assessment and treatment" of a "mentally disordered" patient.
14. Newfoundland (Mental Health Act, 1971, as am., Ss. 6, 7)	Explicit power to impose treatment where the appropriate certificate has been completed or renewed.
15. Nova Scotia (Hospitals Act, S.N.S. 1977, as am., Ss. 46, 43, 44, 50, 52)	No *competent* patient may be treated without his/her consent. If a patient is declared to be incompetent then it is necessary to obtain consent of guardian or (if no guardian exists) of spouse/next of kin. Where spouse or next of kin is not available or "*consent is unable to be obtained*" consent of public trustee is required. Every patient must be examined by a psychiatrist to determine the patient's "capacity to consent to treatment." Psychiatrist must consider the following factors, whether or not the patient being examined: "a) understands the condition for which the treatment is proposed; b) understands the nature and purpose of the treatment; c) understands the risks involved in undergoing the treatment; d) understands the risks involved in not undergoing the treatment; e) whether or not his ability to consent is affected by his condition." Provision is made for review of a declaration of competency (by a review board or the County Court). Restrictions are placed on the performance of psychosurgery. Requires the consent of the patient or, if patient is incompetent, of the guardian/spouse/next of kin/public trustee.
16. Ontario (Mental Health Act, R.S.O. 1980, Ss. 35, 1 (g), 35)	Psychiatric treatment shall not be given to a *competent* patient without his/her consent. If the patient is incompetent, the consent of the nearest relative is required. However, if a patient or a nearest relative (as the case requires) refuses consent or if there is no relative from whom consent may be requested, then the attending physician and two psychiatrists may apply to the Board of Review for an order authorizing treatment. "Mentally competent" means "having the ability to understand the subject matter in respect of which consent is requested and able to appreciate the consequences of giving or withholding consent." An involuntary patient or his/her nearest relative may not consent to psychosurgery.
17. Prince Edward Island (Mental Health Act, R.S.P.E.I. 1974, as am.)	No general, explicit power to impose treatment; such a power must be "implied."
18. Quebec (Mental Patient's Protection Act, R.S.Q. 1977, Divisions II and III)	The power to impose treatment is clearly implied, since the Act refers to the involuntarily committed patient as being in a state of "close treatment."
19. Saskatchewan (Mental Health Act, R.S.S. 1978, as am., S. 26)	The completion of the prescribed certificates by two physicians is "sufficient authority" for a "responsible officer" of a psychiatric institution to "administer such treatment as may be considered necessary."

tia and Ontario has there been a legislative attempt to accord a *competent*, but involuntarily committed, mental health patient a general right to refuse all forms of psychiatric treatment. The Nova Scotia Hospitals Act, R.S.N.S. 1967, c.249 (consld. 1979, c.H-19), boldly states that no competent patient may be treated without his or her consent (Sec. 46). However, the right to refuse treatment may be swiftly overturned if a psychiatrist determines that the patient is incompetent; if such a determination is made, then substitute consent must be obtained. However, the Act provides that if substitute consent is not forthcoming from the guardian, spouse, or next of kin, then the consent of the public trustee will suffice. The Act explicitly requires that every patient must be examined by a psychiatrist to determine the patient's "capacity to consent" (Sec. 43). Furthermore, the Act (Sec. 44) specifies the criteria that the psychiatrist should consider in reaching such a determination. Most of the criteria are conventional in that they relate to the patient's understanding of his or her condition, the nature and purpose of the proposed treatment, and the risks and benefits of being treated or not being treated, as the case may be. However, the last criterion, articulated in the Act, is extraordinarily vague: namely, "whether or not [the patient's] ability to consent is affected by his condition." It might well be argued that the inclusion of such a vacuous criterion effectively turns the issue of competence over to the exercise of unbridled professional discretion. In any event, the existence of this criterion sharply reduces the potential efficacy of the process of reviewing psychiatric determinations of incompetence (Sec. 50 of the Act provides for a review by the review board or the county court).

The approach, adopted by the Ontario Mental Health Act (R.S.O. 1980, c.262), is remarkable for the extent to which it manifests significant internal contradictions in relation to the right to refuse treatment issue. Section 35 provides that psychiatric treatment shall not be given to a competent patient without his or her consent. If the patient is incompetent, then the consent of the nearest relative is required. According to Section 1(g) of the Act, "mentally competent" means "having the ability to understand the subject matter in respect of which consent is requested and able to appreciate the consequences of giving or withholding consent." However, if a patient or the nearest relative (as the case may be) withholds consent to a proposed treatment or if there is no relative from whom consent may be obtained,

then the attending physician and two psychiatrists may apply to the board of review for an order authorizing treatment. The physician and psychiatrists must each examine the patient and be of the opinion

> that the mental condition of the patient will be or is likely to be substantially improved by the specific psychiatric treatment or the specific course of psychiatric treatment [and] that the mental condition of the patient will not or is not likely to improve without the specific treatment or course of treatment. (Sec. 35(5))

The astonishing effect of these provisions is that the board of review is empowered to authorize the compulsory treatment of mental health patients, who are "competent" within the meaning of Section 1(g) of the Act. Furthermore, the imposition of treatment upon a competent patient is not even limited to "emergency" situations. Clearly, what the Ontario legislature has granted with one hand, it has taken away with the other. Although all involuntary patients are accorded a general right to refuse treatment, such a right may be abrogated by a board of review (upon which psychiatrists are represented) even in situations where they are determined to be competent. In this respect, the Ontario Mental Health Act grants a considerably less efficacious right to refuse treatment than its counterpart in the province of Nova Scotia. Although the Ontario government has recently proclaimed Section 33(f) of the Act (which makes provision for an appeal from the board of review's discretion to the county or district court), it may justifiably be contended that the noble attempt to establish a right to refuse treatment is predestined to founder on the shoals of professional discretion.

Although Nova Scotia and Ontario are the sole Commonwealth jurisdictions in which an attempt has been made to enshrine a *general* right to refuse psychiatric treatment in mental health legislation, an increasing number of such jurisdictions have amended their legislation so as to require that the attending mental health professional obtain the patient's consent prior to the administration of specific treatments considered to be particularly hazardous or intrusive. These recent developments will be considered in the broader context of the emerging trend toward the regulation of a variety of aspects of such potentially hazardous or intrusive therapies.

A recent trial court decision in Quebec, *Institut*

Phillipe Pinel de Montreal v. Dion (1983), has perhaps sown the seed for future judicial intervention in this area. This case concerned the forcible treatment of a patient, who was held under a lieutenant governor's warrant after having been found unfit to stand trial. In this particular case, the court ruled that the patient, who was suffering from a psychosis, was incompetent to make treatment decisions, and therefore the court *substituted* its decision for that of the patient. As a consequence, the Institut Pinel was granted the authority to proceed with the appropriate "psychiatric treatment and therapy which the respondent's condition requires, under compulsion if necessary." Of particular note is the fact that the court took great pains to emphasize that such treatment was justified in terms of the accused's "best interests":

> The Court feels that the respondent's refusal to accept the recommended treatment condemns him to detention in perpetuity and the eventual loss of all contact with reality. The court does not believe that a man of healthy mind would do this voluntarily. (pp. 239–241)

The case is of potentially great significance because the court appeared to hold that a *competent* patient cannot be treated against his or her will. Furthermore, it is noteworthy that the court rejected the assertion that a psychiatric institution has the authority to force *any* patient, held under a lieutenant governor's warrant, to undergo psychiatric treatment. Indeed, Durand J. said:

> The court cannot grant this request not only because its decision here is based on an exceptional case, but also because the court believes that each similar case must be considered individually and that the medical decision to disregard the accused's refusal must be examined by the courts. (p. 242)

Significantly, the court also ruled that, in this case, the institution must establish a "special medical committee to review the respondent's case regularly." It remains to be seen whether the court's reasoning will be applicable in the context of involuntary civil commitment as well as in the criminal justice sphere. If so, the case could assume the proportions of a landmark decision in the area of the right to refuse treatment.

It will be recalled that the second principle, identified by Gostin as constituting a critical element in the emergence of the "new legalism," addresses the issue of imposing legal controls upon the administration of certain forms of mental health treatment. There has, indeed, been a significant trend toward adoption of this principle in recent Commonwealth mental health legislation. Without doubt, the most radical manifestation of this trend is the trail-blazing New South Wales Mental Health Act of 1983, recently enacted by that state's parliament. Indeed, the provisions relating to the control of a broad range of treatments are apparently unprecedented both within and outside the Commonwealth. Significantly, these provisions are applicable to both voluntary and involuntary patients.

The Act (part X, division 1) prohibits the performance of psychosurgery upon any involuntary patient unless it is "immediately necessary to prevent death" (Secs. 146(4)(i), 158, 159). Furthermore, psychosurgery may not be performed upon a voluntary patient without his or her informed consent and without the approval of a psychosurgery review board (and, in some cases, the Supreme Court). The Act specifies the requirements for informed consent in considerable detail (Sec. 146(3)). Similar restrictions have been imposed in relation to the administration of ECT (part X, division 2). This procedure cannot be imposed without informed consent except where it is "necessary immediately in order to save the life of a patient" (Sec. 172). Symbolic of the "legalistic" approach espoused by the Act is the requirement that a magistrate determine the validity of a patient's consent (Secs. 168–170). Equally significant is the requirement that at least two medical practitioners (one of whom is an anesthetist) must be present during the administration of ECT (Sec. 165). Such a provision represents a novel legislative exercise in the detailed regulation of psychiatric practice. The Act also provides for the administration of "prolonged deep sleep therapy" and "insulin coma therapy" (Sec. 180).

The New South Wales legislation treads new ground in establishing tentative controls over the most commonly prescribed treatment: namely, drug therapy (part X, division 4). However, the specific controls to be applied are primarily left to the discretion of the psychiatric profession itself. The Act prohibits the administration of doses, which are "excessive or inappropriate" with regard to "professional standards" (Sec. 181). Furthermore, it requires that the medical superintendent establish an internal peer review system within each hospital as a means of closely monitoring the progress of drug therapy (Sec. 182). In an innovative provision, the Act also prescribes that a mental health patient is entitled to detailed information concerning the particulars of his or her treatment with drugs (Sec. 183).

The "legalistic" thrust of the New South Wales Act is strikingly manifested in provisions that regulate the administration of drugs in the period preceding the magisterial hearing, which is an essential component of the civil commitment process in the state. The Act provides that the minimum medication consistent with proper care "be administered prior to the magisterial hearing so as to ensure adequate communication with the patient's representative (Sec. 81). Similarly, the Act states that a magistrate or Mental Health Review Tribunal must, in reviewing a patient's case, consider the impact of the level of medication upon the patient's ability to communicate (Secs. 90(2)(b), 95(2)(a), 169(5)(b)).

The England and Wales Mental Health Act of 1983 furnishes another example of the harnessing of the "new legalism" in relation to the control of specific forms of mental health treatment (see Carson, 1983, pp. 207–209; Gostin, 1983a, pp. 47–55, 1983c, pp. 58–61; Gunn, 1983, pp. 320–323). The Act provides that an involuntarily committed patient's consent is not necessary when he or she is being treated for a mental disorder, provided that the treatment is administered by (or under the direction of) "the responsible medical officer" (Sec. 63). However, the Act also provides for the regulation of two categories of treatment that may be regarded as particularly hazardous or intrusive. The first category of treatments (Sec. 57) requires *both* the informed consent of the patient *and* approval by an independent medical practitioner and two other persons (not doctors) who are appointed by the Mental Health Act Commission. To this point, there are two forms of treatment within this first category: psychosurgery and the "surgical implantation of hormones to reduce male sexual drive." The second category of treatments established by the England and Wales Act (Sec. 58) requires *either* the consent of the patient *or* the approval of an independent medical practitioner (appointed by the Mental Health Act Commission). At this stage, regulations have been passed so as to include two treatment modalities in this category: ECT and the *continued* "administration of medicine" to a patient for a period exceeding 3 months. The Act provides, however, that the restrictions imposed in relation to the two categories for mental health

treatments do not apply in situations of "emergency" (Sec. 62). Significantly, the applicable provision is fairly detailed in setting limits to the exercise of professional discretion in such "emergency" situations. It states that the normal restrictions do not apply to any treatment

(a) which is immediately necessary to save the patient's life; or
(b) which (not being irreversible) is immediately necessary to prevent a serious deterioration of his condition; or
(c) which (not being irreversible or hazardous) is immediately necessary to alleviate serious suffering by the patient; or
(d) which (not being irreversible or hazardous) is immediately necessary and represents the minimum interference necessary to prevent the patient from behaving violently or being a danger to himself or others. (Sec. 62)

Unfortunately, the statutory definitions of the terms "irreversible" and "hazardous" are unmistakably circular in nature: "Treatment is irreversible if it has unfavourable irreversible physical or psychological consequences and hazardous if it entails significant physical hazard" (Sec. 52(3)). It has been contended (Gunn, 1983) that the "emergency" provision leaves too much discretion in the hands of mental health professionals:

It would seem that the exceptions may have gone too far. In particular grounds (c) and (d) seem to allow considerable interference with the individual on grounds which are ill-defined and somewhat permissive. (p. 323)

Nevertheless, this provision is the most comprehensive of its type in the various Commonwealth jurisdictions surveyed in the present study.

A highly significant (and innovative) provision of the England and Wales Mental Health Act of 1983 (Sec. 118) places an obligation upon the Secretary of State for social services to prepare a detailed "Code of Practice" that would, *inter alia*, cover the issues of compulsory admission and treatment. It is envisaged that the independent Mental Health Act Commission will assume the responsibility of preparing this code, which will ultimately be presented to Parliament. No doubt, part of the Code will supplement the existing regulations by expanding the list of treatments, which fall into the two restrictive categories designated in the Act. The members of the Mental

Health Act Commission will be drawn from the ranks of various professions (medical, psychology, nursing, social work, and legal) as well as lay persons. It remains to be seen what form the proposed Code of Practice will ultimately assume. However, it clearly represents a significant advance in the slow march toward external regulation of the administration of potentially hazardous or intrusive therapies.

Despite the fairly dramatic nature of these new controls upon the administration of treatment in England and Wales, it is interesting that Gostin (1983c) has concluded that they represent only a first step toward entrenchment of the "new legalism":

> The consent to treatment provisions, on their face, appear to be a triumph of legalism, they are complex and require the doctor to proceed through a number of procedural obstacles prior to the administration of certain treatments. If closely examined, however, the consent provisions represent a return to legal formalism, but do not provide an effective safeguard for the unconsenting patient, except in respect of treatments requiring consent *and* a second opinion. The form of second opinion is medical with a duty only to consult other professionals. Professional self-regulation is always open to the criticism that it is not sufficiently open, rigorous and dispassionate. (pp. 60–61)

The comprehensiveness of the attempts to impose legal fetters upon the administration of psychiatric treatment in England and Wales and New South Wales is unparalleled in other Commonwealth jurisdictions. However, elsewhere in the Commonwealth, a few tentative steps have been taken in the same direction. In South Australia (Mental Health Act of 1976–1977), two special categories of treatment have been established and extraordinary requirements have been imposed in relation to them (Sec. 19). Category "A" presently covers psychosurgery and requires both the patient's consent (or, if incompetent, the consent of the guardian or nearest relative) and the authorization of the surgeon concerned as well

as two psychiatrists. Category "B" currently covers ECT and requires both the consent of the patient (or substitute consent if he is incompetent) and the authorization of only one psychiatrist. However, the Act contains a vaguely drafted clause that authorizes the imposition of ECT without consent when it is "urgently needed for the protection of the patient or of some other person" and it is "not practicable to obtain consent." Clearly, the somewhat nebulous terms of this emergency clause leaves a potentially broad scope to the discretion of mental health professionals. In the Northern Territory (Mental Health Act of 1979, Sec. 14), it has been provided that treatment may not be administered to an involuntary patient unless (a) it has been authorized by a magistrate; (b) there is an emergency; or (c) it is, in the opinion of the chief medical officer a "recognized standard medical treatment." The practical import of this provision is difficult to assess. However, it may safely be assumed that psychosurgery, for example, would require magisterial authorization as a "nonstandard" treatment. In the State of Victoria (Mental Health Act of 1959, as amended, Sec. 102 and regulation 702), psychosurgery may not be performed without the approval of an "authorized medical officer" (who is, in practice, an independent psychiatrist of the Victoria Health Commission). In Canada, the provinces of Nova Scotia and Ontario, which both have a general requirement of consent in relation to all forms of treatment, have imposed additional restrictions in relation to psychosurgery. The Nova Scotia provision (Hospitals Act, R.S.N.S. 1967, c.249, as amended, Sec. 52) is similar to that of South Australia insofar as it requires the authorization of the attending psychiatrist and two independent psychiatrists. However, the Nova Scotia statute also carves out a significant role for the review board in determining that there has been compliance with the various statutory requirements (including, of course, the requirement of consent). The Ontario approach (Mental Health Act, R.S.O. 1980, c.262, Sec. 35) is identical to that adopted by the New South Wales Parliament in that it proscribes the performance of psychosurgery upon any involuntarily committed patient.[8] However, it might be contended that the "tough" regulation

---

[8]In an action before the Supreme Court of Ontario, in November 1983, it was ruled that E.C.T. was not a form of psychosurgery. Therefore, E.C.T. could be imposed compulsorily upon a competent involuntary patient provided that the board of review issued the necessary approval: see *Re T and Board of Review for the Western Region et al.* (1983), 3 D.L.R. (4th) 442.

of psychosurgery in these provinces represents something of a symbolic sacrifice on the part of the psychiatric profession because in recent years so few operations of this type have been performed throughout Canada. Indeed, Earp (1979, p. 365) found that, in all the provinces (with the exception of Quebec, for which no statistics were available), only five such operations had been performed between January, 1975 and April, 1977.

The preceding review of developments in Commonwealth mental health legislation indicates that in the vast majority of jurisdictions, there is a tacit assumption that all involuntarily committed patients are incompetent to participate in the making of treatment decisions; as a consequence, not even a limited right to refuse treatment exists in such jurisdictions. Only in Nova Scotia and Ontario has such a right been enshrined. In Nova Scotia, however, the right is somewhat precarious given the possibility that it may be overturned by a psychiatric determination of incompetence. The right has been watered down further in Ontario, where the board of review is empowered to approve the forcible treatment even of competent mental health patients. Insofar as Gostin's "new legalism" embraces a general right to refuse treatment, it is clear that, in this respect, very little progress has yet been accomplished in the Commonwealth. On the other hand, at least in a limited number of jurisdictions, there has been considerable progress in relation to a second element of Gostin's "new legalism" — namely, the imposition of controls upon the administration of specific forms of mental health treatment. Indeed, the legislative developments in England and Wales and New South Wales represent an unprecedented invasion of a field whose decisions have traditionally been left to the unlimited discretion of the mental health professionals. Of particular significance is the attempt, in both jurisdictions, to regulate the administration of drug therapy. In each case, the mental health professions will no doubt exercise a dominant influence upon the particular regulations that will be developed. However, the establishment of a peer review system in

New South Wales and the creation of a code of practice in England and Wales should contribute significantly toward the gradual elimination of potential abuses in the treatment of mental health patients with psychotropic drugs. Elsewhere in the Commonwealth, the legislative developments that have been accomplished are considerably less ambitious in their nature and scope. In the few jurisdictions that have controlled such developments, attention has been focused exclusively on the more "dramatic" treatments of psychosurgery and ECT rather than on the more frequently employed treatment of drug therapy. The cautiousness of such legislative approaches may well reflect the continuing hegemony of the mental health professions in those jurisdictions. There is, of course, no doubt that such hegemony persists in the majority of Commonwealth jurisdictions, which have not yet imposed any restrictions whatsoever upon the administration of mental health treatments.

It is quite probable that, over the next few years, the most significant developments in this area will be fashioned in the courts.[9] This is particularly likely to be the case in Canada with the entrenchment of the Charter of Rights and Freedoms in 1982. No doubt, similar considerations will apply in Australia should the Commonwealth government proceed with its declared intention of entrenching a Bill of Rights. Under the Canadian Charter, there are a limited number of options that might be harnessed in a constitutional assault upon provincial mental health statutes. For example, section 7 protects the citizen's "right to life, liberty and security of the person" and the right "not to be deprived thereof except in accordance with the principles of fundamental justice" (see generally Garant, 1982). It could well be argued that, except in cases of genuine emergency, the "principle of fundamental justice" requires a formal determination that an involuntarily committed patient is incompetent before treatment may be administered without consent. Similarly, section 12, which establishes the "right not to be subjected to any cruel and unusual treatment or

---

[9]In the English case, *Freenan v. Home Office* (1983), 3 All E.R. 589 (Q.B.D.), a prisoner serving a life sentence brought an action, for trespass to the person, against the Home Office on the basis of his allegation that he had been administered psychotropic drugs without his consent. On the facts, the court found that the plaintiff had given his consent to the treatment and, therefore, the action failed. McCowan J. (p. 597) addressed the significant issue as to whether a doctor can obtain a "real" consent from a prison inmate: "The right approach, in my judgment, is to say that where, in a prison setting, a doctor has the power to influence a prisoner's situation and prospects a court must be alive to the risk that what may appear, on the face of it, to be a real consent is not in fact so. . . . Essentially, however, the matter is one of fact."

punishment," may be advanced as a means of preserving the right to refuse treatment — particularly in the context of the criminal justice system, where there is the possibility that the more aversive forms of behavioral therapy may be employed without the consent of the offender. Certainly, the (somewhat similarly worded) Eighth Amendment of the U.S. Constitution has been applied in such circumstances in the United States (*Knecht v. Gillman*, 1973; *Mackey v. Procunier*, 1973). However, the provision of the Canada Charter that is most likely to enshrine the right to refuse treatment in Canadian jurisprudence is section 15. This provision, which only came into effect in April 1985, protects the citizens from infringements of their "equality rights." Tarnopolsky (1982, p. 395) has contended that the "equality rights provisions" are the "most likely to be raised most frequently in litigation under the new Charter." Significantly, "mental disability" is a ground of discrimination that is expressly prohibited by section 15. It may well be asserted that the forcible treatment of a *competent* mental health patient (at least in the absence of a genuine emergency) represents a clear infringement of his or her "equality rights" because *competent* patients *outside* the mental health system are unequivocally protected from the administration of medical treatment without their consent. In effect, it could be argued that *competent* mental health patients are being discriminated against on the basis of their "mental disability." It remains to be seen whether such a contention will ultimately prove to be successful before the Canadian courts.

MENTAL HEALTH REVIEW TRIBUNALS

In this area, two issues are immediately relevant to our inquiry: (a) the establishment of new mental health tribunals and (b) the expansion of patients' legal rights in the case of those jurisdictions where tribunals have been in existence for some time. The latter development may have occurred as a consequence of legislative reform, the introduction of new regulations formulated pursuant to principal statutes, and/or judicial decisions. A third issue must also be considered: the extent to which, in practice, review tribunals demonstrate an informal policy of supporting professional dis-

cretion rather than upholding a form of "new legalism." As will be demonstrated, the lack of extensive empirical research into the activities of review tribunals makes this issue the most difficult to investigate.

Review tribunals are certainly not a recent innovation; however, they are not yet established throughout all Commonwealth jurisdictions. In several places, the vestiges of an "old legalism" are still evident; indeed, procedures for assessing the validity of involuntary commitment follow (at least in theory) a model reminiscent of the late 19th century. In New Zealand, for example, there are no mental health review tribunals. However, the Mental Health Act of 1969 provides for a central role on the part of magistrates. Following an involuntary commitment by physicians, a magistrate must hold an "examination" to assess the case. This procedure is also followed where there is an application for a "reception order," which is required for prolonged detention (Secs. 20, 21). Relevant persons may apply to the Minister of Health for a magistrate's inquiry (Sec. 73). The Act (Sec. 74) also provides for an "appeal" to a Supreme Court judge who may, if necessary, "examine" the relevant patient. Initial commitment, continued detention, and discharge are thus subject to *judicial* rather than *administrative* overview. A similar situation can be found in Scotland, where a sheriff's approval is required in the case of involuntary commitments (Mental Health (Scotland) Act of 1960, Secs. 28, 39, 44). The sheriff may hold an inquiry into any case and is also empowered to receive and hear appeals for discharge (Whitehead, 1982; Hoggett, 1976). Likewise, in the Northern Territory of Australia, the new Mental Health Act of 1979 (Secs. 7, 9) provides for a predetention inquiry by a magistrate in the case of involuntarily committed patients.[10]

A noteworthy feature of the Scottish legislation is the Mental Welfare Commission. Among other duties, this body has a protective role vis-à-vis patients and utilizes "official visitors" to fulfill its mandate in this regard (Whitehead, 1982). Official visitors perform a type of review function in that they are required to make themselves available to any patient who may wish to protest his or her commitment and detention. Indeed, in some jurisdictions, this is the main method of review available to patients. In the Australian state of Victoria, no tribunals or initial (and/or

---

[10]Section 34 of the Act also provides for an appeal to the Territory Supreme Court.

automatic) judicial review facilities are available and official visitors provide the only safeguard against abuses or mistakes (Mental Health Act of 1959, no.6605, Secs. 66, 95).[11] Official visitors may recommend discharge, but the final decision rests with the hospital superintendent. Official visitors' powers are thus quite limited, and this situation has attracted a considerable degree of criticism (Gardner et al., 1979; Myers et al., 1981). Similarly, in Western Australia, no tribunals or initial review facilities exist even though the new Mental Health Act of 1981, c.51) is a fairly recent enactment (O'Sullivan, 1981). Each hospital in the state has a "board of visitors" who may, subject to medical discretion, order the discharge of a patient. Patients (and their relatives) have a right to seek an interview with the board, which thereby serves a "review" function (Mental Health Act of 1981, Secs. 18, 54, 58). However, the board's powers are strictly limited, and the conduct of any "interview" is not governed by any requirement that the board adhere to judicially established rules of procedure or fairness.[12] In many respects, the concept of the "official visitor," which clearly has its roots in the Lunacy Act of 1890, can be equated with more recent attempts to introduce hospital ombudsmen. This issue will be discussed in the context of legal services for patients.

Before examining the situation in those jurisdictions, where review tribunals have been established, it is important to consider a "hybrid." In New South Wales, provision has been made for magisterial review of initial commitment, tribunal review of subsequent detention and discharge, and for an official visitor system (Mental Health Act of 1983, Secs. 22–27, 36–62, 88–93). Although the jurisdiction has recently experienced extensive legislative reform, the tripartite review *structure* is not a product of this change. The Mental Health Act of 1958 made provision for a magistrate's hearing prior to permanent detention in an institution, and, once committed, a patient could seek the aid of both a review tribunal and official visitors. Provision was also made for an appeal to the state's Supreme Court (Mental Health Act of 1958, Secs. 12, 18, 35). However, as O'Sullivan (1981) notes, both the hearings and the review process were sharply criticized, stimulating major reforms

to the Act. Although the tribunals had review powers, they had no "teeth." There were no effective rights for patients and the tribunal did not have the power to order the holding of an inquiry. Magisterial hearings were shown to be fully supportive of medical decision-making, did not allow for appeal, and offered minimal legal protections to patients.

The New South Wales Mental Health Act of 1983 (part III) has changed this situation by enhancing tribunal powers, requiring a higher standard of proof (each member must be "satisfied that it is very highly probable that the person is a mentally ill person") and providing for rights of legal representation and for mandatory, 6-month reviews of individual cases. However, hearings are to be conducted informally and the tribunal is not bound by the rules of evidence (New South Wales Mental Health Act of 1983, Sec. 43(2)). On the other hand, a patient has a "right" to appear in person (subject to the tribunal's discretion) and may be represented by a lawyer who may have access to relevant medical records (Secs. 50, 52). The magistrate's hearing has also been strengthened (New South Wales Mental Health Act of 1983, Part V). Detention following the hearing is limited to 3 months, more legal rights are granted to patients (e.g., a right to be represented by a lawyer and a right to an interpreter), patients may not be given medication that may obstruct the process of communication with their representative, and a higher standard of proof ("very highly probable") is required (Secs. 86–93). Thus, although reform has significantly affected the *content* of mental health legislation in the state, the hybrid *structure* (a mixture of initial judicial review, subsequent tribunal review, and the use of official visitors) remains. Events in New South Wales could prove to be useful in evaluating the suitability of the model for other jurisdictions, especially because the model seems to represent a trend toward a "new legalism."

Mental health tribunals (alternatively known as "panels" or "boards") are found in most jurisdictions and, in a number of countries, have recently undergone significant changes — some of which, at first blush, suggest the appearance of a "new legalism." In Australia, tribunals provide the principal

---

[11]Although section 99 of the Act provides for judicial discharge by a Judge of the Supreme Court, this is qualitatively different from the requirement in the New Zealand, Scottish, and Northern Territory statutes that *initial* commitment and continued detention be judicially reviewed in each and every case.

[12]As in the state of Victoria, an appeal against detention may be made to the Supreme Court of Western Australia (Sec. 73).

review mechanism in the states of Queensland, South Australia, and Tasmania.[13] In Canada, review tribunals exist in all the provinces, with the exception of Manitoba, and have been in place for more than 10 years.[14] In England and Wales, mental health review tribunals have been in place since 1959 and, as several writers have noted, the England and Wales Mental Health Act of 1983 expands both the powers of the tribunals and the rights of patients in certain areas (Gunn, 1983; Gostin, 1982a, 1983a; Carson, 1983). The establishment of tribunals and the expansion of powers and rights (through either statutory reform or the introduction of new regulations or rules pertaining to the conduct of tribunals) would seem to suggest an increased desire to control professional discretion. However, on closer examination, some doubts can be raised regarding the extent to which legislation and regulations actually achieve this particular goal.

In a review of the Canadian situation, Gordon (1981a) has shown that the functions, duties, and powers of review tribunals vary considerably.[15] In some jurisdictions, tribunals are concerned only with providing hearings to review patients' cases at specified periods during their involuntary detention. Furthermore, such hearings are provided only if a patient or other party makes an application for review.[16] In other jurisdictions, tribunals have a broader mandate and may review cases automatically. In Nova Scotia (Hospitals Act, R.S.N.S. 1967, c.249; consld. 1979 c.H-19), for example, the tribunal deals with a diverse range of issues affecting patients. It is concerned not only with commitment and continued detention but also with declarations of capacity and competency, determining the appropriateness of psychosurgery, making recommendations in respect of general treatment or care, and "advis-

ing" in relation to the type of treatment that is in the "best interests" of a specific patient. It is obliged to review cases at set periods. Review tribunals in other provinces have a similar (although less extensive) mandate, but only the Ontario legislation (Mental Health Act, R.S.O. 1980, c.262, Secs. 30–35, 43) approximates the Nova Scotia model insofar as the wide scope of tribunal functions and powers is concerned. Commitment, continued detention, and competency matters each fall within the Ontario tribunal's mandate; however, it also considers applications from psychiatrists for the forcible administration of treatment to involuntary patients.[17]

O'Sullivan's (1981) depiction of the Australian situation presents a different image from that presented in Canada; his analysis suggests that tribunal functions are considerably more restricted in scope. In Queensland, for example, tribunals are principally concerned with commitment and detention matters, although they may also make recommendations regarding a patient's "welfare." In Tasmania, the tribunal's powers are also somewhat limited although it does have an additional responsibility in the context of reviewing guardianship orders. The South Australian tribunal — a product of recent legislative reform — is equally limited in its powers, being concerned only with reviewing the cases of those who are compulsorily detained in hospitals and those "protected persons" who are placed in the custody of another person by the state's "guardianship board" (Mental Health Act of 1976–1977, Sec. 35).[18] Thus, in comparison with the Canadian provinces, there is a greater degree of consistency between the legislative provisions establishing review tribunals in the various Australian states. Significantly, such consistency includes a more limited role for the Australian tribunals.

---

[13]Mental Health Act of 1974 (Queensland), sections 14–15; Mental Health Act of 1976–1977 (South Australia), sections 29–39; Mental Health Act of 1963 (Tasmania), sections 43, 76–78.

[14]The absence of review tribunals in Manitoba was sharply criticized in a Manitoba Law Reform Commission report (1979). This report was influential in subsequent legislative reform via the Mental Health Act, S.M. 1980, c.62 which, *inter alia*, established a provincial mental health review board. Prior to this change, review was only possible via a number of (strongly criticized) judicial methods. See, e.g., Katz and Larsen (1975).

[15]The author argues, *inter alia*, that psychiatric perceptions of patients' needs have dominated both legislative reform and the practices of review tribunals even though attempts have been made to expand and reinforce patients' rights in accordance with the perceptions of need, articulated by patients and their advocates.

[16]See, e.g., Mental Health Act, R.S.B.C. 1979, c.256, section 21 (British Columbia); Mental Health Act, S.N. 1971, no. 80, section 17 (Newfoundland).

[17]The tribunals in New Brunswick, Prince Edward Island, Alberta, and Saskatchewan are concerned with issues relating to declarations of incompetency as well as commitment and detention. In the province of Quebec, the equivalent of a review tribunal is provided through the Mental Patients' Protection Division of the provincial Social Affairs Commission.

[18]The tribunal acts as an appeal facility for those wishing to challenge any order of the Guardianship Board (Section 37).

Although an explication of the functions, duties, and powers of tribunals is important in assessing the extent to which professional discretion may be subject to restriction, an evaluation of the rights of patients in relation to tribunals is more revealing. First, however, it is important to note that, generally, an expansion in the use of tribunals can be interpreted as a recognition of the need to increase the degree of control over professional discretion but without recourse to a full legal model. As essentially specialized, *administrative* bodies, tribunals are intended to resolve conflicts without the need to turn to traditional legal mechanisms and as such constitute informal, essentially *nonlegal* alternatives. In this respect, any further creation of tribunals or any expansion in the functions, duties, and powers of existing tribunals may be considered to be indicative of a trend toward *less* rather than *more* legalism (at least in the formal sense).

In this regard, it is interesting to consider briefly the change wrought by the England and Wales Mental Health Act of 1983, this statute being the declared epitome of "new legalism." In the specific context of review procedures, two important changes have been recognized: (a) the creation of the Mental Health Act Commission, and, (b) an enhanced role for existing Mental Health Review Tribunals (Gunn, 1982; Gostin, 1982a, 1983a, 1983b, 1983c). In the first case, the goal appears to be the provision of an umbrella organization charged with the task of providing certain safeguards for detained patients. The commission's specific functions include the investigation of complaints, the review of treatment decisions, the review of decisions to withhold patients' mail, and visiting and interviewing patients. As such, it appears to be an administrative body designed to deal, informally, with a wide range of possible areas of conflict and to this end employs "official visitors." As noted earlier, this is a familiar approach in other Commonwealth jurisdictions that has its roots in the Lunacy Act of 1890 and can be aligned with the "ombudsman" concept. In the second case, an enhanced role for tribunals (Gunn, 1983) points to five major changes. These are as follows: (a) an increase in the number of persons eligible to apply for case review (i.e., those admitted for "assessment," and those detained as "restricted patients"); (b) an increase in the numbers of applications for review that can be made by a patient; (c) the creation of an automatic review process under certain circumstances; (d) an increase in the powers of tribunals, especially in the context of patient discharge (tribunals will be compelled to discharge certain categories of patients if they are not "treatable"); and, (e) an extension of legal aid to cover representation of patients appearing before tribunals. The last development occurred as a consequence of "promised" changes to the regulations created pursuant to the Legal Aid Act of 1974 rather than any new provisions in the England and Wales Mental Health Act of 1983. However, as Gostin (1982a) notes, the Mental Health Review Tribunal Rules will be amended to provide for "assistance by way of representation," subject to a test of "reasonableness."

In light of this, it could be argued that the only change reflecting a "new legalism" is the last one in the previous list. The others merely indicate an expansion of *nonlegal* review mechanisms that will benefit a larger group of patients. If the "new legalism" is to be measured solely by the number of lawyers or advocates involved (or likely to become involved) in the mental health context, then it might well be contended that the recent changes represent a significant increase in the range of legal controls imposed upon the exercise of professional discretion. This cannot, however, be the sole ground for making such an assessment. Certainly, more lawyers will mean a greater degree of representation and the potential for more adversarial hearings. Yet in the absence of a full range of legal rights, enshrined in either the applicable mental health legislation or associated regulations and rules, the mere availability of representation will not be sufficient to sustain the idea that professional discretion has been significantly eroded by legal controls. This point can be further strengthened by an examination of the situation in Commonwealth jurisdictions where tribunal applicants *are* apparently granted a range of important, legal "rights" either by legislation or by regulations and rules.[19]

The conduct of mental health review tribunals

---

[19]In this regard, it is important to note that while legislation is the only forum where legal rights may be formally enshrined, regulations and rules made pursuant to a statute are nevertheless of considerable practical importance. While the latter may not establish statutory rights, they do have the effect of law for all practical purposes. However, they may be amended or removed by executive fiat rather than legislative reform and are thus both easy to remove and easy to expand.

in England and Wales is governed by the Mental Health Review Tribunal Rules (1960, S.I. No.1139). These provide, *inter alia*, for review by "informal determination" and "formal hearing." In the latter case, a number of "legal" entitlements exist, notably, notice of the hearing, appearance at the hearing, opportunity to address the tribunal, give evidence and call witnesses, have the benefit of a representative, and have reasonable access to relevant information necessary to present a case. The same entitlements are granted to those who might seek to oppose the application of release. Broadly speaking, these rules appear to establish a set of legal "rights," although the exercise of some of these rights is left to the discretion of the tribunal. It is important to note that the rules were made in 1960, pursuant to the Mental Health Act of 1959, a statute which is considered a model of professional discretion. The rules' current existence cannot, therefore, be said to reflect the emergence of a "new legalism" although recent changes involving easier access to effective representation may result in an increased use of tribunals and thus a more extensive articulation and examination of the rules by patient advocates. In turn, this may result in changes to the rules where they are found to be in conflict with the fundamental rules of natural justice. As Gunn (1983) notes, regardless of the presence of legal representation, changes in the scope of tribunals will, it is estimated, lead to a fivefold increase in their use. This factor alone can be expected to have an impact on tribunal rules and tribunal behavior. Whether it will lead to a greater or lesser degree of "legalism" is in the realm of speculation. However, it will certainly mean an increased pressure on the tribunals, which may encourage greater informality in the interests of rapid case processing, rather than a preference for lengthy "quasi-legal" proceedings.

Gordon's (1981a) analysis of review tribunals in Canada sought to determine the extent to which patients were accorded a full range of legal rights. He found that although patients have been granted a statutory right to *seek* review in all the provinces, limitations have been placed on the rights that a patient may enjoy once an appeal is placed before a tribunal. The right to *apply* for a hearing is not necessarily accompanied by a right to an actual hearing, and even where a hearing is to proceed, the conduct of the inquiry may be affected by the absence of rights found in conventional, judicial settings. In most provinces, the patient has a right to be present at a hearing unless the tribunal considers that it is not in his or her

"best interests," in which case the patient *may* have a right to be represented. Similarly, legislation in some jurisdictions specifies a right to examine and cross-examine witnesses and make submissions to the tribunal. Such rights are not, however, to be found in all provinces, nor is there any consistent relationship between the right to apply for review, the right to receive a hearing, the right to be present and/or be represented, and the right to test or present evidence before a tribunal. Furthermore, in most provinces there is no established right to appeal the decision of a tribunal to a court.

A brief comparative analysis of the situation in two provinces illustrates this somewhat complex situation. In the province of British Columbia, the Mental Health Act (R.S.B.C. 1979, c.256, Secs. 21, 27) and Regulations (1980, div. 8) grant patients the following rights: to apply for review (at specified times), to receive a tribunal (review panel) hearing, to attend the hearing, to be represented, to make submissions, and to call witnesses. As an alternative, a patient may apply to the provincial Supreme Court for an order prohibiting admission or requiring discharge. Under these circumstances, a full judicial review of the case may occur and the provisions constitute an appeal mechanism vis-à-vis tribunal decisions. The enabling legislation was first proclaimed in 1974 and the Regulations approved and ordered in 1980. The developments have thus occurred over the past 10 years and seem supportive of the idea that the influence of "legalism" is increasing. The pattern of "rights" is consistent even though the "right" to cross-examine witnesses is not granted to the patient (this is invested in the panel alone) and the patient is not allowed access to relevant information (this is also accessible only to the panel, one member of which may be a "representative" of the patient). A patient does, however, have a right to be informed, in writing, of his or her right to review. In British Columbia, the situation is thus close to one where full, conventional legal rights are granted.

This may be compared with the situation in the neighboring province of Alberta, a jurisdiction where considerable reform has been occurring in the mental health law context over the past 15 years (Greenland, 1973; Hellon, 1973; Marshall, 1973; Rhodes-Chalke, 1973). The new Mental Health Act (R.S.A. 1980, c.M-13, Secs. 7–10, 25–29, 32), originally proclaimed in 1972, grants patients the right to review but no corresponding right to a tribunal hearing; this is left to the discretion of the panel. The patient has a right to be present if a hearing is conducted, but this is subject to the panel's discretion. If excluded, the patient must be appointed a representative. Although the patient (or his or her representative) has a right to cross-examine witnesses, there is no corresponding right to make a submission or call witnesses (although the panel may "invite" the applicant to do so). The decision of the tribunal may be appealed to the provincial Court of Queen's Bench, whereupon there shall be a re-hearing of the case in a conventional judicial setting. However, unlike the situation in British Columbia, a patient is not granted the option of a judicial, rather than a tribunal, hearing in the first instance. As will be evident, the situation in Alberta is significantly different despite the introduction of extensive reforms, apparently designed to constrain professional discretion.

As Gordon (1981a) argues, patients' rights, in relation to tribunal decisions concerning commitment and continued detention, are in a confused and inconsistent state across Canada. He contends that an explanation lies in the relative strengths of the psychiatric and patient-group lobbies in each province. However, he also suggests that the continuing dominance of psychiatric perceptions of the needs of patient as well as localized implementation problems (e.g., the costs) may be significant factors. This argument is partly supported by developments in Ontario, where the relatively recent passage of the Mental Health Amendment Act (S.O. 1978, c.50, consld. in Mental Health Act R.S.O. 1980, c.262) was generally heralded as an advance in the protection of patients' rights. From the patients' perspective, a number of gains were made, including reforms to the review process such as the introduction of automatic reviews and a shorter eligibility period before review could be initiated. In this province, patients have a right to review but no right to a tribunal hearing. Attendance is subject to tribunal discretion but, where a patient is excluded, he or she may be represented. An applicant (or his or her representative) may call witnesses and make submissions, but cross-examination is subject to the permission of the chairman (Secs. 30–33). The Mental Health Amendment Act introduced other important provisions. These include the following: a requirement that, upon involuntary admission or further detention, a notice be sent to the local director of the provincial legal aid scheme so that the legal needs of the patient could be canvassed; a limited right of access to relevant information; and a right of appeal, from a review board's decision, to the

county or district court (Secs. 66(30a), 67(33d, 33f)). These, however, were *not* proclaimed immediately and remained "dormant," in part VI of the statute, until the Ontario government finally proclaimed them in March 1984. In seeking the reasons why these provisions remained "in limbo" for more than 5 years, Gordon (1981b) identified two significant factors: (a) the projected increase in expenditure as a consequence of both an increased use of the legal aid scheme and the courts; and (b) the concerns of psychiatrists that the requirement that a legal aid office be advised of an involuntary commitment would involve a breach of patient–physician confidentiality and that allowing patients open access to their files would jeopardize treatment.

O'Sullivan's (1981) review of the legal rights granted to patients applying to Australian review tribunals is also illuminating. In Queensland, patients have a right to apply for review, but it is left to the discretion of the tribunal whether or not a formal hearing will take place. Legal representation is also left to the discretion of the tribunal, and the patient does not have a right to make submissions, present evidence, or cross-examine witnesses. There is no right of appeal to a judicial body, save that the director of a facility may appeal an order to discharge a patient (Mental Health Act of 1974, Secs. 14–15; Mental Health Act Regulations of 1974, regs. 43–50). Although Tasmania has a review tribunal, O'Sullivan's (1981) analysis would suggest that no legal rights of any sort are enshrined in legislation. The situation in South Australia, however, is somewhat more satisfactory. The Mental Health Act of 1976–1977 establishes a review tribunal with a duty to review cases automatically (at specified periods) and provides a right for patients to apply for and receive a hearing. However, the conduct of any hearing is left to the discretion of the tribunal; consequently, full legal rights are not enshrined in the legislation. On the other hand, the Act specifically provides for a patient to be represented by counsel and representation may be supplied by the state's legal aid scheme. The statute also provides for an appeal to the state's Supreme Court against any decision or order of the tribunal (Secs. 29–39). As is the case in Canada, the legal rights of patients appearing before Australian review tribunals appear to be inconsistent and certainly do not reflect a "new legalism." If South Australia and New South Wales can be taken as barometers of reform, then the trend is only toward more lawyers rather than more legal rights. It remains to be seen whether this will constitute an effective challenge to professional discretion.

Although the various statutory and regulatory provisions governing the procedures of Commonwealth review tribunals would seem to be less than helpful to patients and their advocates, it is important to consider developments in the area of administrative law as these tend to act as a counter-balance to the statutory situation. As Gostin and Rassaby (1980) have noted, where they can be said to be acting "judicially" (rather than "administratively"), tribunals of many types are obliged to observe the rules of natural justice. Furthermore, recent developments in jurisprudence have resulted in the emergence of a new legal doctrine — the "duty to act fairly." Significantly, this duty is not limited to situations in which a tribunal or board is acting in a judicial or "quasi-judicial" manner. The history of this duty, beginning with Lord Parker's dictum in *Re K(H) (an infant)*, [1967] 1 All E.R. 226, p. 231, cannot be fully explicated here. Suffice it to note that its impact has been substantial and widespread; in England, for example, in the course of its development, the dictum has been applied to the conduct of bodies resolving disputes, carrying out investigations, and providing "advice" in areas as diverse as soccer, greyhound racing, taxi licensing, gaming, company affairs, and income tax.[20] Its main effect has been to require that, even where a body exercises functions that are not "analytically judicial" but are, instead "administrative," it is still under a duty to observe the rudiments of natural justice; in short, it must act "fairly" (Evans, 1973; Gostin and Rassaby, 1980). However, the requirements of "fairness" have yet to be clearly specified. Lord Denning (*Selvarajan v. Race Relations Board*, 1976, p. 19) has laid down a fundamental rule: "If a person may be subjected to pains or penalties, or be exposed to prosecution or proceedings, or deprived of remedies or redress or in some way adversely affected by the investigations and report (of a body), then he should be told the case against him and be offered a fair opportunity of answering it." However, this does not mean that formal, legal rules of procedure are imposed on a tribunal. It has been held (*Fraser v. Mudge*, 1975, 78), for example, that the duty to act fairly does not include a right to be represented even though such a right would seem to be conducive to granting an affected party a "fair opportunity" of answering a case (particularly where disadvantaged subjects are concerned).

Despite its apparent relevance to the mental health context, there has been surprisingly little application in England of this duty of fairness to the conduct of mental health review tribunals. To begin with, as Gostin and Rassaby (1980) point out, there are no cases "in which a court has considered whether a (tribunal) is under a duty to act *judicially*. But there are strong grounds for saying that a tribunal hearing the case of a patient detained (involuntarily or under a hospital order) is under such a duty" (p. 93). This line of argument, however, has not been favorably received by the one court that has considered a case presented by MIND concerning a "restricted" patient and the conduct of the so-called "Aarvold Board."[21]

It must be noted that other developments in the England and Wales context have a bearing on the issue of the procedural fairness of review tribunals. Britain's ratification of the European Convention of Human Rights has meant that a new arena for legal activity has arisen, and MIND has not been slow in using the Convention to pursue mental health law issues (Gostin, 1982b; Muchlinski, 1980). As Gostin (1982b) reports, the passage of the Mental Health (Amendment) Act of 1982 was spurred by the results of some of the MIND cases, and in 1982, two matters that were concerned with review tribunal practices and procedures were pending before the commission. *Barclay-Maguire v. United Kingdom* (1980) is concerned with the issue of the speed with which review tribunals will come to hear a case and *Collins v. United Kingdom* (1982) focuses on "the right to publicly funded representation and pro-

---

[20]See e.g., *Enderby Town Football Club Ltd. v. The Football Association Ltd.* (1968), 2 All E.R. 545; *In re Liverpool Taxi Owner's Association* (1972), 2 All E.R. 589; *R. v. Gaming Board for Great Britain, ex parte Benaim* (1970), 2 All E.R. 528; *In re Pergamon Press Ltd* (1970), All E.R. 535; *Wiseman v. Borneman* (1971), A.C. 297.

[21]*R. v. Secretary of State for Home Department, ex parte Powell*, unreported, Q.B. Div. Crt. 21 Dec. 1978. The Aarvold Board (the Advisory Board on Restricted Patients) was an extrastatutory body established to *advise* the home secretary regarding the release of "restricted patients." In *theory* it had no *decision-making* powers. In *Powell's* case, the court held that the board had a purely advisory function and was not obliged to comply with the rules of natural justice. See Gostin and Rassaby (1981) for a discussion of the case and the functions of the board.

cedural fairness" (Gostin, 1982b, p. 792). As regards the issue of procedural fairness, the claim is made that the practices of (a) withholding relevant reports, (b) excluding an applicant during the presentation of hospital "evidence," and (c) failing to give detailed reasons for a decision against discharge are contrary to the protections afforded by article 5(4) of the Convention (the entitlement to a review of arrest or detention). As Gostin (1982b) notes, the impact of these cases may be somewhat softened as ameliorative action seems already to have been undertaken through the recent revisions to the Mental Health Review Tribunal Rules but, in any case, they may result in the European court examining and specifying the standards of procedure applicable to bodies such as review tribunals. They thus have a direct bearing on the issue of the duty to act fairly.

Generally, the "duty to act fairly" has been endorsed in other Commonwealth jurisdictions (Taylor 1973, 1974). In Australia, natural justice issues have arisen in the context of Administrative Appeals Tribunals and similar bodies,[22] but as the conduct of these bodies appears to be governed more closely by legislation setting out "fair" rules of conduct than is the case in England,[23] the "duty" has not attracted substantial judicial attention. Certainly, the "duty" has been considered, in passing, by several courts,[24] but no reported cases can be found where it has been applied to the conduct of mental health review tribunals. This is not surprising, given the limited number of states with such tribunals and the lack of active organizations concerned specifically with mental health law issues.

The Canadian situation presents a sharp contrast. In the mental health context, in particular, the duty to act fairly has played an important part in delineating the procedures to be followed by the Lieutenant Governors' Advisory Review Boards, which have been established in each province in order to review the cases of those mentally disordered offenders who are held in institutions under the lieutenant governors' warrants.[25] In in re Abel et al. v. Penetanguishene Mental Health Centre (1979), the Ontario Divisional Court ruled that although the review boards had a purely advisory function, they were nevertheless under a duty to act fairly. This case marked the collapse of any distinction between the role of boards as judicial/quasi-judicial bodies and their role as administrative tribunals; the critical issue is that the boards are, in effect, considered as "decision-makers" regardless of the fact that they are limited to an advisory function vis-à-vis the lieutenant governor. The Ontario Court of Appeal subsequently affirmed the divisional court's ruling.

The Abel decision has been reinforced by parallel and subsequent judgments. In Martineau v. Matsqui Institution Disciplinary Board (1979), the Supreme Court of Canada ruled that a prison disciplinary board has a duty to act fairly even if it is "classified" as an administrative tribunal. This has been extended to cover other "administrative" bodies,[26] and was followed in in re Abel et al. and Advisory Review Board (1980), where the Ontario Court of Appeal stressed not only that boards had a duty to act fairly, but also seemed to extend this duty to encompass the disclosure of relevant information to an appellant's lawyer. This has been recently confirmed in in re Egglestone and Mousseau and Advisory Review Board (1983). The Court ruled that although a patient's lawyer may have access to information, a patient may not see records or files without the tribunal's consent. The case also established that where a tribunal heard the findings of the psychiatric members of the board in the absence of patients, and refused to allow those patients (or their representatives) to be present to question the findings, the tribunal was in breach of its duty to act fairly.

Although far from being specifically stated by

---

[22]See, e.g., Ceskovic v. Minister for Immigration and Ethnic Affairs, 27 A.L.R. 423 (F.C.A.); Sobey v. Commercial and Private Agents Board (1979), 22 S.A.S.R. 70 (S.C.S.A.); Cain v. Jenkins, 28 A.L.R. 219; Hook v. Registrar of Liquor Licences, 35 A.C.T.R. 1.

[23]See, e.g., Administrative Appeals Tribunal Act of 1975 (Cth).

[24]See, e.g., Haj-Ismail (H and M) v. Minister for Immigration and Ethnic Affairs, 36 A.L.R. 516 (F.C.A.).

[25]The Criminal Code does not require that such boards be established pursuant to the code in each province. Where boards are not established under the code, they are not required to follow the prescribed procedures for review. In some provinces (e.g., Ontario), the boards are established under the provincial Mental Health Act. In others (e.g., British Columbia) they are purely ad hoc, administrative committees with no statutory basis. This inconsistency makes an application of the duty an important development vis-à-vis the protection of patient's rights in the criminal law context. See, e.g., Haines (1978); Savage (1981); Schiffer (1982).

[26]Nicholson v. Haldimand – Norfolk Regional Board of Commissioners of Police (1979), 1 S.C.R. 311 (S.C.C.); A.G.: Canada v. Inuit Tapirisat of Canada et al. (1980), 115 D.L.R. (30) 1 (S.C.C.).

the courts, it is becoming increasingly apparent that "acting fairly" means extending an increasing number of conventional legal rights and court procedures to all tribunals and similar bodies. In *in re Brown and Waterloo Regional Board of Commissioners of Police et al.* (1979), a tribunal was held not to be acting fairly when it did not offer an individual a proper hearing, did not give him a statement of the allegations against him, and did not give him a chance to hear the evidence against him, cross-examine witnesses, call his own evidence, or be represented by counsel. In *in re Morgan and Association of Ontario Land Surveyors* (1980), it was held that an individual was entitled to an adjournment of a hearing in order to instruct counsel and prepare a case, especially when given only short notice of a hearing. In *Fry et al. v. Doucette et al.* (1980), it was held that the duty to act fairly encompassed the process of allowing a person to make representations regarding the final disposition. In general, this situation bodes well for the future conduct of review boards in both the criminal and civil contexts. In the case of tribunals dealing with civil commitments, it is clear that such bodies must be considered decision-makers. Although there are, as yet, no reported cases regarding the conduct of these tribunals, it is possible to argue that, if a challenge is mounted, the courts will recognize that they have a duty to act fairly. This may serve to crystallize the issue of patients' rights before Canadian tribunals, where provincial statutes and regulations are ambiguous or inconsistent. The precedents may also be applied in other Commonwealth jurisdictions.

The extent to which Canadian courts seem willing to interpret and apply the duty as an important protective device can be gleaned from recent developments in the criminal law context in British Columbia. In *in re McCann and The Queen* (1982), the British Columbia Court of Appeal held that even though the patient's review board was merely an *ad hoc* committee appointed by the attorney-general to assist him in giving advice to the lieutenant governor, it performed a function analogous to a review board, established under the Criminal Code and was required to observe procedural fairness. The court held that in any situation where the lieutenant governor expresses "his pleasure" on the basis of recommendations

from a board, such recommendations must be reached upon the basis of procedural fairness. In delivering the judgment of the court, Hinkson J.A. stated that it is an accepted common law principle that "a public body or tribunal exercising quasi-judicial or administrative powers or functions that may subject an individual to pains or penalties or in some way adversely affect an individual, is required at least to comply with a duty to act fairly in a procedural sense by telling the party who may be adversely affected the case against him and affording him a fair opportunity of answering it" (*in re McCann*, p. 184). However, this is not etched in stone. Hinkson J. A. was quick to point out that this general principle may always be limited by a statute or regulation germane to the case. [27]

In considering the extent to which statutes and regulations in the various Commonwealth jurisdictions can be said to reflect the emergence of a "new legalism," it is important to take into account developments in administrative law. Although the statutes and regulations per se do not, on the whole, support Gostin's (1983b, 1983c) thesis, the steady growth and application of a "duty to act fairly," with its associated emphasis on introducing conventional legal rights and procedures, would seem to represent a significant trend toward judicial espousal of the new legalism. However, in the mental health context, the "duty" would seem to be at its most refined state only in Canada. Further, it is presently being applied only in the criminal justice context. There do not appear to be any reported cases, in any Commonwealth jurisdiction, where the "duty" has been applied in order to establish standards of procedure for mental health review tribunals exercising their *civil* jurisdiction.

The discussion of the duty to act fairly, with its emphasis on the *actual* procedures adopted and applied by review tribunals, highlights the importance of a third and final issue: namely, the extent to which, in practice, review tribunals follow an informal policy of supporting professional discretion rather than a "new legalism." Although the very existence of the various reported cases discussed above might seem sufficient evidence that some tribunals prefer routinely to follow the advice or recommendations of mental health professionals and, consequently, to eschew the

---

[27]Per Estey J. in *A.G.: Canada v. Inuit Tapirisat of Canada et al.* (1980), 115 D.L.R. (3d) 1 (S.C.C.). For a general review of developments, see Loughlin (1978); Mullan (1975).

canons of procedural fairness, it is perhaps more important to consider the findings of the limited research that has been conducted in the area by social scientists.

The conduct of review tribunals in England and Wales has attracted the interest of several researchers but, as Peay (1981) notes, much of this work has been undertaken by individuals associated with the system rather than by independent social scientists. Of particular merit, however, are (a) Fennell's (1977) history of the tribunal system and critique of the "commonsense," rather than strictly legal, factors that influence tribunal decisions; and (b) Greenland's (1970) extensive analysis of tribunal hearings, his consequent discovery of the marked variability in tribunal decisions between regions, and his finding that legal representation had a marked effect on case outcome by increasing the chances of discharge. The contributions of Cavenagh and Newton (1970, 1971), Cooke (1969), Fleming (1963), Freer (1966), Gostin (1977), Gostin and Rassaby (1980), and Wood (1970) all raise questions about tribunal practices, recruitment procedures and, *inter alia*, the relative efficacy of the lay, compared with the professional, membership. Although all this material is important and raises serious doubts about the practices of the tribunals, Peay's (1981) work is, to date, the most refined, rigorous, and critical contribution to knowledge in this area.

Building upon Fennell's critique, Peay (1981) studied "the factors that influence both the interpretation and application of mental health legislation by tribunal members and the manner in which these individual approaches are qualified by the process of decision-making in a group context" (p. 162). A tripartite method was employed, involving a self-report questionnaire administered to all tribunal members, a statistical analysis of tribunal decisions between 1974–1978, and an experimental study of decision-making in which a videotaped case was used. Following data analysis, Peay concluded that there were significant differences between individual (or lay) members and member groups (legal and medical members) in such areas as their conceptualization of the tribunal's role, their knowledge of the legal criteria relevant to decision-making, and their attitudes toward discharge. For example, discharge rates varied significantly between tribunals and regions and "some individuals (e.g., those with extreme approaches) and some member groups (e.g., legal and medical members) are significantly more likely to influence the outcome of group decisions" (p. 182). In addition, Peay found that communication levels between tribunal members are not sufficient to challenge individual views and that individual decisions are formulated at an early stage in a hearing, regardless of subsequent evidence. As a consequence, Peay rejects the "consensus" model of tribunal decision-making and suggests that the tribunals may be acting arbitrarily. The problem lies, it appears, in the structure of the tribunal system; consequently, "any changes in either the legal criteria or procedural basis for tribunal decisions are unlikely to be either implemented or operated in the intended manner unless further account is taken of the decision-making processes of those individuals who apply the law" (p. 183). Legal reform clearly has its limits in the absence of significant changes vis-à-vis the members of tribunals. In this regard, Peay argues for better training, the strengthening of the "lay" element in decision-making, and procedural changes to offset the bias in favor of detention rather than discharge (e.g., prehearing access to the applicant's argument for discharge).

There can be no doubt that Peay's (1981) research raises serious questions about the procedural fairness of review tribunals in England and Wales. Unfortunately, there is little research available to confirm the suspicion that the same problems exist in other Commonwealth jurisdictions. However, some evidence can be advanced in support of the hypothesis. First, where review tribunals have been established, their composition is basically the same as that in the England and Wales model. In most cases, tribunal membership is composed of one or more medical members, one or more legal members, and one or more lay members (Gordon, 1981a; O'Sullivan, 1981). Thus, on the basis of their composition alone, Peay's observations about the subordinate role of the lay membership could have a wider applicability. This is underscored by evidence presented to the Ontario Standing Social Development Committee in the course of their review of the province's Mental Health Act prior to the 1978 reforms. A legal worker, who had acted as a patients' representative in the presence of tribunals, pointed out the routine imbalance in membership input. Although the tribunals were composed of a clergyman, a psychiatrist, a legal practitioner, and a lay person, the psychiatrist was perceived to dominate the proceedings completely (Gordon, 1981a).

Even where more formal legal review procedures are established, the same kind of behavior has been noted. In New Zealand, for example, Sleek (1980) suggests that, although some examining magistrates may follow the practice of inviting patients to secure the services of a lawyer and may hold a full hearing of the matter (even though this is not required by law), in the main, magistrates do little more than "rubber stamp" medical decisions (Dolan, 1975). As O'Sullivan (1981) points out, a similar situation exists in Australia in the context of both magisterial hearings and tribunal hearings. He argues that "despite the presence of legal members on tribunals it seems unlikely that discharges will often occur against medical opinion" (p. 112). O'Sullivan's argument is based, in part, on the results of some limited research conducted in New South Wales during 1977 as a consequence of criticisms of the arbitrary and medically biased nature and conduct of magistrates' hearings (Institute of Criminology, 1978). The researchers found serious deficiencies in the system of review: notably, the lack of effective patient representation and the absence of the presentation of verbal evidence by physicians seeking involuntary commitment. Magistrates tended simply to affirm medical opinion and there was a strong bias against patients. Patients would often appear in a "drugged" condition, clad in bedtime attire—an observation that led to the proceedings being dubbed "pajama courts." The introduction of an experimental patient representation scheme had a marked effect on proceedings, although it was discontinued, ostensibly for want of funding.

Although these observations may tend to support Peay's (1981) general criticism vis-à-vis the manifest lack of fairness, it also serves to highlight a second issue: While professional discretion may dominate proceedings in the context of the decisions of lay members, it also may influence the decisions of the *legal* members of tribunals. In this regard, Shone's (1976) study of the conduct of Alberta review tribunal hearings is pertinent because it raises questions about the utility of the legal representation of patients in the situation where review tribunal members have a preexisting bias toward informal, rather than formal, review proceedings.

After observing the conduct of tribunals, Shone argues that they were accepting and reinforcing a bias toward a medical model of adjudication that overrode the basic tenets of justice. While lawyers were often present at hearings, they openly expressed doubts about the impartiality of the body, even where they were allowed to present evidence and cross-examine witnesses. Indeed,

the seriousness with which panels view the patient representative's role in such proceedings is demonstrated by one incident observed by Shone. Having excluded a patient from a hearing (in his "best interests"), the tribunal appointed a lawyer from the public trustee's office to act for the patient. This may seem perfectly appropriate until it is realized that the lawyer simply happened to be present by chance, knew nothing of the client, and had no experience in mental health matters beyond those pertaining to estates. He was, in effect, thrown a "dock brief" that he was reluctant to catch. As Shone put it: "No one was more startled than the lawyer himself when the chairman named him to act during the applicant's exclusion. . . . He sat through the medical evidence in self-conscious silence. Not once did he confer with the applicant or endeavour to speak on his behalf. The appointment smacked of pretense" (p. 179). The willingness to engage in pretense reinforced, for Shone, a more serious problem. She felt that, where a tribunal perceived its role as involving informal adjudication, any attempt by representatives to assert a patient's position aggressively might incur the wrath of the tribunal, thereby adversely affecting a patient's case. If this situation can be generalized to other jurisdictions, it points to the possibility that while the "new legalism" may mean "more lawyers," the concrete impact of increased representation may be strictly limited by an existing bias (in favor of informality and professional discretion) held by tribunal members. Clearly, however, further research is needed to confirm or refute this proposition.

This situation is relevant to another issue—"reforms" in the area of providing legal services for patients. Before proceeding to discuss developments and problems in this context, it may be fruitful to summarize the discussion of review tribunals in light of the "new legalism" thesis.

It is contended that the case for a new legalism is not supported at three levels. First, the reforms that have occurred in relation to the creation and expansion of review tribunals point not to more "legalism," but rather to a preference for administrative decision-making in the review context. Certainly, this may be opposed by the claim that regardless of their administrative foundation, the establishment of conventional legal rights and procedures (e.g., through statutory reform) renders these bodies, in effect, "judicial." This, however, can be discounted as a consequence of a second contention. Research indicates that where such rights are extended to a patient, they are applied inconsistently. Further, they are hedged by the broad discretionary powers of the tribunal, and, where there is any "doubt," the benefit will tend to go to the mental health professional rather than the patient. Certainly, it can be pointed out that this situation is being tempered in some jurisdictions by judicial attempts to develop and apply the "duty to act fairly." However, there is no consistent doctrine in this area and, in any case, the duty apparently has not been applied to mental health review tribunals exercising their civil jurisdiction. Finally, the limited research into the actual conduct of review tribunals suggests that, regardless of procedural rules and a duty to act fairly, considerable bias exists in favor of professional discretion.[28] Indeed, any attempt to introduce more "legalism" may have adverse consequences for patients. On this cautionary note, we turn to consider the creation and efficacy of legal services for mental health patients.

LEGAL AND ADVOCACY SERVICES FOR MENTAL HEALTH PATIENTS: STRUCTURAL AND LEGAL CONSTRAINTS

A key feature of Gostin's notion of a "new legalism" is the emergence of professional groups that provide "activist legal services": that is, agencies that actively pursue the provision of effective health care services for patients (e.g., by articulating and pursuing a "right to treatment") and that actively protect patients' liberties and rights in such areas as commitment and treatment (e.g., by articulating and pursuing a "right to refuse treatment" and a right to "due process" before confinement). This statement of mission seems to reflect the general posture adopted by MIND in England. However, in considering the extent to which Gostin's thesis may be generalizable, it is necessary to consider developments in all Commonwealth jurisdictions.

Gordon's (1981a, 1981b, 1982, 1983) analyses of this area provide a clear picture of the evolution of various forms of "legal service," over the past decade and, in so doing, effectively trace the emergence of a mental health law movement in the Commonwealth. As Gordon contends, the growth of legal services can be seen to be closely tied to the evolution of legal aid systems, which have provided fiscal, organizational, and conceptual support and direction. In particular, these systems gave impetus to preexisting, although largely *ad hoc*, services (e.g., those provided by civil liberties groups), provided a selection of service delivery modes (e.g., "duty counsel" schemes), and have spawned the personnel interested in pursuing the legal needs of patients. While some more independent groups have established themselves as key agencies (e.g., MIND in England and NIMR in Canada), formal legal aid systems have been the principal driving force in the Commonwealth as a whole.

The emergence of patients' legal services began in the early 1970s and, over the course of time, five distinct methods of service delivery have crystallized: (a) the "storefront" law center, (b) the specialist advocacy organization or center, (c) the duty counsel system, (d) advice and referral schemes as adjuncts to a "judicare" system, and (e) "ombudsman" schemes. Each method of delivery will be briefly discussed in light of the "new legalism" thesis.

The most significant development of storefront law centers has been in British Columbia (Canada). In 1972 an interdisciplinary group began a limited legal advocacy project in a large psychiatric hospital in Greater Vancouver. This scheme was expanded, under the auspices of the Vancouver Community Legal Assistance Society, into the Mental Patients' Advocate Project. This currently operates from both "storefront" premises on the grounds of the hospital and from the parent agency's inner suburban offices where patients on community release can obtain access to a lawyer. From the outset, the project staff have adopted a "partisan" advocacy approach to patient representation and have offered the types of general services found in more conventional community law centers as well as specialized skills in mental health law matters. In this regard, the project has been aggressive in the pursuit of patients' interests. This factor was established in a federal government evaluation of the project and is reflected in the number of reported cases pursued by project

---

[28]It is interesting to note that, particularly where "bad faith" could be demonstrated, an action might be mounted against the members of a review tribunal in the tort of negligence. This, however, is an uncertain area of law: see Linden (1980).

advocates.[29] Unfortunately, severe economic restraints have meant a cutback in services, and, although the project is still operating, its potential for further activism has been significantly curtailed.

Attempts to provide similar services have occurred in other jurisdictions. In Ontario, for example, the Toronto Community Legal Assistance Service started a patients' legal service in 1974 in a major mental health center. This scheme was designed as an annex to a conventional community law center but ceased operations in 1980. A similar, independent law center opened in the York–Finch General Hospital, in Toronto, in 1974. However, this scheme concentrated only on conventional legal problems and excluded any legal issues pertaining to hospitalization and treatment. The center is still in operation but serves as a location for summary advice and assistance within the Ontario legal aid plan rather than as an independent, community-based legal clinic. In England, where patients' legal needs are principally met by the network established by MIND, at least one attempt at setting up a "storefront" legal service has been reported (Kramer, 1982). Operating as a branch of an independent law center, a representation project has been set up in an office in the grounds of the Springfield Hospital in Tooting, London. Although the casework focus is on the complete spectrum of patients' legal needs (as in the case of the British Columbia project), the actual operations and impact of the agency are yet to be established.

As far as can be determined, there are no other "storefront" services in the Commonwealth. However, it is important to note that some independent community law centers have developed a special interest in mental health law matters even though they have not actually established specific "branch offices" at hospitals or other facilities. In Australia, for example, the Fitzroy Legal Service (Victoria), the Redfern Legal Centre (N.S.W.), and the Macquarie Legal Centre (N.S.W.) have each attempted to develop a specialist interest in mental health services as part of their general operations. Likewise, in Canada, the Dalhousie Legal Aid Service (Nova Scotia) and Parkdale Community Legal Services (Ontario) have sought to pursue mental health law issues. However, these agencies are strictly limited by both personnel and fiscal constraints, particularly as mental health patients constitute only one of the many disadvantaged groups seeking these kinds of legal services (Bottomley, 1983).

Specialist advocacy organizations and centers are, with the exception of MIND's legal department, a relatively recent development. The work of the latter is well known; particularly, its significant impact on mental health law reform in England and Wales and its relatively extensive Mental Health Review Tribunal Representation Service. Although this service (which involves the training of patient representatives) is reported to have limited resources, it is by far the most organized agency of its kind anywhere in the Commonwealth. In Canada, the National Legal Resources Service of the National Institute on Mental Retardation (established in Ontario in 1978) is probably the leading agency in the country although, as the title of the parent agency suggests, its principal interest lies with pursuing the needs of the mentally handicapped rather than the mentally ill per se. Nevertheless, it has had a number of successes in pursuing individual cases of injustice that affect a broad range of consumers of mental health services.[30] It has also made progress in areas such as zoning bylaws and their effects on the establishment of noninstitutional treatment or residence alternatives. In a similar vein, the Advocacy Resource Centre for the Handicapped, in Toronto, is active in pursuing test cases, class actions, and other reformative activities for a broad community of interests. Established in 1980 and funded by the Ontario legal aid plan, this agency is sponsored by a coalition of consumer groups, including mental patients' associations. Recent "successes" include the case of Justin Clark, a *developmentally disabled* person

---

[29]See, e.g., *Rosandik v. Manning* (1978), 5 B.C.L.R. 347 (B.C.S.C.) (establishing a patient's right to apply for release even though his "affairs" were under the control of the public trustee); *Hoskins v. Hislop* (1981), 26 B.C.C.R. 165 (B.C.S.C.); and *Robinson v. Hislop* (1980), 24 B.C.C.R. 80 (B.C.S.C.) (establishing the onus and burden of proof in civil commitment reviews). Other cases have involved such matters as the testing of the legality of "patient labor" in hospitals and, most recently, the legality of the practice of requiring that involuntary patients pay for their hospitalization, *Director of Riverview Hospital v. Andrzejewski* (1983), 150 D.L.R. (3d) 535 (B.C.C.C.). See, generally, Himmelfarb and Lazar (1981).

[30]For example, the case of Emerson Bonnar, an individual held in an institution in New Brunswick for 15 years as "unfit to stand trial." See Endicott (1980), Verdun-Jones (1981), pp. 366–367.

who had been declared to be *mentally* incompetent (*Clark v. Clark*, 1982, see Baker, 1983).

In Australia, progress has been sluggish in this area. At this stage, the Sydney-based Committee on Mental Health Advocacy (an amalgamation of consumer and interest groups established in 1981) appears to be the only agency specifically concerned with organizing mental health reform beyond its home state (New South Wales). However, it is very much in its infancy and although individual members of the organization have been involved in the process of reforming the New South Wales Mental Health Act and in providing legal assistance for patients in local hospitals, its strategy and impact have yet to be clarified. Judging by reports on its formation, it intends to adopt an aggressive and partisan posture in the pursuit of patients' legal needs (C.O.M.H.A., 1981; Bottomley, 1981a, 1981b, 1981c). Although other organizations concerned with patients' rights exist in some states (e.g., the Foundation for the Abolition of Compulsory Treatment, in Western Australia; The Victorian Council of Social Services, in Victoria), these are either small "consumer" groups or general watchdog agencies rather than organized legal or advocacy services. Similarly, the Australian National Mental Health Association (like its Canadian counterpart, the Canadian Mental Health Association) is an important lobbying group and can provide legal representation. However, these kinds of agencies are considerably less organized, in relation to legal representation and law reform activities, than the model upon which they are built—that of MIND.

Apart from law centers and specialized advocacy organizations, a number of "duty counsel" schemes have been established in recent years. In Ontario, for example, duty counsel first appeared in 14 provincial psychiatric hospitals in early 1975, to assist patients on a regular basis with legal problems. Counsel were drawn from a volunteer panel of private practitioners working under the judicare component of the provincial legal aid plan. In Manitoba, a similar duty counsel scheme was also inaugurated in 1975. However, in this scheme, the lawyers are staff members of community legal services offices rather than private practitioners. Regular visits are made to provincial institutions and counsel provide advice and assistance to any patient. A duty counsel scheme of a slightly different nature has also been in operation since 1974 in British Columbia. The provincial Legal Services Society has organized a patient's appointee project to assist those appear-

ing before review panels. A group of interested lawyers has been developed and, on receipt of a request from either a patient or a hospital social worker, the society will refer the matter to one of the practitioners. In addition to these organized schemes, the Legal Services Commissions in Quebec, Newfoundland, and Nova Scotia have set up various systems to *advise* patients of the availability of legal assistance, particularly in relation to review tribunal hearings. Where legal representation is requested, it is handled as a conventional application for legal aid and dealt with in accordance with the policies of the provincial legal aid plan.

In Australia, duty counsel schemes have been established in two states: New South Wales and South Australia. However, although the latter appears to have maintained the service, the former has not. In the case of New South Wales, the Legal Services Commission was reported, in 1981, to be providing two staff lawyers to represent patients at commitment hearings in two Sydney hospitals (C.O.M.H.A., 1981). Yet, by the summer of 1983, the service appeared to have been terminated as a consequence of budgetary cuts. Further plans for the commission to develop a more elaborate advocacy service for patients, in anticipation of major changes to the state's mental health legislation, have also been thwarted. As Bottomley (1983) reports, the promised reforms in the area of mandatory representation at commitment and review hearings have not materialized and, consequently, the principal rationale for a patients' legal service has been removed. This is a surprising development because, of all the Australian states, New South Wales was the first to recognize the need for patients' advocacy services and appeared to be prepared to adopt an innovative posture.

In the course of a review of the state's mental health legislation, in 1975 the Edwards Committee identified legal representation as a principal area in which reform was desirable. As a result, a subcommittee was formed to investigate, operationalize, and evaluate a pilot scheme, in one Sydney hospital, involving experimentation with different representation models (Institute of Criminology, 1975). The scheme operated for 9 months during 1977 and employed three approaches: a duty solicitor (counsel) scheme, a full-time legal officer scheme, and a full-time lay advocacy scheme. An evaluation indicated that, although representation as a whole had a positive impact on the conduct and outcome of commitment proceedings, the outcome was not affected by the *type* of scheme in use; nonlegal advocates were as effective as lawyers (Institute of Criminology, 1978). Nonlegal advocates also reduced the amount of friction between representatives and mental health professionals without necessarily sacrificing patients' interests. Although the results of this pilot scheme were generally well received and the need for a patients' representation service recognized, a formal and organized agency has not been established to date.

In South Australia, however, the situation appears to be more satisfactory to those seeking the establishment of legal services. The Mental Health Act of 1976–1977 improved patients' rights in a number of areas, including the provision of a right to representation when appearing before review tribunals, or when appealing tribunal decisions. Furthermore, indigent patients have been granted a right to have counsel provided under the state's legal aid plan. This plan is administered by the state's Legal Service Commission, which acts as a conduit for applications. A panel of legal practitioners has been established under the judicare component of the plan and thus provides a type of duty counsel scheme. Regrettably, data pertaining to the use of this service are not available although a monitoring scheme has been established (Greycar, 1980).

As can be seen, duty counsel schemes of various types have been established in a number of Commonwealth jurisdictions. In some jurisdictions, the lawyers are concerned primarily with commitment and related matters, whereas in other jurisdictions they appear to provide additional services by way of general legal advice and referral. The schemes may also employ either "staff" lawyers, drawn from the jurisdiction's legal aid offices, or private practitioners, who form a panel and are reimbursed for their services through a judicare system. These schemes do, however, share one common feature: they furnish a patient with immediate access to a lawyer. They are thus to be distinguished from the fourth model of service delivery: advice and referral schemes using nonlawyer personnel to assist patients. An example of this model can be found in Alberta, where in 1975, "community legal-aid interviewers" were appointed to improve the level of access to the provincial judicare system. This method of outreach was designed to benefit all members of the community who were institutionalized or otherwise unable to obtain access to a legal aid office. In the specific context of mental health patients, a regular program of weekly visits to two provincial institutions has been established, complemented by advertising and the utilization of ward social workers who act to channel clients as the need arises.

The fifth, and final, method of service delivery has involved the introduction of a hospital "ombudsman." The first attempt to establish such a scheme in a Commonwealth jurisdiction occurred in Ontario, where a patients' ombudsman experiment was introduced in Toronto's Lakeshore Psychiatric Hospital in the period 1973–1974. As Dobson and Hansen (1976) have reported, this scheme (like other ombudsman schemes) provided an *advocacy* rather than a *legal* service in that it was designed to provide a mechanism for protecting patients' rights in an essentially mediatory context. The goal was to promote patients' awareness of their rights, to resolve conflicts or problems with the hospital's bureaucracy by informal means, to recommend changes in policies and procedures that would avoid conflict, and to educate hospital staff vis-à-vis patients' rights and the patients' perspective on procedures within the hospital. The experiment was reported to have been successful; however, the scheme was phased out with the introduction of the province's duty counsel scheme.

It is interesting to note, however, that the scheme has recently been reintroduced in a more elaborate form. Since the summer of 1983, the province of Ontario has been operating a Psychiatric Patient Advocate Office. Staffed by 11 advocates with different professional backgrounds (lawyers, social workers, and psychologists), the scheme has served 1,500 clients in its first 7 months of operation. Advocates are reported to be assisting patients in all of Ontario's psychiatric facilities (including those detained on lieutenant governor's warrants) in relation to matters concerning treatment, detention, and any other legal issues.[31] The impact of the advocate office is unlikely to be determined for some time. However, it is interesting to note that the work of advocates is already raising criticism from mental health professionals and from patients' rights groups. Whereas the scheme is seen to be threatening and obstructive by the first group, the second

---

[31]"The Struggle for Mental Patients' Rights." The *Globe and Mail*, February 6, 1984.

group is concerned that, because the advocates are funded by the same ministry that operates the institutions (health), they are faced with a conflict of interests and cannot properly pursue patients' rights.

As far as can be determined, there are no other ombudsman schemes in Commonwealth jurisdictions at this time. However, it is clear that, in many respects, they are an extension and elaboration of the old "official visitor" systems that exist (or existed) in many Commonwealth jurisdictions either as the sole mechanism for protecting patients from excesses or as an adjunct to tribunal/judicial review procedures. In this respect, the recent formation of a Mental Health Act Commission in England and Wales, as part of the package of reforms contained in the Mental Health Act of 1983, can be seen as a further extension and variant of ombudsman schemes. In many ways, the commission appears to be similar to the somewhat older Scottish Mental Welfare Commission and may even have its conceptual roots in the scheme set up by the Lunacy Act of 1890: namely, the "commissioners in lunacy." The commission is to provide safeguards for patients by informal, or nonlegal means and, in the course of reviewing various decisions (e.g., in relation to treatment) and investigating complaints, it will employ staff who will both visit and interview patients. The staff, it seems, to some extent will be acting as advocates for the patients. As in the case of the Ontario Advocate Office, any assessment of the procedures and impact of these kinds of commissions will have to wait until they have had a chance to establish routines. However, one thing is becoming clear: ombudsman schemes are popular and may be expected to expand rather than contract. In this respect, and although they do not necessarily support "professional discretion," they seem to reflect a swing away from "legalism" and toward informal dispute resolution and dispute prevention. When coupled with a growth in the use of administrative tribunals (rather than courts) as the medium for reviewing commitment, detention, and treatment decisions and for resolving related disputes, we seem to be witnessing a trend throughout the Commonwealth toward less, rather than more, law in the mental health context. This point can be further illustrated by a brief examination of the actual procedures and impact of the different models of *legal* service delivery.

As Gordon (1982) has demonstrated, although the close ties with legal aid systems have facilitated the emergence of patients' legal services of different types, this marriage has also acted to restrain legal service activities. Service delivery modes and philosophies have been significantly constrained by fiscal considerations as expressed in the eligibility and coverage criteria adopted by the legal aid plans in the various jurisdictions. "Eligibility" criteria are reflected in the process of "means testing" (i.e., determining the level of income below which free assistance will be provided), whereas "coverage" criteria are expressed in terms of the extent to which legal aid will be provided for a range of different circumstances (e.g., only in criminal trials where imprisonment is a possible disposition). In both cases, a patient's access to the resources of a legal service may be limited and, in the absence of appropriate funding, the legal service itself will have only limited resources. As these criteria vary widely from one jurisdiction to another, so the availability and style of patients' legal services also appears to vary. The complexities of this situation await further, empirical exploration but, at this stage, it is apparent that stringent eligibility and coverage criteria act to constrain the activities of patients' legal services.

In addition to this issue of resources, close associations with legal aid plans also means the loss of ideological autonomy in relation to legal service philosophy and tactics. An important aspect of Gostin's "new legalism" is activism on the part of such legal services: that is, aggressive partisan advocacy, designed to establish power for patients in their interactions with mental health systems. Such advocacy involves more than simply providing advice and referral services designed to resolve the problems encountered by individual patients: It encompasses an aggressive assertion of the needs and rights of individuals and, perhaps more important, for mental health patients as a group: for example, for a geographical community (the residents of an institution) and for a community of interest (all clients of the mental health system in a particular jurisdiction). Although this may be the posture of agencies such as MIND and of organizations such as the Mental Patients' Advocate Project in British Columbia, these appear to be the exceptions rather than the rules in Commonwealth jurisdictions as a whole. Instead, the preference appears to be for legal services that have been or can be "tamed," so that they fit within a general welfare system.

In this respect, the alternative models – duty counsel, advice and referral, and ombudsman schemes – seem to be a preferred legal/advocacy service delivery mode, and although they doubtless provide important resources for patients, they are clearly not engaged in partisan advocacy. From what is known of these systems, it appears that they are only marginally concerned with the interests of mental health patients as a group. They are not, for example, schemes designed to pursue law reform activity, whether by way of direct involvement in political processes or by way of test cases and class actions. Instead, they are essentially reactive, mediatory, and oriented toward helping individual clients. Their impact is therefore questionable insofar as pursuing the *collective* interests of patients is concerned. Indeed, as Gordon (1982, 1983) argues, they may in fact be counterproductive in the pursuit of patients' rights issues because they present an illusion that needs are being met and thereby diffuse the demand for the kinds of *activist* legal services that are best equipped and motivated to engage in partisan work.

Closely connected to this general question of the structural constraints imposed on, and the relative effectiveness of, different styles of legal service delivery is the issue of the extent to which legal service practitioners are constrained by the provisions in mental health legislation that limit a patient's access to the courts. The nature and impact of such provisions have been effectively summarized by Gostin (1983c):

> Section 141 of the Mental Health Act 1959 placed a significant impediment on any person seeking to bring civil or criminal proceedings against any person carrying out functions in pursuance of the Act. It required the (aggrieved) person to obtain leave of the High Court before bringing such proceedings, and leave could not be granted unless there were substantial grounds to show that the person to be proceeded against acted in bad faith or without reasonable care. In many important cases, such as wrongful imprisonment, the Act did not simply impede, but effectively prevented a psychiatric patient from

obtaining legal redress because bad faith or lack of reasonable care were not part of the cause of action." (p. 62)

As Gostin (1979b) has shown, this provision has led to many injustices and was clearly introduced to protect mental health professionals rather than to prevent unnecessary or vexatious litigation.[32] For several years, MIND has been attempting to amend or remove this particular provision and, apparently as a consequence of the matter being taken before the European Commission of Human Rights, the new Mental Health Act of 1983 includes a number of changes that limit the circumstances under which leave to bring an action is required. As Gostin notes (1983c), "the Act removed from the scope of Section 141 proceedings against the Secretary of State or a health authority; criminal proceedings are now to be brought with the consent of the Director of Public Prosecutions, instead of by leave of the High Court; and the requirement of showing "substantial grounds" for the claim is removed" (p. 63). Although these developments are important, they clearly still leave some limitations in place.

Restrictive provisions, similar to section 141 of the England and Wales Mental Health Act of 1959, still exist in the mental health legislation of a number of other Commonwealth jurisdictions. In the Canadian provinces of Saskatchewan (Mental Health Act, R.S.S. 1978, c.345, Sec. 52) and Manitoba (Mental Health Act, R.S.M. 1970, c.M-110, Sec. 96), for example, the pursuit of actions against mental health authorities or personnel is limited by the possibility of an action being stayed by a judge of the provincial Court of Queen's Bench. In New Brunswick (Mental Health Act, R.S.N.B. 1973, c.M-10, Sec. 66) and Prince Edward Island (Mental Health Act, R.S.P.E.I. 1974, c.M-9, Sec. 56), similar constraints are imposed in the case of actions against mental health personnel. A further, special time limitation is imposed on actions in these provinces and also in the province of Ontario. In some jurisdictions, an action must commence within 6 months; in others, the period is extended to 12 months. These time limits place a further constraint on patients' lawyers, particularly because

---

[32]See, e.g., *Poutney and Griffiths* (1975), 2 All E.R. 881; *Kynaston v. Secretary of State for the Home Department and Secretary of State for the Department of Health and Social Security* (unreported), Court of Appeal, 18 February, 1981.

alleged wrongdoings may not come to light immediately after they occur. In addition, some Canadian legislation (e.g., Mental Health Act, R.S.B.C. 1979, c.256, Sec. 16) includes a provision specifically protecting persons undertaking duties, in accordance with the statutes, providing they are acting in "good faith and with reasonable care." Overall, only the provinces of Alberta, Quebec, Nova Scotia, and Newfoundland have mental health legislation free of protective provisions, time limits, and restrictive provisions.

This does not mean, however, that patients in these provinces are necessarily free to pursue actions. In addition to mental health legislation, it is also important to consider the impact of related guardianship statutes; that is, the body of legislation dealing with the process of determining the competence or capability of patients to manage their affairs (or estates) and themselves.

Although the overall Canadian situation has yet to be systematically explored,[33] some pilot research indicates that, in general, certificates of incompetency can be and are completed by examining psychiatrists whenever an individual is involuntarily committed to an institution. The effect is to place the patients' estate and/or person under committeeship or guardianship, the committee or guardian frequently being the province's public trustee.[34] When this occurs, legislation usually provides for the surrender of all control to the committee, including control over the process of pursuing legal actions. Under these circumstances, a patient's lawyer may be unable to act on his or her client's behalf because the power to decide whether or not to proceed is held by another person. This may not be a problem where the committee is a private person who shares the lawyer's perspective and sees legal action as important and desirable for a particular patient. However, as is more often the case, where the committee is the province's Public Trustee, and where the issue in hand may ultimately involve action against the trustee, the constraints placed on a lawyer become obvious. Certainly, in at least one jurisdiction — British Columbia — this issue has been raised and resolved in favor of a patient who sought the right to pursue legal action against the wishes of the committee (public trustee). However, this case, *Rosandik v. Manning* (1978), involved an interpretation of a particular section of the British Columbia Mental Health Act and may not be applicable in other jurisdictions.

By all accounts, the situation in Australia is very similar. O'Sullivan's (1981) analysis, for example, indicates that the mental health legislation of most states contains restrictive and protective clauses similar to those found in Canadian jurisdictions. Although the content and effect varies from one jurisdiction to another, one consistent theme is clear; namely, a desire to impose a special set of restraints on patients and their potential representatives presumably to prevent vexatious litigation.[35] Most states also provide for the alteration of faulty documents pertaining to, for example, the commitment of a patient and thereby block a potential area of legal action. Presumably for legislators, encouraging an unfettered exercise of professional discretion, "warts and all," is more desirable than requiring that mental health professionals go through the irksome formality of acting lawfully in the first instance. Furthermore, as is the situation in Canada, Australian states have separate guardianship laws through which a patient may be declared incompetent or incapable. Where this occurs and the patient loses control over his or her affairs, the effects are by and large repeated: With the loss of his or her estate, the patient loses his or her capacity to pursue legal action without the authority of a trustee or guardian.

It is thus apparent that although various types of legal and advocacy services for patients have been established in certain jurisdictions, their work is strictly constrained by both structural and legal factors. As regards the latter, it is important to note that, in addition to the legal factors discussed above, other more deep-rooted constraints exist. For example, unlike the situation in the United States, the doctrine of parliamentary supremacy that dominates in Commonwealth jurisdictions precludes an activist role in law reform on the part of the judiciary. This is compounded by the absence of a constitutionally entrenched bill of rights, the provisions of which

---

[33]Research by the authors is currently in progress under funding from the Canadian Social Sciences and Humanities Research Council. For general comments, see Gordon and Verdun-Jones (1983).

[34]The terms "trustee," "committee," "guardian," and so on, vary from province to province.

[35]The recently enacted New South Wales Mental Health Act of 1983 is generally free from such restrictions. However, police officers who act in good faith are exculpated from liability (Sec. 191).

have been used successfully by mental health advocates in the United States to strike down or amend "unconstitutional" legislative provisions. Certainly, MIND has taken advantage of the European Commission on Human Rights, but its effect has been limited compared with the situation in the United States. Similarly, the impact of Canada's new Charter of Rights and Freedoms[36] has yet to be felt, although a recent development in Manitoba indicates that the charter may be of importance in pursuing patients' rights. In what appears to be the first charter case involving mental health law matters, a High Court judge released an involuntarily committed patient because she was not adequately informed of her constitutional rights and because she was denied "due process."[37] It may, however, be premature to begin celebrating this single case as an indication of the dawn of a new legalism in Canada.

Taken as a whole, developments in the Commonwealth in the area of legal services do not appear to demonstrate a trend toward legalism, new or otherwise. Indeed, the trend seems to be moving rather in the direction of establishing *nonlegal* mechanisms of conflict resolution in relation to the disputes arising between patients and mental health practitioners. It seems reasonable, at this point, to predict the emergence of more services of the advocacy type. No doubt, these services will follow an ombudsman model and they may well be supplemented by various duty counsel schemes. Furthermore, these services will tend to focus their resources upon review tribunal hearings rather than engaging in a broad range of aggressive, partisan legal activities. It can be contended that the latter type of activities are virtually essential if a "new legalism" is to gain a foothold in the mental health field. Because organizations engaging in these adversarial activities appear to exist only in British Columbia and England and Wales, they would appear to be an exception to the general trend toward a preference for informal and individualized mechanisms of mediation. Although a case can be made for a greater emphasis upon the active pursuit of patients' rights and activities — at least until an equality of power is attained for patients interacting with mental health professionals — it would appear that current developments are moving in the opposite direction. Although the present situation cannot be characterized as one that manifests unbridled "professional discretion," equally it cannot be characterized as one that reflects a "new legalism."

MENTAL HEALTH LAW TRENDS IN THE SPHERE OF CRIMINAL JUSTICE

In recent years, an increasing number of Commonwealth jurisdictions have witnessed significant developments in those areas of mental health law that fall within the troubled sphere of criminal justice. Among the more portentous developments in this area are legislative reforms affecting the disposition of mentally disordered offenders and judicial refinements of the case law concerning mental disorder and criminal responsibility. To a considerable extent, many of these developments may be characterized as reflecting a trend toward the adoption of a greater degree of *legalism* — in the sense of the imposition of formal legal controls upon the discretionary processes of the criminal justice system. Unlike its civil law counterpart, the criminal justice system frequently establishes situations in which discretionary decision-making powers are *shared* between mental health professionals and members of the executive arm of government. Therefore, in the sphere of criminal justice, the rise of the new legalism will be examined within the context of the imposition of legal controls upon a broad range of discretionary decision-making processes affecting mentally disordered offenders — whether or not these processes are independently controlled by mental health professionals.

In this section, developments in the following areas of criminal justice will be analyzed:

1. Fitness to stand trial
2. Disposition of mentally disordered offenders: The hospital order
3. Criminal responsibility

FITNESS TO STAND TRIAL

In Commonwealth jurisdictions, there has been universal acceptance of the hoary common-law principle that an accused person, who is suffering from a mental disorder to such an extent that he

---

[36]Constitution Act of 1982; part 1, en. by the Canada Act of 1982 (U.K.) c.11, Sched. B.
[37]"Mental Patient Released by Judge." The *Globe and Mail*, February 14, 1984.

or she is incapable of understanding the nature and object of the criminal proceedings brought against him or her or of participating in his own defense, should not be subjected to the rigors of a criminal trial (see Chiswick, 1978; Freiberg, 1976; Gordon, 1978; Manson, 1982; O'Sullivan, 1981; Prins, 1980; Verdun-Jones, 1981; Walker, 1968).[38] Traditionally, the stated rationale underpinning this doctrine was the evident need to protect the unfit accused from the disastrous consequences emanating from conviction and punishment by a trial court. However, an equally significant — albeit tacit — rationale was the perceived need to protect the community from mentally disordered offenders who were potentially dangerous; hence, the unfit accused, who had been charged with a serious offense, could be incarcerated indefinitely unless he recovered sufficiently to stand trial (an event that, until relatively recently, was somewhat unlikely to occur). Viewed within the modern context, it appears that the inevitable conflict between the goals of protecting society on the one hand and the individual on the other has generally been resolved at the expense of the unfit accused. For example, in Canada, it has been asserted (Verdun-Jones, 1981) that

> despite the many "humanitarian" considerations which have been alleged to be the justification for maintaining the place of the fitness doctrine within the Canadian system of criminal justice, the doctrine has been subjected to a rising wave of criticism in recent years. Far from being a mechanism whose primary concern is the *protection of the accused*, the current legal machinery associated with the fitness issue bears all the indelible hallmarks of a legal device which is equally (if not more concerned) with the *protection of society* from the perceived danger posed by those who have fallen afoul of the criminal law and have suffered the

misfortune of having been diagnosed as "mentally ill." (p. 365)

One of the more dangerous aspects of the traditional procedures, relating to fitness to stand trial, is the possibility that unfit accused may actually spend more time in psychiatric incarceration than they would have spent in prison had they been convicted and sentenced. In 1980, for example, after the exertion of considerable pressure by the Canadian Association for the Mentally Retarded and other community organizations, the province of New Brunswick finally released a man who had been held in a maximum security psychiatric facility for some 26 years. It was revealed that in 1964 he had been charged in connection with an alleged attempt to snatch a woman's purse but had been found unfit to stand trial. Had he been convicted of the offense charged, it is highly unlikely that the accused would have been sentenced to anything more than a relatively brief term of imprisonment (see Savage, 1981; Verdun-Jones, 1981, pp. 366–367; Endicott, 1980).

Given the everpresent threat to civil liberties that is inherent in the traditional procedures relating to fitness to stand trial, it is scarcely surprising that the advent of the new legalism has spawned a number of legislative attempts to redress the historical balance by providing additional safeguards for the unfit accused. Perhaps the most significant legislative trends have manifested themselves in two critical areas: the introduction of equitable procedures for the disposition of the unfit accused and the establishment of "provisional" trials, designed to examine whether the accused has any defense to the charges laid against him or her.

Disposition of the Unfit Accused

In a significant number of Commonwealth jurisdictions, the traditional approach still prevails.[39]

---

[38] Gostin (1983a, p. 30) notes that, in England and Wales, the use of the hospital order has virtually replaced reliance on the plea of unfitness to stand trial.

[39] The "traditional approach," that consigns the unfit accused to an indeterminate period of confinement, still prevails in most Commonwealth jurisdictions in one form or another; in addition to Canada, see section 20B of Crimes Act of 1914–1973 (Commonwealth of Australia); sections 65 and 66 of Lunacy Act (N.S.W.) still applicable in the Australian Capital Territory; sections 613 and 645 of Criminal Code (Queensland) and section 36 of Mental Health Act of 1974 (Qld.); section 293 of Criminal Law Consolidation Act of 1973–1975 (South Australia); sections 380 and 382 of Criminal Code (Tasmania) and section 61 of Mental Health Act of 1963 (Tas.); section 393 of Crimes Act of 1958 (Victoria) and *R. v. Judge Martin; Ex parte the Attorney General* (1973), V.R. 339, in which it was held that the trial judge has no discretion in relation to the disposition of an unfit accused person; section 652 of Criminal Code (W. Australia) and sections 53–54 of Mental Health Act of 1981 (W.A.); Gordon, 1978, 378–379.

For example, in Canada, the Criminal Code provides that, where an accused person is found unfit to stand trial on account of insanity, the judge or magistrate "shall order that the accused be kept in custody until the pleasure of the Lieutenant Governor is known" (Criminal Code, R.S.C. 1970, Sec. 543(6)). Subsequently, the lieutenant governor may issue an order "for the safe custody of the accused in a place and manner directed by him"; alternatively, he may, "if in his opinion it would be in the best interest of the accused and not contrary to the interest of the public," make an order providing for "the discharge of the accused either absolutely or subject to such conditions as he prescribes" (Sec. 545(1)). In practice, persons held "under a lieutenant governor's warrant" are detained in provincial mental health facilities — usually in conditions of "maximum security." If the accused person eventually recovers sufficiently for the purpose of standing trial, the Code provides that he may be returned to court; provided he is deemed to be fit, he will thereupon be tried (Sec. 543(8)). On the other hand, the Crown may well be content to enter a stay of proceedings or to withdraw the charge(s) rather than proceed to trial (Sun, 1974, p. 488). The power associated with the lieutenant governor's warrant, in Canada, are normally exercised by the provincial cabinet or attorney-general, and, in many provinces, they are administered on a day-to-day basis by the provincial health department. A person who is detained by virtue of a lieutenant governor's warrant and remains unfit to stand trial may *only* be released from a psychiatric institution when an order-in-council has been issued by the provincial cabinet (see Verdun-Jones, 1981, pp. 367–373). The Criminal Code provides that conditions may be attached to a person's discharge (Sec. 545(1)(b)) and that a peace officer, who has reasonable and probable grounds to believe that such conditions have been violated, may arrest that person without a warrant (Sec. 545(4)).

It is true that, in Canada, the case of each patient, held under a lieutenant governor's warrant, is automatically reviewed by a provincial board of review.[40] However, it is significant that a patient cannot launch a review of his case on his or her own initiative and, furthermore, that the review board's function is purely *advisory* in nature; the ultimate decision to release can only be made at a *political* level (by the provincial cabinet). In recent years, the only major improvement in the legal status of the unfit accused in Canada has been the judicial application of the evolving "duty of fairness" to the recommendations made by review boards (Verdun-Jones, 1982, pp. xv–135). One recent case witnessed the quashing of an order-in-council, which was issued by the lieutenant governor because the recommendation of the review board (upon which the lieutenant governor's decision was based) had not been made in accordance with the requirements of the duty to be fair (*In re McCann and the Queen*, 1982). Nevertheless, the grim reality remains that the fate of the unfit accused in Canada rests in the hands of the *executive* arm of government, and, in this light, it is perhaps predictable that greater weight has been assigned to the security interests of the community than to the interest of the accused in regaining his or her lost freedom.

Canadian research tends to support the notion that individual civil liberties are, indeed, infringed by the operation of the system of detention under lieutenant governor warrants. For example, a recent study by Roesch, Eaves, Sollner, Normandin, and Glackman (1981) found that the average period of hospitalization served by unfit defendants at the British Columbia Forensic Psychiatric Institute was 6 months. However, it is significant that 50% of the unfit defendants in the sample were charged only with property offenses and other less serious nonviolent crimes. This factor led the authors (1981) to conclude:

> Many of these unfit defendants would, if convicted, likely not be sentenced to prison. Even if incarcerated, it is likely that they would receive relatively short sentences. The concern is that it is quite possible that they could spend a longer time in an institution as unfit . . . than they would have if convicted and sentenced to prison. (p. 155)

An earlier study by Quinsey and Boyd (1974) revealed that unfit patients were a "disadvantaged group" when compared with patients acquitted by reason of insanity (who are also held under lieu-

---

[40]Section 547 of the Code establishes a legislative framework, which permits (but does not mandate) the creation of advisory review boards. Each province has established a review board; however, a number of provinces have established such boards outside of the Criminal Code framework.

tenant governor warrants).[41] Quinsey and Boyd (1974) discovered that unfit patients were held in custody for a *longer* period despite the fact that they were *less* likely to have committed offenses against persons:

> Although these comparative data do not speak directly to the issue of the "unfairness" of unfitness, they lead us to wonder as to whether a court finding of unfitness often leads to unnecessarily lengthy confinement. (p. 274)

In recent years, an increasing number of Commonwealth jurisdictions have moved to extricate the unfit accused from the legal limbo to which the traditional system of fitness procedures has consigned him. Perhaps the spirit of the new legalism is most clearly manifested in legislative amendments recently adopted by the Parliament of New South Wales.[42] These amendments establish fitness procedures that are designed to place stringent limitations upon the periods during which unfit accused may be incarcerated. Furthermore, they provide that an unfit accused may not be compelled to serve time in a *psychiatric* institution unless he or she falls within the criteria for civil commitment; in other words, the amendments respect the autonomy of the individual by requiring consent to psychiatric care, except in the situation where the accused is acutely ill.

The Crimes (Mental Disorder) Amendment Act of 1983 abolished the procedures that required automatic confinement of the accused upon a finding of unfitness. Where an accused person is found to be unfit to stand trial, the court must refer him or her to the Mental Health Review Tribunal (Sec. 428I).[43] In the interim, the court may release the accused on bail or remand him or her in custody. The tribunal is assigned the task of determining "whether, on the balance of probabilities, the person will, during the period of 12 months after the finding of unfitness, become fit to be tried for the offence." If the tribunal arrives at the conclusion that the accused will become fit

within the 12-month period, then it is also required to determine whether or not

> (a) the person is suffering from a mental illness; or (b) the person is suffering from a mental condition for which treatment is available in a hospital and, where the person is not in a hospital, whether or not the person objects to being detained in a hospital. (Sec. 428K)

Where it has been determined that the accused is likely to recover within 12 months, the tribunal must inform the court, which, in turn, may grant him or her bail for a period not to exceed 12 months.

If the tribunal has determined that the accused is "suffering from a mental illness" or is "suffering from a mental condition for which treatment is available in a hospital" and, where the accused is not already in hospital, that he or she does not object to hospitalization, then the court may order that the accused be detained in a hospital for a period not to exceed 12 months. (It should be noted that, under the provisions of the Mental Health Act of 1983, a "mentally ill" person is someone whose condition fulfills the criteria for involuntary commitment.) If the accused is not "mentally ill" or "suffering from a mental condition," etc., or, if he or she is suffering from such a "condition" but objects to hospitalization, then the court may "order that the person be detained in a place other than a hospital" (Sec. 428L).

If the tribunal has determined that the unfit accused is unlikely to recover within 12 months, it must so inform the attorney general (Sec. 428K(4)). The attorney general may decide to proceed no further with the charge(s), in which case the court must release the accused. If the attorney general decides otherwise, then a "special hearing" (or provisional trial) must be conducted in order to determine whether the accused committed the offense(s) charged (Sec. 428M). If it cannot be proved "to the requisite criminal standard of proof" that the accused committed the offense, there must be an acquittal and the accused must

---

[41]Significantly, in *Regina v. Kieling* (April 23, 1983), 9 W.C.B. 471, the Ontario County Court held that the psychiatric incarceration of the unfit accused for a period of 9 months did not violate section 12 of the Charter of Rights and Freedoms (prohibiting "cruel and unusual treatment or punishment") despite the fact that the maximum penalty for the offense charged was only 6 months' imprisonment.

[42]Mental Health Act of 1983 (N.S.W.); Crimes (Mental Disorder) Amendment Act of 1983 (N.S.W.).

[43]The Crimes (Mental Disorder) Amendment Act of 1983 amended the Crimes Act of 1900 (N.S.W.). Section numbers, therefore, refer to those in the Crimes Act.

be released (Sec. 428M(2)). However, if it is established that the accused committed the offense, the court is required to indicate whether, if the accused had been a person who was fit to be tried, it would have imposed a sentence of imprisonment, and, if so, what the length of that term would have been (Sec. 428P(1)). The period nominated by the court now becomes a "limiting term" that operates to fix the parameters for any subsequent period of incarceration (whether it be in a psychiatric facility or elsewhere). Where the court nominates a "limiting term," the accused will be referred to the Mental Health Review Tribunal (Sec. 428P(2)). If the tribunal determines that the unfit accused is "suffering from a mental illness or that the person is suffering from a mental condition for which treatment is available in a hospital" and that, in the latter case, the person (who is not currently detained in a hospital) does not object to hospitalization, then the court may order that he or she be detained in a hospital (Sec. 428Q(a)). Alternatively, where the tribunal determines that the accused is not "mentally ill" or is not suffering from a treatable mental condition, or that although suffering from such a condition objects to hospitalization, then the court may order that the accused be "detained in a place other than a hospital" (Sec. 428Q(b)).

The procedures for review of the detention of unfit accused persons are contained in the Mental Health Act of 1983 (N.S.W.). Within 14 days after the making of a court order providing for the detention of an unfit accused, the Mental Health Review Tribunal must review his or her case and determine;

i) Whether, in its opinion, the person has become fit to be tried for an offense; and ii) whether, in its opinion, the safety of the person or any member of the public will be seriously endangered by the person's release. (Sec. 117(1))

Where the tribunal determines that the accused has become fit to stand trial, it must notify the attorney general (Sec. 117(2)), who will decide whether to proceed with the charge(s); if that decision is in the negative, the unfit accused must be released. If the tribunal determines that the accused remains unfit, it has the option of recommending his release to the minister of health — provided, in its opinion, this action will not compromise the safety of either the accused or the public (Sec. 117(3)). The minister of health must inform the attorney general of such a recommendation, and, provided the latter official does not object, the release of the accused will be implemented (Sec. 117(5)). The tribunal is charged with reviewing the cases of all unfit accused persons at "any time" and, at least, once in every 6 months (Sec. 119(1)).

An unfit accused may not be held for a period greater than the "limiting term" set by the trial court. Such an individual may also be released by the "prescribed authority" at any time, upon the recommendation of the tribunal. Alternatively, the tribunal may reclassify the unfit accused as a "continued treatment patient" (that is to say, a civilly committed patient with all the rights of a person detained on a purely civil basis) (Sec. 127(1)(c)).

Although the New South Wales legislation creates a somewhat complex web of disposition procedures, it cannot be gainsaid that the new safeguards have greatly enhanced the legal status of the unfit accused. It is still possible for such persons to be held for periods that exceed the terms of imprisonment that might have been imposed had they been found fit to stand trial and duly convicted.

The Northern Territory of Australia has also rejected the traditional approach, which mandates automatic and indeterminate incarceration of the unfit accused (Criminal Code Act of 1983). The Criminal Code simply places the issue of disposition within the absolute discretion of the judiciary:

The court may order the accused person to be discharged or may order him to be kept in custody in such place and in such manner as the court thinks fit, or admit him to bail, until he can be dealt with according to law. (Sec. 357(c)).

A more cautious approach has been adopted in New Zealand, where the traditional system of detention at ministerial discretion has been modified by the granting of supervisory powers to the Supreme Court. The Criminal Justice Act of 1954 (R.S.N.Z. 1979, Sec. 39G) provides that a person who is "found to be under disability" shall be detained in a hospital (as a "special patient" under the Mental Health Act of 1969). The effect of this provision is that the unfit accused will remain in a hospital at ministerial discretion. However, certain modifications were made to the system by the Criminal Justice Amendment Act of 1969 (Sec. 2).

These amendments provide that the order, under which an unfit accused is detained in hospital, shall continue in force until the accused is brought forward for trial or his or her status is changed to that of a civilly committed patient. If the appropriate medical personnel certify that the accused is no longer "under a disability," then the minister of justice must either bring the accused to trial or change his or her status to that of an "ordinary" civilly committed patient. If the patient is still "under a disability," the minister of health, in concurrence with the minister of justice, may alter the accused's status to that of a civilly committed patient; however, where the offense charged is punishable with a term of imprisonment of 14 years, only the governor-general-in-council may make such an order (Criminal Justice Act of 1954, Sec. 39H). There is also provision for a Supreme Court judge to order an examination of an unfit accused who remains in psychiatric detention (New Zealand Mental Health Act of 1969, Sec. 74). The judge is granted the power to bring an accused to trial or, if appropriate, may direct that the charge or indictment be dismissed. If the charges are dismissed, the accused must be released unless the judge considers that it is "necessary," either for the patient's "own good" or "in the public interest," that he or she be detained as a civilly committed patient.

In England and Wales, the lot of the unfit accused has been greatly ameliorated by the passage of the Mental Health Act of 1983. As a consequence of the decision of the European Court of Human Rights, in *X v. The United Kingdom* (1981), unfit accused are no longer subject to a regime of detention at the absolute discretion of the home secretary (see Gostin, 1982b). Such persons are in the same position as patient-offenders, who have been placed under a hospital order coupled with a restriction order. The 1983 Mental Health Act provides for the continuation of the home secretary's power to release such patients or to remove restrictions; however, the mental health review tribunals have also been granted a *concurrent* jurisdiction to order an absolute or conditional discharge or to remove restrictions. If restrictions are removed, a patient under a hospital order is then placed on the same legal footing as a civilly committed patient. In England and Wales, the emphasis upon legalism may well become even more marked if the Butler Committee's recommendation that the judiciary have the ultimate discretion to provide for the placement of the unfit accused is ultimately implemented by the government (Butler, 1975).

It appears that other Commonwealth jurisdictions may well decide to abrogate the regime of indeterminate detention at ministerial discretion. The Law Reform Commission of Canada (1976, pp. 17–19), for example, has recommended that the lieutenant governor's warrant be abolished and that, in its stead, the court should control the disposition of the unfit accused. The commission also recommends the adoption of a "limiting term," similar to the device introduced in New South Wales. Such a "limiting term" would prevent an unfit accused person from being detained for a period that exceeds the approximate sentence that would have been imposed had he been fit to stand trial and convicted. In South Australia, the Mitchell Committee advanced somewhat similar proposals (Criminal Law and Penal Methods Reform Committee of South Australia, 1975, pp. 32–38).

Provisional Trials

A potential threat to the civil liberties of the unfit accused lurks in the various Commonwealth statutory provisions that determine *when* the issue of fitness may be raised. The potential danger rests in the possibility that the accused may be found unfit and subsequently be committed to a lengthy period of psychiatric incarceration without having been afforded any opportunity to present a valid defense to the charge(s) against them (see Verdun-Jones, 1981, pp. 376–380). Existing Commonwealth procedures generally provide some degree of protection to the accused in this respect, since the court concerned may postpone trial of the fitness issue until the opening of the case for the defense.[44] However, the scope of this protection is grossly inadequate because it only benefits the accused person, who can obtain his or her acquittal either by asserting that the prosecution has not established a *prima facie* case to answer or by fashioning a successful defense on the basis of the cross-examination of prosecution witnesses. Existing provisions still operate to prevent the accused's counsel from summoning his or her own

---

[44]See, for example, sections 543(4)(a) of the Canadian Criminal Code and section 4 of the Criminal Procedure (Insanity) Act of 1964 (U.K.).

witnesses in order to establish a successful defense. Such an outcome is clearly inequitable in the situation where the accused does, in fact, have a valid defense. In New South Wales, parliament has moved to remedy this potential inequity by establishing the mechanism of a provisional trial.

As noted earlier, where the Mental Health Review Tribunal has determined that it is unlikely that the unfit accused will recover within a period of 12 months and the attorney general decides to proceed with the charge(s), then a "special inquiry" must be conducted (Crimes Act, 1900 (N.S.W.) Sec. 428M(1), as amended in 1983). The court is required to undertake such an inquiry "for the purpose of ensuring, notwithstanding the unfitness of the person to be tried in accordance with the normal procedures, that the person is acquitted unless it can be proved to the requisite criminal standard of proof that, on the limited evidence available, the person committed the offense charged or any other offense available as an alternative to the offense charged" (Sec. 428M(2)). The verdicts available to a court or jury at the conclusion of a special inquiry are (a) not guilty of the offense charged; (b) not guilty on the ground of mental illness; (c) that on the limited evidence available, the accused person committed the offense charged; (d) that on the limited evidence available, the accused person committed an offense available as an alternative to the offense charged (Sec. 428O(5)). A verdict that the accused committed an offense constitutes only a "qualified finding of guilt" rather than a conviction (Sec. 428O(7)). As noted earlier, the court may nominate a "limiting term" that will determine the maximum period of detention. Normally the verdict following a special inquiry will operate as a bar to any subsequent criminal proceedings (Secs. 428O(7)(b) and 428R(1)); however, criminal proceedings may be recommenced prior to the expiration of the "limiting period" provided that the accused has not yet been released from custody as a prisoner or discharged as a forensic patient (Sec. 428R(2)).

The adoption of the device of a provisional trial represents a critical step in the slow march toward ensuring that fitness to stand trial procedures are geared toward protection of the accused person from loss of liberty. Significantly, the Law Reform Commission of Canada (1976, pp. 16–17) has also recommended the introduction of a form of provisional trial into the Canadian Criminal Code. The Butler Committee (1975) in England and Wales has presented a similar recommendation.[45] It remains to be seen whether other Commonwealth jurisdictions will follow suit and expand the scope of the growing trend of legalism that has manifested itself elsewhere in Commonwealth mental health legislation.

DISPOSITION OF MENTALLY DISORDERED OFFENDERS: THE HOSPITAL ORDER

Among the more significant developments that have recently occurred within the complex sphere of criminal justice is the series of major modifications wrought by the Mental Health Act of 1983, in relation to the system of hospital orders that prevails in England and Wales (see Gostin, 1983a, pp. 32–38). The "hospital order" has elicited a considerable degree of interest among criminal justice pundits in the Commonwealth because it affords the courts a valuable measure of flexibility in dealing with the mentally disordered offender (see Law Reform Commission of Canada, 1976, pp. 25–27; Potas, 1982, pp. 11–17, 153–174). In essence, this sentencing option furnishes the judiciary with the power to order that an offender be treated in a psychiatric hospital in lieu of imposing a sentence of imprisonment.

At present, the "hospital order" is available in relatively few of the other Commonwealth jurisdictions;[46] however, this situation may well change in the future. Indeed, there have been a number of advocates (e.g., Potas, 1982, pp. 153–174), who have strenuously urged introduction of the hospital order as a means of extending the range of sentencing options available to the judiciary in other jurisdictions. Among the most

---

[45]See a similar recommendation in the Thomson Report (Scotland); Committee on Criminal Procedure in Scotland (1975), para. 52.18.

[46]Similar legislative provisions exist in Tasmania; Mental Health Act of 1963 (Tas.) as amended, sections 48–49. Elsewhere there are a number of Commonwealth jurisdictions in which there are "close relatives" to the "hospital order" as it has developed in England and Tasmania: Criminal Justice Act of 1954 (as amended), (R. S. New Zealand, 1979, vol. 1, Sec. 39J); Mental Health Act of 1974, No. 2 (Queensland, Part IV); Mental Health Act of 1959 (Victoria), (Sec. 51); Mental Health Act of 1978 (Northern Territory), (Secs. 24–25); Criminal Law Consolidation Act of 1935–1975 (South Australia), Sec. 77a.

prominent of these advocates is the Canadian Law Reform Commission (1976, pp. 25–27), which championed the cause of the hospital order in a report submitted to the federal parliament in March 1976.

The relatively brief history of the hospital order in England and Wales is particularly illuminating insofar as it illustrates the critical problems that inevitably arise when an attempt is made to blend therapeutic with penal measures. It also affords a further example of the gradual legislative shift toward a greater emphasis upon "legalism."

The hospital order came into existence with the passage of the England and Wales Mental Health Act of 1959 (Sec. 60). Briefly, a judge was empowered to make a hospital order as an *alternative* to imposing a routine penal measure, such as imprisonment or a fine (see Prins, 1980, pp. 109–111). In the Crown Court, the offender must have been convicted of an offense other than murder. In a magistrate's court, the offender must have been convicted of an offense punishable by imprisonment upon summary conviction; however, in special circumstances, the magistrate's court was permitted to make an order without recording a conviction.[47] The effect of the hospital order has been succinctly delineated by the "government's white paper," *Review of the Mental Health Act 1959* (Department of Health and Social Security, 1978):

A hospital order enables an offender to be admitted to, and compulsorily detained in, a hospital for treatment for as long as necessary in the interests of his own health or safety or for the protection of other persons. In making the order the court is placing the patient in the hands of the doctors, foregoing any question of punishment and relinquishing from then onwards its own control over him. (p. 45)

In most respects, the offender would be treated in the same manner as a patient admitted to hospital under the ordinary procedures for civil commitment. For example, the offender would have the same rights of appeal to a mental health review tribunal (Gunn, 1979, p. 204). Under the provisions of the 1959 Act, the hospital order was initially valid for a period of 1 year and, thereafter, was renewable every 2 years. The patient-

offender could be released by his or her doctor, the hospital manager, or a mental health review tribunal.

Although the "white paper" blithely asserts that, in making a hospital order, the sentencing court is "foregoing any question of punishment," it would perhaps be more realistic to conceive of the order in terms of a somewhat uneasy union between punitive and treatment-oriented elements. As Potas (1982) has pointed out:

To assume that a hospital order is not punitive is to misconceive the object of this sanction. It shares with imprisonment the consequences of depriving an individual of his or her liberty. Like imprisonment it offers protection to the community by separating inmates from normal societal intercourse. Unlike imprisonment however, the aim of this disposition is to provide remedial action in the form of medical or psychiatric treatment in an attempt to rehabilitate or to retard the deterioration of a mentally disordered person. It is here that the object of rehabilitation assumes most meaning. Unfortunately, it is here also that the rights and liberties of individuals are at greatest risk. (pp. 13–14)

The "mixed" nature of the hospital order is accentuated by the power of the Crown Court to attach a restriction order where it "appears to the court, having regard to the nature of the offense, the antecedents of the offender, and the risk of his committing further offenses, that it is necessary for the protection of the public so to do" (Mental Health Act of 1959, Sec. 65). The restriction order could be imposed for either a fixed or an indefinite period. The practical effect of imposing a restriction order was to prevent the patient-offender's release from hospital, transfer to another hospital, or leave of absence without the permission of the home secretary. The restricted patient could not apply directly to the mental health review tribunal for his or her discharge, although the home secretary possessed the discretion to refer his case at any time to the tribunal and was required to do so, at certain intervals, upon the patient's request. Furthermore, the 1959 Act provided that, even when the patient was ultimately discharged, the home secretary was empowered to impose condi-

---

[47]Mental Health Act of 1959 (U.K.), (Sec. 60 (2)); see *R. v. Lincoln (Kestevan) Justices, ex. p. O'Connor* (1983), *Crim. L. Rev.* 621 (Q.B. Div. Ct.).

tions upon the patient's release and to recall him or her to a hospital at the minister's discretion (see Department of Health and Social Security, 1978, pp. 45–55; Gunn, 1979, pp. 205–209).

Clearly, the combination of a hospital and a restriction order represented a new, and disquieting, ingredient in the amalgamation of penal and therapeutic measures. More specifically, it was evident that a patient-offender could be held indefinitely not only without reference to the gravity of his or her offense but also without access to the discharge procedures that were routinely available to civilly committed patients. Significantly, the Court of Appeal ruled that "since in most cases the prognosis cannot be certain," it was preferable for courts to impose a restriction order without time limit rather than to prescribe a determinate period.[48] Lord Parker, C.J., suggests that the only exception should be "where the doctors are able to assert confidently that recovery will take place within a fixed period when the restriction order can properly be limited to that period."

The potential threat to the civil liberties of the patient-offender was underscored by E. Parker's analysis of restriction orders made by the courts in 1977. Parker (1980, p. 466) notes that the average period of detention under a restriction order was 4 1/2 years and proceeded to compare the proportion of mentally disordered offenders receiving restriction orders with the proportion of "normal" offenders receiving prison sentences of 5 years or more. Parker's conclusion is revealing:

> For each offence, where there are sufficient numbers to warrant a comparison, a greater proportion of mentally abnormal offenders receive restriction orders than do "normal" offenders receive prison sentences of five years or more. This suggests the courts consider that the public needs more protection from mentally abnormal than from normal offenders, even when their offences are similar.

Interestingly, the government "white paper" (Department of Health and Social Security, 1978) conceded that the device of the restriction order had been abused in certain cases: "There can be little doubt that restriction orders have been imposed on occasions where they are not really justified by the nature of the offence or by the offender's previous criminal and medical history" (p. 47).

Perhaps the most striking feature of the English experience with the hospital order has been the marked decline in its use during the last decade. It has been pointed out (Ashworth and Shapland, 1980, p. 633), for example, that the number of hospital orders had, by 1978, dwindled to 71% of the 1973 figure.

It has been contended (Prins, 1980, pp. 335 ff.; Department of Health and Social Security, 1978, pp. 43–44) that the major factor in this decline has been the increasing reluctance of local psychiatric hospitals to receive mentally disordered offenders as patients. The Mental Health Act of 1959 explicitly required that, before a hospital order could be made, the court must be satisfied that a hospital was willing to admit the offender within a period of 28 days. The source of the hospital's reluctance to admit offenders appears to rest in the changing nature of long-term mental health care during the past 2 decades. The vast majority of English mental health patients (88.3% in 1976) are now admitted on a voluntary basis (Department of Health and Social Security, 1978, p. 101), and the period of hospitalization is relatively brief. The creation of a "more open therapeutic environment" has produced a set of circumstances in which very few psychiatric hospitals maintain locked wards. In the words of the government "white paper" (Department of Health and Social Security, 1978, p. 43), these changes have "led to a situation where staff seem to have become increasingly reluctant to assume responsibility for treating patients who are, or whom it is feared may be, disruptive or violent." In many cases, it would appear that mental health professionals had genuine doubts concerning their ability to provide the requisite degree of security in relation to hospital order patients and were, in any event, completely unprepared to return to the "bad old days" of a predominantly custodial regime. It has also been contended (Prins, 1980, p. 337) that some psychiatrists were reluctant to accept patients under a restriction order since they needed the consent of the home secretary before they could discharge such patients or release them on home leave. Similarly, it has been suggested (Department of Health and Social Security, 1978, p. 43) that certain psychiatrists were unwilling to accept such a patient because they feared that

---

[48]R. v. Gardiner (1967), 51 Cr. App Rep 187; see also R. v. Hodge (1979) Crim. L. Rev. 602.

they might be placed in a position in which they would be forced to continue to assume responsibility for the patient, to whom they believed no further treatment should be offered. A final explanation for the decline in use of the hospital order rests in the shortage of beds within the four (maximum security) "special hospitals," in England and Wales that cater primarily to the mentally abnormal offender (see Prins, 1980, pp. 337–342).

It is illuminating to note that there has been a conspicuous decline in the use of hospital orders for patient-offenders diagnosed as "psychopaths." It is probably this group of mentally abnormal offenders that has contributed most to the reluctance of mental health professionals to accept patients under hospital orders. Nursing staff may well perceive such offenders to be particularly violent and disruptive, and psychiatrists may well have concluded that no efficacious modes of treatment exist in relation to many forms of psychopathy. Statistics, compiled by Ashworth and Shapland (1980, p. 633), reveal that between 1973 and 1978, whereas the overall number of hospital orders fell by 29%, the number of orders relating to "psychopaths" fell by some 55%. The authors conclude that:

> Unless one is willing to argue that fewer psychopaths are being convicted of offences, the inferences are either that the classification "psychopath" is being used more sparingly, or that those so classified are being dealt with by non-medical disposals, or both. (p. 633)

The enactment of major changes to the system of hospital orders, by the Mental Health Act of 1983, was preceded by an impressive degree of reflection. Among the more notable examinations of the hospital order are the appropriate sections of the reports of the Butler Committee (1975) and MIND (Gostin, 1977) as well as the government "white paper" (Department of Health and Social Security, 1978).

In its Interim Report, the Butler Committee (1974) addressed the issue of the unavailability of beds in the special hospitals and recommended the immediate establishment of "regional secure units," which would provide a lesser degree of security than the special hospitals but a greater degree than ordinary psychiatric hospitals. Although the government accepted this recommendation and specific funds were allocated for construction, little immediate progress was made. By 1979, some three or four psychiatric hospitals had established interim secure units but, elsewhere, the government's plans were facing a number of major obstacles (see Prins, 1980, pp. 342–344; Faulk, 1979).

Perhaps greater significance should be attached to the various attempts to invest the hospital order with more efficacious legal safeguards. Ironically, the most sweeping reform appears to have been forced upon the government by external events. As noted earlier, one of the more objectionable features of the restriction order was that it deprived the patient-offender of direct access to the Mental Health Review Tribunal and left her or his discharge a matter for absolute ministerial discretion. In X v. The United Kingdom (1981),[49] the European Court of Human Rights ruled that the home secretary's exclusive power to discharge a restricted patient was inconsistent with the provisions of article 5 (4) of the European Convention on Human Rights, which requires that a person detained by reason of "unsoundness of mind" must have a right to periodic judicial review. The court also ruled that the remedy of habeas corpus was too narrow in its scope to provide an adequate safeguard against unjustifiable detention. In response to these rulings, the Mental Health Act of 1983 abrogated the purely advisory functions of the mental health review tribunals and replaced them with the power to order the restricted patient-offender's discharge (either absolutely or conditionally) or to remove restrictions (see Gostin, 1982a). Curiously, this legislative change did not affect the home secretary's existing powers in relation to restricted patients. The Mental Health Review Tribunal and the minister will apparently exercise concurrent jurisdiction in relation to the discharge of such patients.[50] In Gostin's estimation (1982b)

> Future research will indicate whether this change in structure will lead to a significant

---

[49]Judgment delivered, November 5th, 1981.

[50]Gostin (1982b) notes that, although the home secretary and the MHRT will have concurrent jurisdiction to order an absolute or conditional discharge or to remove restrictions, the minister will continue to enjoy exclusive discretion to consent to the transfer of an offender-patient to another hospital.

alteration in the rate of discharge. The primary benefit, therefore, to restricted patients would derive from more open and rigorous procedures with the opportunity for effective representation of their interests. Whether fairer procedures will operate is dependent upon the frequency, speed and quality of tribunal hearings. (p. 791)

In this connection, it is significant that Peay (1981, 1982), on the basis of extensive research, has raised some serious questions concerning the efficacy of mental health review tribunals as safeguards of patients' rights; in her view (1982), "more frequent access to an inadequate safeguard will not improve the effectiveness of that safeguard" (p. 86).

Ironically, in one respect, the Mental Health Act of 1983 has actually curtailed the rights of an offender-patient to review. Under the provisions of the Mental Health Act of 1959, an individual under a hospital order had the right to apply to a mental health review tribunal during the first 6 months of detention. However, under the Act of 1983, this right has been abrogated: According to Gostin (1983a, p. 34), this move was allegedly taken in order to place hospital-order patients upon an equal footing with restricted patients, who never enjoyed this right. However, Gostin has questioned the validity of the government's contention that this consistency is required by the terms of the European Convention on Human Rights.

Apart from these critical modifications to the jurisdiction of the mental health review tribunals, the Mental Health Act of 1983 left the basic structure of the system of hospital orders relatively untouched. Nevertheless, the various changes that *were* introduced may generally be said to reflect the influence of the rising trend of legalism in mental health legislation. For example, an attempt has been made to incorporate some additional safeguards into the restriction order device. In line with a recommendation, made by the Butler Committee (1975, recommendation 108), the Mental Health Act of 1983 adds the proviso that a restriction order may not be made unless it is necessary to "protect the public from serious harm" (Mental Health Act of 1983, Sec. 41). Furthermore, the Act provides that the "responsible medical officer" must provide the home secretary with an annual report in respect of each restricted

patient, also a recommendation of the Butler Committee (1975, recommendation 114).

The criteria for imposition of a hospital order have been modified in accordance with the various changes introduced in relation to the process of involuntary civil commitment. In particular, section 37 of the 1983 Act now specifies that a candidate for a hospital order must be suffering from "mental illness," "psychopathic disorder," "mental impairment," or "severe mental impairment" and that such a condition must warrant detection in a mental hospital. Significantly, where the offender is suffering from "psychopathic disorder" or "mental impairment," it must be established that the proposed treatment is "likely to alleviate or prevent a deterioration of his condition." The initial period of detention has been reduced from 12 to 6 months.[51]

An important innovation, introduced by the 1983 Act, attempts to reduce the likelihood of an offender being sent to prison, rather than a hospital, owing to the difficulty of finding a hospital willing to take him. Section 39 provides that, where a court is considering the imposition of a hospital order, it may request that the regional health authority submit relevant information concerning those hospitals that might have suitable facilities. This provision should be of great assistance to sentencing courts since it will, in effect, require the regional health authority to articulate an explanation as to why a hospital bed cannot be found for any particular offender. Insofar as section 39 represents an attempt to limit the exercise of, hitherto unrestricted, professional discretion, it may well be characterized as an example of the "new legalism."

The 1983 Act (Sec. 38) also blazes a new trail insofar as it creates the mechanism of an "interim hospital order." This "trial order" can be made initially for a period of 12 weeks; thereafter, it may be renewed for periods of 28 days up to a maximum of 6 months. Once the interim order has expired, the court may decide either to make a full-blown hospital order or to impose a routine penal sanction, such as imprisonment. No doubt, the interim hospital order will prove to be an attractive option to the courts since it permits a "trial run" before a full commitment to a hospital order need be made. Similarly, it may well be the case that hospitals will become somewhat more willing to accept mentally abnormal offend-

---

[51]The order may be renewed for a further period of 6 months and, thereafter, for periods of 1 year.

ers once they have been afforded the opportunity both to view a prospective patient at close quarters and to evaluate the potential efficacy of the appropriate treatment modalities. However, Gostin has contended that the interim hospital order may pose a potential threat to the civil rights of an offender, in the situation where the court ultimately decides to impose a term of imprisonment instead of making a full-blown hospital order. More specifically, Gostin (1983a, p. 35) notes that the legislation does *not* provide that any time spent in a hospital shall be discounted from the total term of imprisonment—despite the fact that the offender may have been compulsorily detained in hospital for a period of up to 6 months.

In many respects, it is possible to conclude that the recent modifications to the system of hospital orders have injected a substantial dose of legalism into the process. The inherent tension between the therapeutic and penal dimensions of the hospital order is particularly conspicuous in the situation where it is coupled with a restriction order and it is in this area that the Mental Health Act of 1983 has fashioned its most significant changes. The dramatic expansion of the jurisdiction of the mental health review tribunals, and the tightening up of the criteria that must be satisfied prior to the imposition of a restriction order, are clearly examples of the trend toward the imposition of more specific legal controls upon the operation of the system. Apart from the issue of restriction orders, it is also evident that the patient-offender who is subject to a hospital order will be the beneficiary of the various improvements in the position of the involuntarily committed patient that have been wrought by the 1983 Act. For example, the hospital-order patient will enjoy shorter periods of detention, greater access to the mental health review tribunals, and the narrowing of the criteria for commitment (see Gostin, 1983a, p. 34). There is little doubt that these improvements in the patient-offender's legal position represent a gradual move toward acceptance of a greater degree of legalistic control of the hospital order system.

Curiously, there is a critical issue that has not been addressed in the Mental Health Act of 1983—namely, the right of the competent offender to withhold consent to a hospital order. Once such an order has been made, the patient-offender loses the right to refuse treatment (except in relation to particularly intrusive treatments such as psychosurgery and "chemical castration"), since he or she is subject to part IV of the 1983 Act, which permits compulsory treatment in most instances. In the "ideal" model of legalism, consent of the competent patient to the imposition of a hospital order would constitute a fundamental requirement. Indeed, in recommending the adoption of the hospital order in Canada, the Law Reform Commission of Canada (1976, p. 31) placed great emphasis upon the issue of consent. It recommended that "as a general rule there be no treatment of accused or offenders at any stage of the criminal process without consent." The only exceptions would be where there is a clear need for treatment in an "emergency" situation or an individual has been determined to be "incompetent." Therefore, the commission (1976, pp. 46–47) recommends that the making of a hospital order be predicated upon the consent of the offender. The absence of such a requirement in England and Wales suggests that a considerable distance still remains to be travelled along the road toward the "new legalism."

CRIMINAL RESPONSIBILITY

Within the Commonwealth, there is considerable diversity among the legislative provisions and case law concerning the thorny issue of criminal responsibility. Given this diversity, it is necessary to analyze developments in this area by dividing the relevant jurisdictions into three groups: (a) Canada, (b) Australia and New Zealand, and (c) England and Wales.

Canada

In Canada, there has been no diminution in reliance upon the defense of insanity. Indeed, the 1976 enactment of certain amendments to the Criminal Code (Sec. 669) provided a powerful incentive to its continued use (Webster, Menzies, & Jackson, 1982, pp. 105–106). As a consequence of these amendments, those persons who are convicted of first- or second-degree murder must be sentenced to life imprisonment with parole ineligibility periods of 25 years or 10–25 years, respectively. Just as, historically, the insanity defense developed as a means of evading the noose (Verdun-Jones & Smandych, 1982), so does the modern version of the defense serve as a viable alternative to these minimum terms of imprisonment. Another significant factor that operates to maintain the vitality of the insanity defense is the absence of a formal doctrine of diminished responsibility in the Canadian Criminal Code.[52] Yet a further element in the Canadian insanity brew is the ability of the Crown to raise the issue of insanity over the objections of counsel for the defense (Verdun-Jones, 1979, pp. 45–47).[53] Unlike the situation in England and Wales (see Ashworth, 1979, pp. 482–483), the Crown may pursue this course of action even if the accused has not placed the state of his or her mind at issue. The Crown's power in this respect may well furnish a partial explanation for the use of the insanity defense in relation to a broad range of criminal offenses.

Section 16 of the Canadian Criminal Code represents a modified version of the M'Naghten rules (Verdun-Jones, 1979, pp. 20–25). The precise test of insanity is articulated in section 16(2):

For the purposes of this section a person is insane when he is in a state of natural imbecility or has disease of the mind to an extent that renders him incapable of appreciating the nature and quality of an act or omission or of knowing that an act or omission is wrong.

The most significant divergence from the wording of the M'Naghten rules is to be found in parliament's substitution of the word "appreciating" for the word "knowing" in relation to the phrase, "the nature and quality of an act" (Verdun-Jones, 1979, pp. 26–30). Curiously, it is only in recent years that the Supreme Court of Canada has underscored the importance of this distinction

between the wording of section 16 and the English M'Naghten rules. The leading cases concerning this issue were both decided in 1980. In *Regina v. Barnier* (1980), Estey J. (delivering the judgment of the court) wrote:

The verb "Know" has a positive connotation requiring a bare awareness, the act of receiving information without more. The act of appreciating, on the other hand, is a second state in a mental process requiring the analysis of knowledge or experience in one manner or another. (p. 203)

Similarly, in *Cooper v. The Queen* (1980), Dickson J. (speaking for the majority of the court) stated:

I accept the view that the first branch of the test, in employing the word "appreciates," imports an additional requirement to mere knowledge of the physical quality of the act. The requirement, unique to Canada, is that of perception, an ability to perceive the consequences, impact, and results of a physical act. (p. 147)

In other respects, however, the Supreme Court has preferred the traditionally narrow interpretation of the M'Naghten rules that have long characterized criminal law jurisprudence in England. For example, in *Schwartz v. The Queen* (1977), the court decided that "wrong," in section 16(2), meant "legally" and not "morally" wrong. In *Schwartz* the Supreme Court eagerly embraced the English authorities, *R v. Codere* (1916) and

---

[52]It has been contended that there is a rapidly evolving doctrine of diminished responsibility that has been entirely fashioned by the courts. The Supreme Court of Canada has recognized that mental illness, falling short of insanity within the meaning of section 16 of the Code, may nevertheless operate to negate the specific intent required for conviction of first- as opposed to second-degree murder. See *More v. The Queen* (1963), S.C.R. 522; *McMartin v. The Queen* (1964), S.C.R. 484; *R. v. Mitchell* (1964), S.C.R. 471.

Other courts have found this principle to be applicable to all offenses requiring proof of "specific intent": *R. v. Blackmore* (1967), 1 C.R.N.S. 286 (N.S.S.C., App. Div.); *R. v. Baltzer* (1975), 27 C.C.C. (2d) 118 (N.S.S.C., App. Div.); *R. v. Hilton* (1977), 34 C.C.C. (2d) 206 (Ont. C.A.); *R. v. LeChasseur* (1970), 38 C.C.C. (2d) 319 (Que. C.A.); *R. v. Wright* (1979), 48 C.C.C. (2d) 334 (Alta. S.C., App. Div.); *R. v. Fournier* (1982), 70 C.C.C. (2d) 351 (Que. C.A.); *R. v. Fiddler* (1981), 58 C.C.C. (2d) 517 (Alta. C.A.). See, generally, Gannage, 1981; Topp, 1975; Verdun-Jones, 1979, pp. 42–45.

[53]Recent authorities suggest that the power of the Crown to raise the issue of insanity is subject to the control of the trial judge. In *R. v. Simpson* (1977), 35 C.C.C. (2d) 337 (Ont. C.A.), Martin J. A. ruled that "Where the prosecution seeks to adduce evidence that the accused was insane at the time of the act, the proper test, in my view, is not whether, if advanced by the accused, the evidence would be sufficient to require the defence of insanity to be submitted to the jury by the trial Judge, but whether it is sufficiently substantial and creates such a grave question whether the accused had the capacity to commit the offence that the interest of justice requires it to be adduced." See also *R. v. Saxell* (1980), 59 C.C.C. (2d) 176 (Ont. C.A.); *R. v. Dickie (No. 1)* (1982), 67 C.C.C. (2d) 218 (Ont. C.A.).

Windle (1952), and decisively rejected the decision of the Australian High Court, in *Stapleton v. The Queen* (1952–1953), in which it had been held that "wrong," in the M'Naghten rules, meant "wrong having regard to the everyday standards of reasonable people" (see generally Verdun-Jones, 1979, pp. 30–36).[54]

If there is a consistent theme, underlying the Supreme Court's narrow interpretation of the insanity defense, it may well be found in its resolute determination to ensure that those offenders, suffering only from a personality disorder, do not enjoy the benefit of the defense. In *Chartrand v. The Queen* (1977), for example, the court firmly rejected the notion that irresistible impulse per se could bring an offense within the bounds of section 16 of the Criminal Code (Verdun-Jones, 1979, pp. 36–42). Significantly, Chartrand was alleged to be suffering from a psychopathic personality disorder. In this respect, De Grandpre J. held that:

> Chartrand was therefore able to distinguish between right and wrong, and although he was ill, he was technically sane. What the witness adds on the subject of the inner pathological process cannot be taken into consideration under our criminal legislation, which does not recognize the diminished responsibility theory. (p. 318)

Although the Supreme Court has accepted the view that, for the purposes of section 16, a personality disorder *may* constitute a "disease of the mind," it has also stressed the view that a personality disorder does not generally affect an individual's capacity to appreciate "the nature and quality of an act or omission" or to "know" that it is "wrong." In *Kjeldsen v. The Queen* (1981), the appellant was charged with murder, following the brutal rape and murder of a female taxi driver. Ironically, Kjeldsen committed these acts while on a day pass from a mental hospital in which he had been detained after an acquittal, by reason of insanity, upon charges involving rape and attempted murder. The psychiatric witnesses were unanimous in their diagnosis of Kjeldsen as a "dangerous psychopath with sexually deviant tendencies." However, the medical witnesses disagreed as to whether the accused was capable of

"appreciating the nature and quality" of his acts. The psychiatrists, summoned by the defense, employed a broad definition of this phrase, "which involved not only an ability to foresee the physical consequences of one's acts but, as well, a capacity to foresee and understand the subjective or emotional reactions of those affected" (p. 163).

The defense experts contended that, in light of this definition, a psychopath such as Kjeldsen could not be considered to possess the capacity to appreciate the nature and quality of his acts. On the other hand, the Crown's psychiatric witnesses applied a more restrictive interpretation, which was limited to a consideration of whether the accused had the capacity to "understand and foresee the physical consequences of conduct" (p. 164); in their view, the accused's indifference to the consequences of his acts was irrelevant to the issue of insanity. Ultimately, the Supreme Court ruled that the trial judge had been correct in accepting the interpretation of the Crown witnesses. In the words of McIntyre J., who delivered the opinion of the Supreme Court:

> To be capable of "appreciating" the nature and quality of his acts, an accused person must have the capacity to know what he is doing; in the case at bar, for example, to know that he was hitting the woman on the head with the rock, with great force, and in addition he must have the capacity to estimate and to understand the physical consequences which would flow from his act, in this case that he was causing physical injury which could result in death. (p. 166)

The Court expressly approved a passage from the judgment of the Ontario Court of Appeal in the earlier case of *Regina v. Simpson* (1977). In this passage, Martin J.A. had stated that:

> While I am of the view that s.16(2) exempts from liability an accused who by reason of disease of the mind has no real understanding of the nature, character and consequences of the act at the time of its commission, I do not think the exemption provided by the section extends to one who has the necessary understanding of the

---

[54]For a "generous" consideration of the question of whether the accused knew his act was legally wrong, see *R. v. Budic (No. 3)* (1978), 43 C.C.C. (2d) 419 (Alta. Sup. Ct., App. Div.).

nature, character and consequences of the act, but merely lacks appropriate feelings for the victim or (lacks feelings of remorse or guilt for what he has done, even though such lack of feeling stems from "disease of the mind." Appreciation of the nature and quality of the act does not import a requirement that the act be accompanied by appropriate feeling about the effect of the act on other people. . . . No doubt the absence of such feelings is a common characteristic of many persons who engage in repeated and serious criminal conduct. (p. 355)

Although the Supreme Court's approval of the reasoning employed by Martin J.A. is eminently reasonable, its decision to limit the scope of the insanity defense, by interpreting the phase "nature and quality" as referring exclusively to the *physical* dimensions of the accused's act or omission, smacks of conceptual overkill. Unfortunately, the Supreme Court, in its apparent zeal to exclude psychopaths from the benefits of the insanity defense, has so circumscribed the boundaries of section 16 of the Code that it may now be extraordinarily difficult for an accused person suffering from *any* form of mental illness to establish the defense in Canada. The court's restrictive approach is amply illustrated by the strange case of *Regina v. Abbey* (1982). The accused had been charged with importing cocaine and possession of cocaine for the purpose of trafficking. Both the Crown and defense psychiatrists agreed that he was suffering from a mental illness known as "hypomania," although they disagreed as to whether he was "capable of appreciating the nature and quality" of his acts. The trial judge acquitted Abbey by reason of insanity. The judge found that the accused was suffering from a delusion that he was the recipient of power from an external source and that he was protected from punishment by this mysterious force; therefore, he ruled that Abbey lacked the capacity to appreciate the nature and quality of his acts because his mental illness destroyed his ability to consider an important consequence of his conduct — namely, legal punishment. Applying the restrictive approach, manifested in the *Kjeldsen* case, the Supreme Court ultimately ruled that the trial judge had erred in his interpretation of section 16(2). Dickson J., who delivered the judgment of the Court, reiterated the view that, while section 16(2) requires "an ability to perceive the consequences, impact, and results of a physical act," the word "consequences" refers only to the *physical* consequences of the accused's act:

With respect, the trial judge has confused the "ability to perceive the consequences, impact, and results of a physical act" . . . with a belief, however unjustified, that the legal sanction imposed for the commission of the prohibited act, the "legal consequences," was somehow inapplicable to him. The delusion under which Abbey was supposedly labouring was that he would not get caught, or, if caught, would benefit from some undefined immunity to prosecution. Such a delusion by no means brings him under the first arm of the insanity test in s.16(2) of the *Criminal Code* as developed in the recent cases. (pp. 401–402)

In Canada, the inexorable consequences of an insanity acquittal is indeterminate incarceration at the pleasure of the lieutenant governor. It is clear that the Criminal Code provides that the trial court has absolutely no discretion to release a person acquitted by reason of insanity but, rather, requires that he must be "kept in strict custody" until the pleasure of the lieutenant governor is known (Sec. 542(2)).

Significantly, in *R v. Saxell* (1980), the Ontario Court of Appeal ruled that this legislative scheme did not violate any of the rights, guaranteed by the Canadian Bill of Rights, even in the situation where the question of insanity is raised by the prosecution rather than the defense. Weatherston J.A., in delivering the judgment of the court, proffered a sweeping justification for the regime of indeterminate detention:

Society has a legitimate interest in persons who have committed some serious social harm, but who have been found not to be criminally responsible on account of mental disorder; it is justified in subjecting those persons to further diagnosis and assessment, in exercising appropriate control over them, if necessary, and in providing them with suitable medical treatment. There is an underlying assumption that they may remain a danger to the public because they have, in fact, committed some act which would have been a criminal act had they not been insane when the act was committed. It may well be that in individual cases that underlying assumption is not valid, but that does not mean that the legislative scheme in itself, offends the right of equality before the law or authorizes or effects

CAMROSE LUTHERAN COLLEGE
LIBRARY

arbitrary detention or imprisonment. Parliament must necessarily paint with a broad brush. (p. 187)

It remains to be seen whether a challenge to this legislative scheme would be more successful under the Charter of Rights and Freedoms; however, the approach adopted by the court in *Saxell* suggests that such a challenge would probably fail.[55]

A person who has been acquitted by reason of insanity can only be released from custody when an order-in-council has been issued by the provincial cabinet (Criminal Code, Sec. 545 (1)); hence the ultimate decision as to release is unequivocally "political" in nature. In recent years, the case of each patient, detained under a lieutenant governor's warrant, has been automatically reviewed by a provincial board of review (Criminal Code, Sec. 547). Nevertheless, patients remain in a relatively powerless position since they have no independent right to set the wheels of the review process rolling on their own initiative. Furthermore, it is significant that the review boards' function is purely *advisory* in nature; the final decision to release can only be made by the provincial cabinet.

Although this legislative framework places those acquitted by reason of insanity in a veritable legal limbo, it is significant that Canadian courts have recently mounted an attempt to introduce an element of "legalism" into the control of the review process. The spearhead of this attempt has been the evolving "duty of fairness" that has been applied on a number of occasions to the decision-making processes of the provincial review boards. The first case in which the duty to act fairly was to be upheld by the review board was *In re Abel et al. and Advisory Review Board* (1980). The Ontario Court of Appeal ruled that the chairman of the Ontario Review Board had acted unfairly by ruling that he had no jurisdiction to make hospital reports, submitted to the board, available to the patient-applicants' counsel. By failing to consider the question of release of the records, the chairman had effectively denied the applicants' natural justice in that they had not been afforded an opportunity to ascertain

the nature of the case against them. However, the court also held that the board has a broad discretion as to what information (if any) shall be released, and the court indicated that the board may impose conditions upon any release:

The Board has to obtain the facts to which it is going to apply its mind. If lawyers are going to represent their patient-clients adequately, they need to know the substance of those facts . . . the Board "need not quote chapter and verse." There may be good reason why some of the specific facts should not be revealed. This is for the Board to decide. . . .
What terms, if any, should be imposed when disclosure is made is also a matter for the Board to decide. While it may place the lawyers in an awkward situation, one can envisage cases where information might be disclosed in terms that it not be disclosed to the client. (pp. 167–168)

In *In re Egglestone and Mousseau and Advisory Review Board* (1983), an Ontario divisional court followed the reasoning of the *Abel* case in holding that the chairman of the review board had not acted unfairly in determining that an applicant's hospital and board files could only be viewed by his counsel (and/or a duly qualified psychiatrist) on the basis that disclosure not be made to the applicant without first obtaining the chairman's consent. However, the court also ruled that the board had acted unfairly in relation to a separate issue. It was the practice of the board to make arrangements for the two psychiatric members to conduct private interviews with patients, prior to the formal hearing of their cases. Although patients and their counsel were permitted to be present at the hearing, they were subsequently excluded when the psychiatric members of the board presented their professional opinions to their colleagues. The court (by a 2–1 majority) held that the board's practice was in breach of its duty to act fairly. Griffiths J. held that this duty required that, subject to the discretion of the chairman, the information gathered by the psychiatric members of the board should be disclosed

---

[55]In *R. v. Kieling* (April 23, 1983), 9 W.C.B. 471, the Ontario County Court ruled that the psychiatric incarceration of an *unfit* accused (under a lieutenant governor's warrant) for a period of 9 months did not violate section 12 of the Canadian Charter of Rights and Freedoms (prohibiting "cruel and unusual punishment"), despite the fact that the *maximum* penalty for the offense charged was only 6 months imprisonment. This approach reflects that adopted in the *Saxell* case.

to the patient and his counsel and that the patient and/or his counsel should be present when the psychiatric members proffer their reports to their colleagues on the board. However, Griffiths J. emphasized that there may well be circumstances in which the

> chairman may decide in the exercise of his discretion that counsel alone may be present, on an understanding from counsel, not to disclose any information so acquired to his client. (p. 11)

In *In re McCann and The Queen* (1982), the British Columbia Court of Appeal carried the approach in *Abel* and *Egglestone* a significant step further when it quashed an order-in-council passed by the lieutenant governor. The British Columbia Order-in-Council Patients' Review Board had recommended a substantial variation in the terms and conditions under which a patient was permitted to remain outside the hospital; this recommendation was subsequently adopted by the lieutenant governor. However, the necessary order-in-council was passed without McCann's knowledge and without notice being given to him that the board was considering a recommendation to change his status. Hinkson J.A., delivering the opinion of the court, ruled that the board was under a duty to "observe the requirements of procedural fairness" and that this duty had not been fulfilled in McCann's case. The court's decision may well have the impact of rendering the exercise of the lieutenant governor's discretion considerably less impervious to judicial review than it has been in the past:

> If the Lieutenant-Governor expresses his pleasure by way of other orders in council in the future, upon the basis of recommendations received by him from the Order in Council Patients Review Board, such recommendations must be reached upon the basis of procedural fairness. (p. 188)

So long as the Canadian parliament continues to be loath to tinker with the Criminal Code structure of indeterminate detention, it will remain the function of the courts to introduce principles of fundamental justice into the murky realm of the lieutenant governor's warrant.[56]

In recent years, one of the more troublesome problems facing Canadian criminal courts has been the increasing popularity of the defense of (non-insane) automatism (see generally Campbell, 1981; Holland, 1982; Mewett & Manning, 1978, pp. 235–260; Stuart, 1982, pp. 77–96; Verdun-Jones, 1979, pp. 50–70). Whereas a verdict of "not guilty by reason of insanity" propels an accused person into a regime of indeterminate incarceration, successful reliance upon the defense of automatism results in a total acquittal. Therefore, it is scarcely surprising that the task of distinguishing the boundaries of automatism from those of the insanity defense has assumed major significance. In delimiting these boundaries, the critical issue is the definition of the phrase "disease of the mind," which is contained in section 16(2) of the Canadian Criminal Code. Where it is established that a state of automatism was induced by a "disease of the mind," then the defendant may not be acquitted on the basis of the defense of automatism but must rather be acquitted by reason of insanity.[57] Whether a particular state of mind is capable of constituting a "disease of the mind" is considered to be a matter of law for the trial judge rather than the jury to decide.[58]

Underlying judicial attempts to fashion a satisfactory definition of "disease of the mind" is a major policy consideration; namely, the safety of the community. Because a successful defense of automatism results in a total acquittal, it is possible that a defendant who is perceived to be "dangerous" may be released into the community without any controls (medical or otherwise) on his conduct.

Increased judicial concern with public safety has been manifested in a significant narrowing of the parameters of the defense of (non-insane) automatism and a corresponding expansion of the scope of the insanity defense. The Supreme Court of Canada has achieved this end by adopting a

---

[56]In 1976, the Law Reform Commission of Canada (1976, p. 22) recommended that an acquittal by reason of insanity should be made a "real acquittal," subject only to a "post-acquittal" hearing to determine whether the individual should be civilly detained on the basis of his or her psychiatric dangerousness.

[57]*Bratty v. Attorney-General for Northern Ireland* (1963), A.C. 386 (H.L.); *Rabey v. The Queen* (1980), 54 C.C.C. (2d) 1 (S.C.C.); *R. v. Revelle* (1979), 48 C.C.C. (2d) 267 (Ont. C.A.), affirmed at (1981), 61 C.C.C. (2d) 576 (S.C.C.).

[58]*Rabey v. The Queen* (1980), 54 C.C.C. (2d) 1; *Cooper v. The Queen* (1980), 51 C.C.C. (2d) 129 (S.C.C.); *R. v. Rafuse* (1980), 53 C.C.C. (2d) 161 (B.C.C.A.); *R. v. Rolls* (1981), 62 C.C.C. (2d) 512 (Yuk. Terr. C.A.).

broad interpretation of the concept "disease of the mind." For example, in *Cooper v. The Queen* (1980), Dickson J., speaking for the majority of the court, stated that:

> In summary, one might say that in a legal sense, "disease of the mind" enhances any illness, disorder or abnormal condition which impacts the human mind and its functioning, excluding however, self-induced states caused by alcohol or drugs, as well as transitory mental states such as hysteria or concussion. (p. 144)

This approach set the stage for the court's momentous decision in *Rabey v. The Queen* (1980). This case raised the highly significant issue of whether the subjection of the accused to a "psychological blow" may constitute the basis for a successful assertion of the defense of automatism. Prior to the *Rabey* decision, there had been a number of cases in which Canadian courts had been requested to hold that certain types of emotional stress may produce a state of mind that entitles the accused to be acquitted on the basis of a defense of (non-insane) automatism. The underlying theory of the defense, in these cases, was that such stress should be considered as being analogous to the infliction of a physical blow to the head. Unfortunately, the assertion of the "psychological blow" defense created a situation in which the outcome of cases, often involving the infliction of death or extreme violence, effectively turned upon the ability of expert witnesses to manipulate medical and legal terminology so as to establish that the dissociated state of mind, experienced by the accused, was attributable to the unexpected psychological blow rather than to an ongoing pathological condition (see generally Verdun-Jones, 1979, pp. 57–67).[59] One commentator (Bayne, 1975) advanced the wry observation that:

> The outcome of any given trial seems to vary with the semantic talents of the psychiatrists in avoiding the 'disease of the mind' pigeon-hole or in aiming for it, and with the stakes for, which defence and crown are playing. (p. 281)

It was against this background of conflicting jurisprudence that the issues in *Rabey* took shape. Rabey had severely assaulted a fellow university student after he had discovered a letter, in which the victim expressed a sexual interest in another man and indicated that she regarded Rabey as a "nothing" who kept "bugging" her in class. Rabey testified that he could not remember striking the victim. A psychiatric expert testified, on behalf of the defense, that the accused had been in a "dissociative state" at the time of the violent incident in question. In his view, this dissociative state had been induced by the powerful emotional shock suffered by the accused when his image of the victim was "shattered" by his discovery of her real feelings toward him. The witness went on to contend that a conversation, which the accused had with the victim on the following day, had triggered the dissociative state and that Rabey's condition was comparable to that produced by a physical blow. In the opinion of this expert witness, there was no evidence that the accused suffered from any pathological condition and that it was unlikely that the dissociative state would recur. However, a psychiatric witness, appearing on behalf of the Crown, testified that the accused was not in a dissociative state at the time of the attack on the victim. In his view, the defendant merely went into an "extreme rage" and could probably have formed the specific intent required for the offense. The witness also contended that, if the accused had been in a dissociative state, then he would have been suffering from a "disease of the mind" because such a state is a subdivision of hysterical amnesia, which he regarded as a mental illness. The trial judge nevertheless acquitted Rabey on the basis that there was a reasonable doubt as to whether he was in a state of automatism, as a result of a dissociative state induced by an external cause. In her view, the defendant was, therefore, not insane within the meaning of section 16 of the Criminal Code. However, in *R. v. Rabey* (1977) the Ontario Court of Appeal (1978) allowed an appeal by the Crown and ordered a new trial.

In delivering the judgment of the court, Martin J.A. emphasized that it is the responsibility of

---

[59]The "psychological blow" automatism defense was apparently successful in *R. v. K.* (1971), 2 O.R. 401 (Ont. H. Ct.); *R. v. Cullum* (1974), 14 C.C.C. (2d) 294 (Ont. Cty. Ct.); and *R. v. Gottschalk* (1974), 22 C.C.C. (2d) 415 (Ont. Prov. Ct.). The defense was apparently rejected in *Parnerkar v. The Queen* (1974), S.C.R. 449, *R. v. Sproule* (1975), 30 C.R.N.S. 56 (Ont. C.A.); *R. v. James* (1975), 30 C.R.N.S. 65 (Ont. S.C.); *R. v. Mulligan* (1974), 26 C.R.N.S. 179 (Ont. C.A.), affirmed (1977) 1 S.C.R. 612.

the trial judge to determine which mental conditions fall within the term "disease of the mind," and he suggested that, although it is a legal concept, it nevertheless contains a "substantial medical component":

> The legal or policy component relates to (a) the scope of the exemption from criminal responsibility to be afforded by mental disorder or disturbance, and (b) the protection of the public by the control and treatment of persons who have caused serious harms while in a mentally disordered or disturbed state. The medical component of the term, generally, is medical opinion as to how the mental condition in question is viewed or characterized medically. Since the medical component of the term reflects or should reflect the state of medical knowledge at a given time, the concept of "disease of the mind" is capable of evolving with increased medical knowledge with respect to mental disorder or disturbance. (p. 425)

Martin J.A. proceeded to underscore the principle that whether a particular mental state or condition constitutes a "disease of the mind" is a question of law for the judge, not the medical witnesses, to decide. Significantly, the court rejected the view of Lord Denning, in *Bratty v. A-G. for Northern Ireland* (1961), to the effect that a mental condition must be "prone to recur" before it may be termed a "disease of the mind"; on the contrary, Martin J.A. ruled that "the mental disorder may be permanent or temporary, curable or incurable" (p. 427). On the other hand, the court reaffirmed the principle, articulated in the English case of *Regina v. Quick* (1973), that transient mental states or disturbances, produced by such external causes as drugs or violence (resulting in concussion), do not constitute a "disease of the mind." Martin J.A. proceeded to fashion a "simple" test for distinguishing between insanity and (non-insane) automatism as defenses to a criminal charge:

> In general, the distinction to be drawn is between a malfunctioning of the mind arising from some cause that is primarily internal to the accused, having its source in his psychological or emotional makeup, or in some organic pathology, as opposed to a malfunctioning of the mind, which is the transient effect produced by some specific external factor such as, for example, concussion. Any malfunctioning of the mind or

mental disorder having its source primarily in some subjective condition or weakness internal to the accused (whether fully understood or not) may be a "disease of the mind" if it prevents the accused from knowing what he is doing, but transient disturbances of consciousness due to certain specific external factors do not fall within the concept of disease of the mind. (p. 430)

Martin J.A. concluded that the issue of whether or not any particular transient mental state can be classified as a "disease of the mind" must be decided on a case-to-case basis.

In *Rabey*, the Court of Appeal concluded that the dissociative state, alleged by the accused, could not be categorized as a transient state produced by an external cause. On the contrary, it could only be designated as a "disease of the mind":

> The ordinary stresses and disappointments of life which are the common lot of mankind do not constitute an external cause constituting an explanation for a malfunctioning of the mind which takes it out of the category of a "disease of the mind". . . . The dissociative state must be considered as having its source primarily in the respondent's psychological or emotional make-up. (p. 435)

Significantly, Martin J.A. accepted the view that there may well be some "extraordinary external events," that might affect even the "average normal person" without any reference whatsoever to the subjective make-up of the person exposed to such events. His lordship listed a number of situations in which it might be possible to hold that the dissociative state of mind, which has resulted from an emotional shock, should be classified as an "external cause" entitling the accused to outright acquittal: For example, a situation where the defendant has witnessed the murder of, or a serious assault upon, a loved one (p. 435).

The Supreme Court of Canada (by a 4–3 majority) affirmed the decision of the Ontario Court of Appeal in *Rabey v. The Queen* (1980). Ritchie J., in delivering the brief majority judgment, expressly adopted the critical passages from the judgment of Martin J.A. in the court of appeal. Ritchie J. rejected the view that a finding of insanity in *Rabey* would be unfair to the accused, who would be detained at the pleasure of the lieutenant governor. Ritchie J. once again quoted from the judgment of Martin J.A.:

It would, of course, be unthinkable that a person found not guilty on account of insanity because of a transient mental disorder constituting a disease of the mind, who was not dangerous and who required no further treatment, should continue to be confined. (p. 8)

In essence, the Supreme Court ruled that the device of the lieutenant governor's warrant afforded a considerable degree of flexibility in dealing with a person found not guilty by reason of insanity and that the existence of review boards guaranteed the freedom of such an individual from unnecessary detention.

The approach of the majority of the Supreme Court, in *Rabey*, was soundly criticized by Dickson J., who delivered the judgment of the minority. Dickson J. clearly identified the competing policy considerations that influenced the court's approach to the task of defining the concept "disease of the mind":

There are undoubtedly policy considerations to be considered. Automatism as a defence is early feigned. It is said the credibility of our criminal justice system will be severely strained if a person who has committed a violent act is allowed an absolute acquittal on a plea of automatism arising from a psychological blow. The argument is made that the success of the defence depends upon the semantic ability of psychiatrists, tracing a narrow path between the twin shoals of criminal responsibility and an insanity verdict. Added to these concerns is the *in terrorem* argument that the flood gates will be raised if psychological blow automatism is recognized in law.

There are competing policy interests. Where the condition is transient rather than persistent, unlikely to recur, not in need of treatment and not the result of self-induced intoxication, the policy objectives in finding such a person insane are not served and such a person is not a danger to himself or to society generally. (p. 27)

Dickson J. rejected the implication that, as a matter of law, emotional stress can never constitute an external factor. Furthermore, he questioned why an emotional flaw should be regarded as an external cause of automatism, in some circumstances, and an internal cause, in others:

I cannot accept the notion that an extraordinary external event, i.e., an intense emotional shock, can cause a state of dissociation or automatism, if and only if all normal persons subjected to that sort of shock would react in that way. If I understand the quoted passage [from Martin J.A.'s judgment] correctly, an objective standard is contemplated for one of the possible causes of automatism, namely, psychological blow, leaving intact the subjective standard for other causes of automatism, such as physical blow, or reaction to drugs. (p. 28)

No doubt, Dickson J. was implicitly acknowledging the "psychiatric absurdity" of the notion of a "reasonable dissociative reaction" (Harding, 1981, p. 82).

It remains to be seen exactly what the impact of *Rabey* will be upon the further evolution of the defense of (non-insane) automatism in Canada. However, it is reasonably certain that there will be a significant diminution in the number of automatism defenses based upon an alleged "psychological blow." Similarly, it is fairly clear that the broad definition of "disease of the mind" that was articulated in *Rabey* will have a chilling effect upon the development of new forms of the automatism defense.[60]

Australia and New Zealand

As in other Commonwealth jurisdictions, the dominant feature of the legislative regime relating to mental disorder and criminal responsibility in Australia is the continuing survival of the traditional system, which automatically imposes indefinite incarceration upon an accused person who has been acquitted of a criminal offense by reason of insanity. In effect, the applicable legislation in the various Australian jurisdictions[61] provides that trial judges have no discretion in the disposition of insanity acquittees and that such

---

[60]For example, in *Regina v. MacLeod* (1980), 52 C.C.C. (2d) 193 (B.C.C.A.), it was held, following the *dicta* of Martin J. A. in *Rabey*, that "repressed anxiety" was an "internal factor" and, therefore, a "disease of the mind." See also *Regina v. Fournier* (1982), 70 C.C.C. (2d) 351 (Que. C.A.), in which it was held that "anxiety" constitutes a "disease of the mind."

[61]Section 422 0 of Crimes Act of 1958 (Victoria) as amended; section 292 of Criminal Law Consolidation Act of 1935–1975 (South Australia); sections 647 and 668 of Criminal Code and section 37 of Mental Health Act of 1974 (Queensland); section 653 of Criminal Code and section 54 of Mental Health Act of 1981 (Western Australia); section

persons must be detained indefinitely at the discretion of the appropriate minister of the Crown (Freiberg, 1976, pp. 156–165; O'Sullivan, 1981, pp. 119–126; Potas, 1982, pp. 31–52). Furthermore, a striking feature of this regime is that in many Australian jurisdictions, a significant proportion of insanity acquittees are detained in *penal*, rather than *psychiatric*, institutions (Freiberg, 1976, p. 159; Potas, 1982, p. 69). Only in New South Wales has there been a legislative attempt to introduce a greater degree of "legalism" into this regime.[62] Sec. 428ZB of the Crimes Act, 1900, as amended by the Crimes (Mental Disorder) Amendment Act, 1983, provides that:

> Where, upon the trial of a person charged with an offense, the jury returns a special verdict that the accused person is not guilty by reason of mental illness, the Court shall order that the person be detained in strict custody in such place and such manner as the Court thinks fit until released by due process of law.

Although this provision, at first blush, appears to represent little more than a variation upon the traditional theme, the Mental Health Act of 1983 has introduced significant changes to the process by means of which the detention of insanity acquittees is reviewed. The Mental Health Review Tribunal must now review the case of such persons within 14 days of the making of an order under section 428ZB of the Crimes Act. The tribunal is charged with making either a recommendation as to the appropriate "detention, care or treatment" or a recommendation that the person concerned be released. In the latter case, the tribunal must be satisfied "that the safety of the person or any member of the public will not be seriously endangered by the person's release" (Sec. 118). The Mental Health Act of 1983 also provides that, at least once every 6 months, the tribunal must review the case of every insanity acquittee who is detained in a hospital as a "forensic patient" (Sec.

119). Curiously, however, the Act perpetuates the possibility that an insanity acquittee may be detained in a "prison or other place" (Sec. 118(2)(b)).

The rigidly traditional approach of the great majority of Australian jurisdictions contrasts markedly with the approach enshrined in the New Zealand Criminal Justice Act of 1954 (as amended, R.S.N.Z. 1979, Vol. 1). Indeed, the New Zealand legislation furnishes the trial judge with a considerable degree of discretion in relation to the disposition of an accused acquitted "on account of his insanity." The statute provides that "the Court, having regard to all the circumstances of the case, and being satisfied, after hearing medical evidence, that it would be safe in the interests of the public . . . , may in its discretion: (a) Make an order that the person be detained in a hospital as a committed patient; or (b) Make an order for his immediate release; or (c) If the person is subject to a sentence of imprisonment or detention that has not expired, decide not to make any order under this section." (Sec. 39G(2)). Alternatively, the court may make an order that the accused be "detained as a special patient under the Mental Health Act of 1969" (Sec. 39G(1)). The flexibility afforded to the trial court, under the New Zealand legislation, is unparalleled in the major Commonwealth jurisdictions surveyed in this article.

The substantive provisions relating to mental disorder and criminal responsibility are by no means uniform in the various Australian jurisdictions (see Carter, 1982, pp. 91–97; Harding, 1981; Herlihy & Kenny, 1978, pp. 117–128, 189–192; Howard, 1982, pp. 316–343; O'Regan, 1978a, 1979, pp. 52–67, 89–111). Although the legal tests for insanity are all based – at least to some extent – upon the M'Naghten rules, there are significant differences in wording in the applicable provisions of the so-called "code states" (Queensland, Tasmania, and Western Australia) and the Northern Territory (see Howard, 1982, pp. 316–343).[63] Perhaps the most striking difference is the express inclusion of a form of "irresistible impulse"

---

382 of Criminal Code Act of 1983 (Northern Territory); section 203 of Crimes Act of 1914–1966 (Commonwealth). In the Australian Capital Territory, section 439 of the Crimes Act of 1900 (New South Wales) is applicable. In Tasmania, insanity acquittees are committed to a psychiatric facility and are dealt with in the same manner as hospital order patients, who are subject to restrictions (as is the case in England and Wales): sections 381 and 382 of Criminal Code.

[62]In Queensland, a bill was introduced that would have effected major changes in the disposition of mentally disordered offenders. However, the bill was not passed as a consequence of the dissolution of the legislature prior to the election of 1983. See Campbell, 1983.

[63]See Criminal Code (Queensland), section 27; Criminal Code (W. Australia), section 27; Criminal Code (Tasmania), section 16; Criminal Code (Northern Territory), section 35.

within the definition of insanity. However, other differences include the avoidance of the terms "wrong" and "nature and quality," which have spawned numerous problems of judicial interpretation in other Commonwealth jurisdictions. The code states and the Northern Territory, for example, pose the question of whether the defendant lacked the capacity to know that he "ought not to do" the act in question rather than restating the formulation of the M'Naghten rules, which refer to his knowledge that "he was doing what was wrong." Similarly, instead of referring to the accused's knowledge of the "nature and quality" of the act, the Queensland, Western Australian, and Northern Territory codes focus upon his "capacity to understand what he is doing," whereas the Tasmanian code inquires as to whether he is "incapable of understanding the physical character" of his act or omission. It should also be emphasized that, in New South Wales, Victoria, and South Australia, where the M'Naghten rules are still applicable *in toto*, there has been a broader interpretation of the rules than in other Commonwealth jurisdictions, such as England and Wales and Canada. For example, the High Court of Australia has refused to follow the restrictive interpretation of the word "wrong" that has been adopted in the Mother Country and Canada. In *Stapleton v. The Queen* (1952), the High Court approved the following formulation:

> The question is whether [the defendant] was able to appreciate the wrongness of the particular act he was doing at the particular time. Could this man be said to know in this sense whether his act was wrong if through a disease or defect or disorder of the mind he could not think rationally of the reasons which to ordinary people make that act right or wrong? (p. 367)

The court proceeded to accept the view that "what is meant by *wrong* [emphasis added] is

wrong having regard to the everyday standards of reasonable people." Clearly, the broad approach taken by the High Court of Australia contrasts quite starkly with the restrictive interpretation of the M'Naghten rules, adopted in England and Wales and Canada, where legal orthodoxy has been preserved by defining "wrong" as meaning only "*legally* wrong." The High Court has also indicated that there may be circumstances in which "irresistible impulse" may be a factor that will bring a defendant within the definition of insanity, enshrined in the M'Naghten rules.[64] Given the somewhat generous interpretation of the rules by the High Court, it may well be the case that the differences in wording between the definitions of insanity in the code states and the definition of insanity articulated in the original rules have relatively little significance at the practical level.

In New South Wales, Queensland, and the Northern Territory, there has been an important divergence from the substantive law in force in other Australian jurisdictions — namely, the introduction of diminished responsibility as a partial defense to a charge of murder (Goodman & Connor, 1977; Herlihy & Kenny, 1978, pp. 189–192; O'Regan, 1978b, 1979, pp. 89–111). English experience suggests that the availability of such an alternative is, in no small measure, likely to diminish resort to the defense of insanity.[65]

It has been suggested that reliance upon the defense of insanity in Australian jurisdictions will decline even further in the years ahead. Potas (1982, pp. 63–66) and Freiberg (1976, pp. 160–161), for example, have contended that there has been a steady decline in resorting to the insanity defense ever since the abolition of the death penalty in various Australian jurisdictions. The advent of the defense of diminished responsibility in these jurisdictions is also likely to hasten this trend. In New South Wales it is likely that a major incentive to rely upon the insanity defense will be

---

[64]See Fairall, 1981b, pp. 140-145. In *Stapleton v. The Queen* (1953), 86 C.L.R. 358, at 367, Dixon C. J. stated: "Given a disease, disorder or defect of reason, then it is enough if it so governed the faculties at the time of the commission of the act that the accused was incapable of reasoning *with some moderate degree of calmness* as to the wrongness of the act or of comprehending the nature of significance of the act of killing." (emphasis added). See also, *Brown v. R.* (1959), 66 A.L.R. 808 (H.C.); *A. G. for South Australia v. Brown* (1960), A.C. 432 (P.C.).

[65]In a Case and Comment (1983) concerning the New South Wales case (*R. v. Purdy* [1982], 7 A. Crim R. 122), the author suggests that the Australian experience with the defense of diminished responsibility has been similar to that in England and Wales. In particular, it is noted that the evidence, presented by psychiatrists, is normally not contested in diminished responsibility cases. As in England and Wales, a rule has developed in Australia that uncontradicted medical evidence must be accepted. The author also states (at p. 219) that "(t)he acceptance of guilty pleas in the case of uncontradicted medical evidence (or reduction of murder convictions in similar circumstances) really means that doctors rather than courts are now the usual judges for manslaughter by diminished responsibility."

effectively removed now that the mandatory penalty for murder has been abolished (Crimes (Homicide) Amendment Act of 1982).[66] The trial judge is now able to exercise a sentencing discretion where he is satisfied that there are "mitigating circumstances which significantly diminish the culpability of the person" (see Woods, 1983).

Another factor that may increase the popularity of the defense of diminished responsibility at the expense of its counterpart, the insanity defense, is the critical decision of the Australian High Court in *Veen v. The Queen* (1979). The *Veen* case is of great significance in the evolution of a body of principles concerning the sentencing of mentally disordered offenders in Australia (see Potas, 1982, pp. 200–207; Tomasic, 1981). It was the first case in which the High Court had ever granted leave to appeal against sentence and the first occasion upon which the court relied heavily on the fruits of the social and behavioral sciences (in this instance, the literature concerning the unreliability of psychiatric predictions of dangerousness). At trial, Veen had been acquitted of murder and convicted of manslaughter on the basis of a successfully asserted defense of diminished responsibility. Veen was an aboriginal of some 20 years, and it appeared that he was a homosexual prostitute. The circumstances of the killing were that Veen had spent a weekend in his victim's apartment, and after refusing Veen's request for payment and making some abusive remarks about Veen's racial background, the victim was repeatedly stabbed and subsequently died. Veen had a violent history and the trial judge concluded that he suffered from incurable brain damage. Although the judge was satisfied that Veen's mental responsibility had been substantially impaired, he nevertheless sentenced him to life imprisonment — primarily on the basis that "the community is entitled to be protected from violence" (cited in Potas, 1982, p. 201). In so doing, the trial judge was following a pattern of sentencing that has become well established in

England and Wales[67] and had been adopted in a number of cases in New South Wales and Queensland (O'Regan, 1979, pp. 103–111).[68] The New South Wales Court of Criminal Appeal rejected Veen's appeal against the severity of the life sentence. However, by a 3–2 majority, the High Court of Australia allowed Veen's subsequent appeal and substituted a determinate sentence of 12 years' imprisonment, with no nonparole period. The majority emphasized that the need to protect the community must be placed in a "proper context" because "the protection of the public does not alone justify an increase in the length of sentence" (Jacobs J., p. 313). Similarly, Murphy J. stated that

> if the protection of society requires the applicant to be confined when his imprisonment ends, because he is dangerous, it should only be done (if it can be done lawfully) by methods outside the criminal justice system. (p. 320)

It remains to be seen exactly what the impact of the *Veen* case will be upon the sentencing of mentally disordered offenders in the future. However, it is clear that the courts will no longer be permitted to place exclusive emphasis upon the principle of preventive detention when confronted by such an offender. As one Australian commentator (Tomasic, 1981), has noted:

> The importance of this case lies not so much in taking a bold new course, for no real change of direction will necessarily flow from this case, but rather in the realization evident in the various judgments that no clear-cut answers to sentencing in the area, of preventive detention are available. In essence, this decision was the product of doubt concerning the wisdom of giving priority to any one principle, such as community protection, in cases such as these, and rather, it seeks to reach an uneasy balance between the applicable principles. (p. 266)

---

[66]In the Australian Capital Territory, it appears that, as the consequence of a "legislative oversight," the mandatory sentence for murder has also been abolished: *R. v. Wheeldon* (1978), 18 A.L.R. 619. See, generally, Potas (1982, p. 61).

[67]In England and Wales, it has been possible (since 1961) for the trial court to make a hospital order instead of sentencing a mentally disordered offender to a long term of imprisonment (see *R. v. Morris* (1961) 2 Q.B. 237). However, approximately one-third of those persons convicted of manslaughter (after successful reliance upon the defense of diminished responsibility) are sent to prison — usually for life (Williams, 1978, p. 625). Because the "English-style" hospital order does not exist in New South Wales or Queensland, the courts, prior to *Veen*, appeared to accept the English view that, in the absence of such an order, a life sentence may be appropriate.

[68]See, e.g., *R. v. Dick* (1966), Qd. R. 301; *R. v. Tonkin and Montgomery* (1975), Qd. R. 1.

Ironically, it may be argued that the *raison d'etre* of the diminished responsibility has now been destroyed in New South Wales, with the abolition of the mandatory life sentence for murder (Case & Comment, 1983, p. 221). It remains to be seen whether the New South Wales parliament will formally abrogate the defense or whether the defense will decline into relative disuse.

As in other Commonwealth jurisdictions, there have been no recent legislative attempts to tinker with the wording of the applicable legal tests for insanity in the various Australian jurisdictions. Indeed, it is significant that both the Edwards Committee, in New South Wales, and the Mitchell Committee, in South Australia recommended *against* major changes to the M'Naghten rules (Mental Health Act Review Committee, 1974; Criminal Law and Penal Methods Reform Committee of South Australia, 1977). In these circumstances, recent developments in the criminal law relating to insanity have been fashioned at the hands of the judiciary.

In a recent review of the Australian case law, Harding (1981) has contended:

> Chronic ambivalence has characterized the way in which the criminal justice system has handled issues relating to the mental capacity of defendants for their allegedly criminal acts. Consequently, the operative rules have become anomalous and uncertain.[69] (p. 73)

In Harding's view (p. 77), judicial ambivalence has been, at its most, conspicuous in relation to the plea of non-insane automatism. Along with other Commonwealth jurisdictions, Australian courts have responded to the problem of non-insane automatism "by recognizing the plea with one hand and circumventing it with the other" (Harding, 1981, p. 77).

A conspicuous example of the judicial policy to circumscribe the application of the defense is the erection of an evidentiary hurdle that must be vaulted by the accused. The so-called secondary burden of proof requires that the accused adduce some "credible evidence" (usually medical in nature) if the issue of non-insane automatism is to be considered by the trier of fact. Significantly, this evidential hurdle has been erected in most Commonwealth jurisdictions (Harding, 1981, pp. 77-78).

However, perhaps the most striking application of the restrictive judicial policy is to be found in the case law relating to the demarcation of non-insane automatism from insanity (see generally Fairall, 1981a). As in other Commonwealth jurisdictions, Australian courts have interpreted the phrase "disease of the mind" in an expansive manner. The underlying intent of this approach has apparently been to dissuade defendants from asserting non-insane automatism by raising the specter of their plea being treated as one of insanity. While Australian courts have ruled that a state of automatism caused by a head injury (posttraumatic automatism) entitles the accused to a complete acquittal by virtue of the defense of non-insane automatism,[70] they have also held that automatistic states, induced by epilepsy[71] or such organic defects as arteriosclerosis,[72] must be considered to be the products of a "disease of the mind" and, therefore, entitle the accused only to the qualified acquittal of the insanity defense. As in other Commonwealth jurisdictions, the Australian courts have adopted a particularly restrictive approach toward automatism defenses based upon "hysterical dissociation." The weight of Australian authority now appears to lean heavily toward the type of approach adopted by the Canadian Supreme Court in *Rabey v. The Queen* (1980). Where there is any hint of underlying pathology on the part of the accused, the Australian courts have ruled that hysterical dissociation gives rise only to the defense of insanity.[73] On the other hand, they have apparently left open the possibility of raising the defense of non-insane automatism where the state of hysterical dissoci-

---

[69]Judicial ambivalence toward the insanity defense, in Australia, is well illustrated by the recent case of *R. v. Damic* (1982), 2 N.S.W.L.R. 750. At trial, neither the accused (who represented himself) nor the prosecution adduced evidence relating to insanity. Nevertheless, the trial judge, *on his own motion*, called a psychiatrist to testify as to this issue. Damic was subsequently acquitted by reason of insanity. His appeal against this verdict was dismissed by the N.S.W. Court of Criminal Appeal.

[70]*Wakefield* (1958), 75 W.N. (N.S.W.) 66; *Carter* (1959) V.R. 105; *Cooper v. McKenna* (1960), Qd. R. 407; *Scott* (1967) V.R. 276.

[71]*Meddings* (1966); V.R. 306; *Foy* (1960) Qd. R. 225.

[72]*Holmes* (1960), W.A.R. 122.

[73]*Joyce* (1970), S.A.S.R. 184; *Tsigos* (1964–65), N.S.W.R. 1607; *Williams* (1978), Crim. L.J. 335 (Tasmanian Court of Criminal Appeal). However, c.f. *Pantetic* (1973), 1 A.C.T.R. 1.

ation has been caused by an external triggering force rather than the internal weakness of the accused. Indeed, Harding (1981, p. 83) contends that an Australian inferior court decision "seems to have applied the concept of 'reasonable dissociative reaction'" hinted at in *Rabey*.[74]

In one important respect, the Australian High Court has departed from the general approach adopted by other Commonwealth jurisdictions. More specifically, the High Court has decisively rejected the principle, articulated in the *Regina v. Quick* case (1973), that self-induced (or "culpable") automatism may not excuse a defendant to a criminal charge. Prior to 1980, it appears that Australian acceptance of the culpable automatism doctrine was, at best, mixed. However, in the case of *R. v. O'Connor* (1980), the High Court, in Harding's view (1981, p. 79) left the doctrine "in shreds in Australia." O'Connor had been charged with the offense of stealing and wounding with intent to resist arrest. The accused, in effect, alleged that he could not remember the incidents in question because he was in a state of automatism, induced by a combination of a hallucinogenic drug and alcohol. The orthodox approach to the defense of intoxication was recently restated by the House of Lords in *D.P.P. v. Majewski* (1977) and strongly endorsed by the Supreme Court of Canada in *Leary v. The Queen* (1977). This orthodox approach permits intoxication to be raised as a defense only in relation to crimes of "specific" intent and not in relation to crimes of "basic" intent. In light of this approach, O'Connor's plea of intoxication was, without a doubt, relevant to the charges of stealing and wounding with intent to resist arrest because these were clearly crimes requiring proof of "specific intent"; on the other hand, it would not excuse O'Connor of the (lesser) included offense of unlawful wounding (a crime requiring proof only of "basic" intent). In a surprising move, the High Court of Australia rejected the orthodox approach, so rigorously asserted in England and Wales and Canada, and proclaimed that the distinction between crimes of "specific" and crimes of "basic" intent was not supportable according to the basic principles of the doctrine of *mens rea*. The High Court considered that the critical issue in such cases should be whether the accused's conduct was voluntary; the fact that the accused's state was self-induced is, therefore, irrelevant. Therefore, in *O'Connor's* case, the plea of intoxi-

cation was an issue that should have been considered by the jury in relation to the included charge of unlawful wounding. Harding (1981) has summarized the impact of the *O'Connor* case in the following manner:

> Whether involuntariness arises from intoxication or failure to take a drug to control an epileptic condition or negligently induced hypoglycaemia or from concussion consequent upon negligent driving would seem to be immaterial; it is enough that the prosecution for whatever reason cannot show beyond reasonable doubt that the act of the accused was voluntary. (p. 79)

As will be seen, the English Court of Appeal has significantly modified the doctrine of culpable automatism — at least for cases which do *not* involve self-induced intoxication. In *R. v. Bailey* (1983), the court ruled that a self-induced state of automatism may excuse a defendant from criminal liability, in relation to *all* criminal offenses, unless the Crown can prove, beyond a reasonable doubt, that the accused acted "recklessly." However, in England and Wales, the defense of self-induced intoxication remains subject to the orthodox principles, restated by the House of Lords in *Majewski*. It is clear that, insofar as the issue of self-induced intoxication is concerned, the concrete result of the *O'Connor* case will be a major divergence between the approach taken by Australian and English courts. However, insofar as *other* forms of self-induced automatism are concerned, the approaches maintained in the two jurisdictions will probably be quite similar in practice.

England and Wales

With the availability of less unattractive alternatives, the insanity defense has "fallen into virtually total disuse" in England and Wales (Dell, 1983, p. 431). Indeed, in 1981 the defense was successfully raised in a meagre total of three cases (Wells, 1983, p. 787, n.9). There are a number of potential explanations for this striking phenomenon. In the first place, it is clear that the judiciary's narrow interpretation of the M'Naghten rules has greatly restricted the range of cases in which a defense lawyer may envisage a successful outcome to a plea of insanity (Dell, 1983, pp. 431,437). Second, the inexorable outcome of a

---

[74]*Morris v. Pickett* (1978), 11 A.N.Z.J. Crim. 113.

successful defense of insanity is indeterminate incarceration in a psychiatric hospital. The prospect of such incarceration has traditionally constituted an effective deterrent to the raising of the defense in all cases except those involving a charge of murder (where a life sentence of imprisonment is mandatory).[75] A third reason that may account for the near extinction of the insanity defense is the establishment, in 1957, of a defense of diminished responsibility in relation to a charge of murder.[76] Significantly, Walker (1968, p. 158) has convincingly demonstrated that the introduction of the diminished responsibility defense (which merely operates to reduce the severity of the offense from murder to manslaughter) "has done no more than take over the sort of case which previously would have been accepted by courts as within the McNaghten Rules." Finally, the availability of the hospital order as a sentencing alternative, in all cases other than those involving murder, has greatly diminished the need to establish that an accused person was not legally responsible for his conduct. Williams (1978) has underscored this point in his discussion of the trial judge's discretion to impose a hospital order upon an offender who has successfully raised the defense of diminished responsibility:

> With our national genius for compromise, we have solved the problem of distinguishing legal irresponsibility from responsibility by making almost everyone responsible but entrusting the judge with a wide discretion which is exercised on pragmatic grounds. If there are the requisite medical recommendations the judge will normally make a hospital order. (p. 625)

A highly significant facet of the displacement of the insanity defense by its counterpart of diminished responsibility has been the extent to which reliance upon the latter defense has taken place within a context of consensus. In a fascinating study by Dell (1983), of 194 cases in which the defense had been raised between 1976 and 1977, it was revealed that a striking 80% of such

cases were disposed of by means of a guilty plea (p. 811). Surprisingly, Dell notes that in only 26 of the 194 cases did the Crown challenge the defense before a jury with rebutting medical evidence (p. 809). The study also indicated that the notorious "battle between the experts," which has long plagued the insanity defense in most Commonwealth jurisdictions, has been relegated to a relatively unimportant role within the context of the issue of diminished responsibility; indeed, Dell concluded that there was no disagreement between medical witnesses concerning this issue in all but 13% of the cases, in which the defense of diminished responsibility was raised[77] (p. 813). However, it is important to recognize that, although 70% of successful diminished responsibility defenses result in the imposition of a hospital order, the remainder actually witness the imposition of sentences of imprisonment—usually for a life term (Williams, 1978, p. 625). As Williams (1978, p. 625) has suggested, the "absurdity of reconciling this practice with the notion of substantially diminished responsibility needs no emphasis"; however, he also expresses the view that an indeterminate prison sentence may be justified on the basis of protecting the public from potentially dangerous offenders.

The *de facto* interment of the insanity defense, in England and Wales has not occurred without vociferous protest—particularly from academic quarters (see Walker, 1981; Dell, 1983). For example, Dell has emphasized that the absence of a viable insanity defense severely penalizes mentally disordered offenders because they must bear the potentially crippling consequences of a criminal conviction. According to Dell (1983, p. 434), such consequences may take their toll in a variety of fields—such as employment and immigration and, in her view, "it is hardly desirable to impose these on people who are too disordered for guilt to be attributed to them." It has also been contended (Dell, 1983, p. 434) that, if mentally disordered persons are to be treated as convicted criminals, then they are inevitably liable to imprisonment. Although it is generally possible for

---

[75]The special verdict of insanity results in confinement in a hospital specified by the home secretary. Thereafter, the defendant must be detained indefinitely as though he or she were the subject of a hospital order with restrictions: section 5, schedule 1, Criminal Procedure (Insanity) Act of 1964. Prior to 1983, the defendant could only be released by the home secretary. However, the Mental Health Act of 1983 has improved the lot of such defendants by granting the mental health review tribunal a *concurrent* power to discharge them.

[76]See section 2 of Homicide Act of 1957. As to diminished responsibility in general, see Whitehead, 1982; Williams, 1978, pp. 622–630.

[77]As to the great weight to be placed upon uncontradicted medical evidence of diminished responsibility, see *R. v. Vernege* (1981), 74 Criminal Appeal Reports, 232.

a court to impose a hospital order as an alternative sentence in all cases (other than those involving a conviction of murder), there are certain situations in which implementation of this option is precluded by events that are beyond the control of the courts. For example, an order may not be imposed where the appropriate psychiatric hospitals are unwilling to provide a bed for the mentally disordered offender. In such a case, the offender may well be imprisoned because there is nowhere else to put him or her; as Dell (1983, p. 434) notes, "hospitals refuse to take" such offenders, "knowing that prisons cannot so refuse." Paradoxically, a mentally disordered offender may also wind up serving a prison term because he or she has recovered by the time that the court is considering sentence: Where an offender is no longer mentally disordered, then the sentencing court has no jurisdiction to impose a hospital order. As Dell (1983) has suggested, "this situation is as illogical as it is unjust":

> The irony of cases like these is that if the defendant had recovered a little later, or if his trial had taken place a little sooner, then a hospital order would have been made, and the patient would have been discharged from hospital when he recovered. Recovery in hospital is rewarded by imprisonment. (pp. 435–436)

Walker (1981) has also voiced his disaffection with a "situation in which only defendants accused of murder have recourse to defenses based on their mental state" (p. 596). Along with a number of other commentators, Walker has recommended the implementation of the proposals advanced by the Butler Committee in 1975 (Ashworth, 1975; Butler, 1975; Criminal Law Review, 1975).[78] These proposals call for a significant expansion in the scope of the defense of insanity, as well as the abolition of mandatory commitment following an insanity acquittal. More specifically, the committee recommended that a jury should be instructed

to return a verdict of "not guilty on evidence of mental disorder" if:

> (1) "they acquit the defendant solely because he is not proved to have had the state of mind necessary for the offence and they are satisfied on the balance of probability that at the time of the act or omission he was mentally disordered, or (2) they are satisfied on the balance of probability that at the time he was suffering from severe mental illness or severe subnormality."[79] (para. 18.26)

As far as the disposition of an insanity acquittee is concerned, the committee recommended that the sentencing court should be accorded a broad range of flexible options. Indeed, the committee proposed that in lieu of the current system of mandatory commitment, the court should be empowered to impose a hospital order (with or without a "restriction order"), to order outpatient treatment, or even to grant an absolute discharge. The committee also proposed the creation of a novel form of disposition — namely, a psychiatric supervision order. This order would permit the discharge of the insanity acquittee into the community while providing for his or her recall to the hospital at the discretion of the "supervising officer."

If these proposals should ultimately be adopted, the question would arise as to whether there would be a continued need for a defense of diminished responsibility. The Butler Committee expressed its view that the major raison d'etre for this defense was the mandatory life sentence for murder, which precludes a medical disposition. The "decided preference" of the committee (para. 19.14) was to abrogate both the mandatory sentence and diminished responsibility. The significant expansion in the scope of the "revitalized" insanity defense would probably embrace many of the cases currently disposed of by means of diminished responsibility, whereas the abolition of the man-

---

[78]Not all commentators favor the adoption of the Butler Committee's proposals. See, for example, Wells (1983), who advocates Norval Morris' view that the defense of insanity should be abolished and the issue of mental disorder raised only in relation to sentence.

[79]"Severe subnormality" was a term that was defined in the England and Wales Mental Health Act of 1959. The Mental Health Act of 1983 has replaced the term with "severe mental impairment." The committee would characterize "mental illness" as being "severe" if it has one or more of the following symptoms: "(a) lasting impairment of intellectual functions shown by failure of memory, orientation, comprehension and learning capacity; (b) lasting alteration of mood of such degree as to give rise to delusional appraisal of the patient's situation, his past or his future, or that of others, or to lack of any appraisal; (c) delusional beliefs, persecutory, jealous or grandiose; (d) abnormal perceptions associated with delusional misinterpretations of events; or (e) thinking so disordered as to prevent reasonable appraisal of the patient's situation or reasonable communication with others." (para. 18.35).

datory penalty would permit courts to impose a medical disposition in cases involving a conviction of murder. Not every commentator would argue with this recommendation, however; for example, Walker (1981, p. 597) has embraced the notion that diminished responsibility should actually be expanded to cover offenses other than murder. He has also asserted that, rather than adopting the (potentially illogical) expedient of convicting a "diminished responsibility offender" on a lesser offense, legislative reform should be directed toward providing that diminished responsibility should "limit the choice or severity of the sentence."

As in other Commonwealth jurisdictions, the most significant developments in the English case law concerning mental disorder and criminal responsibility have occurred in relation to the thorny problem of delineating the boundaries of (non-insane) automatism (see MacKay, 1980, pp. 350–361; Williams, 1978, pp. 608–622). In general, English courts have continued to view the defense of (non-insane) automatism with a fair degree of skepticism.[80] This skepticism is perhaps reflected in Williams' (1978) pithy aphorism:

In reality the whole doctrine of non-insane automatism is a dodge for getting out of the mandatory commitment, when it is thought to be an inappropriate outcome. (p. 615)

As in Canada, the critical issue, in the process of demarcating the insanity defense from that of (non-insane) automatism, has been the elaboration of the judicial interpretation of the hoary concept, "disease of the mind." In the last decade, the seminal case has turned out to be Regina v. Quick (1973), in which the question was raised as to whether hypoglycemia was a condition that warranted categorization as "non-insane automatism" or as the product of a "disease of the mind." In Regina v. Quick (1973), the alleged hypoglycemia occurred after the defendant, a diabetic, had taken an injection of insulin, drunk a quantity of alcohol, and eaten little food thereafter. The Court of Appeal ruled that the condition of hypoglycemia should be designated as an instance of (non-insane) automatism. Lawton L.J. asserted that "common sense is affronted" by the spectacle of a diabetic being detained in a psychiatric hospital when, in most cases, the condition of hypoglycemia may readily be alleviated by the simple expedient of placing a lump of sugar in the patient's mouth. In construing the phrase, "disease of the mind," the court stated:

In our judgment the fundamental concept is of a malfunctioning of the mind caused by disease. A malfunctioning of the mind of transitory effect caused by the application to the body of some external factor such as violence, drugs, including anaesthetics, alcohol and hypnotic influences cannot fairly be said to be due to disease. (p. 922)

In the Quick (1973) case itself, the transient hypoglycemic condition was induced by the combination of a number of "external" factors — the administration of an injection, the failure to take nourishment, and the ingestion of alcohol; it could not, therefore, be regarded as the result of a "disease of the mind." Since the Quick case, the "currently accepted" test for distinguishing between the defenses of insanity and (non-insane) automatism has been to inquire whether the defendant's state of mind was caused by an "internal" or "external" factor (Comment, 1983, p. 258).

The potentially harsh consequences that may arise when such a test is applied in a literal manner are well illustrated by the pronouncements made by the House of Lords in R. v. Sullivan (1983). This case raised the issue of whether a defendant, who committed an assault causing grievous bodily harm while in the throes of a psychomotor epileptic seizure, was entitled to claim the benefit of the defense of (non-insane) automatism. At trial, the judge had ruled that if the jury accepted the medical evidence, then the only verdict open to them was that of "not guilty by reason of insanity" because epilepsy, being an "internal" factor, was a "disease of the mind." Both the Court of Appeal and the House of Lords rejected the defendant's appeals. It had been contended, on Sullivan's behalf, that medical opinion no longer regarded epilepsy as "mental illness"; therefore, it should no longer be designated as a "disease of the mind." However, in the House of Lords, Lord Diplock stated that the meaning of "disease of the mind" was a question of law. In his view, the "nomenclature adopted by

---

[80]Judicial skepticism toward the defense of (non-insane) automatism has been manifested, for example, in the requirement that there be expert medical or scientific evidence to support such a defense: R. v. Smith (1979), Crim. Law Rev. 592 (C.A.). See, also, the judicial insistence that the defense not be considered unless there is a medical foundation for it: R. v. Isitt (1978), Crim. Law Rev. 159 (C.A.).

the medical profession may change from time to time... but the meaning of the expression "disease of the mind" as the cause of "defect of reason" remains unchanged for the purpose of the application of the McNaghten rules" (p. 677). According to Lord Diplock, the purpose of the legislation relating to insanity is to protect society against the repetition of dangerous conduct. Lord Diplock expressed considerable reluctance to apply the label of insanity to a defendant suffering from epilepsy; however, in his view, such a result was inevitable so long as parliament failed to enact legislation of the sort recommended by the Butler Committee.

The practical consequence of the approach adopted in *Sullivan* is that any judicial indication that an alleged condition constitutes a "disease of the mind" will almost invariably prompt the accused to change his plea to "guilty"—in order to avoid the drastic outcome of an acquittal by reason of insanity. Indeed, this is exactly what happened in *Sullivan's* case. If an accused person is genuinely "not responsible" for his conduct, it is highly questionable whether he or she should be forced into accepting conviction of a criminal offense in order to side-step the possibility of indeterminate incarceration. The approach maintained by the courts in this respect really makes sense only if there is some certainty that an accused, such as Sullivan, would be speedily released after an insanity acquittal on the basis that he or she was not "mentally ill." It would, perhaps, appear that Sullivan's legal advisor did not have any confidence that his client would be the beneficiary of such a swift release and chose the "lesser evil" of a criminal conviction with its attendant stigma. In this light, it is clear that the courts' move to expand the scope of the definition of "disease of the mind" is aimed not so much at broadening the applicability of the insanity defense as at closing off the possibility of obtaining an acquittal on the basis of (non-insane) automatism.

The *Quick* (1973) case has also generated controversy concerning the issue of "self-induced automatism" (see MacKay, 1982; Williams, 1978, pp. 620–622). In that case, Lawton L.J. (p. 922) made the following remark:

Such malfunctioning, unlike that caused by a defect of reason from disease of the mind, will not always relieve an accused from criminal responsibility. A self-induced capacity will not excuse... nor will one which could have been reasonably foreseen

as a result of either doing or omitting to do something as, for example, taking alcohol against medical advice after using certain drugs, or failing to have regular meals whilst taking insulin.

The issue was squarely raised in *R. v. Bailey* (1983). The accused was charged with wounding with intent or, alternatively, with unlawful wounding. This defense was that he had been acting in a state of (non-insane) automatism caused by a condition of hypoglycemia that had arisen as a consequence of his failure to take sufficient food after a dose of insulin. Apparently following the views of Lawton L.J. in *Quick* (1973), the trial judge ruled that the defense of (non-insane) automatism was not open to the accused since his incapacity had been self-induced. As a consequence, the accused was convicted of wounding with intent. Upon Bailey's appeal, the Court of Appeal ruled that there had been a misdirection to the jury.

In the first place, the court of appeal noted (p. 506) that the leading case of *D.P.P. v. Majewski* (1977) had established the principle that self-induced intoxication may negate the "specific intent" that must be proved as an essential element of certain criminal offenses. In *Bailey* the offense of wounding *with intent to cause grievous bodily harm* was clearly such a "specific intent" offense; therefore, the condition of hypoglycemia could indubitably serve as a defense to this particular charge despite the fact that it had been allegedly self-induced. Otherwise, the self-induced drunkard would be in a more advantageous legal position than the self-induced automation.

The court of appeal then proceeded to deal with the critical question as to whether self-induced automatism may serve as a defense to a charge of an offense that requires only proof of a "basic intent" (such as that of unlawful wounding, which was the alternative charge facing Bailey). In *Majewski*, it had been held by the House of Lords that (voluntary) self-induced intoxication (whether by alcohol or other drugs) would not excuse a defendant charged with a basic intent offense. The *rationale* underpinning this approach is that the necessary *mens rea* for conviction of such an offense is to be found in the accused's *recklessness* in permitting himself to lapse into a state of intoxication. The courts have, therefore, established a "conclusive presumption" against the admission of proof of intoxication for the purpose of disproving *mens rea* in ordinary crimes" (*D.P.P. v. Majewski*, 1977, p. 496). This presumption is apparently founded on the basis that it is "common knowledge" that, for example, an intoxicated person may become violent. In *R. v. Bailey* the court of appeal refused to extend this line of reasoning to those forms of automatism, that have been self-induced by means *other* than alcohol or drugs. In delivering the judgment of the court, Griffiths L.J. asserted:

> It seems to us that there may be material distinctions between a man who consumes alcohol or takes dangerous drugs and one who fails to take sufficient food after insulin to avert hypoglycaemia. (p. 507)

In the court's view, it is not "common knowledge," even among diabetics, that a failure to take food may result in dangerous conduct. Of course, if a particular defendant did, indeed, appreciate that such a failure may lead to such conduct and, nevertheless, deliberately "ran the risk," then he would clearly have been "reckless" and would have no defense to a charge of a basic intent offense, such as assault. However, in any given case, the Crown would have to establish the accused's *subjective* awareness of the inherent risks in his conduct, before a conviction could be entered:

> In our judgment, self-induced automatism, other than that due to intoxication from alcohol or drugs, may provide a defence to crimes of basic intent. The question in each case will be whether the prosecution has proved the necessary element of recklessness. In cases of assault, if the accused knows that his actions or inaction are likely to make him aggressive, unpredictable or uncontrolled with the result that he may cause some injury to others and he persists in the action or takes no remedial action when he knows it is required, it will be open to the jury to find that he was reckless. (p. 507)

Wells (1983) has levelled a number of criticisms at the reasoning articulated in *Bailey*. Perhaps the most significant of those criticisms relates to the "artificiality" of the concepts of "recklessness," when employed in this context:

> The Court of Appeal fails to show an awareness that its use of recklessness is still artificial. The presumptive recklessness of *Majewski* is an artificial one, but it can at least be explained on other ground. . . . *Bailey* does not replace presumptive with

actual recklessness. If it did, all automatons would be acquitted. The recklessness spoken of in *Bailey* itself is still artificial. It is not recklessness at the time of the act; it is recklessness applied before the time of the actual crime. As such it is fraught with problems. (p. 790)

In Wells' view, once the issue of recklessness is pushed back several stages from the dangerous act itself, then "the exercise can only pay lip-service to subjectivism."

The overall picture that emerges in England and Wales is striking. The demise of the insanity defense has created a situation in which a defendant's mental disorder is no longer relevant to the issue of criminal responsibility. Instead, mental disorder has become a relevant factor solely in the process of sentencing — primarily through the operation of the partial defense of diminished responsibility and the imposition of the hospital order. Parallel to these developments, one may discern a resolute judicial attempt to limit the scope of the defense of (non-insane) automatism. For example, the courts have consistently required that defendants negotiate a substantial evidential hurdle before the defense can be considered by the trier of fact. Furthermore, by maintaining a broad definition of "disease of the mind," through the "internal"-versus-"external"-factor test articulated in *Quick*, the courts have effectively fashioned a veritable "Hobson's choice" for many defendants who seek to raise the defense of (non-insane) automatism. Defendants, such as epileptics, whose condition is caused by a so-called "internal" factor, are compelled to choose between a potential insanity acquittal (with the attendant possibility of indeterminate incarceration), on the one hand, and conviction of a criminal offense, on the other. Once again, the trend is toward displacing the relevance of mental disorder from the realm of criminal responsibility to the domain of sentencing.

THE "NEW LEGALISM" IN THE CRIMINAL JUSTICE SPHERE

The preceding review would appear to indicate that elements of the "new legalism" have, indeed, penetrated the sphere of criminal justice. At the legislative level, a number of Commonwealth jurisdictions have taken the first steps toward releasing mentally disordered offenders from a regime in which their fate rests exclusively in the hands of the executive arm of government. Similarly, at the judicial level, it appears that there has been a clearly discernible attempt to limit the role of psychiatrists in the determination of the issue of criminal responsibility.

The New South Wales Mental Health Act of 1983 is manifestly at the forefront of a legislative trend toward increasing the legal protections accorded to those accused persons who have been found unfit to stand trial. This Act greatly improves the position of the long-term unfit accused, who have been afforded the protections of both a provisional trial and the rigid restrictions placed upon the period during which they may be detained. Similarly, the Act ensures that the cases of such individuals are frequently reviewed by a mental health review tribunal. Furthermore, the Act significantly ameliorates the legal status of those unfit accused, whose condition is likely to continue only for a brief period, by placing responsibility for their disposition in the hands of the trial court rather than a minister of the Crown. Although the New South Wales reforms are, by far, the most sweeping yet undertaken in the Commonwealth, the recent legislation in the Northern Territory and New Zealand also reflects a policy of "legalism" insofar as it expands the role of the courts in relation to the disposition of the unfit accused. Similarly, the England and Wales Mental Health Act of 1983 entrenches elements of such a policy through its provision for the release of the unfit accused by a mental health review tribunal.

In England and Wales, there is no doubt that the position of those mentally disordered offenders — who have been placed under the control of a hospital order with a restriction upon their release by medical authorities — has been significantly ameliorated by the provisions of the Mental Health Act of 1983 that grant the Mental Health Review Tribunal the right to release such offenders. Similarly, the requirement that a regional health authority articulate the reasons why a hospital bed cannot be found for an offender may also be perceived as an example of the rise of the "new legalism," in that such a requirement has the potential to limit the exercise of professional discretion to refuse to accept an offender under the terms of a hospital order.

Insofar as the issue of criminal responsibility is concerned, it may be contended that the "new legalism" has exerted its influence in England and Wales, where the Mental Health Act of 1983 has abrogated the situation in which the release of those persons acquitted by reason of insanity was left to the exclusive discretion of the home secretary. Similarly, in New Zealand, the shadow of the new legalism has clearly been cast on the procedures for the disposition of such persons; indeed, the placing of responsibility for making disposition decisions in the hands of the trial court rather than the executive branch of government is a particularly significant example of the trend toward "legalization" of the status of mentally disordered offenders. Finally, in this respect, it may be noted that the New South Wales Mental Health Act of 1983 enhances the legal position of insanity acquittees by granting the Mental Health Review Tribunal a major role in the process of releasing such persons from detention.

The evolving Commonwealth case law in relation to criminal responsibility also bears the imprint of the "new legalism" insofar as it tends to reflect a restriction of the role of psychiatrists in this area. In Canada, the Supreme Court has adopted an increasingly strict interpretation of the Criminal Code provision that defines the nature and scope of the insanity defense. By so doing, the Supreme Court has unequivocally restricted the range of psychiatric evidence that may be considered relevant to the issue of insanity. In England and Wales, the role of psychiatrists in determining the issue of criminal responsibility has been eclipsed by the virtual disappearance of the insanity defense from the courts. No doubt, one of the factors contributing to this situation has been the judicial tradition of interpreting the M'Naghten rules in a consistently narrow manner. Only in Australia has the psychiatric profession retained a potentially broad role to play in the determination of the insanity issue; it has done so primarily as a consequence of the comparatively liberal interpretation of the M'Naghten rules by the High Court (insofar as the rules are applicable in the "non-Code" states) and the expanded legislative definition of "insanity" in those jurisdictions that have codified their criminal law.

In each of the jurisdictions surveyed, the courts have adopted an unmistakable policy of limiting the application of the defense of non-insane automatism. This policy has been implemented through the application of the so-called "internal/external test" (as a means of determining whether a mental condition is caused by a "disease of the mind") and, in most jurisdictions, the associated concept of a "reasonable dissociative reaction." By emphasizing that "disease of the mind" is a *legal* rather than a *medical* concept the Commonwealth courts have underscored their determination to exert strict control over the delicate process of drawing the dividing line between insanity and non-insane automatism. Indeed, it is clear that the courts are not willing to defer to psychiatric determinations concerning this issue. In this sense, the approach of the judiciary may be termed "legalistic."

Paradoxically, the courts, in those jurisdictions that have recognized the partial defense of diminished responsibility, have been willing to give a virtually free rein to psychiatric evidence. As noted earlier, in most cases of diminished responsibility, psychiatric testimony is generally unchallenged. However, the effect of a successful defense of diminished responsibility is not to absolve the offender completely but rather to grant the trial judge a degree of sentencing flexibility in homicide cases. It therefore appears that, in cases where the real issue is one of sentencing, the courts are willing to accept a broad range of psychiatric evidence, whereas in cases involving the potential acquittal of the accused (whether the defense be that of insanity or non-insane automatism), the courts have been keen to circumscribe the scope of such evidence.

CONCLUSION

The foregoing discussion has been lengthy, and the intention here is not to fill these closing pages with a detailed review of the results of this analysis. Rather, we wish to return to our original guiding questions regarding the concept of the "new legalism," to offer some answers in light of our exposition of developments in Commonwealth mental health law, and to suggest some further issues that should be addressed.

The new legalism/"professional discretion" dichotomy identified by Gostin constitutes a dualism, the effects of which resonate throughout many Commonwealth jurisdictions. Although there are problems that relate to the clarity of the two key concepts, the dualism is useful as an analytical construct insofar as it locates the two opposing poles of mental health law reform. However, it is less useful for the purpose of constructing accurate models of mental health law systems in the Commonwealth. Very few jurisdictions have mental health legislation that can be located near either pole. In many respects, the New South Wales Mental Health Act of 1983 is close to the new legalism; however, the statute still preserves a considerable degree of freedom for professional discretion. For example, there is no general right to refuse psychiatric treatment, except in the case of psychosurgery and ECT, and the Mental

Health Review Tribunal still plays a major role in decisions concerning the discharge of involuntary patients. On the other hand, the Victoria Mental Health Act of 1959 is probably the Commonwealth statute that lies the closest to the professional discretion pole. At the same time, the Act does not permit the exercise of unbridled professional discretion.

In general, and when all aspects of the relevant statutes and jurisprudence are considered, it appears that the majority of Commonwealth jurisdictions lie somewhere in the middle of the spectrum (a point most clearly illustrated in our analysis of the interaction between definitions of mental disorder/illness and the criteria for involuntary civil commitment). The situation in these jurisdictions could be described as "quasi-legalistic" in that legal requirements are imposed in relation to such issues as the civil commitment of patients and the periodic review of the status of detained patients. However, the actual *application* of these legislative requirements is left in the hands of mental health professionals; for example, the decision to commit a patient involuntarily rests on the *opinion* of physicians. It is clear, from these and other aspects of legislation and jurisprudence, that there is a preference for leaving mental health professionals alone except in cases of grave abuse. Further, the rise of the Mental Health Review Tribunal symbolizes the quasi-legalistic approach in that it provides an administrative, rather than a judicial, mode of review and is highly susceptible to the influence of psychiatric opinion. This last conclusion is drawn from our review of the membership structure of such tribunals and from the research undertaken to determine the nature of their daily operations.

Insofar as our analysis of the new legalism is concerned, it is clear that developments in a number of Commonwealth jurisdictions have moved legislation *toward* the new legalism pole. However, with few exceptions, these developments have not significantly altered the basic structure of the quasi-legalistic approach. With the notable exception of New South Wales, and to some extent Ontario, professional control over the commitment and treatment processes has been left largely unchallenged, and the hegemony of mental health professionals continues. In short, although there have been a number of developments that introduce certain elements of the new legalism, one must conclude that, with the exceptions noted above, there has been no significant change in the balance of power between patients and professionals.

In the criminal justice sphere, there have been some significant developments. There has been a gradual move away from the situation in which mentally disordered offenders were detained at the pleasure of the executive arm of government which, in most cases, previously acted in accordance with medical advice. In some jurisdictions, the courts have been given powers to release mentally disordered persons (for example, defendants who have been found unfit to stand trial), while, in England, the mental health review tribunals now have the power to discharge mentally disordered offenders. Furthermore, in Canada, the duty to act fairly has been imposed on the lieutenant governors' advisory review boards. These developments have, to some extent, released mentally disordered offenders from the clutches of unbridled discretion. Judicial developments, in relation to criminal responsibility, appear to be aimed at restricting the scope of psychiatric evidence that might be introduced at a criminal trial. In the few jurisdictions that recognize a defense of diminished responsibility, however, the opposite approach has been taken, perhaps because, here, psychiatric evidence is directly relevant to the issue of sentencing rather than the issue of criminal responsibility.

Despite the cautionary notes sounded above, it is nevertheless possible to identify a distinct and significant period of reform occurring throughout the Commonwealth. In terms of its scope and impact, this is akin to the reforms that have occurred in the past (e.g., in the late 1950s to early 1960s), and it deserves careful analysis. Indeed, the results of such an exploration may yield a better understanding of the past periods of reform. In this respect, the use of categories of analysis such as *new legalism*, *quasi-legalism* and *professional discretion* does not advance explanation. They are merely descriptive terms that are rather vaguely formulated at this stage and that appear to be aimed at encapsulating some form of ideological development or change, a discernible set of activities on the part of those advocating patients' rights, and a set of specific policies related to the delivery of mental health services. While such terms aid our understanding, they do not explain *why* changes have occurred, nor do they predict future changes.

It is, therefore, important to examine the reasons that the changes have occurred. As Bean (1980) notes, this requires an examination of the structural conditions of change in this area of law. It is necessary to consider the social, economic, and political forces underpinning reform activities and, in closing, we shall offer some observations pertinent to such an enquiry.

In general, it is apparent that the changes, encompassed by the terms *new legalism* and *quasi-legalism*, do not limit the power of mental health professionals per se. However, the changes do seem to embody an attempt to limit access to public mental health services and might, therefore, be aligned with a policy of constriction of such services. In particular, the following developments and their effects should be noted. Narrower legal definitions of mental illness/disorder appear to introduce greater precision and specificity in the process of initially identifying an eligible group of people within the population of a jurisdiction. This will probably reduce the numbers of such persons falling within the purview of mental health systems. Tighter involuntary civil commitment criteria make such admissions more difficult. The exclusion of treatments and the rendering of treatment decisions subject to review further excludes marginal groups of patients or potential patients. Only those who are "treatable" will be admitted, then detained and treated. Stricter review procedures may result in a reduction in the length of stay in institutions. Legal and advocacy services, which have been introduced or encouraged to operate, serve to facilitate the process of excluding potential patients and reducing the numbers of existing patients. Their presence may be sufficient to curb the enthusiasm of mental health professionals or at least reduce their interest in all but clear-cut cases of mental illness. In many respects, they act to control mental health professionals, but not to the point where such personnel will be subject to negative sanctioning. They act, instead, as deterring watchdogs working to insure that the limitations, imposed by new policies and reflected in legislation, are followed. At the same time, these services are designed in a way that will prevent "disruptive" actions on the part of their staff in areas such as attempting to secure better and more extensive public mental health resources within the current framework.

If it is true that access to public mental health services is being restricted, and that this is a specific policy in many jurisdictions, then an explanation for the current moment of reform may lie with the economics of mental health systems as they are affected by wider economic changes. In this respect, a number of questions need to be answered by researchers:

1. Do fiscal constraints lie behind the reforms?
2. To what extent are the reforms linked to the dismantling of the welfare state?
3. What role is played by legal reform groups in this process — are they truly successful in persuading the state to reform mental health laws only because such laws fail to protect fundamental human rights or are they being co-opted as a convenient vehicle on which to carry the legitimation of a general policy of constriction of mental health services?

Such restraint may have its roots either in a "fiscal crisis" in social welfare systems or in a distinct policy of "fiscal reallocation" in support of monetarist economic policies.

Testing the validity of these questions clearly requires research, research that cannot be even sketched in this essay. However, the importance of such cannot be dismissed — especially in light of two current developments in the area of mental health: deinstitutionalization and privatization. Evidence is mounting to suggest that while public institutions are releasing their residents into the "backstreets" in the name of an enlightened and humanitarian policy of deinstitutionalization, a process of reinstitutionalization via the private sector is occurring. As Scull (1981) argues, a new trade in lunacy is taking shape in which the mental health patient becomes a "commodity" to be bought and sold by the private sector in the welfare marketplace, as this sector assumes the social control and social welfare functions relinquished by the state because of changes in fiscal policy.

An understanding of this process, which probably underpins the developments labeled "new legalism" or "quasi-legalism," is of central importance in understanding the likely face of mental health law in the coming decades. If the thesis sketched above has any validity, the law will be changing further to reflect the shift from the public to the private sectors — particularly in relation to the control of abuses that may occur in private institutions. In this regard, it is possible to predict a revitalized interest in the contents of the Lunacy Act of 1890 and a reexamination of the role of the then commissioners in lunacy who played a key part in the process of regulating, licensing, and inspecting private establishments. Privatization is not new, although we would predict that the legislative response to it in the 1980s and 1990s will suggest otherwise.

AUTHORS' NOTE: This manuscript was submitted for publication in the Spring of 1984. Since that time several changes have occurred in the fabric of Canadian mental health law, as a consequence of the gradually emerging impact of the *Charter of Rights and Freedoms, 1982.* These changes do not affect the substance of the arguments advanced by the authors; however, they are noted here in order to ensure that the context is current.

The Saskatchewan *Mental Health Act* has been reviewed and a new statute, *The Mental Health Services Act* (Bill No. 86, 1984–1985), has been passed by the legislative assembly but has not been proclaimed. It is expected to become law in the spring of 1986. A new *Mental Health Act* has been introduced in the Northwest Territories (Bill 6-85(2)) and reforms are also being contemplated in the Yukon Territory, Alberta and Newfoundland. In each of these jurisdictions, a major goal has been to ensure that the various mental health statutes comply with the legal and equality rights provisions of the *Charter of Rights and Freedoms.* In this regard, Canadian courts have just begun to consider charter cases in the mental health context and there are signs that the charter will figure most prominently in the future (see, e.g., *Lussa v. Health Science Centre and Director of Psychiatric Services* (1983), 5 CHRR D/2203 (Man.Q.B.); *Reference re Procedures and the Mental Health Act* (1984), 5 D.L.R. (4th) 577 (P.E.I.S.C. *in banco*).

REFERENCES

Ashworth, A.J. (1975). The Butler Committee and criminal responsibility. *Criminal Law Review, 1975,* 687–696.

Ashworth, A.J., & Shapland, J. (1980). Psychopaths in the criminal process. *Criminal Law Review, 1980,* 628–640.

Bayne, D. (1975). Automatism and provocation in Canadian case law. *Criminal Records, 31,* 257.

Bean, P. (1980). *Compulsory admission to mental hospitals.* Chichester: John Wiley and Sons.

Beyer, S. (1980). Madness and medicine: The forcible administration of psychotropic drugs. *Wisconsin Law Review, 1980,* 497–567.

Bottomley, S. (1981a). Mental health: The struggle in New South Wales continues. *Legal Service Bulletin, 6,* 209.

Bottomley, S. (1981b). Mental health advocacy. *Legal Service Bulletin, 6,* 31.

Bottomley, S. (1981c). Safeguarding mental patients' rights. *Legal Service Bulletin, 6,* 277.

Bottomley, S. (1983). Mental health: New legislation tabled in New South Wales. *Legal Service Bulletin, 8,* 138.

Briscoe, O.V. (1968). The meaning of "mentally ill person" in the Mental Health Act, 1958–1965 of New South Wales. *The Australian Law Journal, 42,* 207.

Butler, Lord R.A. (1974). *Interim Report of the Committee on Mentally Abnormal Offenders.* London: H.M.S.O. (Cmnd. 5698).

Butler, Lord R.A.B. (Chairman). (1975). *Report of the Committee on Mentally Abnormal Offenders* (Cmnd. 6244) London: H.M.S.O.

The Butler Report (1): Summary of principal recommendations, *Criminal Law Review, 1975,* 673–676.

Cahn, C.H. (1980). Consent in psychiatry: The position of the Canadian Psychiatric Association. *Canadian Journal of Psychiatry, 25,* 78–85.

Cahn, C.H. (1982). The ethics of involuntary treatment: The position of the Canadian Psychiatric Association. *Canadian Journal of Psychiatry, 27,* 67–73.

Campbell, I.G. (1983). Proposed changes to mental health and criminal justice systems in Queensland. *Criminal Law Journal, 7,* 179–206.

Campbell, K. (1981). Psychological blow automatism: A narrow defence. *Criminal Law Quarterly, 23,* 342–368.

Carson, D. (1983). Mental processes: The Mental Health Act 1983. *Journal of Social Welfare Law, 1983,* 195–211.

Carter, R.F. (1982). *Criminal law of Queensland* (6th ed.). Sydney: Butterworths.

Case and Comment. (1983). Purdy. *Criminal Law Journal, 7,* 218–222.

Castel, J.-G. (1978). Nature and effects of consent with respect to the right to physical and mental integrity in the medical field: Criminal and private law aspects. *Alberta Law Review, 16,* 293–356.

Cavenagh, W., & Newton, D. (1970). The membership of two administrative tribunals. *Public Administration, 48,* 449.

Cavanagh, W., & Newton, D. (1971). Administrative tribunals: How people become members. *Public Administration, 49,* 197.

Chiswick, D. (1978). Insanity in bar of trial in Scotland: A state hospital study. *British Journal of Psychiatry, 132,* 598–601.

Clare, A.W. (1978). Therapeutic and ethical aspects of electro-convulsive therapy: A British perspective. *International Journal of Law and Psychiatry, 1,* 237–253.

Committee on Mental Health Advocacy. (1981). *Legal rights for mental patients: The need for change.* Sydney: C.O.M.H.A.

Cooke, J.A. (1969). Mental health review tribunal. *Solicitors Law Journal,* Nov., 843.

Criminal Law and Penal Methods Reform Committee of South Australia. (1975). *Third report on court procedure and evidence.* Adelaide: Ministry of the Attorney-General, South Australia.

Criminal Law and Penal Methods Reform Committee of South Australia (Mitchell Committee). (1977). *Fourth report: The substantive criminal law.* Adelaide: Author.

Dell, S. (1983). Wanted. An insanity defence that can be used. *Criminal Law Review, 1983,* 431–437.

Department of Health and Social Security. (1978). *Review of the Mental Health Act 1959* (Cmnd. 7320) London: H.M.S.O.

Dobson, G., & Hansen, R. (1976). The ombudsman in mental health: Lakeshore's experience. *Canada's Mental Health, 24,* 11.

Dolan, J. (1975). Madness and the law. *Victoria University of Wellington Law Review, 7,* 373.

Draper, G. (1976a). Due process and confinement for mental disorder. *Alberta Law Review, 14,* 266.

Draper, G. (1976b). *The law and mental health* (Vol. 3). Edmonton: Alberta Law Foundation.

Earp, J.D. (1979). Psychosurgery: The position of the Canadian Psychiatric Association. *Canadian Journal of Psychiatry, 24,* 353–365.

Endicott, O. (1980). Will Emerson Bonnar Get His "Day in Court"? *Autonomy, 1,* 1–2.

Fairall, P. (1981a). Automatism. *Criminal Law Journal, 5,* 335–348.

Fairall, P. (1981b). Irresistible impulse, automatism and mental disease. *Criminal Law Journal, 5,* 136–155.

Faulk, M. (1979). Mentally disordered offenders in an interim regional medium secure unit. *Criminal Law Review, 1979,* 686–695.

Fennell, P. (1977). The mental health review tribunal: A question of imbalance. *British Journal of Law and Society, 2,* 186.

Flaherty, B.J., & Hall, W.D. (1981). Psychiatric hospitalization – An empirical study of involuntary and voluntary admission in New South Wales. *Mental Health in Australia, 1,* 17.

Fleming, A.C. (1963). Appeals to mental health review tribunals. *The Lancet, 7275,* 263.

Freer, C.J. (1966). Review tribunals, with special reference to Rampton Hospital. *British Journal of Psychiatry, 7,* 12.

Freiberg, A. (1976). Out of mind, out of sight: The disposition of mentally disordered persons involved in criminal proceedings. *Monash University Law Review, 3,* 134–172.

Gannage, M. (1981). The defence of diminished responsibility in canadian criminal law. *Osgoode Hall Law Journal, 19,* 301–320.

Garant, P. (1982). Fundamental freedoms and natural justice. In W.S. Tarnopolsky and G.A. Beaudoin (Eds.), *The Canadian charter of rights and freedoms* (pp. 258–290). Toronto: Carswell Company.

Gardner, J., Neal, D., & Cashman, P. (1979). *Legal resources book.* Melbourne: Fitzroy Legal Service.

Goodman, E. (1977). Compulsory admission of the mentally ill. *Medical Journal of Australia, 1,* 964.

Goodman, E., & O'Connor, D. (1977). Diminished responsibility – Its rationale and application. *Criminal Law Journal, 1,* 204–213.

Gordon, G.H. (1978). *The Criminal Law of Scotland* (2nd ed.). Edinburgh: W. Green & Son.

Gordon, R. (1981a). *Legal services for mental health patients.* Unpublished M.A. (criminology) thesis. Simon Fraser University.

Gordon, R. (1981b). Legal services for mental health patients: Some Commonwealth developments. *International Journal of Law and Psychiatry, 4,* 171.

Gordon, R. (1982). Legal services for mental health patients: Some practical and theoretical observations on Canadian developments. *Australian Journal of Law and Society, 1,* 101.

Gordon, R. (1983). Legal services for mental health patients: Some observations on Canadian and Australian developments. *Canadian Community Law Journal, 6,* 17.

Gordon, R., & Verdun-Jones, S.N. (1983). The right to refuse treatment: Commonwealth developments and issues. *International Journal of Law and Psychiatry, 6,* 57–73.

Gostin, L. (1977). *A Human Condition* (Vols. 1 and 2). London: National Association for Mental Health.

Gostin, L. (1979a). The merger of incompetency and certification: The illustration of unauthorised medical contact in the psychiatric context. *International Journal of Law and Psychiatry, 2,* 130.

Gostin, L. (1979b). "Unimpeded Access to Court." *New Law Journal*, Vol. 79:213.

Gostin, L. (1982a). A review of the Mental Health (Amendment) Act" (Parts I-III). *New Law Journal, 1982*, 1127-1132, 1151-1155, 1199-1203.

Gostin, L. (1982b). Human rights, judicial review and the mentally disordered offender. *Criminal Law Review, 1982*, 779-793.

Gostin, L. (1982c). Psychosurgery: A hazardous and unestablished treatment? A case for the importation of American legal safeguards to Great Britain. *Journal of Social Welfare Law, 1982*, 83.

Gostin, L. (1983a). *A practical guide to mental health law: The Mental Health Act 1983 and related legislation*. London: MIND (National Association for Mental Health).

Gostin, L. (1983b). The ideology of entitlement: The application of contemporary legal approaches to psychiatry. In P. Bean (Ed.), *Mental illness: Changes and trends*. (pp. 27-54). London: John Wiley.

Gostin, L. (1983c). Contemporary social historical perspectives on mental health reform. *Journal of Law and Society, 10*, 47-70.

Gostin, L., & Rassaby, E. (1980). *Representing the mentally ill and handicapped*. Sunbury: Quartermaine.

Greycar, R. (1980). Legal representation under the South Australian Mental Health Act. *Legal Service Bulletin, 5*, 2.

Greenland, C. (1970). *Mental illness and civil liberty*. London: Bell and Sons.

Greenland, C. (1973). Between the idea and the reality. *Canadian Psychiatric Association Journal, 18*, 339.

Gunn, J. (1979). The law and the mentally abnormal offender in England and Wales. *International Journal of Law and Psychiatry, 2*, 299-214.

Gunn, M.J. (1983). Legislation: Mental Health (Amendment) Act 1982. *Modern Law Review, 46*, 318-329.

Gutheil, T. (1980). In search of true freedom. Drug refusal, involuntary medication, and "rotting with your rights on." *American Journal of Psychiatry, 137*, 327-328.

Haines, E. (1978). Psychiatry and the adversary system of justice. In D. Weisstub (Ed.), *Law and Psychiatry*. Toronto: Pergamon Press.

Harding, R.W. (1981). Sane and insane automatism in Australia: Some dilemmas, developments and suggested reforms. *International Journal of Law and Psychiatry, 4*, 73-87.

Heffey, P.G. (1983). Negligent infliction of imprisonment: Actionable "per se" or "cum damno?" *Melbourne University Law Review, 14*, 266.

Hellon, C.P. (1973). A legislative approach to mental health problems. *Canadian Psychiatric Association Journal, 18*, 335.

Herlihy, J.M., & Kenny, R.G. (1978). *An introduction to criminal law in Queensland and Western Australia*. Sydney: Butterworths.

Hill, B.P. (1977). Civil rights of the psychiatric patient in Quebec. *Revue Juridique Themis, 12*, 503.

Himmelfarb, A., & Lazar, A. (1981). *Legal aid for mental patients: An evaluation report*. Ottawa: Department of Justice.

Hoggett, B. (1976). *Social work and law: Mental health*. London: Sweet and Maxwell.

Holland, W.H. (1982). Automatism and criminal responsibility. *Criminal Law Quarterly, 25*, 95-128.

Howard, C. (1982). *Criminal Law* (4th ed.). Sydney: Law Book Company.

Institute of Criminology. (1975). *Proposed amendments to New South Wales Mental Health Act*. Sydney, N.S.W.: Faculty of Law, University of Sydney.

Institute of Criminology. (1978). *Rights of the mentally ill: Representing patients at mental health act hearings*. Sydney, N.S.W.: Faculty of Law, University of Sydney.

Jones, K. (1960). *Mental health and social policy 1845-1959*. London: Routledge and Kegan Paul.

Jones, K. (1972). *A history of the mental health service*. London: Routledge and Kegan Paul.

Jones, K. (1980). The limitations of the legal approach to mental health. *International Journal of Law and Psychiatry, 3*, 1.

Katz, A. & Larsen, N. (1975). *Guide to the Mental Health Act of Manitoba*. Winnipeg, Manitoba: Legal Aid.

Kaufman, C.L., Roth, L.H., Lidz, C.W., & Meisel, A. (1981). Informed consent and patient decision-making: The reasoning of law and psychiatry. *International Journal of Law and Psychiatry, 4*, 345-362.

Kirby, M. (1981). Mental health law reform: The "second wave." *Medical Journal of Australia, 1*, 421.

Law Reform Commission of Canada. (1976). *A report to parliament on mental disorder in the criminal process*. Ottawa: Information Canada.

Law Reform Commission of Canada. (1979a). *Consent to medical care*. Ottawa: Minister of Supply and Services Canada.

Law Reform Commission of Canada. (1979b). *Sanctity of life or quality of life*. Ottawa: Minister of Supply and Services Canada.

Law Reform Commission of Canada. (1980). *Medical treatment and criminal law*. Ottawa: Minister of Supply and Services Canada.

Linden, A. (1980). Tort liability of psychotherapists, institutions and advisory review boards. Unpublished paper, Conference of Advisory Review Boards, Ottawa.

Loughlin, M. (1978). Procedural fairness: A study of the crisis in administrative law theory. *University of Toronto Law Journal, 28*, 215.

MacKay, R.D. (1980). Non-organic automatism—Some recent developments. *Criminal Law Review, 1980*, 350-361.

MacKay, R.D. (1982). Intoxication as a factor in automatism. *Criminal Law Review, 1982*, 146-156.

MacKinnon, P. (1979). Civil commitment in Saskatchewan: A reform proposal. *Saskatchewan Law Review, 45*, 203-220.

Manitoba Law Reform Commission. (1979). *Report on emergency apprehension, admissions and rights of patients under the mental health act*. Winnipeg: M.L.R.C.

Manson, A. (1982). Fit to be tried: Unravelling the knots. *Queen's Law Journal, 7*, 305-343.

Marshall, C. (1973). A legislative approach to mental health programs. *Canadian Psychiatric Association Journal, 18*, 340.

McCready, J., & Merskey, H. (1981). Compliance by physicians with the mental health act. *Canadian Medical Association Journal, 124*, 719.

McCready, J., & Merskey, H. (1982). On the recording of mental illness for civil commitment. *Canadian Journal of Psychiatry, 27*, 140.

Mental Health Act Review Committee (Edwards Committee) (1974). *Report of the N.S.W. Mental Health Act (1958) Review Committee.* Sydney, N.S.W.: Department of Health, New South Wales.

Meisel, A., Roth, L.H., & Lidz, C.W. (1977). Towards a model of the legal doctrine of informed consent. *American Journal of Psychiatry, 434,* 285–289.

Mewett, A.W., & Manning, M. (1978). *Criminal law.* Toronto: Butterworths.

Monahan, J. (1981). *Predicting violent behavior: An assessment of clinical techniques.* Beverly Hills, CA: Sage.

Morris, G.H. (1981). Dr. Szasz or Dr. Seuss: Whose right to refuse mental health treatment ? *Journal of Psychiatry and Law, 1981,* 283–303.

Muchlinski, P. (1980). Mental health patients' rights and the European Human Rights Convention. *The Human Rights Review,* 5, 95.

Mullan, D.J. (1975). Fairness: The new natural justice? *University of Toronto Law Journal, 25,* 281.

Munetz, M.R., Roth, L.H., & Cornes, C.L. (1981). Tardive Dyskinesia and Informed Consent: Myths and Realities. *Bulletin of the American Academy of Psychiatry and Law,* 1, 77–89.

Myers, D.M., Fitzgerald, D., & Ball, J. (1981). *Report of the Consultative Council on Review of Mental Health Legislation.* Melbourne: Victoria Ministry of Health.

Noble, P. (1981). Mental health services and legislation—An historical review. *Medical Science and Law, 21,* 16.

O'Regan, R.S. (1978a). Automatism and insanity under the Australian State Criminal Codes. *Australian Law Journal, 52,* 208–214.

O'Regan, R.S. (1978b). Diminished responsibility under the Queensland Criminal Code. *Criminal Law Journal, 2,* 183–197.

O'Regan, R.S. (1979). *Essays on the Australian Criminal Codes.* Sydney: Law Book Company.

O'Sullivan, J. (1981). *Mental health and the law.* Sydney: Law Book Company.

Page, S., & Firth, J. (1979). Civil commitment practices in 1977: Troubled semantics and/or troubled psychiatry? *Canadian Journal of Psychiatry, 24,* 329.

Page, S., & Yates, F. (1973). Civil commitment and the danger mandate. *Canadian Psychiatric Association Journal, 18,* 267.

Page, S., & Yates, F. (1974). A note on semantics and civil commitment. *Canadian Psychiatric Association Journal, 19,* 413.

Page, S., & Yates, F. (1975). Power, professionals and arguments against civil commitment. *Professional Psychology,* 6, 381.

Parker, E. (1980). Mentally disordered offenders and their protection from punitive sanctions: The English experience. *International Journal of Law and Psychiatry,* 3, 461–470.

Peay, J. (1981). Mental health review tribunals: Just or efficacious safeguards. *Law and Human Behavior,* 5, 161–186.

Peay, J. (1982). Mental health review tribunals and the Mental Health (Amendment) Act. *Criminal Law Review, 1982,* 794–808.

Pfohl, S. (1978). *Predicting dangerousness: The social construction of psychiatric reality.* Lexington, MA: D. C. Heath.

Plotkin, R. (1977). Limiting the therapeutic orgy: Mental patients' right to refuse treatment. *Northwestern University Law Review,* 72, 461–525.

Potas, I. (1982). *Just deserts for the mad.* Canberra: Australian Institute of Criminology.

Prins, H. (1980). *Offenders, deviants or patients? An introduction to the study of socio-forensic problems.* London: Tavistock Publications.

Quinsey, V.L., & Boyd, B.A. (1974). An assessment of the characteristics and dangerousness of patients held on warrants of the lieutenant-governor. *Crime et/and Justice,* 4, 268–274.

Reitsma, M. (1973). Civil liberties and the mentally ill. *Canada's Mental Health, 21,* 8.

Rhoden, N.K. (1980). The right to refuse psychotropic drugs. *Harvard Civil Rights–Civil Liberties Law Review,* 15, 363–413.

Rhodes-Chalke, F.C. (1973). The Law—A Mouse Trap? *Canadian Psychiatric Association Journal, 18,* 338.

Roesch, R., Eaves, D., Sollner, R., Normandin, M., & Glackman, W. (1981). Evaluating fitness to stand trial: A comparative analysis of fit and unfit defendants. *International Journal of Law and Psychiatry,* 4, 145–157.

Roth, L.R. (1979). A commitment law for patients, doctors, and lawyers. *American Journal of Psychiatry, 136,* 1121–1127.

Roth, L.R., Meisel, A., & Lidz, C.W. (1977). Tests of competency to consent to treatment. *American Journal of Psychiatry, 134,* 279–284.

Rozovsky, L.E. (1973). Consent to treatment. *Osgoode Hall Law Journal, 11,* 103–113.

Savage, H.S. (1981). The relevance of the fitness to stand trial provisions to persons with a mental handicap. *Canadian Bar Review, 59,* 319–336.

Schiffer, M.E. (1982). *Psychiatry behind bars: A legal perspective.* Toronto: Butterworths.

Scull, A.T. (1981). A new trade in lunacy: The recommodification of the mental patient. *American Behavioral Scientist, 24,* 741.

Shannon, P.J. (1976). Coercion and compulsory hospitalization: Some patient attitudes. *Medical Journal of Australia, 1976(2),* 798–800.

Shapland, J., & Williams, T. (Eds.). (1983). *Mental disorder and the law: Effects of the new legislation.* Leicester: British Psychological Association.

Shone, M. (1976). *Confluence of the mental health and legal systems in the process for compulsory civil commitment in Alberta.* L.L.M. Thesis, University of Alberta.

Skegg, P. (1974). A justification for medical procedures performed without consent. *Law Quarterly Review, 90,* 512–530.

Sleek, D. (1980). The rights of mentally disordered children in New Zealand. *Victoria University of Wellington Law Review, 10,* 317.

Stone, A.A. (1981). The right to refuse treatment. Why psychiatrists should and can make it work. *Archives of General Psychiatry, 38,* 358–362.

Stuart, D. (1982). *Canadian criminal law: A treatise.* Toronto: Carswell Company.

Sun, C. (1974). The discretionary power to stay criminal proceedings. *Dalhousie Law Journal, 1,* 482–525.

Tarnopolsky, W.S. (1982). The equality rights. In W.S. Tarnopolsky & G.-A. Beaudoin (Eds.), *The Canadian Charter of Rights and Freedoms* (pp. 315–442). Toronto: Carswell Company.

Toews, J., Prabhu, V., & El-Guebaly, N. (1980). Commitment of the mentally ill. *Canadian Journal of Psychiatry*, 25, 611.

Tomasic, R. (1981). Preventive detention and the High Court. *Australian Law Journal*, 55, 259–266.

Topp, R. (1975). A concept of diminished responsibility for Canadian criminal law. *University of Toronto Faculty Law Review*, 33, 205.

Unsworth, C. (1979). The balance of medicine, law and social work in mental health legislation, 1889–1959. In Parry, Rustin, & Satyamurti (Eds.), *Social Work, Welfare and the State*. London: Edward Arnold.

Verdun-Jones, S.N. (1979). The evolution of the defences of insanity and automatism in Canada from 1843–1979: A saga of judicial reluctance to sever the umbilical cord to the mother country? *U.B.C. Law Review*, 14, 1–73.

Verdun-Jones, S.N. (1981). The doctrine of fitness to stand trial in Canada: The forked tongue of social control. *International Journal of Law and Psychiatry*, 4, 363–389.

Verdun-Jones, S.N. (1982). Fitness to stand trial: Procedural and substantive aspects of a Janus-faced legal doctrine." In J. Atrens, P.T. Burns, & J.P. Taylor (Eds.). *Criminal procedure: Canadian law and practice* (pp. XV-1 to XV-151). Toronto: Butterworths.

Verdun-Jones, S.N., & Smandych, R.C. (1982). Catch-22 in the nineteenth century: The evolution of therapeutic confinement for the criminally insane in Canada, 1840–1900. *Criminal Justice History: An International Annual 2*, 85–108.

Walker, N. (1968). *Crime and insanity in England: The historical perspective*. Edinburgh: Edinburgh University Press.

Walker, N. (1981). Butler v. The CLRC and Others. *Criminal Law Review, 1981*, 596–601.

Webster, C.D., Menzies, R.J., & Jackson, M.A. (1982). *Clinical assessment before trial*. Toronto: Butterworths.

Wells, C. (1983). Whither Insanity? *Criminal Law Review, 1983*, 787–797.

Whitehead, T. (1982). *Mental illness and the law*. Oxford: Blackwell.

Williams, G. (1978). *A textbook of criminal law*. London: Stevens and Sons.

Woods, G.D. (1983). The sanctity of murder: Reforming the homicide penalty in New South Wales. *Australian Law Journal*, 57, 161–166.

Yake, I.B. (1976). *The Law and Mental Health* (Vol. II). Edmonton: Alberta Law Foundation.

TABLE OF CASES

Barclay-Maguire v. United Kingdom, App. No. 9117/80 (1980).

Bratty v. A.-G. for Northern Ireland, A.C. 386 (H.L. 1961).

Chartrand v. The Queen, 1 S.C.R. 314 (1977).

Clark v. Clark, 3 C.R.R. 342 Ont. Co. Ct. (1982).

Collins v. United Kingdom, App. No. 97291/82 (1982), cited in *The Times of London* (1982, February 23).

Cooper v. The Queen, 51 C.C.C. 2d 129 (1980).

Coulombe v. Watier, S.C.R. 673 (1973).

D.P.P. v. Majewski, A.C. 443 H.L. (1977).

Fraser v. Mudge, 3 All. E.R. 78 (1975).

Freeman v. Home Office, 3 All. E.R. 589 (Q.B.D. 1983).

Fry et al. v. Doucette et al., 115 D.L.R. 3d 274 N.S.S.C.A. (1980).

Hopp v. Lepp, 112 D.L.R. 2d 67 (1980).

In re Abel et al. and Advisory Review Board, 56 C.C.C. 2d 153 (1980).

In re Abel et al. v. Penetanguishene Mental Health Centre, 46 C.C.C. 2d 342 (1979).

In re Brown and Waterloo Regional Board of Commissioners of Police et al., 26 O.R. 2d 746 Ont. D.C. (1979).

In re Egglestone and Mousseau and Advisory Review Board, 6 C.C.C. 3d 1 Ont. D.C. (1983).

In re McCann and The Queen, 67 C.C.C. 2d 180 B.C.C.A. (1982).

In re Morgan and Association of Ontario Land Surveyors, 28 O.R. 2d 19 Ont. D.C. (1980).

Institute Phillipe Pinel de Montreal v. Dion, 2 D.L.R. 4th 234 (1983).

Kjeldsen v. The Queen, 64 C.C.C. 2d 161 (1981).

Knecht v. Gillman, 488 F. 2d 1136 (9th Cir. 1973).

Leary v. The Queen, 33 C.C.C. 2d 473 (1977).

Mackey v. Procunier, 477 F. 2d 877 (9th Cir. 1973).

Martineau v. Matsqui Institution Disciplinary Board, No. 2, 50 C.C.C. 2d 353 (1979).

R. v. Bailey, 2 All. E.R. 503 (1983).

R. v. Codere, Cr. App. R. 21 (C.C.A. 1916).

R. v. O'Connor, 54 A.L.J.R. 349 (1980).

R. v. Rabey, 37 C.C.C. 2d 461 (Ont. C.A. 1977).

R. v. Saxell, 59 C.C.C. 2d 176 (1980).

R. v. Sullivan, 2 All. E.R. 673 (1983).

R. v. Windle, 2 Q.B. 826 (C.C.A. 1952).

Rabey v. The Queen, 54 C.C.C. 2d 1 (1980).

Regina v. Abbey, 68 C.C.C. 2d 394 (1982).

Regina v. Barnier, 51 C.C.C. 2d 193 (1980).

Regina v. Quick, Q.B. 910 (C.A. 1973).

Regina v. Simpson 35 C.C.C. 337 (1977).

Reibl v. Hughes, 114 D.L.R. 3d 1 (S.C.C. 1980).

Rosandik v. Manning, 5 B.C.L.R. 347 (1978).

Schwartz v. The Queen, 1 S.C.R. 673 (1977).

Selvarajan v. Race Relations Board, 1 All. E.R. 12 (1976).

Stapleton v. The Queen, 86 C.L.R. 358 (1952).

Tanner v. Norys, 5 W.W.R. 724 (1979).

Tanner v. Norys, 4 W.W.R. 33 (Alta. C.A. 1979).

Veen v. The Queen, 53 A.L.J.R. 305 (1979).

W. v. L., 1 Q.B. 711 (1974).

X. v. The United Kingdom, App. No. 6998/75, European Court of Human Rights; judgment delivered November 5th (1981).

2.
Malpractice in American Psychiatry: Toward a Restructuring of the Psychiatrist–Patient Relationship

Laurence R. Tancredi
David N. Weisstub

ABSTRACT. *The enormous expansion of medical technologies over the past 30 years, augmented by the institutionalization of health care delivery through such devices as health maintenance organizations, primary care centers, and other corporate structures, has had a major influence on the nature of the physician–patient relationship. A major indication of this change is the rate of medical malpractice cases. In the mid-1970s we experienced a major crisis in medical malpractice. This was actually a crisis in the provision of insurance coverage for doctors as the premiums began to escalate rapidly and many companies claimed they were unable to provide coverage. We are now entering what appears to be a second malpractice crisis. The changes that were initiated in the mid-1970s to shore up the existing tort system have obviously been unsuccessful. The annual number of cases is once again rising and this is augmented by many very large awards against physicians, particularly in the specialties of obstetrics and gynecology and surgery. Most of the medical specialties that were the object of the bulk of malpractice actions remain in that same position in the 1980s.*

Nonetheless, the incidence of malpractice actions against psychiatry is also increasing. There are nearly twice as many claims annually against psychiatry than there were up until 1976. Furthermore, and perhaps even more distressing to the profession, there have been many awards to successful plaintiffs of well over a million dollars. With regard to psychiatric malpractice, this was almost unheard of in the mid-1970s. The profile of cases has also undergone some marked changes over the last 20 years, so that in the 1980s the highest frequency claims seem to be for allegations of improper treatment (including improprieties in the psychotherapeutic relationship), followed by drug reactions and, finally, suicide and harm to third parties, including the duty of the psychiatrist to protect third parties who may be potential victims.

The purpose of this examination is three-fold. First, it will be concerned with examining the nature of the psychiatrist–patient relationship. Paradigms that are currently operating, such as the contract, covenant, and tort, are reevaluated in the light of the shifting pattern of psychiatric practice and innovations being proposed for more effectively dealing with compensation and prevention objectives, a system of redress for injuries. The specific psychiatric malpractice actions that are discussed range from informed consent, duty to warn, and dangerousness to third parties to abuses in the psychiatrist–patient relationship, to name a few.

The final section of this paper will focus on alternatives that are being proposed for addressing the inefficiencies of the tort system of medical malpractice. Particular emphasis in this discussion will be on balancing considerations of a social insurance system versus a system predicated on specified events. The details of one such system is closely examined with a particu-

lar eye on the conceptual problems defining specific events, particularly as they relate to psychiatry and the possible advantages that might accrue from implementing such a system in hospital care, particularly the care of psychiatric patients. Finally, a model is proposed for restructuring the psychiatrist–patient relationship in the light of both new technological developments and the emerging concepts regarding the increasing power prerogatives of the consumer in the health care system. These factors compel a reconsideration of the mixture of existing legal paradigms, such as the contract, covenant, and tort, as they address the full range of negotiated issues regarding the patient in psychiatric care.

SOMMAIRE. L'expansion considérable de la technologie médicale au cours des trente dernières années, combinée à l'institutionalisation des soins médicaux par l'intervention des organismes de traitement, des centres de premiers soins et d'autres structures institutionnelles, a profondément marqué la nature de la relation entre le médecin et son patient. Un des principaux indices de ce changement réside dans le taux de poursuites en responsabilité médicale. Au milieu des années 1970, la responsabilité médicale a connu une crise importante au niveau de la garantie d'assurance des médecins à cause de la rapide augmentation des primes et du refus opposé par de nombreuses compagnies d'assurances. Nous entrons maintenant, semble-t-il, dans une deuxième crise car les réformes lancées au milieu des années 1970 pour adapter le régime de la responsabilité délictuelle n'ont évidemment pas abouti. Le nombre de litiges sur une base annuelle est encore en hausse, et ce phénomène est accentué par l'octroi d'indemnités très élevées à l'encontre des médecins, notamment dans des spécialités comme l'obstétrique, la gynécologie et la chirurgie. La plupart des spécialités qui étaient la cible des actions en responsabilité sont restées dans la même situation dans les années 1980.

Néanmoins, l'incidence des actions en responsabilité à l'encontre des psychiatres est aussi en hausse. Le nombre annuel de litiges en psychiatrie est actuellement du double de ce qu'il a été jusqu'en 1976. Qui plus est, et c'est là un élément inquiétant pour la profession, il est arrivé plusieurs fois que des indemnités de bien plus d'un million de dollars soient octroyées à des demandeurs, phénomène tout à fait inconnu dans la responsabilité des psychiatres au milieu des années 1970. Même les types des litiges ont évolué de façon marquée au cours des vingt dernières années de sorte que, dans les années 1980, les actions les plus fréquentes semblent porter sur des allégations de mauvais traitement, notamment d'abus dans la relation psychothérapeutique, suivis d'usage de drogues menant au suicide et à un préjudice à l'encontre de tiers, et sur l'obligation qui incombe au psychiatre de protéger des tiers pouvant être des victimes potentielles.

L'objet de cette étude est triple. Tout d'abord, il s'agit d'examiner la nature de la relation entre le psychiatre et son patient. Il est procédé à la réévaluation de modèles existant actuellement comme le contrat, l'alliance et la responsabilité délictuelle, à la lumière de l'évolution de la pratique et des innovations en psychiatrie qui sont proposées pour mieux accomplir les objectifs d'indemnisation et de prévention, grâce à un régime d'indemnisation du préjudice. Les actions en responsabilité particulières à la psychiatrie qui sont présentées dans ce chapitre posent, entre autres, les problèmes du consentement éclairé, de l'obligation d'avertir, de la dangerosité du patient pour les tiers et des abus dans la relation entre le psychiatre et son patient.

La dernière section de ce chapitre est essentiellement consacrée aux solutions proposées pour redresser le manque d'efficacité du régime de la responsabilité délictuelle en matière médicale. Dans cette discussion, les auteurs insistent notamment sur l'opposition entre les exigences du système de sécurité sociale et celles d'un système fondé sur des litiges précis. Ils examinent ce système en insistant sur les problèmes conceptuels pour la définition de faits particuliers, en particulier liés à la psychiatrie, et les avantages possibles qui peuvent découler d'un tel système dans les soins hospitaliers, notamment pour les patients de psychiatrie. Enfin, ils proposent une conception en vue de restructurer la relation entre le psychiatre et son patient à la lumière des nouvelles technologies et des concepts récemment mis à jour sur le pouvoir croissant des consommateurs dans le régime de la santé. Ces facteurs imposent de reconsidérer la fusion des modèles juridiques actuels comme le contrat, l'alliance ou la responsabilité délictuelle dans la mesure où ils portent sur la gamme complète des questions que pose le traitement des patients en psychiatrie.

INTRODUCTION

In the mid-1970s we experienced a major crisis in medical malpractice. At that time several insurers withdrew coverage of physicians, arguing that the frequency of medical malpractice claims, coupled with the growth in the size of the awards, made it economically impractical to continue insuring health care providers against malpractice. This crisis lasted for a relatively short time. By the end of 1976, malpractice insurers made coverage available again, but with a rise in the average premiums of over 140% from the levels established in 1973, that is, prior to the crest period of the crisis (Adams & Zuckerman, 1984). Since 1976, there appeared to be significant stabilization of the malpractice situation in the United States and, although the rates continued to rise, it seemed that the insurance industry had the problem well in hand. The increases that did occur between 1976 and the early 1980s were claimed to be more reflective of the rate of inflation than of the severity of medical malpractice claims themselves. (Danzon, 1983).

Within the past year, however, there has been renewed concern about the increased rates of medical malpractice premiums. The industry is once again clamoring for permission to increase its premium rates, arguing that during the post-1976 period malpractice claims occurred at a much higher annual rate than they did even prior to 1976. Other statistical indicia seem to support the observation that rates are increasing, that awards are getting higher, and that the crisis of the mid-1970s seems to have returned in 1985. There have been several recent articles in the *New York Times* that have reported substantial increases by various malpractice insurers. In January, 1985, the superintendent of insurance for New York State allowed a rate increase in malpractice insurance premiums of as high as 52% for an insurance company that largely covers physicians in Long Island (*New York Times*, 1985, Jan.) If these rates go into effect, they would increase the amount of premiums for neurosurgeons to as high as $100,000 per year and for obstetrician-gynecologists, nearly $82,000. In April, 1985, the *New York Times* disclosed that the superintendent of insurance granted New York's largest medical malpractice insurer an increase of as much as 55% in malpractice insurance premiums. This medical malpractice insurer covers approximately 16,000 of the 22,000 physicians who are self-insured in the state of New York

(*New York Times*, 1985, Apr.). The average cost of medical liability coverage for physicians will increase to $19,000 a year as compared to $4,000 a year only 10 years ago. Again, the rates for some groups, particularly neurosurgeons and obstetrician-gynecologists, will be most seriously affected.

In addition to the increase in the rates for medical malpractice insurance, there has been a commensurate increase in the indemnity per claim. The increase between the years 1970 and 1975 alone was as much as 160%. In 1975 the indemnity per claim was as high as $16,000, whereas in 1970, only 5 years earlier, it was $10,000 (Blaut, 1977). Before 1976, awards reaching an amount of over $1 million each were relatively rare. However, statistics for the years 1983–1984 alone have shown that there have been at least 250 cases that have settled for awards of over a million dollars each (*New York Times*, 1985, Feb.). With regard to the number of claims there has also been a substantial increase. The American Medical Association (AMA) reported in 1983 that the incidence of claims per 100 physicians annually has increased more than two-fold over the last 5 or more years (Reynolds & Abrams, 1983) and that until 1978 the average annual incidence of claims per 100 physicians was approximately 3.3, whereas from 1978 to 1983 the incidence went up to 8 per 100. When the statistics are further broken down, we discover that some specialties have had conspicuous increases. The highest increase has come in obstetrics and gynecology, which averaged approximately 5.3 claims per every 100 physicians annually before 1978 and reached approximately 15.4 claims per every 100 physicians in 1983 (Adams & Zuckerman, 1984), virtually tripling the number of claims within a 5-year period. Between 1976 and 1981, surgery claims doubled per every 100 surgeons annually. Before 1976 there was an average of 4.5 claims per every 100 surgeons annually, which increased in 1981 to approximately 9 or more claims per every 100 surgeons annually (Adams & Zuckerman, 1984).

According to the statistics of one of the largest providers of malpractice insurance, there has been a major increase in the number of claims between 1979 and 1983. St. Paul Company, which provides malpractice insurance to nearly 15% of the medical market, disclosed that in 1979 there were roughly 2,725 claims against its insurance program. In 1983 the number of claims went up to 5,870, which has been an increase of approximately 116% (American Medical Association, 1984). In contrast to other medical specialties, the annual claims against psychiatrists is still relatively low. Before 1976 there was roughly 1 claim per 100 psychiatrists. Between 1976 and 1981, that incidence of claims increased to approximately 1.7 claims per 100 psychiatrists annually (Adams & Zuckerman, 1984). Though psychiatry remains one of the medical specialties least likely to be litigated, the rate has nearly doubled during the period of 1976 to 1981. Moreover, as we will see shortly, there has been a significant shift and consequent increase in the kinds of cases that are being brought against psychiatrists. For example, cases involving adverse reactions from medication may be expected to continue to increase in the future.

Despite this increase in the numbers of claims against physicians, the tort system, as it now exists, is still quite inefficient and clearly ineffective in providing compensation to injured patients in the medical care system (Institute of Medicine, 1978). If one examines the cost inefficiencies alone, it is clear that the tort system does not result in an equitable distribution of its resources or in an efficient management of the money that is poured into it. Of every premium dollar for medical malpractice insurance paid for by physicians, a relatively small percentage makes its way to injured patients. Some have estimated that as little as 17% of every dollar is received by patients who are injured in medical care; others have claimed that the percentage may be as high as 56% (Joint Legislative Audit Committee, 1975; Williams, 1984), but more than likely it is under 50%. Transactional costs (a large part of which represents the contingency fee system that, in certain instances, provides lawyers with as much as 44% of every dollar in insurance premium) augmented by the administrative costs of the court process, absorb a major amount of the financial resources targeted for the compensation of injured patients (Joint Legislative Audit Committee, 1975).

Furthermore, if one examines the actual practice of the tort system, it is clear that many injured patients never receive any redress for their injuries. In the Report of the Secretary's Commission on Medical Malpractice (Department of HEW, 1973), it was disclosed that an injured patient has a one-in-eight chance of convincing a lawyer to take his or her case in the tort system. Due to the mechanism of the contingency fee, lawyers are influenced to take cases that are likely to produce a major award because that increases the amount of money that they will ultimately receive. Moreover, the percentage of malpractice cases ever

reaching the courts is small. The National Association of Insurance Commissioners (1977) studied this process in 1976 and disclosed that, even in those cases where lawyers are willing to present arguments of claimants, only approximately two thirds of these cases result in any payment to injured parties. That study disclosed that approximately 90.2% of claims are actually settled out of court, and, of those settled out of court, approximately 51% result in some remuneration for the injured party. Of the 7% that actually go to trial approximately 28% come out in favor of patients; the vast majority come out in favor of the defendant. This is largely due to the burden of proof in a malpractice action, which for the most part is placed on the patient. In short, the patient has the burden of establishing injury, duty of care, negligence based on deflection from standards of care, and proximate causation. The two most problematic of these are the establishment of a diversion from customary practice and the determination of proximate cause (which includes not only the element of factual cause but foreseeability).

Recent statistics of the National Association of Insurance Commissioners' survey of claims that closed between July 1, 1976 and June 30, 1978, showed some changes in the percentages of cases that actually reached the court and went to trial (Sowka, 1981). This study disclosed that approximately 16% of all claims that are brought to lawyers actually reach the trial stage. However, if one were to examine the success of those individuals who reached the trial level, some of the statistics are less encouraging than the earlier study indicates. In fact, it looks as though the doctor-owned companies are proving to be far more formidable than other insurance providers in the courtroom setting. They are winning approximately 90% of the cases that actually reach the trial level in contrast to the 75% that was reported in the earlier survey. In a later section of this discussion we will examine some of the more problematic features of the tort system and explore potential alternatives that might successfully resolve these deficiencies.

PHYSICIAN–PATIENT RELATIONSHIP

The medical malpractice crisis, as it was called in 1975, was essentially a crisis in the availability of insurance coverage for medical malpractice. The crisis reflected most conspicuously a straining of the economics of the system of redress or of compensation for medical injuries. The central weakness responsible for this event was a breakdown in the physician–patient relationship. On its most superficial level, this breakdown was illustrated by physicians spending less time explaining to patients the benefits and risks of treatment and by physicians refusing to allow patients to participate actively in decisions of a medical nature, be they diagnostic or treatment-related. As a result, much attention has been given over the past 8 or 9 years to examining the nature of the physician–patient relationship, with a particular eye on the prevention of those infractions that may be responsible for the increasing problem of medical malpractice. More substantive examination has also been conducted over the same period on the essential ingredients in the relationship. This has been brought on by the ethics movement in health care which seemed to have picked up momentum in the late 1960s, a momentum stimulated in large part by the increasingly complex technologies in the diagnosis and treatment of medical diseases. Ethicists have placed particular focus on the nature of that relationship as it comports with covenantal or contractarian principles (Veatch, 1981).

The psychiatrist–patient relationship is a particularly complex one. Not only does it deal with some of the same issues that are generally present in the physician–patient relationship (those issues relevant to the role of the patient in determining what is to be done with his or her body in the medical care process), but the psychiatrist–patient relationship also deals more completely with the emotional and mental processes of the patient. The psychiatrist is more than a physician insofar as one of the focuses of his attention must be the emotional and thinking capacities of the patient. Hence the psychiatrist involves him or herself in the mindset of the patient, and thereby may have an influence well beyond that of determining the appropriate diagnostic and treatment methods. The psychiatrist's influence is more pervasive, impacting on all aspects of the patient's life, particularly those addressing patterns and meanings in relationships generally. To some extent, this complexity in the psychiatrist–patient relationship has been protective of the psychiatrist with regard to medical malpractice. The psychiatrist is more skilled than any other physician in establishing a sense of intimacy with the patient, mainly because the psychiatrist uses the interviewing technique as a principal instrument in his treatment of the patient. To the extent that talking with the patient and creating a relationship is a prophylaxis, not against poor quality of care but against medical malpractice suits, the psychiatrist has a distinct advantage over other medical practitioners. On the other hand, it is because the psychiatrist is so skilled in the use of interviewing techniques and in penetrating the mental and emotional apparatus of the patient that the ethical and even legal obligations of the psychiatrist in the psychiatrist-patient relationship are more complex and deserve greater attention.

The potentialities for abuse in this relationship, and the serious consequences that may ensue, create a greater obligation for the psychiatrist to assure that elements essential to the contractual relationship with a patient are given their proper weight and to assure that the power prerogatives in decision-making are, if not equally balanced, moving strongly in that direction. The argument is very compelling that the nature of the psychiatrist–patient relationship must also be conceptualized as a special type of contract or covenant. This relationship finds its basis not only in the agreement between the psychiatrist and the patient, but it is strongly woven into the fabric of the moral community of people who have some concept of normative ethical principles regarding social relationships (Weisstub, 1985). The contract, therefore, does not exist only between the psychiatrist and the patient; it adheres to some general principles regarding the basic function of the psychiatrist in the social system and some equally general notion of what psychiatric treatment is supposed to achieve. From this perspective, viewing the psychiatrist–patient relationship as a special contract serves an epistemological function. It allows us to understand the terms that are applicable in that relationship to assure that it comports with expected behaviors in the moral community. Hence, the complex layering of qualities such as mutual respect, support, loyalty, and even fidelity are predicated on a basic underlying expectation of what is ethically and morally desirable in social relationships. The contract-covenant paradigms allow for a clear delineation of the duties, responsibilities, and rights of the various parties engaging in an agreement (Veatch, 1981). Inevitably, there are benefits and burdens that apply to both parties, perhaps in uneven amounts. This lack of balance is not problematic to the moral underpinnings of a contractual relationship. In the medical care system, particularly the psychiatrist–patient relationship, it is presumed that some features (medical) may be stronger on the side of the physician than on the side of the patient, whereas other features may be strongly weighted in favor of the patient. Underlying the extent of differences in benefits and burdens of each party are limits set by what is perceived by society as morally acceptable.

Covenant is a concept that publicly represents a particular kind of contract, one resting more strongly on the moral bonds between the parties, whereas *contract* is decidedly more legalistic (Weisstub, 1985). Others have argued that the two notions are really conflatable and, hence, in any pristine sense, indistinguishable (Veatch, 1981). As this is a very complex and basic concept in the nature of the psychiatrist–patient relationship, we will begin this discussion by first viewing contract and covenant as distinguishable. Then we will follow this by examining ways in which they can be viewed as discrete concepts to create a different characterization of the psychiatrist in his or her relationship to patients. In viewing the psychiatrist–patient relationship, the contract model allows us to examine the specific elements that constitute a meaningful relationship. Some of the most significant of these are the presence of fundamental equality and reciprocity in the relationship, the role of faithfulness or loyalty, and the role of autonomy in preserving basic self-determination in the face of the contract.

RECIPROCITY AND EQUALITY

The contract, if it is to be a viable agreement between two parties, must be responsive to the power prerogatives of those entering into the initial agreement (Epstein, 1979). A contract based on inequality becomes less of a contract and more of a coercion, one person's will over the other. A morally acceptable contract or agreement between parties necessitates the presence of equality. Of course, this can potentially conflict with the goals of psychiatric intervention in the care of patients. The psychiatrist's power in influencing the intellectual and emotional state of the patient rests in part on a superior position. The concept of transference, whereby the patient develops intense positive feelings toward the therapist, is the modality through which the psychotherapist can initiate change in the patient's attitudes, emotions, and behavior (Tancredi & Slaby, 1977). In constructing a therapeutic alliance, it is inevitable that the therapist will have an advantage over the patient, certainly to the extent of influencing the way he functions in interrelationships. Often the ostensible goals and desires of the patient will

conflict with those of the psychotherapist. The psychotherapist may have to resort to inducing powerful emotional reactions in order to get the patient to both understand what is happening in his social environment and to be able to change old patterns that keep him attached to unhealthy relationships and behaviors. This altering of the course of his behavioral responses will inevitably involve some pain on the part of the patient. The therapist, in achieving appropriate psychotherapeutic ends, may need to further the patient's progress through unpleasant emotional experiences. If viewed from a purely psychotherapeutic perspective, equality and reciprocity at that level may be virtually impossible. To insist on the presence of equality would vitiate one of the most important tools of the psychotherapy.

But this fact in itself does not necessarily mean that reciprocity and equality cannot be achieved in the psychotherapeutic relationship. When a physician enters into an agreement with a patient to conduct a surgical operation, the patient is at a power disadvantage. At the time of the surgery the surgeon will have control of the instrument that is used to penetrate the body of the patient and bring about the necessary curative activity. But, at the time of the establishment of the agreement, the patient can be placed in a near-equal power relationship. Because other options are available to the patient, including alternative treatments and even alternative physicians, he can achieve a certain degree of freedom in determining which method of treatment and which surgeon he will contract with. Even though at the time of the treatment itself the patient is at a power disadvantage, this does not negate reciprocity and equality at the moment of establishing the contract. A similar analogy can be made with the psychotherapeutic relationship. At the time the patient enters into psychiatric treatment he may be in a near-equal power relationship with the therapist by virtue of informed consent (Tancredi, 1982). The therapist has the obligation to inform the patient (a) of the various modes of treatment that may be available as well as, (b) of the resources in the area the therapist may be considering for the treatment process itself. Ultimately, these decisions may rest on something quite emotional and irrational, and the patient may decide to continue with the therapist based on the quality of the relationship. To some extent, this works adversely on a purely objective assessment of what is being provided by the therapist. On the other hand, this is inevitable in any relationship between a consumer of goods and provider of services.

There is a difference, however, between the surgeon–patient relationship and the psychiatrist-patient relationship. After the initial surgeon-patient agreement is made, the surgeon is no longer dealing with the mental and emotional apparatus of the patient. He has now been contracted to perform a service, presumably an operation or another procedure to relieve the patient of his medical condition. In contrast, the psychiatrist, in his or her relationship with the patient continues to engage with the patient at an intimate mental-emotional level. Once the psychotherapy agreement is made (an agreement that may, in fact, stem from reciprocity and equality), the patient is placing himself in the hands of the psychiatrist for therapeutic ends that involve a continuing engagement with affect, thinking process, and behavior. Hence, the inequality that emerges after the initial agreement, which is inevitable in a psychotherapeutic relationship, may preclude all equality subsequently within the context of that relationship. Transference affects the capacity of the patient to continue on an equal footing. Herein lies the most problematic feature of the psychiatrist-patient relationship, that is, the recognition that, following the initial contractual agreement, the patient may be at an increasing power disadvantage. This power disadvantage is both essential in the therapeutic process and problematic in terms of maintaining the delicate balance in the agreement between the therapist and the patient.

LOYALTY

The second important ingredient of a true contract between a patient and a physician is the presence of faithfulness or loyalty. This refers to the fidelity of individuals to the nature of the contract. Loyalty or fidelity addresses the extent of the commitment of the parties to the elements of the agreement or contract. This means that both parties are respecting each other and demonstrating this by maintaining the terms of the contract in the process of therapy. But the concept of faithfulness or fidelity goes beyond mere loyalty to the terms of the contract; it extends to a faithfulness to the prerogatives of the individuals engaging in the agreement (Veatch, 1981). Hence, if applied to the downstream effects of an agreement, loyalty or fidelity would have to incorporate the engagement of both parties in any alterations of the con-

tract's terms. Consequently, fidelity or loyalty is not strictly limited to the contract terms *per se*; it represents the quality of mutuality and participation in the establishment of what each party is expected to provide in the agreement.

AUTONOMY

Finally, and consistent with the elements of equality and faithfulness, a contract must incorporate the capacity for the patient to maintain autonomy. In fact, it could be argued strongly that autonomy is essential as a logical prerequisite if a system of morality is to be constructed. Autonomy implies responsibility for one's actions. It is essential that the patient be capable of freedom of thought and action in order to enter a contract that is truly reflective of his or her preferences and power prerogatives (Ladd, 1979). This is not to say that autonomy cannot be traded off in the course of the negotiation of a relationship. For example, a patient might be willing to sacrifice some aspects of personal autonomy for the benefits of psychotherapy, but the initial decision is clearly his. It should not be the decision of the profession, nor of society, to sacrifice the individual's autonomy. John Rawls (1973) in A *Theory of Justice*, argues that the first and perhaps most fundamental principle for any contractarian system would have to be liberty. Every individual in the social system should have equal right to the most extensive basic liberty that is compatible "with a similar liberty for others".

Two spin-off aspects of claims of autonomy and liberty are freedom from constraint and entitlement. With regard to the first of these, freedom from constraint potentially affirms the individual's freedom from restrictions or constraints. These are often referred to as liberty rights or even negative rights. These are rights that allow for defining the boundaries of those incursions that may impact on individual autonomy or self-determination (Weisstub, 1985). In contrast, there are other rights called "entitlements," more appropriately termed "positive rights" (Veatch, 1981). These refer to the patient's right to certain duties performed by the professional. For example, in the contract between a psychiatrist and patient, a patient would be entitled to expect a certain level of competency on the part of the therapist. This would be an entitlement in the sense that the competency of the therapist is essential if the patient is to obtain any beneficial results from the relationship. Hence, two types of rights are capable of articulation in the contractual relationship between the therapist and the patient: first, the right against certain kinds of incursions or constraints on individual behavior and the freedom to assert certain options; and, second, the right to certain kinds of entitlements as part of that contractual relationship.

BENEFICENCE

Basic to the dynamics of the therapist–patient relationship is the tension between individual autonomy, particularly that of the patient, and the therapist's tendency toward beneficence. Beneficence as an ethic falls back to some of the basic elements of the Hippocratic Oath, which commands that the physician act for the benefit of the patient (Tancredi & Edlund, 1983). The principle of beneficence, which incorporates notions of paternalism, would conflict with autonomy because the underlying assumption is that there are situations where one can violate the patient's right to autonomy for the patient's benefit. An underlying predicate in malpractice actions is the delicate balance between asserting principles of autonomy and affirming beneficence. The relationship of the psychiatrist and the patient must rely on some notion of superior knowledge and some willingness on the part of the patient to cede over those options for freedom of choice and action. Under certain circumstances, when this balance is seriously affected or when it is shifted off a stable fulcrum, a breakdown in the therapist–patient relationship can occur with the consequences of a malpractice action.

CONTRACTS AND COVENANTS

If one were to take a different position regarding the concepts of contract and covenant, a position that would see them as distinguishable notions, and then apply this to the nature of the psychiatrist–patient relationship, a different calculus would result. We have already discussed several elements that are basic to a contract that deals with two parties who are negotiating ideally, that is, in an equal power balance. Recognizing, of course, that psychiatry on some levels precludes equality in the power balance between the patient and the psychiatrist, it is true, nonetheless, that trends in modern health care generally (due to technological developments, competitive market systems, and increasing consumer awareness)

make the possibilities of equality in a contractual relationship better now than ever before. So perhaps we can maintain the ideal of equality as something attainable in the future as a construct for explicating the nature of the psychiatrist–patient relationship.

From the perspective of the covenant, however, a different historical and formative structure applies. To begin with, the notion of covenant has its origins in the Old Testament. Abraham entered into a covenantal relationship with God. In this agreement, Abraham willingly gave up a certain element of freedom in order to have his prescribed destiny and role in history. In return, God gave up the freedom of having indeterminate choice. That is to say, at that historical point, God had committed himself to the promise of Abraham's actualization as a pivotal, key role in history. When this covenant crystallized into a social fabric, with a bond established between God and the people of Israel, a set of laws emerged.

A critical feature at this moment in history is that the norms and values of the covenant flow essentially in one direction. They are not a mutually agreed upon or negotiated set of values. The values in the covenant that tied the people of Israel to a deity flow from God to the people and are clearly articulated as essential elements in the people of Israel's acceptance of their destiny in the historical process. Hence, synchronically, when freedoms are willingly given up there is also the concommitant application of a higher order of values, a prioritization that is established by the godhead. A second dimension of the covenantal relationship is that which characterizes it as diachronically unfolding. It is a relationship that is dynamic, with a constant interchanging of human and divine intentions, desires, and values. In this diachronic, constantly changing covenantal relationship there is something comparable to what we see in the psychiatrist–patient relationship. If one were to turn to Buber's "I and thou," one sees the establishment of two forms of consciousness interacting, the transference and the countertransference. We perceive the countertransference only by the external manifestation of the values of the choice to move from indeterminancy to determinancy. The transferential relationship, representing that of the people, manifests itself in a variety of theological searchings for definition and meaning made possible by the nature of the covenant, which allows continuous change yet maintains the bonding between the principal parties.

This is very different from the definition of status that Maine (1897) described in his classical work on ancient law. In this work, he addresses the historical movement from status to contract. In the early stages of the development of a society, status manifested itself as predetermined categories. The individual is placed in a position that at the same time defines and limits the extent of his decision-making options. This position not only limits him at the moment of his birth but determines his future and, therefore, limits him in his self-actualization. In the movement from status to contract there is a breaking down of the imprisonment of the initial positioning of the individual. Contract allows, not only for the individual to participate in the decisions that will limit and restrict his options, but also for a concept of equalized power. In contrast to both of these, the covenantal paradigm incorporates both elements of status and those of contract. It is, essentially, a hybrid of the two notions creating certain redefinitions that result in qualities that are more beneficial to both parties in the power balance. The covenantal relationship consists of an open-ended texture. That is, it allows for much flexibility in the renegotiations of its terms over the course of time. It provides a significant amount of movement for discretionary decision-making on the part of both parties involved. It is here that there are significant differences between the nature of a covenant and that of a contract. The open-ended texture of the covenant, with its recognition of disparities in the power prerogatives of the parties allows for some restraining of the decision-making options of the stronger party. A fabric of values surrounds the decision-making that influences both the stronger and the weaker parties in the covenant. There is an assumption that trust rests in the weaker parties because they believe that the stronger will protect them through the values present in this fabric. This allows for greater actualization because the terms are always open for redefinition as more liberty is potentially tolerated. In contrast, the contract model is not open-ended in its texture. It contains categories that are predetermined, which place the duties and responsibilities of the parties at one moment in history, with no opportunity for flexible restructuring of the original terms. Though a contract has the advantage over situations where there is an absence of any terms — providing some notion of entitlement of both parties — from the standpoint of the possibilities for flexible reordering the covenant is far superior.

The covenant paradigm seems particularly relevant to the psychiatrist–patient relationship. First, the psychiatrist can be analogized in terms of being in a superior knowledge position, although, admittedly, with an ill-defined, not-so-obvious fabric of values (as compared to the deity in the previous analogy). The patient, then, would represent the people of Israel. There is the assumption, then, that two elements that are basic to the historical covenant that emerged from the Old Testament are also present in the psychiatrist–patient relationship. The first of these is that there is some value system surrounding the relationship that not only provides for the protection of the patient in the relationship but also gives a definition to the relationship as well as a wedding or bonding to its natural destiny. This natural destiny, as it applies to the psychiatrist–patient relationship, is not a unitary notion, but, in fact, finds itself expressed in many different ways, depending on the epistemological basis of the psychiatric practice. Hence, a Freudian might see natural destiny as a breaking down of resistances and repressions by means of a natural balancing of ego strengths against impulses. A Jungian, in contrast, may see natural destiny as one of accommodation to basic archetypes in one's personality, the ability to deal with "the shadow" and to integrate these factors. And a proponent of Maslow would take a eudaemonistic perspective of the unfolding of the demon within the individual that would result ultimately in self-actualization (Norton, 1976).

The second component of the contract, which was basic to the Old Testament relationship with God, includes some acceptance of random action or punishing behavior, with the understanding that the long-term dedication of the party in a stronger position will lead to the benefit of the weaker party. This is most easily understood in the psychiatrist–patient relationship by the fact that there will be moments in the therapeutic encounter when the patient may be seriously stressed and forced into experiencing pain, which if understood at that point, could be seen as the inflicting of harm. But, arguably, from the psychotherapeutic perspective, this is an essential stage in the growth and development of the patient. Such a deflection would be perfectly consistent with the over-arching values of a covenant to the extent that the diachronic experience demonstrates dedication to the benefit of the parties entering into the agreement.

The two models of the covenantal and the contractual seem to apply to different features of the psychiatrist–patient relationship. The argument could strongly be made that the psychotherapeutic relationship, one based predominantly on the utilization of verbal therapy, lends itself best to the covenantal paradigm. The reasons for this have already been partially discussed but need to be elaborated to the extent that the psychotherapeutic relationship is one that contains, as its principal modus operandi, the use of transference and countertransference. These notions, which include the nature of the power of the bonding, also include the differences in the power prerogatives of the parties and allow for the continuation of dynamic alteration, not only with regard to the terms of the relationship, but even in the nature and the degree of the bonding. This would be consistent with the covenant that has both synchronic and diachronic components of the bonding between the parties. Hence, as patients in the psychotherapeutic relationship develop insight into their own dynamics and into how those dynamics influence their relationship with the psychiatrist, the power of the transference becomes diminished and, similarly, that of the countertransference attenuated. This is a very basic element to both the covenant and the psychotherapeutic relationship. It is the very nature of that relationship as it unfolds that a method of treatment of the patient occurs. The bonding powers of transference and countertransference should undergo change, whereby the terms of the duties and freedoms that are being given up undergo alteration. It is this fact that makes it virtually impossible to apply torts to the determination of infractions of that relationship. The tort is predicated on a more static notion, having at its root the expression of a number of doctrines that are coherent and predictable in a more limited range of possibilities with respect to outcome. Even though tort law may factor in changes over time that would be compatible with psychotherapy, it is categorically fixed in its perceptions of deflection from normative behavior. In contrast, the psychotherapeutic relationship, as with the covenant, lives on the notion of dynamic change and that dynamic change includes the alteration of the criteria for valuing the effectiveness and honesty of the experience. To apply tort law, therefore, is to fall victim to the philosophical quandary of making a category mistake.

This introduces the conceptual problem of applying a system for assessing not only the effectiveness of the psychotherapeutic approach but the determinations of infractions of the covenant. Certain basic questions must be posed about whether or not the duty is well-defined or about whether we can only meaningful speak in terms of an open-ended mutuality of obligation (Ladd, 1979). Furthermore, we have to query whether the notion of foreseeability, as it regards the natural outcome of the terms of the relationship, is a relevant term. The open-endedness, which allows for a continuous alteration of the relationship, includes also the fact that the outcomes to be expected are also alterable. If we are in a continuous system, it becomes virtually impossible to predict with any certainty at all what is to be expected at the end of the tunnel. Thus, one of the most essential elements in the law of tort — foreseeability, which combines with but-for causation — is not at all operative in a covenantal relationship. We are not dealing here with a cause leading to an effect that can be clearly explicated. We are dealing with interactive parties that change themselves at any moment in the trajectory of the process, a process that is expected, but with no foreseeability as to its ultimate destiny.

Within the covenantal relationship there may be aberrations of behavior that can lead to the serious infliction of emotional damage. Given the mortal nature of the participants found in the psychotherapeutic dynamic, the possibility of unjustified regression and manipulation always remains open-ended. Even where we have conceded that the appropriate paradigm is covenantal, we must ask ourselves what the monitoring mechanism should be where the inherent integrity of the dynamic is centrally attacked. These will be instances that are not only counterproductive but are actually destructive to the patient. As we have already pointed out, one can only look at the notion of dedication of purpose in the long term to determine deflections from the terms of the covenant. At any one moment in that experience, there can be the infliction of punishment for a higher end. But the problem remains for those situations where there might occur a systematic breaking down of critical elements of the psychological identity of the patient. Some of those critical elements would be the nature of personal power, the extension of will, or the sense of self-regardedness. If this systematic breaking down occurs, and the covenant produces the opposite of its intent, there is no easy way to determine when such a breakdown actually occurs, thus no easy way to decide redress for the patient. The covenantal model provides merely an understanding of the precise nature of the therapist–patient relationship without providing the means for assessing deflections or infractions of that relationship.

This becomes the central problem of the psychotherapeutic experience, a problem that applies also to the covenant and to the application of tort law. As we will see later in this chapter, there has been no successful appellate court case that has explicitly involved negligence on the part of the psychotherapist without the presence of tangible evidence of harm to the patient (physical harm or the application of unusual or inappropriate treatments in addition to the verbal therapy). Hence, it may be necessary to construct a hybrid model–which though not exactly descriptive of the process of psychotherapy is, nonetheless, relatively close to that process – in order to provide a means for culling out those features of the process that are detrimental and destructive to the patient. This hybrid would have to consist of the combination of covenantal and some contract principles with tort law. The covenantal elements that might be applicable would be evidence in the history of the relationship that suggests the lack of a continuation of dedication on the part of the person in the position of power. This would also include some notion of the extent to which good will has been applied throughout the relationship, even though at specific moments there may be infliction of pain on the patient. If those qualities that can be extracted from the basic ingredients in the covenantal relationship are not sufficient to give us a handle for determining the presence of behavior that is detrimental and destructive to the patient and that would be deserving of some redress, it would then become necessary to apply some principles from the tort of intentional infliction of mental suffering.

This tort establishes the criteria that are based on the particular vulnerability of the person in question, a vulnerability that is known, or should be known, to the actor. It would operate in such a way that there would be an objective assessment of the subjectivity of the therapist, that is, his consciousness regarding the vulnerability of the patient and the extent to which he responded appropriately to those levels of vulnerability. If the therapist's behavior goes beyond an appropriate level that would be consistent with the overall design of the relationship, it would be that profound irregularity that would trigger a legal condemnation according to this tort of intentional

infliction of mental and emotional harm. In intentional tort, the psychotherapist would be potentially at fault even if the damage is temporal rather than sustained over a period of time.

This tort must be distinguished from the lesser moral harm where nervous shock is inflicted, based on the principles of foreseeability and the failure to achieve a standard of care that could be judged according to a set of criteria established by precedent. The distinction here is that in the intentional tort, the value protected is one of the dignitary interests of the patient, and this would be compatible with the overall fabric of values that surround a covenantal relationship. In the latter, because it falls within negligence law, it would require the application of criteria or principles from outside of the covenantal relationship. These criteria – those of negligence – would be derived from the practice of peers, that is, other psychotherapists. Where the practice in question veers significantly from acceptable standards of care, negligence may be established.

But the nature of the covenant is something that extends over and beyond negligence principles. It is an agreement between the parties and, therefore, except in those rare circumstances where the parties are agreeing to behaviors that are totally illegal because they infract some broader social standards of appropriateness or morality, should be respected (Weisstub, 1985). If one respects the terms of the agreements of the parties, then the general principles of negligence law, except for those circumstances of intentional tort, should not be applicable. One does not apply negligence law because it requires the application of an externally defined set of criteria; in contrast examining this from the covenantal as well as the intentional tort model allows for the evaluation of the covenant on the basis of its own terms. In the future, for the proper remedy to occur in verbal therapy cases, the court should turn more to the model of intentional tort, with an eye to protecting patients' dignitary rights, which have been distorted because the very integrity of the bonding relationship has been destroyed by the willful act of the stronger party.

In addition to psychotherapy, psychiatry consists of other modalities of treatment. In contemporary psychiatry, the other modalities of treatment – biological and behavioral – are becoming predominant. There are differences in the nature of the relationship between the patient and the psychiatrist where biological or behavioral modalities are employed. This relationship seems to be more analogous to the traditional physician–patient relationship. It is not based on covenantal principles. That is not to say that one cannot recognize the power imbalances between the physician and the patient. But, methods exist for more carefully equalizing those imbalances, particularly through the application of informed consent principles. Furthermore, the health care system in general has evolved in recent years to include greater information disclosure to consumers of health care. The nonpsychotherapeutic treatments are also more objectively definable. The benefits and risks are delineated and, with a certain exactitude, can be presented to the patient for objective evaluation. A patient, for example, would be informed that when he agrees to take imipramine for a reactive depression the benefits may be improved sleep patterns, with the possibility of amelioration of the depressed feelings within 6 to 8 weeks. But, in addition, he can be informed that the risks might involve periods of hypotensive reactions and the possibility of some cardiac affects. These elements of the treatment can be presented clearly to the patient, such that at the moment of agreement all parties can be nearly equally knowledgeable about the objectives of the treatment and the expectations during the course of it. Covenant would, therefore, be inappropriate as a paradigm for explaining the nature of this relationship. Contract, as a more static agreement that has certainty of entitlement, seems to be more apposite. For the part, the application of contract principles would protect the patients in the course of the physician–patient relationship where these modalities are used.

The only reasonable application of tort law would be in those situations where the terms of the contract are not understood by the patient, either because they have not been properly disclosed or the patient conceivably lacks competency, or in those situations where the relationship is overly paternalistic and the real issue is whether or not the doctor has acted in good faith with respect to his professional responsibilities. If, however, the parties involved approach the ideal model of the contract relationship (which would be a meeting of the minds of parties with equal power prerogatives), then the contract could serve just as adequately as the protective device for the patient. Where there has been a divergence from acceptable standards of care and the patient has been injured, he could either look to the explicit terms of the contract, if such are stated, or to the implicit nature of the contractual relationship, which includes that the patient will pay for the services of the physician, which will be in accordance with an acceptable standard of care. This, therefore, allows for the introduction of externally defined criteria derived from peer examination to the occurrences that lead to the injury or dissatisfactions of the patient.

Arguably, there is a great deal of terrain within psychiatric practice that will not fit neatly into the contractual category. Therefore, it is understandable that the bulk of redress for psychiatric wrongs has historically drifted into the relatively loose categories and principles that sustain the tort system. Some examples of this would be where patients have waived their right to application of the contract and agreed to a paternalistic system of care. It would include the categories of involuntarily committed patients, where competence is in question and where there is no provision for substituted judgment to protect the integrity of the contract for treatment; the treatment of minors, where no parental guardian is available; cases of emergency; and cases where deviation from normal conduct occurs in relatively open-ended situations. These would be cases where an initial contract could not be made meaningfully because the nature of the psychiatric intervention, based on an imperfection of diagnosis or assessment, means that the intervention has to be exploratory and somewhat unpredictable. This covers many cases within psychiatric practice where the prescription of treatment although nonpsychotherapeutic still remains in a hazy category.

The following sections of this discussion will focus first on the profile of various malpractice cases in psychiatry, then move to a description of the specific kinds of interruptions in the psychiatrist–patient agreement that are responsible for psychiatric malpractice. Following this review of types of malpractice in psychiatry, we will examine alternatives to the tort system, most particularly no-fault approaches to medical injury compensation. Along with this we will examine the implications of resorting to contract law as opposed to tort law for resolving malfeasances in the psychiatrist–patient relationship. This shift is not only applicable to the special concerns of psychiatric injuries, but also to the broader area of medical malpractice involving other specialties, and thus is relevant to a whole host of institutional arrangements.

MEDICAL MALPRACTICE
PRINCIPLES

The profile of cases in psychiatric malpractice has changed considerably over the past 20 years. Between 1946 and 1962 there were only 18 psychiatric malpractice cases that reached the appellate courts (Bellamy, 1962). The most frequent cause of actions were brought for adverse reactions resulting from electroshock treatment. In the early days of electroshock treatment, muscle relaxants were not available to prevent some of the injuries to the skeletal system. It was not uncommon for patients to develop fractures of the spine or of the long bones during treatments. With the introduction of succinylcholinesterase, many of the difficulties associated with electroshock treatment were alleviated (*Aiken v. Clary*, 1965). The patient could then be placed in a nearly totally relaxed condition, so that on administration of the shock the convulsive phenomenon was limited to the central nervous system. Fractures became rare, and medical malpractice (with regard to electroshock treatment) only occurred when proper muscle relaxants were not appropriately administered. In addition to untoward outcomes from electroshock treatment, wrongful commitment and patient suicide were also among the most frequent bases for malpractice actions. Actions brought by patients claiming wrongful commitment have been, for the most part, unsuccessful in the court system (Slovenko, 1981). An exception has been where the psychiatrist does not abide by the statutory requirements of a physical examination of the patient but, instead, commits the patient based on a telephone call or on the recommendation of others; or, alternatively, where it could be established that the psychiatrist was in collusion with members of the family to have a patient institutionalized, possibly because of financial benefits to the family. Except for these unusual circumstances, psychiatrists rarely have been sued successfully for wrongful commitment.

Similarly, suits related to suicide have also been relatively rare against individual psychiatrists. Hospital and mental health institutions, on the other hand, have been far more frequently the object of suits alleging malpractice in the care of a patient who subsequently commits suicide. The next most prevalent basis for suit was patients' assaultive behavior, and finally, fee problems.

Between 1971 and 1977 the profile of cases changed somewhat (Hirsh & White, 1978). Malpractice claims in psychiatry were, however, still very infrequent. In fact, of all malpractice claims, psychiatric malpractice claims represented, at most, three percent. The most frequent bases for suit during that period were allegations of improper treatment leading to suicide, followed by negligence in the treatment procedures. With regard to negligence in treatment, electroshock and its adverse side effects represented the most prevalent of these treatment procedures.

Third on the list was the problem of defective informed consent. It is important to realize that informed consent as a legal theory did not really come into existence until the 1950s in the Salgo (1957) *Natanson* (1960) cases. It has only relatively recently become more prevalent as a basis for malpractice actions. Next on the list was inadequate followup where a patient could assert that the psychiatrist did not follow through sufficiently in his care. Such a situation might exist where a psychiatrist goes on a holiday and does not provide for adequate medical backup in the event that the patient enters into a crisis. Wrongful commitment during this period was no longer one of the major bases for a malpractice action.

The profile of cases once again changed between the years 1978 and 1983 (*Psychiatric News*, 1983). The highest frequency of claims during this period was for improper treatment. This might include inappropriate diagnostic and treatment measures or, perhaps more seriously, claims of improprieties in a psychiatrist–patient relationship. Such improprieties have been most conspicuously characterized as sexual contact between psychiatrist and patient. The second highest basis for suit was drug reactions. This has become particularly important since the mid-1950s, when phenothiazines and other neuroleptics were introduced as treatments for serious psychiatric illnesses. One of the most important consequences of drug reactions would be tardive dyskinesia, which are long-term and possibly permanent involuntary movements usually of the upper torso and particularly the buccal region of the face. These suits have become more frequent for several reasons: First, neuroleptics were only relatively recently introduced as effective treatment methods for schizophrenia and other serious psychotic reactions; second, in many cases, it takes some time for the medication to reach the point of developing these long-term and potentially permanent side effects; third, the onset of the patients' rights movement, which has included, in many circumstances, the rights of patients, even psychotic patients, to refuse psychotropic medications; and fourth, in keeping with the move toward patients' rights is the heightened sensitivity to the right not only to determine what is to be done with one's body, even as it applies to psychiatric patients, but also to not be harmed by the treatments that are available. Furthermore, with regard to tardive dyskinesia, there may be limitations on the ability of psychiatrists to determine the susceptibility of any one patient to this condition. On the other hand, if nonneuroleptics could have been used as effectively as neuroleptics to treat the patient's condition, or if it can be established that the drug dosages used were far in excess of those necessary to treat the patient's condition, or finally, that there may have been early signs of the development of a tardive dyskinesia that should have alerted the psychiatrist to pull back on the use of the neuroleptic, then a case may be made for adverse reactions due to medication. Another possible allegation is that the patient did not give an informed consent and was, in fact, competent to do so with regard to the use of psychotropic medications.

Third on the list during 1978–1983 was patient suicide and, fourth and last, harm to third parties. This last basis for psychiatric malpractice might also include failure to properly diagnose a psychiatric condition. This could also mean that the psychiatrist, based on the patient's condition and external manifestations thereof, had sufficient indication that the individual was potentially harmful to others.

At the present time it appears that the major areas for possible suits in psychiatry comprise four kinds of cases: those dealing with side effects of psychotropic medication, those alleging that the therapist infracted his duty to warn third parties that they may be injured by patients, those involving a suicidal patient, and, finally, those asserting improprieties in the relationship between the psychiatrist and the patient, especially allegations of sexual misconduct. Despite this growing cadre of cases addressing these four broad areas, studies suggest that psychiatrists are not frequently sued and, furthermore, that when claims are filed, patients are granted awards infrequently. A recent American Psychiatric Association survey of closed claims filed over the past 10 years disclosed that 80% of the claims brought against an insurance policy sponsored by that organization closed with no payments made to the claimant. An additional

10% settled for awards of a very small amount, approximately $5,000 or less (Taub, 1983). On the basis of this information, one could come to the conclusion that the vast majority of claims were probably of insignificant consequence to the patient. Hence, one could conclude that the vast majority of claims brought against psychiatrists, certainly until recently, are characterized either by doubtful liability or minor or nonexistent injury to patients, or perhaps both of these. Of equal importance, and certainly part of the reason for doubting the existence of *liability*, is the fact that it is often very difficult to establish causation between what the psychiatrist does in the psychiatrist–patient relationship and the harm that is alleged by the patient. We will see this problem as we examine further not only the elements that are essential for a successful medical malpractice action as they apply to psychiatry, but also specific allegations of malpractice.

Several explanations have been given for why psychiatrists are infrequently sued successfully in malpractice actions (Horan & Guerrini, 1981). To begin with, it has been argued that the low incidence of successful claims is attributable to the difficulty of proving the applicable acceptable standard of care. What makes this more difficult in the field of psychiatry than in other areas of medicine is the fact that there are many currently acceptable approaches to the psychiatric treatment of patients. Some therapists present themselves as being predominantly Freudian in their approach; hence, they rely on psychoanalytic methodology. Others would take the position that they believe in behavioral modification as the only effective way to handle a specific patient's condition. And, finally, a third broad category relies predominantly on biological methods for the treatment of patients, using, most predominantly, medication such as antipsychotics and antidepressants for treatment. Even within these three broad classes, there are various approaches to any patient's problem. Psychiatrists who prefer a psychological (or psychotherapeutic) approach may rely on Jungian or even existential psychoanalytic techniques. Some might even take a more eclectic approach and combine various facets of Freudian, Jungian, and existential approaches. Thus, to establish the applicable acceptable standard of care, one might have to rely on experts from specific subsets within the psychiatric treatment community.

Another reason that it is very difficult to establish psychiatric malpractice is, as we have already alluded to, that it is problematic to establish a causal relationship between the breach of an acceptable standard of care and the alleged injury to the patient (Wilkinson, 1982). To begin with, where one is dealing with something as vague and conspicuously nondirective as much of psychotherapy, it is difficult to establish what the applicable acceptable standard of care is for any one individual circumstance in the patient's psychopathology. Even if that problem is resolved, then the second part of that requirement — that of demonstrating a causal relationship — becomes particularly onerous. Unless one is dealing with the application of a procedure such as electroshock or the administration of a medication, it is very difficult, if not impossible, to show a causal nexus between what is done in psychotherapy and the alleged injury to the patient (Bromberg, 1983). In addition to these two scientific problems, there are other issues that are relatively unique to psychiatry. First, the patients are often reluctant to bring a psychiatric malpractice suit because this might mean that deeply personal aspects of their history and psychological difficulties will be made public during the course of the malpractice action. Second, patients may also have a very difficult time conceptualizing and thereby formulating their expectations in the course of psychiatric treatment. Unless such a formulation is successfully achieved, it is hard to assess the results of that treatment, be they psychotherapeutic or due to the use of medications, and thus it is difficult to assess the distortions that might have occurred that could suggest negligence on the part of the psychiatrist. Finally, as we have already suggested, the psychiatrist is particularly adept at establishing a viable professional relationship with patients. A great deal of what constitutes psychiatric treatment rests on interviewing techniques to ferret out from the patient's own history influences from the past which impact on the qualitative interaction with the psychiatrist in question. In the interviewing process the psychiatrist affectively engages the patient in a relationship that makes it very difficult for the patient to pull away and examine the details of his psychiatric treatment objectively and then move to initiate a malpractice action. Hence, very integral to the functioning of psychiatry in the care of patients is the very means whereby medical malpractice actions are essentially averted.

Despite the forces pushing to minimize mal-practice cases, the incidence of claims is increasing. Several reasons have been given for this increase. To begin with, there has clearly been greater societal acceptance of psychiatric treatment. Until 10 years ago, patients who were seeing psychiatrists often hid this fact not only from others in their community but from their own families. There was a stigma attached to the need to seek psychiatric treatment. In large part, this was due to the fact that psychiatry was always closely identified with the care of seriously mentally ill patients, that is, those who required institutionalization. Outside of the seriously mentally ill, psychiatric treatment was seen as a luxury limited to the very wealthy who could afford the high cost of long-term psychoanalysis. With the emergence of community mental health movements, which began to create outreach to communities, psychiatry, as a field of medicine, became more accessible to the average individual. It thereby became increasingly apparent to the public that the psychiatrist and psychotherapist could be useful in a variety of matters affecting individuals in society. Psychotherapy became important in the counseling of adolescents and adults involved in family crises. In its move away from being identified as exclusively associated with the seriously mentally ill, psychiatric treatment became more commonplace. Of course, this open attitude has by no means reached the level of openness surrounding general medical care. Certain employers still discriminate against individuals who require psychiatric treatment. For the most part, however, psychiatry has become more recognized as useful medical treatment in the care of patients with not only serious emotional difficulties but also with general problems of living. This is most frequently manifested by frustrations in interpersonal relationships.

The second major reason for increases in psychiatric claims is that the public has certain expectations regarding the efficacy of psychiatry (Taub, 1983). Over the past 25–30 years, there has been an ever increasing expansion in the application of psychiatry to a variety of interpersonal and social problems in our society. Psychiatrists have, arguably, effectively oversold the societal benefits that could be achieved from psychiatric intervention. Patients often enter into a psychiatrist–patient relationship with great expectations about what is going to be achieved in the course of therapy. Patients who are dissatisfied with their lack of job achievement or with other aspects of their lives may gravitate to a psychiatrist with the expectation that therapy will result in greater actualization of their talents. When the patient does not achieve the expected degree of actualization, dissatisfaction may result, with the consequence that he or she may resort to litigating against the therapist. Furthermore, there are complications associated with the transference process itself, whereby the level of attachment may create patient expectation that the therapist will always be available to support them or to actively enter into their lives and somehow effectively make the decisions that really are their own responsibility. When this does not occur, or when, in fact, the therapist weakens and assumes some of these roles, dissatisfaction may ultimately lead to a malpractice action.

In addition to these personal and social developments, legal changes have occurred that have created an environment rendering it more favorable for malpractice actions. The patient's rights movement in the mental health area in the 1960s, which attained a high degree of momentum in the late 1970s, has given patients a sense of power vis-à-vis their relationships with psychiatrists (Stone, 1975). Institutionalized mental patients, who in the past rarely asserted any legal or ethical rights to their treatment, are now clamoring for a greater role in the decision-making process with regard to not only institutionalization but treatment (such as medication) (*Rogers v. Commissioner of the Department of Mental Health*, 1983). As part of this growing consciousness, patients have become more informed about the nature of psychiatric diagnosis and treatment, and, hence, are able to determine what is to be expected regarding their care (Law & Polan, 1978).

The second legal development relates to the duties that have been articulated in the *Tarasoff* decision, which is relevant to the psychotherapist's obligation to protect third parties (*Tarasoff v. Regents of University of California*, 1976). The *Tarasoff* case, as we will see later, dealt specifically with the situation where the therapist's duty was that of warning a third party that he or she might be victimized by the patient. But, in fact, the court characterized that duty as much broader: that is, the duty to protect third parties. There have been, in the late 1970s, several cases since the *Tarasoff* decision that have expanded the application of that ruling to a wide-range of circumstances, increasing the scope of inactions on the part of the psychotherapist that may be susceptible to psychiatric malpractice.

THE MALPRACTICE ACTION

Before discussing some of the specific types of malpractice actions involving psychiatrists, it would be beneficial to reexamine the nature of malpractice actions generally. For the most part, malpractice law has been characterized as a tort action, that is, the psychiatrist has been negligent in his treatment of the patient and that, as a consequence, the patient has been injured (Furrow, 1980). A malpractice action may also be cast, however, as a breach of contract that arises from the view that the psychiatrist–patient relationship is one based on expressed or implied contract (Epstein, 1979). The psychiatrist, according to this theory, promises to perform his professional services at an acceptable standard of care in exchange for the patient's promise to pay him for his services. By placing himself in the care of the psychiatrist, the patient implies an intent to pay for such services, which automatically places the obligation to perform competently on the psychiatrist. Except in rare circumstances, this arrangement between the psychiatrist and the patient is not the result of an express agreement, but rather an implied one. Physicians generally have become quite cautious about making promises to patients that may be construed as entering into a contract to perform not only a specific service but a service at a specific level of accomplishment. Certainly, in psychiatry, it has been rare that an express promise is made between a physician and a patient.

The vast majority of the cases, however, are not in actions based on contract law. Rather they are actions against physicians that are based on negligence or tort law (Williams, 1984). The exceptions are (a) where the physician has made an express agreement, and the patient can establish that he has relied on that promise to his detriment, and (b) where the statute of limitations in the jurisdiction has passed for tort but not for breach of contract. It is generally the case that the statute of limitations for tort is approximately 2 years and that for breach of contract is 5 or, in some cases, 6 years after the performance of the agreement (Institute of Medicine, 1978). It is possible that a patient who has failed to take action within the limits of the tort statute of limitations is still able to sue for breach of contract. For the most part, these are rather rare circumstances in the field of psychiatric malpractice.

In addition to being the most common forms of malpractice cases against physicians, actions in negligence are often the most difficult for the patient to establish. There are four elements that must be present for a successful tort action (Epstein, 1976). It is usually the patient's obligation and burden to establish that these four elements are operating in any specific case. They are (a) the duty of care; (b) establishment of negligent behavior; (c) presence of injury or harm to the patient; and (d) proximate cause.

DUTY OF CARE

Duty of care has been a relatively easy element to establish in a malpractice action. It emerges essentially from the physician–patient relationship. The patient, therefore, has the duty to establish that a physician–patient relationship exists, because the law, for the most part, does not impose an absolute duty on the physician to treat an injured or sick person (Horan & Guerrini, 1981). The physician usually has the prerogative to refuse to render treatment, and this will not generally give rise to legal liability. On the other hand, if he has agreed to treat a patient, he enters a physician-patient relationship and assumes the duty of care that is created according to the law. Determinations of when the psychiatrist has agreed to treat a patient vary in jurisdictions. Certain jurisdictions would take a conservative position on this question and require more than just a brief interaction between the psychiatrist and patient; they may require something that could be construed as action that implies an agreement on the part of a physician or psychiatrist to continue treating the patient beyond the evaluative stage (Holder, 1978). Other jurisdictions have construed even minimal actions on the part of a physician as creating a duty of care (*O'Neill v. Montefiore Hospital*, 1960).

A distinction has often been made between evaluative and dispositional functions as a determinant of the establishment of duty of care. If a physician or psychiatrist functions merely in an evaluative (third party contracts) role, such as a psychiatrist working for the court to determine whether a patient meets the medical criteria for commitment or an industrial physician performing routine examinations on employees, a physician relationship is not considered to have been established and the physician may not have a duty of care to function competently (Appointment of Independent Medical Experts, 1971). On the other hand, if the physician lapsed at all in affecting the disposition of the patient by treating him directly or referring him to an appropriate specialist, then

a duty of care is established. This distinction, although still operative in many jurisdictions, is beginning to undergo some erosion (*Armstrong v. Morgan*, 1977). A psychiatrist called in on a consultation with a patient on a surgical unit, particularly if he not only informs the primary physician of the patient's psychiatric status but also orders diagnostic measures or treatment consistent with his finding, takes on the obligation of care of the patient. The primary physician, therefore, is usually not held liable for the specialist's malpractice unless he was negligent in selecting him or became active with the specialist in the treatment of the patient's psychiatric problems (Waltz & Inbau, 1971).

ESTABLISHMENT OF NEGLIGENCE

In addition to establishing that the physician has a duty of care, the patient has to show that the physician acted negligently in the provision of medical services (Epstein, 1979). Historically, the standard of negligence was the locality rule, that is, the physician was required to conform to what a physician in his locality would have done under similar circumstances. In time, the locality rule was expanded to include a broader scope than that specific locality, thereby requiring that the physician function as "similarly" situated physicians under similar circumstances. In recent years, the locality rule has been essentially eroded with regard to specialties in medical practice so that, currently, a more general or national standard would be applied to the activities of the psychiatrist (*Christy v. Saliterman*, 1970). Hence, the psychiatrist would be judged by what other specialists in the same field would have done under similar circumstances. This shift to a national standard of care seems reasonable in light of improved and widespread methods of communication through medical journals, society meetings, and conferences, and the recently developed requirements for continuing medical education through both the licensing laws of many states and specialty associations.

Most jurisdictions allow for a "respectable minority" rule (Holder, 1978). This essentially holds that a physician meets his burden of establishing that he practiced according to acceptable standards of care if he can demonstrate that a respectable minority of practitioners find his treatment methods acceptable. Oftentimes, respectable minorities are members of academic institutions who are perhaps engaging in clinical research or who are on the cutting edge of developing new methods for psychiatric practice.

Errors of Judgment Versus Errors of Fact

An important qualification is often made between errors of judgment and errors of fact. This distinction may be difficult, if not impossible, to make in the psychiatric care of patients. It essentially creates an epistemological construct for understanding the decision-making processes of physicians when they treat patients. It creates a distinction between facts of that process, that of obtaining factual information, which of course necessitates some element of judgment as to what information is essential, and that of evaluating the factual information and reaching a decision regarding either a diagnosis of the patient's condition or the next appropriate phase of treatment. This legal distinction means, operatively, that a psychiatrist or any specialist may not be liable for honest errors of judgment if he engages in practices or procedures that are recognized as being within the customary practice of the profession (Bromberg, 1983). If, on the other hand, he fails, for example, to obtain the relevant data regarding either the patient's history or necessary laboratory tests, the law will treat this differently. A lapse in the collection of important data may contribute to the physician's arriving at an improper diagnosis of the patient's condition and, consequently, to the institution of improper measures in the treatment of the patient. The law would view this as an error in fact and likely hold the physician liable for not meeting the acceptable standard of care. Errors in judgment, on the other hand, would not be held actionable when the physician has acted in good faith and has exercised requisite care in obtaining the necessary information to arrive at a diagnosis and treatment of the patient's condition (Holder, 1978).

There are difficulties, however, with the distinction between errors in fact and errors in judgment. To begin with, judgment is inevitably involved in determining what factual material has to be obtained. If it is possible to establish that important factual information was not obtained in arriving at a diagnosis and that negligence has occurred, the error would seem to be more one of judgment than one of fact. That is, one could argue that the reason the relevant factual material was not obtained was that the practitioner misjudged the importance of that factual informa-

tion. Furthermore, by extending this logic, one could argue that even without all of the factual material, it is rarely the case that two competing diagnoses have equal weight. Oftentimes, a psychiatrist is faced with two or three possibilities, one of which clearly stands out as the most accurate, and the others take on secondary diagnostic importance. Even so, once the differential diagnosis is determined, one could argue that two psychiatrists, given the same factual information, may arrive at different diagnostic conclusions, or the diagnosis may still be changed given new information regarding the patient's response to treatment based on the original diagnosis. Hence, various qualifications occur in the trajectory leading to the diagnosis of a psychiatric illness, such that opportunity frequently surfaces for revising one's initial impressions. It is probably the case that rarely is an injury truly the result of an error in judgment which cannot be explained by some deflection from acceptable standards of diagnosis and treatment.

Even so, this distinction is frequently used in particular types of psychiatric malpractice cases. For example, it is often used in cases where the psychiatrist is accused of having discharged from confinement a mentally ill patient who later commits a dangerous act against a third party. The psychiatrist often alleges that the decision to discharge the patient was one of judgment and cannot be shown to have been evidence of negligence simply because subsequent to the discharge the patient goes out and commits a dangerous act. The psychiatrist would argue that, given the factual material available to him at the time he made the decision to discharge the patient, one could go either way, but that no clear-cut basis existed for preferring continued confinement over discharge. In these cases, it may be that the psychiatrist can frequently assert that though his judgment may have been different from others, it is arguably within acceptable boundaries of psychiatric care. Of course, the situation would be much different if one were able to establish that, prior to discharge, the patient engaged in a dangerous act or there was sufficient evidence of dangerousness available that it should have led the psychiatrist to prefer continued confinement.

INJURY AND PROXIMATE CAUSE

Another element that is essential for a successful malpractice action is the presence of an injury or harm to a patient. The physician may engage in improper conduct in his treatment of the patient, but unless it can be established that the plaintiff has been harmed there would be no damages recovered from a malpractice action. The exception might be those circumstances where the conduct of the physician can be shown to be willful and possibly motivated by malicious intent, in which case he or she may be liable for an intentional tort or crime. But, for the most part, the absence of an injury precludes recovery through the tort system.

The last element essential in a malpractice case is the establishment of "proximate cause": a causative connection between what the psychiatrist does and the injury to the patient (Epstein, 1979). It consists of two components: a cause in fact and "foreseeability." Proximate cause refers to the event that, in a "natural sequence unaltered by an intervening event," is a substantial factor in bringing about the injury or harm to the patient and without which the injury would never have occurred (Epstein, 1979). Cause, therefore, refers to something that is immediate and direct and asserts that "but-for" the physician's conduct, the injury would not have occurred. Foreseeability, on the other hand, suggests that the physician knew, or should have known, that his action could bring about the untoward consequences.

It is often exceedingly difficult to establish proximate cause because injuries are usually the result of complex medical events that include many causative factors (Tancredi, 1977). With regard to psychiatry, particularly, some causative factors may be well outside the control of the psychiatrist or the medical care system in general. For example, a patient under the care of a psychiatrist may leave the psychiatrist's office, be provoked by a third party, and become so incensed that he harms the third party. The intervening act or the provocation of the third party is as much, if not more, responsible for the patient's action as the psychiatrist who was aware of the patient's particular weakness or proclivity toward rageful conduct (Gentry, 1980). In psychiatry, where cause and effect relationships are even less clearly defined than in other areas of medicine, it is very difficult to establish probable cause. This is particularly the case where the psychiatrist is engaging in psychotherapy as his principal modality of treatment. Where the psychiatrist uses medication, or physical therapy such as electroshock, the "cause and effect" relationship can be more easily established. Psychotherapy presents particularly difficult problems for the establishment of proximate cause. On

the other hand, the presence of causative factors, other than those related to the psychiatrist's action, do not preclude a determination that the psychiatrist was in the position to have prevented or minimized the patient's injury. It might be that many causative factors have to be present for an injury to occur, but for proximate cause it need only be established that the psychiatrist's conduct was not in accord with customary practice and that it was contributory to, if not wholly responsible for, the untoward outcome for the patient.

PRIMA FACIE AND RES IPSA LOQUITOR CASES

In nearly all cases of malpractice, it is necessary to have an expert testify as to the determination of negligence. Some events may, however, be so egregious that an expert's testimony is quite unnecessary. In these situations, deflection from the standard is so evident by the conduct of the physician that a *prima facie* case of malpractice can be established (Furrow, 1980). When this occurs, the burden of proof shifts to the physician, who must establish that his or her conduct was not negligent. In order to accomplish this, the physician may have to introduce expert testimony to prove that his conduct was absolutely within the scope of proper treatment. This would be particularly the case where the physician might have to rely on the respectable minority rule. The following may be offered as an illustrative example: A psychiatrist administers a medication that is traditionally used for the treatment of manic depressive illness to control episodes of verbal assault. The patient then suffers harmful side effects from the medication and argues that the psychiatrist has been negligent in prescribing this treatment. The psychiatrist may be able to establish that in various academic centers clinicians have been using this treatment for the very purpose for which he himself used it and that it therefore meets acceptable standards of care of this respectable minority of the profession.

A variant of this *prima facie* case occurs under the doctrine of *res ipsa loquitor*, or the "thing speaks for itself" (Furrow, 1980). This doctrine applies when the outcome of a physician–patient interaction would not have occurred in the absence of negligence. An excellent example of a case of *res ipsa loquitor* is the presence of a foreign body in the abdomen of a patient following surgery. Where *res ipsa loquitor* applies the burden of proof shifts to the doctor to establish that his conduct was within the bounds of acceptable diagnosis and treatment. Alternatively, he could establish that the incident was not totally under his control, or that the patient contributed in some way to the injurious treatment. Hence, three ingredients must be present for an untoward event to be classified within the doctrine of res ipsa loquitor: First, it must be the case that the injury would not have occurred without negligence; second, it must be established that the conduct was under the control of the doctor; and third, the patient must not have contributed in bringing about the injury to himself.

Many jurisdictions, Texas for example, do not provide the legal basis for res ipsa loquitor as it applies in medical practice. Where res ipsa loquitor does operate, for example, in California, it is usually applied to cases of foreign bodies left in the patient following surgery, peripheral nerve injuries, and situations where the wrong organ has been removed from the body of the patient.

The application of res ipsa loquitor to the field of psychiatry would be very problematic conceptually.[1] On the other hand, it is possible that at some point in the future the court may select certain injuries as applying to the res ipsa loquitor doctrine. One such injury might be a severe hypotensive reaction from the initial administration of an antidepressant where the patient falls and seriously injures himself while under the care of a psychiatrist. Some might argue that if the antidepressant were properly administered, the severe hypotensive reaction would not have

resulted. The court might determine that this type of reaction would not have occurred in the absence of negligence of the psychiatrist and, barring contributory negligence on the part of the patient, psychiatrists should be held responsible unless they can establish that they have comported with an acceptable standard of care. The doctrine of res ipsa loquitor may be applied to psychiatry more often in the future as medications become more prevalent and we learn more about the prevention of such outcomes as dystonias, akathesias, and the tardive dyskinesias. As it now stands, this doctrine does not seem to be applicable, except rarely, to any area of psychiatric practice.

GROUNDS FOR LEGAL ACTION

The discussion thus far has focused on some basic concepts regarding malpractice laws that apply to medical practice in general. The emphasis has been placed on examining the elements of medical malpractice, the distinction between errors of judgment and errors of fact, and some statistics that suggest that we are in the midst of another crisis in medical malpractice. In addition, much of the discussion has focused on the contractual nature of the physician–patient relationship. In this section, emphasis will be placed on specific instances of psychiatric malpractice. Some of the information, particularly that relevant to the question of informed consent, may be applicable to the full range of malpractice actions in medicine generally. On the other hand, some of the

---

[1] Application of res ipsa loquitor to psychiatry is rare. There was a case in 1932 (Maki v. Murray Hospital, 1932) when this doctrine was applied against the hospital whereby there was a rebuttable presumption of negligence on the part of the defendant for failing to prevent the patient from committing suicide. There is some confusion on the elements that constitute res ipsa loquitor, which is essentially a device that relieves the plaintiff of the burden of proving negligence through measures such as expert testimony. The elements of res ipsa loquitor as described by Prosser (1964) are (a) the event must be of a kind that ordinarily does not occur in the absence of someone's negligence; (b) it must be caused by an agency or instrumentality within the exclusive control of the defendant; and (c) it must not have been due to any voluntary action or contribution on the part of the plaintiff.

Hogan (1979) talks about the application of res ipsa loquitor in the area of psychotherapeutic malpractice and claims that although this doctrine has not been applied to psychotherapy, he could conceive of a situation where public hospitals placed admitted patients on an above-ground floor of a building without window bars. He argues essentially that here psychotherapists would be using unusual or obviously dangerous techniques in the care of the patient. It is not so obvious that the doctrine of res ipsa loquitor should apply in this situation. If one applies the principles described in Prosser, the question would be whether the absence of window bars is sufficient to meet a level of obvious negligence that should trigger res ipsa loquitor. Would the absence of window bars be comparable, for example, to the traditional scope of issues that are usually included in this doctrine, such as leaving a foreign body in a patient (or peripheral nerve injury) following surgery. It would seem that with regard to psychiatric patients and the use of window bars, one would have to consider such issues as the degree of suicidal intentionality, the manifest behavior of the patient, the philosophy of the treatment unit, the accessibility of the windows in relationship to the patient, the application of other restraining devices such as chemotherapy, and the stage of treatment of the patient. A sharper example conceptually might be the presence of certain serious side effects of medication that could be demonstrated medically as very avoidable in a high percentage of cases.

instances discussed in this section are uniquely associated with psychiatric practice.

INFORMATION DISCLOSURE AND CONSENT

Informed consent as a cause of legal action is relatively new in the American tradition (Tancredi, 1982). In fact, the first case involving informed consent occurred in the mid-1950s (*Salgo v. Leland Stanford, Jr. University Board of Trustees*, 1957). Prior to that time, a patient could certainly have brought action against a physician for the unlawful touching of his body. But this action would be frequently presented according to the law of assault and battery, which essentially applies to any harmful or offensive touching of the body of another without that party's consent (Holder, 1978). In an action of assault and battery *per se*, little attention would be devoted to the extent and nature of the disclosure of information regarding the medical justification for touching the body of the patient. The requirement for consent to avoid an action in battery or assault could be satisfied easily by simply showing the most minimal disclosure of intent (if, say, the patient explicitly gave consent to have his or her body touched). The law did not require the disclosure of information *per se*, only that the patient consented to bodily contact.

Informed consent became an issue of particular concern to the medical community during that part of the Nuremberg trials that reviewed the medical atrocities conducted by physicians who experimented on unwilling subjects in Nazi Germany (Katz, 1972). The Nuremberg trials brought forth an articulation of the requirement for informed consent in the area of human experimentation. This was given additional support in the Helsinki Code, which strongly stressed the rights of individuals to have control over what is to be done to their bodies in the course of human experimentation (World Medical Association, 1964). In one of the earliest cases, *Salgo v. Leland Stanford, Jr. University*, the court articulated the nature of information disclosure in the most general terms, and, in fact, created a "duty to warn" the patient of the consequences of his agreement to enter into medical experimentation and/or treatment. This case stated that "all the facts which materially affect his rights and interest and of the surgical risks, hazards, and dangers if any" must be disclosed to patients prior to eliciting their consent to the medical intervention.

The doctrine of informed consent, when introduced in the mid-1950s, was considered to be the cornerstone of patients' rights in the medical care system. Informed consent was viewed as one of the most important doctrines for establishing the autonomy of individual patient decision-making regarding the nature of care and treatment in the health care system. It was viewed as essentially shifting the medical decision in favor of the patient rather than the physician, who had previously enjoyed a strongly paternalistic attitude and prerogative with regard to patient care. Informed consent affirmed individual self-determination and the right of privacy, which includes the right to be left alone (Tancredi, 1982). In fact, it is *such* an important development in the history of patients' rights that it underlies much of what occurred subsequently in the development of the right to refuse medical and psychiatric treatment (*Rogers v. Commissioner of the Department of Mental Health*, 1983). For the most part, the doctrine of informed consent is classified currently under tort or negligence law.

But there are several features about informed consent that make it problematic in terms of its effectiveness as a protective device for patients. To begin with, actions brought by the patient are not successful unless the undisclosed risk actually developed and resulted in injury to the patient (Holder, 1978). There are some exceptions to this requirement, but they are relatively rare. Again, one would apply the standard of proximate cause, which is, that "but-for" the information that should have been disclosed, the patient would not have elected to accept the therapeutic intervention. Furthermore, there is an element of foreseeability that deals with the reasonableness of the physician's divulgence in terms of what he knows or should know to be the informational needs of his patient.

The prevailing standard for informed consent is the physician disclosure standard (Furrow, 1980). A physician is obligated to disclose to a patient any information that a similarly situated physician would disclose under similar circumstances. This standard of informed consent is not unlike the standard for negligence generally applied in medical practice. Hence, a psychiatrist who decides to use for the treatment of schizophrenia a new medication, that does not fit into the general class of phenothiazines, would be obligated to disclose that information, as well as any information that other psychiatrists would have disclosed under similar circumstances. The fact that there may be evidence of a 1% chance of a serious consequence from the medication, such as the development of a cardiac arrythmia, would not be important in a jurisdiction that applied the professional disclosure standard, that is, if other psychiatrists would not have considered this information necessary for disclosure. In *Canterbury v. Spence* (1972), a case in the District of Columbia, the standard for informed consent was changed to what the reasonable person would want to know under similar circumstances. The standard refers to the materiality of the information that must be disclosed about the benefits, risks, and alternatives of treatment. In a jurisdiction that follows the *Canterbury* standard, there is no need for expert testimony to establish the professional custom concerning the nature and extent of disclosure of information. The decision as to whether or not the information should have been disclosed, because it might have materially affected the consent of the patient, is left to an "objective" standard that rests, essentially, on the jury's determination. This determination would be based on two factors: first, that a reasonable person would want to know this information in order to make a rational decision regarding a particular procedure or treatment; and second, that by knowing this information (in the *Canterbury* case it was that there was a 1% chance of paralysis following laminectomy), a patient might reasonably refuse to consent to the treatment.

An important argument can be made against the objective test for determining informed consent as articulated in the *Canterbury* case. This test creates a hardship on the patient to the extent that it ignores the subjective desires and preferences of the individual patient. It is conceivable that one could apply the "reasonable man" test to show that in the *Canterbury* case, had the patient known that there was a 1% chance of paralysis from a laminectomy, he would still have likely accepted the treatment given the alternatives that are available. On the other hand, the "reasonable man" test perhaps should not be applied to Mr. Canterbury. Mr. Canterbury may not have been reasonable on the issue of whether he would have accepted treatment, knowing the possible untoward outcomes.

A strong argument can be made that basic to the contract as an instrument delineating the physician–patient relationship is the extolling of the individual preferences, desires, and needs of the parties involved. When that contract is made, those qualities are essential to its viability. Yet, in the application of the *Canterbury* standards, we are essentially ignoring the individualistic elements of the initial contract by applying a "reasonable man" test. It is clear that every time we deflect from the application of contract principles and instead interpose tort, we burden ourselves with a host of conceptual hurdles with respect to proof, the verification of the subjective intention of the parties, the referencing of peer attitudes, and the credibility of the eccentricities that may have interceded in the relationship. If contract were the exchange model imposed on the system, then patients would be forced to live by their stated agreements of terms and references based on the presentation and acceptance of risk calculi. This would simplify the system of information exchange and support the autonomy of individual decisions.

An extension beyond the "objective" standard, which is based on the materiality of the information, is found in the case of *McPherson v. Ellis* (1982). In this case, the North Carolina Supreme Court took the position that the standard for disclosure should be what that particular patient would have needed to know in order to make a meaningful consent to treatment. This standard would be in the direction of a "subjective" standard because the test would not be based on what the reasonable person would want to know, but rather, on what that specific patient who incurs an injury which can be directly related to information that was not disclosed would *claim* he or she had a right to know. The difficulty with the *McPherson* rule is that it creates problems of proof. It would be very difficult to establish in any one case whether the undisclosed information would have been decisive in that patient's decision. The patient would have to establish that, by knowing this additional information, he would not have accepted the recommended diagnostic or treatment procedures.

Informed consent is a very complex doctrine as it applies to the treatment of patients in medicine generally. It becomes particularly problematic, however, in the mental health field because psychiatrists are not only dealing with the determination of what information should be provided to patients, but they also must address the fact that, in many cases, the patient population is mentally compromised. This compromise of mental status might be due to emotional factors that influence the ability of the patient to understand the information that is presented or might be due to true cognitive difficulties, which might be seen in the case of seriously psychotic patients. Furthermore, the psychiatrist has to deal with the fact that many of his patients may be so emotionally labile that informing them of the particulars of a treatment could be detrimental to their mental and physical condition. A patient may refuse a treatment that would be essential for his care because he could not handle the simple decision-making process. Most of the informed consent cases in psychiatry in the past have involved the physical treatment of patients. There have been cases where patients, injured following electroshock and insulin treatments, have argued that they were not informed of the possibilities of injury, such as fractures of vertebrae or of the long bones of the body (*Lester v. Aetna*, 1957). As has been observed earlier, this is becoming less of a problem due to the introduction of muscle relaxants that essentially avoid these complications in electroshock and insulin treatment.

In the area of medication of patients, informed consent is becoming increasingly important. This is especially the case with respect to the long-term consequences, such as tardive dyskinesias, following treatment with neuroleptics. A case based on an allegation that the patient's family was not provided with information regarding the long-term use of phenothiazines was recently decided in favor of the patient (*Clites v. Iowa*, 1982). The patient, a mentally retarded child, developed several manifestations of a tardive dyskinesia. Informed consent may also become an increasingly important issue with regard to stress therapy and/or the use of encounter groups. In most areas that pertain to the psychotherapeutic intervention of patients, it is hard to establish a malpractice action to begin with, let alone one based on informed consent. However, where one is addressing the issues of stress therapy and/or encounter groups, where the basic characteristic of the intervention is one which creates emotional and mental turmoil for the patient and where the patient may be injured subsequently, an allegation of nondisclosure or of incomplete disclosure may be possible and may lead to a successful informed consent action.

There have been two recent developments in the law of informed consent that have added some new wrinkles to the responsibilities of the physician. Both of these cases may have particular relevance in the area of psychiatric treatment of patients. The first case, *Truman v. Thomas* (1980), creates an affirmative obligation on the part of the physician for informing the patient of the consequences of refusing risk-free diagnostic tests. This

particular case involves a patient who refused pap smears over a period of 5 years. She was in her late 20s and when she entered her early 30s she developed a urinary tract infection, which lead to the discovery of vaginal and cervical irregularities that on subsequent examination revealed a large carcinoma of the cervix. This patient died of cervical cancer at the age of 30, and the family brought a wrongful death suit against the physician claiming that the physician had the obligation to obtain an "informed refusal." The court concluded that, if the patient refuses to submit to a risk-free diagnostic test (and possibly treatment method), the physician has the duty to inform the patient not only of the risks that attend to the procedure itself, but of those risks that might result from the patient's foregoing the recommended diagnostic measure. In the field of psychiatry this might have application to tests that would differentiate organic from functional illnesses or, perhaps, tests such as psychometric examinations that might assist in the differentiation among various functional disorders.

The second case, decided in 1983, is even more applicable to the unique circumstances of the psychiatric treatment of patients, as it places the obligation on the physician to assess the competency of patients to give informed consent. Because in psychiatry patients are often mentally compromised, this legal responsibility could be especially troublesome. The case involved a spinal laminectomy on a congenitally deformed spondylolisthesis infant where consent was obtained from the mother (*Zimmerman, Respondent v. N.Y. Health and Hospital Corp.*, 1983). The mother was informed of the necessity of the surgery in order to prevent the possibilities of paralysis in the patient and was told that one of the untoward consequences of the surgery might be some dysfunction of the bowel and bladder. The mother consented to the procedure and the patient developed some of the adverse consequences that were presented to the mother. Despite these untoward results, there was no question as to the appropriateness of the surgery or that the surgeon's operation in any way deviated from acceptable standards of care. However, the mother later alleged that she was mentally retarded and lacked the capacity to give informed consent. The court pointed out that the doctor knew or should have known that the mother lacked the mental capacity to give consent and that the physician did not describe in detail the procedures or risks from the laminectomy. The court consequently came out in favor of the mother and the patient and awarded $250,000 to the injured patient and $50,000 to the aggrieved mother. On appeal, the damages for the child remained unchanged, but those levied against the mother were reduced to approximately $10,000.

The issue of patients' comprehension of the information presented to them is not limited to psychiatry alone, but extends to all branches of medical practice. Nor is it the case that comprehension is limited merely because the patients are mentally compromised. In fact, studies that have been done in recent years suggest that the general patient population has difficulty understanding the benefits, risks, and alternatives of treatment (Tancredi, 1982). One study that involved 200 women from a highly educated background demonstrated that a large percentage of patients, when presented with medical information, neither understand the nature and purpose of the treatments that are presented nor are able to disclose, even a short time later, the complications of the treatments (Cassileth, Zupkis, & Sutton-Smith, 1980). In addition, that study indicated that 60% of the patients did not read the forms carefully. Other studies conducted on patients who have seen a range of specialists (opthomologists, dentists, etc.), corroborated the results of the Cassileth et al. study (Tancredi, 1982). These studies, including those involving mental patients (Lidz, et al., 1984), strongly suggest that the difficulties surrounding the comprehension of medical information in order to obtain informed consent are by no means limited to the mentally ill and that even patients with no evidence of mental illness and with an average or above average intellectual capacity have problems comprehending medical information. On the other hand, suits dealing with the issue of informed consent in general medical practice are on the increase, and some of them have resulted in rather significant awards for patients (Katz & Capron, 1975). In the informed consent area there is an opportunity for presenting a therapeutic justification for not disclosing information to a patient (Holder, 1978). This qualification of the doctrine of informed consent comes under the concept of therapeutic privilege. It comes into play when a patient is so ill or emotionally vulnerable that the doctor would have reason to believe that the patient would likely be harmed by the disclosure of information. Where the physician asserts this privilege, the onus is placed heavily on him to establish that he acted appropriately.

An alternative to the application of therapeutic privilege would be the use of other surrogate decision-makers. The distinction between emotional lability and cognitive incompetency is not clearcut. The law allows the physician to apply therapeutic privilege essentially in those situations where incompetency is not alleged but emotional vulnerability is. Where, in fact, there is a concern about the competency of the patient, the law will usually rely on surrogate decision-making, which may require the appointment of a *guardian ad litem* or provisions that would allow members of families to make decisions in lieu of the patient. In some respects, the application of a doctrine of surrogate decision-making is not unlike that of therapeutic privilege. It is similar to therapeutic privilege in that it provides a way whereby decisions can be made regarding patients without having to address further the issue of incompetency. It does this by shifting the powerful decisions on to another. However, it is different than the application of the therapeutic privilege in that the *guardian ad litem*, who makes the decision, is not open to the burden of establishing a reason for the decision; he is merely required to show that he acted in the best interests of the patient. In contrast, when the therapeutic privilege is asserted by the physician in cases of emotional lability, the physician has the onus of establishing a justification for the application of the therapeutic privilege. In fact, both of these function in similar ways, that is, by creating a system which would allow for an easier administrative approach to decision-making than forcing the physician and the family into court for each therapeutic issue where patients of compromised mental or emotional conditions are involved.

One issue in law that has not yet been resolved is the question of when one would apply the negligence doctrine to the decisions of surrogate decision-makers (Gutheil & Applebaum, 1980). We have already suggested that when the physician acts as a surrogate decision-maker, as when he relies on "therapeutic privilege" for not disclosing information to a patient, the courts are increasingly shifting the burden on to the physician to justify his decision not to have consulted the patient. Where the physician is not able to give a strong justification for having trumped the rights of the patient by not providing critical information, the physician may be open to an action on grounds of negligence under the informed consent doctrine. With regard to surrogate decision-makers, the issue of negligence has not been clearly resolved except for where one could establish fraud on the part of the surrogate decision-maker — that is, where the decision is made against the best interests of the patient. Here, the decision-maker, a member of a family or a legal advocate, benefits in some way from the decision. There have been no cases in the mental health field with regard to informed consent that have alleged pure negligence on the part of the *guardian ad litem*, although, theoretically, this is quite possible (particularly if it could be shown that the *guardian ad litem* did not carefully assume his responsibilities for evaluating the benefits and risks of the treatment and for making a decision that could be construed as one compatible with the best interests of the patient).

The concept of substituted judgment, in its application to the medical care field, finds its origins in cases dealing with the terminally ill who are also incompetent. The first such case (*In the Matter of Karen Ann Quinlan*, 1976) concerned a young woman who at one time was competent but who entered a comatose state that was diagnosed over a period of time as highly likely to be irreversible. This patient was placed on a respirator and her father petitioned the court for the right to discontinue the use of any mechanical-assist devices. After substantiating that the patient was in an irreversible and terminal state, the court granted the father, as guardian, the right to make the decision to terminate the use of mechanical-assist devices. However, his decision had to be approved by the hospital ethics committee as well as by the physicians treating the patient. This case articulated what has been referred to as the "putative judgment" test for decisions involving incompetent patients. The father, having lived for a long time with Karen Quinlan, knew the cognitive preferences and the affectual qualities of the patient's personality and was therefore able to impute what she would have wanted under these circumstances.

A series of cases following *In the Matter of Karen Ann Quinlan* added some wrinkles to the concept of substituted judgment. The first of these cases, *Superintendent of Belchertown State School v. Saikewicz* (1977), involved a man in his 60s who all his life had been severely mentally retarded (his IQ measured at 10) and who lived in an institution. This patient developed an acute form of leukemia that could be arrested for a very short period of time with the possibility of a remission following chemotherapy treatment. The issue that confronted the court was: How should such a decision be made, given the fact that this patient

was never competent and, therefore, never could have articulated a preference in such situations. The court applied the substituted judgment doctrine, appointing a *guardian ad litem* to "stand in the shoes" of the patient and make a determination of what that patient's preferences would be. The final decision, of course, is to be left to the court, who will make a determination based on the guardian's perceptions of the objective desires of the patient. As there was never a previous state of competency for Saikewicz, the decision would be formed by the *guardian ad litem* who attempted to determine the subjective experience of that patient. Clearly, there was a simpler directive in *Karen Ann Quinlan*, where the father had a relationship with the patient when she was highly competent and her preferences could be known by the guardian.

Saikewicz was followed by a case that also applied substituted judgment, *In the Matter of the Guardianship of Richard Row III* (1981). In that case, the court stated that the decision-maker could not authorize treatment against the desires of the outpatient even where the patient was incompetent. Here, the final decision-maker was the judge, who, consistent with the *Saikewicz* line of cases, would be guided by both the substituted judgment standard and policy considerations such as overriding state interests. The principle of substituted judgment and the use of a judge as final decision-maker was also recently applied in the extension of the *Rogers v. Commissioner of the Department of Mental Health* (1983) decision, *Rogers v. Okin*, 1984.

In all of these cases where there was an attempt to use substituted judgment, the courts were grappling with the insoluble problem of how to make decisions where the patient is incompetent and where, in many circumstances, there is no information available to indicate what these patients' explicit desires would be in such a situation. Yet decisions have to be made. The problem is that these decisions are made by constructing a self without the benefit of any background information. Essentially, the construct is used to obfuscate the fact that there is a vacuum of subjective intentionality. In the final analysis, the device of substituted judgment is really an objectified standard of the incomplete person reconstructed by the values of the surrogate decision-makers. It is a paternalistic model, much in the same way that paternalism exists in the application of therapeutic privilege by the physician, and it is flawed in the sense that there is really no reference point with respect to professional competence in making this judgment. These cases contain a whole set of conflicts and ambivalences because of the emotional proximity that the surrogate decision-maker may have with the patient in question. This emotional aspect does not necessarily have to exist; substituted decision-makers may be appointed by the court. For example, in the *Saikewicz* kind of case the final decision-maker was the judge. Nonetheless, the concept of substitution is a will-o'-the-wisp. Whether the surrogate is in an intimate relationship with the patient or is an objective third party appointed by the court — or is the court itself — the value systems of a party other than the patient are to be imposed.

DUTY TO PROTECT
THIRD PARTIES

Since the mid-1970s, when the California Supreme Court came down with a final decision in the *Tarasoff* case, there has been an ever-increasing number of cases addressing the issue of the psychiatrist's duty to protect third parties from harm that may be inflicted by patients.[2] In the *Tarasoff* case, the court held that a therapist who determines that a patient presents a serious threat of harm to a third party incurs the obligation to

use reasonable measures to protect the intended victim. The duty to protect third parties was to be effected by warning the potential victim or the victim's family that the patient intended to inflict harm on them. Although the obligation was merely one of *warning* the third party, the court in the *Tarasoff* case explicitly stated that the duty was to *protect* third parties who may be victimized by their patients.

In those jurisdictions that have followed the *Tarasoff* ruling there have been various modifications of the original duty to protect third parties. First, the therapist (in some jurisdictions) will not be held liable where the patient made such an explicit threat to harm the victim that the victim or others in the victim's family were aware of the patient's intention (Taub, 1983). Second, many courts have required that the precise identity of the potential victim be known.[3] If the therapist knows that a patient is potentially dangerous, but does not know the precise identity of the victim, then the therapist may not be obligated to issue a warning. On the other hand, the therapist could be held responsible for not having taken whatever reasonable measures necessary to prevent the untoward outcome. In many situations, patients who exhibit such dangerous propensities may be justifiably confined against their will. There are jurisdictions where commitment would not be

---

[2]Some of the recent cases based on *Tarasoff* and duty to protect have unusual scenarios: (a) *Petersen v. State of Washington* (1983). This involved a patient who was discharged from a mental hospital and 5 days later got into an automobile accident, injuring the passenger of another car. The psychiatrist in the case testified that the behavior of the patient was unpredictable and that as such he was potentially dangerous. The psychiatrist made no effort to have the patient committed. Here the court reaffirmed the duty of the psychiatrist to take reasonable precautions to protect third parties; (b) *Lundgren v. Fultz* (1984). This case involved a patient who had been diagnosed as a paranoid schizophrenic. Over the course of several years he had purchased at least five handguns. At one point the police recommended that the guns be removed, which his wife accomplished. The police then refused to return the guns to the patient unless the psychiatrist who was treating the patient could assure that the patient was cured of his disorder. The psychiatrist wrote a letter to that effect, assuming that it was important to have an open relationship with the patient. The patient subsequently killed a woman in a random act, and the court found the psychiatrist negligent for failing to commit the patient and for directing that the guns be returned to him. On appeal the court spoke about certain limits to the professional–patient relationship and indicated that the psychiatrist had exceeded a level of discretion when he recommended the return of the guns to the patient. The case was sent back for reevaluation of negligence in the psychiatrist's decision to have the guns returned.

[3]In a case following the *Tarasoff* decision the California Supreme Court suggested that the presence of a readily identifiable victim is a precondition to liability. This case involved the patient who while on leave from the hospital set fire to his home, injuring members of the family. The court concluded that the psychiatrist who released the patient on a temporary leave of absence had no duty to warn of the patient's dangerous propensities. The court pointed out that the danger that is posed by releasing the patient was no different than that to the general population. Furthermore, members of the family, particularly the mother, had knowledge of the patient's history including similar behavior (*Thompson v. County of Alameda*, 1980). Klein and Glover (1983) assert that one could read *Tarasoff* and *Thompson* together as suggesting that a warning is legally sufficient in cases involving identifiable victims, despite the fact that *Tarasoff* uses the broader obligation of "protect". An Iowa case, *Heltsley v. Votteler* (1982) takes the position that a psychiatrist may have a duty to warn an identifiable victim but does not have the broad duty to protect society from violent patients.

possible, as the patient's expression of intended violence may not be sufficient to justify confinement under the statutes of the state. Third, there are those situations where a patient attacks a third party without ever having made any specific threats ahead of time. Liability for failing to control a patient, whom a therapist knew or should have known had dangerous propensities, would depend on the patient's ability to exercise control and would relate to the responsibility to commit to confinement if the patient's conditions met the criteria for committal in the jurisdiction or, possibly, to the responsibility for medicating the patient (Klein & Glover, 1983). These rules are, at best, very general rules because, as we shall see in some of the subsequent cases flowing from the *Tarasoff* decision, psychiatrists have been held responsible even where the identity of the potential victim is not precisely known and in cases where the potential victim is certainly aware of the danger that the patient presents to him or her but has not been explicitly warned by the psychiatrist (*McIntosh v. Milano*, 1979).

Following the *Tarasoff* case, other cases decided in California somewhat restricted the extent of the duty to protect (Taub, 1983). One case in particular, the *Bellah* case, involved a psychiatrist who had been treating a 19-year-old borderline girl who, over the course of a year, expressed the desire to commit suicide on many occasions (*Bellah v. Greenson*, 1978). The psychiatrist treated this patient on an outpatient basis by psychotherapeutically managing these expressions of suicidal intent. However, at one point in the course of the therapy the patient actually committed suicide, and the parents brought a suit against the psychiatrist, arguing that the psychiatrist had a duty to warn them of their daughter's suicidal potentialities. The court in this case held that the sequences leading to the patient's death did not follow the pattern of responsibility articulated in the *Tarasoff* case, as the patient was the victim and not the parents. Other cases in California have been more explicit regarding the requirement that the identity of the third party victim be known precisely to the psychotherapist in order to trigger the duty to protect that victim (see Footnote 3).

Cases in other states have dealt with unusual circumstances where attempts have been made by the plaintiff to trigger the duty to protect derived from the *Tarasoff* case. One such case, *Cole v. Taylor* (1981) occurred in Iowa and involved a

plaintiff/patient who committed a violent act against a third party. The patient claimed that she had disclosed to her psychiatrist her inclination to kill her husband and that the psychiatrist, therefore, had a duty to intervene and prevent her actions. The case was dismissed by the Supreme Court of Iowa, which took the position that it would be against public policy to allow an individual to maintain a cause of action in court by relying, in whole or in part, on a criminal act to which he/she was a party. A similar case arose in Dallas, in 1982, involving a former mental patient who killed his mother and wounded other members of his family with a shotgun. The patient sued the hospital, claiming that the hospital was negligent in releasing him in his violent condition. Both of these cases highlight the dilemma that has been created by the *Tarasoff* line of decisions. The court in *Cole v. Taylor* (1981) pointed out that the *Tarasoff* case was explicit in its rationale, that is, that the duty to protect or to warn applied only to the intended victim and not to the patient herself. These cases create certain incentives for psychiatrists to avoid the therapeutic posture of forcing the patient to assume the management of his behavior, and, instead, encourage more aggressive control of psychiatric patients.

There was an interesting twist to the *Tarasoff* decision in a recent case in Minneapolis (*Oliver v. Stephens*, 1983). Here, a patient who had undergone a sex change operation brought an action against various members of the staff of the Metropolitan Center of Minneapolis. The patient argued that the staff had an obligation to protect him from undergoing this operation. But the real underlying question is the extent to which the actions of a psychiatric patient can be called voluntary and whether that voluntariness would relieve the therapist of liability. Again, this case, as in the previous two, does not comport with the pattern of protecting the intended victim from being victimized by another party.

Outside of these cases involving the *Tarasoff* decision, two relatively recent cases created additional problems for the psychiatrist in the treatment of patients and in the protection of third parties. The first of these is *Lapari v. Sears, Roebuck, and Company* (1980). This Nebraska case highlights the conceptual difficulties surrounding the duty to warn, particularly as it applies to the nature and scope of potential third parties or victims. The case involved a mentally defective patient who had been released from a Veterans

Administration Hospital a few weeks prior to entering a Sears store for the purpose of purchasing a gun. The store sold the patient a gun. He entered a nightclub in Omaha and began shooting randomly. He killed one person and injured the victim's wife, who subsequently brought a suit against Sears for having sold the gun to the patient. The store, in turn, filed a third-party complaint against the U.S. government for contribution and indemnity, alleging that the Veteran's Administration Hospital had been negligent in the psychiatric care that they provided to this patient. Following the patient's discharge from the Veteran's Administration Hospital, the patient continued psychiatric treatment on an outpatient basis. The store (and the plaintiff) alleged that the psychiatrists treating the patient were negligent in the psychiatric care that they rendered, as they knew, or should have known, of the potential dangerousness of this patient and should have detained him or begun commitment proceedings.

Returning to the original language of the *Tarasoff* case, the court argued that the psychiatrists in the outpatient clinic had an obligation to protect third parties. Similarly, in *Lapari*, the therapist had the duty to initiate whatever protections were reasonably necessary for the safety of third parties. Unlike the scenario of the *Tarasoff* case, the intended victim in *Lapari* was unidentified. It was impossible for the psychiatrist to know who might be injured by the patient's capricious actions. On the other hand, if one relies on the broader obligation in the *Tarasoff* case, which is the duty to protect third parties, then the psychiatrist would have had the affirmative obligation to initiate protective measures, such as confinement of the patient. In this case, both Sears and the U.S. government were held liable. The liability of Sears was due to a violation of a federal statute requiring that prospective gun purchasers be asked certain specific questions, including questions relating to whether the purchaser has a history of mental illness. With regard to the U.S. government, liability flowed from the theory underlying the *Tarasoff* decision.

Another case building on the *Tarasoff* decision is *Jablonski By Pahls v. United States* (1983). In this case, it was alleged that the psychiatrist had not taken the necessary steps to protect the victim from the patient, in spite of the fact that no explicit threats were made against this third party. The patient had been living with the victim for several years, and approximately 4 days prior to

being seen in the emergency room of the Veterans Administration (V.A.) hospital, the patient visited the victim's mother and attempted to rape and harm her. The victim (the woman he was living with) then took the patient to the psychiatrist at the V.A. hospital, who concluded that the patient was not dangerous. The victim, however, expressed her fears and concerns that the patient might attempt to harm her. The psychiatrist responded by suggesting that the victim should move out of the house, which she subsequently did. On one occasion, however, on returning to the apartment, the patient killed the victim, and the victim's daughter brought a suit against Veteran's Administration hospital. The daughter alleged, among other things, that the hospital had shirked its duty to protect and warn the victim. The patient's history, which had been preserved in the records of other V.A. hospitals, had not been obtained by the treating physicians at the V.A. hospital that was the object of the litigation. The records would have disclosed that the patient had attempted to commit serious acts of violence against his former wife and, in fact, had difficulty with women with whom he became intimate. The court determined that the victim was targeted by the patient and decided that, had the records from the prior hospitalization been obtained (augmented by the recent event of the attempted rape on the victim's mother), the treating psychiatrist would have been aware of the extent of this patient's violent propensities. This case, therefore, applied the *Tarasoff* reasoning to the obligation of the V.A. hospital and the treating psychiatrist and did not require the presence of an express threat against the third party, a requirement that was, in fact, required in the *Tarasoff* case.

In addition to the line of cases following the *Tarasoff* decision, there have been suits against psychiatrists for prematurely discharging patients from institutions, where the patients have then gone out and committed dangerous acts (Klein & Glover, 1983). This area of malpractice seems to be on the increase in terms of suits. But again, the distinction is often made between an error in judgment and an error in fact (Taub, 1983). This becomes particularly important if there appears to be no negligence on the part of the psychiatrist who discharges the patient and if there is also nothing explicit in the history of recent behavior to suggest that the patient will be dangerous. Where the psychiatrist, under these conditions, discharges a patient who then goes out and commits a dangerous act, it is likely that the discharge will be perceived as an error in judgment rather than an error in fact. The courts have been liberal in dealing with this issue, a liberalism that may be attributed to modern treatment trends that are directed at returning the patient to the community as soon as possible.

It seems, for the most part, that a psychiatrist may be held liable for prematurely discharging a patient when there is clear evidence that the patient may still be dangerous (Klein & Glover, 1983) or where the therapist has violated a statute, a regulation, or a court requirement in discharging the patient and therefore has abused his discretion (*Williams v. U.S.*, 1978). An improper assessment of dangerousness would be a situation where a patient attempts to assault another patient or a member of a staff and is shortly thereafter discharged in spite of these violent outbursts. If this patient then goes out and commits a seriously dangerous act on a third party, a psychiatrist or treatment facility may be held responsible because the evidence would suggest that he was dangerous at the time of discharge (Bromberg, 1983). Other examples of psychiatrist liability have been cases where patients have been committed by a court on the condition that the court, or a law enforcement officer, be informed of any plans for the patient's release. If, however, the patient is discharged without the therapist having met these requirements and the patient then commits a dangerous act, the therapist would have abused his discretion and might be held liable.

Of course, one of the conceptually difficult aspects of cases involving a psychiatrist's obligation to assess dangerousness is the body of literature that suggests that psychiatrists and other behavioral scientists are relatively poor at this type of assessment. This literature has been particularly pertinent to the case law dealing with the commitment of patients to mental institutions (Stone, 1975). It also has considerable relevance to the issue of a psychiatrist's responsibility for the discharge of patients who then go off and commit dangerous acts. Studies have shown that psychiatrists, as well as other specialists in human behavior, have done relatively poorly in the prediction of violence. [4]

All of these studies (and some of the earlier ones, e.g., the findings reported by Dershowitz, 1969) suggest that psychiatrists, psychologists, and other behavioral scientists are capable of predicting at best one out of three violent behaviors that occur over a period of years following the institutionalization of these patients (Ennis & Litwack, 1974). There are clearly some problems with this research, as was illustrated by Monahan (1981) in his book, *Predicting Violent Behavior*. Monahan points out that, among other things, these studies are not fair tests of the ability of behavioral scientists to measure violent behavior because these patients have all spent periods of time in

---

[4]Some of the important studies directed at assessing dangerousness are the following:

1. Kozol, Boucher, and Garofalo (1972). This study was conducted at the Massachusetts Center for Diagnosis and Treatment of Dangerous Persons. A team of behavioral scientists (two psychiatrists, two psychologists, and a social worker) examined 592 male offenders, most of whom were convicted for violent sex crimes, and determined on the basis of psychological tests and interviews with various friends, members of the families, etc., that 386 should be released. Of the 592 patients, 435 were released. A 5-year follow-up determined that 8% of those diagnosed by the scientists as nondangerous became recidivistic. Of the 49 thought to be high risks for engaging in dangerous behavior, 34.7% actually committed an act during those 5 years. Sixty-five percent committed no dangerous acts during the follow-up period.

2. As a result of *Baxstrom* (1966), over 1,000 patients in New York State were transferred from hospitals for the criminally insane to civil mental hospitals in the community. Steadman and Cocozza (1972) did a follow-up of these patients. They found less violence in civil hospitals following the transfer than anticipated. Only 20% of those transferred to civil institutions became assaultive and only 3% to the extent that they had to be returned to the Institution for the Criminally Insane. This was over a 4-year period. Steadman and Keveles (1972) followed 121 of these same patients who were released into the community for a 2-1/2 year period. Eight percent or 9 of the 121 were convicted of crimes during that period, of which only 1% were violent acts.

3. Cocozza and Steadman (1976) followed 257 defendants found incompetent to stand trial for felonies. Two psychiatrists examined these patients. Forty percent were considered to be nondangerous and 60% were considered to be likely to engage in dangerous behavior. These patients were followed for 3 years. Patients who were designated as likely to be dangerous turned out to be minimally more likely to be assaultive during hospitalization than the other patients. After their release, statistics actually reversed, that is, 49% of the dangerous group, 54% of the nondangerous group were actually rearrested. It was shown that 16% of those who were diagnosed as being nondangerous in the predictive sense turned out to be rearrested for violent offenses as opposed to 14% of those originally assessed as dangerous.

institutions, ostensibly receiving treatment. Furthermore, many of these individuals, who turned out to be false positives, may well have committed violent behavior that just simply was not discovered. In fact, studies of victims of violent acts have suggested that only a small percentage of victims actually report these incidents to the police (Monahan, 1981). One study (Monahan, 1981) showed that as little as 47% of people who claim to have been victimized actually reported this to the police. Finally, these studies may be testing something other than the prediction of dangerousness. Monahan indicates that, in many cases, mental health professionals may not be telling the truth about who they really feel are dangerous and who they feel are not; they may have overdiagnosed people as potentially dangerous in order to attempt to influence their possible release.

What is clear from all of this information is that psychiatrists may not be the best judges of dangerousness and that they may not see or have cause to know of dangerous potential in patients. On the other hand, when you contrast those individuals who have been categorized as dangerous-prone as compared to those who are categorized as a nondangerous prone, the percentage of patients who commit dangerous acts subsequent to release from a mental health facility are usually higher in the former class. The relative figure has been over one third as compared to approximately 7 or 8% (Monahan, 1981). Now whether or not this justifies an assumption that psychiatrists should be held responsible for individuals who are discharged and then go out and commit dangerous acts is another matter. If we look at the decisions in this area, the courts have, for the most part, not held psychiatrists and institutions responsible for discharging patients who subsequently go out and commit dangerous acts except under those unique conditions that have already been discussed in this

section (Wilkinson, 1982). But with the development of the *Tarasoff* duty to protect third parties, and that line of subsequent cases, potentiality for liability may be increasing, even where there is no evidence that counteracts the studies that suggest that psychiatrists and other behavioral scientists have a limited capacity to assess dangerousness.

SUICIDE

The liability associated with suicide is one of the most complex problems in psychiatry. To begin with, the assessment of the suicidal potential of the patient is equivalent in difficulty to the assessment of dangerousness of patients to third parties. Psychiatrists can apply a whole series of parameters for establishing the suicidal potentiality of a patient, but ultimately the degree of certainty is low when associating any or all of the parameters with the actual conduct in question (Slaby, Lieb, Tancredi, 1985). The probability in any one instance is, at best, speculative, though certain behaviors would lead even the lay person to suspect that an individual was suicidal. For example, patients who mutilate themselves or who have a history of recurrent bouts of depression and patterns of suicidal behaviors create a strong presumption in favor of the possibility that they will ultimately commit suicide. But, in fact, the clinical impression in any one case may not be supported by strong epidemiological information. Perhaps the most that can be said is that relying on a psychiatrist's intuitive sense of the patient, the psychiatrist may be able to arrive at the assumption that the patient is highly suicidal. Nonetheless, the court does affix liability in many cases. Generally, three criteria seem to be necessary for determining professional liability (Knapp & Vandercreek, 1983). First, the courts are often preoccupied with the foreseeability of a suicide attempt.[5] For illus-

---

[5]The courts seem to be recognizing in recent years that highly exacting precautions may be anti-therapeutic. In some cases they have actually deferred to the psychiatrist's judgment regarding the benefits of increased freedom for suicidal patients even if it later turns out that the judgment was probably incorrect (*Topel v. Long Island Medical Center* (1981). A similar case is *Johnson v. United States* (1981) where the court recognized the near impossibility of predicting dangerous behavior and did not find the psychiatrist liable for using the open-door approach. Furthermore, they saw this as in accord with good psychiatric practice. A similar holding was decided in *Fiederlin v. City of New York Health and Hospital Corp.* (1981), where a patient was released from the hospital on a temporary pass and then committed suicide. The court pointed to the difficulty of prediction and the importance of according discretion to the psychiatrist to balance the various risks. Some other decisions take this position. See *Bell v. New York City Health and Hospital Corp.* (1982). This case involved a patient who was released from a hospital after a week of hospitalization. He attempted suicide a week later. The court found that the psychiatrist failed to do a proper medical examination by not thoroughly investigating the nature of the patient's delusion. See also *Weatherly v. United States* (1981). The court felt the psychiatrist had been negligent but determined that failure to return the patient to suicide precaution was not a proximate cause of the injury.

tration, a patient who has a history of exhibiting suicidal tendencies suddenly commits suicide, and it is alleged that he was not adequately observed by the professional staff. The court would determine whether the treatment plan did not adequately take into account evidence of the suicidal tendencies. If the court establishes that this is so, then it may well create liability for the physician and other professionals involved with this patient's care by concluding that the threat was foreseeable.

A second criterion of importance is the reasonableness of the judgment of the professional engaged in the treatment of the patient. If a psychiatrist is dealing with a seriously depressed patient, more precautions may be necessary to properly care for him. There may be many approaches to handling this patient. To begin with, the patient should likely be treated with antidepressant medications. Second, it may be that hospitalization would be advisable in order to prevent the patient from successfully committing suicide. Other possibilities might be insuring that the family is highly involved in the care or placement of the patient, under close supervision and observation by mental health personnel if necessary.

The third criteria deals with the thoroughness with which treatment is implemented (*Weatherly v. United States*, 1981). This usually involves the hospitalization of a patient. An illustration of this would be where a physician orders constant observation or frequent observation, but where the staff fails to meet these requirements and the patient commits suicide. Alternatively, there have been situations where paraprofessionals or even residents-in-training have allowed patients to roam freely in an open ward, ignoring the orders of the physician, and the patient escapes and commits suicide. Oftentimes, in these cases, if the physician's orders are ignored by the hospital, the physician may be exonerated in a malpractice action and the hospital may be found liable (Waltzer, 1980).

Most law suits that have been brought in the past as a result of a suicide involve inpatients (Horan & Guerrini, 1981). Of course, anyone who was involved in the care of the patient is vulnerable to litigation: the psychiatrist, the psychologist, nurses, and the hospital itself. Generally, physicians or psychotherapists who use the hospital facilities but who are not employed by the hospital could be viewed as independent professionals and, therefore, independently responsible for their own actions. That is not to say that the hospital cannot be sued if it has been negligent in its prac-

tices regarding the hiring or training of employees who work with psychiatric patients (Waltz & Inbau, 1971). This negligence, however, extends beyond the functions of hiring and training; it also includes the obligations of the hospital to provide proper supervision of the employees and to insure that hazardous circumstances do not exist where patients are being treated. Where it can be shown, for example, that an employee of the hospital has been negligent and that negligent action has led to the conditions that provided the opportunity for the suicide to take place, then the hospital can be sued under the doctrine of vicarious liability (Loggans, 1981). That is, the hospital could be held liable for the actions of its employees. Subsequent to the legal action against the facility, the hospital may choose to sue the employee for the financial loss that was incurred in losing the malpractice action. But, generally, this does not occur, and the hospital insurance policy covers those negligent acts of employees of the hospital.

In the past, hospitals were frequently sued successfully for malpractice in cases involving the suicide of a patient (Loggans, 1981). This occurred primarily because the hospital was perceived to be in a custodial relationship with the patient, which meant, essentially, that the hospital was given the obligation of diagnosing suicidal intent and then instituting close supervision of the patient so that no actual attempt would be possible. As the standard of psychiatric practice has changed regarding the care of suicidal patients, so the standard of strict supervision has been decreased, with the consequence that a more open-door policy has emerged (*Dillman v. Hellman*, 1973). In part, this was brought about by the realization that it would be countertherapeutic to create serious dependency on the part of the patient. A strict hospital environment that promotes this level of dependency may greatly impair the ability of the patient to develop a sense of self-worth sufficient to handle his or her environment in a more positive manner. With this shift toward the therapeutic community, the role of the hospital became less that of a prison and more that of a place for reacclimation of the patient to the outside world. By no means does this reduce the responsibility of the hospital; it simply shifts it so that now the hospital must apply reasonable professional measures in assessing the risk of a certain degree of freedom to the patients and in assessing other changes in the nature of the patient's treatments as regards lessening the extent of supervision (*Johnson v. United States*, 1981).

With regard to outpatient suicide, the psychiatrist is obligated to use reasonable standards of care in diagnosing and treating suicidal behavior (Waltzer, 1980). Again, the possibilities of suicide must be foreseeable, but an equally important factor is the awareness on the part of the court that the psychiatrist has limited control of a patient or of the patient's environment when the patient is being seen on an outpatient basis (*Speer v. U.S.*, 1981). This is very different from the hospital situation, where the psychiatrist and treatment staff can exert a greater degree of control over the actions of the patient (Knapp & Vandercreek, 1983).

The standards of care that are applied in a malpractice suit against a psychiatrist involving the suicide of a patient would be the customary degree of skill and care in the diagnosis and treatment of the patient (Waltz & Inbau, 1971). This would require that proper information be elicited regarding the patient's mental status to determine whether he or she is a suicidal risk. The court would then focus on the foreseeability of the patient's suicide: that is, whether or not at the time that the patient was evaluated and treatment was recommended the psychiatrist knew or should have known of the possibilities and risks that this patient might commit suicide (*Meier v. Ross General Hospital*, 1968). Another issue of concern to the court is the extent to which the patient's self-inflicted injuries are preventable (*Skar v. City of Lincoln, Nebraska*, 1975). For this determination, the court would assess the psychiatrist from the standpoint of the appropriateness of his intervention in handling the suicidal patient. The distinction that is again applicable to this situation, as with many situations involving suicide, is that between errors of fact and errors of clinical judgment (*Fernandez v. Baruch*, 1968). If, after having obtained all the information regarding the patient's history, family history, and mental status, the psychiatrist reasonably concludes that the patient is not a high suicidal risk, then the psychiatrist may be justified in placing the patient in a less restrictive environment. The issue at that point would be one of judgment rather than of fact. There was no negligence in the process of history-taking or in determining the mental status of the patient. If the patient subsequently goes out and commits suicide, a strong argument might be made that, if there was any error, it was an error in judgment as opposed to an error in fact.

As we have discussed earlier in this chapter, an argument might be made that judgment can be relegated to the same kinds of criteria for the establishment of negligence as the fact-gathering process. One could conceivably argue that, given all of the facts, even though the actual diagnosis and foreseeability is not certain, one might be better off taking a more conservative approach (for example, using a "closed ward") than a more liberal one. On the other hand, much of the determination of which approach is appropriate is influenced by the social perceptions of the role of the hospital or of the treating physician. As we have already pointed out, perception with regard to the hospital and its role in the treatment of patients has moved increasingly away from the purely custodial model to one of the open ward (*Knapp & Vandercreek*, 1983). Hence, with regard to the treating psychiatrist, the model may similarly be moving more toward shoring up as much as possible the individual's personal responsibility for behaviors such as suicide (*Dinnerstein v. U.S.*, 1973).

There have been many cases where patients have been discharged from psychiatric facilities because psychiatrists and treatment teams evaluating the patient felt that those patients may do better in a different environment. One case in particular resulted in the patient committing suicide shortly after his release (*Centano v. N.Y. City*, 1975). The court, however, fell into the distinction between error in fact and error in judgment and decided that the psychiatrist's position with regard to discharging the patient was, at best, an honest mistake or error in judgment.

Certain conditions can affect the culpability of the psychiatrist for patient suicide. We have already pointed out that in the outpatient context, a psychiatrist is rarely sued successfully for suicide because he or she has minimal control over the patient's actions. Similarly, where an intervening act occurs, the psychiatrist would also likely be exculpated for a patient's suicide (*Crauverien v. DeMetz*, 1959). For example, let us assume that a patient is discharged from a hospital after an assessment has been conducted, and it has been determined that the patient will be able to function well on the outside with minimal possibilities of resorting to suicidal behavior. Now let us assume the patient leaves the hospital, returns to work, and does quite well in his social interactions, but approximately 3 or 4 weeks later, following an argument with a close female companion, decides to "voluntarily" commit suicide. In a situation like this, it could be argued that there are many intervening facts that are related to the patient's decision to commit suicide. The final responsibility will probably not rest with the psychiatrist who conducted the evaluation and decided to discharge the patient. Too many other factors intervened that could be causally related to the patient's suicide, and, furthermore, it could be argued that enough time elapsed between the discharge and the suicide to provide the opportunity for other intervening factors. There are conceptual problems with determining responsibility insofar as it is very difficult in most cases to determine which factors have the greatest causative effect on an individual's decision to commit suicide. On the other hand, the best that a court can do from the factual pattern is to examine the presence of other factors and the length of time intervening in order to conclude that the discharge from the hospital was not premature. This determination would rest on the following factors: First, that the patient was able to function well for at least 3 to 4 weeks on the outside, and second, that enough time had elapsed for other events to intervene so as to be the primary causative factors in the decision to commit suicide. Again, the issue rests on one of interpretation and these cases do not provide sharp lines of distinction between various potentially causative motives for an individual's behavior.

Certain facts and characteristics should alert the psychiatrist to the possibility that certain patients are suicidal risks. Many epidemiological studies have shown, for example, that if there has been a past history of suicidal attempts on the part of the patient, it is likely that this behavior will continue in the future (Slaby, Lieb, & Tancredi, 1985). Furthermore, a recent loss or death of a loved one in a patient's life may be highly correlated on a statistical basis with that individual's attempt to commit suicide (Slaby et al., 1985). Other factors that may be important are the presence of serious physical illnesses, social or economic difficulties, and alcoholism. These factors become even more significant when they are combined with certain emotional or mental disturbances, such as the presence of command hallucinations, severe insomnia, and profound depression (Slaby et al., 1985).

VICARIOUS LIABILITY

Hospitals can be held responsible for the negligent actions of their employees (Waltz & Inbau, 1971). A distinction is made here between those individuals who are paid on a full-time basis by the hospital as employees and the psychiatrist or psychotherapist who has access to the facilities of the hospital and consequently staff privileges. For the most part, the hospital would not be held liable for the latter's actions, unless, of course, it can be shown that there was gross negligence on the part of the hospital in not requiring proper investigation of the credentials of those using their facility, thereby implying that staff privileges were granted capriciously (Holder, 1978). In general, however, hospitals are held vicariously liable for the negligent acts of those persons working for them. Similarly, psychiatrists can be held vicariously liable for those individuals who are employed by them directly, or who are, in fact, under their supervision. It is not uncommon for psychiatrists to have various paraprofessionals such as physician's assistants and nonmedically trained psychotherapists working with them. The relationship might be symbiotic, whereby the psychotherapist (who is not medically trained) uses the psychiatrist specifically for the purposes of medicating the patient. The psychotherapist, therefore, is not directly employed by the psychiatrist. Under these circumstances it would be unlikely for the psychiatrist to be held vicariously liable for a malpractice action based on the psychotherapist's activities (Horan & Guerrini, 1981). On the other hand, when the psychotherapist or other physician associate is working directly for the psychiatrist, the psychiatrist could be placed in a position of vicarious liability in the event that these employees act negligently (Furrow, 1980).

A more complicated situation presents itself when the psychiatrist is in charge of supervising individuals in training (Waltz & Inbau, 1971). The psychiatrist may be a full-time member of an academic staff or may only be affiliated with a psychiatric department with duties limited to 2–4 hours of supervision a week. Where other mental health workers are involved (be they residents in training or psychotherapists in part of an educational program), psychiatrists can be held liable for negligence when they do not assume their supervisory role and properly oversee the management of patients. The psychiatrist's obligation might involve more than just simply providing supervision; it may involve some direct involvement on the part of the psychiatrist for the care of specific patients. A 1976 New York case emphasized the importance of the psychiatrist's supervisory role. In *Cohen v. New York* (1976), the court addressed the issue of an institution's responsibility for assuring that mental health professionals be supervised by an appropriately qualified psychiatrist. In this case, a 23-year-old medical student in his third year voluntarily admitted himself to a medical center. He was evaluated and diagnosed as paranoid schizophrenic and was placed in an open ward. At the time of admission it was noted that the patient had suicidal potential, but it was felt that an open ward would provide both sufficient structure so that he would not commit suicide and incentive to assume some responsibility for his behavior. Four months after admission, a first-year resident decided that the patient no longer needed to be restricted to the ward. He consequently allowed the patient to wander from the unit. The day that the restriction was lifted, the patient left the unit and killed himself. The patient's wife brought a suit, arguing, among other things, that the hospital and the supervising psychiatrist were negligent in not providing closer supervision and control over the discretionary judgment of the first-year resident. The court concluded that the resident, at least at this stage of training, lacked the requisite skill to provide reasonable psychiatric treatment for the patient. The court then determined that a psychiatrist who places the care and treatment of patients in the hands of those in training has a continuing obligation to be directly involved in their care. This involvement would require proper supervision of the treatment decisions of those in training. When this supervision lags and injury results, the psychiatrist and the hospital can be held liable for the negligence of those under their supervision.

This case and the general thrust of the law in dealing with vicarious liability has important ramifications for the education of psychiatrists and other mental health professionals. The court not only required that those professionals be under supervision during the course of their training, but actually imposes an obligation on the supervisors to have a more direct involvement, if necessary, in the care of the patient. This requirement and the possibility of an action based on vicarious liability means that, at the very least, the supervisory psychiatrist must be ever-aware of the nature of the patient's condition and the treatment that is being provided. The psychiatrist cannot rely wholly on the judgment of the professional, even though that professional may be medically trained, because, in the event of injury, the supervising psychiatrist may be held liable. Some might argue that after 4 or more months of treatment on an open ward it may have been appropriate to provide greater freedom to the patient. There is always the chance, of course, that the patient may go out and commit suicide; on the other hand, the risk of freedom may be perfectly acceptable in the nature of psychiatric practice.

In no case can a psychiatrist or a mental health treatment facility be assured that an individual is not going to go out and commit suicide or injure third parties. The best the profession can do is provide proper treatment for the patient. Ultimately, though, a risk is taken when a patient is given greater responsibilities or is discharged from the institution. The question of whether there was an error in judgment does not enter into this kind of situation because the error in judgment, if it exists, is not that of the supervising psychiatrist; it is that of the first-year resident. In *Cohen*, the first-year resident was simply not at a level of training sufficient to provide the requisite skill to render reasonable psychiatric decisions. Therefore, an honest error in judgment, as an argument against negligence, requires that the individual have the requisite knowledge to be able to make a reasonable decision. The fact that a reasonable decision ends up being wrong, given all the appropriate diagnostic measures to assess the patient, does not automatically result in an attribution of liability for the treating psychiatrist. But the requisite knowledge must be present. In those teaching situations where an error of judgment has been made by a trainee, the fact that the supervising psychiatrist has not been intimately involved in that decision may result in a finding that the psychiatrist and health care institution are responsible for the tort of negligence under the doctrine of vicarious liability.

ABUSES IN THE PROFESSIONAL RELATIONSHIP

There has been considerable controversy in recent years regarding the nature of acceptable social interactions between psychiatrists and their patients. There is little doubt that from a pristine therapeutic perspective, the psychiatrist–patient relationship should be limited to the treatment setting. In a sense, this is a bit restrictive when one considers that many psychiatrists living in relatively small communities are likely to interact with their patients in a variety of settings — religious affiliations, professional organizations, country clubs, and so on. Consequently, it is virtually impossible to avoid some interaction with patients outside of therapy. The difficulties occur, of course, when one attempts to examine the range of types of social interaction, and the point at which the psychiatrist–patient relationship outside of the therapeutic setting becomes problematic. There have been cases such as *Landau v. Werner* (1961), where the courts have clearly recognized that a social relationship was inappropriate outside of the context of treatment, even though this relationship did not result in any overt sexual behavior and began after therapy had been terminated.

Psychiatrists, as a rule, have always considered sexual behavior between therapists and patients inappropriate. Although this only recently became a proscription in the code of ethics of the American Psychiatric Association (1983), few would have recognized any potential benefit in that degree of erosion of the boundaries between the psychiatrist and the patient. Much of the concern about sexual involvement with patients rests on important notions in psychoanalytic theory (Riskin, 1979). A key element of this theory is the transference phenomenon, where the relationship between patient and therapist is at a highly intense level. It is this transference phenomenon that allows the patient to invest the therapist with many of the traits of those persons who played critical roles in the patient's early life. It is not uncommon, for example, for a patient to perceive himself or herself as being in love with the therapist.

Transference is a very important process in the treatment of a patient's psychological difficulties. It is through this attachment that the psychiatrist is able to assist the patient in working through early traumatic experiences as they manifest themselves in current living patterns. Finally, it is only by exploring the nature and operation of the transference phenomenon with the patient, that the patient can ultimately be cured of his most pressing psychological problems. When a patient becomes sexually involved with a psychiatrist, the psychiatrist indulges the historically weighted romantic notions that the patient has about the psychiatrist, notions that are engendered by the transference phenomenon itself. This prevents the patient from working through his or her family modes of developing interpersonal relationships, and preventing intimacy with another human being.

The recognition of the distortion that results from the therapeutically important element of transference when the psychiatrist has sexual relations with a patient has raised not only considerable questions regarding the ethical nature of sexual behavior but also shifted the behavior into the realm of psychiatric malpractice. In some jurisdictions, sexual relations between psychiatrists and patients have resulted in the revocation of licenses (*Salloway v. Department of Professional Regulation*, 1982). Moreover, there have been cases where criminal prosecutions have been brought against psychiatrists under the theory that having sexual engagements is something equivalent to rape (Riskin, 1979). This theory would hold that the transference phenomenon provides a psychiatrist with a powerful tool with which to manipulate the patient into a submissive posture and thereby to psychologically force the patient into a sexual encounter. In several states the statutes are so explicit as to provide that sexual relations with a patient, particularly when they occur under the guise of medical treatment, are to be considered criminal offenses (Burgess, 1981).

In the vast majority of cases where there are allegations of sexual involvement with patients, the therapists are male and the patients are female. Still, until recently there have not been very many cases that have reached the courts. Women are reluctant to bring a cause of action based on sexual involvement because of the publicity that it might create regarding their role in the engagement. Patients may be fearful that too much information will come out into the public eye, information that, although possibly inaccurate, will still influence others' perception of a patient's moral conduct. Equally problematic to many patients is the fear that such information will jeopardize their other relationships or even their careers. Furthermore, many patients are concerned about psychiatrists who have been allegedly involved in sexual behavior with them. They may be fearful that disclosures will result in serious problems for the therapist in his career or perhaps will compromise an otherwise secure marital relationship.

Researchers at the University of California Psychology Department recently sent questionnaires to psychotherapists practicing in California requesting information about patients who report incidences of sexual intimacy (Taub, 1983). These patients were usually sexually involved with previous therapists and were continuing therapy to help them deal with the trauma that was induced by that experience. The questions were open-ended, for the most part. Questionnaires were returned to the researchers by approximately 704 therapists, who provided information about 559 patients who alleged that they engaged in sexual behavior with their previous therapists. The find ings were noteworthy. The overwhelming majority, approximately 90% of these patients, as we have already suggested, were female. Approximately 96% of the therapists were male. Of those patients who engaged in sexual conduct, 90% reported to have suffered ill effects and, in fact, about half of that group had major difficulties recommencing therapy following the incident. Although this study involves the broad class of psychotherapists, which includes others besides psychiatrists, it is one of the most comprehensive studies dealing with the adverse effects of sexual relations between therapists and patients.

In recent years there have been several suits that have received widespread attention. Perhaps the most conspicuous of these was *Roy v. Hartogs* (1976), which took place in New York State in 1976.[6]

Some recent cases have resulted in much more significant awards for the injured plaintiff. Recently, in California, there was the case of *Walker v. Parzen*, in which the jury awarded the injured patient 4.6 million dollars (Wilkinson, 1982). This amount was reduced to 2.5 million in a settlement while the verdict was being appealed to the higher court. These settlements are particularly high because the plaintiff will often be able to substantiate the fact that the sexual relationship with the therapist had the additional effect of resulting in the absence of essential treatment for the patient, which led to a worsening of the patient's mental and emotional disorder. In some cases, patients have also alleged that the sexual interaction with the therapist had other deleterious effects, such as damaging marital or other relationships. Similarly, in Virginia a patient was awarded $650,000 in compensatory damages (*Combs v. Silverman*, 1982). This case involved a 19-year-old woman

who was diagnosed as having schizophrenia when she was 15 years of age and began seeing a psychiatrist at that time. The psychiatrist admitted that he had engaged in sexual behavior with the patient on several occasions. During the course of the trial several psychiatrists testified that not only was this not in comportment with acceptable standards of psychiatric care, but that, had this patient received proper treatment, she would have avoided years of unnecessary hospitalization. The court, in deciding for the plaintiff, took into consideration the bills for previous hospitalization as part of the damages.

Several factors seem to be important in influencing both the prospects of a recovery and the amount of damages (Gentry, 1980). To begin with, the courts would be concerned with the patient's complicity in the sexual behavior. The facts may suggest that the sexual conduct between the therapist and the patient is compatible with an "affair." Along the same lines, the court may determine that the patient knowingly encouraged the psychiatrist's behavior. If these facts are sufficiently convincing, the jury, to some extent, will be unsympathetic to the plaintiff. Underlying the jury's response, obviously, would be the extent to which it perceives the patient as having the capacity to form and exert free will in the decision to enter into sexual behavior with the therapist.

A second factor would be the severity of the patient's psychiatric condition. This factor can be very important and can also apply to the issue of the patient's complicity in the questioned behavior with the therapist. If, for example, the patient is shown to be seriously psychotic or neurotic, the court would recognize the patient's weakened mental and emotional state, perceive the imbalance in the power basis of the two parties, and

---

[6]Following the decision in the *Hartogs* case, the defendant sued the insurance company that provided malpractice coverage arguing that they were obligated to pay the damages assessed against him in the case alleging sexual improprieties. The court in New York in the case of *Hartogs v. Employer's Mutual Liability Insurance Company of Wisconsin* (NY Supp. 1977) held for the defendant that it would be against public policy to allow insurance coverage damages resulting from immoral or improper actions between physicians and patients. The number of suits dealing with sexual propriety is definitely on the increase. (See *Mazza v. Medical Mutual Insurance Company of North Carolina* (1984).) The patient sued the psychiatrist alleging that the psychiatrist engaged in sexual relations with his estranged wife and that the psychiatrist abandoned him at a critical point in his treatment. The patient was awarded $102,000 in compensatory damages, $500,000 in punitive damages on a malpractice count, and $50,670 in compensatory damages on a criminal conversion count. Both the psychiatrist and his insurer appealed regarding the damages for alleged malpractice and the Supreme Court of North Carolina affirmed. The insurer in this case contended that by allowing the insurance coverage to pay for the damage, this would frustrate the purpose for which punitive damages are used, which is to punish the wrongdoer. Here the court found the lower court properly held that the language of the contract for the insurance included the award for punitive and actual damages (unlike the *Hartogs* case). (See also *Omer v. Edgren* (1984).)

likely hold the psychiatrist more responsible for what actually eventuated between the parties. Obviously, if the patient is seriously psychotic, as in the case of an acute schizophrenic disorder, the psychiatrist more than likely would be held responsible for the sexual conduct.

The patient's age is another important factor in the determination of the extent and weight of the psychiatrist's responsibility for conduct (Gentry, 1980). The age factor not only refers to the chronological age of the patient but may also focus on the emotional maturity of the patient. For example, if the psychiatrist engages sexually with a woman in her late 30s or early 40s, and there doesn't appear to be any evidence that the psychiatrist coerced himself physically on the patient, then the court may come out with a very different position regarding responsibility for the sexual conduct. This would be the case particularly if it can be shown that no clinical malpractice occurred, that is, that because of attention being given to sexual relations between the parties, the psychiatrist did not provide care that was essential for the patient's well-being. The extent to which the therapist complies with accepted standards of pharmacological or clinical treatment of the patient is essential to the court's analysis of the degree of culpability of the psychiatrist for the sexual infraction (Furrow, 1980). The polarities, therefore, are between the conceptualizing of a therapist–patient relationship as an affair or as malpractice. The court can be swayed easily based on the age of the patient, the mental and emotional condition of the patient, and the presence or absence of evidence of patient complicity.

It is important to note that in cases involving an allegation of sexual misconduct with the patient, the court will look to the principles of medical ethics of the specialty organization as a test to determine what those acceptable standards of care are. As already suggested, the American Psychiatric Association (1983) clearly forbids sexual activity with patients. The code of ethics of the American Psychiatric Association helps to establish that transference is foreseeable and that the

therapist has an obligation to control his own sexual impulses with regard to the patient; to do otherwise is to act contrary to acceptable standards of psychiatric care and is therefore evidence of negligence.

ADVERSE OUTCOMES OF TREATMENT

Until the early 1970s the most frequent adverse outcomes of treatment were seen in patients who received either electroshock or insulin therapy. As previously discussed, before the advent of muscle relaxant drugs it was not uncommon for patients receiving electroshock treatments and insulin treatments to suffer serious injuries.[7] Similarly, many patients were injured during the 10–15 years when lobotomies were popular, but this patient population, often comprised of chronic schizophrenics who were hospitalized for indeterminate periods of time, was not in the position to initiate court actions against psychiatrists for improper utilization of that technique. In the 1970s, insulin treatment developed a bad name and, as a result, has become nearly obsolete in American psychiatry. Electroshock treatment almost went the same route; however, many psychiatrists have argued in favor of this mode of therapy and, finally, the American Psychiatric Association produced a paper establishing that electroshock treatment is very important for the treatment for certain kinds of refractory depressions (Culver, Ferrell, & Green, 1980). In many patients, where antidepressants or lithium carbonate have minimal effect, electroshock treatment may bring about dramatic changes in the patient's sensorium and affect. In certain forms of depressions, electroshock treatment is clearly preferred to antidepressants or other modes of drug therapy. Until recently, electroshock treatment and other physical procedures were viewed with apprehension by the lay population because they were frequently used to control patient behavior rather than because they were the ideal treatment for the patient.

---

[7]There are a series of cases dealing with patient injuries from electroshock treatment. Some have dealt with patients suffering with fractures (see *Collins v. Hand*, 1968 and *Kapp v. Ballentine*, 1980). Also see cases alleging injuries from disorientation secondary to electroshock (*Brown v. Moore*, 1957), Cert. denied, 1957, and *Adams v. State*, 1967). For cases dealing with alleging failure of the psychiatrist to conform to standard practices, see *Kosberg v. Washington Hospital Center* (1968) and *McDonald v. Moore* (1976). And, lastly, see cases alleging lack of informed consent (*Johnston v. Rodis*, 1958, and *Woods v. Brumlop*, 1962).

In recent years, malpractice actions appear to be increasingly focused on the short-term acute and long-term unremitting side effects of psychotropic medications, particularly neuroleptics (Slovenko, 1980). There are many cases now being considered before the courts, where patients are alleging malpractice in the psychiatrist's use of neuroleptics. The allegations seem to be very similar and center on the argument that the doses are sustained at too high a level for too long a period of time or that the patient's treatment is not frequently reviewed and that he or she is kept on drugs like thorazine, which in the long term bring about serious side effects. The first major suit dealing with this situation was *Clites v. Iowa* (1982). This case was brought in 1982 by the parents of a mentally retarded boy and involved the allegation that the employees of a hospital negligently administered a neuroleptic to the child, bringing about the long-term side effects of tardive dyskinesias. The trial court, in reviewing the information, found that the hospital employees were negligent. To begin with, the court determined that the neuroleptics were used in far greater doses than necessary to control the behavior of the child. Second, the physician who was treating the child neglected to consult with a specialist who was more familiar with the use of these drugs. Third, the multiple drugs that were given to the child should not have been given concurrently. Fourth, when the child began to experience symptoms of tardive dyskinesias, the staff should have altered the regimen of drugs in the treatment plan. They failed to do this. Fifth, there was insufficient observation of the boy's behavior, symptoms, and signs indicating side effects such as the early phases of tardive dyskinesias. The determination as to if and when drugs were to be administered to the child was made to meet the convenience of the staff, ignoring the requirement that these medications were to be used for therapeutic purposes. The trial court, on reviewing the factual material in this case, found for the plaintiffs. The child was awarded $385,165 for future medical expenses that he would have to incur by virtue of his having developed this side effect, and a further $375,000 for past and future pain and suffering (*Clites v. Iowa*, 1982). The Court of Appeal of

Iowa affirmed this judgment and determined that there was substantial evidence in the record to support the trial court's positions on both the damages and the standard of care that applied.

What makes these cases particularly difficult is that neuroleptics sometimes are the only drugs available to control a patient who is either in the acute or chronic stages of a serious psychotic illness. On the one hand, tardive dyskinesias, in addition to being a serious long-term side effect of medication, can be a permanent illness, sometimes causing major disability for the patient. On the other hand, given the advantages that can accrue from this medication, it should not be readily dismissed for the treatment of psychotic patients. It is important to remember that, until the 1950s, when neuroleptics came into existence, patients ended up in institutions for very long periods of time, often under restraint and frequently were subjected to the only treatments that were available at the time — electroshock, insulin, and lobotomies. The advent of the antipsychotic medications was an important landmark development in contemporary psychiatry, even though we now know that these medications do have the long-term, serious side effect of tardive dyskinesias. In a strictly pristine sense, the development of a tardive dyskinesia would be viewed as an iatrogenic complication of psychiatric treatment. But this does not make it presumptive evidence of negligence. It must be proven that the tardive dyskinesia was somehow proximately related to negligent care on the part of the physician (Wettstein, 1983).

A recent review of the claims made against the American Psychiatric Association's insurance firm, which provides coverage for members of APA, has suggested that both sexual improprieties with patients and drug reactions from antipsychotic medications have become increasingly serious problems in a number of claims annually. Several suggestions have been presented for ways of minimizing the impact of tardive dyskinesias, but none of them have proven to be totally satisfactory. Strategies have been employed, such as withdrawing the antipsychotic drugs, which frequently reverse the tardive dyskinesia[8] (Jeste & Wyatt, 1982). One could also decrease the dose of the neuroleptic

---

[8]There is epidemiological information regarding the development of tardive dyskinesias. This information can be very useful in developing a strategy for averting the development of this side effect. These studies have shown that cases of tardive dyskinesias have been estimated at anywhere from 10–20% of patients maintained on neuroleptics. It is potentially irreversible even after efforts are made to decrease or withdraw the medication. It is interest-

given so that it is marginally above the necessary minimum required to bring about certain psychological and behavioral changes, although some patients may develop tardive dyskinesias from very small doses of phenothiazines. What is evident is that these medications cannot be totally eliminated. Moreover, it is essential to follow patients carefully in order to reroute the medication at the first sign of involuntary movements and to present all of the information regarding the difficulties of using these medications to the patient at the outset of treatment, in enough time and over a number of episodes so that the patient is fully informed of the possibilities of something like tardive dyskinesias. What is critically important is that these medications be used only for those conditions that are serious, where it is, by and large, the best treatment available (Cain & Smith, 1982).

INAPPROPRIATE TREATMENT

This is a particularly difficult topic to address in a field like psychiatry. Due to the presence of many schools of psychiatric thought regarding the nature of the diagnosis of psychiatric diseases and the range of appropriate treatments, it is exceedingly difficult to establish when treatments are inappropriate (Horan & Milligan, 1983). Every school seems to set its own standards about what kinds of treatments under what circumstances are appropriate for the mentally and emotionally ill. If, in fact, the psychiatrist resorts to the use of these treatments with a reasonable degree of skill, he will likely be able to avert the consequences of a malpractice action. On the other hand, in spite of the differences in the schools and in the philosophies on the nature of mental illness and the approaches to its resolution, inappropriate treatments do stand out as a phenomenon separate from the psychotherapies. An example of inappropriate treatment might be the use of beating the patient with a whip as a means of placing the patient in a submissive posture and thereby effectively capturing the loyalty of the patient so that he can be pulled through the transference process (*Hammer v. Rosen*, 1960). This type of unconventional treatment is very rarely engaged in, and a

therapist who resorts to physical abuse or even psychedelic medications must expect that, in the event of an injury, there would be little protection from the inevitable argument that the therapist used unconventional and unacceptable methods. As part of the argument about the inappropriateness of unconventional approaches, courts might conclude that an unconventional approach that is dangerous might border on wreckless disregard for the safety and well-being of patients. Under these circumstances, it is not inconceivable for the treating physician to be charged with a criminal offense (Horan & Milligan, 1983).

ABANDONMENT AND INADEQUATE FOLLOWUP

Abandonment is a relatively rare allegation brought by patients against psychiatrists (Furrow, 1980). It can occur, nonetheless, because once the psychiatrist enters into a physician–patient relationship, he assumes certain responsibilities. According to Anglo-American law, a psychiatrist is not obligated to accept a patient into treatment. However, once he sees the patient and agrees to accept him as his own patient, he has created a duty, obligation, or contract with the patient to attend to his psychiatric needs during the period of his illness. Consequently, the psychiatrist has a duty not to abandon the patient during treatment.

There are circumstances in which the psychiatrist may terminate treatment either with or without the consent of the patient (Furrow, 1980). Some of these conditions are the following:

1. The patient may decide to dismiss the psychiatrist. If this occurs and the psychiatrist makes reasonable efforts to contact the patient so as to establish the patient's intent, where this has not been explicitly stated, then it is unlikely that the psychiatrist would be held liable for abandonment.
2. The psychiatrist may terminate service if he provides ample notice to the patient so that the patient can obtain an appropriate substitute therapist. Depending on the resources in the community in which the patient and psychia-

---

ing to note that it is found highest in women between the ages of 40 and 70 and particularly prevalent in an outpatient population. This suggests that these are patients who have been on neuroleptics for long periods of time, perhaps with routine refilling of their prescriptions but without more careful attention to the possibilities of the development of this outcome. See Cain and Smith (1982) and Jeste and Wyatt (1981).

trist live, this period of required notice may be anywhere from a few days to several weeks.

3. The psychiatrist may go one step further and actually furnish the patient with another therapist who will either substitute during the period when the psychiatrist is not going to be available or who will possibly continue treating the patient.

4. If the psychiatrist decides that he can no longer treat the patient, he may discuss this with the patient and obtain his consent to withdraw from continuing to provide treatment to him. When this occurs it is unlikely that he would be held liable for abandonment in the event that the patient subsequently engages in injurious activity. Of course, all of this is under the assumption that the psychiatrist has properly evaluated the patient and determined that the patient is not so seriously mentally and emotionally disturbed that termination of treatment would be precluded.

5. There are situations, particularly with borderline patients, when the psychiatrist may need to use the termination of treatment as a way of truly getting the patient to engage in the treatment process. A patient may be totally uncooperative and refuse to comply with any of the therapist's recommendations for a plan of treatment. The therapist may virtually have no other option but to recommend termination of treatment. Again, it would be wise to provide alternative options to the patient, or, if possible, to obtain the patient's consent to the termination. Where the psychiatrist simply terminates on his own initiative and does not provide any of these alternative channels for the patient to be able to reenter into a treatment context, he may be justified in this approach, but his decision to terminate would be essentially at his own risk. If, for example, he misperceived the seriousness of the patient's problem and the patient is injured subsequent to the termination, it is not then inconceivable that he could be held liable for abandonment.

The fact that a psychiatrist "abandons" or fails to "follow up" on a patient does not, in itself, determine a successful malpractice action. It must also be shown that the patient was injured and that the injury was proximately caused by the abandonment (Epstein, 1979). This would include a requirement that the court determine that had the "abandonment" not occurred a satisfactory result would have been achieved for the patient.

Critical to the determination of abandonment is the presence of a physician–patient relationship. As with other kinds of malpractice actions, this is an element that must be established by the patient. There are situations where a psychiatrist may be involved with a patient and it may not be perceived as part of a physician–patient relationship (Waltz & Inbau, 1971). One example is when a psychiatrist is called in as a consultant to evaluate the patient and present the results to the treating physician. When he completes this task, the responsibility generally shifts to the primary physician to act on the recommendations of the consultant. Other examples would be where a psychiatrist is an agent of the court for the purposes of determining the competency of a patient to stand trial or the appropriateness of commitment proceedings (Holder, 1978). Similarly, if a psychiatrist is hired by a corporation to evaluate employees for the possibility of promotion, he or she does not generally enter a physician–patient relationship but is serving the ends of a third party, which usually does not create an obligation to continue treatment. Once he has completed the task for which he was employed by the primary physician, his obligations to the patient generally end.

WRONGFUL COMMITMENT

Psychiatrists involved in emergency treatment programs or primary care centers frequently express concerns over the possibilities of their being successfully sued for wrongful commitment. Whereas 20–30 years ago suits alleging wrongful commitment were among the most frequent affecting psychiatry (though suits in psychiatry generally were scarce), since the 1960s wrongful commitment has been a rare basis for malpractice action (Horan & Milligan, 1983). This is particularly interesting in light of the fact that since the late 1960s and early 1970s there have been major changes in the criteria for the commitment of patients to mental institutions (Stone, 1975). The *parens patriae* (state as guardian) basis for commitment in the pre-1960s, which included very broadly worded criteria such as the "need for care and treatment," or the patient's "own welfare," allowed for maximum psychiatric discretion and, arguably, protected psychiatrists against wrongful commitment actions. With the pendulum swinging in the direction of more objective criteria — dangerous to self and others, the presence of a serious mental disease or defect — the range of patients who could be committed has been narrowed to specific categories (*Lessard v. Schmidt*, 1974). One would have expected that this would have provided the courts with a better sense of whether negligence was involved in the wrongful commitment of a patient. But, in fact, this has not been the case, and there have been few, if any, successful cases in recent years dealing with wrongful commitment (Slaby, Lieb, & Tancredi, 1985).

The criteria for commitment seem to be slowly shifting back in the direction of including some *parens patriae* justification. Some states, for example, have included as a justification for commitment severe deterioration in functioning. Cases like *Addington v. Texas* (1979) in the late 1970s may be responsible for some of the liberalization of the justifications of commitment. In that case the U.S. Supreme Court stated that the evidentiary standard of proof, which in previous cases was "beyond a reasonable doubt" that a patient is likely to be dangerous to himself or others, would be met constitutionally with a less exacting test of clear and convincing evidence. Furthermore, Justice Berger made clear reference to the lack of certainty in psychiatric diagnosis, a lack that essentially prevents the adoption of a more stringent standard, thereby supporting, to some extent, the notion that psychiatrists should have more latitude in the criteria for determining commitment (*Addington v. Texas*, 1979).

In most cases that have been brought by patients alleging that they have been wrongfully committed to mental institutions, the courts seem to have come out in favor of psychiatrists (Horan & Milligan, 1983). These suits have been brought on a variety of theories, including malicious prosecution, false imprisonment, and defamation of character. The patients, in order to win such actions, must show that the psychiatrist deviated markedly from appropriate standards of care or did not fulfill the statutory requirements that would justify commitment. One of these requirements is that the psychiatrist actually physically examine the patient and not rely on a telephone call or on a family member's opinion. There have been successful cases that allege that the psychiatrist did not examine the patient, and where the patient has been able to establish that this has, in fact, occurred, successful claims for malpractice have ensued (Slovenko, 1981). Other cases that have been successful have alleged that the psychiatrist colluded with the family in having the patient committed, either for the benefit of the family or for the doctor's own benefit. Where fraud or other vested interests could be established, the patient usually won on the basis of wrongful commitment. Except for these rather extraordinary circumstances, if the psychiatrist follows the requirements of the statute and examines the patient and determines that he or she should be committed, the court would likely take the position that if an error could be established, it was one of judgment rather than of fact (Bromberg, 1983).

PSYCHOTHERAPY AND MALPRACTICE

For all the reasons that we have already discussed, it is difficult for a patient to win a malpractice action against a psychiatrist. With respect to psychotherapy those reasons are even more subtle. It is extremely burdensome to establish that psychotherapy was negligently administered to a patient. This is not to say that one could not theoretically conceive of the circumstances where psychotherapy may be negligently administered. For example, there are reasons to believe that there are iatrogenic (treatment-induced) adverse outcomes from therapy such as the inducing of depression, phobias, anxiety, psychosomatic reactions, perhaps even psychosis and, in some cases, suicide. But psychiatrists have been generally protected by the unique nature of the psychiatrist–patient relationship. As in all areas of medical malpractice, a good physician–patient relationship has been shown to be the best prophylactic against malpractice actions. In the psychotherapist–patient relationship, those elements of trust and affective closeness, including transference, are at their most intense, and, consequently, usually provide protection for a psychiatrist against a malpractice claim. In addition to these powerful reasons, it is very cumbersome to establish a nexus between what occurred in psychotherapy and an untoward outcome (Furrow, 1980). It may be possible, on examining the progress notes of a psychiatrist, to show that topics such as suicide loomed prominently during psychotherapeutic sessions or that other highly emotional topics such as sex were discussed frequently, but it would be most difficult to suggest that the psychotherapeutic hour dealing with these topics was in any way responsible for a patient's subsequent decision to overdose on antidepressants. Even if the suicidal act occurred almost immediately following the psychotherapeutic session, it would be hard to arrive at an agreement that there was a proximate cause relationship between what happened in the session and the actions of the patient. Finally, what makes it difficult for a plaintiff to win such malpractice actions is that it is also not clear, from a psychiatric standpoint, what constitutes negligence in psychotherapy (Horan & Milligan, 1983). The customary practice of psychotherapy is so broadly defined and accepted by the profession that almost anything is possible, save the accompaniment of an overt act, such as initiating sexual activity with the patient or resorting to inappropriate treatments that involve physical contact. There is a great diversity of philosophies and techniques involving psychotherapy that nearly preclude the establishment of a bright-line distinction between what is acceptable practice and what is negligent practice.

In the history of malpractice cases involving psychiatry, there has not been one decision reported of an American appellate court holding that the psychiatrist was responsible for negligent conduct of psychotherapy. The exceptions to this, as already discussed, are where psychotherapy is connected with an overt act such as sexual improprieties, where the combination of the two could be characterized as psychiatric malpractice. There have been some cases involving verbal interactions between physicians and patients where it could be established that the physician engaged in egregious misuse of verbal treatment, for example, using obscene or salacious speech during hypnosis (*Shea v. Board of Medical Examiners*, 1978). Except for those egregious deflections the courts have been virtually unable to conceptualize deviations from the customary standard of care. On the other hand, the future of psychiatric malpractice may not be so sparing of psychotherapeutic interactions. One could certainly speculate on three possible areas in psychotherapy where suits may arise. First, it may be possible, given the nature of the dialogue in a psychotherapeutic setting, to arrive at some notion of negligence where a patient leaves a session and commits suicide. It could certainly be argued that the psychiatrist treating the patient has an obligation to be sensitive to the nature of the stress that therapy creates and to the ability of that patient to absorb a certain level of discomfort. One could conceive of a situation where a young woman might be troubled about her sexual identity and the psychiatrist presses her hard on the nature of her sexual impulses. The patient may not have the emotional strength or support system to absorb that crisis, and consequently may resort to a suicide attempt or may seriously decompensate.

A second possibility may exist where it can be established that a psychiatrist became too involved in the personal activities of the patient. For example, a patient may be debating the possibility of getting married and the psychiatrist might take a strong directive position in this regard, say, influencing the patient toward an affirmative decision. If subsequently the patient is dissatisfied with that decision and ends up in a divorce with a significant economic and emotional loss, it is conceivable that the patient could bring a successful malpractice action against the psychiatrist for having taken such a directive approach to the problem. A third and likely possibility is where psychotherapy is used instead of more appropriate biological treatment of patients (Horan & Milligan, 1983). The argument of the psychiatrist might be that he comported with standards of care, certainly with those of other individuals who believe in psychoanalytically oriented psychotherapy, even though biologically oriented psychiatrists would question why a seriously depressed patient was not placed on antidepressants. Because there has been so much evidence in the literature of what can be achieved for seriously depressed patients through the use of antidepressants, courts may increasingly take the position that, even among those psychiatrists who do not believe in medication and prefer the use of verbal treatment, the refusal to provide antidepressants is a significant enough diversion from the main body of psychiatric knowledge to constitute malpractice.

RISK MANAGEMENT IN PSYCHIATRY

As a result of the medical malpractice crisis in the mid-1970s and the fact that well over 70 % of malpractice cases involve hospital treatment, hospitals developed risk-management programs. These programs usually consist of clinical nurses who are hired by the hospital to review the records involving the care of patients. Generally speaking, these nurses will respond to specific issues, for example, they will become involved when a discharged patient contacts a lawyer to bring on a malpractice action. On receiving a letter from a lawyer, a hospital will use its risk-management personnel to evaluate the charts involving that patient's care. The goals of risk management are much broader than simply reacting to patient dissatisfaction. The goals would include identifying and evaluating the frequency, as well as the severity, of risks in the hospital context that bring about financial loss through malpractice (Institute of Medicine, 1978). In addition, a risk-management program would be concerned with eliminating these risks or certainly reducing exposure to them by identifying some of the factors in the care of the patient that may be responsible for adverse outcomes. Many hospitals have begun to establish committees to assist in developing policy to alter medical practices in order to avoid damages.

Little has been done in this regard in the field of psychiatry. Certainly psychiatrists working in general hospitals or mental institutions could benefit from information delineating the risks of treatment to patients entering those institutions. Furthermore, a risk-management analysis of adverse psychiatric outcomes in institutions would provide important clinical information so that certain outcomes could be avoided. Psychiatrists working in private practice are unlikely to be in a position to hire consultants to examine the risks of the patients in their treatment programs. However, if psychiatrists are part of a health maintenance organization or a larger group, it may be economically advantageous to hire consultants to assist in risk reduction to patients. Risk-management programs have established the importance of maintaining proper records of the course of treatment, particularly where major changes have occurred in treatment or where medication is used. Inadequate records can often result in a successful suit against a clinician in a malpractice action.

ALTERNATIVE APPROACHES TO PSYCHIATRIC MALPRACTICE

Thus far in this discussion we have focused on the role of the tort system in psychiatric malpractice. We have pointed out that psychiatric malpractice is still a rather infrequent phenomenon but seems to be on the increase. The elements of malpractice, particularly the establishment of negligence and proximate cause, have made it very difficult for patients to win malpractice suits against psychiatrists. This may be changing in the future as psychiatry moves more and more in the direction of utilizing biological and physical modalities for the diagnosis and treatment of mental illnesses. Where psychotherapy, psychoanalysis, and other verbal therapies have been used, it has been very

difficult to establish a nexus between the actions of the therapist and subsequent injuries to patients.

The following discussion will examine some alternative approaches that have been proposed for dealing with medical malpractice. In part, the concern about alternative approaches has been inspired by the recognition that the tort system leaves a lot to be desired, both from the perspective of the physician and that of the patient (Institute of Medicine, 1978). A number of problems have been identified within the tort system. For one, exorbitant administrative costs associated with it have called into question the efficiency and effectiveness of tort law for dealing with redress of injuries to patients (Williams, 1984). Second, the tort system as it now exists results in haphazard compensation for injured patients (Havighurst, 1984). As we have already pointed out, it is difficult for patients to win in the courts because of the burden of establishing the elements of medical malpractice. A small percentage of those cases that reach the courts actually result in awards to injured patients. Third, it creates high psychic costs for all parties involved. It may take years for a malpractice case to be settled, during which time patients who are injured will receive no compensation for their injuries, and may have to rely on other resources. Physicians will also be kept engaged in a court process that may require significant time from their practice and may result in damaging publicity, which creates a serious stigma to their professional identity.

Finally, the tort system fosters certain perverse incentives, one of the most serious of which is defensive medicine (Havighurst, 1984). There has been no assessment of defensive medicine in psychiatry, and it is unlikely that the fear of malpractice suits is making any significant impact on psychiatric practice. This, again, however, may be changing with the increasing number of suits being brought on grounds of the development of tardive dyskinesias and other side effects from psychotropic medication. But in other areas of medicine, it has been established that defensive medicine practices can be very serious, and some studies have estimated that it creates an annual inflation of health care costs by as much as $3–6 billion (In a Review of Medical Malpractice, 1975). Most recently, the American Medical Association estimated defensive medicine practices may create as much as $15 billion a year of additional expense in health care (AMA Study Reports Sharp Increase in Malpractice Claims Against Physicians, 1983). The studies in the area of defensive medicine, unfortunately, have been inadequately designed to establish the extent of this practice (Tancredi & Barondess, 1978). To begin with, it is hard to differentiate those behaviors that have been induced by the malpractice system, which may be beneficial to patients as against those that are clearly destructive. It is also very difficult to understand the decision-making process of the physician when he or she orders, for example, a large number of psychiatric diagnostic tests. Some of those decisions may be influenced by consumer demand, others by his or her own perceived notions of what quality of care requires without giving any conscious consideration to malpractice as an incentive.

Over the past 8–10 years, efforts have been made to bolster the tort system in medical malpractice so that it functions more effectively. Some states have set ceilings on the amount of awards that a claimant can demand or receive in a successful action (Institute of Medicine, 1978; Department of HEW, 1973). These have been upheld in a few states and overruled elsewhere, where it has been claimed that setting a limit is arbitrary and, therefore, violates that state's constitution (Institute of Medicine, 1978). In some jurisdictions, laws have been enacted to impact on the awards patients receive by minimizing or eliminating collateral recovery to prevent overcompensation or double indemnity. Other states have actually modified the statute of limitations, decreasing the tolling time that would, on that ground alone, eliminate many malpractice actions (Institute of Medicine, 1978). None of these approaches seems to have resolved the problems posed by the tort system. On reflection, the general consensus seems to be that it has functioned inefficiently in achieving its main goals: the compensation of patients who are injured by the negligent actions of physicians and the creation of a system that should provide incentives for the prevention of injuries (Williams, 1984).

In the late 1970s, the Institute of Medicine of the National Academy of Sciences set up a committee to examine the malpractice situation in the United States. After deliberating for a few years, the committee published a report, "Beyond Malpractice: Compensation for Medical Injuries," in which it clearly defined what it considered to be the three major goals that should underlie a malpractice system (Institute of Medicine, 1978). The first of these would be the fair and equitable distribution of resources or compensation for those suffering losses associated with health care. The second goal would be efficiency in the distribution and availability of these resources to all injured patients. This would essentially be concerned with the administrative simplicity and minimization of costs of a system for patient redress. The third goal, which is very important, would be a compensation system for injured patients that functions to conserve resources by preventing injuries. Of these three main goals articulated by the committee, two seemed particularly important: widespread compensation for those injured in the medical care system and the avoidance of injuries.

The various approaches to handling the medical malpractice system can be conceptualized as fitting along a spectrum that, on one end, would be the tort or fault system and, on the extreme other end, a system of social insurance. The tort or fault system would include some administrative alternatives to courts, such as arbitration and screening panels. These alternatives have already been implemented in many jurisdictions. With regard to screening panels, the general consensus is that they have simply added to the administrative bureaucracy rather than actually making that bureaucracy more effective or efficient (Mediation Isn't Cure, 1980). For the most part, such panels do not have the power to come to a final adjudication on the merits of the action. Hence, a patient could still continue to go through the tort system in spite of a recommendation by a screening panel that the cause of action lacks sufficient merit. Arbitration has been shown to make some difference in the time that it takes to bring an action to resolution, but the long-term effectiveness of arbitration remains somewhat questionable (Ladimer, Solomon, & Mulvihil, 1981). In the middle of this system, which includes the two poles of fault and total no-fault (the latter of which represents social insurance), would be a system that is based on specified events. In short, this would be a third alternative involving the identification of certain outcomes of medical care that would be perceived by professionals as avoidable and at the same time acceptable for automatic compensation when they occur in the treatment of a patient (American Bar Association Commission on Medical Professional Liability, 1979).

We have already dealt with one end of this spectrum, which is the tort system, and have shown the conceptual problems involved with it. Some of the benefits, however, have not been articulated. These benefits seem to be mostly derived from the substantive due process rights of individuals who gain access to courts. Because of rules on hearsay and other evidentiary rules, the tort system does control prejudicial or unreliable testimony through its formal rules of evidence (Williams, 1984). This does not apply to alternative systems such as social insurance or a system based on specified events, but it also does not apply strongly to arbitration or screening panels. The traditional tort system can also claim that it maintains impartiality, which is created by judges and juries on individual case-by-case decisions. What it does not do effectively is achieve its goals of compensating injured patients and preventing injuries.

Before examining the alternatives of social insurance, which essentially is automatic compensation for injury, and specified events, it is important to discuss what little we know about the nature of medical injuries, especially as they apply to hospitals and other treatment programs. Then we will return to examining the implications of a social insurance system versus a specified event system as these would affect psychiatric malpractice.

To begin with, the area of medical injuries deserves serious investigation. It is generally felt that in the medical treatment of patients there are far more injuries occurring than have ever surfaced in the tort system, which requires the establishment of negligence (Furrow, 1981). Most of the studies that have attempted to determine the incidence and prevalence of medical injuries have focused on injuries that occur in hospitals. This has been done for the practical reason that the environment is easier to control, thus it is easier to arrive at some meaningful data. In addition, the vast majority of malpractice cases involve hospital-based injuries. No such studies of medical injuries have been conducted in the area of psychiatry, particularly in the hospital treatment of psychiatrically disturbed patients. There have been various studies conducted dealing with medical injuries generally, and these will be discussed shortly. The relevance of this information to psychiatry is that it strongly suggests that there is a wide universe of adverse outcomes likely in the hospital care of psychiatric patients. These outcomes, referred to as medical or psychiatric injuries, represent three possible classes of events. First, they may be outcomes that result from behaviors on the part of the psychiatrist that would fit the definition of negligence. Second, they may be outcomes that represent iatrogenesis, in which case they could be either negligently induced or unavoidable, given the trade-off deci-

sions that must be made when treatment is administered. Third, these medical injuries may be simply unavoidable, that is, they may be more representative of problems of life or the condition of the patient that exists when he enters the psychiatric hospital system. Although no studies have been conducted in psychiatry, a great deal of information on the potential categories of adverse outcomes can be gleaned by examining the empirical literature involving medical injuries generally.

There are some very significant studies involving medical injuries. There was a study that was conducted in the mid-1970s by the California Medical Association-California Hospital Association (1977), which involved the review of 21,000 hospital records. Three physician–lawyers were enlisted to examine the records for the purpose of determining the incidence of medically related injuries. They discovered that the rate of injury was approximately 4.65% for all hospital admissions. Approximately .8% of the records indicated clear evidence of provider liability. This amounted to nearly 1,155 events, which, if one applied prevailing legal principles, could have justifiably become successful malpractice actions against health care providers. Other studies were conducted around the same time with similar, and perhaps higher, results of the incidence of medically related disabilities (Pocincki, Dogger, & Schwartz, 1974).

Two recent studies have become particularly important in supporting the notion that medical errors are widespread in the hospital system. The first of these studies involved 815 patients who were monitored over a 5-month period with regard to the general medical services at a university hospital (Steel, Gertman, Crescenzi, & Anderson, 1981). Of these patients 290 (approximately 36%) suffered one or more iatrogenic illnesses, 76 (approximately 9%) suffered major complications, and 15 patients actually died during the course of the study. The mortality rate was approximately 2% of all patients, or approximately 5% of all of those who suffered any complications. Although not the only reason for the death of these patients, iatrogenic illness was considered to be a contributing cause.

The second study involved surveying the avoidable injuries that seemed to be secondary to colonic surgery (Couch, Tilney, Rayner, & Moore, 1981). In this study, 56 types of errors were delineated, of which 31 were considered to be related to unnecessary or negligent surgery. For the patient, the consequences of these adverse outcomes were serious. Patients who suffered injuries had 10 times the mortality in contrast to those patients who underwent colonic surgery and had no complications. The authors also determined that the length of hospitalization of those who were injured, as compared to those who were not, was approximately 4 times as long, and the overall average cost for treatment of the injured patients was 7 times that of the cost for the uncomplicated cases. The conclusion of this study was that there are many severe iatrogenic events in colonic surgery that can be associated with errors in physician judgment. The authors argue that with improved data collection and improved communication among those involved on the surgical team or those in any way associated with the operation, many of these errors of judgment can be rectified.

The importance of these studies, however poorly constructed methodologically, is that they address the fact that not only does the tort system, which is the prevailing system in the United States, not seem to be preventing injuries that would make it successful according to its own criteria, but it seems to be having minimal impact on medical injuries that are occurring in hospitals generally. Furthermore, these studies establish that medical injuries, particularly iatrogenically induced injuries, are far more prevalent than anybody considered possible in the treatment system (Steel, 1984). The tort system has clearly not been effective in avoiding these untoward outcomes.

One approach that has been suggested for resolving the inefficiencies of the tort system, an approach that would also consider the broad scope of medical injuries that occur in medical practice, would be a social insurance system (Institute of Medicine, 1978). A variant of that might be a national health insurance system. It would certainly assure that individuals who are injured will be compensated to the extent of medical care expenses and loss of wages. Such a system would meet the important goals of widespread compensation to injured patients and would absorb the broader, more pervasive scope of those individuals who are injured in health care generally, but who may find it virtually impossible to establish provider negligence so as to succeed in a malpractice action. The major problem with such a social insurance system, unfortunately, is that there would be little incentive for injury avoidance. If patients are automatically compensated for any injury, then it becomes virtually impossible to identify provider negligence or behavior that, if

corrected, would result in injury avoidance. All injuries would be compensated, so virtually none would be delineated as potentially avoidable or as requiring that modifications be made in the delivery of health services. A social insurance system would, however, have the benefit of ameliorating the perverse incentives that now exist in the tort system. There would be virtually minimal reason for defensive medical practices. Such practices are not only problematic because they result in an inflation of the costs of health care but because they create many more diagnostic tests than may be necessary for determining the best treatment of a patient's condition and, in the process, create additional risks. These diagnostic tests may involve invasive procedures such as angiography or the use of radio isotopes for determining blood flow or the presence of lesions. With invasive procedures there is always a potential risk of serious injuries to patients.

The third alternative, which is a compromise between the tort system that is based totally on the fault of the individual provider and a social insurance system which obviates any need for fault-finding, would be a specific events system (Institute of Medicine, 1978). Such a system would require the listing of designated compensable events (DCEs), that is, those events which, if they occur, would result in automatic compensation to patients. In psychiatry, for example, it may be that a group of psychiatrists would be willing to conceptualize such a listing to include tardive dyskinesias, severe dystonias, or suicide while in the hospital, to list a few. This listing of course would be subject to continuous updating as new technologies emerge and enter into the practice of psychiatry, technologies that unfortunately offer the opportunity for potential injuries and risks to patients. To some extent a system based on designated compensable events would be a no-fault system (Havighurst & Tancredi, 1973). Determination as to whether items would be listed on the DCE system would be based on more than just a relative avoidability of the untoward outcome. Relative avoidability would be an important factor but this would be conceptualized in statistical terms, not in terms of avoidability in any one specific case. A group of psychiatrists acting consensually may determine that in many cases it may be virtually impossible to prevent tardive dyskinesias. However, when taken in the statistical sense, the group may determine that tardive dyskinesias is relatively avoidable. That is to say that if certain techniques were instituted, such as closer follow up of the patient, including periodic neurologic examinations and reassessments of the amount and duration of the medication that is provided, it may be possible to avoid a certain percentage of cases of tardive dyskinesias (Jeste & Wyatt, 1982). Relative avoidability would include more than just preventing the outcomes, it would also include the concept of being able to intervene early enough in treating the first manifestations of an untoward outcome so as to avoid the largest proportion of medical care expenses and loss of wages that would result from the full-blown adverse event. Another factor that might go into establishing DCEs in psychiatry would be the administrative simplicity of including a certain outcome (Havighurst & Tancredi, 1973). It could be argued that as tardive dyskinesias becomes increasingly the object for malpractice suits, it would be easier to have the patient automatically compensated than to go through the administrative and transactional costs of the tort system. Furthermore, by listing tardive dyskinesias on a listing of untoward outcomes, it would create incentives in the direction of finding new ways to avoid the undesirable outcome.

The third factor, which is especially important in determining this listing, would be the impact of listing the event on quality of psychiatric care (Stevens, 1981). Returning to the example of tardive dyskinesia, it could be claimed that placing this condition on the list for automatic compensation may enhance the quality of care. This will result because it would create incentives for providers to alter their behaviors to minimize the use of medications, to be more vigilant in determining when to terminate the use of neuroleptics, and finally, to be more careful about using them in borderline cases, where arguably other tranquilizers or other medications could be used in lieu of neuroleptics (Wettstein, 1983). The issue that remains unresolved would be the equivalent opposite impact of including tardive dyskinesias on such a listing (Calabresi, 1970). The question would be: To what extent would such an inclusion alter the behavior of the psychiatrist in ways that may be more damaging to patients? Would incentives be created so that psychiatrists would be disinclined to use neuroleptics where they would be necessary for the care of seriously disturbed and psychotic patients, and instead use other kinds of medications that may produce untoward outcomes of equal or more serious impact?

The advantages of a DCE system are that it combines elements of the fault system because it includes some provider responsibility in the notion of relative avoidability, and, at the same time, combines elements of the no-fault system in that it creates a system of automatic compensation in all cases without an individual case-by-case determination of responsibility (American Bar Association Commission on Medical Professional Liability, 1979). Thus constructed, it creates pressure through economic incentives on the nature of provider behavior so as to hopefully improve the quality of outcomes. But at the same time, the no-fault component of a DCE system avoids such behaviors as defensive medicine, impediments to the widespread compensation of injured patients, and serious delay in providing compensation for those who need it to cover related expenses.

The conceptually difficult part of this no-fault approach has been the question of the feasibility of defining such events. The American Bar Association (1977) undertook a study to establish the feasibility of defining compensable events in medicine. Two specialties of medicine were used in this study, orthopedic and general surgery, both of which are among the most frequently sued medical specialties. Events were identified in a preliminary listing from the National Association of Insurance Commissioner's study in the mid-1970s, which itemized over 90% of the claims that were filed during a 2–3-year period and provided a large number of adverse outcomes. The most economically prominent of these constituted the tentative listing that was distributed to panels of orthopedic surgeons and general surgeons who then agreed upon a certain number as being sufficiently avoidable and of meeting the other criteria of easy detectability and administrative simplicity. No such examination of psychiatric injuries has yet occurred, though it would be quite simple to apply this methodology to the area of psychiatry.

The anatomy of a designated compensable event is complex. It consists of three principle elements that relate in various ways so as to narrow or widen the scope of those adverse outcomes that should be incorporated in any listing of DCEs. The first critical element in understanding a DCE that would apply to psychiatry is the nature of psychiatric intervention. For the most part, this would be described as an affirmative act, that is, that a psychiatrist or therapist has intervened in the patient's condition either through a diagnostic or therapeutic procedure. The latter would include not only the administration of some physical treatment but also medications. An example of an affirmative act in psychiatry would be the administration of electroshock treatment that resulted in an injury, such as organic changes in the patient. Negative acts or acts of omission should also be considered because they are clearly present in the psychiatric treatment of patients (American Bar Association Commission on Medical Professional Liability, 1979). However, they are far more problematic to prescind and to constitute as a DCE. By a negative act we mean some diagnostic or treatment measure that, although appropriate, is omitted, resulting in an injury to the patient. An illustration of this would be where a patient comes into a mental institution and presents symptoms that border between something that could be functional or organic in nature. On the basis of the ambiguous symptoms, it may be appropriate at some point to employ Computerized Axial Tomography (CT Scan) to rule out the presence of a lesion of the temporal lobe. This diagnostic test is, however, not ordered even though it would be essential for a definitive diagnosis. As a result, the patient is diagnosed clinically as suffering from schizophrenia and treated accordingly. A patient with a lesion of the temporal lobe may present with fugue states that are not unlike certain forms of schizophrenic reactions. Because of the clinical diagnosis that was arrived at without the use of this important diagnostic tool, the patient is treated with antipsychotic medications. These may enhance the possibility of seizure, which could be quite detrimental to a patient who suffers from an organic disturbance. Where an injury occurs, there would be a strong case for establishing negligence on the basis that all necessary diagnostic tests had not been conducted. The patient, therefore, would likely succeed in an action in tort for this omission. But it may be very difficult in conceptualizing a DCE that could articulate omissions that are narrow enough and specific enough in focus to avoid the inclusion of other events that would not be appropriate for coverage as a DCE. In most cases of psychiatric treatment, it would be very difficult to establish that an omission has occurred or that a particular omission has a direct causative effect, even though this notion of causation is statistically determined in establishing DCEs or the evolution of an adverse outcome.

In the research that was done in the late 1970s to establish the feasibility of a listing of DCEs, the National Association of Insurance Commissioners' study of closed claims does not include many illustrations of negative acts or acts of omission. It certainly would be a failure of the system to ignore the importance of the concept of omission; ultimately, this must be included as part of the definition of psychiatric intervention. This would require that we gain sophistication regarding particular treatments for specific ailments or diseases in psychiatry. Once this occurs, it will be possible to begin to demarcate psychiatric interventions that have not occurred, which have resulted in relatively specific outcomes that could be appropriately conceptualized in a listing of DCEs. Obviously, for a listing of DCEs to be complete in any conceptual way, and thereby effective as a method of compensation and quality assurance, it would have to include some notion of negative acts to provide for maximum flexibility in this application.

The second critical element in understanding a designated compensable event in psychiatry would be an examination of the nature of the physiological mechanism. Here, we are dealing with what has occurred in the psychiatric intervention that has led to the injury that the patient experiences (American Bar Association Commission on Medical Professional Liability, 1979). By physiological mechanism we mean that which happens biologically or physiologically that creates the patient's disability. For instance, a patient enters a hospital with severe anxiety, and it is decided that the appropriate way to handle this is to inject the patient with a minor tranquilizer. Valium, one of the most frequently used minor tranquilizers, is found not to be effective in treating this patient's acute reaction, so the psychiatrist decides to use an injectable form of a phenothiazine. The patient fits into that rare category of patients who react with the development of a blood dyscrasia from the injectable major tranquilizer. Disability, therefore, is the development of the outcome of the blood dyscrasia, which may be severe weakness, susceptibility to infections, or immunological inadequacy. The physiological mechanism is the process of the development of the blood dyscrasia. The procedure or the psychiatric intervention, as we have already pointed out, was the injection of the major tranquilizer.

The third element important for conceptualizing DCEs is the disability or injury (American Bar Association Commission on Medical Professional Liability, 1979). This would essentially refer to the adverse outcome that is the final result of the medical intervention and of the ensuing biological process.

There are a few features of disability that would be important in considering a compensation system for psychiatric adverse outcomes. The first important feature would be the nature of the abnormality. This would essentially deal with the type of injury or damage that has resulted from the psychiatric treatment. An example of such damage might be injury to an organ such as the brain where certain medications are used or electroshock applied. Another abnormality might be fractures of the long bones as a reaction to insulin convulsive therapy. A third abnormality might be the development of a tardive dyskinesia.

The second important feature of the disability would be its severity. This is important because, in a compensation system, the extent of economic redress would be based on the severity of the injury, be it temporary or permanent. For example, a patient, who develops a severe hypotensive reaction from an antidepressant, falls on the floor of a psychiatric ward, bangs his head against the table, and develops motoric weakness on the left side, may sustain a permanent disability. Severity also would refer to the degree of impairment or functional loss. In the case of the brain-damaged patient who has fallen on the floor, the injury would be of major severity and consequent serious functional loss.

The importance of conceptualizing the elements of a DCE rests on the fact that the way the event is characterized would either cause a narrowing or a broadening of what injuries are to be included, if terms from each of these three categories are used in varying degrees of intensity. For example, it may be that a group of psychiatrists would be willing to accept the development of tardive dyskinesia following the administration of a major tranquilizer for depression. Mellaril, a phenothiazine, has been believed to have antidepressant qualities. Obviously, as a major tranquilizer, it also possesses the potentialities (though some argue less than others) of causing tardive dyskinesia. Where Mellaril is given for the purposes of treating a depressed patient, the psychiatrist might be willing to conceptualize the subsequent development of tardive dyskinesia as highly avoidable, particularly since other antidepressant agents exist which do not have the likelihood of causing this condition. If the DCE system incorporates as an item on its listing the development of tardive dyskinesia, then all cases where that condition occurs (many of which may be relatively unavoidable given the psychiatric exigencies of treating psychotic patients) would be included

for automatic compensation. Where the definition of the injury is linked with a specific physiological process or a specific type of medical intervention, it becomes narrowed in its scope and consequently potentially more acceptable as an outcome for automatic compensation, once it can be demonstrated that statistically it is relatively highly avoidable (Kane & Smith, 1982).

The integration of the features of psychiatric intervention, physiological mechanism, and disability is essential in the development of these outcomes. It is that integration that provides for that method of calibration, not only horizontally of the number of DCEs, but of the narrowness and sharpness of the scope of those outcomes to be included on a listing. Hence in this discussion the emphasis has been on demonstrating that anatomically such DCEs or specific outcomes must be carefully analyzed along these three important gradients. Once these gradients are applied to a range of adverse outcomes in psychiatry, then a fourth principle can be introduced that would assure some limitation on the nature of outcomes that are compensated. That fourth principle would be some notion of the minimum threshold of significance of the impact of the patient's injury to justify its inclusion in a listing for automatic compensation. If one is dealing specifically with a system that although cannot be complete for all adverse outcomes in psychiatry, is geared principally to culling out those that would be most economically prominent and most likely to lead to enhancement in the quality of care by affecting the behavior of psychiatrists, then many events that result in little economic loss to patients should be excluded from a final list. One reason for this would be that the existing medical insurance of that patient would probably absorb the additional necessary treatment created by a minor injury.

It must be noted that the application of no-fault to the medical care system is not a new concept. It was first articulated in a law review article published by the late Professor Albert Ehrenzweig (1964) in the early 1960s. He conceptualized a system whereby patients would receive compensation for all untoward events that occur during the course of their hospital care. In so structuring the system, he explicitly excluded from consideration those outcomes that may be referable to the disease process that brought the patient to the hospital to begin with. However, he did not define the nature of the accidents or the adverse outcomes that should be compensated. He provided no guidelines for making distinctions between the regular risks of life, including the nature of the disease process, and those that may be more referable to the treatment. But this has been an important paper because it introduced the concept of no-fault for the first time as a consideration for the health care system.

In the early 1970s two no-fault proposals emerged that attempted to address some of the pitfalls of the Ehrenzweig system. The first of these was referred to as elective no-fault and was developed by Professor Jeffrey O'Connell (1985). According to this system, health care providers, be they physicians or hospitals, are given the discretion to decide which adverse outcomes they would be willing to have automatically compensated by insurance policies. The problem with this program is that it would not result in uniformity among various providers of health care, and, consequently, would not provide a systematic way of assessing the individual experiences of providers to get at critical information that would be helpful for risk avoidance. According to the elective no-fault system, those events that are not provided by the physician would be subject to the regular tort system.

Recently Professor O'Connell (1985) designed a modification of this proposal, which has been incorporated in the Moore–Gephardt strategy (a bill currently before the U.S. Congress). This system would utilize the private contract as a way of creating limitations on the current malpractice system. Essentially, when the patient becomes aware of an injury that may be due to treatment from a health care provider, the strategy would allow the provider to tender an offer to cover the patient's net economic losses. This offer would last for anywhere from 60 to 90 days and, should the patient elect to accept the tender, he would enter into a contract with the health care provider that would then foreclose a law suit for the medical injuries. It has been suggested that the main advantages of this system are that the patient would be certain of compensation if he accepts the tender. He would not have to wait for a long period of time, often years, to receive any compensation for his injuries, and would not have to face the uncertainty of waiting for a court's decision. For the provider, it would eliminate the expenses of the tort system and allow for ready redress so as to preclude wastage of time and the stigma that applies to malpractice trials.

The second alternative approach to no-fault would be the medical adversity insurance system

(Havighurst & Tancredi, 1973). This would rely on the outlining of DCEs, which would be agreed upon by physicians in their various specialties. The insurance policies of the health care provider would automatically compensate patients when they are injured with an adverse outcome that fits into that already listed in the DCE system. For those events that have not been listed, the patient still has the option of going through the tort system to establish that medical malpractice has occurred. The advantages of the medical adversity insurance system is that it provides uniformity across the specialties which allows for experience rating of the premiums of physicians and other providers. If a health care provider has a larger number of adverse events automatically compensated for than other providers in that specialty, the insurance policy premiums could be raised to create economic incentives against the practicing physician. Obviously, if such claims persist, professional peer review groups can be constructed to examine the claims record against various health care providers and possibly use unfavorable review findings to coerce the physician to return to school or perhaps to suspend licensing privileges.

In psychiatry, for example, the DCE system could be linked with the American Psychiatric Association or local medical societies so that it creates not only an economic bite in the direction of altering provider behavior, but also the possibilities of peer review pressures. This system would be put into place to cull out from general medical malpractice injuries a large number that would be automatically handled through medical adversity insurance. Administrative and transactional costs would be minimized, yet a system would be implemented that allows for widespread compensation and provides incentives in the direction of injury avoidance. The other advantage of this designated compensable event system is that it can be calibrated so as to meet the economic exigencies of a compensation system. Hence, if too many injuries are being compensated through the medical adversity insurance system, resulting in a strain on the economics of a compensation program, then one could eliminate some of the injuries for automatic compensation and let them continue to be dealt with through the tort process (Institute of Medicine, 1978).

The medical adversity insurance system, as originally conceived, relied on a compulsory or mandatory no-fault approach. The ideal system would be one where every health care provider would be required to resort to DCEs when injuries occur. Disclosure requirements would be present, perhaps statutorily defined, and patients would be automatically compensated where injured. Furthermore, a mandatory system allows for the most efficient approach to quality assurance because all physicians would be vulnerable to assessment in terms of their own individual claims of adverse events. If this ideal system is not possible at the present time, an alternative system would be the use of contract as a method for instituting a similar program (Epstein, 1979). Accordingly, such an approach would be in keeping with other developments in the health care system, such as the importance of shoring up the physician–patient relationship. A psychiatrist could enter into a negotiation with a patient that, in the event of an adverse outcome, his premiums would cover the economic losses for the patient. This would allow the patient to have some choice in either selecting or rejecting a system of automatic compensation. Also, the advantage of the contract approach is that it reaffirms the importance of the dialogue between the physician and the patient, and the extent to which the patient is given increasing power in decisions, not only regarding the way he will be treated in the health system but also regarding the method that will be provided for compensating injuries that might occur (Havighurst, 1984).

One of the major criticisms of the application of a no-fault system in medical malpractice, especially one based on designated compensable events, is that it would create an economic strain on the health care system. There is some basis to the argument that such a system would expand considerably the number of adverse outcomes that would result in compensation to patients (Institute of Medicine, 1978). At the present time, as we have already described in the earlier discussion on medical injuries, significantly more injuries occur in the hospital than ever get handled through the tort system for medical malpractice actions. Many of these injuries would not succeed in the courtroom because it would be difficult, if not impossible, to establish that the physician or health care provider actually engaged in malpractice based on principles of negligence. But some of those medical outcomes that would be adversive to the patient would also succeed through the fault system for compensation. However, patients are often unaware of these injuries, or they may be relatively trivial economically, or the patient may

be locked into a good, if not protective, psychiatrist–patient relationship, so that he does not desire to bring a malpractice action.

Although the automatic compensation of those injured under a DCE system would be limited to economic loss with some fraction of the money for pain and suffering, some concern has been expressed that, in the aggregate, medical injuries would require larger amounts of money to be channeled through the malpractice insurance system (Havighurst, 1975). Though this may be true, one cannot ignore the fact that these costs are being absorbed in any event by someone in society. A large part of the patient population in this country is covered by some insurance policy — employment-covered insurance, Medicaid, Medicare, and so on. Second, even if the patient is not covered by any insurance policy, including disability insurance, someone is still absorbing the costs incurred by the medical injury, most likely the patient himself (Havighurst & Tancredi, 1973).

In addition to the fact that the overall societal costs of a no-fault system is probably not greater than the combination of the existing tort system and other social insurance programs, the no-fault system offers an opportunity to use a mechanism of financing compensation for medical injuries as a way of creating maximum incentives for improvement of health care. If we apply Professor Guido Calabresi's (1970) notions, the maximum deterrent effect would be created by designating the provider of health care (the physician or health care institution) as the risk-bearer because he is in the best position (lowest cost avoider) of either directly avoiding the untoward outcomes from medical intervention or creating the means for developing information that would ultimately decrease the incidence of untoward outcomes. The health care provider, therefore, as the lowest cost avoider, would be in the best position to positively affect the universe of accidents that occur in the health care system. Therefore, though it would appear that the costs of a medical compensation system would be considerably increased by a specific event system, if one considers the existing distribution of costs for medical injuries and the potential quality-enhancing benefits of such a system, the overall costs would be significantly less than the existing tort system. An additional feature that would impact positively on the cost of the system would be the elimination of collateral sources that also compensate injured patients. This would not only result in reducing double indemnification, but could be structured so that the insurer's malpractice policy would be obligated to compensate other insurance programs covering the injured patient. Therefore, the provider's policy would absorb the maximum, if not the full, economic impact of the designated compensable event. This would have both the advantages of adding an additional cost-saving feature and of empowering the incentives for the provider to enhance the quality of care.

There is another wrinkle to the social-cost problem associated with the designated compensable event system that deserves attention. In an earlier discussion, it was argued that the tort system has had a weak effect on one of the most important objectives of compensation—injury avoidance. The DCE system offers the opportunity of improving, in the long term, the incidence and prevalence of medical injuries. The history of health care over the last 30 years has demonstrated that new technologies are being developed and diffused into medical practice at an ever-increasing rate. The DCE system is sufficiently flexible so that information on the risks associated with newly developed technologies can be incorporated into the designated compensable event listing. In spite of the accelerating problems of medical malpractice, there has been little attention directed to developing a taxonomy of adverse outcomes in medical care (Havighurst & Tancredi, 1973). Instead, the thrust of medical research activity has been focused on improving diagnostic and treatment methods. A system that is predicated on designated compensable events offers the opportunity for the first time of developing a classification of adverse outcomes. This listing could provide incentives for initiating medical research on injury avoidance which, over time, should have a major economic impact in the operation of a compensation system (American Bar Association Commission on Medical Professional Liability, 1979).

CONCLUSION

Several important concepts have been treated in this discussion of medical malpractice that extend beyond the simple structural features of a malpractice system. The first and possibly foremost of these is that medical malpractice, when applied to psychiatry, forces us to analyze the basis of the physician–patient relationship. Earlier, this chapter discussed the three competing paradigms for explicating the central nature of that relationship. The first of these was the covenant, which appears to be the most fitting model for comprehending the psychiatrist–patient relationship. The very definition of covenant includes a dynamic interactionism that is both synchronic and diachronic and that coincides with the fundamental elements of interaction in the psychotherapeutic process. The second model, the contract, is distinguishable from the covenant primarily because the contract is a static instrument that fixes the responsibilities and duties of a relationship at one point in time for the duration of the association. As a result, it fails to reflect the dynamics that dominate the psychotherapeutic process. In contrast to both the contract and covenant, the tort paradigm does not attempt to elucidate the nature of the relationship. It is concerned only with the undesirable consequences that flow from the interaction of two or more individuals. It is not a paradigm in the strict sense; it is instead a mechanism for returning those who are injured by accident to the whole position.

Besides the economic and quality-of-care reasons for questioning the effectiveness and appropriateness of the tort system in handling psychiatric malpractice, negligence seems utterly inappropriate as a measuring device to be applied to psychotherapy. It is virtually impossible, perhaps with the exception of the most egregious of circumstances, to establish what is negligent conduct. The tort system creates a burden on the profession through its definition of negligence, which the profession can often fail to meet. For example, as we have seen in our discussion of psychiatric malpractice cases, an increasing number of cases resulting in very high awards are concerned with the complex problems of prediction of dangerousness. In spite of the fact that many studies have been conducted that establish the difficulties that psychiatrists and other behavioral scientists have in the prediction of dangerousness, the tort law is holding these professionals responsible for failing to warn potential victims of their patient's dangerousness and for "negligently" discharging patients who then go out and harm others. Based on what we know scientifically of the profession's capacity to predict or avoid these injuries in any one situation, it seems clear that the tort system is more responsive to public and societal needs than it is to the realities of what psychiatrists can and cannot do.

The contract and covenant in various ways offer an opportunity not only to restructure the nature of the compensation system for injured patients but to be in alignment with the actual process of psychiatric intervention in the care of patients (Alexander & Szasz, 1973). None of these approaches, however, seems to be sufficient in itself. In the restructuring of a compensation system, adverse outcomes in psychiatry will necessarily involve all three of these approaches in varying degrees. Because it most precisely defines the process of psychiatric treatments, the covenant as a model should be the dominant approach to handling infractions in the psychiatrist–patient relationship. On the other hand, as we have already discussed, this model relies on the integrity of a bonding over time and therefore provides little in the way of criteria for external assessment when it diverts from its initial goal. This is not to say that certain kinds of actions in the context of that covenant could not be selected as evidencing a breakdown of the initial transaction between the patient and the psychiatrist, but the conceptual difficulty occurs in the fact that even the infliction of pain or harm on the patient may be consistent with the overarching intention of the covenant. Nonetheless, because it is such an important model for enhancing the benefits that are to be derived by all parties in the psychotherapeutic relationship, it must be given preference as the primary model of identification of that relationship, even in terms of the establishment of untoward consequences. The limitations of the covenant and its failure to establish objectively defined criteria, can be resolved by supplementing it with the contract and intentional tort for specific purposes.

The way in which this new mosaic model would operate would be as follows. The covenant would predominate with regard to the outlining of the affirmative features of the psychotherapeutic process. As it is embedded in broad social values, it creates the framework, the healing process of psychiatric intervention. The contract seems to be most appropriate as the "instrument" to be used by the parties to negotiate what compensation mechanism should be employed when an untoward outcome occurs. The psychiatrist and patient can negotiate on the acceptance of specific outcomes as automatically compensable. This allows for freedom of choice among the parties. The patient, for example, may wish to have the adverse effects of psychotropic medications be covered under an automatic compensation system. Other events which have been selected by a con-

sensus of psychiatrists as appropriate compensable outcomes may also be the object of negotiation by both the patient and the psychiatrist. Once the contract has been agreed upon, if one of the parties ignores its terms, the aggrieved party would then have an action according to contract principles without any need to resort to the inefficient tort system.

Tort law would still have a role in this new relationship between the psychiatrist and patient. Its role, however, would be limited to a form of intentional tort that would be consistent with maintaining the dignity of the covenant between the parties. The nature of this intentional tort would be that of infliction of emotional and mental harm in the event that the patient is psychologically broken down through the malicious and intentional acts of the therapist. The advantage of an intentional tort of this nature is that it averts all of the difficulties associated with defining standards of care and negligence. In addition, punitive damages are most readily associated with intentional tort where the infraction has a dignitary base. As the tort system has emerged in recent times it has been distorted in its objectives to the extent that the goal of compensation seems to dominate in many situations, even over the attribution of professional responsibility. Intentional tort would be directed specifically at professional responsibility for highly unacceptable conduct.

The hybrid arrangement constituted by elements of covenant, contract, and intentional tort facilitates the implementation of a creative alternative to the existing malpractice system. The no-fault system based on specific events allows for maximum flexibility to the extent that a patient may decide that it is not necessary to have all adverse outcomes automatically covered for compensation. He may be willing to take risks along the lines of the contractual portion of his relationship with the therapist but, at the same time, demand that the covenant maintain the higher order of objectives consistent with the psychiatric treatment that is being provided. In the event that either party refuses to accommodate to the negotiations around a DCE system, the injured party can choose to continue with the existing negligence system. An important side benefit of the DCE system includes experience-rated premiums on the incidence and prevalence of DCEs claimed against individual psychiatrists. This provides a method for quality control of psychiatric practice. Insurers would have statistical information available to assess in broad terms the performance of an individual provider or health care institution. This information could ultimately become very important for informing the consumer of the DCE incidence of individual practitioners with regard to adverse outcomes in their practice.

Because of the social and economic developments in medical care generally, not simply the increasing incidents and prevalence of psychiatric malpractice, there is a critical need for constructing alternative models for understanding the psychiatrist–patient relationship. This discussion, therefore, has dealt not only with traditional categories of injuries in psychiatry that are the subjects of malpractice actions, but it has also attempted to look at ways whereby adverse outcomes can be more appropriately handled so as to create a system that maximizes injury avoidance while it recognizes the losses that are being incurred by patients. The statistical information surrounding psychiatric malpractice still suggests that it is among the least vulnerable specialties in terms of frequency of malpractice actions. To some extent this information is deceiving because, based on the incremental changes that have occurred over the past 3–4 years, it is apparent that psychiatric malpractice is becoming increasingly problematic to the profession. The awards have been getting decidedly larger, many have reached into the millions of dollars, and certain types of actions are becoming subjects of frequent suits. This chapter is an attempt to design an approach for dealing with these problems before they reach crisis levels in psychiatry. This approach has relied on a more creative restructuring of the essential elements dealing with the rights of patients and on what actually occurs in the psychiatric treatment process.

REFERENCES

Adams, E.K., & Zuckerman, S. (1984). Variation in the growth and incidence of medical malpractice claims. *Journal of Health, Policy and Law, 9*, 475–488.

Adams v. State, 71 Wash. 2d 414, 429 P 2d (1967).

Addington v. Texas, 99 S. Ct. Rptr. 1804 (1979).

Again, the malpractice crunch. (Feb. 4, 1975). *New York Times*, A18, col. 1–2.

Aiken v. Clary, 396 S.W. 2d 668 (1965).

Alexander, G.J., & Szasz, T.S. (1973). From contract to status via psychiatry. *Santa Clara Lawyer, 13*, 537–559.

AMA Special Task Force on Professional Liability and Insurance and Professional Liability in the 80s. (1984, October) Chicago: American Medical Association, 1–24.

AMA study reports sharp increase in malpractice claims against physicians. (1983, December) *Med. Liab. Adv. Serv.*, pp. 1–2.

American Bar Association, Commission on Medical Professional Liability (1979). *Designated compensable event system: A feasibility study.* Chicago: American Bar Association.

American Psychiatric Association. (1983). *Opinions of the ethics committee on the principles of medical ethics.* Washington, DC: Author.

APA malpractice claim types constant but frequency costs have doubled. (1983, Nov. 4) *Psychiatric News, 18*, 3–4.

Appointment of independent medical experts. (1971). *Journal of the American Medical Association, 216*, 207–212.

Armstrong v. Morgan, 545 S.W. 2d 45 (1977).

Baxstrom v. Herold, 383 U.S. 107 (1966).

Bell v. New York City Health and Hospital Corp., 90 App. Div. 2d 270, 456 N.Y.S. 2d 787 (1982).

Bellamy, W.A. (1962). Malpractice risks confronting the psychiatrist: A nationwide 15-year study of appellate court cases, 1946–1961. *American Journal of Psychiatry, 119*, 269–273.

Bellah v. Greenson, 146 Cal. Reptr. 535 (1978).

Blaut, L. (1977, January). The medical malpractice crisis, its causes and failures. *Insurance Council Journal, 44*, 114–126.

Brown v. Moore, 247 F. 2d 711 (3rd Cir., 1977).

Bromberg, W. (1983). The perils of psychiatry. *Psychiatric Annals, 13*, 219–236.

Burgess, A.W. (1981). Physicians, sexual misconduct, and patients' responses. *American Journal of Psychiatry, 138*, 1335–1342.

Cain, J.M., & Smith, J.M. (1982). Tardive dyskenesia. *Archives of General Psychiatry, 39*, 473–481.

Calabresi, G. (1970). *The costs of accidents: A legal and economic analysis.* New Haven, CT: Yale University Press.

California Medical Association-California Hospital Association. (1977). *Report on the medical insurance feasibility study.* San Francisco, CA: Sutter Publications.

Canterbury v. Spence, 464 F. 2d 772 (D.C. Cir.), cert. denied, 409 U.S. 1064 (1972).

Cassileth, B.R., Zupkis, R.V., & Sutton-Smith, E. (1980). Informed consent — why are its goals imperfectly realized? *New England Journal of Medicine, 302*, 896–900.

Centano v. N.Y. City, 369 NYS 2d 710 (1975).

Christy v. Saliterman, 288 Minn. 144, 179 N.W. 2d 288 (1970).

Clites v. Iowa, 322 N.W. 2d 917 (Iowa App., 1982).

Cobbs v. Grant, 8 Cal. 3d 229, 104 Cal. Reptr. 505, 502 P. 2d 1 (1972).

Cocozza, J., & Steadman, H. (1974). Some refinement in the measurement and prediction of dangerous behavior. *American Journal of Psychiatry*, 1012–1020.

Cocozza, J., & Steadman, H. (1976). The future of psychiatric predictions of dangerousness: Clear and convincing evidence. *Rutger's Law Review, 29*, 1084–1101.

Cohen v. N.Y., 382 N.Y.S. 2d 128 (1976).

Cole v. Taylor, 301 N.W. 2d 766 (Iowa, 1981).

Collins v. Hand, 431 PA 378, 236 A. 2d 398 (1968).

Combs v. Silverman, No. LE596 (Richmond, Virginia Circuit Court, February 5); cited in ATLA Law Reporter 25: 98 (April, 1982).

Commission on Medical Professional Liability. (1979). *American Bar Association designated compensable event system: A feasibility study.* Washington, DC: American Bar Association.

Couch, N.P., Tilney, N.L., Rayner, A.A., & Moore, F.D. (1981). The high costs of low-frequency events. *New England Journal of Medicine, 304,* 634–637.

Crauverien v. DeMetz, 20 Misc. 2d 144, 188 N.Y.S. 2d 627 (1959).

Culver, C.M., Ferrell, R.B., & Green, R.M. (1980). ECT and special problems of informed consent. *American Journal of Psychiatry, 137,* 586–591.

Danzon, P. (1983). The economic analysis of the medical malpractice system. *Behavioral Sciences and the Law, 1,* 39–54.

Department of Health, Education, and Welfare. (1973). *Report of the Secretary's Commission on Medical Malpractice.* (DHEW Publication No. OS 73-88).

Dershowitz, A. (1969, February). The psychiatrist's power in civil commitment. *Psychology Today,* 47–53.

Dillman v. Hellman, 383 So. 2d 288 (Fla App., 1973).

Dinnerstein v. U.S., 486 F. 2d 34 (2nd Cir., 1973).

Doctors' insurance with 52% rate rise. (1985, January 15). *New York Times,* A1, col. 2, and B4, col. 2.

Ehrenzweig, A. (1964). Compulsory "hospital accident" insurance: A needed first step toward the displacement of liability for "medical malpractice." *University of Chicago Law Review, 31,* 279.

Ennis, B.J., & Litwack, T.R. (1974). Psychiatry and the presumption of expertise: Flipping coins in the courtroom. *California Law Review, 62,* 693–752.

Epstein, R.A. (1979). *Medicine malpractice: The case for contract.* (Occasional Paper Series No. 9). New York: The Center for Libertarian Studies.

Fernandez v. Baruch, 52 N.J. 127, 244 A. 2d 109 (1968).

Fiederlin v. City of New York Health and Hospitals Corp., 80 App. Div. 2d 821, 437 N.Y.F. 2d (1981).

Furrow, B. (1980). *Malpractice in psychotherapy.* Lexington, MA: Lexington Books.

Furrow, B.R. (1981). Iatrogenesis and medical error: The case for medical malpractice litigation. *Law, Medicine and Health Care, 9,* 5–11.

Gentry, W.C. (1980). Psychiatric liability of the therapist–patient relationship. *Trial, 16,* 26–35.

Gutheil, T.G., & Applebaum, P.S. (1980). Substituted judgment and a physician's ethical dilemma: With special reference to the psychiatric patient. *Journal of Clinical Psychiatry, 41,* 303–305.

Hammer v. Rosen, 7 N.Y. 2d 376 (198 N.Y.S. 2d 65, 165 NE 2d 756) (1960).

Harris, M. (1973). Tort liability of the psychotherapist. *University of San Francisco Law Review, 8,* 405–436.

Hartogs v. Employer's Mutual Liability Insurance Company of Wisconsin, 391 N.Y.S. 2d 962, 89 Misc. 2d 468 (N.Y. Supp. 1977).

Havighurst, C. (1984, winter). Reforming malpractice through consumer choice. *Health Affairs,* 64–85.

Havighurst, C., & Tancredi, L. (1973). Medical adversity insurance—A no-fault approach to medical mal-

practice and quality assurance. *Health and Society* (Milbank Memorial Fund Quarterly), *51,* 125–168.

Havighurst, C.C. (1975). Medical adversity insurance—Has its time come? *Duke Law Journal, 197,* 1233–1242.

Heltsley v. Votteler, 327 N.W. 2d 759 (Iowa, 1982).

Hirsh, H.L., & White, E.R. (1978, January). The pathological anatomy of medical malpractice claims. *Legal Aspects of Medical Practice, 6*(1), 25–32.

Hogan, D.B. (1979). *The regulation of psychotherapists, Vol. III: A review of malpractice suits in the United States* (p. 10). Cambridge, MA: Ballinger Publishing Co.

Holder, A.R. (1978). *Medical malpractice law* (2nd ed.). New York: John Wiley & Sons.

Horan, D.J., & Guerrini, M.E. (1981). Developing legal trends in psychiatric malpractice. *Journal of Psychiatry and the Law, 9,* 65–78.

Horan, D.J., & Milligan, R.J. (1983). Recent developments in psychiatric malpractice. *Behavioral Sciences and the Law, 1,* 23–38.

In a review of medical malpractice: Problem in the United States. (1975). Washington, DC: Health Insurance Association of America.

In the matter of Karen Quinlan, An alleged incompetent, 70 N.J. 10, 355 A. 2d. 647 (1976).

In the matter of the guardianship of Richard Row III, 421 N.E. 2d 40 (Mass., 1981).

Institute of Medicine (1978). *Beyond malpractice: Compensation for medical injuries.* Washington, DC: National Academy of Sciences.

Jablonski By Pahls v. U.S.A., 712 F. 2d 391 (1983).

Jeste, D.V., & Wyatt, R.J. (1981). Changing epidemiology of tardive dyskinesia: An overview. *American Journal of Psychiatry, 138,* 197–309.

Jeste, D.V., & Wyatt, R.J. (1982). Therapeutic strategies against dyskensias. *Archives of General Psychiatry, 39,* 803–816.

Johnson v. United States, 409 F. Supp. 1283 (1981).

Johnston v. Rodis, 251 F. 2d 917 (D.C. Cir., 1958).

Joint Legislative Audit Committee, Office of the Auditor General, California Legislature (1975, September). *Doctors' malpractice insurance: An interim report.*

Kane, J.M., & Smith, J.M. (1982). Tardive dyskinesia. *Archives of General Psychiatry, 29,* 473–481.

Kapp v. Ballentine, 402 N.E. 2d 463 (Mass., 1980).

Katz, J. (Ed.). (1972). *Experimentation with human beings.* New York: Russell Sage Foundation.

Katz, J. (1980). Disclosure and consent in psychiatric practice: Mission impossible. In C. K. Hoffling (ed.), *Law and Ethics in the Practice of Psychiatry* (p. 91). New York: Brunner/Mazel.

Katz, J., & Capron, A.M. (1975). *Catastrophe diseases: Who decides what?* New York: Russell Sage Foundation.

Klein, J.I., & Glover, S.I. (1983). Psychiatric malpractice. *International Journal of Law and Psychiatry, 6,* 131–137.

Knapp, S., & Vandercreek, L. (1983). Malpractice risks with suicidal patients. *Psychotherapy: Theory, Research and Practice, 20,* 274–280.

Kosberg v. Washington Hospital Center, 394 F. 2d 947 (D.C. Cir., 1968).

Kozol, H., Boucher, R., & Garofalo, R. (1972). The

diagnosis and treatment of dangerousness. *Crime and Delinquency, 18,* 371–392.

Ladd, J. (1979). Legalism and medical ethics. *Journal of Medicine and Philosophy, 4,* 70–80.

Ladimer, I., Solomon, J.C., & Mulvihill, M. (1981). Experience in medical malpractice arbitration. *The Journal of Legal Medicine, 2,* 433–470.

Landau v. Werner, 105 Sol. J. 257, 105 Sol. J. 1008 (1961).

Lapari v. Sears Roebuck and Company. (D.C. Neb.) 497 F. Supp. 185 (1980).

Law, S., & Polan, S. (1978). *Pain and profit: The politics of malpractice.* New York: Harper and Row.

Lessard v. Schmidt, 379 F. Supp. 1078, vacated 94 S. Ct. 713 (1974).

Lester v. Aetna, 240 F. 2d 676 (5th Dist. Cir. Ct. La., 1957).

Lidz, C.W., Meisel, A., Zerubavel, E., Carter, M., Sestak, R.M., & Roth, L.H. (1984). *Informed consent: A study of decision-making in psychiatry.* New York: The Gilford Press.

Loggans, S. (1981). Psychiatrists and hospitals: Liability for patients' self-inflicted injuries. *American Journal of Trial Advocacy, 5,* 1–13.

Lundgren v. Fultz, 354 N.W. 2d 25 (Minn. Sup. Ct., 1984).

Maine, H.S. (1897). *The early history of institutions.* London: Oxford University Press.

Maki v. Murray Hospital, 91 Mont. 251, 7 P. 2d 228 (1983).

Mazza v. Medical Mutual Insurance Co. of North Carolina, 319 S.E. 2d 217 (N.C. Sup. Ct., 1984).

McDonald v. Moore, 323 So. 2d 635 (Fla. App., 1976).

McIntosh v. Milano, 168 N.J. Super. 466, 403 A 2d 500 (1979).

McPherson v. Ellis, 287 SE 2d 892 (N.C., 1982).

Mediation isn't cure for patient's claims. (1980, February 4). *The National Law Journal, 1,* 218.

Meier v. Ross General Hospital, 69 Cal. 2d 420, 71 Cal. Reptr. 903, 445 P. 2d 519 (1968).

Monahan, J. (1981). *Predicting violent behavior.* Beverly Hills, CA: Sage Publications.

Natanson v. Kline, 186 Kan. 186, 354 P. 2d 670 (1960).

National Association of Insurance Commissioners (1977). Malpractice claims (Vol. 1, No. 4). Milwaukee. WI: Author.

Norton, D.L. (1976). *Personal destiny: A philosophy of ethical individualism.* Princeton, NJ: Princeton University Press.

O'Connell, J. (1985). The "new no-fault" alternative. *Virginia Medical, 112,* 239–243.

Oliver v. Stephens, cited in *National Law Review, 5*(19), 1 (1983, January 17).

Omer v. Edgren, 685 P. 2d 635 (Wash. Ct. of Appeals, July 26, 1984; rehearing denied August 21, 1984).

O'Neill v. Montefiore Hospital, 202 N.Y.S. 2d 436 (1960).

Peterson v. State of Washington, 671 P. 2d 330 (Wash. Sup. Ct., 1983).

Physicians' insurer granted 55% malpractice rise. (1985, April 5). *New York Times,* A10, col. 1.

Pocincki, L., Dogger, S.J., & Schwartz, B.P. (1974). The incidence of iatrogenic injuries. In *Secretary's Commission Report on Medical Malpractice.* Washington, DC: DHEW Government Printing Office.

Prosser, W.L. (1964). *Handbook of the law of torts* (3rd ed.), pp. 218. St. Paul, MN: West Publishing Co.

Rawls, J. (1973). *A theory of justice.* Boston, MA: Harvard University Press.

Rennie v. Klein, 720 F. 2d 266 (3rd Cir. 1983).

Reynolds, R.A., & Abrams, J.B. (1983). *Socio-economic characteristics of medical practice.* Chicago, IL: American Medical Association.

Riskin, L. (1979). Sexual relations between psychotherapists and their patients: Towards research or restraint. *California Law Review, 67,* 1000–1027.

Rogers v. Commissioner of the Department of Mental Health, 390 Mas. 489 (Mass. Supp. Jud. Ct. December 2, 1983).

Rogers v. Okin, 738 F. 2d 1 (1984).

Roy v. Hartogs, 366 NYS 297 (Civ. Ct. NY. Af. on condition of remitter 381 NYS 2nd 587) Sup. Ct. NY (1976).

Salgo v. Leland Stanford, Jr. University Board of Trustees, 154 Cal. App. 2d 560, 31 F.P. 2d 170 (1957).

Salloway v. Department of Professional Regulation, 421 So. 2d 573 (Fla. Dist. Ct. App. 1982).

Schwartz v. United States, 226 F. Supp. 84 (D.D.C. 1964).

Shea v. Board of Medical Examiners, 81 Cal. App. 3d 564 (1978).

Skar v. City of Lincoln, Nebraska, 599 F. 2d 253 (8th Cir. 1975).

Slaby, A.E., Lieb, J., & Tancredi, L.R. (1985). *Handbook of psychiatric emergencies* (3rd ed.). New York: Medical Examination Company.

Slovenko, R. (1980). On the legal aspects of tardive dyskinesia. *Journal of Psychiatry in the Law, 7,* 295–310.

Slovenko, R. (1981). Malpractice in psychiatry and related fields. *Journal of Psychiatry in the Law, 9,* 18–25.

Sowka, R. (1981). The medical malpractice of closed claims study conducted by the National Association of Insurance Commissioners. *Connecticut Medicine,* 91–114.

Speer v. U.S., 512 F. Supp. 670 (1981).

State of Maryland (1978). *Maryland's defective delinquency statute — A progress report.* Unpublished manuscript. Department of Public Safety and Correctional Services, Annapolis, MD.

Steadman, H. (1972). The psychiatrist as a conservative agent of social control. *Social Problems, 20,* 263–271.

Steadman, H., & Cocozza, J. (1972). *Careers of the criminally insane.* Lexington, MA: Lexington Books.

Steadman, H., & Keveles, C. (1972). The community adjustment and criminal activity of the Baxstrom patients: 1966–1970. *American Journal of Psychiatry, 19,* 304–310.

Steel, K. (1984). Iatrogenic disease on a medical service. *Iatrogenic Disease, 32,* 445–449.

Steel, K., Gertman, P.M., Crescenzi, C., & Anderson, J. (1981). Iatrogenic illness on a general medical service at a university hospital. *New England Journal of Medicine, 304,* 638–642.

Stevens, C.M. (1981). Medical malpractice: Some implications of contract and arbitration in HMOs. *Health and Society* (Milbank Memorial Fund Quarterly), *59,* 59–88.

Stone, A. (1975). *Mental health and law: A system in*

transition. Rockville, MD: National Institute of Mental Health.

Superintendent of Belchertown State School et al. v. Joseph Saikewicz, 370 N.E. 2d 417 (1977).

Tancredi, L.R. (1977). No-fault and medical malpractice: The causation issues of defining compensable events. *Inquiry*, *14*, 341–351.

Tancredi, L.R. (1982). Competency for informed consent: Conceptual limits of empirical data. *International Journal of Law and Psychiatry*, *5*, 51–63.

Tancredi, L.R., & Barondess, J. (1978). The problem of defensive medicine. *Science*, *200*, 879–882.

Tancredi, L.R., & Edlund, M. (1983). Are conflicts of interest endemic to psychiatric consultation? *International Journal of Law and Psychiatry*, *6*, 293–316.

Tancredi, L.R., & Slaby, A. (1977). *Ethical policy in mental health care: The goals of psychiatric intervention*. New York: Watson Academic Press.

Tarasoff v. Regents of University of California, 131 Cal. Rptr. 14, 551 P. 2d 334 (1976).

Taub, S. (1983, June). Psychiatric malpractice in the 1980s: A look at some areas of concern. *Law, Medicine and Health Care*, 97–135.

Taylor, V.J., & Wagner, N.N. (1976, November). Sex between therapists and clients: A review and analysis. *Professional Psychology*, *2*, 593–598.

Thompson v. County of Alameda, 167 Cal. Rptr. 70. 17 Cal. 3d 741, 641 P. 2d 728 (1980).

Topel v. Long Island Medical Center, 55 N.Y. 2d 682, 446 N.Y.S. 2d 293, 431 N.E. 2d 393.

Truman v. Thomas, 27 Cal. 3d 285, 62 P. 2d 902 (1980).

Veatch, R. (1981). *A theory of medical ethics*. New York: Basic Books.

Walker v. Parzen, See Wilkinson, A. (1982, December). Psychiatric malpractice: Identifying areas of liability. *Trial*, *18*, 72–77.

Waltz, J.R., & Inbau, F.E. (1971). *Medical jurisprudence*. New York: Macmillan Publishing Company.

Waltzer, H. (1980). Malpractice liability in patient's suicide. *American Journal of Psychotherapy*, *34*, 89–102.

Weatherly v. United States, 109 Misc. 2d 1024, 441 N.Y.S. 2d 319 (Ct. Cl. 1981).

Weisstub, D. (1985). Le droit et la psychiatrie dans leur problematique commune. *McGill Law Journal*, *30*, 221–261.

Wettstein, R.N. (1983). Tardive dyskinesia and malpractice. *Behavioral Sciences and the Law*, *1*, 85–107.

Wilkinson, A.P. (1982). Psychiatric malpractice: Identifying areas of liability. *Trial*, *18*, 73–77.

Williams, P.C. (1984). Abandoning medical malpractice. *The Journal of Legal Medicine*, *5*, 549–594.

Williams v. U.S., 450 F. Supp. 1040 (D.C. SC 1978).

Woods v. Brumlop, 71 N.M. 221 (1962).

World Medical Association (1964). Declaration of Helsinki. *New England Journal of Medicine*, 271–473.

Zimmerman, Respondent v. N.Y. Health and Hospital Corporation, (1st Dept.), 91 App. Div. Repts. 2d 1 (1983).

3.
Men Who Have Sex with Children

Vernon L. Quinsey

ABSTRACT. Child molestation is common in modern Western societies, as it has been historically and in other cultures; there are even cultures in which sex with young boys is obligatory. In modern Western societies, a sizeable proportion of child molestations involve physical
coercion, but a very small proportion result in physical injury. In view of the incidence of
these behaviors, however, the absolute numbers of physical injuries are substantial. Heterosexual, homosexual, and incestuous offenders differ from each other in important ways, including recidivism. Homosexual offenders are the most likely to recidivate and incestuous offenders
the least. There is ample evidence that repetitive child molesters, particularly those who select
unrelated victims, prefer children as sexual partners. Sometimes, however, children are selected
as surrogates; in these instances, opportunity, alcohol, and difficulties in relations with adults
play an important role. The behavioral treatment of child molesters has made a promising
beginning and comparative studies of different treatment methods are now in order. Much
more knowledge is needed about the development of both normal and inappropriate sexual
age preferences.

SOMMAIRE. L'agression sexuelle à l'encontre des enfants est un phénomène courant dans les
sociétés occidentales modernes comme il a toujours été dans l'histoire et dans d'autres cultures;
il existe même des cultures où il est obligatoire d'engager des relations sexuelles avec les jeunes
garçons. Dans notre société, une proportion importante des agressions sexuelles à l'encontre
des enfants fait intervenir la coercition physique mais une très petite proportion entraîne un
préjudice corporel. Vu l'incidence de ces comportements, les nombres absolus des agressions
physiques demeurent importants malgré tout. Les délinquants hétérosexuels, homosexuels et
incestueux diffèrent les uns des autres à plusieurs égards et, en particulier, sur le plan de la
récidive. Les délinquants homosexuels sont ceux qui ont le plus de probabilités de récidive tandis
que les délinquants incestueux en ont le moins. Il existe une preuve importante que les auteurs
d'agressions sexuelles répétées à l'encontre d'enfants, en particulier ceux qui choisissent des
victimes qui n'ont pas de lien entre elles, préfèrent les enfants comme partenaires sexuels.
Cependant, il arrive parfois que les enfants soient choisis à la place d'adultes et, dans ces cas-là,
le caractère occasionnel, l'alcool et les difficultés dans les relations avec les adultes sont des
facteurs importants. Le traitement behavioral des agresseurs d'enfants a eu un succès remar-
quable et des études comparatives sur les différentes méthodes de traitement s'imposent maintenant. Il est nécessaire de faire des études plus approfondies sur le développement des
préférences sexuelles liées à l'âge qui seraient à la fois normales et anormales.

The author thanks Christopher Earls, Grant Harris, and Marnie Rice for their critical reading of an earlier version of this paper. Thanks also to Catherine Cormier, who located many of the articles, and Marlean Quinsey, who
discovered some important anthropological work for this chapter.

INTRODUCTION

Sexual behaviors, like any others of social importance, are complex and are determined in a multidimensional fashion. This multidimensionality of determining events causes major methodological and interpretive problems when particular sexual behaviors are to be explained theoretically. The occurrence of the behaviors themselves are seldom sufficient for inferences about their causation. Although these problems are perhaps obvious, their effects are often not, particularly concerning a topic such as sexual interactions with children, which is laden with a priori assumptions and value judgments. I will, therefore, begin this review by attempting to clarify certain conceptual issues before turning to substance.

Sexual behaviors are species-typical and consummatory in nature; there is, therefore, an almost irresistable inclination to ascribe the adjective "natural" to those behaviors that are related to procreation and the adjective "unnatural" to those that are not. Clearly, from an evolutionary viewpoint, it would be strange indeed if behaviors that led to the continuation of the species did not have some advantages. We might think, for example, that, for males, there is something inherently attractive about sexual activities with reproductively viable women. Regardless of the truth or falsity of this proposition, however, it should be clear that sexual acts of various kinds can be motivated in a variety of ways simultaneously. In particular, it is probable that most sexual acts are determined simultaneously by a mix of environmental contingencies and organismic variables.

To clarify this matter, consider an experiment in animal behavior. Rats in an experimental chamber are given the opportunity to drink sweet water out of a drinking tube. If the rats are sufficiently hungry, they will lick the tube in a burst-like manner with a species-specific frequency. They do not have to be taught this response. It can be arranged, however, for this licking response to have a variety of additional consequences; for example, licks can be consequated with an aversive event such as electric shock. One could arrange a positive relationship between response occurrence and shock (punishment), a noncontingent relationship between licking and shock, or a schedule in which licks avoid shocks that would otherwise be delivered (free operant avoidance). These contingencies of reinforcement can be thought to lie on a continuum based on the degree and type of their correlation with the behavior of interest. Such a situation, involving two schedules targeted on the same response (in this case, shock and sweet water consequating licking), is termed a "conjoint schedule." Conjoint schedules affect species-typical behaviors in a lawful manner (Quinsey, 1972).

The methodological point that the previous experiment illustrates is that by looking at the licking behavior of these animals alone, we in fact cannot tell what is motivating their responses. Because of the experimental arrangement, however, we know that some animals are licking in spite of shock and some animals are licking both because of their hunger and to avoid shock. In the area of socially important behaviors, such as sexual activity, multiple determination is ubiquitous and extremely complex; as we shall see, different societies have imposed complicated rules that reward, punish, or ignore sexual interactions between men and children. Furthermore, we often do not know what the contingencies actually are (or were) for a given individual or group. This problem has spurred a variety of approaches to the problem of sexual motivation in recent years.

A related issue concerns inclusive fitness: Because sexual behaviors are so clearly linked with evolutionary success, it is natural to think of sexual motivation as being part of "human nature" and to be relatively invariant (Ford, 1960). Unfortunately, the elements of sexual behavior that are invariant are not well understood. In addition, such an approach is ill-suited when we wish to examine individual differences in sexual behavior and what causes them (e.g., Buss, 1984).

The primary focus of the present paper is on men who have sexual interactions with children in modern Western societies. Because these behaviors are criminal offenses, in addition to being viewed for the most part as immoral, the latter part of this chapter treats sexual behaviors with children as crimes and focuses on the modification and prevention of these behaviors. In order to have a less parochial theoretical view of these behaviors, however, the first part of the chapter is concerned with the description of societies and periods of history in which these behaviors were more or less accepted.

ANTHROPOLOGICAL STUDIES

There have long been scattered reports of sexual behavior between adult men and children in a variety of cultures (Carstairs, 1964). For example,

Henry (1964) reports that, among the Kaingang of the Brazilian highlands, "The growing child's sexual experience is primarily humorous, often illicit, administered by adults, and apt to be violent in the case of girls" (p. 18). The anthropological literature on homosexuality has been particularly sparse and of uneven quality (Fitzgerald, 1977).

More recently, however, adult sexual behavior with children has received some attention from anthropologists with the systematic study of ritualized and obligatory homosexual activities with male children occurring in parts of Melanesia. Homosexuality in this part of the world is ritualized in that it involves male initiation rites, has religious connotations, is condoned or prescribed by broader social roles and rules, and is structured by age and kinship rules and taboos (Herdt, 1984a). Herdt estimates that 10–20% of Melanesian societies practice ritualized homosexuality or have practiced it in the recent past. This institution is characteristic of Papuan-speaking societies of the southwestern New Guinea coastal fringe and certain islands to the east of New Guinea (it also occurs in parts of Australia but that area has not received much systematic study in this connection).

Perhaps the most outstanding feature of societies that have institutionalized homosexual eroticism between men and boys is the degree of gender polarity and antagonism. Males belong to secret societies and gain prestige from warfare and head-hunting. Women's status is very low. There is a strict separation of labor along gender lines and residential separation as well. Women do not participate very much in public affairs, often have no choice in the selection of a marriage partner, and have little control over their economic products. In addition, beliefs about the polluting effects of women's bodies are common, as are negative images of women in myth and idiom (Herdt, 1984a).

The Sambia of the fringe highlands of eastern New Guinea practice obligatory homosexual fellatio in secret male societies (Herdt, 1984b). The practice is strictly age-graded, with boys starting at age 7, or somewhat older, by performing fellatio on older men. These homosexual behaviors are promiscuous within certain limits: Homosexual contacts are not permitted among age-mates, fellow clansmen, matrilateral kin, or ritual sponsors. It is noteworthy that homosexual taboos are closely related to heterosexual (incest) taboos, as ritual sponsors are viewed as "parents." In addition, the taboo on age-mates reflects the asymmetry of heterosexual relations between the stronger male and a weaker female. As a boy becomes older and further initiated, he switches from fellating to being fellated. This homosexual activity continues until he fathers children. Similarly, marital relations are begun with fellatio, which continues until the woman is "strong enough" for vaginal intercourse and the bearing of children. Marital sexual intercourse is, in general, viewed as procreative work.

There is an elaborate belief structure concerning the value of semen, which is seen as a scarce resource. Semen is necessary for a boy's growth and for his own later use in fathering children. Relations with women are seen as particularly semen-depleting, and this semen must be replenished by drinking the white sap of certain trees. The growth-inducing properties of semen are reflected in myths that equate the penis with secret flutes and women's breasts.

Perhaps not surprisingly, there is a great deal of cross-gender antagonism in Sambian society.

Erotic attraction plays an important role for the older partners in ritualized homosexuality. The boys must often be coerced into their initial homosexual contacts and they do not achieve orgasm, although they do become erect when performing fellatio as they become older. Men find boys more sexually arousing the younger they are and some men have difficulty switching to exclusive heterosexuality when they have children. Herdt believes that the primary motive for these activities is simply homoerotic play and that the beliefs concerning the fellator's growth are primarily rationalizations.

These homosexual contacts may have an important social function, of which more will be said later. Because the groups that have homosexual relationships also exchange sisters for marriage, the homosexual relationships can cement social contacts between potential enemies, which may become affines (related through marriage) and later kin (Herdt, 1984b).

Other societies that practice ritualized homosexuality exhibit different features within a similar cultural framework. Among the Marind-Anim of southern New Guinea, boys are taken to live in the men's house when just past infancy (Van Baal, 1984). As the boy's puberty approaches, he is introduced to anal intercourse by his mother's brother who "feeds him" anally for 3-4 years. There is also ritual homosexual promiscuity in connection with various rites. The Marind-Anim are very concerned with fecundity, which was very low even before the arrival of venereal disease. Part of the difficulty has been female sterility caused by vaginal irritation. This irritation, ironically, is associated with the fertility rite of having a woman copulate with large numbers of men in succession at marriage and at the first menstruation following pregnancy. The mixture of semen and vaginal fluids is gathered on these occasions and is thought to be a potent medicine. Although women have higher status among the Marind-Anim than among the Sambians, the males appear to Van Baal to be dissatisfied with their gender role; hence their belief that semen is the source of all fertility and growth and their preoccupation with male activities such as head-hunting.

Among the Big Nambas of North Vanuatu (an island near New Guinea), ritualized homosexuality also occurs in a context of extreme male ideology (Allen, 1984). The situation is somewhat different, however, in that the leading man of each village has an almost complete monopoly on the labor and sexual services of the women and the teenaged boys of the village.

The Kimam Papuans of southern New Guinea also exhibit ritualized homosexuality involving anal intercourse with young boys (Serpenti, 1984). The boy's mother's younger brother is the preferred mentor who performs this task. They also preferentially select young girls (as young as 8 years of age) for sexual activities designed to produce semen to be used as medicine. Girls of marriageable age are tested sexually by many men in succession to be sure they are ready for marriage. There is also promiscuous male–female intercourse associated with mourning rites.

There are other societies in this area that practice ritualized homosexuality or that employ homosexuality as a mythic theme. In general, all of these societies perceive sperm as creating growth and strength in prepubertal boys. It is of interest, however, that the method of "sperm-feeding" varies over these societies. Some employ anal intercourse, some fellatio, and some masturbation and the smearing of sperm on the boy's skin. Different societies do not always approve of their neighbor's methods (Sorum, 1984).

Enough has been said to illustrate the nature of the "variations on a sociosexual theme in Melanesia" as Lindenbaum (1984) has described it. How is this ritualized homosexual theme to be explained? Herdt (1984a) suggests that a number of elements combine in these societies to produce

the phenomenon. First, he notes that these societies are ecologically marginal and involve small populations. Surprisingly, within these small populations there are markedly imbalanced sex ratios at birth in favor of males; this initial imbalance is then exacerbated by polygamy and late menarche. To this shortage of women, Herdt adds taboos on sexual activity with women, heterosexual restrictiveness, and residential separation of the genders. Second, there are beliefs concerning the undesirability of women and the efficacy of semen in the promotion of growth. Finally, Herdt notes the sexual attractiveness of boys: For example, among the Wogeo it is well recognized that some boys are more attractive than others and, among the Sambians, some boys are seen as more attractive by the bachelors, as are some bachelors by the boys.

Schwimmer (1984) emphasizes somewhat different issues in the explanation of ritualized homosexuality. He notes that the status of women in these societies is not always low and that ritualized homosexuality may well be a result of gender competition rather than gender dominance. Because marriage partners are closely related, and women owe some loyalty to their brothers (who are often potential enemies), women are in fact a threat. This threat is dealt with by the creation of male secret societies that use homosexual relations to create bonds within their warrior group.

Lindenbaum (1984) has attempted to integrate and extend the explanations offered by Herdt and Schwimmer. She observes that the occurrence of ritualized homosexuality is far from random in Melanesia and contrasts societies which do and do not practice ritualized homosexuality in order to find explanations. In the New Guinea highlands, there are exchanges of shells, feathers, and pigs in initiation ceremonies as opposed to the exchange of semen. Where the exchange is most elaborate, there is no initiation. The concern is with the production of men of status, not so much the production of "men" per se. These societies do not have ritualized homosexuality. The eastern highlands are intermediate in that homosexuality is a symbolic theme but is not practiced. In the lowlands, ritualized homosexuality is very common. These lowland societies are small and live in precarious environments. Marriage is by sister exchange and there is no bride price. Sister exchange is a difficult way to obtain wives because it must involve equity or debt on the part of one of the parties. This problem of inequity or potential inequity is addressed by ritualized homosexuality in which the ideal inseminator is a boy's sister's husband. Semen, therefore, is, like bride service, a covenant which keeps the sister-exchange mechanism intact. Bride price makes its appearance as sister exchange and ritualized homosexuality disappears (Lindenbaum, 1984).

The phenomenon of ritualized homosexuality illustrates the complex interweaving of variables at the societal and individual levels. In the context of the animal experiment mentioned in the introduction, these are complex conjoint schedules indeed; clearly, however, in these exotic societies, sexual behavior with boys is encouraged in a variety of ways. We can observe, therefore, an interaction between sexual behaviors and positive societal sanctions that is not found elsewhere in contemporary societies. The anthropological data indicate that any explanations of sexual behaviors between adult men and children will involve not only sexual attractiveness but also societal constraints and supports, not to mention the beliefs and attitudes of the participants.

HISTORICAL STUDIES

The historical literature concerning sexual activities occurring between men and children is very small; de Mause (1974) notes that children's lives have not been recorded well and that historians have in general ignored the history of childhood. From what literature there is, however, it appears that the level of child care deteriorates as one goes back in time (de Mause, 1974). The literature concerning sex with children appears much better developed in the case of boys (see Jones, 1982) than in the case of girls, about whom there is little literature. (From what is available, the lack of commentary appears to reflect its acceptance and ubiquity.) For purposes of exposition, the sexual use of boys will be considered first.

It is well known that boys were the subject of a great deal of sexual attention in the ancient Mediterranean societies. In Crete and Boetia "pederastic marriages and honeymoons" were common. There were child brothels in every large city. Sexual use of boys was common by their teachers and their masters. In Greece and Rome, infant boys were sometimes castrated because intercourse with castrated boys was thought to be particularly arousing (de Mause, 1974; Rush, 1980).

The best known sexual activities between men and boys occurred in ancient Greece, where it was normative among the upper classes (Vanggaard,

1972). Despite the frequent allusions to "Greek love," however, most of our information comes from a fragmentary Athenian literature during the period 490–323 B.C. (Ungaretti, 1978). Homosexual relationships in ancient Greece were strongly hierarchical in that the boy, preferably postpubescent but yet unbearded, was pursued, loved, and subjected to anal intercourse by a warrior-hero. The boys involved in these activities received instruction from their mentor/lover. The boys were expected to be sexually passive and were valued for their sexual attractiveness (Ungaretti, 1978); specific attributes such as buttocks and thighs were mentioned in this regard (Vanggaard, 1972). Men who were sodomized by boys were held in contempt. Warriors would take their boy-lovers with them during military campaigns and would capture enemy women for sexual purposes as well, when possible. The status of women in ancient Greece was low, although some courtesans were of high social status. In general, however, women were sequestered in the home; adultery was punishable by death (Ungaretti, 1978).

Ungaretti (1978) has concluded that, because the ancient Greek family was dominated by the male head of the household and marriage was seen as an economic and reproductive unit, the institution of homosexual relations between men and youths kept the emotional, sexual, and intellectual needs of the men from burdening the marital relationship. Because relationships among men were so fiercely competitive, homosexual relations among age peers were an impossibility. Aristotle's contemporaneous views on this phenomenon are intriguing; he thought that homosexual relationships kept men from being dominated by their wives (Ungaretti, 1978) and that boys who had been used sexually by men from a young age would grow up to become homosexuals (de Mause, 1974).

The parallels between ritualized homosexuality in Melanesia and homosexuality in ancient Greece are striking. In both cultures the status of women is low, there is a great deal of sexual restrictiveness, the men are organized into warrior groups, male machismo is prized, male youths are valued for their sexual attractiveness, the homosexual relationships are age-graded and asymmetrical, and the boys receive tutoring from their lover/mentors.

Opinions about homosexual relations between men and youths changed over time and, indeed, were changing in ancient Greece. Increasingly, sexual relations between adults and children were viewed negatively. Essentially, the Western world went from a set of environmental or cultural contingencies that encouraged sexual interactions with boys to one that discouraged it. There is no doubt, however, that such behaviors continued.

After the 12th century, European law conformed increasingly to the Christian ethic (Goodich, 1976). Evangelical fervor condemned Jews, usurers, apostates, heretics, prostitutes, magicians, and sodomites. There was a close connection in medieval law between heresy and sodomy (heretical sects were often accused of sodomy and sexual libertinage). The theological justification for the prosecution of homosexuals was provided by the biblical destruction of Sodom and Gomorrah. The penalty for heresy and sodomy was death by burning. Torture to obtain confessions was common by the Inquisition, which investigated both heresy and sodomy. Despite all of this prosecution, however, such illicit sexual activities continued to occur and to be punished. In the 1300s, for example, boys were being prostituted in Florence. The boys were not treated as harshly under the law as older men (Goodich, 1976).

In the 15th century, there was the infamous case of Giles de Rais, who raped and murdered more than 40 peasant boys in his Brittany castle. At his trial in 1440, he claimed to have been influenced by written accounts of the Caesars, such as Caligula (Brownmiller, 1975).

The Marquis de Sade (1785/1966) wrote the first detailed account of sexual fantasies involving children. His unfinished but very lengthy "The 120 Days of Sodom" was written in the Bastille in only 37 days; he considered it his masterpiece and he was convinced it had been lost during the French Revolution. The book reappeared much later, however, and has given us an unusual look at sexual fantasy involving children. The book contains detailed descriptions of every bit of sexual nastiness that can be imagined and makes modern sadistic literature appear rather inoffensive. Simone de Beauvoir (1951/1966), in a perceptive essay, asserts that Sade's chief value is in his ability to disturb us. Sade is disturbing and is so deliberately; his method is to invert the values of the society in which he lived. For example, sex with a boy would be better than sex with a girl because it is more unnatural; it would be better yet if the boy suffered and was later killed; having the offender be a bishop would improve the story further, particularly if he were not caught and punished for the crime. Other details, like

having the parents watch the torture and suggesting that these sexual murders occur very frequently and will continue forever would be worked into the plot whenever possible. Sade does not want us to like his "heroes" and goes out of his way to make them contemptible rather than grandly evil; the sexual acts themselves are treated in the same way, partly through endless repetition.

It is not clear which, of all of the sexual activities Sade describes with such gusto, he himself found sexually arousing. Apparently, he did enjoy being the recipient of anal intercourse and enjoyed inflicting pain but there is no evidence that he was sexually involved with children. The historical value of Sade's work in the present context is that it clearly shows the psychological availability of sadistic fantasies involving children at the time of the French Revolution. The theoretical questions raised by the wide variety of sexual misbehaviors that Sade describes are several. Chief among these pertains to the connection among these widely different fantasies. Preferred sexual fantasies are usually thought to be idiosyncratic and limited in number for any one individual. Is Sade an anomaly, or is it common for others to be sexually aroused by all manner of sexual misbehaviors? In short, can naughtiness per se be a sexual cue? Can something be erotically attractive only because it is forbidden? At present we have no answers to these questions but they are at the heart of an explanation of sadism. We will return to these questions when we consider research on the sadistic use of children.

In the 18th century, there was widespread use of boys as passive sexual objects in many parts of the world: China, Japan (among the Samurai), subSaharan Africa, and the Islamic areas of Turkey, Egypt, Arabia, and India (Trumbach, 1977). These homosexual behaviors were practiced quite openly and did not arouse public indignation or incur punishment as they did in Europe at this time. Although England was perhaps the most punitive of the European countries in the 18th century concerning these matters, there was a flourishing homosexual underground in London involving a specialized argot and illicit meetings between men of all social classes in latrines, parks, and brothels. Young boys often sold themselves as prostitutes (Trumbach, 1977).

In view of this punitive climate of English opinion, it is of considerable interest that a literature appeared in England in the late 1800s which attempted to justify and glorify sexual interactions with young boys. This literature was written by the "Uranian" poets (Taylor, 1976), of whom the best known was Oscar Wilde. Taylor concludes:

> The Uranians, in their poetry, constructed and amplified an image of their sexual orientation as God-given and divinely-sanctioned, as a means of overcoming or of ameliorating class barriers, as erotically and aesthetically superior to other affective attachments, and as a means of recapturing their own lost youth. Add to that their recognition of the inevitable transience of its availability, and we can see that these poets managed to formulate a set of motives for conventionally negatively-sanctioned sexual activity which enabled its enactment as guilt-free behaviour. (p. 108)

What little historical literature there is on the sexual use of young girls has been reviewed by Rush (1980). The phenomenon was essentially seen as unremarkable. In Sumerian tablets of 5,000 years ago, the goddess Ninlil is depicted as refusing intercourse on the grounds that she was too young and too small. From the Book of Numbers in the Bible and from Talmudic tradition until the 12th century, it is clear that a girl 3 years of age plus a day could be betrothed by intercourse. Rapes of boys under 9 years of age and girls under 3 years of age were not punished as they were viewed under the law as "invalid." In Roman times the sexual use of young, particularly slave, girls was common.

In sixth-century Christian society, 12 years of age was the age of marriage for girls and 13 for boys, although marriages were arranged for girls who were much younger. Consent was thought to be desirable but penetration was binding; sex with a female under 7 years of age, however, was not considered to be valid in a legal sense (Rush, 1980).

Good criminal records exist for Venice in the early Renaissance of the mid-1300s (Ruggiero, 1975). These records indicate the frequency of certain crimes and their punishments; sometimes descriptive material is available as well. Many crimes were dealt with extremely harshly; for example, a man who had sexual relations with a boy was burned. Heterosexual rape, however, was dealt with far more leniently. An examination of the penalties indicates that rapes of females under 12 years of age were punished on average by about 2 years in jail, rapes of unmarried but marriageable women by less than 6 months in jail, and rapes of married women by approximately 1 year in jail. Penalties were often in the form of fines and so strongly favored the upper class, who appeared to commit more than their share of rapes. Rapists apparently did not rape above their class, as the females were almost exclusively of the same or lower class than the rapists.

In the 13th century, England began to recognize sex with a female under 12 years of age as statutory rape (Rush, 1980). Unfortunately, the effect of this ruling is unknown as it was interpreted ambiguously for a very long time. With the industrial revolution in Victorian England, the prostitution of female children was recognized as an important and increasing social problem. There was a flourishing international "white slave" trade and it was not uncommon for girls to be kidnapped and coerced into prostitution in England and the United States. The exploitation of these girls and their resultant severe health problems was a scandal (Rush, 1980).

It was not only in Western countries that female children were commonly used sexually. In India, child marriage was legal until 1955. Hindu religion prescribed child marriage and there were numerous health problems caused by the sexual intercourse to which very young girls were subjected (Rush, 1980).

This historical summary has documented the widespread occurrence of sexual activities between men and children in cultures and periods of history that vary widely in their attitudes toward the behavior. Because of the incompleteness of the data, many questions remain unanswered; in particular, it would be interesting to know how common it was in various times and places for men to engage in sexual activities with children exclusively, instead of intermittently, and how this phenomenon varies with societal regulation of sexual behavior.

The ubiquity of sexual behaviors with children and the persistence of these activities in the face of strong punishments in certain societies are the most salient features of this review. We can conclude, therefore, that sexual activities with children are inherently attractive, at least to some men, and that an interest or preference for these sorts of behaviors are easily learned under a wide variety of circumstances.

INCIDENCE

Turning to Western contemporary society, many researchers who have investigated sexual crimes perpetrated against children have made various estimates of their frequency. Unfortunately, however, these estimates are extremely difficult to evaluate. A number of important methodological issues must be borne in mind before the difficulty of the problem becomes apparent (e.g., Elliott, Ageton, Huizinga, Knowles, & Canter, 1983). First, authors have frequently confused prevalence with incidence. Prevalence refers to the proportion of individuals in a given population who have engaged in a particular behavior within a specified period of time (e.g., a year or a lifetime). Incidence, on the other hand, refers to the numbers of behaviors of a particular type which occur in a specific population in a given time. Obviously, prevalence figures must be lower than incidence figures for the same populations and the same time intervals. A further complication ensues when the at-risk population is defined (e.g., all males or all males over 16 years of age). The problem becomes more acute in estimating the incidence of crimes such as incest, where part of the definition of the crime involves the relationship of the offender and victim (number of families having children of certain ages or number of families in which the biological father is present).

The magnitude of the difficulties increases severalfold when the definition of the offense is considered. Many of the offenses are in fact quite minor and involve exposing the genitals or the fondling of nongenital areas through the victim's clothes. Often the offense occurs among social intimates. Given the well known vagaries of recall, such incidents will often not be reported by victims or offenders.

Data on the number of offenses can be gathered from three sources: police data, offender reports, or victim reports. Each source of data is subject to its own problems of interpretation; conversely, each source of data sheds additional light on the subject.

Considering police report data first, one must not confuse crimes known to the police, arrest data, and conviction data. With respect to crimes known to the police, there is also the distinction to be made between founded (where the police believe a crime has been committed) and unfounded crimes (where the police believe that the allegation is spurious). Depending upon one's purpose, any of these sorts of police data may be appropriate. When one is most concerned that the crime actually occurred and wants a conservative estimate, conviction data should be employed. It is of interest that convictions for sex offenses are

less common than often believed; for example, Chiswick (1983) indicates that offenders found guilty or cautioned for sex crimes in England make up less than 1% of offenders found guilty of indictable offenses for that entire country.

The problems inherent in using police data are many. Police reporting and arrest policies vary over both time and jurisdiction. In addition, there is a very poor correspondence between legal category or charge and actual behaviors; it is often not even possible to distinguish sexual from nonsexual crimes against the person. Court records or police descriptions of the behaviors are far superior to simply using "rap sheets" because of these ambiguities. There is also the well known problem of the victim's failure to report offenses that do occur. This failure to report is, of course, very likely when the victim is a child and is more likely the more minor the offense. It is highly probable that such under-reporting varies directly with the socio-economic status of the child and the relationship of the offender to the victim.

Offender reports can be gathered in several ways. The most common is in interviews with convicted offenders. These data often suffer from the offender seeking to conceal the frequency and specific nature of his crimes because of the very real possibility that such information will lead to an increased sentence, a longer time which he will spend in a correctional or psychiatric institution, or poorer treatment at the hands of fellow inmates or custodial personnel. Persons who have volunteered for treatment and have been guaranteed anonymity are likely to be more forthcoming in this regard. The difficulty, however, in interpreting data from known offenders, whether institutionalized or not, is in knowing how typical they are of some population. It would be better, of course, to ask some large and demographically stratified population of males the same questions under conditions of anonymity. The problem in all of this self report revolves around the nature of the behaviors themselves. It requires very special circumstances for a person to admit that he has, for example, buggered a child, when that offense is not already known to the police or questioner. Finally, there are the methodological issues involved in any retrospective interview technique, such as differential recall. These latter problems can be addressed, if not eliminated, by providing specific temporal anchor points and careful structuring of the questions.

Many of the same issues apply to victim reports. The problems of accuracy are compounded, however, by the young age of the victims, who often do not have the vocabulary necessary to describe what has happened to them, and by the long time that has elapsed if older persons are asked about their childhood victimization. The same issue as in the offender case arises as to whether only known victims will be interviewed or whether demographically stratified populations of at-risk individuals will be interviewed. The ethical problems in asking children such questions are not to be underestimated.

Before proceeding with a discussion of the incidence of the behaviors that are the subject of this chapter, it is necessary to describe them in more detail. Broadly speaking, we are interested in sexual interactions between adult men and prepubertal children; this definition can be operationalized as a sexual interaction between a male who is 16 years of age or older and at least 5 years older than the child, who, in turn, is 13 years of age or younger. Varying definitions have been used in the literature but the papers which will be reviewed more or less conform to this operationalization. The men who engage in these sexual behaviors have been termed "child molesters" or "pedophiles" and the children involved have been called "victims." Although these terms carry evaluative baggage, they are so common in the literature that they will be employed in the remainder of the review. The sexual behaviors of concern to this review involve touching of the genitals, buttocks, or breasts or those behaviors involving exposure of the genitals. The sexual behaviors will be considered in more detail the more that they involve coercion and aggression.

This chapter is concerned primarily with the characteristics of sexual offenders against children. However, this concern only makes sense if some men are more likely to commit sexual offenses against children than others; if men are equally likely to commit these offenses, then we should be interested exclusively in situational variables, such as differential opportunities or societal sanctions.

Sexual interactions between men and children are a common occurrence in Western societies. In 1953 Kinsey et al. (cited in West, 1981) interviewed over 4,000 normal females in the United States. Their prevalence figures indicate that 24% of the sample had been approached sexually by a man over 15 years of age and at least 5 years older than themselves when they were under 14 years of age. Nearly half of the men involved were acquaintances or relatives. The sexual behaviors seldom involved coitus (3%) and were

often minor (31% involved petting and fondling without touching of the genitals). Only one of the respondents indicated that she had received serious injury but many reported having been upset by the experience.

More recently, Finkelhor (1979) gathered interview data from 530 female and 266 male American college students regarding their childhood sexual experiences with adults and older adolescents. Females reported that they had had a sexual experience with an adult when under age 12 in 11% of the cases, whereas males reported such sexual contact in 4% of the cases. When young adolescents and sexual contact by older adolescents was included, the figures rose to 19% for females and 9% for males. For females, family members were involved in 43% of the cases, acquaintances in 33%, and strangers in 24%. The situation was quite different for boys, where the corresponding figures were 17, 53, and 30%. For females, 37% of the sexual contacts occurred at 9 years of age or younger, 47% between ages 10 and 12, and 16% between ages 13 and 16. For males, 27% of the contacts occurred before 10 years of age, 41% between ages 10 and 12, and 32% between ages 13 and 16. A regression analysis indicated that use of force and partner's age best predicted how much trauma females said they experienced.

Much more extensive information has recently become available from a Gallup poll based on a national probability sample of Canadians over 18 years of age. (Committee on Sexual Offences, 1984a; 1984b). There were 2,008 persons who provided complete information under anonymous conditions; this represents 94% of those contacted. Fifty-four percent of the females and 31% of the males had received unwanted sexual attention at some time in their lives. The majority of these events took place before the respondents were 18 years of age. Females were victimized twice as frequently as males.

Of those persons who reported having been victimized, the age of the first unwanted sexual contact was recorded and the type of contact was noted. For persons who reported being victimized before age 13, the types of acts involving female victims were: offender exposure (41%), threatening (7%), touching (30%), and assault or attempt (22%). For males, the corresponding figures were: 37% (exposure), 6% (threat), 42% (touch), and 15% (assault or attempt). Of those sexual behaviors involving physical contact before age 16, 1 male reported being victimized for every 2.6

females. For males, 56% of this contact involved physical coercion and 6% threats; for females, 58% involved physical coercion and 3% threats. With respect to injury incurred during the first unwanted sexual contact, 4% of males and 20% of females reported physical injury and 7 and 24% of males and females reported emotional or psychological trauma. The finding that more than half of the sex offenders against children used coercion to achieve physical contact was also obtained by De Francis (1969), who also observed an inverse relation between the amount of force employed and the degree of the relationship between the offender and victim.

For victims younger than 15 years of age, where the offense involved physical contact, the distribution of offenders by their relationship to the victim was noted. Strangers were involved in only 18% of the cases. Friends and acquaintances made up 48% of the offenders. The remainder were incest (10%), other relatives and family (11%), guardians or persons in a position of trust (4%), and other known persons (9%). Over half of the assaults on children occurred in the victim's home.

Only 11% of the male victims and 24% of the female victims reported the first instance of unwanted sexual attention to another person. Victims were much more likely to report an incident the more serious it was.

It was of interest that there was no effect of respondent age on the reported frequencies of childhood victimization. This null finding supports the view that the frequency of sexual assaults did not change over time (it must be remembered, however, that because all of the respondents were over 18 years of age, the recent past was not covered).

The estimates that can be derived from this Gallup survey are the best that can be made at the present time. It is one of the few that have asked detailed questions pertaining to sexual assault against children. The aspects of the results that are most important are the frequency with which boys are molested, the large numbers of sexual assaults against children in general, and the sizeable minority of victims who report physical and emotional damage occasioned by the assaults.

Central to the present review is the question of differential incidence over offenders. It is very clear, on the basis of child molester self-reports, that at least some men commit very large numbers of offenses. Bernard (1975) gave a questionnaire to members of the Dutch "Working Group of Pedophilia." Of the 50 pedophiles polled, 96% preferred boys (this figure does not, of course, reflect the proportion of homosexual child molesters among child molesters in general). These respondents indicated that they were quite young when they became aware of their pedophilic tendencies (8% at less than 10 years of age) and had had their first contact with a child at a young age (6% at less than 10 years of age). The preferred partner age ranged broadly but peaked at ages 11 and 12. The number of children contacted by each pedophile ranged from less than 10 (30%) to 10–50 (28%), to 50–300 (14%); some respondents answered some (6%) or many (24%). Fifty-four percent reported that they had a regular child partner at the time they filled out the questionnaire. Many of the pedophiles had traveled to other countries for boy prostitutes with whom to perform anal intercourse; Mediterranean Europe and North Africa were favored locations. Most of the respondents used various forms of erotic material that related to their preferences (e.g., magazines, photos). Over half of the pedophiles had been sentenced for pedophilia and 38% had received psychiatric treatment for their behavior but, interestingly, 90% of this admittedly select sample had no wish to abandon their sexual behaviors with boys.

Additional self-report data have been collected by Abel, Mittelman, and Becker (in press); these reports, however, were obtained from outpatients voluntarily seeking treatment for their sexual problems in New York City and Memphis, Tennessee. An elaborate system for protecting subject confidentiality was in place. The 232 child molesters who were interviewed reported a mean of 238 attempts to molest children under 14 years of age and 167 completed molestations; they reported an average of 76 victims. The men who committed acts of child molestation also reported the commission of a variety of other sexual crimes: 30% had exposed themselves to children and adults, 17% had committed adult rape, 14% voyeurism, and 9% frottage. The sexual behaviors of 85% of the child molesters involved physical contact; usually fondling or oral sex. Most of these men started becoming aroused to children at young ages; over half of the homosexual and 30% of the heterosexual pedophiles reported such arousal before age 15. There was often a lengthy period before this inappropriate sexual arousal was acted upon. Over 60% of the child molesters received no psychiatric diagnosis and showed no signs of psychopathology (other than paraphilia, a diagnostic term applied when an unusual act or image is required for sexual excitement). Most of the child molesters were primarily heterosexual in their orientation.

Both the Bernard and the Abel, Mittelman, and Becker samples were questioned under conditions that would guarantee anonymity to the respondents. The very high incidence rates which were obtained in these studies are undoubtedly due to this fact. Such high frequencies are occasionally reported by child molesters whom this author has interviewed in maximum security psychiatric institutions, but they are common neither in his experience nor in the literature more generally. Although the representativeness of the samples interviewed in these two studies may be questioned, it is clear that there are some child molesters who commit offenses very frequently. Even in prison settings under conditions of anonymity, child molesters ($n = 54$) report an average of 11 sexual offenses for which they were never charged (Groth, Longo, & McFadin, 1982). The modal age at first reported offense was 16 years.

As an aside, it is of interest to consider to which of the many possible populations these samples should be related: all men, all men who have been sexually aroused by children, all sex offenders, all men who have molested children, all men who have molested unrelated children, men who have coerced children into having sex, men who have been incarcerated for a sexual offense with a child, men who have committed more than one sexual offense involving a child under conditions of societal disapproval, and so on. The population that is selected says a great deal about how the problem is viewed.

In view of the methodological difficulties outlined earlier (see, Freund, Heasman, & Roper, 1982), it would be fruitless to attempt to provide accurate estimates of the incidence of sexual crimes against children, of the number of victims, or of the number of offenders. It is sufficient for our purposes to note that sexual crimes against children are common and that some offenders commit large numbers of such crimes.

FOLLOW-UP STUDIES

Much of what we know about child molesters comes from studies of known groups of offenders; these offenders are often institutionalized. The most important type of study that has been performed on these individuals concerns their post-release commission of new sexual offenses against children. These studies are important because they are directly related to issues of social policy, such as the need for and the efficacy of treatment interventions, and the adequacy of release decision-making. The studies reviewed in this section will be those that do not compare different treatment conditions and do not attempt to predict outcome from measures of therapeutic change. Studies that study child molesters primarily as part of larger groups of sexual offenders (e.g., Christiansen, Elers-Neilson, Le Maire, & Sturup, 1965) will not be reviewed.

In an early English study, Radzinowicz (1957) studied 1,985 sex offenders before the courts and their 1,994 victims. The offenders were followed up for a 4-year period subsequent to their conviction or release from prison. Sixty-nine percent of the victims were female. Of these, 25% were under 8 years of age and a further 44% were under 14 years of age. For the males, 20% were under 8 years of age and 53% were between 8 and 14 years of age. Eight-two percent of the victims of an indictable sex offense were under the age of 16. Of the offenders, 50% were convicted. Seventy percent of the offenders were strangers or casual acquaintances of the victims. Sixty percent of the offenses were classified as minor from the police reports. Of the 1,985 offenders, 83% had never been convicted for a sexual offense previously; however, about one-fourth admitted to having committed previous sexual offenses. The proportion of offenders who had had previous convictions was higher for men offending boys than girls.

Despite the short follow-up period from conviction or release from prison, 20% of the sample was reconvicted of a sexual offense. Of the heterosexual child molesters, 13% were reconvicted; the comparable figure for homosexual child molesters was 27%. New sexual offenses usually involved the same type of victim. Sexual recidivists were more likely to reoffend.

In a more recent English study, Gibbens, Soothill, and Way (1981) followed 48 men charged in 1951 with unlawful sexual intercourse with an unrelated female of under 13 years of age as well as a similar sample of 62 men charged in 1961. Sixty percent had had no previous serious offenses and 11% had been previously convicted for sex crimes. Many of the previous offenses involved property. In the 24-year follow-up period for the 1951 group, 46% were reconvicted and 19% were convicted for a new sexual offense. These calculations were adjusted for opportunity to reoffend.

In the 1961 group, the comparable figures for the 15-year follow-up were 35 and 5%. Gibbens et al. observed that these offenders continued to commit new sexual offenses for very long periods after their index offense and conclude that sex crimes against young children do not show the fast drop in frequency with age that is characteristic of property offenses. In a separate study, Gibbens, Soothill, and Way (1978) followed the criminal careers of men convicted of father–daughter incest; there was a very low rate of sexual recidivism among these men.

Fitch (1962) studied 139 men who were convicted of sex crimes against children and sent to a British prison. Of these, the index offense was homosexual for 45% of the sample and heterosexual for the remainder. Of those offenders who had committed more than one sexual offense, 82% had remained constant with respect to victim gender. The homosexual child molesters had committed more nonsexual and sexual offenses previously than had the heterosexual offenders. More important, homosexual offenders were twice as likely to be convicted of a new sexual offense upon their release from prison. Sexual reoffenders had committed more previous sexual offenses and had committed their first sexual offense at an earlier age than nonrecidivists.

Perhaps the best follow-up study has been conducted by Frisbie and Dondis (1965). They studied "sexual psychopaths" who had been treated in a maximum security psychiatric institution in California and discharged to the court as improved. Based upon the relation of the victim to the offender and the victim gender, the sample consisted of 1,035 heterosexual, 428 homosexual, and 49 bisexual child molesters. Of the heterosexual sample, there were 318 cases of father–daughter or father–stepdaughter incest. The victims in the incest cases tended to be older (8–17 years of age) than the unrelated victims who were usually under 11 years of age. The homosexual offenders were more frequently younger, better educated, single, and diagnosed as sociopathic than the heterosexual offenders.

The incest offenders had a cumulative 6-year recidivism rate of 10%, the heterosexual offenders against children less than 13 years of age had a recidivism rate of 22%, and the recidivism rate for homosexual child molesters was 35%. Most reoffenders maintained the gender of the victim involved in the index offense. The recidivism rate of the bisexual offenders was similar to that of the heterosexual offenders. Recidivists tended to be

younger and were more frequently diagnosed as sociopathic.

In a sequel to the Frisbie and Dondis study, Frisbie (1969) conducted a followup of 887 men 18 years of age or older who had been convicted of a sexual offense involving bodily contact with a minor under 18 years of age; 75% of the offenders were heterosexual. An effort was made to interview offenders whose victims were less than 14 years of age and offenders who were already sexual recidivists. Of the 617 offenders who were released, 15% were convicted of a new sexual offense within 3.5 years. Frisbie concluded on the basis of the follow-up interviews that economic stress, overcrowding and lack of privacy, unsatisfactory familial relationships, difficulties in occupational or social situations, health problems, and aging were all unrelated to recidivism. Instead, the following variables were found to be important: alcohol abuse, unorthodox ethical values, problems in establishing meaningful relationships with adult females, and the desire for physically immature females as sexual objects.

Taken together, these data indicate that recidivism increases with the number of previous sexual offenses, the selection of male victims, and the selection of unrelated victims.

CHARACTERISTICS OF CHILD MOLESTERS

This section concerns the issue of how and whether child molesters are different from other males. It should be clear from the material already reviewed, however, that the commission of an act of child molestation cannot, in itself, be used to infer much about the personal characteristics of the offender because the motivation of the behavior can be controlled by a variety of extrinsic factors. In the same way, we could not reliably deduce why the animals in the drinking experiment were drinking when we were not aware of the environmental contingencies (see Swanson, 1968). In this connection, the early literature exhibits an astonishing naivete in postulating predictable character types primarily on the basis of offense characteristics (e.g., Kopp, 1962).

Conceptually, it is not clear—without some sort of articulated theory—from what sorts of persons child molesters should be expected to differ. This is the same issue of comparison-group choice that was raised in the section on incidence. Investigators have, in general, taken an atheoretical approach and looked for differences between institutionalized child molesters and other known groups, which they then try to interpret. Unfortunately, such differences that are found may be attributable more to the vagaries of criminal justice policy and admission procedures than to differences between offender types.

The study of institutionalized or other highly selected populations of child molesters is far from useless, however. The data are directly relevant to similar populations of offenders and are the first step toward program evaluation efforts within the institution itself. Moreover, if similar findings emerge over institutions and settings which vary widely in their characteristics, we can have some confidence that the differences are true of some larger population. Finally, we should expect that institutionalized samples will be biased in useful ways by differential recruitment of more serious offenders (e.g., those who cause physical damage) and more repetitive offenders (those who have more opportunities to be apprehended). In terms of interventions designed to lessen the frequencies of child molestation based on the alteration of offender variables, it is obviously the more serious and repetitive offenders in whom we should be most interested.

DESCRIPTIVE STUDIES

There are a number of studies that are primarily descriptions of various intact groups of child molesters. They primarily involve institutionalized samples of varying sizes and present demographic, diagnostic, and some offense description data. The results of these studies reflect in part the different admission and referral systems that determine the availability of the offender population. These papers are part of a larger body of literature in which sex offenders are not necessarily classified by offense type. Reports that describe child molesters as a separate entity include those by Earls, Bouchard, and Laberge (1984); Gebhard and Gagnon (1964); Henn, Herjanic, and Vanderpearl (1976); Law (1979); Mandel, Bittner, Webb, Collins, and Jarcho (1965); McGeorge (1964); Myers and Berah (1983); Revitch and Weiss (1962); Shoor, Speed, and Bartlet (1966); and Swanson (1968).

It would be pointless to compare and contrast the findings of all of these various studies; however, in order to give some flavor of the findings, the Earls, Bouchard, and Laberge (1984) investigation will be described in more detail because it is one of the few to perform some statistical anal-

yses and interrater reliability checks on data coded from files. The sample was comprised of men incarcerated in Quebec federal penitentiaries, all of whom had sentences of over 2 years. Of 165 men, 112 had been sexually aggressive against adult women, 34 were child molesters (44% with male victims), and 19 were sexual murderers. In the context of the dangerousness of child molesters, it was of interest that the mean victim age for the sexual murderers was 16 years with 21% of the victims under 11 years of age. The victims of the child molesters were hospitalized at least one night in 5% of the cases, but there was mention of at least some injury in 32% the cases.

The child molesters, like the other offenders, came from multiproblem, low socio-economic status homes; had completed little formal schooling; and were often unemployed. They were much more likely to have been victims of sexual aggression themselves as children or adolescents (53%) than the other offenders; it was of interest that 63% of these childhood victimizations were perpetrated by nonfamily members. Eighty-two percent of the child molesters had had a previous conviction and 50% had had a previous conviction for a sex offense. Fewer of the child molesters had abused alcohol or drugs. The child molesters averaged 36 years of age at the time of the index offense, significantly older than the other offenders.

Turning to the offenses themselves, the child molestations were different than the other sexual offenses in that there were never accomplices involved, they were more frequently premeditated (91%), and seldom involved alcohol or drugs (26%). The victims (all under 14 years of age) averaged 11 years of age; of these, 38% were close relatives and 28% were strangers. Considering the index conviction, there were more victims involved in the child molestations (an average of 2.7) than in the other sex crimes.

Considered in the light of the victimization surveys, we can see that a sample of offenders sentenced to a penitentiary term of 2 years or more is not representative of child molesters in general, as child molestation is characterized by greater offense severity.

There is a large separate body of literature concerning father–daughter incest (e.g., Finkelhor, 1978; Frude, 1982; Meiselman, 1978; Russell, 1983; Vander Mey & Neff, 1982). Father–son incest appears to be a much rarer phenomenon (Dixon, Arnold, & Calestro, 1978; Langsley, Schwartz, & Fairbairn, 1968). Included in this literature are victimization surveys, a large number of reviews that express a variety of very strong opinions, and some descriptive studies of incest offenders (e.g., Gebhard, Gagnon, Pomeroy, & Christenson, 1965). A description of 78 German incest cases presented by Maisch (1972) will be reviewed here because of the detailed manner in which his results were presented and integrated with the previous literature. Maisch begins with a review of the relevant European and American laws concerning incest and properly notes that, for a behavior that is supposedly subject to a universal taboo, there is tremendous variance in the amount of past and present legal tolerance for father–daughter incest. Turning to the description of the incest cases themselves, the principal difference between incest and other forms of child molestation was in the extended duration of the sexual relationship (see De Francis, 1969). It was rare for the sexual behaviors to occur only once or twice; indeed, the behavior often began when the female approached puberty and continued until she was 15 or 16 years of age. The nature of the behavior varied as a function of victim age; fondling at younger ages was followed by coitus as the daughter became older. Quite often, the father precipitated the severance of the relationship by his jealousy of the daughter's contact with her male peers.

The incest offenders tended to come from lower socio-economic strata but typically did not live in overcrowded housing. Similarly, De Francis (1969) found in a comparison of incestuous and nonincestuous cases in New York City that the greater the degree of family disorganization and pathology, the greater the probability that the offender would be related to the victim. De Francis also observed that the victims in both incest and nonincest cases were poor; half of the families involved were receiving welfare. In a comparison of the literature on child familial physical abuse and familial sexual abuse, Avery-Clark, O'Neil, and Laws (1981) have noted that families which are involved in either form of abuse were subject to frequent crises and lived in chaotic circumstances (see Patterson, 1982). In the Maisch study, most of the offenders appeared to be normal in a psychiatric sense and had fewer previous criminal convictions than other groups of sex offenders. There were a number of factors that appeared to be predispositional on the basis of their frequency of occurrence; in order of descending importance, these were: prior family disorganization, disturbed marital relationship,

disturbed marital sexual relationship, "psychopathological personality" of the offender, and heavy offender drinking. A large percentage of alcoholics among incest offenders has also been observed by Virkkunen (1974). In agreement with other surveys, Maisch found the recidivism rate of incest offenders to be low.

TYPOLOGICAL SCHEMES

As pointed out earlier, typologies of child molesters can have immediate practical relevance if they are related to recidivism rates or to the selection of treatment methods or targets for specific intervention (Quinsey, 1977). To this can be added the possible heuristic use of such typological schemes in guiding subsequent research. Typological schemes, given real heterogeneity among child molesters, represent an initial step toward theoretical explanation. We have seen that a simple grouping of child molesters into heterosexual and homosexual and related and unrelated victim classes represents a large increase in our ability to predict recidivism. It is not difficult to see that such a classification scheme could relate directly to treatment interventions as well (if only in the sense that one is attempting to alter the selection of particular types of victims).

Other differences have been noted between heterosexual and homosexual child molesters as well. The average victim age of homosexual child molesters is older than that of heterosexual child molesters (Mohr, Turner, & Jerry, 1964). Heterosexual incest is much more frequently reported than homosexual incest (Dixon, Arnold, & Calestro, 1978; Langsley, Schwartz, & Fairbairn, 1968; Quinsey, 1977). Fewer homosexual than heterosexual child molesters report drinking at the time of the offense and, although both groups of child molesters have extensive histories of alcohol abuse, there is a trend for more heterosexual child molesters to have such a history (Rada, 1976). Homosexual child molesters report different sexual histories (for example, earlier onset of puberty) than heterosexual child molesters (Nedoma, Mellan, & Pondelickova, 1971).

The proportion of child molesters who choose male victims is surprisingly high. Estimates of the proportion of men who prefer adult men to those who prefer adult women as sexual partners cluster around 5% (Freund, Heasman, Racansky, & Glancy, 1984). However, a number of reports that describe the proportions of heterosexual, homosexual, and bisexual child molesters in a variety of settings indicate that homosexual child molesters are at least one third of the total (Freund, Heasman, Racansky, & Glancy, 1984). A finding of this magnitude is probably not an artifact of differential offense frequency, and we are left to speculate as to why such a large percentage of child molesters are homosexual when such a small percentage of men who prefer adults are homosexual. Lest there be confusion, it must be pointed out that most homosexual are not child molesters.

A typology based on victim gender and relatedness represents the null hypothesis in that a more elaborate typology would have to do better with respect to treatment issues or prediction of recidivism. None of the more elaborate typologies which have been advanced so far meet these criteria.

Categorical schemes have involved offender age (Mohr, Turner, & Jerry, 1964; but see Wilson & Cox, 1983), adequacy of social skills (Cohen, Seghorn, & Calmas, 1969), or a combination of victim type and presumed etiology (Gebhard, Gagnon, Pomeroy, & Christenson, 1965; Groth, Hobson, & Gary, 1982; McCaghy, 1967; 1968). The Gebhard et al. scheme is typical of many and involves classifying offenders by victim age and relationship and by type of act (e.g., aggressive) and then within these categories into subcategories: pedophiles, sociosexually underdeveloped, amoral delinquents, situational cases, mental defectives, psychotics, drunks, and senile deteriorates. These typological schemes have not been empirically related to recidivism or treatment outcome.

Rather than present a detailed review of the typologies mentioned above or the many similar schemes that have been presented in the literature (e.g., Fitch, 1962; LaMontagne & Lacerte-LaMontagne, 1977; West, 1965), some general methodological problems will be described which will indicate why such efforts have not and will not prove useful. The interested reader can find a complete review of these typologies in Knight, Schneider, and Rosenberg (in press). The basic problem with most of these efforts is that interjudge reliability of the categorizations have not been assessed; we have no way of knowing whether independent observers would agree on the classification of a given offender. Many (but certainly not all) of the variables employed are highly inferential, for example, whether an offender is viewed as "situational." Such a judgment often depends on an offender's luck in not being caught more than once and on how convincing a storyteller he is. Because much offender verbal

behavior in this situation is basically exculpatory, one has to be extremely skeptical. It is, of course, likely that a situational cause will be "found" when no other cause presents itself.

A further problem arises when the classification is dependent primarily on the offender's history: For example, offenders are often classified as psychopathic or sociopathic. Such a classification can be made in a variety of ways but usually rests on the number of previous offenses and the absence of major mental illness. Investigators will then sometimes turn full-circle by demonstrating empirically that the sociopathic offenders have committed more previous offenses than nonsociopathic offenders (e.g., Virkkunen, 1976). *Quelle surprise!*

A somewhat more amusing example of a similar phenomenon was provided by an author (who shall remain anonymous) who succeeded in demonstrating that offenders who were judged to be "immature" were younger than those who were not. As an aside, and to further witness the abysmal weakness of much of this literature, "psychological immaturity" is often advanced as an explanatory principle for pedophilia in general, based upon the resemblance of the looking, exposing, and fondling behaviors often indulged in by child molesters to those exhibited by children. In view of what pedophiles say about themselves and their concerns (e.g., Bernard, 1975; Rossman, 1976), such behaviors are more parsimoniously viewed as the result of offenders' desiring to avoid charges of rape, desiring not to hurt the victim, victim noncompliance, and the physical difficulty involved in penetrating small children. At the very least, one needs some corroborative data to support the conclusion that child molesters are immature.

Other problems in classification arise because of a lack of mutual exclusiveness among the categories; for example, "drunk" offenders could presumably overlap with every other category of offender. An overlapping categorical scheme (fuzzy sets) is workable but only with explicit decision rules. Finally, the coverage of these schemes has seldom been investigated and has never involved cross validation.

All of these difficulties stem from the conspicuously casual manner in which these schemes are derived. Basically, investigators gather some summary demographic statistics and some interview material and relate them in some intuitive fashion to offense descriptions. Although this is a sound strategy before one begins a research project, it is not the desired end-product. As pointed out elsewhere (e.g., Quinsey, 1984a), the sensible approach involves theory-driven or empirical-clustering algorithms on large multivariate data sets. These clusters can be tested on or, indeed, are partially derived from recidivism data.

Recently, some investigators have begun to approach the taxonomical problem from a clustering perspective. Knight, Schneider, and Rosenberg (in press) subjected 33 variables gathered on 125 rapists and child molesters to factor analysis to obtain four factor scores (substance use, social competence, antisocial behavior, and offense impulsivity) that were used together with a sexualized aggression scale in a cluster analysis. These data, although preliminary, revealed interpretable subtypes. Additional similar work with larger samples of child molesters should bring order to the repeatedly observed heterogeneity of these men.

This section on typologies has implications for what follows. As noted above, offenders vary in some important ways according to the gender and relationship of their victims. Clinical impressions suggest that a variety of other differences exist among these men. With this thought in mind, it can be appreciated why attempts to differentiate child molesters from other sorts of persons have often not proved fruitful. Differences may not be found between groups of child molesters and other persons because there really are no differences or because the heterogeneous nature of the child molester group chosen for comparison masks differences which are in fact there.

PSYCHOLOGICAL TESTS

Psychological tests are, in essence, highly structured interviews. As in less structured interviews, the perception of the interview situation by the interviewee is of the utmost importance. Often the testing or interviewing situation is perceived by a sex offender as one in which he must portray a particular image of himself. Sometimes this image is portrayed in terms of an account of the deviant activity. Accounts can have self-presentational functions even under conditions where the interviewer is not asking for an account. Even when the offender is not deliberately lying, the accounts that are provided are affected by a variety of factors in the interview or testing situation. McCaghy (1907, 1968), for example, has described how child molesters will attribute their offense to alcohol in order to disavow sexual devi-

ance and how offenders will adopt the language of their therapists in order to secure their release. Taylor (1972) obtained 86 accounts offered by sex offenders for their crimes from a variety of sources and classified them into types. In terms of the decreasing degree of voluntary control implied by the accounts, they were: breakdown in mental functioning ($N = 41$), inner impulse ($N = 12$), defective social skills ($N = 12$), victim implication ($N = 6$), desire for special experiences ($N = 7$), wish to frighten or hurt ($N = 3$), and refusal to accept normative restraint ($N = 5$). Which sort of explanation an offender proffers can have important consequences for him. Taylor found that magistrates were more likely to rate an account as highly believable, the less voluntary it was (importantly, however, the least voluntaristic accounts were both highly accepted and rejected as plausible explanations by the magistrates). When considering the literature on psychological testing as well as interview data on child molesters, the possible self-presentational strategies of the respondents, who are certainly in social predicaments, must constantly be borne in mind.

The literature on the psychological testing of child molesters has been reviewed several times previously (Langevin, 1983; Lester, 1975; Quinsey, 1977); it is reviewed here in some detail not because of the importance of the findings but because child molesters are so frequently assessed by means of psychological tests. This literature is rather poor scientifically (for example, there is the persistent problem of investigators using multiple univariate tests instead of multivariate techniques in studies employing tests with many subscales), although some of the more recent studies reflect increasing sophistication. One of the primary problems in this area is that investigators have not always appreciated the strategy that persons who have been charged with a sex offense against a child are most apt to employ; these persons are likely to attempt to appear contrite, compliant, and reformed. These attempts are likely to be more marked on the part of child molesters than other offenders because there is little in the way of subcultural support for such offenses available in the offender's immediate environment. Remarkably, this problem sometimes escapes the grasp of even very sophisticated behaviorally oriented scientists (e.g., Cliffe & Parry, 1980).

Occasionally, clinicians employ psychological tests, such as projectives, which are more or less opaque to the subject, to circumvent problems of dissimulation. Unfortunately, the very properties that make these tests difficult for the subject to interpret render them difficult for anyone else to interpret as well. It would be expected that a subject would adopt a very guarded response style when responding to ambiguous stimuli under these conditions. This expectation has been confirmed by Stricker, who analyzed semantic differential ratings of Rorschach cards (Stricker, 1964) and the Blacky pictures (Stricker, 1967). More promising results, however, have been obtained by Schlesinger and Kutash (1981), who elicited interpretations of ambiguous pictures by asking sex offenders and drug abusers to describe the "crimes" involved. Subjects produced stories that were related to the types of crimes they had committed and went far beyond the information given. More work on this criminal fantasy technique might prove useful.

Not surprisingly, perhaps, the instrument most commonly used to assess child molesters is the MMPI (Minnesota Multiphasic Personality Inventory); it has been said that, in view of the proliferation of these investigations, every man, woman, and child on earth will have published an MMPI study by the year 2000. Early studies (e.g., Marsh, Hilliard, & Liechti, 1955) developed special scales to discriminate mixed populations of sex offenders from other groups of known composition (see Atwood & Howell, 1971). The first study to examine child molesters as a separate group was conducted by Toobert, Bartelme, and Jones (1958). They obtained MMPI data on 120 California prison inmates who had committed a sex offense against a child less than 12 years of age and on 160 inmates who had not committed a sex offense. The child molesters were significantly different from the prison controls and a sample of normal men from Minnesota on 27 items. Cross validation indicated that the 27-item scale differentiated a new sample of child molesters from a new sample of nonsex offender inmates but not from a group of neurotics. The sex offenders scored highly (in descending order) on the psychopathic deviate, depression, femininity, and paranoia scales. Toobert and his colleagues concluded that sex offenders who scored low on the scale were simply psychopathic, whereas those who scored highly were religious, sexually dissatisfied, interpersonally inadequate, experiencing guilt, and highly sensitive to others' judgments. Such a grouping of traits is hardly unexpected, given the offenders' circumstances, and a perusal of the items indicates very clearly that most involve the offenders' arrested and incarcerated

status. The items include: "I enjoy children" (scored false), "I have never indulged in any unusual sex practices" (scored false), "I believe that I am a condemned person" (scored true), and so on.

Subsequent research has confirmed the finding that child molesters typically peak on the psychopathic deviate scale (e.g., Panton, 1979); however, it has been found that the more violent offenders tend to score next highest on the schizophrenia MMPI scale (Armentrout & Hauer, 1978; Panton, 1978), as do recidivistic child molesters (McCreary, 1975). Unfortunately, such a pattern of response is not only common among institutionalized child molesters but also among a wide variety of other offenders as well (Quinsey, Arnold, & Pruesse, 1980).

Langevin, Paitich, Freeman, Mann, and Handy (1978) reported data from the MMPI and 16 personality factor (PF) tests gathered from 27 father or stepfather incest offenders, 29 heterosexual child molesters, and 22 homosexual child molesters. Their results emerged from discriminant analyses of data from the aforementioned groups, a group of normal controls, and a variety of other groups of sexually anomalous men who were outpatients or incarcerated awaiting trial. The homosexual child molesters presented an emotionally disturbed pattern on the MMPI, scoring more highly than the controls on the depression, schizophrenia, psychopathic deviate, paranoia, and social introversion scales. On the 16 PF, they were more conservative and shrewd but less intuitive and group-dependent. The heterosexual child molesters exhibited a "tense" profile, scoring highly on the MMPI hypochondriasis scale and the tension scale of the 16 PF. They scored highly on 16 PF scales measuring reservedness and shyness but differed from the homosexual child molesters only in being less conservative. They also produced considerable evidence of emotional disturbance. The incest cases, in contrast, appeared more emotionally stable than the other groups but were the least assertive. None of the child molester groups showed high femininity scores.

Incarcerated child molesters have also been studied with the Edwards Personal Preference Schedule (Fisher, 1969; Fisher & Howell, 1970) and semantic differential tests involving ratings of their real and ideal selves (Dingman, Frisbie, & Vanasek, 1968; Frisbie, Vanasek, & Dingman, 1967; Vanasek, Frisbie, & Dingman, 1968). In general, these studies have produced findings interpretable in terms of their respondents' living conditions and attempts to impress the examiners.

Howells (1979) compared the responses of 10 nonsex offenders and 10 heterosexual child molesters undergoing group therapy on the Repertory Grid test, which requires the subject to specify the manner in which one stimulus is different from two others. Subjects were given the concepts of males and females of varying ages to evaluate. In the case of the child molesters, the female children were described as victims. The constructs elicited in the two samples were similar but there were some differences; the child molesters tended to view both men and women in terms of dominance and submission and to be preoccupied with small body builds. They saw their victims as passive and nondominant. Howells recommends further investigation of child molesters' perceptions of children in the areas of low dominance, physical slimness, and "innocence."

In summary, incarcerated child molesters produce test responses suggesting psychopathy (as do many other institutionalized samples), exhibit signs of emotional disturbance, respond in a very guarded style, and, in the Howells study, we see the first indication of a preference for immature body shapes. There are, in addition, some indications that heterosexual, homosexual, and incestuous child molesters respond differently on these tests. Overall, however, the yield from this line of investigation has been meager. Many of the differences that have been found are plausibly related not to enduring personality characteristics but to simple details of the offenders' histories (e.g., admitting having committed a sexual offense) or the response of the offender to arrest and surveillance. It is of interest that none of these studies attempted to predict recidivism or treatment outcome.

Fortunately, some of the findings produced by studies of incarcerated samples have also been obtained in a study of 77 members of an English pedophile self-help club (Wilson & Cox, 1983). Although this sample is clearly biased, it is at least biased in a different manner than the studies reported on above. About half of the club members agreed to take the Eysenck Personality Questionnaire and another specially constructed questionnaire. In agreement with the picture obtained in other studies, these child molesters (most of whom were interested in boys) presented themselves as introverted, shy, sensitive, lonely, depressed, and humorless. They did not, however, report guilt, as has been observed in other studies.

CLINICAL ASSESSMENT

Psychological tests are often used in broader clinical assessments of child molesters that are performed for various purposes, such as sentencing, deciding on the appropriateness or type of treatment, and release decisions. Thus, the questions that are at issue can relate to the presence of a specifiable mental illness, the responsiveness of an offender to any treatment or a particular treatment, and the dangerousness of the offender. The issue of diagnosis and the presence of a particular mental illness is no different with child molesters than with any other persons and will not be commented on further here; suffice it to say, as mentioned earlier, that a minority of child molesters have major mental illnesses and most are diagnosed as personality disordered. The issue of how clinicians decide on the treatability of child molesters has not received systematic study, but there is reason to believe, from studies of the assessment of treatability of heterogeneous groups of offenders, that clinicians would, in general, be pessimistic as to outcome and exhibit a high degree of disagreement among themselves with respect to offender treatability and to the applicability of particular treatment modalities (Quinsey & Maguire, 1983). More research is required on this point.

The assessment of dangerousness of child molesters has received some study. Dix (1975) attended ward conferences in a maximum security psychiatric institution in which recommendations were made about the continuing dangerousness of sex offenders (most of whom were child molesters). Dix's impression was that eight variables were related to a judgment of lessened dangerousness: verbalized acceptance of guilt and personal responsibility, development of an ability to articulate resolution of stress-producing situations, no report of deviant sexual fantasies, responsible behavior, having served "long enough" for the particular crime, achievement of maximum benefit from hospitalization, favorable changes in community circumstance, and the potential seriousness of a new offense should one be committed. Dix thought that very little time was spent in specifically addressing how dangerous the patients were; the probability of an offender getting in trouble again was never discussed with any precision.

Unfortunately, when clinicians are asked to specify the probability of a child molester reoffending upon release, the data are not encouraging. Quinsey and Ambtman (1979) had four experienced forensic psychiatrists and nine high school teachers study the psychiatric assessments (including relevant data from the patients' stay in a maximum security psychiatric institution), histories, and offense descriptions of 9 child molesters, 10 property offenders, and 11 serious offenders against adults. The three types of patient data were presented both separately and together on separate occasions to each judge. Ratings were made of the likelihood of a property offense, likelihood of an assaultive offense, and the seriousness of an assault, should one occur. Raters also judged whether a patient should be released from maximum security institutions. Agreement among judges within occupational categories was very low both in the ratings and in the release decisions, but the teachers and psychiatrists made, on average, very similar judgments. Ratings of the combined data were very well predicted from a linear combination of the three data types. Psychiatric and psychological assessment data and the patients' progress in the hospital made little contribution to the appraisal of the overall file. These data indicate that clinical assessments of dangerousness in these cases are determined primarily by offense severity and secondarily by patient history and are of very low reliability.

It may be comforting, in view of these data, to learn that processing decisions in the criminal justice system are quite often affected only trivially by clinical judgments. Konecni and Ebbesen (1984) studied the processing of mentally disordered offenders in California. Persons who engaged in abnormal sexual activities or offenses were interviewed by three court-appointed psychiatrists, who filed a presentence report containing a diagnosis and a classification of "mentally disordered sex offender" or "not a mentally disordered sex offender." In brief, it was found that if an offender had committed a previous sexual offense, he was diagnosed as a sexual deviant and classified as a mentally disordered sex offender. The judge almost invariably followed the psychiatrists' recommendations. In one sense, therefore, the clinical appraisal had an effect on the decision. When the basis of the appraisal is considered, however, it is apparent that it was entirely superfluous.

SEXUAL AGE PREFERENCES

Because the behaviors under discussion are sexual in nature, sexual preferences for children would be expected to be of great significance. We would expect, for example, that persons who choose a particular type of partner exclusively would have an erotic preference for that type of person. Given that one cannot always obtain what or whom one wants, an even clearer indication of preference is the imagining of certain sorts of persons during sexual or masturbatory fantasies. Of course, people would be expected to vary in the narrowness of their preferred categories of imaginary partners, and some persons might prefer several categories of partners. It would be better, therefore, to speak of relative erotic or sexual preference. For example, men who repeatedly seek sexual contact with young boys would be expected to report sexual fantasies involving exactly those sorts of activities and partners and to have fantasies involving other sorts of persons less frequently, in addition to finding them less arousing. Under conditions of anonymity or trust, child molesters often do report sexual fantasy material that is in accord with their histories of victim choices.

It would not be difficult to imagine, however, that on occasion, partners would be selected from a nonpreferred category because of special circumstance, such as the unavailability of persons with the preferred attributes. Such a phenomenon is common in prison, for example, where ordinarily heterosexual men become involved in homosexual relationships. This observation is not novel; many years ago, the noun "bugger" was defined as a term of endearment used among sailors.

Although the importance of sexual attractiveness might seem obvious on the basis of common observation, and perhaps even tautological, the idea that child molesters prefer sexual interactions with children because they find them sexually appealing has not won universal acceptance. The very fact that some child molesters exclusively choose boys and others girls would appear to be difficult to explain without invoking the concept of sexual preference. These observations notwithstanding, it has been argued that child molestation is not a sexual act. Groth, Hobson, and Gary (1982) assert, for example, that

> as with other forms of sexual assault (rape, indecent exposure, obscene telephone calling, and the like), sexual desire or passion does not appear to be the primary determinant of such behavior. Child molestation is the sexual expression of non-sexual needs and unresolved life issues. Pedophilia goes beyond sexual need and is, ultimately, a pseudo-sexual act. (p. 137)

Of course, as the animal experiment described at the beginning of this paper illustrates, consummatory behavior can be motivated by a number of contingencies simultaneously. It is not clear, however, whether multiple incentives would qualify a sexual act to be designated as pseudosexual. Operationally, the question becomes one of whether child molesters (particularly repetitive child molesters) are differentially sexually aroused by prepubertal children. The answer to this question, as will be seen below, is unequivocally "yes."

The scientific work on sexual preference measurement was begun by Dr. Kurt Freund. Over the course of many years, Freund developed and validated a means of measuring erotic preference among child molesters. His early work demonstrated that child molesters could be discriminated from nonchild molesters on the basis of a physiological measure of sexual arousal (Freund, 1965). Freund developed a means of measuring penis volume changes that occurred in response to slides of persons varying in age and sex. The rationale for the use of this measure was that changes in the state of appetence should be reflected most clearly in the relevant consummatory organ (Freund, 1977). Subsequent research using the phallometric method has employed circumferential gauges as well as volumetric devices. Methodological reviews can be found in a number of sources (Earls, 1984; Earls & Marshall, 1983; Freund, 1981; Laws & Osborne, 1983).

In an important study of sexual preference, Freund (1967a, 1967b) presented slides of males and females of varying ages to 35 heterosexuals, 25 homosexuals who preferred adult males (androphiles), 27 heterosexual child molesters, 23 homosexuals who preferred 13–17-year-olds, and 20 homosexual child molesters. As has been found by others, the homosexual child molesters' average victim age was older than the heterosexual child molesters' average victim age (11 years of age versus 8 years of age). Group assignment was based on previous choice of sexual partners because quite a number of these men claimed to prefer adult females as sexual partners. Each of the groups showed the largest erectile responses to the category of persons who matched their history of victim/partner choice. The heterosexual men responded less as the female stimuli decreased in age, although all of the female stimuli elicited a response; there was little and no differential response to the male series. Among the other subjects, however, the amount of sexual arousal elicited by persons of the nonpreferred gender varied

over age in the same relative order as the amount of response elicited by the preferred gender. Thus, for example, among female stimuli, androphiles showed the largest response to slides of adult women, and homosexual child molesters responded most to slides of female children. This finding suggests that body size and body shape as it varies over age is a critical determiner of sexual attractiveness.

Phallometric investigations have found that the age preferences for stimulus persons of the preferred gender are nearly identical for heterosexual and homosexual men who prefer adult partners (Freund, Langevin, Cibiri, & Zajac, 1973). In addition, it has been shown that men who report bisexual preferences for adults are indistinguishable on phallometric measures from homosexual men (Freund, Scher, Chan, & Ben-Aron, 1982). Bisexual preferences have been found in phallometric investigation, however, among groups of heterosexual and homosexual child molesters defined by victim choice (Freund & Langevin, 1976; Freund et al., 1982).

The finding that child molesters can be discriminated from nonchild molesters on the basis of their penile responses to slides of persons varying in age and gender has been replicated. Quinsey, Steinman, Bergersen, and Holmes (1975) compared 20 child molesters and 10 nonsex offender patients from a maximum security psychiatric institution with 11 heterosexual noninstitutionalized control subjects. Heterosexual child molesters responded most to slides of female children, homosexual child molesters most to slides of male children, and bisexual child molesters most to slides of little girls. The child molesters were discriminable from the groups of nonsex offenders (who did not differ from each other) on the basis of penile tumescence measurements but not on the basis of their rankings of the slides in terms of sexual attractiveness.

Incestuous child molesters appear less frequently to have inappropriate sexual age preferences. Quinsey, Chaplin, and Carrigan (1979) matched incestuous child molesters with child molesters who had selected unrelated victims on the basis of victim age and gender and the offender's age at the time of testing. One group of incestuous offenders had victimized either daughters or stepdaughters and another had chosen other relatives as victims. Incestuous subjects with daughter or stepdaughter victims showed more appropriate age preferences than their matched controls, but there was no significant differences among the other groups. This finding makes sense because it would be expected that men would shift to their next preferred category of person when there was difficulty in obtaining a person from their preferred partner category; thus in disturbed marriages, some men might be expected to shift their sexual attentions to their pubescent daughters because men prefer pubescent girls next to adult females (Freund, McKnight, Langevin, & Cibiri, 1972). This "surrogate hypothesis" of incest fits in with the low recidivism of incest cases, the differential involvement of pubescent female victims, the frequent prior marital unhappiness observed in incestuous families, and the commonly observed disturbances of the father's sexual relations with his wife together with opportunities for sex with his daughter (Maisch, 1972). This hypothesis is not inconsistent with data indicating that some incestuous fathers have inappropriate sexual preferences (Abel, Becker, Murphy, & Flanagan, 1981); obviously, some child molesters have children. It would be expected, however, that incestuous men with inappropriate sexual age preferences would be likely to victimize their children at earlier ages, sometimes choose their sons, and to molest children who are not related to them as well.

As with other measures applied to child molesters, the possibility of faking must be considered in interpreting penile response data. Freund, Chan, and Coulthard (1979) assessed a large group of men who had a history of child molestation. In addition to replicating the finding that most men with a repetitive history of such offenses exhibit inappropriate sexual preferences, they found that men who admitted their preference for children were more likely to exhibit such a preference phallometrically. That this result was likely due to faking instead of a real preference for adults was demonstrated by an increase in the proportion of "correct diagnoses" when the testing procedure was altered with the addition of a priming technique. The priming technique involved the presentation of a stimulus which the person claimed to prefer prior to the presentation of the target stimulus (a stimulus person from the category which the person is suspected of preferring on the basis of his history of victim choice).

Freund has concluded on the basis of this and his earlier studies (Freund, 1971, 1976, 1977, 1981) that several procedural issues are important in dealing with faking. First, the presentation of stimuli should be brief, unpredictable, and impressive. Second, only "admitters" should be used for theoretical work on the structure of sexual preferences. Third, the measurement of change in a therapeutic situation is extremely problematic because subjects gain experience in the measurement situation in a setting with very strong demand characteristics. Fourth, more work needs to be done on the prevention of faking using techniques such as priming.

Other investigators have shown that some, but by no means all, men can voluntarily influence their penile responses both by suppression or inhibition and by facilitation or production in accord with instructions (Henson & Rubin, 1971; Laws & Holmen, 1978; Laws & Rubin, 1969; Quinsey & Bergersen, 1976; Quinsey & Carrigan, 1978; Rosen, Shapiro, & Schwartz, 1975). The implications of these findings are clear. The measurement of sexual arousal by penile response is, at present, the best technology available for the investigation of age preferences. This technology, however, cannot be applied blindly because the testing situation is psychologically complex. Unfortunately, a test result indicating inappropriate preferences is more easily interpretable than one which indicates appropriate preferences because in most situations offenders claim nondeviance; test results, therefore, often indicate deviance or are difficult to interpret. Because these measures are the best available, they are becoming more commonly used; this raises the disturbing probability that strategies for self-presentation in phallometric testing situations will become part of the institutional offender culture. The irony of all this is the greater the weight assigned to these measures by persons who decide on the disposition of offenders, the less will be such measures' validity.

DANGEROUSNESS OF CHILD MOLESTERS

The issue of the dangerousness of child molesters is perhaps the most confused in the literature. In the present discussion the term "dangerousness" will designate the probability with which a person can be expected to commit an act that physically damages a child. Thus, "dangerousness" is a prediction of the probability of future behavior and a "dangerous person" is one who is expected to inflict future physical injury when unconstrained. In this scheme, the most dangerous child molester would be a person who is expected to kill a child. None of this is meant to deny the psychological suffering which can be inflicted on victims; the restriction on the concept of dangerousness is made to impose some order on the literature by means of an unambiguous definition. Physical injury is more easily measured than psychic trauma and, in addition, is of great importance in its own right.

A persistent problem in the literature is the confusion of the probability with which a child molester will commit a future offense and the probability with which he will commit a future violent offense involving injury (Quinsey, 1977). The respective likelihoods of these two phenomena are vastly different.

Turning first to child murder, the statistics make it abundantly clear that sexual homicides involving children are extremely rare. Compared to automobile accidents, the most common cause of violent death among children, death by sexual homicide is a statistical oddity. Even among child murders, sexual murders are very rare. Myers' (1967) 25-year survey of prepubescent homicides in Detroit found that 3 out of 83 victims had been killed in a sexual assault. Most of the murders were intrafamilial; mothers were the assailants in 43% of the cases. In New York City, Kaplun and Reich (1976) found similarly that the mother was the most frequent assailant in child homicide. Of the 112 victims killed between 1968 and 1969, 2% were killed as part of a sexual assault. Both of these studies linked child homicide to ongoing child abuse, poverty, and chaotic living conditions.

We have seen from the survey literature that a relatively small proportion of persons report having been injured during a sexual assault and that most of these injuries are minor. In fact, Gebhard, Gagnon, Pomeroy, and Christenson (1965) reported that none of the 18,000 persons interviewed by the Kinsey group claimed to have been sadistically victimized as a child.

These data, nevertheless, do indicate that the physical injury of children as a result of sexual assault should be regarded as a significant problem. Small proportions of samples become very large absolute numbers when extrapolated to entire populations. When the very high incidence of coercion and threat in sexual assaults on children are considered (Committee on Sexual Offences, 1984a, 1984b; De Francis, 1969), the magnitude of the problem increases considerably.

In summary, a small proportion of child molesters commit sexual acts causing injury and a small proportion of children are physically injured by child molesters. However, the absolute numbers of injuries, particularly minor injuries, and the number of assaults involving coercion and threat is substantial.

In view of the public concern about dangerous child molesters, the amount of research that has been done on them is astonishingly slight. Much of what has been done is at the anecdotal and case report level (see Quinsey, 1977, for a review of this literature). We have already seen in the section on clinical assessment that clinicians are not particularly good at predicting dangerousness among child molesters.

Recently, however, there has been a small amount of work in this area. Most of this research, of course, concerns child molesters who have been institutionalized. Such groups of institutionalized men are likely to be differentially comprised of dangerous offenders for several reasons. Men who have inflicted injury on their victims are more likely to have the crime reported, more likely to be charged, more likely to be prosecuted with vigor, and more likely to receive long sentences or other incapacitating dispositions. A cross section of institutionalized men will contain a differentially large proportion of serious offenders simply on the basis of sentence length alone. In addition, child molesters who have high offense densities will be differentially represented because of their greater opportunity to be arrested.

We must concern ourselves with two questions in connection with dangerousness. First, are some child molesters more dangerous than others or are physically injurious sexual acts distributed at random over offenders and occasions? Second, if some offenders are more likely than others to commit physically injurious acts, how can we identify who they are? These empirical questions have to be addressed through systematic follow-up or longitudinal research. The difficulties in the prediction of dangerous behavior are well known and include the difficulty in predicting a phenomenon having a low base rate of occurrence (e.g., see Quinsey, 1984b). There are situations, however, particularly with offenders confined in situations where there is considerable discretion concerning release, in which the base rate might increase for persons who have been repeatedly passed over or turned down (Quinsey, 1980). Because of the low base rate of physically injurious behaviors among child molesters, follow-up studies would have to employ enormously large samples in order to identify predictive variables or to select a sample with a high base rate on the basis of what is already known. In any event, the type of large-scale research with long follow-up periods, which would be necessary to address these issues, has not been accomplished (Quinsey, 1977). At present, the best that can be done is to examine postdictive studies, that is, studies that attempt to discriminate among child molesters who are known to have committed physically injurious acts from those who are not.

Even if such a discrimination could be achieved and be shown subsequently to have predictive validity, our problems would not necessarily be over. As the section on follow-up studies and recidivism has demonstrated, most of the variables that are known to be related to postrelease offenses relate to the offender's history of offending and, therefore, cannot change. From this perspective, we know all that we will ever know about an offender's dangerousness the moment that he commits his offense (Quinsey, 1977). What is required to circumvent this problem is the identification of groups of offenders with high base rates using static historical variables and the further identification of dynamic variables which can reflect lessened dangerousness within this group as a result of some intervention.

There are a variety of ways in which injury to a child could arise in the commission of a sexual assault. Because child molesters frequently resort to threats and physical force to effect sexual contact, injury could result from the child's struggle or escalation could ensue if the child refused to be intimidated. Injury could also occur from the type of sexual act employed, for example, intercourse with very young children. Child molesters might also attempt to eliminate the witness to the sexual assault in panic or as a result of premeditation. Finally, some child molesters might derive sexual pleasure from the infliction of pain, degradation, and fear. Injuries to victims that occur as a result of physical intimidation and penile penetration are described more frequently in the criminal histories of institutionalized child molesters than has been assumed (Marshall & Christie, 1981).

It has also been found that some child molesters are differentially sexually aroused by descriptions of sexual acts with children that involve force or sadism. Marshall and Christie (1981) present some data for individual child molesters that demonstrate such arousal. Abel, Becker, Murphy, and Flanagan (1981) have found, with a small sample of child molesters who were treated as outpatients, that the greater the amount of sexual arousal (measured phallometrically) to audiotaped descriptions of coercive sex with children (as opposed to "consenting" sex with children), the more violent the child molester's previous offenses against children. Avery-Clark and Laws (1984) have replicated and extended this basic finding. They studied 15 institutionalized child molesters judged to be quite dangerous on the basis of their offense descriptions together with 16 who were

judged to be less dangerous. Elements of the offense leading to the more dangerous categorization were: the use of more force than required to obtain victim compliance, the use of aggressive behaviors, and unresponsiveness to victim expressions of discomfort or pain. The stimuli were audiotaped descriptions of interactions between a man and a child (male or female depending on the history of the offender), which varied according to the type of sexual activity and the amount of force described. The more dangerous child molesters did not differ from the less dangerous in their penile responses to descriptions of consenting fondling and intercourse or nonconsenting intercourse but did show more arousal to the stories involving aggressive sex and assault. These data clearly indicate that some child molesters have sadistic sexual preferences and that these preferences are related to the commission of more injurious sexual assaults against children.

A similar conclusion has been reached in the study of offenders against adult women (Quinsey, 1984a). In cases of extremely violent rape against women, sadistic fantasies are known to be very important. MacCulloch, Snowden, Wood, and Mills (1983) have found among highly violent institutionalized sex offenders that most not only fantasized about sadistic sexual activities before the index offense but that most had actually carried out behavioral rehearsals before the violent act itself.

The relevance of sadistic fantasies in the prediction of dangerousness is obvious. In rare and extreme cases these fantasies relate to sexual murder. Very little research, particularly follow-up research (for obvious reasons), has been conducted on child molesters with histories of sadistic violent behaviors resulting in victim death. What little is known from clinical experience suggests that once these fantasies are established, they do not dissipate with time (e.g., Freund, 1976).

TREATMENT OF CHILD MOLESTERS

Because of our incomplete knowledge concerning the etiology of child molesting and the historically nonempirical approach to intervention, it is perhaps not surprising that the treatment of such offenders has been marked by confusion and failure. The early treatment literature consists almost completely of case reports, vague descriptions of group therapy, and assertions of treatment success without documentation (Quinsey, 1977). In many jurisdictions, special legislation has been implemented, which provides for the indeterminate detainment of dangerous child molesters. These efforts have either failed or remain controversial; sometimes the wrong sorts of individuals have been admitted, and often no one knows what to do with the offenders once they are incarcerated (Greenland, 1977, 1984; Meeks, 1963). Under the best of circumstances, admission, treatment, and release decisions are extremely difficult (Kozol, Cohen, & Garofalo, 1966).

There are, however, signs that the situation is improving rapidly (Crawford, 1981). The more recent literature on the treatment of child molesters is more empirical in nature, much more humble in its claims, and attempts to tailor the treatments to theoretically relevant aspects of the offenders' behaviors. The number of studies, reviews, and investigators have also increased, leading to the possibility of replication, joint follow-up efforts, and the comparison of different treatment techniques — all of which are necessary for the accumulation of clinical knowledge. Doubtless, this new activity will lead to disappointment and frustration as well as to new leads. However, given the variety of treatments that have been used for sex offenders, it is almost as important to demonstrate conclusively that something does not work as it is to demonstrate efficacy.

Intervention to eliminate child molestation can take a variety of forms. There are preventative measures that focus on limiting opportunities or on teaching children resistance and/or avoidance strategies (e.g., Brassard, Tyler, & Kehle, 1983; Poche, Brouwer, & Swearingen, 1981). These approaches, although important, will not be considered further here because they are outside the purview of a study concerned with offenders.

Traditionally, the state has relied on the incapacitation, deterrence, and punishment provided by incarceration. The incarceration of child molesters has never been formally evaluated as an intervention technique by being compared to some other forms of intervention, although the conviction rates for this type of offense do not encourage optimism. It seems clear, however, that incarceration will continue to be used for the foreseeable future because of societal reactions to these offenses and because of the undeniable incapacitation of aggressive offenders that confinement provides.

Efforts to modify child molesters themselves have focused on a number of variables either singly or in combination. The variables chosen for intervention are those conditions that clinicians judge to be either etiologically relevant or necessary for the commission of the offense for child molesters in general or for specific offenders. Efforts have been made to teach offenders self-control through guilt induction, empathy training, the acceptance of personal responsibility (e.g., Groth, 1983; Longo, 1983), and specific strategies for the avoidance of high risk situations (e.g., Pithers, Marques, Gibat, & Marlatt, 1983). Disinhibitory factors, such as alcohol abuse and high stress, have also been addressed. In cases of incestuous offenders, curtailment of opportunity through removal of the offender from the home is a technique used frequently (Finkelhor, 1983), as is marital and family therapy (Giarretto, 1976). Values and beliefs that facilitate child molesting have been treated through sex education and direct confrontation of the validity of these beliefs (Abel, Mittelman, & Becker, in press).

The sexual nature of these acts is also reflected in treatment approaches. Difficulties in obtaining gratification from adult partners have been approached through sex education, social skills training, and treatment for sexual dysfunction. Sexual preferences for children have been targeted by attempts to make children less attractive as sexual objects through the association of child molesting with aversive consequences (aversion therapy), as well as other techniques. Attempts have also been made to eliminate sexual arousal, which is a necessary condition for sexual performance, by alterations of the hormone system through castration or medication (Berlin, 1983). Drugs to reduce overall sexual arousal have been used as temporary expedients (while other treatments are being applied) or as long-term treatments in themselves. There have been some reports of success with these treatments but long-term follow-ups of treated child molesters are seldom reported, and treatment dropouts are a problem.

Most of the recent programs that have received evaluative attention are comprised of several modules which are offered to offenders on the basis of their individual needs. These modules commonly include: sex education (with an emphasis on values), social skills training, a program for the elimination of inappropriate sexual arousal (age preferences or sadistic sexual interests), and training in self-control techniques. Descriptions of these types of programs can be found in several sources (e.g., Abel, Becker, & Skinner, in press; Abel, Rouleau, & Cunningham-Rathner, 1984; Marshall, Earls, Segal, & Darke, 1983; Quinsey, Chaplin, Maguire, & Upfold, in press).

Two kinds of outcome data are relevant to the evaluation of these programs: the achievement of proximate goals and the achievement of ultimate or distal goals. With respect to proximate goals, an effort is made to determine whether offenders change on variables that the intervention targets. The evaluative data on this point have been very positive. Whitman and Quinsey (1981) demonstrated that child molesters can be taught to interact more skillfully with adult females with a brief heterosocial skill-training intervention involving modeling, coaching, and videotaped feedback; similarly, sex offenders very readily acquired sexual knowledge from a sex education course offered in a lecture and group-discussion format. With respect to inappropriate sexual age preferences, aversion therapy has been shown to make significant changes in the relative arousal elicited by adult and child slides (Quinsey, Chaplin, & Carrigan, 1980). This latter finding is in agreement with a substantial literature (Quinsey & Marshall, 1983).

Before turning to the literature on outcome, some problems in this literature should be addressed. The short-term changes produced by these programs are quite impressive, as we have seen; in addition, they appear to be specific to the type of program that has been implemented. There are, however, variations in the efficacy of these treatments—particularly in the modification of deviant sexual arousal—which are not at all well understood (Quinsey & Marshall, 1983). In addition, the theoretical interpretation of changes in penile responses to the stimuli used in treatment is moot. Do these changes reflect the offender's implementation of a strategy to control his sexual arousal, which we hope will generalize to nonlaboratory situations, or do they reflect a fundamental realignment of sexual preference structure? If the former, then the only difference between successful training and faking is in our opinion as to the offender's attributions about the nature of the strategy and its generalizability.

Turning to outcome data, Kelly (1982) reviewed 32 behaviorally oriented treatment studies of which 26 reported data from follow-up periods ranging from 2 weeks to 6.5 years. A total of 176 child molesters were treated in this series. Nearly 90% of these treatment efforts attempted to decrease urges to molest children (mostly through some variant of aversion therapy), and half tried to increase sexual behaviors directed toward adults. Most of the studies targeted more than one behavior. All of the studies reported at least some success; in particular, there was a reported reduction (as indexed by various measures) in urges to molest children in 95 of the 121 offenders for whom this was attempted.

There have been a number of recent studies that have presented follow-up data on child molesters as a separate group. Maletzky (1980) treated 38 child molesters with assisted covert sensitization. This procedure is a form of aversion therapy that involves pairing thoughts of child molestation with aversive imagery (covert sensitization) and assisting this procedure with the pairing of aversive odors with thoughts of child molestation (olfactory aversion therapy). Twenty-four weekly sessions were given, followed by 12 booster sessions over the next 3 years. Outcome data included police reports, client self-reports of fantasies and behavior, and penile plethysmography. Nearly 90% of the child molesters achieved a 75% reduction in overt and covert pedophilic behaviors and maintained this over a 30-month followup. No difference in outcome was obtained between self- and court referrals.

One of the important factors responsible for Maletzky's encouraging results may be the provision of continued follow-up and treatment. Quinsey, Chaplin, & Carrigan, 1980) found that, among subjects given aversion therapy, posttreatment sexual preference for children was related to subsequent recidivism over an average 29-month follow-up period. However, this relationship was lost with a longer follow-up period (Quinsey & Marshall, 1983). Penile circumference assessment data of two subjects who had recidivated indicated that their pretreatment sexual arousal pattern had returned. None of the subjects in these studies had received behavioral treatment subsequent to their release from maximum security institutions.

Abel, Rouleau, and Cunningham-Rathner (1984) have reported preliminary outcome data on an outpatient treatment program that included social skills training, confrontation of deviant beliefs concerning sexual misbehaviors, and methods to reduce deviant sexual arousal. Reduction of deviant arousal was accomplished with covert sensitization and satiation (the latter is a procedure involving the extensive rehearsal of deviant fantasies in a nonsexually aroused state). Of a mixed group of self-referred sex offenders, 89% of 44 offenders who were contacted at 6 months and 79% of 19 offenders who were contacted at 12 months reported, under confidential conditions, no further deviant activity. Incest offenders and heterosexual child molesters recidivated very seldomly; recidivism, when it did occur, was primarily among homosexual child molesters.

Davidson (1984) evaluated a behavioral program involving the modification of deviant arousal patterns, group psychotherapy, and social skills training, which was conducted in a maximum security penitentiary. Thirty-six treated men whose victims were under 12 years of age were matched on victim age, gender, and relationship with 36 men who had been released from prison before the treatment program was established. Over a follow-up period with a maximum of 60 months, the treated group averaged .0124 convictions per man-year at risk, whereas the untreated group averaged .0562 convictions — a clinically and statistically significant difference.

Taken as a whole, these treatment studies provide grounds for cautious optimism. Practically, they suggest that brief, focused treatments can be effective, particularly when combined with continuing community intervention. Thus, for child molesters who have high densities of offending, such interventions appear cost-effective and socially beneficial. Theoretically, these studies support the idea that inappropriate sexual arousal is a central etiological element in sexual behaviors directed toward children.

This area of investigation now requires some comparisons of different treatment techniques so that a better theoretical understanding of the therapeutic process and critical therapeutic elements can guide the improvement of future treatment methods.

THEORIES OF CHILD MOLESTATION

A complete and satisfactory theory of child molestation is, of course, beyond our grasp at present because of limitations in our factual knowledge. We can see, however, from the material that has been reviewed thus far, the general form such a theory might take and some important observations that a theory must explain. This section will attempt to bring together the principal observations and discuss their implications for an etiological theory. No attempt will be made to review the very limited and often fanciful theoretical statements that have been made in the literature (the interested reader is referred to Howells, 1981).

In order to facilitate the discussion that follows, a brief recapitulation of the major findings in the literature is in order. Child molestation has been observed in a wide variety of temporal and cultural contexts. Where it is common, it is accompanied by cultural beliefs that support and structure its practice. It is important to note, however, that child molestation has persisted in societies which condemn and punish it severely. In contemporary Western societies, child molestation is a common occurrence. Physical coercion and threat are often involved in these offenses, but serious physical injury to children occurs in but a very small percentage of offenses. Child molesters who are or have been incarcerated, however, are much more likely to have injured their victims. Some child molesters contact many victims over long periods of time but are seldom arrested. Homosexual child molesters prefer older victims, are less likely to be incestuous, and have higher sexual recidivism rates than heterosexual child molesters. Incestuous offenses are more often repeated over long periods of time but incest offenders have lower recidivism rates than other child molesters. Psychological test data indicate that child molesters score highly on psychopathy and tend to be shy individuals. Clinicians show poor agreement about the dangerousness of child molesters. Although treatment approaches for child molesters must be considered experimental, behavioral methods appear promising.

The principal difference between child molesters and other people is that child molesters are more sexually responsive to children. Most men are, however, to a lesser extent, responsive to younger females as well, such that they exhibit an age preference gradient. We might infer, therefore, that children are chosen because they are either preferred as sexual partners or are surrogates or second choices. We would expect phallometric testing to indicate inappropriate preferences whenever a person reports being attracted to children, exclusively chooses children as sexual partners, and goes to great lengths to contact children sexually. Inappropriate sexual age preferences would be considered more likely when male victims are chosen (because most nonsex offenders show little interest in male children) and where the victims are very young. It is more likely that inappropriate age preferences are involved in causing sexual interactions with children in modern Western societies than in times and places where this behavior is normative. Simply put, when the behavior occurs in spite of the penalties and contempt that can result from sexual interactions with children, we should conclude that it is more attractive. Nabokov (1955) provides a compelling fictional account of a child molester's struggle to conceal his preference for little girls in order to avoid the negative consequences of discovery. In this connection, it would be of great interest to study the sexual age and gender preferences among men from societies which practice ritualized homosexuality.

What might lead a person who prefers adult partners to choose a child as a sexual object in the face of extremely aversive contingencies? The temporary or permanent unavailability of the preferred type of partner would, of course, be a necessary condition for this type of interaction (Frude, 1982). Thus, we would expect this type of child molester to be experiencing marital discord and a poor sexual relationship with his wife or to be unattached. We would expect that he would have difficulty attracting and keeping adult partners because of homeliness (Berman & Freedman, 1961), real or self-perceived lack of social skills (Segal & Marshall, in press; Wilson & Cox, 1983), and excessive shyness (Wilson & Cox, 1983). Relatively low intelligence or organic defect has also been sporadically reported in the literature, but because these diagnoses often lead to placements in institutions where sex offenders are seldom studied, no definitive statement is possible. In addition, we would expect such a person to be relatively unresponsive to aversive societal sanctions because of poor socialization, as reflected in high psychopathic deviate scores on the MMPI and by the frequent commission of property crimes. Alcohol abuse would be expected to lead to the same result, and such a history is often marked among child molesters (Henn, Herjanic, & Vanderpearl, 1976; Marshall & Christie, 1981; Rada, 1976). Opportunity would also play an important role in this type of offense, particularly when it involves a low probability of discovery. Such opportunity can be provided by familial living conditions or by seductive behavior on the part of the victim (Virkkunen, 1975, 1981; Yates, 1982).

It is of interest that these behaviors are often accompanied by a complex of justificatory beliefs; this was observed in Melanesian societies that practice ritual homosexual pedophilia, in ancient Greece, among the Uranian poets, and among many present-day child molesters (e.g., Abel, Rouleau, & Cunningham-Rathner, 1984). A good guess is that such beliefs arise as a consequence of the behaviors rather than as their cause, but there are no data on the issue one way or the other.

In summary, there are two issues in the genesis of sexual behavior with children. One involves a continuum of relative sexual preference for children and the other a variety of reasons why children are chosen as sexual expedients. These two phenomena are, of course, not mutually exclusive but additive. Aside from the issues involving sexual preference, an explanation for child molesta-

tion can be expected to come from general criminology and behavior theory; thus, these phenomena need not detain us further and we can turn our attention to the acquisition of sexual preferences for young children. The development of sexual interest in sadistic activities is probably similar in child molesters and rapists, and the reader is referred to Quinsey (1984a) for a detailed discussion of this topic.

From an evolutionary viewpoint, it would appear that an exclusive preference for young children is a very costly error in male reproductive strategy. Because of this and related observations (Quinsey, 1984a), it seems plausible that such preferences are learned. However, because of the importance of sexual preferences in reproductive success, it is unlikely that they would be entirely unconstrained by natural selection. We don't, after all, observe persons who prefer trees as sexual partners. As argued elsewhere (Quinsey, 1984a), some preferences are likely to be much more easily learned than others. Stimuli that are associated with reproductively viable females are plausible candidates for "prepared" or easily conditionable status: These would include youthfulness, primary sexual characteristics, signs of good health, and secondary sexual characteristics (see Symons, 1979). It is not difficult to imagine circumstances in which youthfulness might become the dominant cue, particularly because a viable male reproductive strategy might involve forming a long-term relationship with an immature female. This account is obviously highly speculative, but it does lead to the prediction that female children should be more commonly selected as victims than male children, that bisexual preferences should be more common among child molesters (because youth is more important than primary sexual characteristics), and that age preferences should be similar for preferred and nonpreferred genders. As we have seen, Freund's research supports these predictions.

A great deal of research is yet required before a theoretical account can be given for the development of inappropriate sexual age preferences. There are a few leads, however. The first lead involves the age at which inappropriate sexual preferences are first reported or noted. We know that, among men who prefer adult males as sexual partners, these preferences are reported to be manifest at very early ages (Bell, Weinberg, & Hammersmith, 1981). Similarly, child molesters report becoming aroused by children at young ages, although these reports show considerable variance (Abel, Mittelman, & Becker, in press); it should be noted in this connection that the detection of "inappropriate" sexual attraction for young children becomes increasingly difficult and then impossible as the informant reports about his earlier and earlier ages. Child molesters sometimes report that their fantasies concerning children precede their overt behaviors by a considerable period of time; this temporal gap may be a period in which the behavior is uniquely susceptible to intervention.

A second lead is provided by the very high frequency with which child molesters report being sexually victimized themselves as children. From a social learning perspective, one has no difficulty with such a finding. One possible source of inappropriate sexual interest has not been supported, however; child molesters report having been exposed to less pornography at young ages than normal subjects (Goldstein & Kant, 1973).

Our understanding of the development of inappropriate sexual age preferences is, however, extremely handicapped, as there is little known about the development of normal sexual age preferences despite the well documented interest children have in sexual activities (Goldman & Goldman, 1982; Langfeldt, 1981). It is unknown whether the development of normal sexual age and gender preferences involve the acquisition of sexual interest in particular age- and gender-related cues, the inhibition of already existing interests, or some combination of both. Several hypothetical scenarios present themselves for consideration: A preference for adult females exists from birth or from a very early age, this preference for adults develops slowly over the course of childhood; there is a preference for same-age female peers that shifts upward with age; and there is an initial preference for age peers and older females but the interest in younger females is progressively inhibited. In the absence of empirical work in this area, other scenarios could doubtless be advanced.

There may be ways to approach the subject of the development of sexual age preferences indirectly which have not yet been tried. Sheer physical attractiveness is related to sexual attractiveness in a general way, but the relationship between esthetics and sexual arousal is at present unclear; equally unclear is how this relationship might vary with age. It is known that physical attractiveness has profound effects on person perception (Berscheid & Walster, 1974) and is a principal determiner of dating desirability (Berscheid,

Dion, Walster, & Walster, 1971; Walster, Aronson, Abrahams, & Rottman, 1966). Cross and Cross (1971) studied preferences for facial photographs that varied in age and gender among subjects from 7 years of age to adult. Males of all ages preferred to look at pictures of 17-year-olds. The preferences of adult men declined in the following order: 17-year-old girls, adult females, 17-year-old males, 7-year-old girls, 7-year-old boys, and adult males. The preferences of the 7-year-old boys, on the other hand, declined in the order: 17-year-old boys, 17-year-old girls, 7-year-old girls, adult men, 7-year-old boys, and adult females. Although some of these differences in ratings were small, they are nonetheless suggestive in the present context. It would be of great interest to know how ratings of attractiveness would vary over age and gender with full-body photographs of people in bathing suits. Further research on the relation of esthetic judgment to sexual preference may prove fruitful.

In conclusion, an explanation of the development of inappropriate sexual age preferences is probably best approached from the study of appropriate sexual age preference development. Such a theory would go a long way toward an explanation of child molesting. Among child molesters themselves, comparisons of sadistic and nonsadistic offenders and further comparisons of homosexual, bisexual, and heterosexual child molesters may provide important practical and theoretical insights.

REFERENCES

Abel, G.G., Becker, J.V., Murphy, W.D., & Flanagan, B. (1981). Identifying dangerous child molesters. In R.B. Stuart (Ed.), *Violent behavior: Social learning approaches to prediction, management, and treatment* (pp. 116–137). New York: Brunner Mazel.

Abel, G.G., Becker, J.V., & Skinner, L.J. (in press). Treatment of the violent sex offender. In L.H. Roth (Ed.), *Clinical treatment of the violent person* (Crime and Delinquency Issues: A monograph series). Washington: National Institute of Mental Health.

Abel, G.G., Mittelman, M.S., & Becker, J. (in press). Sexual offenders: Results of assessment and recommendations for treatment. In M.H. Ben-Aron, S.J. Hucker, & C.D. Webster (Eds.), *Clinical criminology: The assessment and treatment of criminal behavior.* Toronto: Butterworth.

Abel, G.G., Rouleau, J., & Cunningham-Rathner, J. (1984). Sexually aggressive behavior. In W. Curran, A.L. McGarry, & S. Shah (Eds.), *Modern legal psychiatry and psychology.* Philadelphia: Davis.

Allen, M.R. (1984). Homosexuality, male power, and political organization in North Vanuatu: A comparative analysis. In G.H. Herdt (Ed.), *Ritualized homosexuality in Melanesia* (pp. 83–126). Berkeley: University of California Press.

Armentrout, J.A., & Hauer, A.L. (1978). MMPIs of rapists of adults, rapists of children, and non-rapist sex offenders. *Journal of Clinical Psychology, 34,* 330–332.

Atwood, R.W., & Howell, R.J. (1971). Pupillometric and personality test score differences of female aggressing pedophiliacs and normals. *Psychonomic Science, 11,* 115–116.

Avery-Clark, C., & Laws, D.R. (1984). Differential erection response patterns of sexual child abusers to stimuli describing activities with children. *Behavior Therapy, 15,* 71–83.

Avery-Clark, C., O'Neil, J.A., & Laws, D.R. (1981). A comparison of intrafamilial sexual and physical child abuse. In M. Cook & K. Howells (Eds.), *Adult sexual interest in children* (pp. 3–39). Toronto: Academic Press.

Bell, A.P., Weinberg, M.S., & Hammersmith, S.K. (1981). *Sexual preference: Its development in men and women.* Bloomington, IN: Indiana University Press.

Berlin, F.S. (1983). Sex offenders: A biomedical perspective and a status report on biomedical treatment. In J.G. Greer & I.R. Stuart (Eds.), *The sexual aggressor: Current perspectives on treatment* (pp. 83–123). New York: Van Nostrand Reinhold.

Berman, L.H., & Freedman, L.Z. (1961). Clinical perception of sexual deviates. *Journal of Psychology, 52,* 157–160.

Bernard, F. (1975). An enquiry among a group of pedophiles. *The Journal of Sex Research, 11,* 242–255.

Berscheid, E., Dion, K., Walster, E., & Walster, G.W. (1971). Physical attractiveness and dating choice: A test of the matching hypothesis. *Journal of Experimental Social Psychology, 7,* 173–189.

Berscheid, E., & Walster, E. (1974). Physical attractiveness. In L. Berkowitz (Ed.), *Advances in experimental social psychology* (Vol. 7, pp. 157–215). New York: Academic Press.

Brassard, M.R., Tyler, A.H., & Kehle, T.J. (1983). School programs to prevent intrafamilial child sexual abuse. *Child Abuse and Neglect, 7,* 241–245.

Brownmiller, S. (1975). *Against our will: Men, women, and rape.* New York: Simon and Schuster.

Buss, D.M. (1984). Evolutionary biology and personality psychology: Toward a conception of human nature and individual differences. *American Psychologist, 39,* 1135–1147.

Carstairs, G.M. (1964). Cultural differences in sexual deviation. In E. Rosen (Ed.), *The pathology and treatment of sexual deviation: A methodological approach* (pp. 419–434). London: Oxford University Press.

Chiswick, D. (1983). Sex crimes. *British Journal of Psychiatry, 143,* 236–242.

Christiansen, K.O., Elers-Neilsen, M., Le Maire, L., & Sturup, G.K. (1965). Recidivism among sexual offenders. In K.O. Christiansen (Ed.), *Scandanavian Studies in Criminology* (Vol. 1, pp. 55–85). London: Tavistock.

Cliffe, M.J., & Parry, S.J. (1980). Matching to reinforcer value: Human concurrent variable-interval performance. *Quarterly Journal of Experimental Psychology, 32,* 557–570.

Cohen, M.L., Seghorn, T., & Calmas, W. (1969). Sociometric study of the sex offender. *Journal of Abnormal Psychology, 74,* 249–255.

Committee on Sexual Offences Against Children and Youths. (1984a). *Sexual offences against children* (Vol. 1). Ottawa: Supply and Services Canada.

Committee on Sexual Offences Against Children and Youths. (1984b). *Sexual offences against children* (Vol. 2). Ottawa: Supply and Services Canada.

Crawford, D.A. (1981). Treatment approaches with pedophiles. In M. Cook & K. Howells (Eds.), *Adult sexual interest in children* (pp. 181–217). Toronto: Academic Press.

Cross, J.F., & Cross, J. (1971). Age, sex, race, and the perception of facial beauty. *Developmental Psychology, 5,* 433–439.

Davidson, P.R. (1984). *Behavioral treatment for incarcerated sex offenders: Post-release outcome.* Unpublished manuscript.

de Beauvoir, S. (1966). Must we burn Sade? In A. Wainhouse & R. Seaver (Eds. and Trans.), *The 120 days of Sodom and other writings* (pp. 3–64). New York: Grove Press. (Original published in 1951 and 1952).

De Francis, V. (1969). *Protecting the child victim of sex crimes committed by adults.* Denver, CO: American Humane Association, Children's Division.

de Mause, L. (1974). *The history of childhood.* New York: Psychohistory Press.

de Sade, M. (1966). The 120 days of Sodom. In A. Wainhouse & R. Seaver (Eds. and Trans.), *The 120 days of Sodom and other writings* (pp. 189–674). New York: Grove Press. (Original work written in 1785.)

Dingman, H.F., Frisbie, L., & Vanasek, F.J. (1968). Erosion of morale in resocialization of pedophiles. *Psychological Reports, 23,* 792–794.

Dix, G.E. (1975). Determining the continued dangerousness of psychologically abnormal sex offenders. *Journal of Psychiatry and Law, 3,* 327–344.

Dixon, K.N., Arnold, E., & Calestro, K. (1978). Father-son incest: Underreported psychiatric problem? *American Journal of Psychiatry, 135,* 835–838.

Earls, C.M. (1984). *Analyse critique des metholodologies utilisees pour mesurer les reactions sexuelles chez les hommes.* Cahier de Recherche No. 8, Institut Philippe Pinel de Montreal.

Earls, C.M., Bouchard, L., & Laberge, J. (1984). *Etude descriptive des delinquants sexuels incarceres dans les penitenciers Quebecois.* Cahier de Recherche No. 7, Institut Philippe Pinel de Montreal.

Earls, C.M., & Marshall, W.L. (1983). The current state of technology in the laboratory assessment of sexual arousal patterns. In J.G. Greer & I.R. Stuart (Eds.), *The sexual aggressor: Current perspectives on treatment* (pp. 336–362). Toronto: Van Nostrand Reinhold.

Elliott, D.S., Ageton, S.S., Huizinga, D., Knowles, B.A., & Canter, R.J. (1983). *The prevalence and incidence of delinquent behavior: 1976–1980* (National Youth Survey Report No. 26). Boulder, CO: Behavioral Research Institute.

Finkelhor, D. (1979). Psychological, cultural and family factors in incest and family sexual abuse. *Journal of Marriage and Family Counseling, 4,* 41–49.

Finkelhor, D. (1983). Removing the child–prosecuting the offender in cases of sexual abuse: Evidence from the National Reporting System for Child Abuse and Neglect. *Child Abuse and Neglect*, 7, 195–205.

Fisher, G. (1969). Psychological needs of heterosexual pedophiliacs. *Diseases of the Nervous System*, 30, 419–421.

Fisher, G., & Howell, L.M. (1970). Psychological needs of homosexual pedophiliacs. *Diseases of the Nervous System*, 31, 623–654.

Fitch, J.H. (1962). Men convicted of sexual offences against children: A descriptive followup study. *British Journal of Criminology*, 3, 18–37.

Fitzgerald, T.K. (1977). A critique of anthropological research on homosexuality. *Journal of Homosexuality*, 2, 385–397.

Ford, C.S. (1960). Sex offenses: An anthropological perspective. *Law and Contemporary Problems*, 25, 225–248.

Freund, K. (1965). Diagnosing heterosexual pedophilia by means of a test for sexual interest. *Behaviour Research and Therapy*, 3, 229–234.

Freund, K. (1967a). Diagnosing homo- or heterosexuality and erotic age-preference by means of a psychophysiological test. *Behaviour Research and Therapy*, 5, 209–228.

Freund, K. (1967b). Erotic preference in pedophilia. *Behaviour Research and Therapy*, 5, 339–348.

Freund, K. (1971). A note on the use of the phallometric method of measuring mild sexual arousal in the male. *Behavior Therapy*, 2, 223–228.

Freund, K. (1976). Diagnosis and treatment of forensically significant anomalous erotic preferences. *Canadian Journal of Criminology and Corrections*, 18, 181–189.

Freund, K. (1977). Psychophysiological assessment of change in erotic preferences. *Behaviour Research and Therapy*, 15, 297–301.

Freund, K. (1981). Assessment of pedophilia. In M. Cook & K. Howells (Eds.), *Adult sexual interest in children* (pp. 139–179). Toronto: Academic Press.

Freund, K., Chan, S., & Coulthard, R. (1979). Phallometric diagnosis with "nonadmitters." *Behaviour Research and Therapy*, 17, 451–457.

Freund, K., Heasman, G., Racansky, I.G., & Glancy, G. (1984). Pedophilia and heterosexuality vs. homosexuality. *Journal of Sex and Marital Therapy*, 10, 193–200.

Freund, K., Heasman, G.A., & Roper, V. (1982). Results of the main studies on sexual offences against children and pubescents (a review). *Canadian Journal of Criminology*, 24, 387–397.

Freund, K., & Langevin, R. (1976). Bisexuality in homosexual pedophilia. *Archives of Sexual Behavior*, 5, 415–423.

Freund, K., Langevin, R., Cibiri, S., & Zajac, Y. (1973). Heterosexual aversion in homosexual males. *British Journal of Psychiatry*, 122, 163–169.

Freund, K., McKnight, C.K., Langevin, R., & Cibiri, S. (1972). The female child as a surrogate object. *Archives of Sexual Behavior*, 2, 119–133.

Freund, K., Scher, H., Chan, S., & Ben-Aron, M. (1982), Experimental analysis of pedophilia. *Behaviour Research and Therapy*, 20, 105–112.

Frisbie, L.V. (1969). *Another look at sex offenders in California* (California Mental Health Research Monograph, No. 12). State of California Department of Mental Hygiene.

Frisbie, L.V., & Dondis, E.H. (1965). *Recidivism among treated sex offenders* (California Mental Health Research Monograph, No. 5). State of California Department of Mental Hygiene.

Frisbie, L.V., Vanasek, F.J., & Dingman, H.F. (1967). The self and the ideal self: Methodological study of pedophiles. *Psychological Reports*, 20, 699–706.

Frude, N. (1982). The sexual nature of sexual abuse: A review of the literature. *Child Abuse and Neglect*, 6, 215–223.

Gebhard, P.H., & Gagnon, J.H. (1964). Male sex offenders against very young children. *American Journal of Psychiatry*, 121, 576–579.

Gebhard, P.H., Gagnon, J.H., Pomeroy, W.B., & Christenson, C.V. (1965). *Sex offenders: An analysis of types*. New York: Harper & Row.

Giarretto, H. (1976). Humanistic treatment of father-daughter incest. In R.E. Helfer & C.H. Kempe (Eds.), *Child abuse and neglect: The family and the community* (pp. 143–158). Cambridge, MA: Ballinger.

Gibbens, T.C.N., Soothill, K.L., & Way, C.K. (1978). Sibling and parent-child incest offenders. *British Journal of Criminology*, 18, 40–52.

Gibbens, T.C.N., Soothill, K.L., & Way, C.K. (1981). Sex offences against young girls: A long-term record study. *Psychological Medicine*, 11, 351–357.

Goldman, R., & Goldman, J. (1982). *Children's sexual thinking*. Boston: Routledge & Kegan Paul.

Goldstein, M.J., & Kant, H.S. (1973). *Pornography and sexual deviance*. Berkeley: University of California Press.

Goodich, M. (1976). Sodomy in medieval secular law. *Journal of Homosexuality*, 1, 295–302.

Greenland, C. (1977). Psychiatry and the dangerous offender. *Canadian Psychiatric Association Journal*, 22, 155–159.

Greenland, C. (1984). Dangerous sexual offender legislation in Canada, 1948–1977: An experiment that failed. *Canadian Journal of Criminology*, 26, 1–12.

Groth, A.N. (1983). Treatment of the sexual offender in a correctional institution. In J.G. Greer & I.R. Stuart (Eds.), *The sexual aggressor: Current perspectives on treatment* (pp. 160–176). New York: Van Nostrand Reinhold.

Groth, A.N., Hobson, W.F., & Gary, T.S. (1982). The child molester: Clinical observations. *Journal of Social Work and Human Sexuality*, 1, 129–144.

Groth, A.N., Longo, R.E., & McFadin, J.B. (1982). Undetected recidivism among rapists and child molesters. *Crime and Delinquency*, 28, 450–458.

Henn, F.A., Herjanic, M., & Vanderpearl, R.H. (1976). Forensic psychiatry: Profiles of two types of sex offenders. *American Journal of Psychiatry*, 133, 694–696.

Henry, J. (1964). *Jungle people: A Kaingang tribe of the highlands of Brazil*. New York: Random House.

Henson, D.E., & Rubin, H.B. (1971). Voluntary control of eroticism. *Journal of Applied Behavior Analysis*, 4, 37–44.

Herdt, G.H. (1984a). Ritualized homosexual behavior in the male cults of Melanesia, 1862–1983: An introduction. In G.H. Herdt (Ed.), *Ritualized homosexuality in Melanesia* (pp. 1–81). Berkeley. University of California Press.

Herdt, G.H. (1984b). Semen transactions in Sambia culture. In G.H. Herdt (Ed.), *Ritualized homosexuality in Melanesia* (pp. 167–209). Berkeley: University of California Press.

Howells, K. (1979). Some meanings of children for pedophiles. In M. Cook & G. Wilson (Eds.), *Love and attraction* (pp. 519–526). New York: Pergamon.

Howells, K. (1981). Adult sexual interest in children: Considerations relevant to aetiology. In M. Cook & K. Howells (Eds.), *Adult sexual interest in children* (pp. 55–94). Toronto: Academic Press.

Jones, G.P. (1982). The social study of pederasty: In search of a literature base: An annotated bibliography of sources in English. *Journal of Homosexuality, 8*, 61–95.

Kaplun, D., & Reich, R. (1976). The murdered child and his killers. *American Journal of Psychiatry, 133*, 809–813.

Kelly, R.J. (1982). Behavioral reorientation of pedophiliacs: Can it be done? *Clinical Psychology Review, 2*, 387–408.

Knight, R.A., Schneider, B.A., & Rosenberg, R. (in press). Classification of sexual offenders: Perspectives, methods, and validation. In A. Burgess (Ed.), *Research handbook on rape and sexual assault.* New York: Garland.

Konecni, V.J., & Ebbesen, E.B. (1984). The mythology of legal decision-making. *International Journal of Law and Psychiatry, 7*, 5–18.

Kopp, S.B. (1962). The character structure of sex offenders. *American Journal of Psychotherapy, 16*, 64–70.

Kozol, H.L., Cohen, M.I., & Garofalo, R.F. (1966). The criminally dangerous sex offender. *New England Journal of Medicine, 275*, 79–84.

LaMontagne, Y. & Lacerte-LaMontagne, C. (1977). *L'attentat sexuel contre les enfants.* Ottawa: Les Editions La Presse.

Langevin, R. (1983). *Sexual strands: Understanding and treating sexual anomalies in men.* London: Erlbaum.

Langevin, R., Paitich, D., Freeman, R., Mann, K., & Handy, L. (1978). Personality characteristics and sexual anomalies in males. *Canadian Journal of Behavioural Science, 10*, 222–238.

Langfeldt, T. (1981). Sexual development in children. In M. Cook & K. Howells (Eds.), *Adult sexual interest in children* (pp. 99–120). Toronto: Academic Press.

Langsley, D.G., Schwartz, M.N., & Fairbairn, R.H. (1968). Father-son incest. *Comprehensive Psychiatry, 9*, 218–226.

Law, S.K. (1979). Child molestation: A comparison of Hong Kong and Western findings. *Medicine, Science, and Law, 19*, 55–60.

Laws, D.R., & Holmen, M.L. (1978). Sexual response faking by pedophiles. *Criminal Justice and Behavior, 5*, 343–356.

Laws, D.R., & Osborne, C.A. (1983). How to build and operate a behavioral laboratory to evaluate and treat sexual deviance. In J.G. Greer & I.R. Stuart (Eds.), *The sexual aggressor: Current perspectives on treatment* (pp. 293–335). Toronto: Van Nostrand Reinhold.

Laws, D.R., & Rubin, H.B. (1969). Instructional control of an autonomic response. *Journal of Applied Behavior Analysis, 2*, 93–99.

Lester, D. (1975). *Unusual sexual behavior: The standard deviations.* Springfield, Illinois: Thomas.

Lindenbaum, S. (1984). Variations on a sociosexual theme in Melanesia. In G.H. Herdt (Ed.), *Ritualized homosexuality in Melanesia* (pp. 337–361). Berkeley: University of California Press.

Longo, R.E. (1983). Administering a comprehensive sexual aggressive treatment program in a maximum security setting. In J.G. Greer & I.R. Stuart (Eds.), *The sexual aggressor: Current perspectives on treatment* (pp. 177–197). New York: Van Nostrand Reinhold.

MacCulloch, M.J., Snowden, P.R., Wood, P.J.W., & Mills, H.E. (1983). Sadistic fantasy, sadistic behaviour, and offending. *British Journal of Psychiatry, 143*, 20–29.

Maletzky, B.M. (1980). Self-referred vs. court-referred sexually deviant patients: Success with assisted covert sensitization. *Behavior Therapy, 11*, 306–314.

Mandel, N.G., Bittner, M.L., Webb, R.L., Collins, B.S., & Jarcho, P. (1965). The sex offender in Minnesota. *Journal of Sex Research, 1*, 239–248.

Maisch, H. (1972). *Incest* (C. Bearne, Trans.). New York: Stein and Day.

Marsh, J.T., Hilliard, J., & Liechti, R. (1955). A sexual deviation scale for the MMPI. *Journal of Consulting Psychology, 19*, 55–59.

Marshall, W.L., & Christie, M.M. (1981). Pedophilia and aggression. *Criminal Justice and Behavior, 8*, 145–158.

Marshall, W.L., Earls, C.M., Segal, Z., & Darke, J. (1983). A behavioral program for the assessment and treatment of sexual aggressors. In K.D. Craig & R.J. McMahon (Eds.), *Advances in Clinical Behavior Therapy* (pp. 148–174). New York: Brunner Mazel.

McCaghy, C.H. (1967). Child molesters: A study of their careers as deviants. In M.B. Clinard & R. Quinney (Eds.), *Criminal behavior systems: A typology* (pp. 75–88). Toronto: Holt, Rinehart, and Winston.

McCaghy, C.H. (1968). Drinking and deviance disavowal: The case of child molesters. *Social Problems, 16*, 43–49.

McCreary, C.P. (1975). Personality differences among child molesters. *Journal of Personality Assessment, 39*, 591–593.

McGeorge, J. (1964). Sexual assaults on children. *Medicine, Science, and Law, 4*, 245–253.

Meeks, W.M. (1963). Criminal sexual psychopaths and sexually dangerous persons. *Corrective Psychiatry and Journal of Social Therapy, 9*, 22–27.

Meiselman, K. (1978). *Incest.* San Francisco: Jossey-Bass.

Mohr, J.W., Turner, R.E., & Jerry, M.B. (1964). *Pedophilia and exhibitionism.* Toronto: University of Toronto Press.

Mohr, J.W. (1981). Age structures in pedophilia. In M. Cook & K. Howells (Eds.), *Adult sexual interest in children* (pp. 41–54). Toronto: Academic Press.

Myers, R.G., & Berah, E.F. (1983). Some features of Australian exhibitionists compared with pedophiles. *Archives of Sexual Behavior, 12*, 541–547.

Myers, S.A. (1967). The child slayer. *Archives of General Psychiatry, 17*, 211–213.

Nabokov, V. (1955). *Lolita.* Toronto: Longmans, Green.

Nedoma, K., Mellan, J., & Pondelickova, J. (1971). Sexual behavior and its development in pedophilic men. *Archives of Sexual Behavior*, *1*, 267–271.

Panton, J.H. (1978). Personality differences appearing between rapists of adults, rapists of children and non-violent sexual molesters of female children. *Research Communications in Psychology, Psychiatry, and Behavior*, *3*, 385–393.

Panton, J.H. (1979). MMPI profile configurations associated with incestuous and non-incestuous child molesting. *Psychological Reports*, *45*, 335–338.

Patterson, G.R. (1982). *Coercive family process.* Eugene, OR: Castalia.

Pithers, W.D., Marques, J.K., Gibat, C.C., & Marlatt, G.A. (1983). Relapse prevention with sexual aggressives: A self-control model of treatment and maintenance of change. In J.G. Greer & I.R. Stuart (Eds.), *The sexual aggressor: Current perspectives on treatment* (pp. 214–239). Toronto: Van Nostrand Reinhold.

Poche, C., Brouwer, R., & Swearingen, M. (1981). Teaching self-protection to young children. *Journal of Applied Behavior Analysis*, *14*, 169–176.

Quinsey, V.L. (1972), Lick–shock contingencies in the rat. *Journal of the Experimental Analysis of Behavior*, *17*, 119–125.

Quinsey, V.L. (1977). The assessment and treatment of child molesters: A review. *Canadian Psychological Review*, *18*, 204–220.

Quinsey, V.L. (1980). The baserate problem and the prediction of dangerousness: A reappraisal. *Journal of Psychiatry and Law*, *8*, 329–340.

Quinsey, V.L. (1984a). Sexual aggression: Studies of offenders against women. In D. Weisstub (Ed.), *Law and mental health: International perspectives* (Vol. 1). New York: Pergamon.

Quinsey, V.L. (1984b). Politique institionnelle de liberation: Identification des individus dangereux. Une revue de la litterature. *Criminologie*, *27*, 53–78.

Quinsey, V.L., & Ambtman, R. (1979). Variables affecting psychiatrists' and teachers' assessments of the dangerousness of mentally ill offenders. *Journal of Consulting and Clinical Psychology*, *47*, 353–362.

Quinsey, V.L., Arnold, L.S., & Pruesse, M.G. (1980). MMPI profiles of men referred for a pretrial psychiatric assessment as a function of offense type. *Journal of Clinical Psychology*, *36*, 410–417.

Quinsey, V.L., & Bergersen, S.G. (1976). Instructional control of penile circumference in assessments of sexual preference. *Behavior Therapy*, *7*, 489–493.

Quinsey, V.L., & Carrigan, W.F. (1978). Penile responses to visual stimuli: Instructional control with and without auditory sexual fantasy correlates. *Criminal Justice and Behavior*, *5*, 333–342.

Quinsey, V.L., Chaplin, T.C., & Carrigan, W.F. (1979). Sexual preferences among incestuous and nonincestuous child molesters. *Behavior Therapy*, *10*, 562–565.

Quinsey, V.L., Chaplin, T.C., & Carrigan, W.F. (1980). Biofeedback and signaled punishment in the modification of inappropriate sexual age preferences. *Behavior Therapy*, *11*, 567–576.

Quinsey, V.L., Chaplin, T.C., Maguire, A.M., & Upfold, D. (in press). The behavioral treatment of rapists and child molesters. In E.K. Morris & C.J. Braukmann (Eds.), *Behavioral approaches to crime*

and delinquency: Application, research, and theory. New York: Plenum.

Quinsey, V.L., & Maguire, A. (1983). Offenders remanded for a psychiatric examination: Perceived treatability and disposition. *International Journal of Law and Psychiatry*, *6*, 193–205.

Quinsey, V.L., & Marshall, W.L. (1983). Procedures for reducing inappropriate sexual arousal: An evaluation review. In J.G. Greer & I.R. Stuart (Eds.), *The sexual aggressor: Current perspectives on treatment* (pp. 267–289). Toronto: Van Nostrand Reinhold.

Quinsey, V.L., Steinman, C.M., Bergersen, S.G., & Holmes, T.F. (1975). Penile circumference, skin conductance, and ranking responses of child molesters and "normals" to sexual and nonsexual visual stimuli. *Behavior Therapy*, *6*, 213–219.

Rada, R.T. (1976). Alcoholism and the child molester. *Annals of the New York Academy of Sciences*, *273*, 492–496.

Radzinowicz, L. (1957). *Sexual offences: A report of the Cambridge Department of Criminal Science.* Toronto: Macmillan.

Revitch, E., & Weiss, R.G. (1962). The pedophiliac offender. *Diseases of the Nervous System*, *23*, 73–78.

Rosen, R.C., Shapiro, D., & Schwartz, G.E. (1975). Voluntary control of penile tumescence. *Psychomosomatic Medicine*, *37*, 479–483.

Rossman, G.P. (1976). *Sexual experience between men and boys.* London: Temple Smith.

Ruggiero, G. (1975). Sexual criminality in the early Renaissance: Venice 1338–1358. *Journal of Social History*, *8*, 18–37.

Rush, F. (1980). *The best kept secret: Sexual abuse of children.* Englewood Cliffs, NJ: Prentice-Hall.

Russell, D.E.H. (1983). The incidence and prevalence of intrafamilial and extrafamilial sexual abuse of female children. *Child Abuse and Neglect*, *7*, 133–146.

Schlesinger, L.B., & Kutash, I.L. (1981). The criminal fantasy technique: A comparison of sex offenders and substance abusers. *Journal of Clinical Psychology*, *37*, 210–218.

Schwimmer, E. (1984). Male couples in New Guinea. In G.H. Herdt (Ed.), *Ritualized homosexuality in Melanesia* (pp. 211–246). Berkeley: University of California Press.

Segal, Z., & Marshall, W.L. (in press). Heterosexual social skills in a population of rapists and child molesters. *Journal of Consulting and Clinical Psychology.*

Serpenti, L. (1984). The ritual meaning of homosexuality and pedophilia among the Kimam-Papuans of South Irian Jaya. In G.H. Herdt (Ed.), *Ritualized homosexuality in Melanesia* (pp. 318–335). Berkeley: University of California Press.

Shoor, M., Speed, M.H., & Bartelt, C. (1966). Syndrome of the adolescent child molester. *American Journal of Psychiatry*, *122*, 783–789.

Sorum, A. (1984). Growth and decay: Bedamini notions of sexuality. In G.H. Herdt (Ed.), *Ritualized homosexuality in Melanesia* (pp. 337–360). Berkeley: University of California Press.

Stricker, G. (1964). Stimulus properties of the Rorschach to a sample of pedophiles. *Journal of Projective Techniques and Personality Assessment*, *28*, 241–244.

Stricker, G. (1967) Stimulus properties of the Blacky to

a sample of pedophiles. *Journal of General Psychology*, 77, 35-39.

Swanson, D.W. (1968). Adult sexual abuse of children: The man and circumstances. *Diseases of the Nervous System*, 29, 677-683.

Symons, D. (1979). *The evolution of human sexuality.* New York: Oxford.

Taylor, L. (1972). The significance and interpretation of replies to motivational questions: The case of the sex offender. *Sociology*, 6, 24-39.

Taylor, B. (1976). Motives for guilt-free pederasty: Some literary considerations. *Sociological Review*, 24, 97-114.

Toobert, S., Bartelme, K.F., & Jones, E.S. (1958). Some factors related to pedophilia. *International Journal of Social Psychiatry*, 4, 272-279.

Trumbach, R. (1977). London's sodomites: Homosexual behavior and Western culture in the 18th century. *Journal of Social History*, 11, 1-33.

Ungaretti, J.R. (1978). Pederasty, heroism, and the family in classical Greece. *Journal of Homosexuality*, 3, 291-300.

Vanasek, F.J., Frisbie, L.V., & Dingman, H.F. (1968). Patterns of affective responses in two groups of pedophiles. *Psychological Reports*, 22, 659-668.

Van Baal, J. (1984). The dialectics of sex in Marind-anim culture. In G.H. Herdt (Ed.), *Ritualized homosexuality in Melanesia* (pp. 128-165). Berkeley: University of California Press.

Vander Mey, B.J., & Neff, R.L. (1982). Adult-child incest: A review of research and treatment. *Adolescence*, 27, 717-735.

Vanggaard, T. (1972). *Phallos: A symbol and its history in the male world.* London: Cape.

Virkkunen, M. (1974). Incest offences and alcoholism. *Medicine, Science, and the Law*, 13, 124-128.

Virkkunen, M. (1975). Victim-precipitated pedophilia offences. *British Journal of Criminology*, 15, 175-180.

Virkkunen, M. (1976). The pedophilic offender with antisocial character. *Acta Psychiatrica Scandanavica*, 53, 401-405.

Virkkunen, M. (1981). The child as participating victim. In M. Cook & K. Howells (Eds.), *Adult sexual interest in children* (pp. 121-134). Toronto: Academic Press.

Walster, E., Aronson, V., Abrahams, D., & Rottman, L. (1966). Importance of physical attractiveness in dating behavior. *Journal of Personality and Social Psychology*, 5, 508-516.

West, D.J. (1965). Clinical types among sexual offenders. In R. Slovenko (Ed.), *Sexual behavior and the law* (pp. 413-424). Springfield, IL: Thomas.

West, D.J. (1981). Adult sexual interest in children: Implications for social control. In M. Cook & K. Howells (Eds.), *Adult sexual interest in children* (pp. 251-270). Toronto: Academic Press.

Whitman, W.P., & Quinsey, V.L. (1981). Heterosocial skill-training for institutionalized rapists and child molesters. *Canadian Journal of Behavioural Science*, 13, 105-114.

Wilson, G.D., & Cox, D.N. (1983). Personality of paedophile club members. *Personality and Individual Differences*, 4, 323-329.

Yates, A. (1982). Children eroticized by incest. *American Journal of Psychiatry*, 139, 482-485.

4.
Psychobiological Factors in the Relationship Between Crime and Psychiatric Illness

Terrie E. Moffitt
Sarnoff A. Mednick
Jan Volavka

ABSTRACT. This chapter begins by demonstrating that there is good evidence for a genetic relationship between parental antisocial behavior and the antisocial behavior of offspring. The possibility is presented that, in addition to the heritable contribution from parental criminal behavior, some forms of parental mental illness may genetically predispose offspring to behave antisocially. Studies of the incidence of both serious mental illness and antisocial behavior within individuals and within families are presented. Both environmental and genetic effects could be advanced to explain results of the family studies, but psychobiological factors are of primary emphasis in this chapter; thus, much of the research focuses on genetically oriented research efforts.

Twin and adoption studies that provide evidence for heritable components of serious mental illness are reviewed and then followed by a discussion of investigations of a genetic contribution to antisocial behavior. The possibility is entertained of a genetically influenced spectrum of disorders involving both serious mental illness and antisocial behavior, but the important problem posed by the phenomenon of cross-assortative mating is acknowledged and some recent unpublished work that begins to address this problem is reviewed.

The chapter later reviews the research on two biological correlates of antisocial behavior which show promise of being among the heritable characteristics that may account for the positive results of genetic investigations in criminal behavior: autonomic nervous system responsiveness and neurophysiological status.

SOMMAIRE. Dans la première partie de ce chapitre, les auteurs commencent par démontrer qu'il existe des preuves manifestes d'une relation génétique entre le comportement anti-social des parents et le comportement anti-social des enfants. Il serait possible qu'outre la contribution héréditaire provenant du comportement criminel des parents, certaines formes de maladies mentales de ces derniers prédisposent leurs enfants sur le plan génétique à se comporter de façon anti-sociale. Des études ont été faites à propos de l'incidence à la fois de la maladie mentale grave et du comportement anti-social sur les personnes et sur les familles. Les résultats des études sur les familles pourraient être expliqués à la fois par des effets du milieu et des effets génétiques mais, dans ce chapitre, les auteurs mettent l'accent sur les facteurs

The writing of this chapter was supported by U.S.P.H.S. Grant No. 31353 from the Center for the Study of Crime and Delinquency and by the National Institute of Justice Graduate Research Fellowship No. 83-IJ-CX-0030.

psycho-biologiques de sorte que le reste de la section est centré sur des efforts de recherche orientés vers la génétique.

Après un examen des études faites sur des jumeaux et des enfants adoptifs, lesquelles mettent en évidence l'existence de composantes héréditaires dans la maladie mentale grave, les auteurs se livrent à une discussion sur les enquêtes en matière de contribution génétique au comportement anti-social. Ils envisagent qu'une gamme de troubles, à la fois du point de vue de la maladie mentale grave et du comportement anti-social, pourrait être influencée par des causes génétiques, mais ils reconnaissent le problème d'interprétation important que pose le phénomène de l'accouplement d'êtres à caractéristiques différentes; ils examinent donc les récents travaux non publiés qui commencent à traiter de cette question.

La deuxième section du chapitre porte sur la recherche de deux correlats biologiques du comportement anti-social qui pourront figurer dans les caractéristiques héréditaires susceptibles d'expliquer les résultats positifs des recherches génétiques en matière de comportement criminel: la réponse du système nerveux autonome et le statut neurophysiologique.

GENETICS AND ANTISOCIAL BEHAVIOR

SERIOUS MENTAL ILLNESS AND ANTISOCIAL BEHAVIOR: IS THERE A RELATIONSHIP IN GENETIC PREDISPOSITION?

Traditionally there has been very little overlap of research efforts in the areas of serious mental illness and antisocial behavior, although both are deviances that present similar problems to society. This lack is probably due in part to the disciplinary boundaries between psychology or psychiatry and the more sociologically oriented criminology. However, findings described in this review suggest that a significant number of individuals afflicted with serious mental illness or antisocial behavior apparently do not adhere to these disciplinary boundaries. It seems that some individuals have symptoms of both mental illness and antisocial behavior, and that both deviances often tend to run in the same families. This evidence that serious mental illness and antisocial behavior often emerge in close proximity, coupled with recent demonstrations from research on twins and adopted children that each separately has some heritable component, suggests that a genetic approach to the analysis of their interrelationship may prove profitable.

Definition of Terms

Throughout this review we will refer to the defined concepts of serious mental illness and antisocial behavior. Rosenthal (1971) points out that problems in the replication of diagnostic procedures are a great impediment to schizophrenia

research. This comment might well also be made of research into antisocial behavior. Primarily in the interest of maintaining some stability of conceptualization, we have chosen to refer to the most generic of terms when attempting to assimilate results from a number of studies, each of which has used a different operational or research definition of the behavioral syndrome under examination. We do not, however, wish to obscure important methodological or clinical differences in syndromes by using these generic terms, so we retain the research definition terminology when reviewing individual studies.

Studies presented here under the heading of antisocial behavior have assessed maladjustment in school, juvenile delinquency, adult police contacts, conviction records, imprisonment on felony charges, diagnosis of antisocial personality disorder, and psychopathy, among others. We have taken the liberty of including psychopathy (or sociopathy) under antisocial behavior rather than under serious mental illness because of the writings of Feldman (1977), Hare, Frazelle, and Cox 1978), Lewis and Balla (1976), and Schulsinger (1974). These researchers have noted that the psychopathy diagnosis is most often inferred from a long history of illegal or antisocial behaviors. The assessment of other less observable factors, such as absence of remorse or egocentrism, is often difficult to make and subject to cultural biases.

Studies discussed under the heading of serious mental illness are primarily studies of schizophrenia. However, there appears to be quite a range in the terms that define "schizophrenia," including *schizoid, borderline, possible schizophrenic, reactive schizophrenic, process schizophrenic, hospitalized schizophrenic,* persons judged *schizophrenic from case history or interview data*, and sometimes simply *admission to a psychiatric hospital*. Some studies include depressive and manic-depressive psychoses, and in the course of the research it became apparent that childhood hyperactivity, personality disorders, and substance abuse disorders need also be considered.

SERIOUS MENTAL ILLNESS AND ANTISOCIAL BEHAVIOR WITHIN INDIVIDUALS

As early as 1892 Lombroso, one of the first to look for biological causes of crime, differentiated five types of criminals; occasional criminals, habitual criminals, criminals motivated by passion, born criminals, and insane criminals (Lindesmith & Dunham, 1941). Rosenthal (1971) mentions that both Kraeplin and Bleuler noted an overlap in patients with schizophrenia and psychopathy.

Studies of Prisoners and Psychiatric Patients

Thompson (1937) reported that of 1,380 recidivistic criminals seen in court in New York City in 1935, 5.6% were psychopaths and only 0.6% were psychotic. In another study, Bromberg and Thompson (1937) searched records of 10,000 convicted criminals seen in the psychiatric clinic of the court of general sessions of New York City. Of these, 1.5% were psychotic, 6.9% were psychopaths, and 6.9% were neurotic. Oltman and Friedman (1941) examined 100 criminals committed consecutively to a psychiatric facility for observation and found 26% to be psychotic, 14% psychopathic, and 3% neurotic. They noted that, despite the large number of psychotics, only 9% of the sample could confidently be diagnosed "schizophrenic." Glueck's (1918) analysis of 608 consecutive admissions to Sing Sing prison revealed that 59% of the men were psychiatrically ill in some way, 12% were psychotic, and 6% were schizophrenic. A more recent survey of imprisoned offenders (Smith, 1971) found 10% of the prisoners to be "describable by formal diagnostic labels." Kloek (1968) reviewed the evidence and concluded that there was no special relationship between schizophrenia and crime; in fact, he estimated that only 1 in 500 criminals are clearly schizophrenic, a rate far below the general population rate of 1 schizophrenic per 100 persons. Kloek did note, however, that criminals are afflicted with other psychiatric disturbances in large numbers.

Wiersma (1966) agreed with Kloek. In a review of European studies on crime rates among psychiatric patients Wiersma concluded that criminals are not found more frequently among schizophrenics than among normals. Roth (in press) has concluded that the majority of surveys show the extent of general psychiatric pathology found among prison inmates to be in the range of 15-20% and that less than 5% of inmates exhibit severe psychotic mental disorders. However, numerous studies (Durbin, Pasework, & Albers, 1977; Rappeport & Lassen, 1965; Zitrin, Hardesty, Burdock, & Drosman, 1976) have concluded that mental patients are much more likely to engage in criminal behavior than are members of the general population, especially in serious offenses such as rape, assault, and robbery. Ribner and Steadman (1981) have analyzed record data from Albany County, New York, to find that the arrest rate of released mental patients in 1975 was 111 per 1,000 while the 1975 arrest rate among the county's general population was 32.5 per 1,000. (It may be useful, however, to evaluate the mental patients' arrest rate, which seems comparatively large, against the rate of 695 per 1,000 found for excriminal offenders.) Steadman, Cocozza, and Melick (1978) reported from the same database that the rate of arrest for violent crimes among discharged mental patients (12.03 per 1,000) was almost four times larger than the rate of arrests for violent crimes among the general population (3.61 per 1,000). Individuals psychiatrically hospitalized for personality disorders and substance-abuse disorders were the most frequently arrested.

Results of these studies are uncomfortably conflicting. The reported rate of general mental illness among prisoners ranges from 6.2% to 59%. The rate of psychosis ranges from 0.6% to 26%, and the rate of schizophrenia ranges from .2% to 9%. The highest rates should be expected from the studies of criminals referred for psychiatric evaluation, but some of the highest rates reported are from Glueck's study of unselected admissions to a prison. It is more likely that differences reported in rates of mental illness among prisoners are ascribable mainly to differences in methods of obtaining psychiatric data or differences in diagnostic criteria. The preponderance of studies did, however, find evidence that many prisoners suffer from some form of serious mental illness and that some types of mental patients are likely to engage in illegal behaviors. It seems very probable that, as Guze (1976) has posited, the psychiatric problems experienced by criminals are more often antisocial personality disorder, drug abuse, and alcoholism than the psychoses. In concluding reviews of this topic, several authors point to a need for adequate epidemiological level studies (Mesnikoff and Lauterbach, 1975; Roth, in press; Taylor, 1982).

Studies of Antisocial Adolescents

In addition to these studies of adult prisoners, several studies have been done on the relationship between mental illness and antisocial behavior in adolescents. Healy and Bronner (1926, 1936) have provided rich case studies of mentally ill delinquents. They reported that "mental abnormalities and peculiarities" were a main factor in the delinquent behavior of 455 of 823 children they evaluated. Loney, Kramer, and Milich (1979) and Satterfield (in press) have found significant connections betweeen hyperactivity (minimal brain dysfunction) and juvenile delinquency.

Bender (1958) has introduced the concept of "pseudopsychopathic schizophrenia," in which adolescents initially labeled antisocial for their unusual delinquent behaviors are later found to be schizophrenics as young adults. Bender proposes that this change is the result both of symptom picture responses to age-specific social demand characteristics and of age biases in likelihood of diagnostic applications. In support of Bender's concept, Silverman (1946) reported that 22% of 500 psychotic criminals studied retrospectively had records of aggressive behavior or petty thievery from childhood. Watt (1972) also noted that unsocialized aggression is characteristic of many preschizophrenic males (preschizophrenic females are "inhibited"). Lewis and Balla (1976) searched adult records at two state psychiatric hospitals for 689 men who were known to juvenile courts since their boyhood, 25 years previously. Twelve percent had received psychiatric treatment, a rate significantly higher than for normal men their age and socioeconomic level. Of this 12% (82 men), 21 men were schizophrenic and had adult criminal records. These subjects had been arrested for their first juvenile offense a mean 13 months earlier than had juveniles who did not later receive treatment. In another follow-up study, Morris, Escoll, and Wexler (1956) found that, of 66 children with an aggressive behavior disorder, 20% became schizophrenic as adults. O'Neal and Robins (1958) followed up two groups of children referred to a clinic for problem behavior. Group

1 was composed of delinquents with a court record, while Group 2 children were guilty of theft, runaway, truancy, assault, sexual misbehavior, and destruction of property but had no records of court action. At follow-up, 6% of the apprehended delinquents were psychotic and 37 percent were sociopathic. Of the "delinquents" who had not been officially processed, 30% were psychotic and 6% sociopathic. The smaller number of sociopaths in Group 2 may be explained by the reluctance of diagnosticians to establish sociopathy in the absence of a juvenile offense record. It is not known why relatively more Group 2 children became psychotic. It is conceivable that the two groups were not consonant for the types of juvenile offenses committed and that such a dissimilarity may contribute to the discrepant outcomes in observed psychosis.

Retrospective follow-up studies are known to be susceptible to problems in accuracy of data (Moffitt, Mednick, & Cudeck, 1983), but some prospective studies of children at risk for schizophrenia also yield support for Bender's concept. Rieder (1973) reviewed studies by Beisser, Glasser, and Grant (1967), Mednick and Schulsinger (1968), and Ricks and Berry (1970). Rieder concluded that children who later develop schizophrenia are of two behavior types: the withdrawn anxious ones (who may be early labeled schizoid or inadequate personality), and the aggressive ones (who may be labeled hyperactive, delinquent, or psychopathic). It appears that Bender's concent of pseudopsychopathic schizophrenia in adolescence may accurately describe a development from early onset antisocial behavior to adult mental illness overlapping antisocial behavior.

Problems in Interpretation

Despite wide ranges in the reported rates of mental illness among imprisoned offenders, most of the studies found that many prisoners evidenced some type of serious mental illness. A number of studies of persons displaying antisocial behavior in adolescence found that significant numbers of these adolescents later became psychotic. One problem with the studies on this subject is the problem of nonrepresentative sampling. In each study discussed, subjects selected were already incarcerated or hospitalized, had received treatment for childhood behavior problems, or were known to be at risk for serious mental illness. One would be hard-put to find a study of the prevalence of serious mental illness and antisocial behavior among individuals representative of the general population. Nevertheless, the findings from available studies imply that some individuals do indeed evidence both serious mental illness and antisocial behaviors. There are many explanations for the presence of serious mental illness among criminals or of antisocial behaviors among persons who are seriously mentally ill. Feldman (1977) proposes the following reasons why the apparent relationship may be artifactual. Serious mental illness may not be associated with increased probability of committing antisocial behaviors, but of being detected; disturbed persons may plan and carry out offenses less carefully and increase their risk of detection. The police may more readily detain and charge a disturbed person, whether because of community pressure or the altruistic aim of securing professional help for the person. Guilty pleas may be made more frequently by mentally disturbed persons, whether out of lack of understanding of court procedure or as a means to plea bargain for psychiatric treatment in place of imprisonment. All of these events would inflate the official records of mental illness in criminal populations. Guze (1976), in contrast, points out that seriously disturbed offenders are often diverted to psychiatric facilities immediately when detected by police and never enter judicial system records, thereby deflating the mental illness rate among apprehended criminals.

Feldman (1977) also proposes that stressful penal institution conditions may increase the incidence of psychological disorders among incarcerated offenders. Such a situation may have special relevance to Bender's (1958) concept of early delinquency that later emerges into mental illness. It is these possibly confounding factors in the association of mental illness and antisocial behavior that make it important to consider the presence of both serious mental illness and antisocial behavior within family groups.

SERIOUS MENTAL ILLNESS AND ANTISOCIAL BEHAVIOR WITHIN FAMILIES

History

Francis Galton (1869) was the first to use the family-study method to examine whether human social "eminence" was subject to the laws of heritability espoused in Darwin's *On the Origin of Species* (1859). In this method a "proband" is selected who evidences the trait in question, and members of either preceding or succeeding generations (or both) are examined for evidence of the trait or of other traits that seem to accompany it. Dugdale (1877) first adapted Galton's method to the study of less desirable traits when he announced that criminal activities had been prevalent among members of the Jukes family for more than 130 years. Goddard (1912) expanded on the methodology when he reported data from the Kallikak family. During the American revolutionary war Martin Kallikak had begun two families, one illegitimate with a "mentally deficient and morally degenerate" tavern maid, the other with his "well-bred, intelligent" young wife. For several generations the family members from the illegitimate union far surpassed those from the marriage in mental retardation, criminal behavior, and general degenerate character.

Kallman (1938) conducted a more sophisticated study of three generations of descendants of 1,087 unselected schizophrenic probands. He found that adult criminality rates far surpassed the normal population rates but in only the probands and their children. Within these groups almost all of the excess in criminality was ascribable to the most chronic schizophrenic subjects, leading Kallman to conclude that the elevation in criminality was a function of the crimes committed by individuals in a psychotic state.

Recent Studies

In a more recent family study, Lewis and Balla (1976) found that of 223 schizophrenic proband parents, 17% had at least one child with a juvenile delinquency record. Only 6% of control parents had a delinquent child. It is possible that some of the delinquent children of these schizophrenic parents were themselves future schizophrenics and thus victims of Bender's (1958) pseudopsychopathic schizophrenia in adolescence. In such a case, Lewis's results would agree with Kallman's findings with adult subjects.

In a companion study of general mental illness, Lewis and Balla (1976) examined the records of 478 parents of children referred to a Connecticut court psychiatric clinic and 261 parents of children seen in court but not referred for psychiatric evaluation. Fifteen percent of "clinic parents" and 10% of "court parents" had psychiatric records, a significantly greater incidence than for a sample similar in socioeconomic status in Connecticut. A large number of parents with psychiatric records also had criminal records.

Paternal psychiatric treatment related to a significantly earlier age of child's first arrest; the mean first arrest age of children whose fathers were psychiatrically treated was 9.4 years as opposed to 12.7 years for the remaining delinquents. The relationship of parental psychiatric status to early onset of offspring delinquent behavior is an important one; individuals who begin their criminal careers earlier are known to engage in a greater number of criminal acts over the course of their careers (Van Dusen & Mednick, 1984; Wolfgang, Figlio, & Sellin, 1972). Parental psychiatric treatment was not related to the severity of the child's crimes or to the number of crimes committed, but the boys were under age 16 at the time of the study so severity and recidivism measures may have been tempered by the youth of the subjects.

Cloninger and Guze (1973), Guze (1976), and Guze, Wolfgram, McKinney, and Cantwell (1967) reported results from a study of 223 consecutive male felons and 66 female felons in Missouri along with 807 of their first-degree relatives. Of the male felons, 78% were sociopaths, 1% schizophrenics, 54% alcoholics, and 12% had anxiety neuroses. Of their relatives, 7% were sociopathic, none were schizophrenic, 15% were alcoholic, and 8% had anxiety neuroses. Four percent of their female relatives had diagnoses of hysterical personality, and if female relatives were removed from consideration, the percentage for sociopathy and alcoholism rose significantly. For the female felons, percentage rates were 65% sociopaths, 47% alcoholics, 41% hysterical personalities, 1.5% schizophrenics, and 11% anxiety neuroses. The percentages for their relatives were all twice those of the male felons' relatives. Again, there were no schizophrenic relatives. Thus, in this family study, sociopathy, alcoholism, hysterical personality, and anxiety seem to be related to felon status. Guze (1976) noted that many felons were diverted to the mental health system after arrest and this practice would have precluded their eligibility for his study. Therefore, he examined a sample of 50 offenders who had been diverted in this way. Psychoses were more prevalent in this group; 22% were schizophrenic and 10% were manic-depressive. If these subjects had been included in the earlier study, the psychotic rate would have been 6%, significantly above the population prevalence rate. The rate of psychoses among relatives of the additional 50 subjects was not reported. Cloninger and Guze (1973) interpreted this study to suggest both a genetic relationship between sociopathy and hysteria, and a stronger genetic contribution to sociopathy in females than in males. However, Feldman points out that the large numbers of deviant relatives of the female felons provided these women with more environmental influence toward sociopathy as well as more genetic influence. Actually, both Cloninger and Guze's and Feldman's interpretations assume that males and females have an equal probability of being diagnosed as sociopaths, but it is probable that there are sex biases in the criterion symptoms for diagnosis. It is also possible that even if Guze's (1976) female psychopaths evidenced the same antisocial behaviors as the males, these behaviors represented relatively greater deviance because they violated the relatively less-lenient social norms for female behavior. An elevated number of deviant family members might be expected in the families of more deviant psychopaths.

Robins (1966) combined the follow-up and family methods in a study of female probands who had been referred to a clinic for antisocial behavior as children. She found 48% of their mothers and 23% of their fathers to be psychiatrically disturbed or intellectually handicapped. Twenty-six percent of the girls were later diagnosed as hysterics in adulthood.

In summary, family studies have yielded conflicting results with regard to the relationship between schizophrenia or psychotic mental illness and antisocial behavior. These differences may be ascribable in part to methodological differences between studies, specifically in the age at which subjects' behaviors are assessed and in whether subjects are omitted from study who are initially diverted from the judicial system to the mental health system. Some carefully done studies revealed family patterns connecting antisocial behavior, alcoholism, sociopathy, and hysterical personality. In light of these results and the findings reported in an earlier section relating hyperactivity and delinquency (and later schizophrenia) in children, it is pertinent to report the results of two studies of the families of hyperactive probands (Cantwell, 1972; Morrison & Stewart, 1971). In both studies, fathers of probands evidenced greater sociopathy than fathers of controls, and mothers of probands were more often hysterics than mothers of controls.

Problems in Interpretation

Although family studies are important in delineating possible patterns of heritability, the problem for interpretation is that people generally share their socialization environments with their families as well as their genes. No conclusions can be drawn concerning any genetic relationship between serious mental illness and antisocial behavior from studies discussed thus far. Toward examining the possibility of such a relationship, studies designed to test genetic hypotheses about serious mental illness and antisocial behavior will be presented in the following sections. The majority of genetic studies fall solely within one domain of interest or the other. A few studies do, however, consider both serious mental illness and antisocial behavior. Results of these studies will be presented within one of the two following sections according to whether the probands of the study were selected for serious mental illness or antisocial behavior.

A PRIMER IN BEHAVIOR GENETICS METHODOLOGY

Determination of genetic contribution to behavioral phenotypes is always complicated by the fact that learning processes and environmental influences play such a large role in shaping the expressed behaviors that even Mendelian inheritance patterns may be obscured. Strictly speaking, there are no behaviors that are *completely* ascribable to either nature or nurture; even syndromes caused "entirely" by genetic variation, such as phenylketonuria, depend on environmentally determined nutritional states for expression. Behaviors that are probably completely determined by learning, such as preferences for soda-pop flavors, depend on proper genetic coding for the development of taste receptors. This ever-present interaction between genetics and environment makes the problem of research design in behavior genetics one of discerning the relative amount of influence on a phenotypical characteristic that is genetic. There are two approaches to this problem: twin studies and adoption studies.

Twin Studies

In twin studies, a concordance rate is calculated, which reflects the proportion of twin pairs where one twin (the proband) is affected with a syndrome in which the other twin is also affected. Any concordance of less than 100% in monozygotic (MZ) twins, who share the same genetic endowment, can be attributed to environmental factors and/or error. Often concordance rates are compared for groups of MZ and dizygotic (DZ) twin pairs (who share no more genes than nontwin siblings). If the rate for MZ pairs is signif-

icantly greater, the inference can be made that the trait is inherited. This method is based on the assumption that MZ twins do not experience more similar rearing environments than DZ twins, an assumption that is increasingly questioned (Feldman, 1977) but probably remains tenable (Loehlin & Nichols, 1976). Studies comparing concordance rates in MZ twins reared apart and MZ twins reared together can avoid this problem, but it is not often easy to obtain such subjects.

Adoption Studies

The adoption method is best suited for separation and comparison of environmental and genetic effects because children adopted at birth have one family that contributes only environmental influence, and another that contributes only genes. In actuality, some environmental influence is provided by the biological family in the form of perinatal phenomena. Also, not all adoptive children are removed from their biological families at birth. These factors may weaken the adoption study design; it is desirable to obtain data on the subjects' adoption schedules and perinatal environments and conduct analyses of the possible contributions of these factors.

In the adoptees' family method, adoptee probands are selected who have trait x (these probands form the index group) and who do not (these probands become the control group). Rates of trait x among biological relatives of index and control adoptees are compared, and if biological relatives of index adoptees have rates significantly higher than the biological relatives of control adoptees, a genetic effect for trait x is inferred. In the adoptees study method, the probands are biological parents who gave up children for adoption. Index adoptees whose biological parents were afflicted with trait x are compared to control adoptees whose biological parents were normal. If index adoptees have higher rates of x, a genetic contribution is demonstrated. The cross-fostering method has been adapted to human behavior genetics from animal studies. To compare the relative contributions of genetics and rearing environment, we form one group of adoptees who have a biological parent afflicted with trait x but who also have normal adoptive parents. The second group is formed by finding adoptees who have an adoptive parent with trait x but normal biological parents. Rates of trait x in the two groups of adoptees are compared to assess the contribution of genetics relative to the environmental contribution. The possibility of interaction between genetics and environment in producing trait x can be examined by adding two groups to the cross-fostering design. One group has both biological and adoptive parents with trait x, the other group is made up of adoptees with normal biological and normal adoptive parents. If the group with both sets of parents afflicted has higher rates of trait x than the other three groups, some interaction exists between genes and rearing.

There are practical methodological problems with the adoptee method (Mednick & Volavka, 1980). Adoptees may vary in the age at which they were removed from their biological parents and in the amount of time spent in institutions prior to being adopted. Adoption agencies may have had policies of matching adoptive parents and biological parents for characteristics such as socioeconomic status or of informing adoptive parents about deviance in a child's biological family. Children with seriously deviant parents or noticeable health or behavior problems may be screened from the adoptee population and remain unadopted, perhaps in orphanages. Mothers who plan to have their infants adopted may be motivated to invest relatively less effort in prenatal health care, contributing to effects which, though biological in nature, are perinatal rather than genetic in etiology. (However, mothers who put their infants up for adoption are usually younger as a group than mothers who keep their infants, and younger mothers tend to deliver infants characterized by fewer perinatal complications (Moffitt & Mednick, 1979).) Finally, the identities of biological fathers of many illegitimate adoptees may not be known, and it is possible that the fathers who are not available for study may be different on some variables from the fathers who are included in analyses.

Neither twin nor adoptee studies can provide direct information about the mechanisms by which a behavioral deviance is produced from genetic coding, but they are useful for establishing the extent to which a genetic propensity toward a behavioral syndrome exists.

EVIDENCE FOR A GENETIC CONTRIBUTION TO SERIOUS MENTAL ILLNESS

Genetic studies have been done of mental illnesses such as manic-depressive affective disorder (see Kringlen, 1967; Mendlewicz, Fleiss, & Fieve, 1975; Winokur, Clayton, & Reich, 1969 for reviews), neuroses (see Rosenthal, 1971 for review),

alcoholism (see Goodwin, 1977; Reich, Winokur, & Mullaney, 1975; Rosenthal, 1971 for reviews), and Down's syndrome (Lejeune, Gautier, & Turpin, 1959) with varying degrees of success in demonstrating the presence of a genetic contribution. This chapter will review genetic studies of schizophrenia, which is the most serious of mental illnesses and accounts for the preponderance of genetic studies in mental illness. The present review is not an exhaustive one and draws heavily on more detailed writing by Crowe (1975), Gottesman (1978), Gottesman and Shields (1976), McClearn and DeFries (1973), Rosenthal (1971), and Slater and Cowie (1971).

Twin Studies

Rosenthal (1971) reviewed 11 major twin studies spanning 40 years and nine countries. He concluded that these studies yielded three important points (p. 118):

1. The concordance rate for MZ twins is always less than 100%, sometimes much less, which indicates that nongenetic factors are playing an important role with respect to who develops schizophrenia and who does not.
2. The concordance rate is always greater for MZ than for DZ pairs, with the possible exception of Tienari's (1963) study. The MZ–DZ concordance ratio is appreciable, mostly between 3:1 and 6:1. These findings afford strong but not conclusive evidence of a genetic contribution to schizophrenia.
3. There is a considerable range in the rates reported for both MZ and DZ pairs.

Rosenthal went on to illustrate how the between-study differences in concordance rate "can be traced to factors like sampling procedure, diagnostic preferences, methods of zygosity determination, and possibly cultural-geographical differences" (p. 118). Rosenthal also considered a total of 16 pairs of MZ twins reared apart for eight different studies. The concordance rate for schizophrenia in these twins was 62.5% (higher than the median rate for MZ twins reared together), leading Rosenthal to conclude that MZ twin concordance for schizophrenia certainly cannot be attributed to similar rearing of MZ twins.

Adoption and Fostering Studies

Crowe (1975) has reviewed all adoption studies of schizophrenia. The first adoptees study followed 47 index adoptees (30 males and 17 females born between 1915 and 1945) who were separated from their hospitalized schizophrenic mothers in the first days of life and reared in a variety of institutions and foster or adoptive homes (Heston, 1966). (This study cannot strictly be called an adoption study; not all of the probands were actually taken into adoptive homes.) The index adoptees evidenced significantly more schizophrenia than controls (11% v. 0%) but also rated twice as high as the controls in neurotic personality disorder (28%), antisocial personality or sociopathy (19%), and mental deficiency (9%). Index adoptees were higher than controls on number of felonies committed, number of psychiatric or behavioral army discharges received, years spent in prison, and musical talent. A total of 26 of the 47 index adoptees were found to be mentally disturbed. Heston's study was one of the first indications that the inherited disorder may be considerably broader than overt schizophrenia. This study has reported some of the highest rates of deviance among separated offspring of schizophrenics. The study may reflect a truer rate than studies of only adoptees because children considered "defective" or unsuitable for adoption remained in Heston's sample.

Rosenthal, Wender, Kety, Welner, and Schulsinger (1971) interviewed 76 Danish adoptees of biological parents diagnosed as having an illness within the schizophrenia "spectrum": schizophrenia, doubtful schizophrenia (borderline), or manic-depressive psychosis. In all, 32% of the index adoptees fell within this spectrum as compared to 18% among control adoptees, a significant difference suggestive of a heritable component for illnesses within the spectrum. No subjects were found to be antisocial.

Three studies from Iceland of children separated from schizophrenic parents and reared in foster homes have been reported by Karlsson (1966, 1970). Of a total of 137 children from the studies, 10.2% have developed schizophrenia, a rate comparable to that expected among children reared by their schizophrenic parents. Karlsson did not assess antisocial behavior.

Another Danish study conducted by Kety, Rosenthal, Wender, and Schulsinger (1968) is an adoptees family study of 33 schizophrenic adoptee probands and controls. Hospital records and interviews were used to follow up biological and adoptive relatives. Of index biological relatives, 21% fell within a schizophrenia spectrum of process or borderline schizophrenia and inadequate or schizoid personality, significantly more than

control biological relatives or adoptive relatives. Kety et al. (1968) also found a higher prevalence of cases of psychopathy and character disorder among index biological relatives than among control biological relatives, suggesting that these antisocial disorders also share some heritable factors with schizophrenia spectrum disorders.

A cross-fostering analysis of schizophrenia has been attempted by Wender, Rosenthal, Kety, Schulsinger, and Welner (1974). Twenty-eight adoptees were found who were born to normal parents and reared by schizophrenic parents. They were compared with 79 adoptees with both normal biological and adoptive parents and 69 adoptees born to schizophrenic parents and reared by normal parents. The adoptees with schizophrenic biological parents were significantly more likely to become schizophrenic than the other two groups, which did not differ in rate of schizophrenia. The results suggest that having a schizophrenic rearing parent does not facilitate development of schizophrenia in a child unless he has a genetic predisposition.

In combination, twin and adoption studies have demonstrated appreciable evidence for a genetic contribution to serious mental illness. In addition, two studies have found a significant rate of antisocial behavior among biological relatives of schizophrenic adoptees, although one other study (Rosenthal et al., 1971) that looked for this relationship did not find it.

EVIDENCE FOR A GENETIC CONTRIBUTION TO ANTISOCIAL BEHAVIOR

In the years since Dugdale's (1877) study of criminality in the Jukes family, several studies have demonstrated that one of the best predictors of a person's antisocial behavior is the presence of antisocial behavior in his family. Robins, West, and Herjanic (1975) found, in a study of 76 black St. Louis males, that for fathers with a juvenile record, 46% of their sons also had a juvenile record. Reich, Cloninger, and Guze (1975) reported elevation in sociopathy among relatives of male and female sociopaths. Lewis and Balla (1976) reported that increasing seriousness of parents' crimes related significantly to early-age first arrest in their children. Osborn and West (1979) reported records of the fathers of boys in the Cambridge Study of Delinquent Development. Of criminal fathers, 51% had delinquent sons, significantly more than the 24% of noncriminal fathers with delinquent sons. Of criminal fathers, 38% had a recidivistic son, and these recidivists accounted for 52% of the convictions in the sample. When boys with juvenile convictions were ruled out, there was no family effect for sons whose criminal careers began after age 18. Osborn and West matched two groups of 10-year-old boys with criminal fathers and without criminal fathers on the four variables that had been the best statistical predictors of delinquency: low I.Q., large family, low income, and inadequate parental behavior. The significant effect remained; 51% of criminal fathers had criminal sons, whereas 28% of matched but noncriminal fathers had criminal sons. Osborn and West concluded that the link between sons' and fathers' criminal behaviors could not be fully explained by "background adversity."

XYY Studies

Interest in the genetic determination of antisocial behavior was encouraged when Sandberg, Koepf, Ishihara, and Hauschka (1961) first discovered that it was possible for human males to have an extra Y chromosome. Speculation that the extra Y might yield a super-aggressive male led to a flurry of poorly executed and conflicting studies of the incidence of XYY prisoners (see Owen, 1972, for review). Sarbin and Miller (1970) called for a definitive study that would eliminate sampling bias by drawing XYY subjects from the general population. Witkin et al. (1977) executed this study and found 12 XYY men by karyotyping all the men taller than 183 cm (6 feet) who were born in Copenhagen from 1944–1947 (n = 4,139). Although these XYY men had committed more crimes than matched controls, they did not commit violent crimes. The study clearly demonstrated the rarity of XYY men in the general population; they account for only a fraction of antisocial behavior and their behavior is not violent. The following studies have been designed to examine the possibility of a more general genetic effect in antisocial behavior.

Twin Studies

Christiansen (1977a) has ably reviewed all twin studies of antisocial behavior, and the present review draws heavily from his writings. Nine twin studies from four countries were reported between 1929 and 1963 (Borgstrom, 1939; Kranz, 1936, 1937; Lange, 1929; Legras, 1934; Rosanoff,

Handy, & Plessett, 1934; Stumpfl, 1936; Tienari, 1963; and Yoshimasu, 1961, 1965). All were problematic in that their proband twins were selected from institutional populations where it is probable that concordant MZ twins attracted an unusual amount of attention. The concordance rates varied widely, of course, but in general the MZ concordance rates hover around 67% whereas DZ rates hover around 33%. It is interesting that the six studies reporting the highest MZ concordance were done in Germany during the Nazi era.

More recently, two careful studies were done that found lower concordance rates than the early studies. Dalgaard and Kringlen (1976) examined 139 unselected Norwegian male twin pairs. Concordance rates were 26% for MZ pairs and 15% for DZ pairs. Noting that MZ twins may be reared more similarly than DZ pairs, Dalgaard and Kringlen compared MZ and DZ pairs with strong "intrapair interdependence" (having been dressed alike, treated similarly by parents, and expressing a subjective sense of mutual identity). In this comparison, concordance rate differences were not significant: 23.2% of MZ pairs were concordant and 21.4% of DZ pairs were concordant. Mednick and Volavka (1980) have noted that "this group of Norwegian twins seems to have been disproportionately drawn from the lower classes" (p. 97), and they point out that MZ-DZ concordance differences were found by Christiansen (1977b) to be considerably lower in lower class twin pairs. They propose that Dalgaard and Kringlen sample additional twin pairs to overcome this social skew.

Christiansen (1977b) executed the most ideal study. He examined the records of an unselected complete birth cohort of 3,586 Danish twin pairs, where in 799 pairs one or both twins had been registered for criminal behavior. He found 35% concordance among male MZ pairs and 13% concordance among male DZ pairs.

Christiansen (1977a) also reports concordance rates for a total of eight MZ twin pairs (reared apart) who were gathered from five separate studies. Four of the pairs were concordant, a rate of 50%, but two of the pairs were not separated before 8 years of age and one pair was also concordant for schizophrenia.

Although strongly suggestive, the twin literature remains inconclusive with regard to genetic effects on antisocial behavior, primarily due to the problem suggested by Dalgaard and Kringlen (1976) of greater intrapair similarity in rearing among MZ pairs than among DZ pairs. Feldman

(1977) has pointed out that the identical twin of a person known to the police as a previous offender may be more likely to attract arrest; in fact, one brother may suffer from the "labeling" of his MZ twin (Lemert, 1951).

Adoption Studies

Some Scandinavian countries maintain detailed central registers of all their citizens who are submitted for adoption. Such a register made possible an adoptees family study of 2,324 adoptees born between 1930 and 1949 in Sweden (Bohman, 1978). Registered criminal behavior was elevated in biological fathers, biological mothers, and female adoptees. However, adoptees whose biological parents were registered for criminal convictions did not appear in the criminal registers more often than other adoptees, except in cases where alcoholism (registered by the Swedish Temperance Board) was present in the biological parents. Bohman (1978) suggested that criminal behavior may only appear to have heritable components because it is often a consequence of alcoholism. One problem with this study is that alcoholics are more likely to come to the attention of the Swedish Temperance Board if they commit antisocial acts, thus building in an association between *registered* alcoholism and crime in Sweden. After further research with this Swedish population, Bohman, Cloninger, Sigvardsson, and von Knorring (1982) set aside the assumption of "criminality as a unitary trait" and examined subgroups of criminal adoptees. They found that specifically violent and chronic offenders clustered in the biological "families" characterized by heritability of alcoholism. In contrast, among biological "families" without alcohol involvement, a tendency to commit property crimes was notably heritable. Recently, Mednick and Volavka (1980) have reported that Bohman has conducted further analyses of these data, distinguishing between levels of severity of biological parents' crimes. These analyses are yielding subgroups of adoptees whose criminal behavior is partly explained by their biological parents' criminal status.

Bohman (1971, 1972), in an earlier study, also reported on 163 Swedish adoptees. These subjects were 10 and 11 years of age at the time of the study, and adoptive parents' reports of maladjustment in school were assessed. Results were equivocal. There were several methodological problems in this study, primarily the result of placement policies held by the Swedish adoption agency at the time these children were submitted for adoption. However, it is very likely that the subjects were simply too young to have evidenced much antisocial behavior and that the method of questioning parents about their childrens' adjustment at school did not adequately appraise the true incidence of antisocial behavior.

Schulsinger (1974) has conducted a third adoptees family study using data from Danish adoption and psychiatric registers. Beginning with a population of 5,483 children who were adopted between 1924 and 1947, Schulsinger reviewed the case records of the 507 with psychiatric hospital records and found 57 adult psychopaths (40 males and 17 females) characterized by a long history of impulsive or acting-out behavior. Any cases with full or borderline psychoses were excluded. Fifty-seven control adoptees with no mental illness recorded were matched to the psychopaths on sex, age, age of transfer to the adoptive home, and social class of the adoptive parents. Records were searched for a total of 854 biological and adoptive relatives of the adoptees. The use of official records should underestimate the true prevalence of psychopathology, but equally for all subject groups. The biological relatives of the psychopathic adoptees evidenced significantly more general mental illness than either of the other three groups of relatives, who were about equal in prevalence. Relatives of psychopaths had significantly more drug abuse, alcoholism, hysterical character disorder, criminal behavior, and psychopathy, which prompted Schulsinger to refer to these diagnoses as a "psychopathy spectrum." Nine percent of the male relatives of psychopaths were themselves psychopaths, $2\frac{1}{2}$ times more than among control relatives. Schulsinger examined the roles of pregnancy and birth complications and age of transfer to the adoptive home in the etiology of psychopathy for his subjects. Neither factor was found to account for psychopathy in the index adoptees or the frequency of psychopathology among their biological relatives. Schulsinger's work produces results not inconsistent with studies reviewed above; there appears to be a genetic relationship between antisocial behavior (defined as psychopathy), drug and alcohol abuse, and hysterical personality disorder.

Crowe (1972, 1974) has followed up 27 male and 25 female adoptees who were born to female offenders in correctional institutions in Iowa. The adoptees ranged from 16–46 years of age at follow-up. Based on official records of arrest and psychiatric hospitalization, 13% of the index adoptees (4 males and 4 females) had been convicted of an offense, 12% had been incarcerated for offenses, and 15% had been admitted to psychiatric hospitals. These rates were significantly higher than those for control adoptees, of whom 2% had been convicted, none incarcerated, and 4% admitted to psychiatric hospitals. Three raters made independent blind diagnoses based on both official record and personal interview data. Of the index adoptees, 13% were diagnosed as certain antisocial personalities, whereas only 2% of the controls were diagnosed as probable antisocial personalities. This study has demonstrated a very likely genetic effect for antisocial behavior associated with antisocial personality disorder.

It was noted that 72% of the antisocial index adoptees had spent over 12 months in temporary care between birth and transfer to their adoptive homes. They were significantly different from the other index adoptees in this respect. However, control adoptees who had also spent over 12 months in temporary care had not become antisocial. Crowe suggests that these data indicate a gene–environment interaction in which institutionalization is more detrimental to children who have a genetic predisposition toward antisocial personality. Subjects with delays of over 12 months were too few to allow statistical testing of the interaction.

Another American adoptee study has been reported by Cadoret, Cunningham, Loftus, and Edwards (1975) and Cunningham, Cadoret, Loftus, and Edwards (1975). These investigators interviewed by telephone the adoptive parents of 59 adoptees (aged 12-24) who had at least one biological parent noted (in the child's file at the adoption agency) to be in some way socially deviant. Adoptive parents had not been informed of this deviance. Fifty-four control adoptees whose parents were not noted as deviant were matched to index adoptees for age of biological mother at time of the child's birth. Thirty-five percent of the sample was lost to Cadoret's study when adoptive parents refused to be interviewed. It is possible that inclusion of their reports may have altered the results of the study. One of the investigators diagnosed the cases blindly from telephone interview data.

Of the 59 index parents, 22 had been diagnosed as having antisocial personalities. Significantly more index adoptees than control adoptees had behavior disorders and had received professional treatment. Most of them were hyperactive, and

hyperactivity occurred most often among the offspring of the antisocial biological parents. The index adoptees had also been placed later with their adoptive families than controls, but within the index group, age at placement did not correlate with extent of psychopathology. Cunningham et al. (1975) noted that the delay was the result of more testing being done by the agency for children whose biological parents were known to be deviant.

Cadoret (1978) has also reported findings from a similar study of 246 adoptees in Iowa. Biological parents were again diagnosed from adoption agency files. Of these parents, 190 were disturbed and 28 had antisocial personalities. The adoptees ranged from 10–37 years of age. Adoptive parents were interviewed for adoptees under 18 years of age, and older adoptees were interviewed personally, with their parents' permission.

There were no differences in behavior problems between control and index adoptees under 18 years of age, nor was there any relationship between a child's behavior and biological parent's diagnosis. However, results for the adult adoptees are quite different. Antisocial adult adoptees were significantly more likely than controls to have an antisocial biological parent. Adult adoptees with an antisocial biological parent were also more likely to report symptoms such as wide mood swings and audible thoughts. Female adoptees with an antisocial biological parent reported a large number of psychosomatic illnesses of the sort typical of hysterical personality disorder. Regression analyses were performed with antisocial biological parent, other diagnoses of biological parent, socioeconomic level of adoptive family, time adoptee spent in temporary care, deviance in adoptive parents or siblings, and sex of adoptee as independent variables. Antisocial biological background remained a significant predictor of number of antisocial behaviors committed by the adoptee and was the *only* significant predictor of psychosomatic symptoms for female adoptees. Alcoholic biological background was also predictive of the adoptees' antisocial behaviors.

The absence of findings among the adoptees under 18 in this study has interesting implications for the studies reported previously, which relied on reports by adoptive parents of the behavior problems of young adoptees. It is possible that significant amounts of antisocial behavior had not emerged because of the youth of the subjects. It is also possible that more accurate data concerning psychopathology was obtained when the adult adoptees themselves were interviewed than when their parents were asked to describe the children.

Hutchings and Mednick (1977). These authors executed a study in Denmark using an unselected birth cohort of adult adoptees and official records of their criminal activities. (This work served as a pilot study for the later study of the expanded Danish Adoption Cohort. The pilot work by Hutchings and Mednick will be reviewed first, followed by a review of the full study by Mednick, Gabrielli, and Hutchings, 1984.) They matched 1,145 male adoptees ranging from 30–44 years of age to 1,145 nonadopted controls for sex, age, occupational status of their fathers, and residence. Official police records of arrest for serious criminal offenses were searched for biological and adoptive fathers, adoptees, and the controls and their fathers.

The lifetime risk for criminal registration for males in Denmark is 8.9%. Of controls, 9% were registered, and 16% of adoptees were registered. No effect was found for age at transfer to adoptive home. Thirteen percent of adoptive fathers, 11% of control fathers, and 31% of the adoptees' biological fathers were registered. Considering the criminal adoptees, 22% of their adoptive fathers and 49% of their biological fathers were registered. Because contact between the adoptees and their biological fathers was "in most cases nonexistent," the data seem to demonstrate a genetic effect. However, the increase in number of adoptive fathers who were registered if their adoptive sons carried this genetic predisposition must be accounted for. It is possible that adoption agencies matched adoptive and biological parents on at least some vague indicators of social functioning that may be related to criminal status. That this may indeed have happened is supported by the finding of a significant correlation of .22 in the social class levels of the adoptees' adoptive and biological fathers. A multiple regression analysis was performed with adoptive father's criminal behavior, and social class was entered prior to biological father's social class and criminal behavior. Two results were obtained. Social class and paternal criminal behavior had independent effects, and the criminal behavior of the biological father had a significant effect even when the contribution from the adoptive father had been accounted for.

The authors next conducted a proband study of the 143 criminal adoptees, matched to 143 non-criminal control adoptees for age and occupational status of the adoptive father. Criminal and psychiatric records of biological and adoptive parents were searched. The criminal adoptees had larger numbers of criminal adoptive and biological parents than did controls, and also more mentally ill biological parents than did controls. A multiple regression analysis of criminal outcome in the adoptees was performed with criminal record in adoptive or biological mother or father, psychiatric hospitalization in adoptive or biological mother or father, social class, severe birth complications, and "several of the more promising interactions" as independent variables. All variables were dichotomized. Three factors contributed significantly to the regression analysis and accounted for about 10% of the variance. They were criminal status in at least one biological parent, criminal status in at least one adoptive parent, and psychiatric diagnosis for the biological mother. Most of these mothers had received diagnoses of psychopathy and depressive neurosis rather than psychosis.

Hutchings and Mednick (1977) presented a cross-fostering interaction study of antisocial behavior. When neither the adoptive nor biological father were registered criminals, 10.5% of the adoptee sons were criminals. This rate was increased to only 11.5% if the adoptive father was criminal but the biological father was not. However, if the biological father was registered but the adoptive father was not, the rate of criminal status in the sons doubled to 22%. If both adoptive and biological father were registered, 36.2% of the sons were also registered, suggesting an interactive effect of adoptive fathers' influence in the presence of a genetic predisposition but negligible effects of adoptive father's criminal behavior in the absence of such a predisposition.

Hutchings and Mednick were aware of possible methodological problems presented by the Danish adoption agency's policy of screening children from adoption because of criminal or psychiatric complications in the child's biological background. They also were concerned about the possibility that adoptive parents may have been informed of deviance in their adoptive child's background. Therefore, Mednick and Hutchings (1977) report a comparison of criminal registration rates among adoptees whose biological fathers committed their first offenses before the birth of the child and adoptees whose fathers did not become criminal until a year after the birth of the child (thus criminal status information could not have been relayed to adoptive parents). In each group, 23% of the adoptees became criminals. The possibility that adoptive parents had knowledge of a biological father's criminal status does not seem to be related to the probability of offending in adoptees.

Mednick, Gabrielli, and Hutchings (1984). Following the Hutchings and Mednick pilot study, two additional pertinent reports have been yielded from this Danish adoption project. Mednick, Gabrielli, and Hutchings (1984) report their work using the updated and expanded version of the adoption data, which contains a cohort of all nonfamilial official adoptions that took place in Denmark between 1924 and 1947 ($n = 14,427$). Court conviction records were utilized as the index of criminal involvement. Characteristics of the population were similar to those reported earlier in Hutchings and Mednick's (1977) description of the subset of the cohort, with adoptees and their biological parents evidencing higher rates of conviction than adoptive parents or the general Danish citizenry. The analyses reported were conducted using the male adoptees and their biological and adoptive parents. Cross-fostering analysis was repeated for this large cohort and Table 4.1 presents the results. If *both* the biological and adoptive parents were convicted, we observe the highest level of conviction among the sons (24.5%). Note that these findings refer to court convictions.

A log-linear analysis of the data in Table 4.1 is presented in Table 4.2. Adoptive parent criminality is not associated with a significant increment in the son's criminality. The effect of the biological parents' criminality is marked. Study of the model presented in Table 4.2 reveals that considering only the *additive* effect of the biological parent and the adoptive parent, the improvement in the chi square leaves almost no room for improvement by an interaction effect.

Figure 4.1 presents the relationship between property crime and violent crime in the sons and degree of recidivism in the biological parent. Log-linear analyses reveal that the relationship is highly significant for property crimes and not statistically significant for violent crimes. This property-crime specific genetic effect closely replicates the findings of Bohman et al. (1982). Mednick et al. (1984) tested the notion that genetic predisposition might play an especially important role in the cases characterized by "chronic" recidivistic offending. They selected as chronic offenders the 4.09% of the male adoptees with

Table 4.1. "Cross Fostering" Analysis: Percentage of Adoptive Sons Who Have Been Convicted of Criminal Law Offenses

Criminal Adoptive Parents	Criminal Biological Parents	
	Yes	No
Yes	24.5% (of 143)	14.7% (of 204)
No	20.0% (of 1226)	13.5% (of 2492)

Note: The number in parentheses are the total *n*s for each cell. From "Genetic Factors in Human Behavior: Evidence from an Adoption Cohort" by S.A. Mednick, W.F. Gabrielli, and B. Hutchings, 1984, *Science, 224,* 891–894. Copyright 1984 by American Association for the Advancement of Science. Reprinted by permission.

PERCENT MALE ADOPTEE PROPERTY OFFENDERS AND VIOLENT OFFENDERS BY BIOLOGICAL PARENT CONVICTIONS

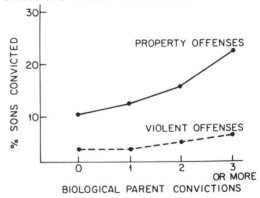

Figure 4.1. Percentage of male adoptee property offenders and violent offenders by biological parent criminality (cases in which adoptive parents are noncriminal). From "Genetic Factors in Human Behavior: Evidence from an Adoption Cohort" by S.A. Mednick, W.F. Gabrielli, and B. Hutchings, 1984, *Science, 224,* 891–894. Copyright 1984 by American Association for the Advancement of Science. Reprinted with permission.

three or more court convictions. This small group of recidivists accounted for 69.4% of all of the court convictions for all of the male adoptees. The proportion of these chronic offenders was found to increase as a function of level of recidivism in the biological parents. The increase is not monotonically linear, however. The rate of conviction among sons of very recidivistic biological parents jumps to twice the conviction rate found for the sons of biological parents with two convictions.

Table 4.2. Log Linear Analysis: The Influence of Adoptive Parent and Biological Parent Criminality upon Male Adoptee Criminality

Model	Model Chi-Square	df	p	Improvement Chi-Square	df	p
Baseline (S, AB)	32.91	3	.001			
Adoptive Parent (SA, AB)	30.71	2	.001	2.20	1	ns
Biological Parent (SB, AB)	1.76	2	.415	31.15	1	.001
Combined Influence (SB, SA, AB)	0.30	1	.585	32.61	2	.001
Biological Parent given Adoptive Parent (SB/SA, AB)				30.41	1	.001
Adoptive Parent given Biological Parent (SA/SB, AB)				1.46	1	ns

Note: S = adoptee son effect; A = adoptive parent effect; B = biological parent effect; ns = not significant. From "Genetic Factors in Human Behavior: Evidence from an Adoption Cohort" by S.A. Mednick, W.F. Gabrielli, and B. Hutchings, 1984, Science, 224, 891–894. Copyright 1984 by American Association for the Advancement of Science. Reprinted by permission.

Thus, Mednick et al. (1984) have demonstrated that the genetic factor seems to be strongest for chronic recidivistic offenders and for property offenders, but biological father's criminal offense record was not a good predictor of adoptees' violent behavior. It is difficult to assess the relationship of these findings to those of Bohman et al. (1982) because alcoholism data are not recorded in Denmark as they are in Sweden, by a national temperance board.

Mednick et al. (1984) also report interesting results from a study of sibling adoptees. There were a number of instances in which a biological mother and/or a biological father contributed more than one of their children to this population. These offspring were, of course, full- and half-siblings; they were usually placed in different adoptive homes. It was predicted that the separated full siblings would show more concordance for criminal convictions than the separated half-siblings. Both of these groups would show more concordance than two randomly selected, unrelated, separately-reared male adoptees. The predictions were confirmed by the data. The probability of any two randomly paired unrelated male adoptees being concordant (pairwise) for having at least one conviction was .085. The concordance rate for the 126 male half-sibling pairs reared apart was 12.9% and the concordance rate for the 40 male full-sibling pairs placed in different adoptive homes was 20%. When the biological father of the sibling pairs had been convicted (n = 45), this rate rose to 30.8%. Although the numbers of subjects were small, they represented all the cases, as defined, in a total cohort of adoptions. The results show that as degree of genetic relationship increases, the level of concordance for criminal conviction increases, especially in the cases in which the biological father was a criminal.

Mednick et al. (1984) conducted analyses to evaluate the possible effects of several factors upon their results. The historical period in which the adoption took place, the age at which the child was transferred from an orphanage to the adoptive home, the presence of subjects whose court records could not be identified, and the possibility that the adoptive parents might have been informed of convictions in their adoptee's biological parents were all tested as possible confounding factors. None were found to alter the results. Thus, the results of this study may be construed as positive evidence for a genetic predisposition toward criminal behavior.

Using this same adoption cohort, Van Duzen, Mednick, Gabrielli, and Hutchings (1983) were able to demonstrate that some portion of the variance in criminal behavior traditionally ascribed to social class is probably accounted for by genetic factors associated with lower class membership (if adoptive social class is controlled). Also, incidentally, by controlling for genetic factors, this group is the first to demonstrate that there are effects of social class on crime which are solely the result of the environmental experience of growing up in the lower social classes.

Conclusions From Adoption Studies

The work of five adoption research groups was reviewed, and all found a relationship between antisocial behavior in adoptees and antisocial behavior in their biological parents. Despite this agreement, any attempt to compare results across studies is beset with problems. Such a problem is the varying definitions of "antisocial", which ranges from psychopathy, to conviction for felony offenses, to maladjustment in school. A closely related problem is the means of assessment of antisocialness, with studies which used official records showing stronger results in most cases than studies relying on parental report. The large numbers of subjects lost to the studies done in the United States may have affected the results in some way. The age of the adoptees affected results strongly; the two analyses including children as young as 10 years of age did not support a genetic relationship. The possibilities that adoption agencies may have matched biological and adoptive parents for social class or deviance, or that adoptive parents were informed of deviance in a child's background, were not addressed in most of the studies, but Hutchings and Mednick (1977) and Mednick, Gabrielli, and Hutchings (1984) were able to demonstrate genetic effects even after accounting for these problems.

Delay of adoption or time spent institutionalized did not seem to have a strong impact on the genetic findings. Bohman (1978), Hutchings and Mednick (1977), Mednick et al. (1984), and Schulsinger (1974) found no effect at all. Cunningham et al. (1975) reported that children of deviant parents were held longer before adoption for testing, but the delay was not correlated with antisocial behavior in the adoptees.

Some of the studies were able to demonstrate that genetic effects on antisocial behavior were independent of social class or environmental rearing effects. Although initial analyses of a small subset of the Danish adoption data by Hutchings and Mednick (1977) seemed to provide evidence for a gene-environment interaction, this effect, in the same direction, was not significant when analyzed using criminal conviction data for the entire cohort (Mednick et al., 1984).

IMPLICATIONS FROM GENETIC FINDINGS FOR GENETIC RESEARCH

The Possibility of a Genetic Tie Between Serious Mental Illness and Antisocial Behavior

Separate reviews of genetic studies of both schizophrenia and antisocial behavior have demonstrated that genetic factors do operate in the etiology of each of these deviances. Two of the previously discussed adoption studies of serious mental illness found elevated rates of antisocial behavior among biological relatives of schizophrenics (Heston, 1966; Kety et al., 1968). No evidence of a connection between antisocial behavior and specific psychotic illness was shown in any of the adoption studies of antisocial behavior reviewed in the last section. However, Crowe (1972) reported elevated rates of general psychiatric admission in adoptees with criminal mothers, Hutchings and Mednick (1977) found biological mothers' psychiatric diagnosis to be predictive of adoptees' criminal status, and Schulsinger (1974) found drug and alcohol addiction and hysterical character disorders to be elevated in the relatives of psychopaths. Bohman et al. (1982) demonstrated a genetic relationship between alcoholism and more serious and recidivistic crime. Cadoret (1978) found that biological fathers' antisocial personality predicted strongly to psychosomatic symptoms in young female adoptees, symptoms which are often used in the diagnosis of hysterical personality in adult females. Hyperactivity accounted for most of the behavior problems in the Cunningham et al. (1975) adoptees from antisocial biological parents. In consideration of these results, and those relating substance abuse, hysterical personality, hyperactivity, and antisocial behavior within individuals and within families (reported in an earlier section), we cannot discount the possibility of some genetic relationship between these illnesses.

The two schizophrenia adoption studies suggest that even psychoses cannot be eliminated from consideration as part of this relationship. At present, the "spectrum" concept is so ill-defined and beset by contradictory research findings that it remains an intriguing set of hypotheses in need of testing.

Assortative Mating

It is reasonable to assume (genetics aside) that being reared by two deviant parents will bode even worse prospects for a child's behavior than being reared by one parent who provides a deviant influence.

We have seen that there are some genetic contributions to both serious mental illness and antisocial behavior. What outcome might we expect from a child given a share of genetic predisposition to deviance from not only one parent, but both parents?

The mating of individuals who are phenotypically more similar (or less similar) with regard to a trait than would be expected if mating were entirely at random is called assortative mating. There is evidence that assortative mating does occur in humans for a variety of characteristics. For example, humans have been found to mate assortatively for similarity on age and I.Q., and for dissimilarity on number of illnesses and pulse rate (see Spuhler, 1967, 1968; Vandenberg, 1972, for reviews). Some data exist that suggest that humans also mate assortatively for a combination of serious mental illness and antisocial behavior. Greater than random mating for two different phenotypes is called cross-assortative mating. Lewis and Balla (1976) noted that 30% of the criminal fathers in their family study had wives who had received psychiatric treatment. Guze (1976) also examined the wives of the 223 male felons in his family study. Six percent were sociopathic, 14% had anxiety neuroses, 4% were hysterical personalities, 7% were alcoholics, and 1% were schizophrenics. In assessing the fathers of Danish children chosen for a high-risk study because their mothers were schizophrenics, Mednick (1978) found that 49.6% of these fathers were known to the police and 39.6% had been convicted at least once. Fowler and Tsuang (1975) interviewed spouses of schizophrenics and found that although few of the husbands were schizophrenic themselves, 39% of them were psychiatrically disturbed. Alcoholism and personality disorders accounted for 70% of disturbed husbands. Rosenthal (1974) also interviewed the mates of the schizophrenic index parents in his adoptee study of the schizophrenia spectrum. He discovered that whereas 45% of the mates of male schizophrenics were diagnosed within the schizophrenia spectrum, the diagnoses for 56% of the mates of female schizophrenics were divided evenly between the schizophrenia spectrum and psychopathy. Erlenmeyer-Kimling, Wunsch-Hitzig and Deutsch (1980) have explained that although some older studies using hospital diagnosis records as the criterion found little evidence of cross-assortative mating, more recent studies such as those of Fowler and Tsuang (1975) and Rosenthal (1974), in which interview data were used as the criterion, have found good evidence that cross-assortative mating does occur. The extent of agreement between studies on a rate of cross-assortative matings hovering between 22% and 39% is notable. In addition, there appears to be a sex-specific pattern, with antisocial men often mating with mentally ill women.

Implications for an Adoption Study

What are the implications of cross-assortative matings of this type for study of the genetics of serious mental illness, antisocial behavior, or the relationship between the two? Rosenthal (1974) writes of adoption studies of schizophrenia available to date:

> No effort was made to determine the diagnostic status of the second parent. Such a research strategy may be useful, but from a genetic standpoint, it is equivalent to Gregor Mendel beginning his investigation with one selected type of sweet pea plant in the F_1 generation, crossing it with other plants whose characteristics he knew nothing about, and then trying to relate all the characteristics he finds in the F_2 generation to those of the F_1 parent whose special characteristics were known to him. Imagine the confusion and folly of this procedure. A proper genetic study must be based on who mates with whom. In fact, although genetics has been defined in various ways, the simplest and perhaps best definition of genetics is: *the science of matings.* (p. 168)

A study such as Heston's (1966), which begins with a proband schizophrenic mother and finds an elevated rate of psychopathic disorders in the offspring, cannot conclude that the psychopathy is genetically associated with schizophrenia unless he can show that the male coparents were not psychopaths themselves (p. 171).

Only 3 of the 11 adoption research groups whose work was reviewed here considered both antisocial behavior and serious mental illness in tandem with collecting data on both biological mothers and fathers. Kety et al. (1968) noted that the biological relatives of their schizophrenic adoptees showed elevated rates of psychopathy as well as schizophrenia. Schulsinger (1974) found both psychopathy and other mental illnesses elevated in the biological relatives of his psychopathic adoptees. Do these results reflect a true spectral genetic relationship between serious mental illness and antisocial behavior, or are they artifacts of cross-assortative mating? Hutchings and Mednick (1977) found that mental illness in the biological mother predicted criminal conviction in their adoptees independently of biological fathers' conviction. Thus, some grounds have been found for a genetic link between mental illness and antisocial behavior that may not be explained by cross-assortative mating.

An Appropriate Study

Evidence has been presented that some individuals suffer from both serious mental illness and antisocial behavior, and that these deviances also tend to run in the same families. Genetic components have been shown to exist in the etiology of each deviance. A number of studies have indicated that a genetic spectrum including both serious mental illness and antisocial behavior may also exist. It is not known to what extent cross-assortative mating of mentally ill women with antisocial men has affected the findings of such a spectrum in studies to date.

In addition to the neglect of the possibility of cross-assortative mating, other methodological problems were found in the studies reviewed. Inconsistencies in the findings of studies using telephone interviews or parental reports of adoptees' deviance point to a need for a reliable source of data, such as official records of deviant behavior by the subjects. Some studies assessed children who were too young to have developed either serious mental illness or serious antisocial behavior; subjects are needed who have reached at least young adulthood. Lifetime data of the incidence of deviance for subjects are desirable for analysis of any developmental changes, for example, the change from early antisocial behavior to later mental illness. The study of a large unselected birth cohort will avoid problems of representative sampling and should provide enough subjects to make even cross-fostering interaction analyses possible. It is desirable to obtain data for all possible psychiatric diagnoses received by the subjects so that the entire range of diagnoses that have been intimated to belong in the genetic spectrum may be considered. Finally, data must be available for both adoptive and biological mothers and fathers as well as for the adoptees in order to evaluate the implications of cross-assortative matings for any spectrum relationships discovered.

In short, what is needed is an adoption study of a large unselected birth cohort of adult adoptees in which both lifetime records of criminality and psychiatric illness (for a number of diagnoses) are available for the adoptees, each of their biological parents, and each of their adoptive parents. The database originally described in the study by Hutchings and Mednick (1977) and Mednick et al. (1984) has been expanded so that it now fits these qualifications, and we next report some preliminary results from examinations of this database.

Ongoing Analyses in the Expanded Danish Adoption Project

The authors of this chapter are currently investigating the implications of mental illness in the biological parents for criminal outcome of their adopted-away offspring. The aspects of criminal outcome which are being investigated are violent offending and recidivistic offending. We are asking these questions in the context of the Danish adoption dataset: Are violent individuals more likely to have serious mental illness in their biological backgrounds than other adoptees? Are persons with biological backgrounds including mental illness more likely to be repeatedly convicted for criminal acts? How does the picture of the two dependent measures change when the biological background contains frequent criminal offending in addition to mental illness?

Positive Findings. We began our investigation of the possibility of a genetic contribution from mental illness to recidivistic and violent criminal behavior by demonstrating that there is some basis in the data for a genetic relationship between mental illness in general, as represented by the presence of a psychiatric hospitalization record and criminal conviction. Figure 4.2 presents a histogram of the percentage of adoptees convicted for any criminal offense as a function of biological parent hospital admission status. To simplify interpretation, in these analyses only the male adoptees whose adoptive parents were free of criminal conviction and psychiatric hospitalization are used as subjects.

The risk of conviction for any criminal offense among the 5,182 male adoptees whose conviction records could be searched is 15.09%. If the biological parents were never admitted to a psychiatric hospital, the risk of adoptee conviction is 14.45%. However, if at least one of the two biological parents was admitted to a psychiatric hospital, the risk of adoptee conviction rises to 19.23%, a difference that is significant (chi-square = 10.50, $df = 1$, $p < .01$).

Figure 4.2 also depicts the risk of adoptee conviction as a function of psychiatric hospitalization separately for the biological mothers and biological fathers. The biological mothers' psychiatric hospitalization can be seen to contribute slightly more strongly than the biological fathers' psychiatric hospitalization to adoptee conviction outcome. The biological fathers' contribution, although only slightly less notable than the biolog-

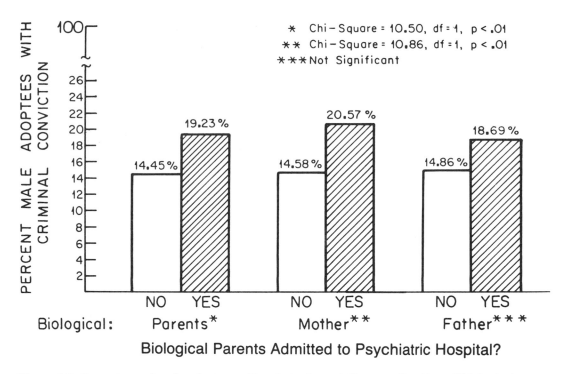

Figure 4.2. Percentage of male adoptees with criminal conviction as a function of biological parent psychiatric hospital admission.

ical mothers' contribution as depicted in Figure 4.2, was not significant when tested by chi-square.

Analyses subsequent to this investigation of the fundamental relationship between parental mental illness and offspring criminal conviction have addressed the specific adoptee outcomes of conviction for violence and multiple recidivistic nonviolent conviction. These analyses have yielded a number of positive findings:

1. Increasing levels of offspring nonviolent criminal recidivism are associated with increasing prevalence of psychiatric illness among biological parents.
2. When mental illness and *recidivistic* criminal behavior are present together in the genetic background, they interact to increase the likelihood of conviction for violent offenses and the likelihood of multiple conviction for nonviolent offenses.
3. The genetic relationships described above between mental illness and criminal outcome may be ascribed specifically to parental disorders of personality and disorders of substance abuse. Endogenous psychoses are not geneti-

cally related to criminal behavior in this adoption cohort.
4. The heritable factors associated with these "antisocial" diagnoses (drug and alcohol abuse and antisocial personality disorder) are distinct from those which account for the previously reported genetic association between parental *crime* and offspring *crime*.

The analyses are described fully in Moffitt (1984).

Although parental cross-assortative mating patterns have yet to be explored in these data, the analyses that have produced the findings listed previously are strongly suggestive that parental mental illness has its greatest effect upon adoptee criminal behavior when it is found in combination with parental multiple criminal recidivism. In view of the importance of this interaction between parental crime and mental illness, questions arose concerning the outcomes of adoptees whose genetic backgrounds were characterized by both mental illness and criminal behavior. In order to address these questions in a preliminary way, the percentages for certain outcome variables available in the Danish adoption data set were com-

Table 4.3. Deviant Outcomes for Male Adoptees by Varying Combinations of Biological Parent Psychiatric Hospitalization and Conviction Status

Biological Background Status	n	Nonviolent Criminal Convictions*	3+ Nonviolent Criminal Convictions*	Violent Convictions	More Than 6 Mos. Incarcerated*	Onset of Convictions Before Age 19*	Psychiatric Hospitalization*
				Percent of Male Adoptees			
(0) No deviance	2236	10.08	2.06	3.20	2.95	3.66	5.28
(1) Criminal conviction only	1004	14.81	3.95	3.39	3.98	5.65	6.87
(2) Psychiatric admission only	319	14.03	1.80	4.47	2.56	5.43	7.84
(3) Criminal conviction and psychiatric admission	248	20.45	5.45	3.90	7.05	7.20	10.08
(4) Mother's or father's conviction records not identified**	1852						
Total	5659						

*p < .01.
**These cases excluded from biological parent status rows 0 and 2.

piled and are presented in Table 4.3. In 248 adoption family cases, both psychiatric hospitalization and criminal conviction were present in the biological parents. Note that the combination of parental hospitalization and conviction does not represent cross-assortative mating alone; there are numerous ways in which this combination might occur in a set of two parents, and no distinctions by sex of parent associated with type of social deviance is made in Table 4.3.

Table 4.3 allows comparison of adoptees with genetic backgrounds containing no parental deviance, parental conviction only, parental psychiatric hospitalization only, or a combination of the two parental deviances, for six outcome measures of adoptee social deviance. It can be seen that adoptees with genetic contributions from both parental mental illness and parental crime are significantly more likely to become convicted for nonviolent offenses, to become convicted three or more times, to spend more than 6 months in prison or jail, to become convicted relatively early in life (under age 19), and to themselves be psychiatrically hospitalized. (Although the lack of increased violent convictions for this group may at first seem to contradict point 2, listed earlier, elevated rates of violence were found only when *high* levels of biological parent recidivism were in combination with biological parent hospitalization; Table 4.3 includes nonrecidivistic convicted

biological parents as well.) Thus, although the convicted male with parental mental illness and parental conviction in his family background is a rare individual, he comprises 1% of this male adoptee population, he seems to account for a proportionately large share of social deviance (as defined), and he seems to require a large share of societal resources for social control. This 1% of the adoptees accounts for 12.24% of the adoptee convictions in the present study and for 9.39% of the total months of imprisonment for the cohort.

Methodological Considerations. The findings described above lead us to the conclusion that there is a genetic relationship between crime and certain forms of psychiatric disorder: alcoholism, drug abuse, and personality disorder. However, as discussed previously in this chapter, there are a number of methodological imperfections in the adoption design which need be addressed before we may confidently make inferences from these findings. Analyses have been conducted (described in detail by Moffitt, 1984) that have ruled out possible confounds from (a) missing data, (b) the adoptee's age at transfer from the orphanage to his adoptive home, (c) the possibility that adoptive parents were informed of biological parent deviance by adoption agency personnel, (d) perinatal and birth complications in the biological mother's pregnancy, and (e) historical period in which the adoption took place. None of these factors were demonstrated to significantly alter the relationships found between parental mental illness and adoptee criminal outcome.

Overview

So far this chapter has presented the evidence that heritable factors exist which serve to increase the likelihood of criminal involvement among the offspring of individuals who themselves are characterized by criminal behavior, personality disorder, and substance abuse. Thus, to date we know that knowledge of one or more of these three characteristics in a child's biological parents is an indicant of the presence of his predisposition toward development of serious antisocial behavior. The chapter will now move on to discuss the efforts of biological criminologists to identify the precise heritable factors underlying these markers, that is, the transmissible physiological substrates that account for the heritable contribution to crime which we have thus far observed at the epidemiological level.

AUTONOMIC NERVOUS SYSTEM AND NEUROPHYSIOLOGICAL FACTORS

IMPLICATIONS FOR FUTURE RESEARCH

The first part of this chapter has demonstrated that some factors that produce a tendency toward criminal antisocial behavior are inherited from biological parents who behave antisocially or exhibit some forms of mental illness. What implications are there from these findings for future psychobiological research into criminal behavior? We know, of course, that it is not criminal behavior per se that is inherited, but some polygenic combination of biological processes and factors which act to predispose some individuals to behave antisocially.

The implications of these findings for future research have been discussed by Gabrielli and Mednick (1983). Their discussion takes the form of a set of suggestions:

1. What is transmitted in some biological factor or factors. Such biological factors should be found to be differentially characteristic of individuals who have evidenced antisocial behavior.
2. In order to include these biological factors among possible causes of antisocial behavior,

these variables should be investigated in prospective, longitudinal studies.
3. The heritability of the biological factors should be determined.
4. Nongenetic influences (e.g., family, peers, school, perinatal events, societal change) which modify or interact with the biological predispositions should be identified.
5. The biological predispositions and the nongenetic influences (Point 4) should be integrated in a comprehensive theory of the development of antisocial behavior.
6. Guided by the theory (Point 5), methods of primary intervention should be tested. These methods should reduce the likelihood of antisocial outcome in otherwise predisposed individuals. When all six steps have been successfully accomplished, the research questions will have been answered.

We are, of course, at the very beginning of stages of this series of steps. But there are some biological factors that are characteristic of antisocial individuals, are predictive in prospective studies, and are heritable, that can be included in a biobehavioral theory of the origins of criminal behavior. This section of the chapter reviews the research literature on two of these variables, autonomic nervous system function and neurophysiology, for which research on Point 3, evidence of heritability, has been productive. We will also present a biobehavioral theory including genetic (autonomic nervous system) and nongenetic (family) factors.

Heritability of Autonomic Nervous System Factors: Skin Conductance

The possibility that components of the skin conductance response may be genetically determined using twin methodology has been investigated by Hume (1973), Jost and Sontag (1944), Lader and Wing (1966), Rachman (1960), and Vandenberg, Clark, and Samuels (1965), with varying results. Although each study found one or more components of the response to be heritable, we should note Hume's statement: "Lamentably few of these studies can be regarded with any degree of credibility" (p. 88). Bell, Mednick, Gottesman, and Sergeant (1977) noted this state of the literature and conducted a study of 10 monozygotic and 13 dizygotic twin pairs, which accounted for many of the problems of the earlier studies. This study showed that significant genetic factors seem to be present in the response components of rise time and recovery time (this latter variable is critical in the biobehavioral theory). This finding was strongest when data were recorded from the left (typically nondominant) hand.

Heritability of Neurophysiological Factors: The EEG

Notably consistent support for a genetic factor in the etiology of variants in EEG activity has been found in several twin studies. Dustman and Beck, 1965; Vogel, Schalt, Kruger, and Klarich (1982); and Young and Fenton (1971), among others, report closer relationships in EEG patterns for monozygotic twin pairs than from dizygotic twin pairs or unrelated pairs of control subjects.

AUTONOMIC NERVOUS SYSTEM STUDIES (SKIN CONDUCTANCE)

The psychopath is described by Hare (1978a) as among the most aggressive, dangerous, and recidivistic clients of a prison. Although there is low agreement about the diagnosis, most clinicians describe the psychopath as unsocialized and callous: He feels no guilt, remorse, or shame; lacks emotion; and is incapable of love. He does not alter his behavior as a result of punishment and fails to learn from punishing experiences. He is unable to control impulses and cannot anticipate consequences (American Psychiatric Association, 1968; Buss, 1966; Cleckley, 1976; Craft, 1965). Many of these symptoms describe a lack of emotional expression (no guilt, no emotionality, incapable of love, callous, etc.). Other symptoms relate to emotion-mediated learning (failure to learn from punishment, inability to anticipate negative consequences or to be socialized).

Psychophysiologists have techniques appropriate to systematic study of emotions and emotional learning. Inevitably, some psychophysiologists are curious as to whether this clinically described psychopathic lack of emotion is expressed in lower levels of objectively measured physiological indices of emotional expression such as heart rate, blood pressure, respiration, and skin conductance. This section reviews physiological research of antisocial individuals relating to three of these clinical characteristics: absence of emotionality or emotional responsiveness (or callousness), absence of ability to anticipate negative consequences, and failure to learn from punishment.

The discipline of psychophysiology is most concerned with studying peripheral signs of autonomic nervous system (ANS) activity. The ANS mediates physiological activity associated with emotions; hence, it is important to the study of psychopathy. Examples of peripheral manifestations of ANS activity include changes in heart rate, blood pressure, respiration, muscle tension, pupillary size, and electrical activity of the skin.

The measurement of electrical properties of the skin—called galvanic skin response (GSR), or skin conductance—is the most commonly used peripheral indicant of ANS activity, both in psychophysiology and in criminology. The skin conductance response, as it is usually measured, is most heavily dependent on the activity of the sweat glands of the palms. Individuals who are often emotionally aroused, anxious, and fearful tend to have clammy, wet handshakes because their emotional responsiveness is reflected in the overactive sweat glands of their palms. Such emotional individuals usually exhibit high skin conductance even when they are not stimulated. Very calm, unemotional types typically have very low skin conductance. (This "emotional" perspiration is also abundant in the soles of the feet but is typically less evident, because people we encounter are usually wearing shoes. The soles and palms are called volar areas.)

When frightened or otherwise emotionally aroused, normally calm individuals will evidence episodes of volar sweating. This sweating moistens the skin with a salt solution that increases its electrical conductivity. (More detailed information can be found in Venables & Christie, 1975). If a weak current (generated by a battery) is leaked through the fingers we can monitor the electrical resistance (or its inverse, conductance) of the skin to the passage of this current. If we stimulate the individual to become emotionally aroused (e.g., shoot off a gun behind his back) his ANS will activate his volar sweat glands. The skin will be suffused with perspiration, which will increase its conductance; if we are monitoring this conductance on a polygraph, we will see an excursion of the pen that (all other things being equal) will be proportionate to the extent of ANS arousal experienced by our subject. Subjects who are relatively unaroused by stimulation will produce little or no pen excursion. Individuals who are highly aroused by the gunshot will evidence a substantial pen excursion. The extent of pen excursion can be calibrated so that it can be expressed in electrical units of conductance. This process yields an objective score that reflects, at least to some substantial extent, the subject's degree of emotional arousal via ANS activation. There is a considerable body of methodological literature describing application of this technique; despite some complaints on details in the literature, there is good standardization of technique, which makes it possible, with due caution, to compare results from different laboratories.

Skin conductance is the most frequently measured psychophysiological characteristic of antisocial individuals. The pattern of results reported regarding certain conductance characteristics of antisocial persons has been relatively consistent across many laboratories, nations, experimental procedures, and definitions of antisocial behavior. For these reasons, this discussion is restricted, in the main, to skin conductance.

Much of the reported work used prisoners as subjects. The prisoners are typically divided and compared on the basis of assessed psychopathy level, seriousness of criminality, recidivism, or some combination. Nonprisoner controls are rarely assessed. Studies on the skin conductance of either prisoners or nonincarcerated criminals must be interpreted with considerable caution. The criminal life and the prison experience very likely affect a person's emotional response patterns (D'Atri, 1978). Thus, skin conductance deviance in antisocial individuals may be the result of their criminal careers or incarceration. Etiological interpretations of such data must be very cautiously proffered. However, some tiny beginnings of prospective research have been undertaken in which young people are assessed and the results related to their delinquency later in years. Assessments of prisoners have also been related to their subsequent recidivism. These few prospective studies will be emphasized in this review.

Emotionality and Emotional Responsiveness

The descriptions of the callous, remorseless, unfeeling psychopath present a challenge to the psychophysiologist to produce an objective measure that might make it possible to subject this clinical description to analytic study. The psychophysiologist has responded to this challenge rather productively by investigating the psychopath's customary or *basal level* (relatively unprovoked) of emotionality and his emotional *responsiveness* when provoked by a variety of challenging stimuli.

Basal-Level Emotionality. To measure basal-level emotionality, the subject is brought into the laboratory and appropriate electrodes are applied; his skin conductance level is then continuously re-

corded under conditions of no special stimulation. The psychopathic prisoner tends to evidence a slightly lower level of skin conductance than the nonpsychopathic prisoner. For some studies, this difference is statistically significant (Blankenstein, 1969; Dengerink & Bertilson, 1975; Hare, 1965, 1968; Mathis, 1970; Schalling, Lidberg, Levander, & Dahlin, 1973). In other studies, the difference, while not statistically significant (perhaps in part because of the low reliability of the diagnosis), is usually in the direction of a lower skin conductance for the psychopath (Borkovec, 1970; Fox & Lippert, 1963; Hare, 1972, 1975; Hare, Cox, & Frazelle, in press; Hare & Craigen, 1974; Hare et al., 1978; Hare & Quinn, 1971; Lippert & Senter, 1966; Parker, Syndulko, Maltzman, Jens, & Ziskind, 1975; Schalling et al. 1973; Schmauk, 1970; Sutker, 1970). Hare (1978b), noting this consistent but weak tendency, combined the results from eight independent studies in his laboratory. In most of these studies, statistically significant basal-level skin conductance was *not* observed, although in each study psychopaths had lower skin conductance. The combined results are statistically significant.

Loeb and Mednick (1977) report on a 10-year follow-up and delinquency assessment of a group of 104 normal Danish adolescents. In 1962, these adolescents were subject to a skin conductance examination; in 1972, their officially recorded delinquency was ascertained from the Danish National Police Register, which has been described by Wolfgang (1977) as "probably the most thorough, comprehensive and accurate in the Western world . . . .The reliability and validity of the Danish recordkeeping system are almost beyond criticism" (p. v). At 10-year follow-up, 7 males of the 104 adolescents had been registered for mildly delinquent acts. Seven of the other boys were matched to these mild delinquents for social factors and age. The predelinquency basal skin conductance level of 6 of the 7 delinquents was below that of all the controls (*t* tests between the delinquents and nondelinquents were not significant). Note that in this study, mild registered delinquency, not psychopathy, defined the groups.

Spontaneous Skin Conductance Phenomena. After a subject is attached to the skin conductance recording device, he is usually permitted a 5–10-minute rest. During this time, continuous recording of skin conductance takes place. Although no stimulation is being systematically provided by the experimenter, the subject will almost always exhibit episodic increases in skin conductance that produce pen excursions. These are called spontaneous responses. They may be instigated by thoughts, images, sounds outside the laboratory, or unknown factors. Subjects who are more aroused and anxious tend to exhibit more spontaneous responses (Szpiler & Epstein, 1976).

As in the case of basal level, the results of several experiments are inconclusive but suggest that psychopaths have fewer spontaneous responses during a pre- or postexperimental rest period (Hare, 1968; Hare & Quinn, 1971; Schalling et al., 1973). Fox and Lippert (1963) observed that antisocial psychopaths exhibit less spontaneous activity than do inadequate psychopaths. Lippert and Senter (1966) did not find significant differences between psychopaths and controls. Hemming (1977) found no differences between prisoners and students. Siddle, Nicol, & Foggit (1973) report no spontaneous response differences between groups varying in degree of delinquency. Hare (1978b) combined the results of several studies from his laboratory in which the psychopath tended to evidence fewer spontaneous responses but still did not obtain statistically significant differences.

If this review had found consistent evidence of a lower skin conductance basal level and fewer spontaneous responses for the psychopath, this would have suggested that the psychopath continuously experiences an underaroused, unemotional state of being. The picture, unfortunately, is inconsistent. The cumulative impression of the studies suggests that if indeed the basal skin conductance of the psychopathic prisoner *is* relatively low, the differences from the nonpsychopathic prisoner are not very great or consistent. Inspection of the reported variances in some studies suggests that the psychopathic group may have a greater range of basal levels and a greater number of spontaneous responses. This may reflect the possibility that a subgroup of psychopaths consistently lowers the group's mean.

It is a pity that these studies do not include nonprisoner comparison groups. This would give us a frame of reference for evaluating the results. The differences within prisoner populations may be totally dwarfed by the differences between prisoners and noncriminal populations. Evidence for such a difference has been mentioned by Hare (1978b).

The assumption underlying both the basal level and the spontaneous response studies is that the observed skin conductance behavior is unstimulated. Actually, as each experimenter fully realizes, the subject is rather heavily stimulated by being introduced and attached to the apparatus. These skin conductance measures may be heavily influenced by such situational characteristics.

Skin Conductance Responses to Stimulation. Cleckley (1976) has described the psychopath as evidencing a general poverty of emotional reactiveness. Psychophysiologists have attempted to confirm this description by use of physiological recordings of psychopath's skin conductance responses to stimuli, such as simple tones, loud noises, electric shock, insertion of a hypodermic needle, and slides of horrible facial injuries. The results of most of these studies are rather consonant: The psychopath, the prisoner, the criminal, and the delinquent are decidedly emotionally hyporeactive to stimulation. (Aniskiewicz, 1973; Blankenstein, 1969; Borkovec, 1970; Hare, 1972; Hare, 1975; Hare & Craigen, 1974; Hare & Quinn, 1971; Hemming, 1977; Hinton & O'Neill, 1978; Hodgins-Milner, 1976; Mathis, 1970; Schalling, 1975; Siddle et al., 1973; Sutker, 1970).

Hare et al. (in press) report that psychopaths evidence only diminished responsiveness to exceptionally loud noise (120 decibels). Their research is carried out in a prison. Subjects were selected by inviting 250 prisoners to participate in the research. Of these, 87 volunteered and 64 were finally tested. The investigators are aware of the difficulty of generalizing from such a selected population. In addition, it should be emphasized that all of the subjects (both psychopaths and controls) were recidivistic criminals. Perhaps this is the reason that differences between psychopaths and nonpsychopaths were apparent only under extreme stimulus conditions. In another study, using similar subject selection methods, Hare (1975) reports no differences between psychopaths and nonpsychopaths. Lippert and Senter (1966) also report no differentiation of psychopaths by skin conductance amplitude (size of response).

In the one published prospective study mentioned previously (Loeb & Mednick, 1977), skin conductance amplitude was measured on a group of 104 Danish adolescents some 10 years before delinquency was ascertained. Predelinquent skin conductance amplitude of the 7 delinquents was markedly (and statistically significantly) lower than that of controls. In 1962, the nondelinquent controls evidenced a mean response amplitude that was 5–10 times as great as that of the boys who eventually evidenced delinquency. The transgressions involved were mild.

Cleckley's clinical description is consistent with

the physiologically assessed emotional responsiveness of not only the psychopath but also the criminal and the delinquent. The finding is substantially consistent across a considerable variety of national settings, laboratory procedures, levels, and definitions of antisocial behavior. The single prospective study has a pitifully small group (7) of mild delinquents, but the results do not contradict the hypotheses and are bolstered considerably by the other cited literature.

The robustness of the cross-sectional findings encourages the inclusion of skin conductance responsiveness among the reliable characteristics of individuals who are officially noted as having transgressed. The single prospective findings suggests that ANS responsiveness should not be excluded from the group of variables showing potential etiological significance in the *development* of antisocial behavior.

Anticipation of Negative Experiences

The psychopath is marked by his inability to foresee the negative consequences of his acts. This includes negative consequences for himself and for his victims. Psychophysiologists have attempted to create laboratory situations in which foreseeable negative consequences (e.g., electric shock, very loud noises) would result from designated behavior. Skin conductance responses are then monitored to test whether antisocial individuals evidence normal emotional (skin conductance) apprehension in anticipation of the shock or noise.

In 1957, Lykken reported that psychopaths evidence relatively small skin conductance responses in anticipation of electric shock. Hare (1965) presented prisoners with numbers (1–12) in serial order and warned them that they would experience an electric shock at Number 8. The nonpsychopathic prisoners evidenced strong electrodermal responses early in the number sequence preceding Number 8. The psychopaths evidenced little or no anticipation until just before Number 8. The nonpsychopaths also demonstrated greater responsiveness immediately before the electric shock. In a more recent study (Hare et al., 1978), prisoners were warned that they would experience a very loud (120 decibels) aversive "blast" of noise after a 12-second countdown. The psychopathic prisoners did not begin to show anticipatory skin conductance response until just before the blast and even then their responses were rather weak. The nonpsychopathic prisoners were evidencing substantial skin conductance anticipation after 3 seconds. The psychopathic subgroup reached the

highest level of skin conductance anticipation just before the blast (12 seconds), the same as the level reached by the nonpsychopaths after just over 6 seconds.

This lack of the psychopath's emotional response to anticipated pain or aversive stimulation is well documented (Hare & Craigen, 1974; Hodgins-Milner, 1976; Lippert & Senter, 1966; Schalling, Levander, & Dahlin-Lidberg, 1975). Tharp, Syndulko, Maltzman, and Aiskind (1978) repeatedly presented trials consisting of a countdown followed by a very loud noise (95 decibels). After a few countdown-noise trials, the psychopaths showed no skin conductance response whatsoever in anticipation of the aversive loud noise. The controls (nonprisoners in this study) continued to evidence skin conductance anticipation of the impending noise.

There are other ways to measure ANS functioning in anticipation of stress that do not deal with skin conductance. Lidberg, Levander, Schalling, and Lidberg (in press) observed catecholamine levels in the blood of Swedish men just before they were to appear in criminal court to be tried. Catecholamine levels in normals are highly elevated during ANS excitation, such as states of anxiety or fear; it would be expected that men just before such a trial would have elevated levels. The pretrial men were divided into high- and low-psychopathy groups. The more psychopathic men evidenced no heightening of their catecholamine levels just prior to the trial. The less psychopathic men had strongly elevated levels. The anticipation of the court trial evoked no physiological inkling of anxiety or fear in the psychopaths.

A second nonskin conductance study concerned delinquents in a sample of 5,362 single-born, legitimate, live births drawn from all 13,687 births occurring between March 3rd and March 9th in England, Wales, and Scotland in 1964 (Wadsworth, 1976). This classic longitudinal birth cohort study was begun by Douglas (Douglas & Bloomfield, 1958). Wadsworth (1975) described the cumulative officially recorded delinquency in this birth cohort at 21 years of age and then examined the relationship of this delinquency to a predelinquency measure of ANS response to anticipation of stress. The survey members were subjected to a school medical examination at 11 years of age. The period during which they waited for this examination was designed to be somewhat stressful. Their pulse rates were measured to assess the effects of this anticipation. Delinquents were defined as those who "either made a court appearance or were formally cautioned by the police between the ages of 8 and 21 years" (p. 249). Those who were *later* registered as delinquents had a lower anticipatory pulse rate. The delinquent–nondelinquent differences were significant for those committing indictable offenses and sexual and violent offenses.

The Wadsworth (1975, 1976) study is important because it is based on a large, national birth cohort and the results must be seen as representative. The data on pulse rate were gathered by hundreds of different physicians in different schools using rather primitive methods. Not all of these measurements were equally accurately taken. About 10 years intervened between the recording of the pulse rates and the ascertainment of the sexual and violent offenses. The hypothesized results emerged despite these conditions — which in most studies do not tend to inflate positive findings. The violent individuals evidenced a low level of emotional, physiologically measured anticipation of an aversive experience. Those who did not suffer anticipatory "fear" before the examination were those boys who later were more likely to become delinquent. Perhaps this anticipatory fear was also lacking before they committed the act (or acts) that placed them in the delinquent group.

One other feature of the Wadsworth study (1975, 1976) warrants emphasis. The low anticipatory pulse rate was observed 10 years before the delinquency was assessed. It is unlikely that the delinquency experience produced the low pulse rate. The prospective nature of the study establishes low pulse rate in anticipation of stress as a variable worthy of consideration as a potential etiological factor in delinquency.

How salient a predictive factor is pulse rate? Not very. In the Wadsworth study it predicts delinquency about as well as the "broken home" variable. It is naive to expect that any variable alone (whether biological or social) will explain large amounts of delinquency variance. Delinquency is likely to be as complex in its causation as it is in its manifestation.

In some studies the subjects have the opportunity to anticipate that others are about to be shocked or blasted with noise. Sutker (1970) studied noninstitutionalized psychopaths and controls while they observed an individual experiencing an electric shock when a countdown from "1" to "12" reached "4". The psychopaths displayed no or minimal skin conductance response in anticipation of the other's pain. This result has been replicated by House and Milligan (1976) in a study on prisoners. Similar results have been obtained by

Aniskiewicz (1973) and Hare and Craigen (1974).

Psychopaths, prisoners, and delinquents evidence minimal or no physiological signs that they are apprehensive about a forthcoming painful or aversive stimulus to themselves or to others. Nonpsychopathic (or less psychopathic) prisoners, and individuals not officially registered as delinquent, do evidence physiological anticipation of such events. The intended analogy of these laboratory confrontations to the development of "real-life" acts of lawlessness is clear. Of course, most elements of criminal acts in the "field" are only remotely modeled by this laboratory paradigm. Yet the relatively consistent confirmation of the hypotheses that instigated these studies cannot be ignored. These studies give no reason to reject the hypothesis that lack, or diminution, of a "normal" ANS fear reaction anticipating negative or painful consequences may be partly responsible for the relative ease with which certain individuals commit deviant acts.

As pointed out above, the evidence in support of this hypothesis is all correlative. A more rigorous examination of the role of this variable in the etiology of antisocial behavior can only be carried out in the context of a prospective, *experimental-manipulative* project (primary or secondary prevention). Training techniques that improve the young person's emotional ability to foresee the aversive consequences of his acts could be tested. The more effective the training techniques (taking into consideration social factors and initial level of emotional anticipation), the greater should be the reduction of delinquency. Given use of an adequate control group in such a study, this experimental-manipulative approach (as opposed to the traditional weak correlative approach) would improve our capacity to test this hypothesis.

Failure to Learn From Punishment: A Biosocial Theory of Antisocial Behavior

The clinical characteristic of the psychopath that is perhaps most critical to understanding the origins of his condition is his reputed inability to learn from punishment. This lack certainly relates to his hectic recidivism; even more important, it suggests a mechanism that would make the young psychopath-to-be relatively unresponsive to one of society's important moral training forces, namely, family and peer punishment for transgressive acts.

This section presents a minitheory of the bases and consequences of some individuals' inability to learn from punishment. Viewed inversely, the theory is an explanation of the development and learning of morality and law abidance. The theory postulates the interaction of specific social factors and specific ANS aptitudes. After presenting the theory, skin conductance evidence relating to the theory and to the examination of the antisocial individuals' abilities to learn from punishment in laboratory situations is presented.

We will begin with a discussion of how morality is defined. An early publication of this topic was chipped in stone and brought down from Mount Sinai. The major thrust of that message was negative: "Thou shalt *not* . . . ." Although subsequent moral authorities have added *some* positive acts as prescriptions of moral behavior (e.g., "Love thy neighbor"), they have retained the original basic inhibitory definitions of moral acts. Very few will denounce you if you do not love your neighbor; but if you seduce your neighbor's wife, steal from him, or kill him, you may be certain that your behavior will be classified as immoral. Statements of moral behavior that are critical for everyday activities are essentially negative and inhibitory. That these strictures were enumerated and then carved onto stone tablets suggests that, at some point, there must have been a strong need for insistence on these inhibitions.

How are these inhibitions taught to children? Simple instruction suffices for some; for others the instructions must be reinforced. There seem to be three learning mechanisms that could help parents teach children civilized behavior: modeling, positive and negative reinforcements, and punishment. Positive acts such as loving neighbors, helping old ladies across the street, and cleaning the snow and ice from the front walk can be learned by modeling. But for the more inhibitory moral commands, modeling appears impracticable. Artificial arrangements can be imagined in which modeling is used to teach children not to be adulterous or aggressive, but if our civilization had to depend solely on modeling, it is likely that things would be even more chaotic than they are today. It is also possible to use positive reinforcement (rewards) to teach inhibition of forbidden behavior; but again, reinforcing a child 24 hours a day because he is *not* stealing seems both inefficient and unfocused.

Following the excellent exposition of Gordon Trasler (1972), we would suggest that the avoidance of transgression (that is, the practice of law-abiding behavior) demanded by the moral commandments is probably learned through punishments administered by society, family, and peers. The critical inhibitory morality-training forces in childhood that are likely to be important are (a) the punishment of antisocial responses by family, society, and friends, and (b) the child's individual capacity *to learn to inhibit* antisocial responses.

Here is one explanation of how children learn to inhibit aggressive impulses. When child A is aggressive to child B, child A is often punished by a peer or a parent. Eventually, after enough punishment, just the thought of aggression should produce a bit of anticipatory fear in child A. If the fear response is large enough, the aggressive attempt will cease and the aggressive impulse will be successfully inhibited.

This theory suggests that what happens in this child after he has successfully inhibited such an antisocial response is critical for his learning of civilized behavior. Let us consider the situation again in more detail.

1. Child A contemplates aggressive action.
2. Because of previous punishment or the threat of punishment, he suffers fear.
3. Because of fear he inhibits the aggressive response.
4. *Because he no longer entertains the aggressive impulse, the fear will begin to dissipate.*

Fear reduction is the most powerful, naturally occurring reinforcement that psychologists have discovered. The reduction of fear (which immediately follows the inhibition of the aggression) can act as a reinforcement for this *inhibition* and will result in learning aggression inhibition. The powerful reinforcement associated with fear reduction increases the probability that the inhibition of the aggression will occur in the future. After many such experiences, the normal child will learn to inhibit aggressive impulses. Each time such an impulse arises and is inhibited, the inhibition will be strengthened by reinforcement, since the fear elicited by the impulse will be reduced following successful inhibition.

What does a child need in order to learn social norms effectively?

1. A censuring agent (typically family or peers)
2. An adequate fear response
3. The ability to learn the fear response in anticipation of an antisocial act
4. Fast dissipation of fear to provide a natural reinforcement for the inhibitory response

We have already summarized evidence in this essay that suggests that the antisocial individual exhibits an abnormally diminished ANS response to frightening (or neutral) stimuli (Point 2 above) and is relatively unable emotionally (ANS) to anticipate negative events (Point 3). The discussion now turns to Point 4, the antisocial individual's ability to experience a normally fast dissipation of an ANS fear response and to be reinforced for inhibiting the antisocial response.

The speed, size, and quality of a reinforcement determines its effectiveness (Mednick, 1973). An effective reinforcement is one that is delivered immediately after the relevant response. The faster the reduction of fear, the faster the delivery of the reinforcement. The fear response is, to a large extent, controlled by the ANS. ANS activity can be estimated by use of peripheral indicants such as skin conductance.

A child who has an ANS that characteristically recovers very quickly from fear will receive a quick and large reinforcement for inhibiting the aggression response and will learn inhibition quickly. If he has an ANS that recovers very slowly, he will receive a delayed, small reinforcement and will learn to inhibit aggression slowly, if at all. This theory would predict that (barring constant family training; critical variables such as social status, criminal associations, poverty level; and similar factors) many of those who commit antisocial acts should be characterized by slow autonomic recovery. The slower the recovery, the less the learned inhibition and the more serious and repetitive the antisocial behavior predicted.

Some semicontradictory evidence has come from Hare's experiments. Hare finds reliable differences only between his psychopathic serious criminals and nonpsychopathic serious criminals under specific (usually, in some way, extreme) stimulus conditions. As he himself suggests, the minitheory just described relates only to moral training and subsequent law abidance. The theory is not confounded by the discovery that it is difficult to observe recovery differences between two groups that have exhibited behavior reflecting somewhat negatively on the adequacy of their moral training. In addition, Hare has only reported on recovery. Within such prisoner groups it would be wise also to examine ANS responsiveness (another critical aspect of the theory).

Quite a number of studies have tested the hypothesis that antisocial behavior is associated with slow ANS recovery. Not one study unequivocally refutes this hypothesis. There are tentative indications from two prospective studies that slow ANS recovery precedes the onset of recorded delinquency and predicts recidivism. Consequently, slow ANS recovery must be included among the factors that may be etiologically related to antisocial behavior.

Conditioning Studies Using Punishment

The classic research in the field of ANS factors in antisocial behavior is the 1957 study by Lykken. In the Lykken study, one type of maze error caused a red light to flash, thus indicating to the subject that he had made a mistake; another type of maze error subjected the subject to an unpleasant electric shock. Antisocial individuals as well as controls learned to negotiate the push button maze to avoid the red light. The controls quickly learned to avoid the buttons which resulted in shock. The antisocial individuals showed little evidence of learning to avoid the shock button.

Schachter and Latane (1964) and Schmauk (1970) replicated the Lykken findings. Schmauk's study demonstrated that the psychopath has normal ability to learn with positive reinforcement (rewards). When shock or social censure (i.e., punishment) was involved, the psychopath evidenced relatively poor skin conductance conditioning. In other words, the psychopath's deficiency is most apparent when an ANS response is needed to mediate learning. This result has been observed by several investigators (Hare, 1970; Hare & Quinn, 1971; Rosen & Schalling, 1971; Schoenherr, 1964). The Loeb and Mednick (1977) prospective study also found that those boys who later became delinquent evidenced poor skin conductance conditioning to noxious stimuli.

Several explanations for the psychopath's deficit in ANS-mediated learning have been mentioned in the literature. It is known, for example, that conditioning of skin conductance response is facilitated if the subject is consciously aware that the conditioned stimulus tone will be followed by an electric shock (Dawson, 1973; Dawson & Faredy, 1976). It has been argued that the psychopath is simply not able to verbalize this contingency. Studies by Syndulko, Parker, Jens, Maltzman, and Ziskind (1975) and Ziskind, Syndulko, and Maltzman (1978), however, indicate that even when the psychopaths were clearly aware of the contingencies and could verbalize them, they still evidenced a deficit in skin conductance conditioning.

It has also been suggested that the psychopaths have such a low level of arousal that they are immune to conditioning. It is not clear why this low arousal level does not affect learning involving positive reinforcement. In support of this interpretation, Schachter (1971) has demonstrated that imprisoned psychopaths who evidence poor skin conductance conditioning will show normal conditioning under the influence of an injection of adrenaline. The adrenaline will, of course, increase the subject's state of ANS arousal. Hare (1973) has offered some cogent criticisms of the basis of this study. Chesno and Kilman (1975) noted that psychopaths who evidence poor ANS conditioning under low background-noise stimulation will learn normally under high background-noise stimulation. If background noise increases level of ANS arousal, perhaps recidivism would be decreased by administration of a drug that would increase arousal. They report that a pilot trial with subjects seemed exceptionally promising.

The antisocial individual evidences relatively poor skin conductance conditioning. This finding is reliable and not contradictory. In discussions of this literature there has been a tendency to imply that the psychopath simply cannot learn an ANS-conditioned response. Perhaps it would be more accurate to say that at a given level of aversive stimulation (noise or electric shock), the antisocial individual evidences a deficit in ANS conditioning. This deficit has generated hypotheses regarding the etiology of a failure in moral learning. It also suggests that if rehabilitation or prevention programs are contemplated, consideration should be given to arousal manipulations to improve emotional learning.

Skin Conductance Recovery

There was little precedent for measuring skin conductance recovery when researchers began examining its functioning characteristics in 1962 (Mednick & Schulsinger, 1964). It was a critical element in a theory of inhibition-learning in schizophrenia (Mednick, 1962, 1974). Loeb and Mednick (1977) examined 104 normal adolescents (controls for children at high risk for schizophrenia) with a variety of assessment devices, including skin conductance. Of the 104, 7 adolescents who later were registered for mild delinquent acts had a distinctly and significantly slower rate of skin conductance recovery than their controls.

Siddle et al. (1973) examined skin conductance responsiveness of 67 English borstal inmates, divided into high-, medium-, and low-antisocial groups. When Siddle learned of the recovery hypothesis, he rescored his data for skin conductance recovery; speed and rate of recovery varied inversely as a function of antisocial behavior levels. Recovery measured on a single trial was surprisingly effective in differentiating the three groups (Siddle, Mednick, Nicol, & Foggitt, 1977). Bader-Bartfai and Schalling (1974) also reana-

lyzed skin conductance data from a previous investigation of criminals, finding that criminals who tended to be more "delinquent" on a personality measure tended to have a slower recovery. Hare (1975) reports slow recovery (for a novel tone) for psychopaths among prison inmates. There have been other supportive findings reported (Eisenberg, 1976; Hemming, 1977; Hinton, O'Neill, & Webster, 1977; Plovnick, 1976; Waid, 1976). Hare et al. (in press) and Hare et al. (1978) found that prison psychopaths evidence slow recovery both in anticipation of a loud noise (120 decibels) and to the noise itself. Bader-Bartfai and Schalling (1974), Levander, Lidberg, Schalling, and Lidberg (1977), and Lidberg, Levander, Schalling, and Lidberg (1977) report slow skin conductance recovery in psychopathic criminals and delinquents.

Hare's studies find that psychopaths from prison populations evidence slow ANS recovery under extreme stimulus conditions. In one study (1978a) he compared prisoners with college students. There are serious difficulties of interpretation in such comparisons, but it is nevertheless interesting that the students' average recovery speed was more than twice that of the prisoners.

> Thus, while it may be possible to differentiate between psychopathic and nonpsychopathic inmates in terms of electrodermal recovery to intense stimuli, it may be easier to differentiate between criminals and noncriminals or between groups who show marked differences in asocial behavior. (p. 128)

In 1964, Hare examined skin conductance in prisoners (all in a maximum security prison). He checked 10 years later to see how seriously recidivistic the prisoners subsequently became. Skin conductance recovery was used to predict the degree of recidivism. As might be expected, the extent of the relationship between skin conductance and recidivism within this group composed exclusively of serious offenders is not great ($r = .24$, $p < .05$, in a one-tailed test). Interestingly enough, a small group of the slowest recoverers was almost entirely composed of individuals repeatedly convicted of fraud (Hare, 1978a). This attempt to link specific antecedents with specific types of offender characteristics is a research mode worth emulating.

The theory assumes that skin conductance recovery is mediated by central ANS processes. Bundy (1977) has argued that recovery is *not* mediated by central ANS processes. He suggests that recovery reflects peripheral sweat-gland activity. In a recent report, Levander, Schalling, Lidberg, Bader-Bartfai, and Lidberg (1980) present evidence relevant to this point; their results suggest that recovery is, in large part, mediated by central ANS processes.

The relationship between slow recovery and antisocial behavior seems rather robust across national boundaries, experimental procedures, and definitions of "antisocial." There are small prospective studies (which gain some credence from the cross-sectional findings) that do not contradict the hypothesis. Siddle (1977) states:

> The results concerning skin conductance recovery and antisocial behavior appear to be quite consistent. Subjects who display antisocial behavior (psychopaths, adult criminals and adolescent delinquents) also display significantly slower SCR recovery than do matched controls.

Skin Conductance Recovery and Serious Mental Illness. This chapter began with an argument in support of a genetic contribution of parental mental illness to antisocial behavior. It was noted that recent adoption work provides some evidence that the offspring of biological parents diagnosed as drug abusers, alcohol abusers, and having personality disorders are more likely than the general population to be convicted for violent criminal offenses. In contrast, offspring of schizophrenic biological parents seemed to be less likely to be criminally convicted for violent behaviors. A number of studies (Ax & Bamford, 1970; Gruzelier, 1973; and Gruzelier & Venables, 1972) have reported that schizophrenics demonstrate considerably faster skin conductance recovery than other deviant and nondeviant controls. In addition, Mednick and Schulsinger (1968) have found a rapid rate of skin conductance recovery among the offspring of schizophrenic mothers in a high-risk study. We already know that cross-assortative mating of schizophrenic mothers and antisocial fathers is not uncommon. Assuming that each parent contributes a genetic predisposition toward opposite extremes of ANS responsiveness, what could be the diagnostic outcome for this child? Will one or the other predisposition dominate, producing a child likely to become *only* criminal or *only* schizophrenic, or will the genes somehow combine effects, perhaps producing the individual described by Bender (1958), who is both psychotic and criminal? Yet another (hopeful) possibility, perhaps they will cancel each

other out, producing a child protected from deviant involvement. Perhaps the latter outcome is the most likely target for further research; there are some findings suggestive of a "protection from deviance" hypothesis.

In Mednick's (1978) investigation of children at risk for schizophrenia, the children who had a criminal father as well as a schizophrenic mother were found to have slower skin conductance recovery than the children with schizophrenic mothers and noncriminal fathers. Venables (in press) reports similar impacts on childrens' heart rates of maternal schizophrenia and paternal antisocial behavior. Recently Talovic (1981) has analyzed follow-up data on these subjects and found that the high-risk subjects who have not yet suffered psychiatric breakdown seem to be primarily the subjects with criminal fathers. Kirkegaard-Sorensen and Mednick (1975) discuss the possibility that for a child with a schizophrenic mother, inheriting some of the autonomic hyporesponsiveness of a criminal father could tend to be protective against schizophrenia. The finding from the Danish adoption project, that adoptees convicted for violent behavior were less likely to have schizophrenia in their biological parents than were nonviolent adoptees, suggests that the inverse of Talovic's findings may also be true. If inheriting ANS hyporesponsiveness from a criminal father helps protect against schizophrenia, inheriting ANS hyperesponsiveness from a schizophrenic mother may also help protect against serious antisocial behaviors. These possibilities remain quite tentative, and are in need of further systematic investigation.

NEUROPHYSIOLOGICAL STUDIES

A variety of assessment strategies have been used to examine central nervous system (CNS) functioning in antisocial individuals. Many of these studies are based on electroencephalographic (EEG) evaluation of CNS functioning. This aspect of brain activity has generated considerable violence-related research. In addition to providing a relatively simple method for evaluation of intact CNS activity, the EEG provides reliable and culture-free assessment of function.

Electroencephalographic Features

Because some of the research reviewed in this report relies on electroencephalographic findings, a brief presentation of facts concerning the EEG is in order. Electrochemical processes in the living human brain produce periodic voltage oscillations that can be detected by scalp recordings. The detected brain activity is described in terms of its amplitude (size), and its frequency (rhythmicity). EEG amplitudes are generally 20–100 microvolts (1/1,000 of a volt). Frequency of EEG activity usually discussed in current literature ranges between .5 and 40 hz (cycles per second). For descriptive convenience, the frequency range is, by convention, classified according to the following scheme: delta, .5–3 hz; theta, 4–7 hz; alpha, 8–12 hz; beta, 13–40 hz (Kooi, Tucker, & Marshall, 1978).

The occurrence and amplitudes of activity within these frequency ranges are known to be dependent on characteristics (such as age and sex) as well as behavioral state (asleep or awake) of the subject. Clinically, EEG evaluation has proven most useful in the diagnosis of epilepsy (Kooi et al., 1978). Much current research is directed toward elucidating associations between EEGs, subject characteristics, and behavioral states. Current research is also underway to discover the specific relationship between EEG and neuronal activity.

EEG records can be evaluated in two ways. First, they can be inspected visually by an electroencephalographer and rated according to some classification scheme. Usually, such ratings result in EEG records being classified as normal, abnormal, or "borderline." Second, EEGs can be quantitatively analyzed, typically by computers. Such a procedure results in a set of parameters with numeric descriptors that can be used for direct comparison of EEGs. These two methods of analyses are complementary.

Quantitative computer analysis is not as effective as the human eye in detection of aberrant wave complexes (as are found in epilepsy). Estimates generated by quantitative computer analysis of EEG parameters (e.g., of frequency and amplitude) are more precise than is possible by qualitative evaluation.

Prevalence of EEG Abnormality Among Violent Individuals

Research has been conducted to establish prevalence of EEG abnormalities in criminal (usually violent) individuals. For this purpose, visual ratings have been widely used for EEG evaluations; quantitative computer EEG analyses have rarely been reported.

The earliest reports are based on studies of murderers (Hill & Pond, 1952), and subsequent studies provide estimates of EEG abnormalities in violent prisoners (Okasha, Sadek, & Moneim, 1975; Sayed, Lewis, & Brittain, 1969; Winkler & Kove, 1962). Hill and Pond (1952) report that about half of 105 murderers had EEG abnormalities. Sayed et al. (1969) examined 32 murderers and reported that 65% of their EEGs were abnormal. Winkler and Kove (1962) studied 55 persons convicted of manslaughter or murder and reported that 24% had EEG abnormalities.

More recent reports have not limited the scope of study to murderers. Williams (1969) studied 333 persons incarcerated for crimes of violence and reports that about half exhibited EEG abnormalities. Bach-y-Rita, Lion, Climent, and Ervin (1971) also report that approximately half of 79 outpatients who were having difficulty controlling their violent tendencies were characterized by EEG abnormalities. Mark and Ervin (1970) reviewed EEGs of over 400 violent adult prisoners and report that approximately one third were abnormal. These results suggest that the prevalence of EEG abnormalities in violent individuals ranges 25–50%. Qualitative evaluation of EEG abnormalities among normal populations ranges 5–20% (Kooi et al., 1978).

Two studies have reported much lower incidences of EEG abnormalities among violent individuals. Riley (1979) found 6.7% EEG abnormalities among a group of 212 violent individuals referred for outpatient treatment of violent behavior and episodes of rage. Riley's low percentage may be related to the fact that he screened out subjects with any neurological history. Knott, Lara, Peters, and Robinson (1975) report that only 4% of 73 people accused of murder evidenced EEG abnormality. It is not clear why Knott et al. (1975) report such low incidence.

Several studies reported no EEG differences between criminal and noncriminal populations (Driver, West, & Faulk, 1974; Gibbs, Bagchi, & Bloomberg, 1945; Jenkins & Pacella, 1943). To some extent, these negative findings resulted from misinterpretation of data.

The Gibbs et al. (1945) study in particular was taken by many authors (De Baudouin, Haumonte, Bessing, & Geissman, 1961; Forssman & Frey, 1953; Hill, 1963; Knott, 1975) as an example of a disagreement in the literature regarding the abnormality of EEG in criminals. This widely cited study compared the EEGs of 452 prisoners with those of 1,432 nonprisoner controls. The subjects were divided into three age groups. Comparisons did not yield significant differences between prisoners and controls. The rationale for the age grouping was that "in both prisoners and controls, normal EEGs were commoner in the young than in the older groups" (Gibbs et al., 1945, p. 296). This rationale does not receive much support from their Table III: The percentage of normal EEGs in young, middle-aged, and older control groups is 82%, 81%, and 82%, respectively. Furthermore, the differences between the criminals and the controls show the same tendency in all three age groups. We therefore collapsed the three age groups into one and found a significant difference between prisoners and controls ($x^2(3) = 10.5$, $p < .02$). Most of the difference was due to the greater proportion of abnormally fast EEGs among the prisoners. Moreover, the percentages of normal recordings in the control groups used for this study were quite low. Using the same method of EEG evaluation, Gibbs and Gibbs (1950) found 84.2% normal EEGs in 1,000 controls. Even that percentage is low compared with other estimates (Cobb, 1963; Williams, 1969). Thus a spuriously high percentage of EEG abnormalities in the control groups might have reduced the contrast with the criminals. We conclude that Gibbs, Bagchi, and Bloomberg have collected a large amount of interesting material that was misinterpreted.

The weight of research findings strongly supports a conclusion that criminals' EEGs are more frequently classified as abnormal than those of noncriminal control subjects. In order to explore the implications of this finding, we have to review the type of EEG abnormalities reported to occur in criminal populations and try to trace the relation of these electrical abnormalities to specific types of antisocial behavior.

Specific EEG Features

Subgroups of criminal individuals can be based either on degree of violence or according to frequency of past aggressive behaviors. Early results (Arthurs & Cahoon, 1964; Levy & Kennard, 1953) did not suggest that estimates of EEG abnormalities differ for more — as compared to less — violent individuals. However, when subgroups of violent individuals are formed on the basis of frequency of aggressive activity, a slightly different picture emerges. In these studies, recidivist aggressors are compared to persons who have committed only one or two violent acts. Wil-

liams (1969) reports that EEG abnormalities are four times as great in habitual aggressors. Nezirogly (1979) found that rates of EEG abnormalities were twice as high in a habitually aggressive group. Monroe et al. (1977) cite evidence that 88% of recidivist adolescent aggressors exhibit EEG abnormalities.

Findings that recidivist aggressors have higher rates of EEG abnormalities suggest underlying organic dysfunction. Two specific types of EEG abnormalities have been identified. The EEG may be characterized by an excess of slow activity (usually in the theta range) or by an excess of fast activity (in the beta range).

Hill (1952) noted that approximately half of the psychopaths who persistently commit aggressive acts have increased theta in their EEGs. Williams (1969) also reported that 80% of 333 violent prisoners exhibited excess slow activity in the theta band. Hill (1952) as well as others (Monroe, 1970; Williams, 1969) have interpreted this EEG slowdown to reflect a maturational lag in cerebral development. Hare (1978b) has offered an alternative to the maturational lag hypothesis in accounting for increased theta activity. Hare suggests increased EEG theta may reflect a low level of cortical excitability and a tendency toward drowsiness during rather dull experimental settings.

Blackburn (1975) provides evidence relevant to these hypotheses. Quantitative EEG analysis was used to compare theta and alpha activity of 80 subjects divided into two groups, based on frequency of assaultive behavior. There were no statistically significant differences in amounts of theta or alpha activity that distinguished more-from less-habitual aggressors. However, when exposed to a painful stimulus, habitual aggressors manifested greater reductions in alpha activity, indicating a *greater* arousal.

It is certainly conceivable that subgroups of violent individuals may be characterized by different EEG features. Lorimer (1972) studied violent individuals and identified two subgroups. One subgroup was characterized by excess slow activity (6–8 hz); the second subgroup was characterized by excess fast activity (beta, 30–40 hz). Earlier reports do not comment on EEG beta (Blackburn, 1975; Hill, 1952; Monroe, 1978). It is difficult, therefore, to assess the likelihood that slow (theta) and fast (beta) activity characterize distinct subgroups of violent individuals. The possible association of specific EEG features to subgroups of violent individuals deserves more rigorous attention, particularly by quantitative EEG assessment.

Two additional EEG patterns have frequently been associated with violent behavior. These syndromes are 14-and-6 spikes and temporal lobe epilepsy.

The 14-and-6 EEG Pattern. An EEG wave form characterized by a fast spike followed by a slow wave is termed a "14-6" pattern. Perhaps early reports of this EEG pattern in bizarre murderers (Schwade & Geiger, 1960) promoted association of the 14-6 pattern and violence. Schwade and Geiger reviewed findings in over 1,000 children and adolescents and report that the majority of those who behaved violently also display the 14-6 pattern. However, in view of the high prevalence of this pattern (20%) in normal children (Gibbs & Gibbs, 1964), it seems unlikely that the 14-6 pattern is specifically related to violence.

Temporal-lobe epilepsy. Probably the EEG syndrome most extensively investigated with regard to antisocial behavior is temporal-lobe epilepsy (also known as psychomotor seizures). Probably the earliest link to violence appeared in a description of an individual case: A male who had committed an unmotivated murder had paroxysmal EEG features (Hill & Sargant, 1943). Since that time, much evidence has been collected toward clarifying the association between psychomotor seizures and violence.

Some reports examine the prevalence of temporal-lobe epilepsy in violent individuals. For example, Mark and Ervin (1970) report that temporal-lobe epilepsy is 10 times higher in a sample of 400 violent adult prisoners than would be expected in the general population. Hill and Pond (1952) estimate that between 17 and 26% of the murderers they studied were epileptic. Lewis (1976) reported that 72% of 78 violent juveniles experienced symptoms indicating psychomotor seizures. Bender (1959) reported that 10% of juvenile murderers subsequently developed epilepsy. However, none of the 32 Sayed et al. (1969) murderers was epileptic. Gunn and Bonn (1971) compared epileptic with nonepileptic prisoners and failed to obtain differences on the basis of their violent behaviors.

These findings are not entirely inconsistent with the notion that violence and temporal-lobe epilepsy are associated. The results suggest that

perhaps this relationship could be clarified by examining the prevalence of violent behavior among temporal-lobe epileptics. However, this evidence is also equivocal in outcome. Falconer et al. (1958) report that 38% of temporal-lobe epileptics exhibit "pathological aggressiveness." Currie, Heathfield, Henson, & Scott (1971) report that 29% of the temporal-lobe epileptics they studied behaved aggressively. Among 100 children studied by Ounsted (1969), none of the 36 that demonstrated outbursts of rage received a diagnosis of temporal-lobe epilepsy. Rodin (1972) reviewed over 700 psychomotor-seizure patient's histories and identified only 5% who had committed aggressive acts.

No definitive conclusions for the association of temporal-lobe epilepsy to violence are possible, since the results of the studies are quite contradictory. There are two important methodological considerations that hamper investigation of this association. Diagnosis of temporal-lobe epilepsy (or psychomotor seizures) on the basis of EEG is complicated by the fact that paroxysmal discharge occurrences in the temporal region are not always accurately reflected in the scalp-recorded EEG (Bach-y-Rita, Lion, & Ervin, 1970). Further complications arise because visual EEG assessments are not perfectly reliable (Sayed et al., 1969).

Methodological problems involved in subject sampling and in definitions of aggressive behavior and temporal-lobe epilepsy have been reviewed by Klingman and Goldberg (1975). These problems are so overwhelming that their review does not provide any conclusion as to whether temporal-lobe epilepsy is associated with aggressive behavior either during seizures or between them. Temporal-lobe epilepsy appears to be a heterogenous group of disorders; aggressive behavior may of course be determined by a very large number of factors.

At this point the relationship of temporal-lobe epilepsy to violence remains unresolved. The evidence has been interpreted both in support of the association (Pincus, 1980) and against it (Goldstein, 1974).

Activation Techniques

In order to increase the sensitivity of EEG as a measure of underlying brain dysfunction, activation techniques to trigger EEG abnormalities can be used. Typical procedures designed to elicit abnormalities include administration of drugs, exposing subjects to flashing lights, and asking subjects to breathe deeply or go to sleep.

EEG patterns subsequent to specific drug administration have been evaluated in violent individuals. Kido (1973) studied 186 male juvenile delinquents. The subjects were divided into groups on the basis of criteria such as the number of times they had been detained and whether they had committed murder or physical assault that (unintentionally) resulted in death. Pentamethylenetetrazol (PMST) or diphenhydramine (DIPH) were administered intravenously to trigger possible EEG abnormalities. Individuals in the group of subjects with the most recidivistic tendencies and the group of subjects who had committed murder exhibited the most vulnerability to these drugs. None of the subjects in the group that had committed physical violence (unintentionally) resulting in death manifested sensitivity to these drugs. These results provide support for the notion that quite different subgroups of violent individuals may be identified.

Monroe (1970) reviews evidence that another pharmacological agent, alpha chloralose, induces EEG abnormalities in many epileptics and in patients with histories of neurological disease or head trauma. Alpha chloralose is considered an experimental drug by the U.S. Food and Drug Administration (FDA); this may explain the paucity of research with this drug. The most obvious side effects are certain types of seizures.

Monroe (1978) administered alpha chloralose to 93 male prisoners. Most were convicted of aggressive crimes at least six times. Each subject underwent EEG testing twice. Between 40 and 49% abnormal EEGs were obtained on the basis of routine EEG assessments, which included sleep and hyperventilation as activators. However, when alpha chloralose was administered, detection of EEG abnormalities increased to approximately 82-88%. This result demonstrates the potential utility of alpha chloralose as a routine activator, especially in assessment of potentially violent behavior. It should be noted that approximately 15% of normal individuals demonstrate EEG abnormalities after alpha chloralose (Monroe, 1978).

Kido's (1973) report indicates that PMST and DIPH are effective activators in juvenile males, especially those with violent and recidivistic tendencies. Monroe's (1978) results demonstrate the potential utility of including alpha chloralose activation in EEG assessment of violent male offenders. The use of these activators in the study of the EEG of violent offenders seems promising.

Prospective EEG Research

Prospective studies that examine features of brain functioning as potential predictors of criminality are few. To our knowledge, only two such studies have been conducted. The incidence of violent behavior is low in both reports.

Subjects examined in the first study were drawn from a Danish birth cohort. The cohort consists of all children born between September 1st, 1959 and December 31st, 1961 at Rigshospitalet in Copenhagen, Denmark (Mednick, Volavka, Gabrielli, & Itil, 1981). During 1971-1972, a prospective study of delinquency was initiated, and EEG measures on 265 Danish children (11-13 years of age) were obtained. By 1978, many of these 265 children had been arrested for a variety of offenses. (The Danish Police Register maintains official records of individuals apprehended for criminal behavior.) In this way, the EEG measures obtained in 1971-1972 could be examined in relation to a child's delinquency status in 1978.

Each subject was classified as belonging to one of three groups: noncriminal (no official contacts with police), one-time offender, or multiple offenders. Only males were included ($n = 129$). These three groups were then compared on the basis of EEG measures in the delta, theta, alpha, and beta frequency bands.

Statistical analyses revealed that future multiple offenders (especially thieves) exhibited slower alpha frequencies (8-10 hz) than either noncriminals or one-time offenders (Mednick et al., 1981). Of the 129 boys examined, 72 were selected because they had psychiatrically disturbed parents and thus an elevated risk of delinquent behavior. In order to "remove" the influence of the parents' psychiatric condition, statistical analyses were undertaken separately for the 57 normal male controls included in this investigation. The results of these analyses indicate that slow alpha affords greater predictability of delinquent behavior among boys with normal parents than among boys with parents with psychiatric involvement. Delinquent offenses committed by psychiatrically deviant boys may tend to be an expression of their psychiatric problems rather than an indicant of persistent antisocial tendencies.

Mednick, Volavka, Gabrielli, and Itil (1981) conducted a second data analysis on these same subjects. In the fall of 1981, the police registers were again searched to determine what additional offenses had been committed by the subjects. A number of individuals who had not been arrested by 1978 (17–18 years of age) were included in the police files by 1981 (about 21 years of age). Many of the earlier delinquents had continued to commit crimes as adults, while a number were not registered for any criminality after reaching adulthood. Using the same EEG data collected in 1972, we again tried to discriminate the repeat offenders from the one-time offenders and the nonoffenders. We found that the percentage of slow alpha activity in the 1972 EEGs still discriminated the recidivistic property offenders as of 1981, even though there had been a substantial increase in the number of individuals in that group. When we considered "chronic" offenders (defined by Wolfgang et al., 1972, as individuals arrested five or more times), we observed that they showed the greatest increase in relative percentage of slow alpha power.

Our finding that slow alpha characteristics may predict criminal behavior was replicated by a similar analysis on an independent sample in Sweden (Petersen, Matousek, Volavka, Mednick, & Pollock, 1983). In 1967, EEG measures on 571 healthy Swedes (1–21 years of age) were obtained. In 1980, 22 recidivistic criminal offenders were identified by access to the Swedish National Police Register. The registered offenses for which these 22 persons had been apprehended consisted chiefly of thievery. EEG characteristics of the 22 multiple offenders were compared to age-matched controls. In 1967, average alpha frequency was lower among multiple offenders (9.07 hz) than among noncriminals (9.25 hz). Certain EEG abnormalities (e.g., paroxysms during sleep) were also more prevalent among multiple offenders. These results indicate that neurophysiological deviance, such as slow alpha, characterizes persons *before* they begin criminal behaviors. Some subgroup of violent offenders comprises recidivistic property offenders; this fact suggests that EEG evaluations may be useful measures in prospective studies of violent offenders.

CONCLUSIONS

The first half of this chapter reviewed the literature providing evidence for the inheritance of biological characteristics that are predisposing to

criminal involvement. In an adoption sample, criminal conviction histories of the biological parents was related to property offenses in the offspring but not to violent offenders. In addition, studies of the genetics of certain forms of mental illness were reviewed, and the possibility that some of these psychiatric illnesses may be related genetically to criminal behavior was proposed. Results from a recent investigation of the Danish adoption cohort were presented, demonstrating that parental personality disorders, drug abuse, and alcohol abuse, when found in combination with parental criminal behavior, are associated with elevated rates of *violent* and *recidivistic* criminal behavior in adopted-away sons.

The second half was directed at illuminating the nature of these specific heritable factors. A 6-step plan for research into the genetically influenced, biosocial determinants of criminal behavior was proposed. Two biological variables of current interest to criminologists have shown promising results of fulfilling the requirements of the earliest research steps. These factors are autonomic nervous system functioning (as measured by skin conductance) and neurophysiological activity (EEG). Twin studies that have shown twins to each have some heritable components were noted. The literature linking skin conductance and EEG to criminal behavior was reviewed. We conclude that these two heritable biological characteristics are potential genetically-influenced candidates for entry into a theoretical structure descriptive of the etiology of criminal behavior. Such a theory, incorporating both biological and social variables, was also presented.

IMPLICATIONS FOR INTERVENTION

It is first important to delimit the importance of the findings presented in this chapter. The research reviewed has shown that genetic factors are probably not involved in predisposing to the relatively mild or infrequent criminal behaviors of the majority of offenders. However, because of the well-known concentration of criminal acts among the relatively few serious offenders, it is appropriate to be concerned about the implications of the findings described herein for intervention in criminal behavior. For example, Wolfgang et al. (1972), in an important American birth cohort study, found that 6% of the offenders had committed 52% of the offenses. Similarly, Mednick et al. (1984) noted that, in the Danish adoption cohort, 4% of the male adoptees were responsible for 69% of the cohort's convictions. Thus, preventive intervention efforts aimed at the very few persons who *do* seem to evidence some biological predisposition to serious criminal involvement could conceivably result in a very substantial reduction in crime rates.

Many criminologists are reluctant to acknowledge the facts presented here because it is assumed that these facts yield a pessimistic prognosis regarding intervention. But, as has been demonstrated in the field of psychiatric treatment of mental illnesses, treatment modes based on known biological deficits often have far more optimistic expectations than many nonbiological modes of psychiatric intervention.

Observers who are sensitive to issues of social justice have historically-based fears of the moral and legal implications of the fact that criminal behavior has biological as well as social determinants (Sagarin, 1980). Their basic fear seems to be that if the offender is seen to be distinguishable biologically, this will be seen as an excuse for mistreatment of individuals guilty of crimes. It is worth pointing out that the prevailing notion of social causality of crime has not transformed our criminal justice system into a humane and therapeutic societal agency. In fact, widespread acknowledgement of some etiological role of biological factors in producing criminal behavior may serve to create general attitudes of greater understanding and tolerance for the criminal individual. The punitiveness of interventions applied to offenders by society may actually lessen if it is more widely understood that biological factors (which are beyond the control of the offender) are partially responsible for his acts.

The authors of this chapter, at scientific meetings, have frequently noted a certain attitude on the part of many of those involved in criminology. In its most positive manifestation, some criminologists wish to see any research that smacks of biology totally ignored. There is also a vocal minority that would eagerly block any support for biocriminology research and would like to see existing results from biocriminology research suppressed. Despite the undoubtedly positive motives of such individuals, their efforts only serve to postpone the time when knowledge of the biosocial bases of criminal behavior will permit us to effectively prevent and treat, alleviating much human suffering.

REFERENCES

American Psychiatric Association. (1968). *Diagnostic and statistical manual for mental disorders.* Washington, DC: American Psychiatric Association.

Aniskiewicz, A. (1973). *Autonomic components of vicarious conditioning and psychopathy.* Unpublished doctoral dissertation, Purdue University, Lafayette, IN.

Arthurs, R.G.S., & Cahoon, E.B. (1964). A clinical and electroencephalographic survey of psychopathic personality. *American Journal of Psychiatry, 120,* 875.

Ax, A.F., & Bamford, J.L. (1970). The GSR recovery limb in chronic schizophrenia. *Psychophysiology, 7,* 145–147.

Bach-y-Rita, G., Lion, J.R., Climent, C.E., & Ervin, F. (1971). Episodic dyscontrol: A study of 130 violent patients. *American Journal of Psychiatry, 127*(11), 1473–1478.

Bach-y-Rita, G., Lion, J.R., & Ervin, F.R. (1970). Pathological intoxication: Clinical and electroencephalographic studies. *American Journal of Psychiatry, 127*(5), 698–703.

Bader-Bartfai, A., & Schalling, D. (1974). *Recovery time of skin conductance response as related to some personality and physiological variables.* Stockhold: Psychological Institute, University of Stockholm.

Beisser, A., Glasser, N., & Grant, M. (1967). Psychological adjustment in children of schizophrenic mothers. *Journal of Nervous and Mental Disease, 145,* 448–492.

Bell, B., Mednick, S.A., Gottesman, I.I., & Sergeant, J. (1977). Electrodermal parameters in male twins. In S.A. Mednick & K.O. Christiansen (Eds.), *Biosocial bases of criminal behavior.* New York: Gardner Press.

Bender, L. (1958). The concept of pseudopsychopathic schizophrenia in adolescents. *American Journal of Orthopsychiatry, 29,* 491–509.

Blackburn, R. (1975). Aggression and the EEG: A quantitative analysis. *Journal of Abnormal Psychology, 84*(4), 358–365.

Blankenstein, K.R. (1969). *Patterns of autonomic functioning in primary and secondary psychopaths.* Unpublished master's thesis, University of Waterloo, Ontario.

Bohman, M. (1971). A comparative study of adopted children, foster children, and children in their biological environment born after undesired pregnancies. *Acta Paediatrica Scandinavica* (Supplement 221).

Bohman, M. (1972). A study of adopted children, their background, environment, and adjustment. *Acta Paediatrica Scandinavica, 61,* 90–97.

Bohman, M. (1978). Some genetic aspects of alcoholism and criminality. *Archives of General Psychiatry, 35,* 268–276.

Bohman, M., Cloninger, R., Sigvardsson, S., & von Knorring, A. (1982). Predisposition to petty criminality in Swedish adoptees. *Archives of General Psychiatry, 39,* 1233–1247.

Borgstrom, C.A. (1939). Eine serie von kriminelleen zwillingen. *Archiv fur Rassenbiologie.*

Borkovec, T. (1970). Autonomic reactivity to sensory stimulation in psychopathic, neurotic, and normal juvenile delinquents. *Journal of Consulting and Clinical Psychology, 35,* 217–222.

Bromberg, W., & Thompson, C.B. (1937). The relation of psychosis, mental defect, and personality types to crime. *Journal of Criminal Law and Criminology, 28,* 70–89.

Bundy, R.W. (1977). *Electrodermal activity as a unitary phenomenon.* Paper presented at the meeting of the Society for Psychophysiological Research, Philadelphia.

Buss, A. (1966). *Psychopathology.* New York: John Wiley.

Cadoret, R.J. (1978). Psychopathology in adopted-away offspring of biological parents with antisocial behavior. *Archives of General Psychiatry, 35,* 176–184.

Cadoret, R.J., Cunningham, L., Loftus, R., & Edwards, J. (1975). Studies of adoptees from psychiatrically disturbed biologic parents II. *The Journal of Pediatrics, 87*(2), 301–306.

Cantwell, D.P. (1972). Psychiatric illness in the families of hyperactive children. *Archives of General Psychiatry, 27,* 414–418.

Chesno, F., & Kilman, P. (1975). Effects of stimulation intensity on sociopathic avoidance learning. *Journal of Abnormal Psychology, 84,* 144–150.

Christiansen, K.O. (1977a). A review of studies of criminality among twins. In S.A. Mednick & K.O. Christiansen (Eds.), *Biosocial bases of criminal behavior.* New York: Gardner Press.

Cleckley, H. (1976). *The mask of sanity* (5th ed.). St. Louis: C.V. Mosby.

Cloninger, C.R., & Guze, S.B. (1973). Psychiatric illnesses in the families of female criminals: A study of 288 first-degree relatives. *British Journal of Psychiatry, 122,* 697–703.

Cobb, W.A. (1963). The normal adult EEG. In J.D.N. Hill and G. Parr (Eds.), *Electroencephalography* (2nd ed.). London: MacDonald.

Craft, M.J. (1965). *Ten studies into psychopathic personality.* Bristol: John Wright.

Crowe, R.R. (1972). The adopted offspring of women criminal offenders, a study of their arrest records. *Archives of General Psychiatry, 27,* 600–603.

Crowe, R.R. (1974). An adoption study of antisocial personality. *Archives of General Psychiatry, 31,* 785–791.

Crowe, R.R. (1975). Adoption studies in psychiatry. *Biological Psychiatry, 10*(3), 353–371.

Cunningham, L., Cadoret, R.J., Loftus, R., & Edwards, J.E. (1975). Studies of adoptees from psychiatrically disturbed biological parents I. *British Journal of Psychiatry, 126,* 534–549.

Currie, S., Heathfield, K., Henson, R., & Scott, D. (1971). Clinical course and prognosis of temporal lobe epilepsy: A survey of 666 patients. *Brain, 94,* 173.

Dalgaard, O.S., & Kringlen, E. (1976). A Norwegian twin study of criminality. *British Journal of Criminology.*

Darwin, C. (1859). *On the origin of species by means of natural selection, or the preservation of favoured races in the struggle for life.* London: John Murray.

D'Atri, D.A. (1978). *Psychophysiological responses to crowding determinants of criminal behavior.* (L. Otten, Ed.). Rosslyn, VA: Mitre Corporation.

Dawson, M. (1973). Can classical conditioning occur without contingency learning? A review and evaluation of the evidence. *Psychophysiology, 10,* 82–86.

Dawson, M., & Faredy, J. (1976). The role of awareness in human differential autonomic classical conditioning: The necessary gate hypothesis. *Psychophysiology, 13,* 50–53.

DeBaudouin, Haumonte, Bessing, & Geissman, P. (1961). [Study of a population of 97 confined murderers] *Annales Medico-Psychologiques, 119*(1), 625–686.

Dengerink, H.A., & Bertilson, H.S. (1975). Psychopathy and physiological arousal in an aggressive task. *Psychophysiology, 12,* 682–684.

Douglas, J.W.B., & Blomfield, J.M. (1958). *Children under five.* London: Allen & Unwin.

Driver, M.V., West, L.R., & Faulk, M. (1974). Clinical and EEG studies of prisoners charged with murder. *British Journal of Psychiatry, 125,* 583–587.

Dugdale, R.L. (1877). *The Jukes.* New York: G.P. Putnam's Sons.

Durbin, J.R., Pasework, R.A., & Albers, D. (1977). Criminality and mental illness: A study of arrest rates in a rural state. *American Journal of Psychiatry, 134,* 80–83.

Dustman, R.E., & Beck, E.C. (1965). The visual evoked response in twins. *EEG Clinical Neurophysiology, 19,* 570–575.

Eisenberg, J. (1976). *Criminality and heart rate: A prospective study.* Unpublished doctoral dissertation, New School for Social Research, New York.

Erlenmeyer-Kimling, L., Wunsch-Hitzig, R.A., & Deutsch, S. (1980). Family formation by schizophrenics. In L.N. Robins, P.J. Clayton, & J.K. Wing (Eds.), *The social consequences of psychiatric illness.* New York: Brunner/Mazel.

Falconer, M.A., et al. (1958). Clinical, radiological, and EEG correlations with pathological changes in temporal lobe epilepsy and their significance in surgical treatment. In M. Baldwin & P. Bailey (Eds.), *Temporal Lobe Epilepsy.* Springfield, IL: Charles C Thomas.

Feldman, M.P. (1977). *Criminal behavior: A psychological analysis.* New York: John Wiley & Sons.

Forssman, H., & Frey, T.S. (1953). Electroencephalograms of boys with behavior disorders. *Acta Psychologica et Neurologia Scandinavica, 28,* 61–73.

Fowler, R.C., & Tsuang, M. (1975). Spouses of schizophrenics: A blind comparative study. *Comprehensive Psychiatry, 16,* 339–342.

Fox, R., & Lippert, W. (1963). Spontaneous GSR and anxiety level in sociopathic delinquents. *Journal of Consulting and Clinical Psychology, 27,* 368.

Gabrielli, W.F., & Mednick, S.A. (1983). Genetic correlates of criminal behavior: Implications for research, attribution, and prevention. *American Behavioral Scientist, 3,* 1–23.

Galton, F. (1869). *Hereditary genius: An inquiry into its laws and consequences.* London: Macmillan.

Gibbs, F.A., Bagchi, B.K., & Bloomberg, W. (1945). Electroencephalographic study of criminals. *American Journal of Psychiatry, 1022,* 294–298.

Gibbs, F.A., & Gibbs, E.L. (1950). *Atlas of electroencephalography, Vol. I: Methodology and controls* (2nd Ed.). Cambridge, MA: Addison-Wesley.

Glueck, B. (1918). A study of 608 admissions to Sing Sing Prison. *Mental Hygiene, 2,* 85–151.

Goddard, H.H. (1912). *The Kallikak family.* New York: Macmillan.

Goldstein, M. (1974). Brain research and violent behavior: A summary and evaluation of the status of biomedical research on brain and aggressive violent behavior. *Archives of Neurology, 30*(1), 1–35.

Goodwin, D.W. (1977). Family and adoption studies of alcoholism. In S.A. Mednick & K.O. Christiansen (Eds.), *Biosocial bases of criminal behavior.* New York: Gardner Press.

Gottesman, I.I. (1978). Schizophrenia and genetics: Where are we? Are you sure? In L.C. Wynne, R.L. Cromwell, & S. Matthyse (Eds.), *The nature of schizophrenia.* New York: John Wiley & Sons.

Gottesman, I.I., & Shields, J. (1976). A critical review of recent adoption, twin, and family studies of schizophrenia. *Schizophrenia Bulletin, 2,* 360.

Gruzelier, J.H., & Venables, P.H. (1972). Skin conductance orienting activity in a heterogeneous sample of schizophrenics. *The Journal of Nervous and Mental Disease, 155,* 277–287.

Gunn, J., & Bonn, J. (1971). Criminality and violence in epileptic prisoners. *British Journal of Psychiatry, 118,* 33f.

Guze, S.B. (1976). *Criminality and psychiatric disorders.* New York: Oxford University Press.

Guze, S.B., Wolfgram, E.D., McKinney, J.K., & Cantwell, D.P. (1967). Psychiatric illness in the families of convicted criminals: A study of 519 first-degree relatives. *Diseases of the Nervous System, 10,* 651–659.

Hare, R.D. (1965). Temporal gradient of fear arousal in psychopaths. *Journal of Abnormal Psychology, 70,* 442–445.

Hare, R.D. (1968). Psychopathy, autonomic functioning and the orienting response. *Journal of Abnormal Psychology* (Monograph Supplement) 73, 1–24.

Hare, R.D. (1970). *Psychopathy: Theory and research.* New York: John Wiley.

Hare, R.D. (1972). Psychopathy and physiological responses to adrenalin. *Journal of Abnormal Psychology, 79,* 138–147.

Hare, R.D. (1973). The origins of confusion. *Journal of Abnormal Psychology, 82,* 535–536.

Hare, R.D. (1975). Psychophysiological studies of psychopathy. In D.C. Fowles (Ed.), *Clinical applications of psychophysiology.* New York: Columbia University Press.

Hare, R.D. (1978a). Psychopathy and crime. In L. Otten (Eds.), *Colloquium on the correlates of crime and the determinants of criminal behavior.* Rosslyn, VA: Mitre Corporation.

Hare, R.D. (1978b). Electrodermal and cardiovascular correlates of psychopathy. In R.D. Hare & D. Schalling (Eds.), *Psychopathic behavior: Approaches to research.* New York: John Wiley & Sons.

Hare, R.D., Cox, D.N., & Frazelle, J. (in press). Psychopathy and electrodermal responses to nonsignal stimulation. *Biological Psychology.*

Hare, R.D., & Craigen, D. (1974). Psychopathy and physiological activity in a mixed-motive game situation. *Psychophysiology, 11,* 197–206.

Hare, R.D., Frazelle, J., & Cox, D.N. (1978). Psychopathy and physiological responses to threat of an aversive stimulus. *Psychophysiology, 15,* 165–172.

Hare, R.D., & Quinn, M.J. (1971). Psychopathy and autonomic conditioning. *Journal of Abnormal Psychology, 77,* 223–235.

Healy, W., & Bronner, A.F. (1926). *Delinquents and criminals, their making and unmaking: Studies in two American cities.* New York: Macmillan.

Healy, W., & Bronner, A.F. (1936). *New light on delinquency and its treatment.* New Haven, CT: Yale University Press.

Hemming, H. (1977). *Comparison of electrodermal indices theoretically relevant to antisocial behavior in a selected prison sample and students.* Paper presented to the British Psychophysiological Association, Exeter.

Heston, L.L. (1966). Psychiatric disorders in foster home reared children of schizophrenic mothers. *British Journal of Psychiatry, 112,* 819–825.

Hill, E. (1952). EEG in episodic psychotic and psychopathic behavior. *Electroencephalography and Clinical Neurophysiology, 4*(4), 419–442.

Hill, D. (1963). The EEG in psychiatry. In J.D.N. Hill & G. Parr (Eds.), *Electroencephalography* (2nd ed.). London: MacDonald.

Hill, D., & Pond, D.A. (1952). Reflexions on 100 capital cases submitted to electroencephalography. *Journal of Mental Science, 98*(410), 23–43.

Hill, D., & Sargant, W. (1943). A case of matricide. *Lancet, 244*(1), 526–527.

Hinton, J., & O'Neill, M. (1978). Pilot research on psychophysiological response profiles of maximum security hospital patients. *British Journal of Social and Clinical Psychology, 19,* 103.

Hinton, J., O'Neill, M., & Webster, S. (1977). Electrodermal indices of psychopathic recidivism and schizophrenic abnormal offenders. *British Journal of Social and Clinical Psychology, 19,* 257–269.

Hodgins-Milner, S. (1976). *Psychopathy: A critical examination.* Unpublished doctoral dissertation, McGill University, Montreal, Quebec.

House, T.H., & Milligan, W.L. (1976). Autonomic responses to modeled distress in prison psychopaths. *Journal of Personality and Social Psychology, 34,* 556–600.

Hume, W.I. (1973). Physiological measures in twins. In G.S. Claridge (Ed.), *Personality differences and biological variations: A study of twins.* Oxford: Pergamon Press.

Hutchings, B., & Mednick, S.A. (1977). Registered criminality in the adoptive and biological parents of registered male adoptees. In S.A. Mednick & K.O. Christiansen (Eds.), *Biosocial bases of criminal behavior.* New York: Gardner Press.

Jenkins, R.L., & Pacella, B.L. (1943). Electroencephalographic studies of delinquent boys. *American Journal of Orthopsychiatry, 13,* 107–120.

Jost, H., & Sontag, L.W. (1944). The genetic factor in autonomic nervous system function. *Psychosomatic Medicine, 6,* 308–310.

Kallman, F.J. (1938). *The genetics of schizophrenia.* New York: J.J. Augustin.

Karlsson, J.L. (1966). *The biologic basis of schizophrenia.* Springfield, IL: Charles C Thomas.

Karlsson, J.L. (1970). The rate of schizophrenia in

foster-reared close relatives of schizophrenic index cases. *Biological Psychiatry, 2*, 85.

Kety, S.S., Rosenthal, D., Wender, P.H., & Schulsinger, F. (1968). The types and prevalence of mental illness in the biological and adoptive families of adopted schizophrenics. In D. Rosenthal & S.S. Kety (Eds.), *The transmission of schizophrenia.* London: Pergamon Press.

Kido, M. (1973). An EEG study of delinquent adolescents with reference to recidivism and murder. *Folia Psychiatrica et Neurologia Japonica, 27*, 77–84.

Kirkegaard-Sorensen, L., & Mednick, S.A. (1975). Registered criminality in families with children at high risk for schizophrenia. *Journal of Abnormal Psychology, 84*, 197–204.

Klingman, D., & Goldberg, D.A. (1975). A temporal lobe epilepsy and aggression. *Journal of Nervous and Mental Disease, 160*, 324–341.

Kloek, J. (1968). Schizophrenia and delinquency. In Rueck and Porter (Eds.), *The mentally abnormal offender.* Boston: Little, Brown.

Knott, J.R. (1975). Electroencephalograms in psychopathic personality and in murderers. In W.P. Wilson (Ed.), *Applications of electroencephalography in psychiatry.* Durham, NC: Duke University.

Knott, J.R., Lara, R.T., Peters, J.F., & Robinson, M.D. (1975). EEG findings in 73 persons accused of murder. In B. Burch & H.I. Altschuler (Eds.), *Behavior and brain electrical activity.* New York: Plenum Press.

Kooi, K.A., Tucker, R.R., & Marshall, R.E. (1978). *Fundamentals of electroencephalography,* (2nd ed.). Hagerstown, MD: Harper & Row.

Kranz, H. (1936). *Lebenschicksale krimineller zwillinge.* Berlin: Springer-Verlag OHG.

Kranz, H. (1937). Untersuchungen and zwillingen in fursorgeer-zaiehung sanstalten. *Induktive abstammungs-vererbumgslehre,* 508–512.

Kringlen, E. (1967). Heredity and environment in the functional psychoses: *An epidemiological-clinical twin study.* London: William Heinemann Medical Books.

Lader, M.H., & Wing, L. (1966). *Physiological measures, sedative drugs, and morbid anxiety.* Oxford: Oxford University Press.

Lange, J. (1929). *Verbrechen als schicksal.* Leipzig: Georg Thieme Verlag.

Legras, A.M. (1934). Psychose en criminaliteit by tweelingen, utrect, 1932 (cited in Rosanoff, A. J., et al., *American Journal of Psychiatry, 91*, 247–286).

Lejeune, J., Gautier, M., & Turpin, R. (1959). Etude des chromosomes somatiques de neuf enfants mongoliens. *Comptes Rendus de l'Academie des Sciences, Paris, 248*, 1721–1772.

Lemert, E.M. (1951). *Social Pathology.* New York: McGraw-Hill.

Levander, S.E., Lidberg, L., Schalling, D., & Lidberg, Y. (1977). *Electrodermal recovery time, stress, and psychopathy.* Unpublished manuscript.

Levy, S., & Kennard, M.A. (1953). A study of the electroencephalogram as related to personality structure in a group of inmates of a state penitentiary. *American Journal of Psychiatry, 109*, 832.

Lewis, D.O. (1976). Delinquency, psychomotor epileptic symptomatology and paranoid ideation. *American Journal of Psychiatry, 133*, 1395.

Lewis, D.O., & Balla, D.A. (1976). *Delinquency and psychopathology.* New York: Grune and Stratton.

Lidberg, L., Levander, S., Schalling, D., & Lidberg, Y. (1977). Necker cube reversals, arousal, and psychopathy. *British Journal of Social and Clinical Psychology.*

Lidberg, L., Levander, S., Schalling, D., & Lidberg, Y. (in press). Urinary catecholamines, stress, and psychopathy — A study of arresting men awaiting trial. *Psychosomatic Medicine.*

Lindesmith, A.R., & Dunham, H.W. (1941). Some principles of criminal typology. *Social Forces, 19*, 307–314.

Lippert, W.W., & Senter, R.J. (1966). Electrodermal responses in the sociopath. *Psychonomic Science, 4*, 24–26.

Loeb, J., & Mednick, S.A. (1977). A prospective study of preductors of criminality: 3 electrodermal response patterns. In S.A. Mednick & K.O. Christiansen (Eds.), *Biosocial bases of criminal behavior.* New York: Gardner Press.

Loehlin, J.C., & Nichols, R.C. (1976). *Heredity, environment and personality.* Austin: University of Texas Press.

Loney, J., Kramer, & Milich, R. (1979). *The hyperkinetic child grows up: Predictions of symptoms, delinquency, and achievement at follow-up.* Paper presented at the Annual Meeting of the American Association for the Advancement of Science, Houston, TX, January 7.

Lorimer, F.M. (1972). Violent behavior and the electroencephalogram. *Clinical Electroencephalography, 3*, 193.

Lykken, D.T. (1957). A study of anxiety in the sociopathic personality. *Journal of Abnormal and Social Psychology, 55*, 6–10.

Mark, V.H., & Ervin, F.R. (1970). *Violence and the brain.* New York: Harper & Row.

Mathis, H. (1970). *Emotional responsivity in the antisocial personality.* Unpublished doctoral dissertation, George Washington University, Washington, DC.

McClearn, G.E., & DeFries, J.C. (1973). *Introduction to behavioral genetics.* San Francisco: W.H. Freeman and Co.

Mednick, S.A. (1962). Schizophrenia: A learned thought disorder. In M. Nielsen (Ed.), *Clinical psychology: Proceedings of the XIV International Congress of Applied Psychology.* Copenhagen: Munksgaard.

Mednick, S.A. (1973). *Learning* (2nd Ed.). Englewood Cliffs, NJ: Prentice-Hall.

Mednick, S.A. (1974). Electrodermal recovery and psychopathology. In S.A. Mednick, F. Schulsinger, J. Higgins, & B. Bell (Eds.), *Genetics, environment and psychopathy.* Amsterdam: North-Holland.

Mednick, S.A. (1978). Berkson's fallacy and high-risk research. In L.C. Wynne, R.L. Cromwell, & S. Matthyse (Eds.), *The nature of schizophrenia.* New York: John Wiley & Sons.

Mednick, S.A., Gabrielli, W.F., & Hutchings, B. (1984). Genetic factors in criminal behavior: Evidence from an adoption cohort. *Science, 224*, 891–894.

Mednick, S.A., & Hutchings, B. (1977). Some considerations in the interpretation of the Danish adoption studies in relation to antisocial behavior. In S.A. Mednick & K.O. Christiansen (Eds.), *Biosocial bases of criminal behavior*. New York: Gardner Press.

Mednick, S.A., & Schulsinger, F. (1964). A preschizophrenic sample. *Acta Psychiatrica Scandinavica, 40*, 135–139.

Mednick, S.A., & Schulsinger, F. (1968). Some premorbid characteristics related to breakdown in children with schizophrenic mothers. In D. Rosenthal & S.S. Kety (Eds.), *The transmission of schizophrenia*. London: Pergamon Press.

Mednick, S.A., & Volavka, J. (1980). Biology and crime. In N. Morris & M. Tonry (Eds.), *Crime and justice: An annual review of research* (Vol. 2). Chicago: University of Chicago Press.

Mednick, S.A., Volavka, J., Gabrielli, W.F., & Itil, T. (1981). EEG as a predictor of antisocial behavior. *Criminology, 19*, 219–231.

Mendlewicz, J., Fleiss, J.L., & Fieve, R.R. (1975). Linkage studies in affective disorders: The Xg blood group and manic-depressive illness. In R.R. Fieve, D. Rosenthal, & H. Brill (Eds.), *Genetic research in psychiatry*. Baltimore: Johns Hopkins University Press.

Mesnikoff, A.M., & Lauterbach, C.G. (1975). The association of violent dangerous behavior with psychiatric disorders: A review of the research literature. *The Journal of Psychiatry and Law, 3*, 415–445.

Moffitt, T.E. (1984). *Genetic influence of parental psychiatric illness on violent and recidivistic criminal behavior*. Unpublished doctoral dissertation, University of Southern California, Los Angeles.

Moffitt, T.E., & Mednick, S.A. (1979). Unpublished analyses of the Plum Perinatal Birth Cohort.

Moffitt, T.E., Mednick, S.A., & Cudeck, R.A. (1983). Methodological issues in high-risk research: The prospective longitudinal approach. In R.E. Tarter (Ed.), *The child at risk*. New York: Oxford University Press.

Monroe, R.R. (1970). *Episodic behavioral disorders: A psychodynamic and neurophysiologic analysis*. Cambridge, Harvard University Press.

Monroe, R.R. (1978). *Brain dysfunction in aggressive criminals*. Toronto: Lexington.

Monroe, R.R., Hulfish, B., Balis, G., Lion, J., Rubin, J., McDonald, M., & Barcik, J.D. (1977). Neurological findings in recidivist aggressors. In C. Shagass, S. Gershon, & A.J. Friedhoff (Eds.), *Psychopathology and brain dysfunction*. New York: Raven Press.

Morris, H.H., Escoll, P.J., & Wexler, R. (1956). Aggressive behavior disorders of childhood: A follow-up study. *American Journal of Psychiatry, 112*, 991–997.

Morrison, J.R., & Stewart, M.A. (1971). A family study of the hyperactive child syndrome. *Biological Psychiatry, 3*, 189–195.

Nezirogly, F. (1979). Behavioral and organic aspects of aggression. In J. Obiols, C. Ballees, E. Dongalex, M. Monclus, & J. Pujol (Eds.), *Biological psychiatry today* (Vol. B). Amsterdam: Elsevier North-Holland.

Okasha, A., Sadek, A., & Moneim, S.A. (1975). Psychosocial and electroencephalographic studies of Egyptian murderers. *British Journal of Psychiatry, 126*, 34–40.

Oltman, J.E., & Friedman, S. (1941). A psychiatric study of one hundred criminals. *Journal of Nervous and Mental Disease, 93*, 16–41.

O'Neal, P., & Robins, L.N. (1958). The relation of childhood behavior problems to adult psychiatric status: A 30-year follow-up study of 150 subjects. *American Journal of Psychiatry, 114*, 961–969.

Osborn, S.G., & West, D.J. (1979). Conviction records of fathers and sons compared. *British Journal of Criminology, 2*, 120–133.

Ounsted, C. (1969). Aggression and epilepsy. *Journal of Psychological Researches, 13*, 237.

Owen, D.R. (1972). The 49 XYY male: A review. *Psychological Bulletin, 18*, 209.

Parker, D.S., Syndulko, R., Maltzman, I., Jens, R., & Ziskind, E. (1975). Psychophysiology of sociopathy: Electrocortical measures. *Biological Psychology, 3*, 198–200.

Petersen, I., Matousek, M., Volavka, J., Mednick, S.A., & Pollock, V.E. (1983). EEG antecedents of thievery. *Acta Psychiatrica Scandinavica*.

Pincus, H.H. (1980). Can violence be a manifestation of epilepsy? *Neurology, 30*, 305.

Plovnick, N. (1976). Autonomic nervous system functioning as a predisposing influence on personality, psychopathy and schizophrenia. Unpublished doctoral dissertation, New School for Social Research, New York.

Rachman, S. (1960). Galvanic skin response in identical twins. *Psychological Reports, 6*, 298.

Rappeport, J.R., & Lassen, G. (1965). Dangerousness — Arrest rate comparisons of discharged patients and the general population. *American Journal of Psychiatry, 121*, 776–783.

Reich, T., Cloninger, C.R., & Guze, S.B. (1975). The multifactoral model of disease transmission: I., II., & III. *British Journal of Psychiatry, 127*, 1–32.

Reich, T., Winokur, G., & Mullaney, J. (1975). The transmission of alcoholism. In R.R. Fieve, D. Rosenthal, & H. Brill (Eds.), *Genetic research in psychiatry*. Baltimore: Johns Hopkins University Press.

Ribner, S.A., & Steadman, H.J. (1981). Recidivism among offenders and ex-mental patients. *Criminology, 19*(3), 411–420.

Ricks, D.F., & Berry, J.C. (1970). Family and symptom patterns that precede schizophrenia. In M. Roff & D. Ricks (Eds.), *Life history research in psychopathology*. Minneapolis, MN: University of Minnesota Press.

Rieder, R.O. (1973). The offspring of schizophrenic parents: A review. *The Journal of Nervous and Mental Disease, 3*, 179–190.

Riley, T.L. (1979). The electroencephalogram in patients with rage attacks or episodic violent behavior. *Military Medicine, 144*(8), 515–517.

Robins, L.N. (1966). *Deviant children grown up*. Baltimore: Williams & Wilkens.

Robins, L.N., West, P.A., & Herjanic, D.L. (1975). Arrests and delinquency in two generations: A study of black urban families and their children. *Psychology and Psychiatry, 16*, 125–140.

Rodin, E.A. (1972). Psychomotor epilepsy and aggressive behavior. *Archives of General Psychiatry, 29*, 210–213.

Rosanoff, A.J., Handy, L.M., & Plessett, I.R. (1934).

The etiology of manic-depressive syndromes with special reference to their occurrence in twins. *American Journal of Psychiatry, 91*, 247–286.

Rosen, A., & Schalling, D. (1971). Probability learning in psychopathic and non-psychopathic criminals. *Journal of Experimental Research in Personality, 5*, 191–198.

Rosenthal, D. (1971). *Genetics of psychopathology*. New York: McGraw Hill.

Rosenthal, D. (1974). The concept of subschizophrenic disorders. In S.A. Mednick, F. Schulsinger, J. Higgins, & B. Bell (Eds.), *Genetics, environment and psychopathology*. New York: North-Holland, Elsevier.

Rosenthal, D., Wender, P.H., Kety, S.S., Welner, J., & Schulsinger, F. (1971). The adopted-away offspring of schizophrenics. *American Journal of Psychiatry, 128*, 307.

Roth, L.H. (in press). Treating violent behaviors in prisons, jails, and other special institutional settings. In L.H. Roth (Ed.), *Clinical treatment of the violent person*. (NIMH Crime and Delinquency Issues: A Monograph Series).

Sagarin, E. (Ed.) (1980). *Taboos in criminology*. Beverly Hills: Sage Publications.

Sandberg, A.A., Koepf, G.F., Ishihara, T., & Hauschka, T.S. (1961). An XYY human male. *The Lancet*, 488.

Sarbin, T.R., & Miller, J.E. (1970). Demonism revisited: The XYY chromosomal anomaly. *Issues in Criminology, 5*, 195–207.

Satterfield, J. (in press). Childhood diagnostic and neurophysiological predictors of teenage arrest rates: An eight year prospective study. In S.A. Mednick & T.E. Moffitt (Eds.), *The new biocriminology*. New York: Cambridge University Press.

Sayed, A.A., Lewis, S.A., & Brittain, R.P. (1969). An electroencephalographic and psychiatric study of thirty-two insane murderers. *British Journal of Psychiatry, 115*, 115–124.

Schachter, S. (1971). *Emotion, obesity and crime*. New York: Academic Press.

Schachter, S., & Latane, B. (1964). Crime, cognition and the autonomic nervous system. In M.R. Jones (Ed.), *Nebraska symposium on motivation*. Lincoln: University of Nebraska Press.

Schalling, D. (1975). The role of heart rate increase for coping with pain as related to impulsivity. Unpublished manuscript, University of Stockholm.

Schalling, D., Levander, S., & Dahlin-Lidberg, Y. (1975). A note on the relation between spontaneous fluctuations in skin conductance and heart rate, and scores on the Gough delinquency scale. Unpublished manuscript, University of Stockholm.

Schalling, K., Lidberg, L., Levander, S.E., & Dahlin, Y. (1973). Spontaneous autonomic activity as related to psychopathy. *Biological Psychology, 1*, 83–97.

Schmauk, F.J. (1970). Punishment, arousal and avoidance learning in sociopaths. *Journal of Abnormal Psychology, 76*, 325–335.

Schoenherr, J.C. (1964). Avoidance of noxious stimulation in psychopathic personality. Unpublished doctoral dissertation, University of California, Los Angeles.

Schulsinger, F. (1974). Psychopathy, heredity, and environment. In S.A. Mednick, F. Schulsinger, J. Higgins, & B. Bell (Eds.), *Genetics, environment, and psychopathology*. New York: North-Holland, Elsevier.

Schwade, E.D., & Geiger, S.G. (1960). Severe behavior disorders with abnormal EEGs. *Diseases of the Nervous System, 21*, 616.

Siddle, D.A.T. (1977). Electrodermal activity and psychopathy. In S.A. Mednick & K.O. Christiansen (Eds.), *Biosocial bases of criminal behavior*. New York: Gardner Press.

Siddle, D.A.T., Mednick, S.A., Nicol, A.R., & Foggitt, R.H. (1977). Skin conductance recovery of antisocial adolescents. In S.A. Mednick & K.O. Christiansen (Eds.), *Biosocial bases of criminal behavior*. New York: Gardner Press.

Siddle, D.A.T., Nicol, A.R., & Foggitt, R.H. (1973). Habituation and over-extinction of the GSR component of the orienting response in antisocial adolescents. *British Journal of Social and Clinical Psychology, 12*, 303–308.

Silverman, D. (1946). The psychiatric criminal: A study of 500 cases. *Journal of Clinical Psychopathology, 8*, 301–327.

Slater, E., & Cowie, V. (1971). *The genetics of mental disorders*. London: Oxford University Press.

Smith, C.E. (1971). Recognizing and sentencing the exceptional and dangerous offender. *Federal Probation, 3*, 25–27.

Spuhler, J.N. (1967). Behavior and mating patterns in human populations. In J.N. Spuhler (Ed.), *Genetic diversity and human behavior*. Chicago: Aldine.

Spuhler, J.N. (1968). Assortative mating with respect to physical characters. *Eugenics Quarterly, 15*, 128–140.

Steadman, H.J., Cocozza, J.J., & Melick, M.E. (1978). Explaining the increased arrest rate among mental patients: The changing clientele of state hospitals. *American Journal of Psychiatry, 135*(7), 816–820.

Stumpfl, F. (1936). *Die ursprunge de verbrechens am lebenslauf von zwillingen*. Leipzig: Georg Thieme Verlag.

Sutker, F. (1970). Vicarious conditioning and sociopathy. *Journal of Abnormal Psychology, 76*, 380–386.

Syndulko, K., Parker, D.A., Jens, R., Maltzman, I., & Ziskind, E. (1975). *Central and autonomic nervous system measures of conditioning in sociopaths and normals*. Paper presented at the Science Fair of the Society for Psychophysiological Research, Toronto, Canada.

Szpiler, J.A., & Epstein, S. (1976). Availability of an avoidance response as related to autonomic arousal. *Journal of Abnormal Psychology, 85*, 73–82.

Talovic, S. (1981). Personal communication, August.

Tharp, V., Syndulko, K., Maltzman, I., & Aiskind, E. (1978). Skin conductance and heart rate measures of the gradient of fear in non-institutionalized compulsive gambler, socio-paths.

Thompson, C.B. (1937). A psychiatric study of recidivists. *American Journal of Psychiatry, 94*, 591–604.

Tienari, P. (1963). *Psychiatric illness in identical twins*. Copenhagen: Munksgaard.

Trasler, G. (1972). Criminal behavior. In H.E. Ensenck (Ed.), *Handbook of abnormal psychology* (2nd Ed.). London: Putnam.

Vandenberg, S.G. (1972). Assortative mating, or who marries whom? *Behavior Genetics*, 2, 127–157.

Vandenberg, S.G., Clark, P.J., & Samuels, I. (1965). Psychophysiological reactions of twins. *Eugenics Quarterly*, 12, 7–10.

Van Dusen, K.T., Mednick, S.A., Gabrielli, W.F., & Hutchings, B. (1983). Social class and crime in an adoption cohort. *The Journal of Criminal Law and Criminology*, 74, 249–269.

Van Dusen, K., & Mednick, S.A. (1984). *A comparison of delinquency in Copenhagen and Philadelphia*. Final Report to the National Institute of Justice (Grant No. 79-NI-AX-0087).

Venables, P. (in press). Autonomic nervous system factors in criminal behavior. In S.A. Mednick & T.E. Moffitt (Eds.), *The new biocriminology*. New York: Cambridge University Press.

Venables, P.H., & Christie, M.J. (1975). *Research in psychophysiology*. New York: John Wiley.

Vogel, F., Schalt, E., Kruger, J., & Klarich, G. (1982). Relationship between behavioral maturation measured by the "Baum" test and EEG frequency. A pilot study on monozygotic and dizygotic twins. *Human Genetics*, 62, 60–65.

Wadsworth, M. (1975). Delinquency in a national sample of children. *British Journal of Criminology*, 15, 167–174.

Wadsworth, M. (1976). Delinquency, pulse rates and early emotional deprivation. *British Journal of Criminology*, 16, 245–256.

Waid, W.M. (1976). Skin conductance to both signalized and unsignalized noxious stimulation predicts level of socialization. *Journal of Personality and Social Psychology*, 34, 923–929.

Watt, N.F. (1972). Longitudinal changes in the social behavior of children hospitalized for schizophrenia as adults. *Journal of Nervous and Mental Disease*, 155, 42–54.

Wender, P.H., Rosenthal, D., Kety, S.S., Schulsinger, F., & Welner, M.D. (1974). Crossfostering: A research strategy for clarifying the role of genetic and experiential factors in the etiology of schizophrenia. *Archives of General Psychiatry*, 30, 121.

Wiersma, D. (1966). Crime and schizophrenics. *Exerpta Criminologica*, 6, 168–181.

Williams, D. (1969). Neural factors related to habitual aggression — Consideration of differences between those habitual aggressives and others who have committed crimes of violence. *Brain*, 92, 503–520.

Winkler, G.E., & Kove, S.S. (1962). The implication of electroencephalographic abnormalities in homicide cases. *Journal of Neuropsychiatry*, 3, 322.

Winoker, G., Clayton, P.J., & Reich, T. (1969). *Manic depressive illness*. St. Louis: C.V. Mosby.

Witkin, H.A., Mednick, S.A., Schulsinger, E., Bakkestrom, E., Christiansen, K.O., Goodenough, D.R., Hischhorn, K., Lundsteen, C., Owen, D.R., Philip, J., Rubin, D.V., & Stocking, M. (1977). Criminality, aggression, and intelligence among XYY and XXY men. In S.A. Mednick & K.O. Christiansen (Eds.), *Biosocial bases of criminal behavior*, New York: Gardner Press, 1977.

Wolfgang, M.E. (1977). Foreword. In S.A. Mednick & K.O. Christiansen (Eds.), *Biosocial bases of criminal behavior*. New York: Gardner Press.

Wolfgang, M.E., Figlio, R.M., & Sellin, T. (1972). *Delinquency in a birth cohort*. Chicago: University of Chicago Press.

Yoshimasu, S. (1961). The criminological significance of the family in the light of the studies of criminal twins. *Acta Criminologie et Medicinae Legalis Japonica*, 27.

Yoshimasu, S. (1965). Criminal life curves of monozygotic twin-pairs. *Acta Criminologie et Medicinae Legalis Japonica*.

Young, J.P.R., & Fenton, G.W. (1971). The measurement of autonomic balance in children: Method and normative data. *Psychosomatic Medicine*, 5, 241–253.

Ziskind, E., Syndulko, K., & Maltzman, I. (1978). Aversive conditioning in the sociopath. *Pavlovian Journal*, 13, 199–205.

Zitrin, A., Hardesty, A.S., Burdock, E.T., & Drosman, A.K. (1976). Crime and violence among mental patients. *American Journal of Psychiatry*, 133, 142–149.

5.
The Psychotherapist–Patient Privilege: A Search for Identity

Michael J. Churgin

ABSTRACT. *The basic function of rules of evidence is to insure that trustworthy testimony or other evidence be made available to the trier of fact in a proceeding. A rule of privilege thwarts the truth-finding process in that relevant, indeed often crucial, evidence is withheld from the decision-maker. This suppression of evidence is balanced and trumped by certain societal values that are considered even more important than the presentation of reliable testimony and accurate factfinding. This survey focuses on American law, but also includes some material from other jurisdictions.*

During the past 25 years, there has been a concerted effort in the United States to create a psychotherapist–patient privilege. The common adopted physician–patient privilege has become discredited since few believe that patients confide or withhold information from doctors based on any notion of fear of a possible court appearance by the doctor. Rather than repeal an already enacted privilege, jurisdictions simply riddle the privilege with exceptions.

There has been a considerable body of thought, however, that confidentiality of communications is crucial to treatment by a psychotherapist and that without that promise of secrecy, treatment could not take place. Various states have adopted special statutes for psychotherapists, psychiatrists and/or psychologists. Today, about 45 states within the United States have some form of special statute.

No statute, however, is absolute in practice. Either through judicial interpretation or by statutory exception, certain communications have been placed outside the privilege. The standard exceptions include civil commitment proceedings, court-ordered examinations for a specific purpose, and situations where the patient was a litigant using his mental condition as part of the underlying claim or defense. More recently, an exception has been added for child abuse and neglect cases. Each jurisdiction interprets the privilege and accompanying exceptions in a different manner.

The balancing that takes place varies widely. Some courts are hostile to the notion of a privilege and take a very narrow view in construing it. Others look to the underlying purpose of the privilege and restrict the exceptions to limited situations, analyzing each claim separately. Criminal cases pose a particularly difficult situation since a defendant has a right, guaranteed by the United States Constitution, to confront witnesses. This includes attacking the credibility of a witness based on prior psychiatric treatment if the mental condition of the witness might affect one's ability to perceive events accurately.

This work was supported in part by grants from the University Research Institute, University of Texas at Austin, and the Hogg Foundation for Mental Health. The author wishes to acknowledge the research assistance of Leah Bisk, Patti Ogden, and Kay Shafer, former law students at the University of Texas. Statutes and cases reported through late 1984 have been reviewed to prepare this chapter.

The United States has not adopted a privilege for federal proceedings. The Supreme Court promulgated a psychotherapist–patient privilege in 1972, but Congress refused to allow it to take effect. Federal courts analyze each claim of privilege on a case-by-case basis; most are not supportive. However, the proposed Supreme Court rule became a model for many states, and it has been adopted with modifications by many state legislatures and courts.

Outside of the United States, the psychotherapist–patient privilege has not developed. Common-law countries traditionally have rejected the notion of a privilege. Canadian jurisdictions, however, have been experimenting in this area and there have been efforts to create a privilege in some form. Civil-law countries recognize a strong physician–patient privilege, backed with penal sanctions, but limited consideration is given to nonphysicians who might be involved with therapy.

SOMMAIRE. Les règles de preuve ont pour fonction essentielle d'assurer que des témoignages fiables ou d'autres preuves soient mis à la disposition du juge du fait lors du procès. La règle de la confidentialité fait obstacle à la recherche de la vérité parce que des éléments de preuve parfois même cruciaux ne sont pas portés à l'attention de celui qui prend la décision. La dissimulation de la preuve est compensée par certaines valeurs sociales qui sont considérées comme plus importantes que la présentation de témoignages fiables et la recherche des faits exacts.

Au cours des vingt-cinq dernières années, on a assisté à un effort concerté aux États-Unis en vue de l'institution du principe de la confidentialité des relations entre le psychothérapeute et son patient. Le critère de confidentialité le plus communément adopté entre le médecin et son patient était devenu discrédité parce que l'on doutait que les patients confient ou cachent des renseignements au médecin parce qu'ils craignent une comparution éventuelle du médecin devant un tribunal. Au lieu d'abroger un privilège déjà existant, les juridictions l'ont simplement accompagné d'exceptions.

Il existait cependant toute une école de pensée selon laquelle la confidentialité des communications était cruciale en psychothérapie parce que, sans cette promesse de secret, le traitement ne pouvait pas aboutir. Différents États commençaient à adopter des lois spéciales pour les psychothérapeutes, les psychiatres ou les psychologues. Aujourd'hui, environ 45 États américains se sont dotés d'une forme de loi particulière.

Cependant, aucune loi n'est absolue dans la pratique. Que ce soit par le biais de l'interprétation judiciaire ou par voie d'exception législative, certaines communications ont été exemptées du privilège de confidentialité. Les exceptions standards sont notamment les procédures d'internement civil, les interrogatoires ordonnés par la Cour pour un but précis et les cas où le patient était partie au litige et faisait valoir son état mental dans sa demande ou dans sa défense sous-jacente. Plus récemment, une exception a été adjoutée pour les cas de mauvais traitement et de négligence à l'égard d'enfants. Chaque juridiction interprète ce principe de confidentialité, et les exceptions dont il est assorti, d'une manière différente.

L'équilibre s'établit de façon très variée. Certains tribunaux sont hostiles à la notion de privilège et adoptent un point de vue très étroit dans leur interprétation. D'autres se fient à l'intention sous-jacente visée par la règle de la confidentialité et restreignent les exceptions à des cas limités en analysant chaque litige séparément. Les affaires criminelles posent un problème particulièrement difficile puisqu'un défendeur a le droit (garanti par la Constitution américaine) de confronter les témoins. Ce droit signifie notamment qu'il peut attaquer la crédibilité d'un témoin si ce dernier a reçu un traitement psychiatrique, lorsque son état mental était de nature à modifier sa capacité de percevoir les événements de façon exacte.

Les États-Unis n'ont pas admis la confidentialité dans le cadre des procédures fédérales. La Cour suprême a promulgué un privilège de confidentialité pour les psychothérapeutes et leurs patients, mais le Congrès a refusé de l'entériner dans une loi. Les Cours fédérales analysent chaque revendication de confidentialité au cas par cas, et la plupart d'entre elles ne sont pas en faveur d'une telle exception. Cependant, la règle proposée est devenue un modèle dans de nombreux États, et elle a été adoptée avec des modifications dans bon nombre de législatures et de tribunaux des États.

À l'extérieur des États-Unis, le principe de la confidentialité des communications entre le psychothérapeute et son patient n'a pas été établi. Les pays de Common Law ont traditionnellement rejeté la notion d'un tel privilège. Cependant, les tribunaux canadiens ont tenté des expériences dans ce domaine et ont fait des efforts pour instituer une certaine forme de con-

fidentialité. Les pays de droit civil reconnaissent le caractère confidentiel des relations entre le médecin et son patient de façon très nette et assortissent ce privilège de sanctions pénales, mais le cas des personnes qui pourraient administrer la psychothérapie sans être médecins n'est pratiquement pas envisagé.

In declaring that the president of the United States had an obligation to present evidence, the U.S. Supreme Court reiterated the basic tenet that " 'the public . . . has a right to every man's evidence,' except for those persons protected by a constitutional, common-law, or statutory privilege. . . . Whatever their origins, these exceptions to the demand for every man's evidence are not lightly created nor expansively construed, for they are in derogation of the search for truth" (*United States v. Nixon*, 1974). Jeremy Bentham (1827) aptly described the application of this basic rule:

Are men of the first rank and consideration, are men high in office, men whose time is not less valuable to the public than to themselves, — are such men to be forced to quit their business, their functions, and what is more than all, their pleasure, at the beck of every idle or malicious adversary, to dance attendance upon every petty cause? Yes, as far as it is necessary, — they and everybody! What if, instead of parties, they were witnesses? Upon business of other people's, everybody is obliged to attend, and nobody complains of it. Were the Prince of Wales, the Archbishop of Canterbury, and the Lord High Chancellor, to be passing by in the same coach while a chimney-sweeper and a barrow-woman were in dispute about a halfpennyworth of apples, and the chimney-sweeper or the barrow-woman were to think proper to call upon them for their evidence, could they refuse it? No, most certainly. (p. 320)

The attorney–client privilege developed over the centuries in common-law jurisdictions. Other privileges had a long gestation period. The physician–patient privilege, in some ways the parent of the psychotherapist–patient privilege, is a creature of statute, not of common law. In a trial before Parliament in 1776, a physician objected to testifying about information "that has come before me in a confidential trust in my profession," but Lord Mansfield rejected the claim (*Duchess of Kingston's Trial*, 1776), noting that

a surgeon has no privilege, where it is a material question, in a civil or criminal cause. . . . If a surgeon was voluntarily to reveal these secrets, to be sure he would be guilty of a breach of honor, and of great indiscretion; but, to give that information in a court of justice, which by the law of the land he is bound to do, will never be imputed to him as any indiscretion whatever. (pp. 572–573)

The New York Legislature enacted a statute (N.Y. Revised Statutes, 1829) providing for a physician-patient privilege in 1828 and became the first jurisdiction to reject the common-law disapproval of such a privilege. Its provisions were absolute:

No person authorized to practice psychic or surgery shall be allowed to disclose any information which he may have acquired in attending any patient, in a professional character, and which information was necessary to enable him to prescribe for such patient as a physician, or to do any act for him as a surgeon.

The basic assumption of this and subsequent statutory provisions is that an individual would not seek medical attention without the privilege. Today, the privilege is common in most jurisdictions. However, the long list of exceptions attached to its application result in it having only limited impact (Goode & Sharlot, 1983).

With the lessening in impact of a physician-patient privilege, there has been a corresponding rise in the attention given to the creation of a psychotherapist–patient privilege. Some jurisdictions that have rejected the doctor–patient privilege or have rendered it of little substance have embraced the psychotherapist–patient privilege. It is narrower than the physician–patient privilege in terms of the type of information that is protected, but it is broader in many jurisdictions because communications to mental health professionals other than physicians are also covered.

THE CREATION OF A PRIVILEGE

Most commentators in the field of evidence turn to Wigmore's (1961) four-part formulation to determine whether or not a privilege should exist. All conditions must be satisfied to warrant the establishment of a new privilege:

(1) the communications must originate in a confidence that they will not be disclosed; (2) this element of confidentiality must be essential to the full and satisfactory maintenance of the relation between the parties; (3) the relation must be one which in the opinion of the community ought to be sedulously fostered; (4) the injury that would inure to the relation by the disclosure of the communications must be greater than the benefit thereby gained for the correct disposal of litigation. (Vol. 8, Section 2285)

In his seminal article 25 years ago, Professor Ralph Slovenko reviewed each of Wigmore's fundamental requirements and concluded that a psychotherapist–patient privilege satisfied each (Slovenko, 1960). Perhaps the most quoted statement about the psychotherapist–patient relationship is from the Group for the Advancement of Psychiatry (1960), which states:

Among physicians, the psychiatrist has a special need to maintain confidentiality. His capacity to help his patients is completely dependent upon their willingness and ability to talk freely. This makes it difficult if not impossible for him to function without being able to assure his patients of confidentiality and, indeed, privileged communication. Where there may be exceptions to this general rule . . . , there is wide agreement that confidentiality is a *sine qua non* for successful psychiatric treatment. The relationship may well be likened to that of the priest–penitent or the lawyer–client. Psychiatrists not only explore the very depths of their patients' conscious, but their unconscious feelings and attitudes as well. Therapeutic effectiveness necessitates going beyond a patient's awareness and, in order to do this, it must be possible to communicate freely. A threat to secrecy blocks successful treatment. (p. 242)

The United States Court of Appeals for the District of Columbia Circuit, an active court concerning issues of law and psychiatry, emphasized a special need for a privilege because of the very nature of the disclosures by a patient to a psychotherapist and the trust that is necessary in order for treatment to exist (*Taylor v. United States*, 1955, p. 401, quoting M. Guttmacher and H. Weihofen, p. 272):

Many physical ailments might be treated with some degree of effectiveness by a doctor whom the patient did not trust, but a psychiatrist must have his patient's confidence or he cannot help him. "The psychiatric patient confides more utterly than anyone else in the world. He exposes to the therapist not only what his words directly express; he lays bare his entire self, his dreams, his fantasies, his sins, and his shame. Most patients who undergo psychotherapy know that this is what will be expected of them, and that they cannot get help except on that condition. * * * It would be too much to expect them to do so if they knew that all they say — and all that the psychiatrist learns from what they say — may be revealed to the whole world from a witness stand."

The California Supreme Court, describing the intimate nature of the disclosures by a patient to a psychotherapist, recognized a constitutional underpinning for a privilege:

We believe that a patient's interest in keeping such confidential revelations from public purview, in retaining this substantial privacy, has deeper roots than the California statute and draws sustenance from our constitutional heritage. . . . [W]e believe that the confidentiality of the psychotherapeutic session falls within one such zone [of privacy guaranteed by the Bill of Rights]. (*In re Lifschutz*, 1970, p. 564)

The Pennsylvania Supreme Court, relying on its own state constitution as well as the United States Constitution, created a privilege. "In laying bare one's entire self, however, the patient rightfully expects that such revelations will remain a matter of confidentiality exclusively between patient and therapist" (*In re B.*, 1978, p. 426).

Although perhaps overstated, Krattenmaker's (1973, p. 89) rationale for a privilege emphasizes the societal interest in having some relationships beyond the reach of government-compelled examination and disclosure of the communications:

THE PSYCHOTHERAPIST-PATIENT PRIVILEGE

Democracy requires both individual growth, creativity and responsibility, and an inner zone of personal security which the state cannot penetrate. Privacy provides both that zone of impenetrable individuality and the means by which public contributions can flow from responsible individual control over oneself. . . . Testimonial privileges, through fostering this control, help to provide a context for the development of personal autonomy, emotional release, self-evaluation, and limited and protected communication. None of these ends is attainable solely by oneself; successful pursuit of any one of them apparently requires at least some disclosure to another, but that must occur in a situation which permits individual control over the breadth of disclosure.

The difficult question is balancing the injury to the patient by disclosure against the societal benefit of accurate truth-finding by our courts. Slovenko (1966, p. 169) has asserted that

without the legal sanctity of a privilege, treatment may be effectively fettered by the fear of the patient that what is said in therapy may be compelled on subpoena in the courtroom. Weighing the conflicting values, the benefit of preserving the confidence inviolate seemingly outbalances the possible benefit of permitting litigation to prosper, significant as is that consideration.

When faced with this same balancing test, the Alaska Supreme Court focused on both the patient and the psychiatrist:

Finally, in balancing injury to the relation, by fear of disclosure, against the benefit to justice by compelling disclosure, the scales weigh heavily in favor of confidentiality. We believe that the goals of therapy may be frustrated if the privilege does not attach. Reason indicates that the absence of a privilege would make it doubtful whether either psychotherapists or their patients could communicate effectively if it were thought that what they said could be disclosed compulsorily in a court of law. We are also aware of the delicate position occupied by the psychotherapist himself. Because of the special nature of a patient's confidences, the psychotherapist is subject to an even more stringent honorable obligation not to disclose, under any circumstances, than are other professionals. We do not wish psy-

chotherapists to be faced with the dilemma of either violating this extraordinary trust or being incarcerated. (*Allred v. State*, 1976, p. 418)

One justice of the Alaska court went so far as to make a special claim for psychiatry (*Allred v. State*, 1976, p. 429), noting that

often the purpose of the psychotherapist–patient relationship is the prevention and curing of antisocial behavior, such as the therapy in the instant case [involving a murder]. If this type of activity is successful, then many potential crimes will not be committed. The prevention of a number of similar defendants being prosecuted in future cases is more than an adequate balance for the hampering of the truth-finding function in an individual case.

Advocates of a constitutionally based psychotherapist–patient privilege suspect that a statutory privilege would be riddled with exceptions following the route of the physician–patient privilege (Smith, 1980, p. 60):

Although a privilege fashioned out of constitutional principles of privacy would not necessarily be absolute, it would assure patients of protection in all but the most narrow and compelling circumstances. Successful psychotherapy advances the interests of both individual patients and society. Because successful therapy depends upon confidentiality between patient and psychotherapist, the protection of individual and societal interests requires the recognition of a principle that will surround the communications of therapy with a nearly impenetrable veil. . . . Constitutional protection for the confidences of therapy will have a considerable impact on persons beyond those who actually invoke a privilege. Few patients will need to invoke the privilege to prevent the disclosure of information regarding therapy. Knowledge that the privilege is available, however, will protect all psychotherapy patients, who will know that they can be fully open and honest in therapy.

A constitutional underpinning, however, would not eliminate the exceptions. The question of privilege is one of balancing, and courts will still override the privilege when some pressing interest in revealing the information at stake exists.

Other commentators have pointed to a moral and ethical basis for the psychotherapist–patient privilege. Perhaps the most prominent advocate of this position was the late David Louisell, a prolific writer on the subject of privilege. Louisell (1957, p. 750) claimed that

> any values to judicial administration inherent in attempts to force the psychotherapist to disgorge the secrets of his patients are over-balanced by: (1) the inducement to perjury implicit in such attempts and (2) the harm to the human personality, and hence to freedom, in governmental forcing of a serious conflict of conscience.

To Louisell (1956, p. 101), the constant focus on the effect of privileges on litigation "deprecates their social and moral significance and worth." The ethical norms of the American Psychological Association and the American Psychiatric Association emphasize the duty of confidentiality to protect the interests of the client/patient.

Despite the widespread support for the psychotherapist–patient privilege, some observers have noted that it is not intuitively obvious that the privilege is necessary to preserve the psychotherapist–patient relationship. Justice Matthew Tobriner observed in one case (*In re Lifschutz*, 1970, p. 564) that

> although petitioner has submitted affidavits of psychotherapists who concur in his assertion that total confidentiality is essential to the practice of their profession, we cannot blind ourselves to the fact that the practice of psychotherapy has grown, indeed flourished, in an environment of non-absolute privilege. . . .Whether psychotherapy's development has progressed only because patients are ignorant of the existing legal environment can only be a matter for speculation; psychotherapists certainly have been aware of the limitations of their recognized privilege for sometime.

A study conducted in Texas (Shuman & Weiner, 1982) also lends support to the doubters. Most individuals were not aware if a privilege did exist, and when questioned, they indicated that the existence or lack thereof would not affect their decision to seek therapy. When the members of the sample group were told to assume that no privilege existed, they indicated a lesser willingness to disclose. However, the authors—a law professor and a psychiatrist—concluded that non-disclosure by clients "probably has little relationship to fear disclosure, and would therefore probably not be greatly enhanced by a statutory privilege. The basic reason why patients withhold items is because they fear the judgment of their therapist" (p. 926).

Critics of the privilege have pointed out that the discussion appears based on an assumption that psychotherapy is conducted on a Freudian model. Goode and Sharlot (1983) state:

> Other therapies for dealing with mental and emotional distress such as chemotherapy or neurology would not necessarily require this baring of personal intimacies. Indeed, in the case of group therapy, an offshoot of traditional psychotherapy, confidentiality can rarely be guaranteed, yet it is perceived as nonetheless effective. . . . Whether traditional psychotherapy, whatever the level of confidentiality achieved, actually is effective in treating mental illness, and therefore deserving of encouragement through the protection of a privilege, is itself a matter of serious dispute. (p. 348)

THE DEVELOPMENT OF A PRIVILEGE: THE FEDERAL EXPERIENCE

In order to understand the operation and extent of the psychotherapist–patient privilege, it is necessary to examine an example in detail as to its applicability, scope, assertion, and exceptions. A useful model is the one proposed by the U.S. Supreme Court in 1972 (Rules of Evidence, 1972) for use in all federal courts. Although Congress ultimately rejected the privilege, the proposal has been adopted in various forms by states and has become a basic component of the process to determine whether a privilege should be applied to a specific case in federal court. The proposed federal rule follows:

(a) Definitions.
  (1) A "patient" is a person who consults or is examined or interviewed by a psychotherapist.
  (2) A "psychotherapist" is (A) a person authorized to practice medicine in any state or nation, or reasonably believed by the patient so to be, while engaged in the diagnosis or treatment of a mental or emotional condition, including drug addiction, or (B) a person licensed or certified as a psychologist under the

laws of any state or nation, while similarly engaged.

(3) A communication is "confidential" if not intended to be disclosed to third persons other than those present to further the interest of the patient in the consultation, examination, or interview, or persons reasonably necessary for the transmission of the communication, or persons who are participating in the diagnosis and treatment under the direction of the psychotherapist, including members of the patient's family.

(b) General rule of privilege. – A patient has a privilege to refuse to disclose and to prevent any other person from disclosing confidential communications, made for the purposes of diagnosis or treatment of his mental or emotional condition, including drug addiction, among himself, his psychotherapist, or persons who are participating in the diagnosis or treatment under the direction of the psychotherapist, including members of the patient's family.

(c) Who may claim the privilege. – The privilege may be claimed by the patient, by his guardian or conservator, or by the personal representative of a deceased patient. The person who was the psychotherapist may claim the privilege but only on behalf of the patient. His authority so to do is presumed in the absence of evidence to the contrary.

(d) Exceptions.

(1) Proceedings for hospitalization. – There is no privilege under this rule for communications relevant to an issue in proceedings to hospitalize the patient for mental illness, if the psychotherapist in the course of diagnosis or treatment has determined that the patient is in need of hospitalization.

(2) Examination by order of the judge. – If the judge orders an examination of the mental or emotional condition of the patient, communications made in the course thereof are not privileged under this rule with respect to the particular purpose for which the examination is ordered unless the judge orders otherwise.

(3) Condition on element of claim or defense. – There is no privilege under this rule as to communications relevant to an issue of the mental or emotional condition of the patient in any proceeding in which he relies upon the condition as an element of his claim or defense, or, after the patient's death, in any proceeding in which any party relies upon the condition as an element of his claim or defense. (pp. 240–241)

Although formally promulgated by the Supreme Court, this proposal, like all similar rules, actually was drafted by an advisory committee of judges, law faculty, and lawyers in practice. One interesting aspect about the psychotherapist–patient proposal is that there is no accompanying physician–patient privilege. The advisory committee concluded that "doubts attendant upon the general physician–patient privilege are not present when the relationship is that of psychotherapist and patient. While the common law recognized no general physician–patient privilege, it had indicated a disposition to recognize a psychotherapist–patient privilege, . . . when legislatures began moving into the field" (Rules of Evidence, 1972).

The definition of psychotherapists includes all licensed doctors "while engaged in the diagnosis or treatment of a mental or emotional condition," and therefore is not limited only to those who are psychiatrists. The advisory committee did not wish to exclude the general practitioner who might well be involved in the treatment of mental or emotional conditions. An early and frequently cited law review note (Note, 1952) points out the difficulties with such a broad definition:

It is very common for the general practitioner of medicine to use the methods of the psychotherapist . . . in the process of treating one of his patients – e.g., in simply discussing with the patient his personal problems. In such a case, most of the same considerations supporting a privilege for the psychiatrist and psychologist are applicable here. But two distinctions should be noted: a) the general practitioner ordinarily has not had special training in psychotherapy, and presumably is not as competent in this area as the psychotherapy specialist; b) the general practitioner ordinarily deals with less serious cases than the psychotherapy specialist. It would seem that the public interest – the ultimate basis of any testimonial privilege – does not compel the same legal protection for the general practitioner when acting in the capacity of a psychotherapist as it does for a psychotherapy specialist. . . . Moreover, from the standpoint of judicial administration, it would be difficult to determine just when a physician is acting as a psychotherapist and when he is not. The only basis for such a determination would be the word of the physician himself, who presumably would prefer not to reveal damaging information about a patient. (p. 388)

Strong advocates of the psychotherapist–patient privilege fear that the broader the definition of the term "psychotherapist," the weaker the privilege would become as courts and legislatures carve out exceptions to prevent too much undercutting of the fact-finding process.

Psychologists, properly licensed or certified, are also included within the ambit of the privilege. However, psychiatric social workers, counsellors, or others are not included. A rationale for this exclusion is not discussed by the advisory committee. One court (*Allred v. State*, 1976) noted that any broadening of the privilege would be inappropriate because of numerosity as well as a substantial difference between medical doctors and clinical psychologists on the one hand and counsellors and psychiatric social workers on the other. To this court, the term "psychotherapy"

implies treatment by medical personnel, or treatment by non-medical professionals, clinical psychologists, who are as well trained as physicians to employ psychological methods of treating emotional and personality disturbances. . . . Counselling most often refers to psychological efforts of a non-medical nature, administered by non-medical personnel. Counselling is aimed not primarily at uncovering deep psychological processes but at enabling the client to make more effective use of his present resources. . . . Moreover, counselling is considerably more superficial and less searching than what we understand to be included within the term "psychotherapy." (pp. 418–419)

Other states have been more generous in their outlook toward persons who are neither doctors nor licensed clinical psychologists. These statutes will be discussed in a subsequent section.

The definition of a confidential communication is not exceptional and is modeled largely on the attorney–client privilege. There is one problem worth mentioning, although it is beyond the scope of this chapter. Third-party payment is used frequently as a method of compensating mental health professionals. This often involves disclosure of personal information concerning the patient to insurance companies and other like organizations. Neither the patient nor the psychotherapist has control over the dissemination of this information by the third party, and some might find that the privilege has been lost once the material is disclosed.

The scope of the privilege is restricted to communications made for the purpose of diagnosis and treatment. However, recognizing that the psychotherapist might wish to involve other people in the process of therapy, the proposed rule also includes those participating in the diagnosis or treatment. The rule specifically mentions members of the patient's family, but the rule would also encompass persons involved in group therapy.

As with privileges generally, the claim of protection is to be made by the individual who has made the confidential communication or that person's representative. Any claim by the psychotherapist can be made solely on behalf of the patient; any waiver by the patient would bind the psychotherapist. Attempts by mental health professionals to assert the privilege, even over the objection of the patient, have routinely been rejected. One Alaska judge took a contrary position, stating, "I believe that circumstances may well exist where the psychiatrist should be permitted to assert the privilege — even in the face of an abandonment or waiver of the privilege by the patient — for the best welfare of the patient" (*Allred v. State*, 1976, p. 430), but this position has not found support in legal circles.

The advisory committee that drafted the rules of evidence permitted three exceptions to the privilege, following the drafters of the 1961 Connecticut statute who had concluded that in these instances "the need for disclosure was sufficiently great to justify the risk of possible impairment of the relationship" (Rules of Evidence, 1972). The first exception concerns commitment proceedings, but disclosure is only permitted when the psychotherapist has determined that hospitalization is necessary. Thus, disclosure would not be permitted where a relative files an application for commitment without the support of a treating psychotherapist — unless the patient waived the privilege so the psychotherapist could testify against commitment. The second exception is for a court-ordered examination. This might include competency evaluations in criminal proceedings or custody-related evaluations in a divorce. The examinations are for a specific purpose, and disclosure is so limited. The third exception preserves basic fairness. If the patient relies on his or her emotional condition as part of the claim or defense, the opposing party would be able to question the patient's psychotherapist concerning these matters. Once again, both civil and criminal proceedings are covered. Therefore, an assertion of an insanity defense might result in the compelled disclosure of confidential communications to the defendant's psychotherapist.

As noted earlier, Congress decided not to adopt the psychotherapist–patient privilege. In fact, Congress chose not to adopt any specific privilege; rather, the question "shall be governed by the principles of the common law as they may be interpreted by the courts of the United States in the light of reason and experience" (*U.S. Code Congressional and Administrative News*, 1974 p. 7053). The exception to this common-law approach for federal actions concern matters tried in federal court where the law of a specific state provides the basic rule of decision; in these instances, state law would also determine the privilege issue. The Senate Report described the rationale for this congressional decision (*U.S. Code Congressional and Administrative News*, 1974, p. 7059):

> It should be clearly understood that, in approving this general rule as to privileges, the action of Congress should not be understood as disapproving any recognition of a psychiatrist–patient . . . or any other of the enumerated privileges contained in the Supreme Court rules. Rather, our action should be understood as reflecting the view that the recognition of the privilege based on a confidential relationship and other privileges should be determined on a case-by-case basis.

Congress also chose to prohibit the Supreme Court from adopting any privilege on its own without first seeking congressional approval. Representative William Hungate, now himself a federal judge, emphasized the legislative component (Congressional Record, 1974):

> Rules of privilege keep out of litigation relevant and material information. They do so because of a substantive policy judgment that certain values — such as preserving confidential relationships — outweigh the detrimental effect that excluding the information has on the judicial truthfinding process. In short, rules of privilege reflect a substantive policy choice between competing values, and this policy choice is legislative in nature.

The federal courts have now had over a decade in which to develop their own common law of a psychotherapist–patient privilege. As could be expected, the results have not been uniform and the debate continues. Some courts have been hostile; others have been somewhat supportive of a psychotherapist–patient privilege. The United States Supreme Court has yet to address the issue.

In construing the local District of Columbia statute providing for a physician–patient privilege, the United States Court of Appeals noted that "in regard to mental patients, the policy behind such a statute is particularly clear and strong. Many physical ailments might be treated with some degree of effectiveness by a doctor whom the patient did not trust, but a psychiatrist must have his patient's confidence or he cannot help him" (*Taylor v. United States*, 1955, p. 401). Over a strong dissent, the majority excluded statements made by a defendant asserting the insanity defense to his treating psychiatrist at a government facility. The proposed federal privilege would have permitted the admission of these statements since the defendant placed his mental condition at issue by asserting the insanity defense. In a somewhat similar case, the United States Court of Appeals for the Ninth Circuit simply assumed, along with the parties, that a privilege existed. However, the psychiatrist was allowed to testify as to statements made by the defendant because the court concluded that the examination itself was not within the scope of the privilege (*Ramer v. United States*, 1969). Subsequently, the same court recognized a "conditional right of privacy encompassing the psychotherapist–patient relationship" (*Caesar v. Mountanos*, 1976, p. 1070). However, in that case, the plaintiff had placed her own mental and emotional condition at issue and therefore "the patient and her psychiatrist should not now be permitted to rely upon an absolute privilege which would preclude a proper determination of the truth of the plaintiff-patient's allegations." Thus, the privilege did not assist the psychiatrist.

In a rather summary opinion, the United States Court of Appeals for the Fifth Circuit rejected a claim by a defendant that testimony and records of a psychiatrist should not have been admitted at his criminal trial because of a privilege. "At common law, no physician–patient privilege existed and, therefore, we recognize no such privilege in federal criminal trials today." The court did not engage in any analysis as to whether the common law would now recognize a psychotherapist–

patient privilege (*United States v. Meagher*, 1976, p. 753). Rather, the court treated the question of a psychotherapist privilege as part of a physician–patient privilege. In addition, the court did note that even if the proposed Rule 504 had been adopted, because the defendant had raised the insanity defense, the privilege would not have applied. Subsuming the psychotherapist–patient privilege under the physician–patient privilege would always prove to be a death-knell for any recognition of a privilege. Courts historically have viewed the physician–patient privilege with alarm as have most commentators on the subject. By refusing to recognize a difference between the physician–patient privilege and the psychotherapist–patient privilege, this court and others never subject the psychotherapist–patient privilege to the independent analysis that it deserves.

In a recent case (*United States v. Lindstrom*, 1983), a government witness had a psychiatric history. The defense counsel attempted to obtain access to the psychiatric materials, but the district court refused permission. The court of appeals reversed, pointing out a basic difficulty in applying any rule of nondisclosure against a defendant in a criminal case:

> The government strenuously argues that the privacy interest of a patient in the confidentiality of her medical records and the societal interest in encouraging the free flow of information between patient and psychotherapist require affirmation of the trial court's rulings. While we recognize the general validity of those interests, they are not absolute and, in the context of this criminal trial, must "yield to the paramount right of the defense to cross-examine effectively the witness in a criminal case." (p. 1167)

The government also noted the question of privilege, but once again an appellate court analyzed the question in terms of a doctor–patient relationship rather than the more specialized and protected psychotherapist–patient relationship:

> Rule 26 of the Federal Rules of Criminal Procedure states that in federal criminal trials the admissibility of evidence is to be governed by the principles of the common law, except as modified by Act of Congress. At common law there was no physician–patient privilege. There is no federal statute creating such a privilege. Therefore, testimony concerning the doctor–patient relationship is admissible in federal court. (p. 1167 n. 9)

Once again, this simplistic analysis dooms even the possibility of recognition of the psychotherapist–patient privilege. While the privilege probably should not apply in this case, the better analysis would be to recognize the possibility of its existence and then show the compelling need to override it.

The Confrontation Clause of the Bill of Rights of the United States Constitution will always trump any privilege as long as the evidence sought is relevant. In the *U.S. v. Lindstrom* case:

> The cumulative evidence of the psychiatric records suggest that the key witness was suffering from an ongoing mental illness which caused her to misperceive and misinterpret the words and actions of others, and which might seriously affect her ability "to know, comprehend and relate the truth." . . . Broad-brushed assertions of the societal interest in protecting the confidentiality of such information cannot justify the denial of these defendants' right to examine and use this psychiatric information to attack the credibility of a key government witness. A desire to spare a witness embarrassment which disclosure of medical records might entail is insufficient justification for withholding such records from criminal defendants on trial for their liberty. (pp. 1166–1167)

Thus, the right of confrontation will always be paramount to any other state interest at issue.

The key question often will be one of relevance, and courts would be well-advised to review materials *in camera* rather than disclose materials to the parties. However, if the relevance question is resolved in favor of the defendant in a criminal case, disclosure will be mandatory. The only exception will be a constitutionally based privilege of special weight such as the right against compelled self-incrimination. Otherwise, any privilege or special statutory rule will fall. The conclusion of the court of appeals emphasized the importance of this particular evidence for the truth-finding process (*United States v. Lindstrom*, 1983):

> We hold that the jury was denied evidence necessary for it to make an informed determination of whether the witness' testimony was based on historical facts as she perceived them or whether it was the product of a psychotic hallucination. The jury was denied any evidence on whether this key witness was a schizophrenic, what schizophrenia means, and whether it affects one's

perception of external reality. The jury was denied any evidence of whether the witness was capable of distinguishing reality from hallucinations. Such denial was reversible error. (p. 1168)

What advocates of a psychotherapist-patient privilege would find disappointing about this case is not necessarily the result, but rather the method of analysis. Few, if any, serious commentators could argue that there should ever be an absolute psychotherapist-patient privilege. However, in order for the basic balancing test to have any meaning, the privilege first must be recognized as having some weight. In this case, as in the previous ones, the appellate court simply dismissed the question of privilege by saying one did not exist. It would have been far preferable for the court to have recognized the existence of a privilege, but noting that it could not prevail in the face of the Confrontation Clause of the Bill of Rights of the United States Constitution.

In certain cases where psychiatrists have asserted the privilege on behalf of their patients, the revulsion of courts to the particular fact situations has undercut the value of the privilege. One psychiatrist allegedly participated in a fraudulent medical clinic whose sole function was the sale of Quaaludes (*In re Doe*, 1983). A subpoena was issued for his patient files, and he asserted a psychotherapist-patient privilege as a reason for nondisclosure. He was found in contempt and appealed. First, the court of appeals confused the psychotherapist-patient privilege with the physician-patient privilege, citing a Supreme Court observation concerning the many exceptions to the physician-patient privilege for the proposition that this was the case with the psychotherapist-patient privilege. However, the court then went on to determine whether a psychotherapist-patient privilege should exist in this particular case. The negative result is not surprising. The court accepted for purpose of argument the notion that a psychotherapist-patient privilege might satisfy the four criteria enunciated by Wigmore

> but the relationship in this case does not meet all four conditions. Presumably those visiting the Jorum clinic wanted the fact and purpose of their visit kept in confidence, but there was hardly any relationship of trust since it appears that Dr. Doe did not even recognize his 'patient' of two weeks earlier. The 17-patient per day assembly-line technique involving only a brief interview is scarcely a psychiatrically

nurturing event for a patient, much less one worth fostering. (p. 1193)

A grand jury proceeding investigating possible insurance company fraud by a psychotherapist was the subject of another analysis of the psychotherapist-patient privilege (*In re Pebsworth*, 1983). The record sought here included names of patients, claim submission records, and some diagnostic information. The court of appeals assumed the existence of a privilege for sake of argument, and then held that there had been a patient waiver as to the specific records in question:

> Well-settled principles of testimonial privilege compel the conclusion that any arguable psychotherapist-patient privilege as to these specific kinds of billing and administrative records was intentionally and knowingly relinquished through the patients' assent to the publicizing aspect of the reimbursement and claims procedure. . . . [A] reasonable patient would no doubt be aware that routine processing of reimbursement claims would require these records to be brought into the hands of numerous anonymous employees within a large corporation. (pp. 262–263)

The court concluded that this waiver did not mean that all information disclosed to the psychotherapist in question could now be revealed, but "such limited information as is present here was no longer protected in view of the patients' explicit authorization of disclosure and the easily anticipatable and important purposes to which the disclosed information is now sought to be put." In response to a claim that patients would rather forego treatment than have this material revealed, the court noted that courts and the grand jury would be careful to limit the disclosure (*In re Pebsworth*, 1983).

This is a particularly sensitive area and one that has not received the attention it deserves in the literature. A judge concurring in the opinion noted that traditional waiver doctrine might be inappropriate and that consent for disclosure for one particular purpose did not necessarily mean that the patient had consented to anything else. Some jurisdictions have taken special measures to insure that disclosures to insurance companies do not result in widespread release of private information.

In yet another grand jury investigation into possible fraud in billings by a psychiatrist, a court of appeals did an extensive analysis of the privilege (*In re Zuniga*, 1983). While reaching the same result as other courts, that the privilege did not apply in this specific case, this court followed the recommended procedure for evaluating claims of privilege. First, the court determined whether or not a psychotherapist–patient privilege should exist. Second, the court looked at whether the particular information sought was privileged:

> The interests promoted by a psychotherapist–patient privilege are extensive. As the Advisory Committee Notes stated: "confidentiality is the *sine qua non* for successful treatment." . . . The inability to obtain effective psychiatric treatment may preclude the enjoyment and exercise of many fundamental freedoms, particularly those protected by the First Amendment. Mental illness may prevent one from understanding religious and political ideas, or interfere with the ability to communicate ideas. Some level of mental health is necessary to be able to form belief and value systems and to engage in rational thought. . . .
>
> The interest of the patient in exercising his rights is also society's interest, for society benefits from its members' active enjoyment of their freedom. Moreover, society has an interest in successful treatment of mental illness because of the possibility that a mentally ill person will pose a danger to the community.
>
> This Court has evaluated these interests, taking into account the aforementioned position of the states, the Judicial Conference Advisory Committee and various commentators, and finds that these interests, in general, outweigh the need for evidence in the administration of criminal justice. Therefore, we conclude that a psychotherapist–patient privilege is mandated by "reason and experience." Rule 501. (p. 639)

The information sought in this case consisted of name, dates of treatment, and duration of each treatment. As a general rule of privilege, identity is not within the scope of the privilege. However, the court acknowledged "that some persons would be hesitant to engage the services of a psychiatrist if confronted with the prospect that the mere fact of their treatment might become known. This consideration is not insubstantial" (p. 640). However, the court concluded that as to this information, the "interest of society in obtaining all evidence relevant to the enforcement of its laws"

has higher priority. "The essential element of the psychotherapist–patient privilege is its assurance to the patient that his innermost thoughts may be revealed without fear of disclosure. Mere disclosure of the patient's identity does not negate this element" (p. 640). The court agreed with other courts which had concluded that basic identity information is waived by seeking third-party payment.

The analysis of the court in *Zuniga* is a model of what courts should be doing when confronted with an assertion of a psychotherapist–patient privilege. Unfortunately, the conduct of the several courts noted earlier is far more common. Recently, one appellate court went so far as to refer to the "well-settled federal rule that such [psychiatric] communications are not privileged" (*Slakan v. Porter*, 1984). The basic reason for this hostility to the psychotherapist–patient privilege by appellate courts has little to do with this particular privilege, but rather reflects an overall hostility to keeping evidence away from the fact finder. As the Supreme Court stated in 1980 (*Trammel v. United States*, 1980) when cutting back on the exercise of the long-recognized common-law spousal privilege:

> Testimonial exclusionary rules and privileges contravene the fundamental principle that "the public . . . has a right to every man's evidence." . . . As such, they must be strictly construed and accepted "only to the very limited extent that permitting a refusal to testify or excluding relevant evidence has a public good transcending the normally predominant principle of utilizing all rational means for ascertaining truth." (p. 50)

This aversion to the recognition of privilege by most federal appellate courts has, of course, extended to the district courts as well.

One notable exception among the trial courts has been Judge Jack Weinstein of the United States District Court in Brooklyn, New York. The author of the major treatise on the Federal Rules of Evidence 501 (1974), Judge Weinstein has had occasion to wrestle with the psychotherapist–patient privilege in cases before him. His method of analysis is illustrative of what federal trial courts should be doing when faced with an assertion of privilege. In one case, the plaintiffs in a civil rights action asserted that black and Hispanic children were assigned to special schools in a racially discriminatory manner. To establish their claim, the plaintiffs requested 50 randomly selected anonymous files which contained diagnostic information. The defendants asserted a privilege as well as numerous constitutional challenges to disclosure. As a starting point in considering the issue of privilege, Judge Weinstein immediately drew the distinction between the psychotherapist–patient relationship and that normally covered by the physician–patient privilege. As noted previously, the physician privilege has been roundly condemned by courts and commentators. In order for the psychotherapist–patient privilege to be recognized, a sharp distinction from the general physician–patient privilege must be maintained. He also declared that "it is desirable as a matter of social policy to protect psychotherapist–patient confidences by an evidentiary privilege, at least to the extent that this may be done consistently with other social requirements."

One error commonly made by those analyzing privileges, according to Judge Weinstein, is the failure to recognize the basic balancing component involved:

> Balancing of competing interest is permissible and in fact required, to determine whether a federal evidentiary privilege should be extended to particular communications as a matter of social and legal policy. This flexible nature of rules of privilege is often overlooked. They are sometimes mistakenly characterized as conferring "absolute" or "unqualified" immunity.

One reason for this frequent error is that claims of privilege are often made in absolute terms. The more strident and uncompromising the argument, the easier it is for a court to reject such a claim.

In this particular case, Judge Weinstein balanced the interests at stake and concluded that certain material may be disclosed, but only under certain conditions. These included coding the record so that names do not appear, restricting use of the material, confidentiality enforcement through the contempt power of the court, limiting the copying of material, sealing records in court files, and the return of all files following the completion of the litigation. To evaluate his application of the privilege, Judge Weinstein used the proposed Supreme Court rule.

Although "Rule 504, along with other specific privilege rules, was rejected by Congress in favor of the more general Rule 501, it still provides a useful standard from which analysis can proceed" (Lora v. Board of Education, 1977, p. 584). Under the proposed rule, the material at issue would not have been privileged. Similarly, in another case, Judge Weinstein employed the same basic analysis to find that no privilege existed with regard to a defendant who had placed his mental condition at issue by raising the insanity defense (Edney v. Smith, 1976). This is a common exception even in those jurisdictions which have strong privilege statutes.

In sum, the past decade has not seen any consensus by the federal courts concerning the existence of the psychotherapist–patient privilege. Called on by Congress to look at such a privilege on a case-by-case basis in light of the common law, the courts have had difficulty wrestling with the problem. Most seem to wish to ignore it. The question of a psychotherapist–patient privilege is not discussed independently but rather is pigeonholed with the discredited physician–patient privilege. Interestingly, there has been little reference to state statutes on the subject. Although technically correct in all but those cases where state law provides the rule of decision, the federal courts are shortsighted to ignore this more developed body of law on the question of privilege. As Judge Weinstein indicated:

> We acknowledge that "a strong policy of comity between state and federal sovereignties impells federal courts to recognize state privileges where this can be accomplished at no substantial cost to federal substantive and procedural policy." . . . If the state holds out the expectation of protection to its citizens, they should not be disappointed by a mechanical and unnecessary application of the federal rule. (Lora v. Board of Education, 1977, p. 576)

Other federal courts do not seem to be in agreement. The more normal course of action is to note that there is no recognized psychotherapist–patient privilege in common law and therefore none exists in federal court. Some recent decisions, such as Zuniga, show that a thoughtful analysis is possible. However, I think it unlikely that there will be any widespread adoption of the psychotherapist–patient privilege by the federal judiciary. The basic climate is against the extension of privileges, and unless Congress creates one, case-by-case development will continue to be skeptical of the recognition that such a privilege should become part of the common law.

There are two special federal statutes that affect the psychotherapist–patient privilege in all jurisdictions. The Federal Child Abuse Prevention and

Treatment Act (U.S. Code, 1976) and the accompanying regulations (Code of Federal Regulations, 1984) require every state to have a child abuse reporting mechanism in order to qualify for federal funds. The reporting statutes usually require abrogation of the psychotherapist–patient privilege to a certain extent. The operation of specific statutes is discussed in the following section on a state-by-state basis where appropriate.

The second statute has an opposite effect (U.S. Code, 1984, Supp.). It provides for confidentiality of records of patient identity, diagnosis, prognosis, or treatment in federally assisted drug and alcohol rehabilitation programs. There is an exception that provides for disclosure

> if authorized by an appropriate order of a court of competent jurisdiction granted after application showing good cause therefor. In assessing good cause, the court shall weigh the public interest and the need for disclosure against the injury to the patient, the physician–patient relationship, and to the treatment services. (U.S. Code, Section 290dd–3)

The statute and regulations are exclusive and preempt any state law to the contrary. In one case, the United States Supreme Court assumed, without deciding, that the statutory scheme would prevent a counselor at a federally supported facility from reporting a participant's confession of rape and murder to the police (*Minnesota v. Murphy*, 1984).

States have not been uniform in enforcing the federal statute. For example, a sharply divided Montana Supreme Court held that the exclusive remedy for a violation of an individual's confidentiality would be the statutory fine rather than the exclusion of the improperly revealed statement (*State v. Magnuson*, 1984). The Minnesota Supreme Court was faced with a situation where the child abuse reporting statute, enacted as a result of federal pressure, was in conflict with the drug treatment and confidentiality provisions. The court abrogated the medical privilege "only to the extent that it would permit evidentiary use of the information required to be contained in the maltreatment report" (*State v. Andring*, 1984, p. 133). An Alabama appellate court refused to permit a defendant to obtain access to prior treatment records of the victim's wife in a murder prosecution. The defendant had established no overriding necessity for the disclosure of the rec-

ords and the victim's wife's admitted drug abuse was already before the jury (*Bell v. State*, 1980).

STATE PRIVILEGES

The vast number of trials in the United States, both civil and criminal, take place in state court. Federal proceedings constitute a minute percentage. Although federal courts and federal rules provide models for state courts and legislatures, basic decisions are left to the states. In the area of privileges, states have taken the lead. As Justice Louis Brandeis stated in another context: "It is one of the happy incidents of the federal system that a single courageous State may, if its citizens chose, serve as a laboratory; and try novel social and economic experiments without risk to the rest of the country" (*New State Ice Co. v. Liebmann*, 1932, p. 31).

The psychotherapist–patient privilege was first recognized as a separate entity less than 30 years ago. Today, some form of privilege exists in 45 states. The scope and applicability vary widely; exceptions dot the landscape. To properly understand the psychotherapist–patient privilege, it is necessary to look at state statutes, court rules, and judicial interpretation on a state-by-state basis. The current trend is to provide exceptions conforming to the proposed federal privilege and a special one for child abuse and neglect cases. What follows is a brief analysis of each state's efforts in the field. The focus is on psychiatrists and psychologists. Others, such as school counselors, have special statutory privileges, but these are beyond the scope of this chapter.

ALABAMA

Psychologists in Alabama were able to obtain legislative protection for their practice in 1963. Faced with this situation, the Alabama Supreme Court indicated that the privilege would also apply to psychiatrists (*Ex parte Day*, 1979), and the Alabama legislature recognized the anomalous situation and changed the statute. On its face, the Alabama privilege is one of the broadest:

> For the purpose of this chapter, the confidential relations and communications between licensed psychologists and licensed psychiatrists and clients are placed upon the same basis as those provided by law between attorney and client, and nothing

in this chapter shall be construed to require any such privileged communications to be disclosed. (Alabama Code, 1982, Sec. 34-26-2)

Despite the broad sweep of the statutory language, the courts have carved out certain exceptions to the privilege to insure accurate fact-finding. An assertion of insanity by a defendant is such an example:

> There are states which hold that by pleading insanity, a criminal defendant waives his statutory privilege against disclosure of a "psychotherapist–patient communication." The better-reasoned cases hold, however, that there must be some presentation of evidence of insanity in addition to the plea, in order for the question of "waiver" to arise. (*Ex parte Day*, 1979, p. 1162)

As the Alabama Court of Criminal Appeals noted, any other result would give license to the defendant to call only his experts and prevent rebuttal witnesses of the prosecution from testifying (*Magwood v. State*, 1982).

Recently, the Alabama court carved out an exception for a custody dispute. Noting the importance of the privilege, the court indicated, however, that it must yield when the question would be the best placement for a child. In the course of the same case, the court did note that a mere release authorizing exchange of information from medical records at a mental hospital did not waive the privilege (*Van Goyt v. Alabama*, 1984). This is in contrast to the standard doctrine for other privileges that once a waiver has taken place, all communications involved lose their privileged status. Many courts have been careful to limit waivers to the purpose for which they were executed.

ALASKA

Few states have been as conscientious as Alaska in evaluating the issue of the psychotherapist–patient privilege. As noted earlier, Alaska did not have an adequate statutory provision. There was a statute concerned with confidentiality of communications, but the Alaska Supreme Court termed this merely an "anti-gossip" provision. Faced with the question of whether a defendant in a criminal case could assert a psychotherapist–client privilege to prevent a psychiatric social worker from testifying, that court created a common-law privilege after carefully reviewing the available literature (*Allred v. State*, 1976).

In two subsequent cases, the Alaska courts carved out certain exceptions for criminal defendants. First, the court held that the common-law psychotherapist–patient privilege is waived when the defendant asserts an insanity defense (*Post v. State*, 1978), and applied the same rationale to defendants who claim diminished capacity (*Loveless v. State*, 1979).

A recent decision illustrates Alaska's sensitivity to the question of the psychotherapist–patient privilege. A clinical psychologist was subpoenaed to appear before a grand jury investigating charges that a father had sexually molested his daughter. The parents began therapy immediately prior to the state's filing a petition in family court for the daughter's custody. Subsequently, the state charged the father with a variety of criminal violations, including rape, sexual abuse, and sexual assault. The psychologist declined to testify before the grand jury based on the psychotherapist–patient privilege. The Alaska Court of Appeals affirmed the decision of the trial court which upheld the privilege (*State v. R. H.*, 1984).

By this time, Alaska had adopted a statutory privilege based on the Uniform Rules of Evidence, which tracks basically with the proposed federal standard discussed earlier in this chapter. In addition, following practice in many jurisdictions, Alaska has a special statute for child abuse cases. "Neither the physician–patient nor the husband–wife privilege is a ground for excluding evidence regarding a child's harm, or its cause, in a judicial proceeding related to a report made under this chapter" (Alaska Statute, 1983, Sec. 47.17.060). The question before the court was whether Rule 504 had been superseded in this case by the special child abuse disclosure statute. First, the court assumed that the privilege applied to psychologists, even though the privilege rule only included medical doctors. It then determined that criminal proceedings were not covered by the term "judicial proceeding"; only child protection proceedings would abrogate the privilege. In addition to basing its decision on a close reading of the statutory scheme, the court also noted special privacy interests at stake. Child protection proceedings are

essentially confidential. Only the immediate participants are aware of what transpires. Testimony by a psychologist or psychiatrist in the context of such a proceeding would not amount to general publication of his patient's problems. In addition, the nature of the proceedings are corrective rather than punitive. A psychologist or psychiatrist testifying in such a proceeding might well be perceived as helping rather than harming his patient. In contrast, in a criminal proceeding the psychologist would necessarily be cast as an adversary of his former patient. (*State v. R. H.*, 1984, p. 281)

The court also suggested that the special child protection statute might not apply to the psychotherapist–patient privilege, but only the physician–patient privilege. The court left the matter to further resolution by the legislature and the Alaska Supreme Court in its rulemaking function, but noted that certain constitutional questions might exist.

The sensitive balancing of interests by the Alaska appellate court in this case is a model of how the question of privilege should be approached. Careful drafting is important in this area, and so is careful judicial determinations. Although the privilege barred the testimony of the psychologist in a criminal prosecution, the daughter who made the initial accusation could still testify.

ARIZONA

Certified psychologists have special statutory protection in Arizona. Confidential relations and communications "are placed on the same basis as those provided by law between attorney and client" (Arizona Revised Statutes, 1983, Sec. 32-2085). There are two statutory exceptions to the privilege — child abuse and adult protection cases. The Arizona Court of Appeals was faced with an interesting, and common, situation in which both parties to a divorce had been seeing a psychologist. There was an ensuing custody battle and one party called the psychologist and a claim of privilege was made. Because the statutory protection is worded in terms of attorney and client, the court looked to developed law concerning two individuals seeking counsel from the same attorney. Finding that no privilege would exist as between the parties, the court extended this to the custody situation. The privilege would still hold against the outside world, but when the husband and wife had chosen to have counseling with the same psychologist, that psychologist could testify

in a dispute between them (*Hahman v. Hahman*, 1981).

The importance of the certification for the psychologist was illustrated in another court of appeals decision (*State v. Howland*, 1982). Under Arizona procedure, a doctorate degree is necessary in order to be certified by the state. In this particular case, the marriage counselor only had a master's degree in psychology. Therefore, the court held that no privilege would exist and that the marriage counselor could testify over the objection of the client. Although the decision is correct under the terms of the statute, the holding does pose some danger to clients because laypersons rarely are familiar with certification rules. Some state statutes focus on the belief of the client rather than the actual existence of certification.

ARKANSAS

The Uniform Rules of Evidence provision governs in Arkansas, but it has been interpreted rather narrowly (Arkansas Statutes, 1979). In a criminal case, a key government witness had been under treatment by a psychologist. When defense counsel attempted to question the psychologist at a pretrial hearing, the psychologist asserted the psychotherapist–patient privilege and refused to discuss any of the witness's psychological history. The trial court sustained the privilege, but the court of appeals reversed. The Supreme Court in a previous case had "rejected a notion that Rule 503, the physician and psychotherapist–patient privilege, protected 'any information' exchanged between doctor and patient; instead the Court construed the privilege narrowly to protect only *confidential communications between doctor and patient*" (*Horne v. State*, 1984, emphasis in original). The defendant sought to show that the witness "suffered from a histrionic personality, causing her to fantasize events that never happened. In short, appellant's inquiry to the psychologist was directed towards his diagnosis of Shelley's mental condition and not his confidential communications with her."

The court of appeals acknowledged that Arkansas has a more restrictive interpretation of Rule 503 than other jurisdictions. The court also noted a constitutional underpinning for its position that the psychologist must testify. The judge must "give full range to the accused's constitutional right to confront and cross-examine witnesses against him." Preventing the psychologist from testifying might run afoul of the defendant's basic constitutional rights.

There is one interesting aspect of the case that was irrelevant for the decision. The defense counsel sought permission to call the psychologist at trial and force him to invoke the privilege in front of the jury. The trial court refused this request. The basic purpose would have been to emphasize to the jury that there was some material being kept from them with the hope that the jurors would infer that the testimony would be contrary to the government's case. Forcing the invocation of a privilege in front of the jury generally is not favored by courts. It leads to speculation by the trier of fact and burdens the exercise of the privilege.

CALIFORNIA

A state with a long history of supportive judicial interpretation of the privilege is California. At one time, California had a broad privilege for psychologists, but psychiatrists could only claim the benefit of the weaker and somewhat discredited physician–patient privilege. When California overhauled its Evidence Code in 1965, it created one psychotherapist–patient privilege to cover both physicians and psychologists. Subsequently, licensed clinical social workers, credentialed school psychologists, and licensed marriage, family, and child counselors were also included within the ambit of the privilege:

> [The] patient, whether or not a party, has a privilege to refuse to disclose, and to prevent another from disclosing, a confidential communication between patient and psychotherapist if the privilege is claimed by: (a) the holder of the privilege; (b) the person who is authorized to claim the privilege by the holder of the privilege; or (c) the person who was the psychotherapist at the time of the confidential communication, but such person may not claim the privilege if there is no holder of the privilege in existence or if he is otherwise instructed by a person authorized to permit disclosures. (California Evidence Code, 1966, Sec. 1024)

The impetus for the broad psychotherapist–patient privilege was a study conducted by the California Law Revision Commission. The proposal of the commission would have extended the privilege to all medical doctors because

> many medical doctors who do not specialize in the field of psychiatry nevertheless practice psychiatry to a certain extent. Some patients cannot afford to go to specialists and must obtain treatment from doctors who do not limit their practice to psychiatry. Then, too, because a line between organic and psychosomatic illness is indistinct, a physician may be called upon to treat both physical and mental or emotional conditions at the same time. Disclosure of a mental or emotional problem will often be made in the first instance to a family physician who will refer the patient to someone else for further specialized treatment. In all of these situations, the psychotherapist privilege should be applicable if the patient is seeking diagnosis or treatment of his mental or emotional condition. (California Law Revision Commission, 1964, pp. 239-240)

However, the legislature was not as generous, and restricted it to a doctor "who devotes, or is reasonably believed by the patient to devote, a substantial portion of his time to the practice of psychiatry (Sec. 1010(a)). It is unclear what effect this has had.

The commission favored and the legislature adopted a much broader privilege than is accorded the physician. The psychotherapist–patient privilege applies in criminal proceedings with certain limited exceptions, civil commitment other than when disclosure is necessary to prevent a threatened danger, and other civil actions including those arising out of the patient's criminal conduct. The commission's comment on the privilege has been recited in many jurisdictions by those advocating similar provisions:

> Adequate psychotherapeutic treatment is dependent upon the fullest revelation of the most intimate and embarrassing details of the patient's life. Unless a patient can be assured that such information will be held in utmost confidence, he will be reluctant to make the full disclosure upon which his treatment depends. The Commission has received several reports indicating that persons in need of treatment sometimes refuse such treatment from psychiatrists because the confidentiality of their communications cannot be assured under existing law. Many

of these persons are seriously disturbed and constitute threats to other persons in the community. Accordingly, the Commission recommends that a new privilege be established that would grant to patients of psychiatrists a privilege much broader in scope than the ordinary physician–patient privilege. Although it is recognized that the granting of the privilege will operate to withhold relevant information in some situations where such information would be crucial, the interests of society will be better served if psychiatrists are able to assure patients that their confidences will be protected. (California Law Revision Commission, 1964, pp. 239–240)

The California Senate Report on the bill and judicial opinions construing the Evidence Code echo the commission's comments.

California is one of the few states that does not have a broad exception for civil commitment proceedings as part of the psychotherapist–patient privilege. At the same time, there is an exception to the physician–patient privilege. This distinction was intentional:

A patient's fear of future commitment proceedings based upon what he tells his psychotherapist would inhibit the relationship between the patient and his psychotherapist almost as much as would the patient's fear of future criminal proceedings based upon such statements. If a psychotherapist becomes convinced during a course of treatment that his patient is a menace to himself or to others because of his mental or emotional condition, he is free to bring such information to the attention of the appropriate authorities. The privilege is merely an exemption from the general duty to *testify* in a proceeding in which testimony can ordinarily be compelled to be given. The only effect of the privilege would be to enable the patient to prevent the psychotherapist from testifying in any commitment proceedings that ensue. (California Law Revision Commission, 1964, pp. 239–240)

As noted, disclosure is permitted "if the psychotherapist has reasonable cause to believe that the patient is in such mental or emotional condition as to be dangerous to himself or to the person or property of another and that disclosure of the communication is necessary to prevent the threatened danger."

This exception, permitting disclosure in situations where patients are dangerous, played a role in the well-known *Tarasoff* case (*Tarasoff v. Regents*, 1976). The California Supreme Court indicated that a therapist would be liable for the death of an individual killed by his patient when the therapist had determined that a serious danger of violence to the deceased existed and failed to exercise reasonable care to protect the victim from that danger. Representatives of the psychiatric profession argued vociferously that such a ruling would deter individuals from seeking therapy and would constitute a breach of trust by the psychotherapist. The court majority rejected these notions, observing that in a previous case the same groups had claimed that if the privilege were not absolute, individuals would not seek treatment:

We rejected that argument, and it does not appear that our decision in fact adversely affected the practice of psychotherapy in California. Counsel's forecast of harm in the present case strikes us as equally dubious. . . . We cannot accept without question counsels' implicit assumption that effective therapy for potentially violent patients depends on either the patient's lack of awareness that a therapist can disclose confidential communications to avert impending danger, or upon the therapist's advanced promise never to reveal nonprivileged threats of violence. (*Tarasoff*, p. 26)

The court concluded that the exception to the psychotherapist–patient privilege for dangerous patients reflected a careful legislative balance of the competing interest:

We realize that the open and confidential character of psychotherapeutic dialogue encourages patients to express threats of violence, few of which are ever executed. Certainly a therapist should not be encouraged routinely to reveal such threats; such disclosures could seriously disrupt the patient's relationship with his therapist and with the persons threatened. To the contrary, the therapist's obligations to his patient require that he not disclose a confidence unless such disclosure is necessary to avert danger to others, and even then that he do so discreetly, and in a fashion that would preserve the privacy of his patient to the fullest extent compatible with the prevention of the threatened danger. . . . Amicus suggests that a therapist who concludes that his patient is dangerous should not warn the potential victim, but institute proceedings for involuntary detention of the patient. The giving of a warning, however, would in many cases represent a far lesser inroad upon the patient's privacy than would involuntary commitment.

The revelation of a communication under the above circumstances is not a breach of trust or a violation of professional ethics; as stated in the Principles of Medical Ethics of the American Medical Association (1957), section 9: "A physician may not reveal the confidence entrusted to him in the course of medical attendance . . . *unless he is required to do so by law or unless it becomes necessary in order to protect the welfare of the individual or of the community."* We conclude that the public policy favoring protection of the confidential character of patient–psychotherapist communications must yield to the extent to which disclosure is essential to avert danger to others. The protection privilege ends where the public peril begins.

Our current crowded computerized society compels the interdependence of its members. In this risk-infested society we can hardly tolerate the further exposure to danger that would result from a concealed knowledge of the therapist that his patient was lethal. If the exercise of reasonable care to protect the threatened victim requires the therapist to warn the endangered party or those who can reasonably be expected to notify him, we see no sufficient societal interest that would protect and justify concealment. The containment of such risks lies in the public interest. (*Tarasoff v. Regents,* 1976, p. 27, emphasis added)

One commentator has noted that under the California Evidence Code there is a provision for a pretrial judicial review of claims of privilege.

By interposing informed judicial consideration of the necessity for disclosure between the allegation of negligence and the grant of discovery, the dangerous-patient exception can preclude unwarranted intrusions into therapist–patient confidentiality as well as prevent obstructive claims of privilege. (Olander, 1978, p. 285)

I think the author is somewhat optimistic; even preliminary discovery skirmishes might well do some harm to the relationship. However, use of the special pretrial hearing could resolve many issues.

The California Supreme Court has interpreted the exceptions to the psychotherapist–patient privilege quite narrowly. The basic maxim is that "the psychotherapist–patient privilege is to be liberally construed in favor of the patient" (*Roberts v. Superior Court,* 1973). In this particular case, an automobile accident victim filed an action for personal injuries and indicated that because of the defendants' conduct, she had become "sick, sore, lame, and disabled" and sought damages. After several preliminary discovery skirmishes, the trial court compelled production of the records of the plaintiff's psychotherapist, holding that the psychotherapist–patient privilege had been waived by the patient-litigant exception. The plaintiff then sought a writ of prohibition to challenge the discovery order. An initial question concerned the appropriateness of an interlocutory appeal. As a general rule, such piecemeal approaches to litigation are disfavored. The desired procedure is for the entire case to be tried followed by an appeal. However, the California Supreme Court indicated that

the need for the availability of the prerogative writs in discovery cases where an order of the trial court granting discovery allegedly violates a privilege of the party against whom discovery is granted is obvious. The person seeking to exercise the privilege [the psychiatrist] must either succumb to the court's order and disclose the privileged information, or subject himself to a charge of contempt for his refusal to obey the court's order pending appeal. The first of these alternatives is hardly an adequate remedy and could lead to disruption of a confidential relationship. The second is clearly inadequate as it would involve the possibility of a jail sentence and additional delay in the principal litigation during review of the contempt order. (*Roberts v. Superior Court,* p. 312)

Some courts in other jurisdictions have not been as sympathetic to the need for an interlocutory appeal.

Turning to the merits, the court indicated that the trial judge had interpreted the exception to the psychotherapist–patient privilege too broadly, for "even where the patient files a claim for mental suffering and damage, disclosure can be compelled only with respect to communications which are directly relevant to the specific conditions placed at issue by the patient's pleadings. 'Disclosure cannot be compelled with respect to other aspects of the patient-litigant's personality even though they may, in some sense, be "relevant" to the substantive issues of litigation' " (p. 313).

The patient-litigant claimed that her suit for injury was limited to pain in her neck, back, and legs. The psychiatric treatment was related to an overdose of pills. The defendants, however, asserted that there was some possibility of a "mental component" because the complaints seemed in excess of what was normal. The supreme court met this issue head-on:

> We must of course recognize that any physical injury is likely to have a "mental component" in the form of the pain suffered by the injured person, at least insofar as he is conscious of the physical injury. Presumably, the perception of pain from a particular injury will vary among individuals. Thus, in every lawsuit involving personal injuries, a mental component may be said to be at issue, in that limited sense at least. However, to allow discovery of past psychiatric treatment merely to ascertain whether the patient's past condition may have decreased his tolerance to pain or whether the patient may have discussed with his psychotherapist complaints similar to those to be litigated, would defeat the purpose of the privilege. (p. 314)

Merely indicating that she had received psychotherapy also did not waive the privilege. In fact, this disclosure was necessary "to avoid the application of the patient-litigant exception to the privilege" (p. 315). In addition, the records of the psychotherapy had been sent to other physicians involved with the plaintiff's treatment. This did not waive the privilege either. The plaintiff had also signed a consent form at the behest of the defendant's insurance company which referred to "the medical history, physical condition, and treatment" (p. 317). The court refused to construe the waiver so broadly as to include past psychiatric treatments. This sensitive approach to exercise of the psychotherapist–patient privilege in a routine automobile case evidences the special position held by the psychotherapist–patient privilege in California. Other jurisdictions often use an "all-or-nothing" approach and do not consider the possibility that exceptions could be narrowly drawn to effectuate the basic purpose of the underlying privilege.

A divorce case presented another facet of the privilege. Believing that her husband, a psychiatrist, was underreporting his income, the wife sought the identity and fee payment of all his patients during a 17-month period. The trial court ordered disclosure indicating that the privilege did not exist as to identity. The question for the appellate court was whether such information was part of the definition of "confidential communication." The court of appeal held that

> the identity of petitioners' clients is protected under the psychotherapist–client privilege. When a patient seeks out the counsel of a psychotherapist, he wants privacy and sanctuary from the world and its pressures. The patient desires in this place of safety an opportunity to be as open and candid as possible to enable the psychotherapist the maximum opportunity to help him with his problems. The patient's purpose would be inhibited and frustrated if his psychotherapist would be compelled to give up his identity without his consent. Public knowledge of treatment by a psychotherapist reveals the existence and, in a general sense, the nature of the malady. (*Smith v. Superior Court*, 1981, p. 148)

This is one of the few areas where the breadth of the psychotherapist–patient privilege is more extensive than the attorney–client privilege.

In another divorce case, the mother had custody of the children and opposed the father's right to visitation. To buttress her claim, she subpoenaed the records of his psychiatrist. The trial court indicated that requesting standard visitation placed in issue the father's mental condition. The appellate court rejected this broad notion and indicated that a mere claim of visitation did not waive the psychotherapist–patient privilege (*Simek v. Superior Court*, 1981).

As discussed earlier, there has been a trend in the United States to create a special exception to all privileges for the reporting of child abuse. When analyzing the effect of such a statute on the psychotherapist–patient privilege, the California Supreme Court carefully balanced all interests at stake. An individual had been involved in sexual activities with his stepdaughter over a 15-month period. Upon learning of this situation, the mother arranged for counseling with a clinical psychologist for both her husband and her daughter. During the course of a counseling session, the daughter revealed the sexual activity with her stepfather. The psychologist immediately reported this information to the appropriate child welfare agency. California law provides that "there is no privilege . . . [where] the patient is a child under the age of sixteen [and] the psychotherapist has reasonable cause to believe that the patient has been the victim of a crime and that disclosure of the communication is in the best interest of the child" (California Evidence Code, 1984, Sec. 1027). The father saw the clinical psychologist as well. A deputy from the sheriff's office spoke to the psychologist and indicated that a provision of the Child Abuse Reporting Act permitted the psychologist to relate to authorities the details of the psychotherapy session with the father, including his confession that he had indeed had sexual relations with his stepdaughter. When the psychologist was called to testify during the criminal trial of the father, the defendant's assertion of the psychotherapist-patient privilege was overruled.

On appeal, the California Supreme Court concluded that all that was necessary to comply with the reporting statute was the call to the child welfare agency immediately following the interview with the stepdaughter. No further action was necessary since the conversation with the father concerned the same incidents of child abuse mentioned by the stepdaughter. The obligation to report was complete once the initial disclosure took place (California Penal Code, 1984).

In explaining its rationale for the decision, the court stated:

We have recognized the contemporary value of the psychiatric profession, and its potential for the relief of emotional disturbances and of the inevitable tensions produced in our modern, complex society. . . . That value is bottomed on a confidential relationship; but the doctor can be of assistance only if the patient may freely relate his thoughts and actions, his fears and fantasies, his strengths and weaknesses, in a completely uninhibited manner. If the psychiatrist is compelled to go beyond an initial report to authorities regarding a suspected child abuse and must thereafter repeat details given to him by the adult patient in subsequent sessions, candor and integrity would require the doctor to advise the patient at the outset that he will violate his confidence and will inform law enforcement of their discussions. Under such circumstances it is impossible to conceive of any meaningful therapy. Ironically, in this case medical help was initially what this distraught family sought as a result of these tragic events. (*People v. Stritzinger*, 1983, pp. 437–438)

A concurring member of the court felt that the psychologist's conversation with the father would have to be considered privileged unless it could be shown that the patient had been made aware of the therapist's possible duty under the Child Abuse Reporting Act to testify against him.

COLORADO

Like many other states, Colorado covers psychiatrists within the physician–patient privilege, with all its exceptions, but gives certified psychologists broader protection (Colorado Revised Statutes, 1973); in addition, there is a special privilege for communications made by a client to a social worker (Colorado Revised Statutes, 1978). Part of the psychologist privilege explicitly includes group therapy. Despite the separate statutes, the Colorado Supreme Court has construed the physician and psychologist privileges as one:

The purpose of the psychologist–client privilege, as is obvious from the plain meaning of its statutory terms, is identical to that of the physician–patient privilege. These privileges, once they attach, prohibit not only testimonial disclosures in court, but also pretrial discovery of information within the scope of the privilege. (*Clark v. District Court*, 1983, p. 8)

In the *Clark* case, the plaintiff sought recovery against Clark and his employer, claiming among other things that Clark's long history of mental illness was known to his employer and that he should not have been hired as a manager of a bar. In the course of his employment, Clark had shot and killed the father of the plaintiff. In his response to the suit, Clark denied any liability and never raised his physical or mental condition as a defense. The plaintiff sought access to Clark's treatment records, and the trial court overruled an objection based on the various privileges. Recognizing the importance of the issues at stake, the Colorado Supreme Court found the trial judge's order immediately reviewable: "If Clark's treatment records are indeed protected from disclosure by statutory privileges, then the damage to him will occur upon their disclosure regardless of the ultimate outcome of any appeal from a final judgment (*Clark v. District Court*, 1983, p. 7).

The plaintiffs argued that the statutory privileges are qualified, meaning that the trial judge would balance one party's need for access against the other party's interest in confidentiality. The Colorado Supreme Court indicated that the legislature had not chosen that route. Rather, "once these privileges attach, therefore, the only basis for authorizing a disclosure of the confidential information is an express or implied waiver" (p. 9). Finding that Clark had not injected his physical or mental condition into the litigation, the court refused to find any implied waiver.

In another case, *Bond v. District Court* (1984), the plaintiffs were seeking recovery in a personal injury action for mental pain and suffering as well as for past and future psychiatric expenses. The trial court indicated that the privilege had been waived and refused to consider issuing any protective orders to limit the disclosure of materials that ordinarily would be privileged. Although agreeing that the privilege had indeed been waived, the Colorado Supreme Court indicated that the application for a protective order should be considered by the trial judge with appropriate balancing of the respective interests of the parties. Noting that the "privilege encourages and protects the person seeking treatment," the court asserted that

> this policy consideration is even more compelling in the therapist–patient relationship than in the physician–patient relationship. A physical ailment may be treated by a doctor whom the patient does not trust, but if a psychologist or psychiatrist does not have the patient's trust, the therapist cannot treat the patient. . . . The mental health therapist's ability to help his patient is completely dependent upon the patient's willingness and ability to talk freely. (*Bond v. District Court*, 1984, p. 38)

In remanding the matter back to the trial judge, the court acknowledged "the sensitive nature of the therapist–patient communications and the possible adverse effects of disclosure upon the course of therapy. . . . [The plaintiff's] interest in protection from or restrictions upon disclosure [is] particularly weighty" (p. 40). It suggested that the trial judge might review the records in private and then fashion an appropriate way to protect the interests of all concerned.

CONNECTICUT

One of the earliest statutes providing for a psychotherapist–patient privilege was enacted in Connecticut in 1961. At the time, Connecticut had no physician–patient privilege. The Group for the Advancement of Psychiatry, which initially had supported a model statute placing the relationship between the psychiatrist and patient on the same basis as that between the attorney and client, adopted the Connecticut statute as its model following a devastating critique by Professors Goldstein and Katz of Yale Law School (Slovenko, 1966).

Connecticut now has separate privilege statutes for psychologists and psychiatrists. The psychologist privilege is limited to those engaged in the practice of clinical psychology and applies to both civil and criminal cases. Where a court-ordered examination has been ordered, the privilege does not apply as long as the person being examined has been told that the communication would not be privileged. In addition, admission is limited to those issues involving the person's psychological condition. There is one remaining exception which is applicable only to civil proceedings. If an individual raises his psychological condition as an element of claim or defense, there is a qualified waiver of the privilege. It is waived if "the judge finds that it is more important to the interests of justice that the communications be disclosed than that the relationship between the person and psychologist be protected" (Connecticut General Statutes Annotated, 1984, Sec. 52-146c).

The psychiatrist privilege is more elaborate. The scope, for example,

> means all oral and written communications and records thereof relating to diagnosis or treatment of a patient's mental condition between the patient and his psychiatrist, or between a member of the patient's family and a psychiatrist, or between any of such persons and a person participating under the supervision of a psychiatrist in the accomplishment of the objectives of diagnosis and treatment, wherever made, including communications and records which occur in or are prepared at a mental health facility. (Connecticut General Statutes Annotated, Sec. 52-146c).

Disclosure is permitted without the patient's consent in certain limited situations. These include discussions among professionals as long as the disclosure is necessary for diagnosis or treatment, and the patient must be informed. The privilege also does not apply when the psychiatrist believes commitment is necessary or if it is determined that "there is substantial risk of imminent physical injury by the patient to himself or others." In addition, there is a limited fee-dispute exception as well as one for court-ordered examinations where the patient has been informed that communications would not be confidential. This applies to both criminal and civil proceedings. Finally, there is only a qualified privilege in civil proceedings similar to that provided for psychologists (Connecticut General Statutes Annotated, 1984, Sec. 52-146d–f).

The Connecticut Supreme Court has construed the psychiatrist–patient privilege to favor nondisclosure. In a murder prosecution, the state offered the testimony of its psychiatrist based on an examination of the defendant to refute a claim of insanity. The defendant objected because the examination had not been court ordered as provided for under the exceptions to the psychiatrist–patient privilege. The trial court admitted the testimony, but the supreme court reversed. The state attempted to argue an implied waiver because of the insanity defense, but the court noted that a "necessary element to waiver is the requisite knowledge of the right, and a waiver presupposes a full knowledge of an existing right or privilege and something done designedly or knowingly to relinquish it" (*State v. Toste*, 1979, p. 295). Without the waiver, the testimony could not be admitted.

In the same case, the state called a clinical psychologist who had examined the defendant on behalf of the defense. Agreeing with the majority of jurisdictions which have reached the question, the court concluded that

> where a psychiatric expert, whether psychiatrist or psychologist, is retained by a criminal defendant or by his counsel for the sole purpose of aiding the accused and his counsel in the preparation of his defense, the attorney–client privilege bars the state from calling the expert as a witness. (*State v. Toste*, 1979, p. 294)

There is a minority view, articulated by New York courts, that once a defendant places his mental condition in question by raising the insanity defense, the defendant also waives the attorney-client privilege.

In two recent cases, the Connecticut Supreme Court was faced with the question of whether the Confrontation Clause of the Bill of Rights overrode the state-created privilege. In the first case, the trial court refused to grant the defendant access to certain psychiatric and social agency records of the victim who testified at trial. The

supreme court noted that *in camera* inspection of the records by the court was appropriate to determine whether the records would be relevant evidence on the question of the ability of the witness to recollect or communicate. Without such a finding by the trial court, no disclosure was necessary and the right of confrontation was not denied (*State v. Storlazzi*, 1983). Refining this decision, the supreme court recently indicated that the trial court has the discretion to review psychiatric records *in camera*. If relevant material is not present in the records, they should be resealed. However, if relevant evidence is found, the witness must then be given the opportunity to decide whether to consent to the release of the material to the defendant or face having testimony stricken (*State v. Esposito*, 1984). If the victim-witness declined to waive the privilege following the *in camera* inspection, the prosecution could not go forward. This strong view of the Connecticut court is not followed by many of its sister courts in other states.

DELAWARE

By rule of the supreme court, a psychotherapist–patient privilege was adopted in Delaware in 1980. The privilege provision tracks the federal proposal but adds a specific exception for child abuse cases (Delaware Rule of Evidence, 1981). The Delaware Supreme Court has had an opportunity to construe the psychotherapist–patient privilege recently. In one case, two parents who had voluntarily placed their children with a social service agency sought visitation rights; the agency petitioned to terminate parental rights. The trial court admitted psychological records concerning the parents despite their claim of the privilege. The supreme court indicated that the petition for visitation interjected their emotional condition as an issue in the case and therefore the material was not privileged. In addition, the court concluded that any privilege must be a qualified one in a termination proceeding.

> When otherwise inaccessible and privileged information becomes pertinent to an issue vital to the future well-being of the child, the parent's right to privacy and confidentiality must yield. . . . Whenever one seeks to resist the termination of her parental rights over a child, the emotional health of such person is put in issue within the meaning of Rule 503. (*Betty J. B. v. Division of Social Services*, 1983, p. 531)

In a criminal case (*McKinney v. State*, 1983), a court-ordered examination was conducted on the defendant to determine present competency to stand trial. During trial, however, the state introduced the testimony of the clinical psychologist to show the defendant's consciousness of guilt concerning a murder. The trial court admitted the testimony, but the supreme court reversed. Under the court-ordered examination exception to the psychotherapist–patient privilege, the scope of communications is limited "to the particular purpose for which the examination is ordered unless the court orders otherwise" (p. 360). In this particular case, since the testimony had nothing to do with the purpose of the examination, the privilege did apply and the testimony should not have been admitted.

DISTRICT OF COLUMBIA

Congress adopted a physician–patient privilege in 1963 and then expanded it to cover psychologists plus other mental health professionals. For civil proceedings, the privilege is quite broad barring disclosure of

> any information, confidential in its nature, that he has acquired in attending a client in a professional capacity and that was necessary to enable him to act in that capacity, whether the information was obtained from the client or from his family or from the person or persons in charge of him. (District of Columbia Code, 1981)

One case concerned the interesting question of who possessed the privilege once the individual died. There was a dispute as to testamentary capacity and the statute stated that the legal representative is the successor of the decedent with regard to the privilege. The executor declined to waive the privilege but the heirs who had been excluded asserted their right to waive the privilege. After reviewing the state of the law, the court concluded that a literal interpretation of "legal representative" was inappropriate and that because the legislature had provided a procedure to challenge wills, it would not make sense to exclude the best evidence on the subject, namely the testimony of doctors who had treated the decedent (*In re Estate of Wilson*, 1980).

The privilege contains no exceptions such as one for the patient–litigant. In wrestling with this problem, one court indicated that in a product liability action in which the plaintiffs had placed their mental condition at issue, the privilege must be considered waived:

> The privilege was never intended, however, to be used as a trial tactic by which a party entitled to invoke it may control to his advantage the timing and circumstances of the release of information. . . . The court concludes that it would be an abuse of privilege to allow it to be used in such a manner which has no relation to the purposes for which it exists. (*Doe v. Eli Lilly & Co.*, 1983, pp. 128–129)

In criminal matters, the privilege is only a qualified one. The court is to determine if disclosure would be required in the interests of public justice when a defendant is charged with injuring another human being. In addition, the privilege is waived in any situation in which the insanity defense is raised (*White v. United States*, 1980).

FLORIDA

Two previous statutes providing for a psychiatrist–patient and psychologist–patient privilege were combined to establish one psychotherapist–patient privilege based on the proposed federal provision. Florida never had a separate physician–patient privilege (Florida Statutes, 1979). Most of the litigation concerning the privilege in recent years has involved family matters. In a series of cases involving divorce, the various Florida district courts of appeal have indicated

> that a parent, by seeking child custody in a dissolution proceeding, did not automatically thereby waive the psychiatrist–patient privilege. . . . [T]he testimony of a treating psychiatrist could not be compelled, but the court retained the authority to order psychiatric examination of a parent seeking custody because the mental health of a parent is a proper factor to be considered in a custody determination. (*Davidge v. Davidge*, 1984, p. 1052)

However, if a party puts his mental condition at issue, then the privilege disappears. A husband sought to set aside a prior settlement based on his mental condition at the time of the contract. At trial, the court did not allow the wife to call the psychiatrist who had treated both parties near the time of the contract based on the privilege. The appellate court reversed, noting that the husband could not put his mental condition at issue without waiving the privilege. Otherwise, he could present his side of the case and then foreclose the best evidence available as to his mental condition at the time of the contract — the testimony of the psychiatrist both parties had been seeing (*Davidge v. Davidge*, 1984).

In an adoption proceeding, the trial court had directed that records concerning the psychiatric treatment of the adoptive mother be disclosed. The appellate court concluded that although "the mental and physical health of a party seeking to adopt a child are relevant considerations[,] . . . that does not make the mental health of a person seeking to adopt an element of her claim or defense" (*Manner of Adoption of H.Y.T.*, 1983, p. 252). The trial court could require a court-appointed examination that would not be covered by the privilege, similar to the procedure advocated for dissolution proceedings, but could not invade the privilege. Proceedings involving child abuse, however, stand on another ground. By statute, the psychotherapist-patient privilege is specifically abrogated in situations "involving known or suspected child abuse or neglect" (Florida Statutes Annotated, 1984 Supp., Sec. 827.07). There is no balancing; the privilege simply does not apply (*E.H. v. State*, 1984).

The major case decided by the Florida Supreme Court concerning the psychotherapist-patient privilege involved an individual applying for admission to the Florida Bar Association. A question on the standard form requested information concerning treatment for "any form of insanity, emotional disturbance, nervous or mental disorder"; the applicant refused to fill out the question and asserted his psychotherapist-patient privilege. The court summarily rejected the claim, noting that by applying to the bar the applicant placed his mental and emotional fitness at issue and therefore any communications with psychiatrists were not privileged under the exception concerning "communications relevant to an issue of the mental or emotional condition of the patient in any proceeding in which he relies upon the condition as an element of his claim or defense" (*Florida Board of Bar Examiners re Applicant*, 1983, p. 77).

GEORGIA

A psychologist-patient privilege was adopted in 1951 placing communications "upon the same basis as those provided by law between attorney

and client" (Georgia Code, 1971, Sec. 84-3118). Special protection is afforded psychiatrists, as opposed to other physicians. The statute is quite simple, declaring "admissions and communications [between psychiatrists and patients] excluded from consideration of public policy." The physician-patient privilege contains an exception for proceedings in which the patient has placed his mental condition at issue, but the exception explicitly does not apply to psychiatrists (Georgia Code, 1971, Sec. 38-418).

The Georgia Supreme Court has given full force to the privilege. For example, in a divorce case in which custody was one of the issues, the husband sought to depose the wife's psychiatrist. The trial court sustained an objection based on the psychiatrist-patient privilege. Noting that the wife "went to the psychiatrist on her own volition for the purpose of gaining professional psychiatric assistance thus creating the requisite confidential relationship of psychiatrist and patient," the court upheld the privilege (*Kimble v. Kimble*, 1977). There is no discussion of how this might affect the obtaining of evidence for a proper custody determination. However, since the focus is on the creation of the confidential relationship, when a court appointed a psychiatrist to examine a parent, one might assume that such communications would not be covered by the privilege.

In another civil action, the plaintiff was seeking to recover damages for injuries of a mental and emotional nature. The appellate court held that psychiatric testimony concerning the plaintiff was inadmissible. "The existence of a 'voluntary' psychiatrist-patient relationship renders any testimony whatsoever by the psychiatrist excludable from evidence at the election of the patient" (*Wilson v. Bonner*, 1983, p. 142). This is perhaps the broadest application of the privilege imaginable. However, I wonder if a court would take such a broad view if crucial evidence would be excluded; in this case, the wrongful admission of the psychiatrist's testimony was considered harmless as plaintiff would have lost anyway.

In a criminal prosecution of a wife for the death of her husband, the defendant sought to call her psychiatrist to the stand to testify about joint counselling sessions that she and the victim had attended to seek assistance with their marital problems. The state asserted the psychiatrist-patient privilege. (Neither side raised the issue of the state's standing to do so, and the court declined to do so itself. However, it did observe that some jurisdictions indicate that the privilege is

personal to the patient or the patient's representative or the psychiatrist at death, whereas others
find that the trial court has an independent discretion to invoke the privilege.) The defendant
claimed that her presence at the sessions would
destroy the privilege between the decedent husband and the psychiatrist. In response, the court
noted "a strong public policy in favor of preserving
the confidentiality of psychiatric–patient confidences where a third party is present as a necessary or customary participant in the consultation
and treatment" (*Sims v. State*, 1984, p. 165). The
court concluded that both husband and wife were
necessary participants and that the communications to the psychiatrist by the victim-husband
were entitled to protection; the privilege survives
the husband's death. This is an odd decision. The
defendant had testified that some of her conduct
on the date of the murder was the direct result of
advice from the psychiatrist, and now the jury
was being deprived of this evidence. There is no
claim by the defendant of a constitutional deprivation, but it would not be difficult to fashion a
theory that withholding the psychiatrist's testimony might have deprived her of a fair trial.

HAWAII

The proposed federal rule served as a model for
Hawaii, which adopted a general physician–patient privilege that by definition includes psychiatrists and a special psychologist–client privilege
(Hawaii Revised Statutes, 1980 Special Rules
Pamphlet, Rules 504, 504.1, 1980). Both track the
proposed federal rule and have the standard
exceptions. Under prior Hawaii law, the patient
had a privilege to prevent the psychiatrist from
testifying but could be compelled to testify about
what he or she had indicated to the psychiatrist.
With the enactment of the rules, the privilege
covers the patient as well (*Doe II v. Roe II*, 1982).
In another context, the Hawaii Supreme Court
has indicated that the rules have full applicability to both civil and criminal proceedings (*State
v. Swier*, 1983).

IDAHO

There is a general statute covering confidential
relations and communications which has provisions for doctors, psychologists, certificated counsellors, or psychological examiners employed by a
school for the purpose of counselling students

(Idaho Code, 1979, Secs. 9-203.4, 9-203.6). There
is a separate statute for psychologists which
appears to be broader.

> A person licensed as a psychologist under
> the provisions of this act cannot, without
> the written consent of his client, be exam-
> ined in a civil or criminal action as to any
> information acquired in the course of his
> professional services in behalf of the client.
> The confidential relations and communica-
> tions between the psychologist and his cli-
> ent are on the same basis as those provided
> by law between an attorney and client, and
> nothing in this article shall be construed
> to require any such privileged communica-
> tion to be disclosed. (Idaho Code, 1979,
> Sec. 54-2314)

Although the physician–patient privilege has various exceptions of the common variety, the psychologist–client privilege appears to have none.
Unfortunately, there are no reported cases construing the psychologist–client privilege.

Prior to filing for divorce, a husband and wife
had been seeing a psychiatrist, together and separately. In the divorce proceeding, the issue of
custody of two daughters was raised, but the court
upheld the invocation of the privilege to prevent
the psychiatrist from testifying concerning his
evaluation of a parent. Unless there was some evidence of abuse or neglect — a statutory exception
to the privilege — the issue of custody was not sufficient to eliminate the privilege (*Barker v. Barker*,
1968). One might assume that if the court desired,
it could order an examination of the parties to
assist it in a custody decision. Such an evaluation
would not be privileged because the information
acquired was not for the purpose of treatment.

ILLINOIS

The Mental Health and Developmental Disabilities Confidentiality Act probably is the most
elaborate and comprehensive effort by a state to
protect communications between psychotherapists
and patients (Illinois Annotated Statutes, 1984).
As articulated in *Laurent v. Brelji* (1979), p. 931,
"to meet the avowed purpose of protecting the
confidentiality of the records and communications
of those receiving mental health services, the
Act is premised on a general prohibition against
the disclosure of such information except where
specifically provided for in the Act." The term
"therapist" under the act includes psychiatrists,

physicians, psychologists, social workers, or nurses providing services. It also includes any other person "not prohibited by law from providing such services or from holding himself out as a therapist if the recipient reasonably believes that such person is permitted to do so." Therefore, one court indicated that a marriage counsellor was covered by the statutory scheme. Consent to disclose may only be in writing and must include specific identification of the material to be disclosed, the consequence of a refusal to disclose, a fixed period for disclosure, and a right to revoke. Once disclosure takes place, the privilege does not end and redisclosure is prohibited. There are special provisions concerning disclosure for application of benefits, insurance services, funding and accreditation of facilities, and training and administrative review.

The key provision of the Act provides "in any civil, criminal, administrative, or legislative proceeding, or in any proceeding preliminary thereto, a recipient, and a therapist on behalf and in the interest of a recipient, has the privilege to refuse to disclose and to prevent the disclosure of the recipient's record or communications" (Illinois Annotated Statutes, ch. 91 1/2, Sec. 810). The exceptions are narrowly drawn. For example, the standard exception for the patient's introduction of a claim or defense concerning a mental condition is limited. Before disclosure is to be permitted, the trial court must hold an *in camera* proceeding and determine that the proffered evidence "is relevant, probative, not unduly prejudicial or inflammatory, and otherwise clearly admissible; that other satisfactory evidence is demonstrably unsatisfactory as evidence of the facts sought to be established by such evidence; and that disclosure is more important to the interests of substantial justice than protection from injury to the therapist-recipient relationship or to the recipient or other whom disclosure is likely to harm" (Illinois Annotated Statutes, ch. 91 1/2, Sec. 810). The only general exception is for the insanity defense in criminal proceedings. One's mental condition is not introduced into a proceeding merely by requesting damages for pain and suffering or by filing for divorce. Rather, a party would first have to testify as to a record or communication before that party's privilege would be at risk. With regard to court-ordered examinations, the court must determine that the recipient of services had been fully informed that the communications would not be confidential. Admissibility is also limited to the issues for which the examinations were ordered. There are further lim-

ited exceptions for homicide investigations, initiation of civil commitment, provision of emergency care, and for reporting of child abuse and neglect.

The statute also recognizes the possibility that a recipient might wish to waive the privilege, but that a therapist might feel it is not in that individual's best interest. In such a situation, the court can hold an *in camera* hearing to resolve the issue. In addition, at the suggestion of any party, the court is to conduct an *in camera* proceeding concerning the scope of the privilege. Finally, the court has broad authority to issue protective orders to preserve the confidentiality even when disclosure would be mandated under the Act.

Issues concerning the rights of defendants have given the courts the most difficulty in construing the act. In one case, there was a civil service discharge proceeding concerning an employee who allegedly had abused a patient at a mental health facility. The employee sought access to the records concerning the particular patient, and the facility superintendent refused to comply with a subpoena, claiming that the records were privileged. The Civil Service Commission asserted a right to review all relevant material and this included the patient's records. The court rejected this notion:

> The creation of a statutory privilege is a legislative balance between the encouragement and protection of confidential relationships and the interest of disclosure of relevant information before an investigatory body. The inquiry of whether given information is subject to disclosure does not end with the determination that it is relevant. Implicit in every testimonial privilege is the assumption that the privileged matter may indeed be highly probative of the issues in dispute. Despite any relevance, however, the promotion and protection of certain relationships is deemed to be of greater value than the unqualified disclosure of pertinent information incident to individual disputes.

Presumably, the patient in psychotherapeutic treatment reveals the most private and secret aspects of his mind and soul. To casually allow public disclosure of such would desecrate any notion of an individual's right to privacy. At the same time, confidentiality is essential to the treatment process itself, which can be truly effective only when there is complete candor and revelation by the patient. Finally, confidentiality provides proper assurances and inducement for persons who need treatment to seek it. (*Laurent v. Brelji*, 1979, p. 931)

The court found it possible to construe the patient–litigant exception to be broader than actions that involve the patient. Because the records would be disclosed if the patient had filed a civil action against the employee, the court reasoned that the record should be disclosed in an administrative proceeding where the employee could lose his job.

> Our conclusion that the records of L. S. are subject to disclosure in no manner implies that a person, merely by presenting himself as a witness, must run the risk of having his entire mental history drug out and exposed before a public hearing for the ostensible purpose of questioning his perceptive abilities. . . . We merely hold that in defending against the accusations of this witness there is no discernible distinction between the proceeding here and a personal action by the recipient based on the same allegations. (*Laurent v. Brelji*, 1979, pp. 932–933)

The court went on to note that a court would have to hold an *in camera* proceeding to determine what information would be appropriate for the administrative hearing, and the employee would have to show a "compelling need" for the record. By so construing the statute to permit the possibility of disclosure, the court avoided a basic due process question: Would a proceeding in which the employee could lose his job have been fundamentally fair without access to at least part of the records of the key witness?

The Illinois appellate courts have wrestled with this special problem facing criminal defendants when they try to obtain arguably privileged records concerning witnesses against them. In one case (*People v. Phipps*, 1981), the defendant was charged with the maltreatment of and cruelty to mentally retarded persons in a state facility. He sought the records of the witnesses against him. The court was faced with pronouncements of the U.S. Supreme Court, which held that the right of confrontation entitled a defendant to question a witness concerning matters that were privileged under that jurisdiction's statutory scheme. The right of confrontation was referred to as "paramount." Balancing the right of confrontation with the strict Illinois privilege, the appellate court found that when "a statutory evidentiary privilege comes in direct conflict with a defendant's constitutional rights of confrontation and due process, we hold that the former must give way so that the fundamental protections of our criminal justice

system will not be abrogated" (*People v. Phipps*, 1981, p. 730). Subpoenas were to be issued to obtain the records; upon invocation of privilege, the trial court was to hold an *in camera* proceeding with the attorneys for the state and defendant present to determine which information would be relevant and material.

In a subsequent case (*People v. Dace*, 1983), the key witness against the defendant (charged with burglary) was an alleged codefendant. Her testimony was the only evidence of the defendant's participation. The defendant knew that she had been committed to a mental hospital and sought the records of her hospitalization. The trial court, at the urging of the state, ruled that the defendant had not demonstrated the relevance and materiality of the commitment records. However, as the appellate court noted, without seeing the records it would be difficult, if not impossible, to make the requisite showing:

> The court had no information as to her diagnosis, treatment or release. The trial court could not reasonably conclude, from the absence of this information, that the mental health history of the witness was irrelevant and immaterial. Confronted with articulable evidence that raises a reasonable inquiry of a witness's mental health history, a court should permit a defendant to discover that history. If either the witness or the therapist wish to invoke the privilege, the trial court should conduct an in camera hearing in the presence of counsel for the State and the defendant, to determine which information would be relevant and material to the witness's credibility. This approach balances a defendant's sixth and fourteenth amendment rights with a witness's right to confidentiality of his mental health records. (*People v. Dace*, 1983, p. 1035)

Having an *in camera* hearing protects the person asserting the privilege to some extent. Because courts uniformly have indicated that an individual's mental condition is relevant to the question of credibility, it is hard to imagine how a privilege could be made absolute when faced with the demands of the confrontation clause. The Illinois courts have required some showing prior to subpoenaing records and witnesses to avoid a fishing expedition. However, where the witness for the state has been committed because of mental illness or has been seeing a psychiatrist on a regular basis, it is likely that the privilege cannot be maintained in the face of a defendant's constitutional demands.

INDIANA

There is a special privilege for certified psychologists with limited exceptions (Indiana Code, 1976, Sec. 25-33-1-17). Psychiatrists must rely on the statutorily strong physician–patient privilege which indicates that physicians are not competent witnesses (Indiana Code, 1976, Sec. 34-1-14-5). There is also an exception for cases involving possible child abuse (*Hunter v. State*, 1977). There has been almost no case law of any significance interpreting either privilege.

IOWA

The focus of the Iowa statute is the giving of testimony. There is no broad privilege as to communications in general, but only as to what is said in court or in pretrial depositions. Initially, the statute did not include psychologists. However, following court rulings that clinical psychologists are not barred from testifying by the physician–patient privilege (*State in Interest of O'Neal*, 1981), nor by the counsellor–client privilege (*In re Marriage of Ganmer*, 1981), the statute was amended to include all mental health professionals (Iowa Code, 1983). The standard patient-litigant exception applies. The Iowa Supreme Court has indicated that court-ordered examinations are not covered by the privilege:

> Three elements must be established in order for the privilege to be applicable: the relationship of doctor-patient; the acquisition of the information or knowledge during this relationship; and the necessity of the information to enable the physician to treat the patient skillfully. . . . We have held that the third requirement of the privilege is lacking in court-ordered evaluations: the communication is not for the purpose of treatment, but to evaluate the mental condition for the benefit of the court. (*Snethen v. State*, 1981, pp. 14–15)

While investigating possible Medicaid fraud, a county attorney subpoenaed the records of a clinic that provided psychological services. The subpoena did not seek diagnostic information, but the requested records contained such information. Upon failing to turn over the material, the custodian was held in contempt; the supreme court

affirmed. Although acknowledging the salutary purpose of a privilege, the court repeated its earlier comments that the Iowa statute is a limited testimonial privilege. The clinic also asserted a claim based on the constitutional right of privacy. This too was unavailing:

> We need not here decide the precise reach of the patient's constitutional privacy right. Whatever that reach, the privacy interest must be balanced against society's interest in securing information vital to the fair and effective administration of criminal justice. . . . [Investigation of Medicaid fraud] is a specific application of the general principle that society has a strong interest in allowing official investigators of criminal activity broad authority to conduct thorough investigations. (*Chidester v. Needles*, 1984, p. 853)

However, the court noted that the subpoenaed records would be confidential until charges were filed and then the trial court could issue appropriate protective orders.

KANSAS

Psychiatrists are covered solely through the standard physician–patient privilege with all its exceptions (Kansas Statutes, 1980, Sec. 60-427). Certified psychologists have a privilege analogous to the attorney–client privilege (Kansas Statutes, 1980, Sec. 74-5323). The case law is quite limited. In criminal cases, the physician privilege does not apply to felony cases (*State v. Parson*, 1979).

Certain statutes concerned with children waive the physician–patient privilege and the psychologist–client privilege. For example, a Kansas appellate court indicated that the child protection act waived the privilege in a parental severance proceeding. The court refused to permit the natural parent, who was the subject of the proceeding, to claim the privilege. Only the guardian ad litem would have that power (*In the Interest of Zappa*, 1981). For divorce cases, the privileges are deemed waived in all matters of child custody, with the exception of court-ordered marital counselling (Kansas Statutes, 1980, Sec. 60-1610).

KENTUCKY

The psychiatrist–patient privilege is modelled on the proposed federal statute (Kentucky Revised Statutes, 1983, Sec. 421.215), whereas the psychologist–client privilege is separate and is based on the attorney–client relationship (Kentucky Revised Statutes, 1983, Sec. 319.111). The Kentucky courts have construed the privileges broadly and have noted that they are absolute in the absence of specific statutory or recognized exceptions. For example, a community mental health center did not have to turn over records concerning the defendant in a criminal case for the purpose of preparation of the presentence investigation report. No exception was applicable and therefore the privilege applied (*Southern Bluegrass MHMR v. Angelucci*, 1980).

However, the Kentucky courts have carved out an exception for custody matters based on the patient-litigation provision of the privilege statute. Holding that custody specifically placed the mental condition of family members at issue, a court indicated that a parent had waived the privilege by participating in the litigation (*Atwood v. Atwood*, 1976). Similarly, in a case concerned with termination of parental rights, when the mother indicated she had been under the care of a psychiatrist but was still able to provide for her children, the court found that she had placed her mental condition at issue and was precluded from asserting the privilege (*Allen v. Department for Human Resources*, 1976). Where children are not at issue, the privilege will hold. For example, an ex-husband sought all information concerning the treatment of his former wife who was not a party to the particular action. Because her mental condition was not in issue or an element of claim or defense, there was no exception to the privilege. The court also noted that the privilege extended to those who participate in diagnosis or treatment under the supervision of a psychiatrist (*Amburgey v. Central Kentucky Regional Mental Health Board*, 1983).

LOUISIANA

There is a broad statute covering communications between a health care provider and the patient. Within its ambit are psychiatrists, nurses, psychologists, and other professionals. The patient has a privilege

> to refuse to disclose and to prevent a health care provider from disclosing any communication, wherever made, relating to any fact, statement, or opinion which was necessary to enable that health care provider or

> any other health care provider to diagnose, treat, prescribe, or act for the patient. (Louisiana Revised Statutes, 1983 Supp., Sec. 13.3734)

The statutory exceptions are the standard ones.

The privilege applies to both criminal and civil actions. However, when a defendant claims an insanity defense, this places the mental condition at issue and the privilege does not apply (*State v. Aucoin*, 1978). The privilege also does not apply when there is a court-appointed psychiatrist (*State v. Felde*, 1982).

There is a substantial body of case law concerning divorce and custody matters. The crucial issue appears to be which party instigated the action. For example, where the father filed a custody action, the mother was protected by the privilege from having to produce hospital records. A child custody case is not a statutory exception (*Wing v. Wing*, 1980). In a divorce action brought by a wife, the court properly refused to permit her to depose her husband's psychiatrist. The patient-litigant exception in the statute for actions to recover damages was not applicable (*Vincent v. LeMaire*, 1979). In a recent case, a father sought to have a prior custody order amended to provide for joint custody. In opposing the application, the mother subpoenaed hospital records concerning the father. The court first indicated that the father's physical and mental condition were essential elements to his action for custody. Therefore, he had waived the privilege. In addition, the appellate court noted that the civil code provision concerned with joint custody provided for consideration of the mental and physical health of the parties. Therefore, any action concerned with joint custody automatically interjected the parties' mental condition into question (*Dawes v. Dawes*, 1984).

MAINE

Two previously existing one-sentence statutes providing a privilege for psychologists and psychiatrists were replaced by adoption of a rule similar to the proposed federal psychotherapist–patient privilege; however, Maine chose to include all physicians (Maine Revised Statutes, 1978). In a criminal case under the previous privilege statutes, the trial court was faced with a situation where the defendant asserted the insanity defense but then claimed the privilege to prevent a psychologist and two psychiatrists, who had examined the defendant subsequent to the crime, from testifying. The Maine Supreme Judicial Court agreed with the trial judge that the privileges were inapplicable. In evaluating the claim of privilege, the court carefully weighed the interests at stake:

> The reason motivating the Legislature to establish either the psychologist–patient privilege or the psychiatrist–patient privilege obviously was to create an atmosphere of confidence between the parties and to encourage patients to communicate freely with these people for the purpose of securing a proper diagnosis of their condition. Such public policy would be so promoted with the legal assurance that any information the patients did pass on which might result in humiliation, embarrassment or disgrace to them may not be disclosed, but will remain confidential.
>
> On the other hand, the public interest in ascertaining the true condition of persons accused of crime who seek to avoid legal responsibility for their criminal activity by reason of their mental deficiencies is very strong. If a defendant is permitted to escape punishment for his criminal acts on the basis of expert testimony tending to establish that his behavior was the product of mental disease or defect, and the State may not introduce impeaching testimony of other experts who have examined him, on the ground that the privilege prevents the disclosure of such evidence, then the cause of justice would be brought into extreme ridicule. . . .
>
> Furthermore, where, as here, the patient at his trial, first fully discloses the evidence of his affliction which he could have kept secret by the exercise of the privilege, it is only reasonable to believe that the Legislature viewed such revealment by the patient as tantamount to an implied waiver of the privilege within the intendment of the legislation. Once the evidence of his mental condition has been fully aired at the instigation of the patient–defendant, there is no need to protect further disclosures by other psychologist or psychiatrist witnesses called by the State. Any other rule would simply be an unreasonable and unnecessary obstruction to public justice. (*State v. Lewisohn*, 1977, p. 1211)

Under the current rule, the result should be the same.

MARYLAND

Communications between patients and both psychiatrists or psychologists are covered by the Maryland privilege statute. Psychiatrists are defined only to include a doctor "who devotes a substantial proportion of his time to the practice of psychiatry." Under the statute, where the patient is incompetent to assert the privilege, the court is to appoint a guardian. The exceptions provided for under the statute are the standard ones and apply to both civil or criminal proceedings (Maryland Courts, 1983). One interesting Maryland case concerned a *Tarasoff* situation. The court indicated that a psychiatric team was not liable to the plaintiff for failure to warn of an individual's violent condition because had they done so, it would have been a violation of the psychotherapist–patient privilege (*Shaw v. Glickman*, 1980). The relatively unique provision providing for the appointment of a guardian for somebody who is incompetent to assert the privilege has particular applicability in custody situations. Parents are not given the authority to assert or waive the privilege (*Nagle v. Hooks*, 1983).

The difficult situation that has faced Maryland courts concerns the limits of cross-examination in criminal cases where a key witness of the state has a background of psychiatric problems.

> The right to discredit an accuser being one of constitutional dimension can be but limitedly circumscribed. It appears that only to the extent that the examination strays from extracting from a witness that which discredits the credibility of his testimony, and embarks upon an effort rather to humiliate his person, that the duty to protect at the other end of the spectrum arises. (*Reese v. State*, 1983, p. 496)

Sensitive to the effect cross-examination could have on a particular witness, the appellate court noted that the

> inquiry must be carefully limited to that which is relevant to credibility. The trial judge's duty to which we have alluded is to quickly curtail lapses from that limitation, the effect of which may be merely to annoy, harass, or humiliate. The stress factor also may be tested by proper cross-examination of relevant facts but may not be pressed by emotional tangents solely geared to seek a breaking point. The balance in permitting

the exposure of credibility gaps and protecting an unstable mentality from improper pressure is a delicate one. (*Reese v. State*, 1983, p. 496)

MASSACHUSETTS

The statute adopting a psychotherapist–patient privilege is more limited than most. In order for a psychologist to be within the coverage of the statute, the individual must have a doctoral degree in the field of psychology (Massachusetts Annotated Laws, 1983 Supp.). This restriction has been the subject of several court cases, and communications have been declared unprivileged because of the lack of the proper credentials. A staff psychologist at a community health center testified as to conversations he had with the defendant following an alleged murder. The defendant met with the psychologist that evening, and the next day the psychologist arranged for the admission of the defendant into treatment following an overdose of antihistamine pills. However, the claim of privilege was rejected. The staff member was not licensed to practice psychiatry or psychology and did not have a doctorate, although he was educated in the field and was employed as a staff psychologist. Noting that the psychotherapist–patient privilege had not been recognized at common law, the Massachusetts Supreme Judicial Court refused to extend it beyond the limits set in the statute. As an alternative position, the defendant claimed that the staff psychologist was an agent for the psychiatrist who worked at the center. Referring to the statute, the court looked at the definition of "patient" and held that there had to be some confidential relationship between the patient and credentialed psychotherapist before the privilege could be established (*Commonwealth v. Mandeville*, 1982).

Massachusetts does not have the standard patient-litigant exception. Rather, a qualified privilege is created and the trial judge must consider whether "it is more important to the interests of justice that the communication be disclosed than that the relationship between patient and psychotherapist be protected." There also is a special exception for child custody cases. If "upon a hearing in chambers, the judge, in the exercise of his discretion, determines that the psychotherapist has evidence bearing significantly on the patient's ability to provide suitable custody, and that it is more important to the welfare of the child that

the communication be disclosed than that the relationship between patient and psychotherapist be protected" (*Petition of Catholic Charitable Bureau*, 1984, p. 869), the privilege is abrogated. Construing the statute, the court held that the exception did not apply to an adoption proceeding.

MICHIGAN

Separate statutes exist for the licensed psychologist and the psychiatrist. The psychologist and an individual under supervision "shall not be compelled to disclose confidential information acquired from an individual consulting the psychologist in his or her professional capacity and which information is necessary to enable the psychologist to render services" (Michigan Compiled Laws, 1980). No exceptions are provided in the statute. Psychiatrists must rely on the standard physician–patient privilege (Michigan Compiled Laws, 1968, Sec. 600-2157). Neither privilege is applicable in matters involving intentional injury to children (Michigan Compiled Laws, 1968, Sec. 722-574). There are few cases interpreting these statutes. In a criminal appeal, the defendant asserted that a child psychologist's testimony concerning his treatment of the defendant's son should have been inadmissible under the psychologist–patient privilege statute. The court rejected the argument on procedural grounds, but then considered the merits.

> The purpose of the privilege statute is to protect the confidential nature of the psychologist–patient relationship. . . . Defendant would assert the privilege in this case not to preserve the confidentiality of the child's statements to the psychologist, but to exclude potentially harmful testimony in a murder trial. Even assuming that defendant was the child's guardian, we conclude that defendant was not entitled to assert the statutory privilege in this case. (*People v. Lobaito*, 1984, pp. 240–241)

In another criminal case, a psychiatrist examined the defendant at the prosecutor's request shortly after arrest. The defendant was informed that information would be released to the prosecutor for use in court. The court held that no privilege existed because the communications were not for the purpose of treatment (*People v. Boucher*, 1983).

MINNESOTA

In one omnibus statute, Minnesota has created a series of privileges, including a licensed physician privilege as well as a psychologist–client privilege. The statute itself does not contain exceptions, but the courts have construed the privileges to provide for the standard ones. (Minnesota Statutes, 1984, Sec. 595.02). For example, a court noted that the only way an adverse party can force pretrial discovery of testimony relating to a patient's mental condition is for the patient to place his health in issue, thus waiving the privilege (*Wenninger v. Muesing*, 1976). In a commitment hearing, there was an objection to the report by a court-appointed psychiatrist. The court held that because the examination was provided for in the commitment statute and that the examination itself was not for the purpose of diagnosis or treatment, the privilege did not apply (*In the Matter of Skarsten*, 1984). In a criminal case, the defendant's sole defense against a charge of false imprisonment was that he was attempting to prevent the complainant from committing suicide. As a result, the court directed that prior psychiatric records of the victim be disclosed. To sustain the privilege would mean denial of the defendant's constitutional right of confrontation (*State v. Hembd*, 1975).

Recently, the Minnesota Supreme Court had occasion to wrestle with the conflict between the privilege statute and a special statutory scheme concerning the reporting of child abuse. A defendant was charged with sexual contact with two minors. Pending trial, he voluntarily entered therapy, including one-on-one counselling and group therapy sessions. The state moved for discovery and disclosure of the records of the psychotherapy. These communications clearly were covered by the privilege statute. However, Minnesota has a specific statute concerned with child abuse which provides in part that "no evidence regarding the child's injuries shall be excluded in any proceeding arising out of the alleged neglect or physical or sexual abuse" (Minnesota Statutes, 1984, Sec. 626.556). The question facing the Minnesota Supreme Court was the extent of the exception to the privilege:

> The legislature may well have decided that the need to discover incidents of child abuse and neglect outweighs the policies behind the medical privilege. Once abuse is discovered, however, the statute should not be construed, nor can the legislature have in-

tended it to be construed, to permit total elimination of this important privilege. The central purpose of the child abuse reporting statutes is the protection of children, not the punishment of those who mistreat them . . . . This policy, which recognizes that the child may return to the same home environment in which the maltreatment occurred, is best effectuated by continued encouragement for child abusers to seek rehabilitative treatment. . . .

> We hold that the medical privilege is abrogated only to the extent that it would permit evidentiary use of the information required to be contained in the maltreatment report — the identity of the child, the identity of the parent, guardian, or other person responsible for the child's care, the nature and extent of the child's injuries, and the name and address of the reporter. (*State v. Andring*, 1984, pp. 132–133)

The remaining issue facing the court was whether communications at group therapy sessions were covered by the privilege. Standard privilege law would provide that if third parties heard the communications, the privilege would not exist. However, as the court noted:

> participants in group psychotherapy sessions are not casual third persons who are strangers to the psychiatrist/psychologist/nurse-patient relationship. Rather, every participant has such a relationship with the attending professional, and, in the group therapy setting, the participants actually become part of the diagnostic and therapeutic process for co-participants. (*State v. Andring*, 1984, p. 133)

The court observed that group therapy is cost-effective in that several individuals could be treated by one psychotherapist and, furthermore, that the group setting encourages some persons to discuss matters once they hear others doing so.

> Because the confidentiality of communications made during group therapy is essential in maintaining its effectiveness as a therapeutic tool, . . . we hold that the scope of the physician–patient/medical privilege extends to include confidential group psychotherapy sessions where such sessions are an integral and necessary part of a patient's diagnosis and treatment. (*State v. Andring*, 1984, p. 134)

This sensitive balancing of the interests at stake by the Minnesota Supreme Court is a model of proper analysis in the privilege area.

In a subsequent case, the court was confronted with the situation where law enforcement authorities first found out about criminal sexual conduct through the operation of the child abuse reporting statute. During the course of therapy, the defendant revealed to the therapist that he had abused the 4-year-old niece of a neighbor. This information was in turn reported by the clinic staff to the proper authorities. The court held that the limited disclosure of the clinic staff was authorized by the special child abuse statute and therefore there was no violation of the defendant's privilege. "Information which is sheltered by the statutory medical privilege loses its privileged status to the extent its disclosure is authorized by the Child Abuse Reporting Act" (State v. Odenbrett, 1984, p. 268).

MISSISSIPPI

Separate statutes concern psychologists and psychiatrists. The psychologist statute contains no exceptions and has a phrase common to most such statutes providing "nor shall a psychologist's secretary, stenographer, or clerk be examined without the consent of his employer concerning any fact, the knowledge of which he has acquired in such capacity" (Mississippi Code, 1973). Psychiatrists are covered by the standard physician–patient privilege statute. A patient-litigant exception became effective in 1983; filing a lawsuit against a physician "shall constitute a waiver of the medical privilege and any medical information relevant to the allegation upon which the cause of action or claim is based shall be disclosed upon the request of the defendant" (Mississippi Code, 1984 Supp.).

MISSOURI

Separate privileges exist for psychologists (Missouri Annotated Statutes, 1983, Sec. 337.055) and physicians (Missouri Annotated Statutes, 1983, Sec. 491.060). Although the statutes contain no exceptions, the Missouri courts have applied the standard ones. The privileges apply in both criminal and civil cases (Gonzenbach v. Ruddy, 1982) and the courts are not hesitant to apply the privilege in appropriate situations. For example, by simply

seeking custody of his children, a husband did not place his mental health at issue and did not waive his physician–patient privilege as to the contents of his medical records (Husgen v. Stussie, 1981); however, the privilege did not cover the name of the doctor nor the time and place of treatment. A police doctor's opinion as to the mental state of a policeman was inadmissible since the officer had consulted the doctor for treatment of depression and anxiety and thus the situation came within the privilege (Jones v. Sayad, 1983). Turning over medical records to an insurer in order to obtain payments did not constitute an implied waiver of the physician–patient privilege because there was no clear unequivocal act amounting to waiver (State v. Eberwein, 1983).

Like other states, Missouri has adopted a special child abuse reporting statute. By its express terms, the privileges covering psychotherapists are abrogated:

> Any legally recognized privileged communication, except that between attorney and client, shall not apply to situations involving known or suspected child abuse or neglect and shall not constitute grounds for failure to report as required or permitted . . . or to give or accept evidence in any judicial proceeding relating to child abuse or neglect. (Missouri Annotated Statutes, 1983, Section 210.140)

A defendant consulted a psychologist concerning sexual contact with a foster child. The psychologist informed the family that she would have to report any suspected abuse. Counselling ensued and the defendant sought to bar the psychologist's testimony at his criminal trial for deviate sexual assault. The Missouri appellate court indicated that even absent the warning given by the psychologist, the psychologist–client privilege would not apply because of the child abuse reporting statute. The court made no attempt to distinguish child abuse and neglect proceedings from criminal trials, but held that the privilege was totally abrogated.

> The contention that these statutes are intended for child protection and not as tools for criminal prosecution so as to prevent statements given in such course for use as confessions also misreads the legislative policy. It may be that the predecessor enactments — as well as the Model Act and

the federal prototype — served a more pristinely sociological purpose: to report incidents of child abuse and to provide for prevention of recurrence by therapy. To those features the present law adds the possibility of punishment. (*State v. Brydon*, 1981, p. 451)

MONTANA

An early doctor–patient privilege was enacted by Montana in 1867. The basic statutory provision remains the same: "A licensed physician or surgeon cannot, without the consent of his patient, be examined in a civil action as to any information acquired in attending the patient which was necessary to enable him to prescribe or act for the patient" (Montana Code, 1983, Sec. 26-1-805). In addition, there is a psychologist–client privilege of the attorney–client variety (Montana Code, 1983, Sec. 23-1-807). However, there is a more recent statutory scheme concerning the confidentiality of health care information that would appear to include both psychiatrists and psychologists as well as other mental health professionals within its coverage.

Confidential health care information is not subject to compulsory legal process in any type of proceeding, including any pretrial or other preliminary proceedings, and a person or his authorized representative may refuse to disclose and may prevent a witness from disclosing confidential health care information in any proceeding. (Montana Code, 1983, Sec. 50-16-314)

There is a patient-litigant exception as well as one for court-ordered examinations. By its terms, this provision applies to both criminal and civil cases. It is unclear how the various provisions will be harmonized. No privilege applies in child dependency and neglect proceedings (Montana Code, 1983, Sec. 41-3-404).

There is no statutory exception for civil commitment hearings. However, when faced with the issue, the Supreme Court of Montana judicially created one:

Indeed, to uphold the assertion of the privilege in commitment proceedings would be to frustrate the state interests involved in the commitment procedure, rendering a patient's true mental condition incapable of proof. The sole persons qualified to render

an educated psychological or medical opinion as to the mental condition of a patient and its actual and potential manifestations are those psychologists and psychiatrists who have been engaged in evaluation and treatment of that patient. Neither judges nor administrative personnel are as qualified as psychologists and psychiatrists to render judgments concerning a patient's mental condition. . . . We conclude that mental health professionals on the hospital staff qualify as "neutral factfinders." Accordingly, we recognize an exception to the privilege in cases such as the instant one. (*Matter of Sonsteng*, 1977, p. 1154)

In a criminal case, a state psychiatrist had examined the defendant and testified on rebuttal to refute certain testimony by a defense expert concerning the mental illness of the defendant. There was an objection to the testimony based on a special statute which provides that a statement made during an examination or treatment would only be admissible when the defendant's mental condition was in issue (Montana Code, 1983, Sec. 46-14-401). In this particular case, there was no insanity defense. However, an expert for the defendant had testified concerning treatment programs and diagnosis. According to the court, this placed the defendant's mental condition at issue (*State v. Clark*, 1984).

NEBRASKA

Adapting the proposed federal rule to its needs, the Nebraska legislature adopted a broad privilege that includes all doctors as well as licensed or certified psychologists. In addition to the standard exceptions, one was added "regarding injuries to children, incompetents, or disabled persons" for neglect and abuse proceedings "or in any criminal prosecution involving injury to any such person or the willful failure to report any such injuries" (Nebraska Revised Statutes, 1979). In a case concerned with the placement of a minor with the Welfare Department, the court determined that the mental condition of the parents was an issue within the child injury exception to the privilege and admitted the testimony of the parents' treating psychiatrists (*In re Interest of Spradlin*, 1982). Mere testimony mentioning the fact of treatment does not waive the privilege; a waiver must be "clear, voluntary, and intentional" (*Branch v. Wilkinson*, 1977).

NEVADA

Using the proposed federal psychotherapist–patient privilege proposal as a guide, the Nevada legislature broadened it to include all doctors, psychologists, psychiatric social workers, or persons under their guidance, direction, and control. The exceptions follow the standard model with the addition of one to cover persons who might use the privilege to shield them from prosecution for procuring drugs (Nevada Revised Statutes, 1981). The only reported case construing the privilege concerned a situation where a defendant in a criminal case had been the subject of a court-ordered examination for the purpose of sentencing following a guilty plea. However, the guilty plea was withdrawn, and at trial, the prosecutor impeached the defendant with statements made to the psychiatrist during that examination. The Nevada Supreme Court reversed the conviction, noting that "a subject being examined by a court-appointed physician should feel free in such a clinical climate to discuss all the facts relevant to the examination without the guarded fear that the statements may be later used against him. Fair play dictates nothing less" (*Esquivel v. State*, 1980, p. 587). The exception to the privilege did not apply because the questioning had nothing to do with the purpose of the court-ordered examination.

NEW HAMPSHIRE

Parallel statutes exist in New Hampshire placing physician–patient and psychologist–client communications on the same basis as that between attorney and client (New Hampshire Revised Statutes, 1981). In considering the privileges, the New Hampshire Supreme Court seems to apply an analysis based on whether or not the privileged information would be essential for a fair trial. If yes, the privilege would yield. For example, a defendant was not allowed to impeach a state's witness testimony by a comment made to a psychiatric nurse. The court noted that the privileged information was not essential (*State v. Thresher*, 1982). However, in a situation where access to certain privileged information was necessary to cross-examine a state witness, the supreme court indicated that the privilege would be abrogated. However, the trial court was to hold an *in camera* proceeding with counsel to determine which materials should be disclosed (*State v. Farrow*, 1976).

In commitment proceedings, the supreme court seems quite willing to find it essential to void the privileges (*In re Field*, 1980). Similarly, in a neglect proceeding, the testimony of the therapist and physician at a mental health clinic concerning their counselling of the parents was essential evidence and therefore not privileged (*In re Brenda H.*, 1979).

NEW JERSEY

The psychologist–client privilege is of the attorney–client variety (New Jersey Statutes, 1983 Supp., Sec. 45-14B-28) and includes "confidential relations and communications between and among a licensed practicing psychologist and individuals, couples, families, or groups in the course of the practice of psychology." Psychiatrists are covered by the physician–patient privilege. In order to be asserted, the judge must find that the communication was confidential, that the patient or physician reasonably believed the communication necessary or helpful for diagnosis or treatment, that the witness is the holder of the privilege or a proper person who received the information, and finally, that the claimant is the holder of the privilege (New Jersey Statutes, 1976). There is also an extremely broad marriage counsellor privilege (New Jersey Statutes, 1983 Supp., Sec. 45-8B-29).

There are few appellate court decisions interpreting the New Jersey statutes. In one case, concerning statements made by an alleged juvenile delinquent at group sessions in an institution, the appellate court noted that the psychologist–client privilege would not apply because the individual leading the sessions was not a licensed psychologist. However, because there was an assurance of confidentiality and failure to cooperate entailed sanctions, the court concluded that it would be fundamentally unfair to allow the prosecutor to use the statements made (*In re J.P.B.*, 1976). The broad marriage counsellor privilege has caused some lower courts considerable difficulty in custody matters. One trial court went so far as to hold the privilege violative of the constitutional right of a child to have a fair determination concerning the custodial arrangement. Without abrogating the privilege, material evidence relevant to the determination of the child's best interest was impossible. There is no reported appeal (*M. v. K.*, 1982).

NEW MEXICO

The proposed federal psychotherapist privilege was adopted by New Mexico in toto (New Mexico Statutes, 1978). The New Mexico Court of Appeals has construed the privilege narrowly. A letter written by a defendant while in jail to the psychiatrist who had previously conducted an evaluation of his mental condition was not privileged because the psychiatrist had been acting under court order (State v. Milton, 1974). Similarly, the court found that to the extent that a psychologist's testimony concerning a mother's mental condition was based on a court-ordered examination, the privilege could not apply in the parental termination hearing (State Health and Social Service Department v. Smith, 1979).

In a more recent case, the court first determined that a mother had placed her mental condition at issue in opposing the termination of her parental rights. Therefore, she could not use the privilege to prevent the testimony of two psychologists concerning her "chronic, inadequate personality which was unlikely to change." Narrowly construing the definition of "confidential," the court concluded that no confidential communications with the psychologists had been disclosed by their testimony. Analyzing the situation, the court gave its theory of the privilege:

> Communications between psychotherapists and patients are not ipso facto confidential. To be confidential, two conditions must be present: [1] the patient "intended" the communications to be undisclosed; and [2] that non-disclosure would further the interest of the patient.
> A communication includes: [1] verbal communication of patient to psychotherapist; [2] information or knowledge gained by observation and personal examination of the patient; [3] inferences and conclusions drawn thereform; and [4] exhibiting the body or any part thereof to the psychotherapist for an opinion, examination or diagnosis....
> No objective standard exists to determine a person's state of mind. It is not sufficient for a patient to say that in the patient's mind the communications were confidential and furthered her own interest. It must be manifested in some fashion with words or words and conduct which lead a psychotherapist to understand or believe that the information obtained was intended to be confidential.

The purpose of this rule is to encourage persons who need medical consultation, examination or interview to seek the advice and opinion of a psychotherapist without fear of betrayal. Fear of betrayal, which is a state of mind, must induce a person to communicate this thought to the psychotherapist who in turn will understand the thought conveyed. During consultation, examination or interview, a psychotherapist may inquire about confidentiality but is under no duty to do so. The psychotherapist is ordinarily neutral on this issue until non-disclosure is conveyed. The patient is not neutral because disclosure or non-disclosure may further the patient's interest in the consultation examination or interview. (Matter of Doe, 1982, pp. 514–515)

It is unclear how a person asserting the privilege is to prove the intent that the communication be undisclosed. An assurance of confidentiality by the psychotherapist would not seem to be sufficient to establish the patient's intent that the communication be confidential.

NEW YORK

The statutory terms of the privileges in New York do not reflect their full extent. Neither the psychologist–client privilege, which is of the attorney–client variety (New York Civil Practice Law, 1983 Supp.), nor the physician–patient privilege, which covers psychiatrists (New York Civil Practice Law, 1963), reflect the many exceptions grafted onto the privileges by the judiciary. The only statutory exceptions are contained in the physician–patient privilege, mandating disclosure when a "patient who is under the age of sixteen years has been the victim of a crime" as well as a special provision concerning deceased patients.

New York is among the minority of states that provide that once a defendant has asserted an insanity defense, statements made to any psychiatrist, including those hired by defense counsel to evaluate the defendant, are admissible to establish the basis of the psychiatrists's opinion as to sanity. In other jurisdictions, the attorney–client privilege protects from disclosure statements made to defense psychiatrists who are not called to testify by the defense. New York's position is that once the issue is raised by the defendant, all related information on the issue of sanity should be admissible, and courts have found this procedure to be constitutional (Edney v. Smith, 1976).

In a recent decision, a New York appellate court further broadened the patient-litigant exception to the privileges in criminal cases. A licensed clinical psychologist had interviewed the defendant at a hospital to determine whether he was suicidal. During the trial, the psychologist was called as a rebuttal witness by the state and testified as to statements made by the defendant concerning his wounds. The defendant had never asserted an insanity defense nor had he placed his mental condition at issue. However, to the court, once the defendant stated his version of his injuries, "at least as to the nature and cause of his wounds, preventing further disclosure would no longer have served the statutory purpose, and 'would simply be an obstruction to public justice.'" *(People v. Wilkins*, 1984, p. 708). The two dissenting judges would have applied the privilege.

During the course of its discussion, the majority explained the interrelationship between the two privileges. "The psychologist–client privilege is no broader than the doctor–patient privilege. The principles under which confidentiality is deemed to be waived are equally applicable to both privileges. The overriding, and here controlling, principle of waiver is that a litigant may not use the privilege as 'both a sword and a shield' " *(People v. Wilkins*, 1984, p. 708). By its terms, the psychologist–client privilege seems broader in its protection. However, the courts of New York have placed a judicial gloss on both privileges to provide all the standard exceptions and more.

A state worker was charged with misconduct based on physical assaults on several patients at a state facility. In order to defend himself at an arbitration proceeding, the employee sought and received a court order directing the state to turn over the medical records on these patients. The state claimed they were privileged by the physician–patient, social worker–client, and psychologist–client privileges. The appellate court affirmed the order of disclosure: "Here the need for maintaining the confidentiality of the patients' records must be balanced against the concern for respondent's rights and any adverse impact on his reputation, livelihood and future employment. Clearly, confidentiality, on these facts, must yield to respondent's right to conduct an effective defense to the disciplinary action" *(Office of Mental Retardation v. Mastracci*, 1980, p. 948). The court, however, did make some concession to the privileges. Disclosure would be limited to issues of competency and credibility where the patient was a witness as well as information as to physical con-

dition and propensity for violence. The identity of the individual patients could remain confidential.

The New York Court of Appeals, the state's highest court, rejected a claim of privilege by a psychiatrist who was resisting a state subpoena issued in an investigation of Medicaid billing practices. Referring to the physician–patient privilege as "a purely statutory creation, in derogation of the common law rule," the court noted that there were already several exceptions, including statutory provisions "to effectuate some other public policy, such as the detection and prevention of child abuse or the treatment of narcotic addiction" *(Camperlengo v. Blum*, 1982, p. 698). Although there was no explicit statutory provision providing an exception for Medicaid records, one was "necessary to satisfy the important public interest in seeing that Medicaid funds are properly applied." Redisclosure for any other purpose would not be permitted.

In most cases, it is the psychiatrist or psychologist who joins the patient in seeking to uphold the privileges and prevent disclosure of confidential information. In an interesting case, a former patient sued his psychiatrist for divulging information to the patient's wife without consent. It was the task of the court to determine whether such an action is acceptable. The appellate court created a cause of action both in contract and in tort.

> This physician–patient relationship is contractual in nature, whereby the physician, in agreeing to administer to the patient, impliedly covenants that the disclosures necessary to diagnosis and treatment of the patient's mental or physical condition will be kept in confidence. *(MacDonald v. Clinger*, 1982, p. 802).

In addition, wrongful disclosure is "a violation of a fiduciary responsibility to plaintiff implicit in and essential to the doctor-patient relation." The court recognized an exception to the rule of confidentiality for countervailing public interest such as the *Tarasoff* situation where the patient may be a danger. However, it rejected the psychiatrist's claim that there should be a spousal exception as well:

> Although the disclosure of medical information to a spouse may be justified under some circumstances, a more stringent standard should apply with respect to psychiatric information. One spouse often seeks counselling concerning personal problems that may affect the marital relationship. To per-

mit disclosure to the other spouse in the absence of an overriding concern would deter the one in need from obtaining the help required. Disclosure of confidential information by a psychiatrist to a spouse will be justified whenever there is a danger to the patient, the spouse, or another person; otherwise, information should not be disclosed without authorization. *(Mac-Donald v. Clinger*, 1982, p. 805)

The defendant's psychiatrist would have to bear the burden of proof to justify any disclosure.

NORTH CAROLINA

There are no privileges in the traditional American sense in North Carolina for either psychologist or psychiatrist. The statutory provisions provide for only qualified privileges: "The court, either at the trial or prior thereto, . . . may compel such disclosure, if in [its] opinion the same is necessary to a proper administration of justice" (North Carolina General Statutes, 1983). There also is a blanket exception to the physician–patient privilege for cases involving child abuse *(State v. Elfird*, 1983). Although the statutory exception does not mention the psychologist–client privilege, the North Carolina courts have construed both to have the same meaning *(In re Albemarle Mental Health Center*, 1979).

There appear to be no North Carolina Supreme Court decisions detailing how the trial judge is to determine whether or not disclosure would be necessary to the administration of justice. In a divorce action, the wife's psychiatrist was permitted to testify concerning her treatment over an objection based on the privilege. There was no waiver nor an implied waiver (she did not place her mental condition at issue). In addition, there was no explicit finding by the trial judge concerning the necessity of disclosure for the proper administration of justice. Therefore, the appellate court concluded that the testimony should not have been admitted. The trial judge's overruling of the objection to the testimony was not an implicit finding that the interests of justice required the privilege to be withheld *(McGinnis v. McGinnis*, 1984).

NORTH DAKOTA

The physician– and psychotherapist–patient privileges are combined in one rule, which tracks the uniform rule but broadens the proposed federal psychotherapist privilege to include all physicians (North Dakota Rules, 1983 Supp.). In addition, there is the standard abrogation of the privilege with regard to reports of child abuse and neglect *(Interests of R.D.S.*, 1977). In a proceeding to terminate parental rights, the parents sought to exclude the testimony of a psychologist who performed a court-ordered evaluation. The parents claimed that the purpose of the evaluation was to assist them in becoming better parents. However, the North Dakota Supreme Court held that there were no confidential communications involved under the privilege *(In the Interest of M.R.*, 1983).

As part of a class action lawsuit, the named plaintiff sought the name and address of all state employees who had received treatment for alcoholism. The trial court directed disclosure based on the state's civil procedure rules, and the supreme court reversed. The appellate court noted that

> the spirit of the law . . . clearly implies that such information is to be treated as confidential out of respect for the individual. The laws and rule of evidence would be of little value if the information can be obtained by other means. Even in instances where an individual wished to object to disclosure, such action would in effect amount to a disclosure. *(Holloway v. Blue Cross of North Dakota*, 1980, p. 908)

The supreme court directed the trial court to fashion a remedy that would permit those wishing to disclose treatment to come forward through newspaper advertisements or some other method. This decision represents a very sensitive approach to a difficult question involving third parties to a lawsuit.

OHIO

The psychologist–client privilege is defined in terms of the physician–patient privilege, which in turn is quite broad. Only the patient-litigant exception is mentioned, although courts have grafted the standard exceptions onto the exercise of either privilege (Ohio Revised Code, 1981). For example, in a case that did not involve a psychotherapist, the Ohio Supreme Court noted that the privilege is not absolute and that when weighed against certain public interests the privilege must bow to sensible administration of criminal justice *(State v. Dress*, 1982).

There is no exception for civil commitment hearings. However, an Ohio appellate court analyzed the situation by focusing on whether or not there was a voluntary consultation with the psychiatrist:

> Whether the institution is public or private or whether the physician is appointed by the state or retained by the family is not determinative. The crucial prerequisite for creation of the privilege is the voluntary consultation by the patient. This must be present to create the privilege in the patient, for if the patient is not voluntarily seeking help, then the underlying rationale for the privilege is not present, i.e., the promotion of free and full discourse between physician and patient. Thus, there is no reason to exclude the relevant and material testimony of such physician. (*In re Winstead*, 1980, pp. 945–946)

The court put off to another day the question of whether a relationship that developed involuntarily could eventually become a voluntary relationship for the purpose of the privilege. Similarly, in another case, the court found that the psychologist–client privilege did not apply where parents consulted with a psychologist at the behest of the local child welfare agency as part of a custody proceeding (*In re Smith*, 1982).

OKLAHOMA

The legislature adopted a combined physician- and psychotherapist–patient privilege that follows the proposed federal and uniform rule with minor modifications. A "psychotherapist" also includes persons reasonably believed by the patient to be licensed or certified as psychologists as well as persons who are actually licensed. This statute includes the standard exceptions (Oklahoma Statutes, 1984 Supp.). There have been few cases that even mention the privilege. In one criminal case, a defendant gave permission to his psychotherapist to speak with investigators, but a few days later withdrew permission. The Oklahoma Court of Criminal Appeals held that the waiver was a valid one and noted that the magistrate did not permit the psychotherapist to testify about conversations held with investigative officers following the withdrawal of the waiver. However, the appellate court did not disturb the trial court's refusal to hold an *in camera* hearing to question the psychotherapist and investigators about the time and subject matter of each conversation to ensure that there would be no testimony about periods when the waiver was not in effect (*Driskell v. State*, 1983).

OREGON

Under the Oregon adaptation of the proposed federal rule, the term "psychotherapist" is given a broad meaning: "a person who is licensed, registered, certified or otherwise authorized under the laws of any state to engage in the diagnosis or treatment of a mental or emotional condition, or reasonably believed by the patient so to be, while so engaged" (Oregon Revised Statutes, 1981). There are a few cases interpreting the privilege. In one, a defendant called a witness to testify concerning his problems with alcohol and its effect on him. The court held that because the defendant had made a voluntary disclosure and had introduced evidence as to his condition, he fell within the patient-litigant exception to the privilege (*State v. Corgain*, 1983). In another decision by the intermediate appellate court, the focus was on whether or not a confidential communication had been made. The court held that neither the receptionist at the state hospital nor a psychiatrist had engaged in privileged communication with the defendant who had called the hospital to say that he had killed a man (*State v. Miller*, 1984).

PENNSYLVANIA

According to the statutes, psychiatrists must depend on a very weak physician–patient privilege that concerns only civil matters. In addition, the only information covered is that which "shall tend to blacken the character of the patient" (Pennsylvania Consolidated Statutes, 1982, Sec. 5929). Communications between licensed psychologist and clients are privileged in both civil and criminal matters; the provision is of the attorney–client variety (Pennsylvania Consolidated Statutes, 1982, Sec. 5944).

The Pennsylvania courts have wrestled with the privilege on several occasions. As part of its effort to determine the proper placement of a juvenile delinquent (*In re B.*, 1978), the trial court directed that the mother's psychiatric records be released. Upon the psychiatrist's refusal to comply, the court held him in contempt. In reviewing the case, the Pennsylvania Supreme Court concluded that the privilege statutes provided no protection for the psychiatrist. However, the court determined that the communications between the psychiatrist and patient were covered by a constitutional right of privacy recognized by both the Pennsylvania and U.S. Constitutions:

> We conclude that in Pennsylvania, an individual's interest in preventing the disclosure of information revealed in the context of a psychotherapist–patient relationship has deeper roots than the Pennsylvania doctor–patient privilege statute, and that the patient's right to prevent disclosure of such information is constitutionally based. *(In re B.*, 1978, p. 425)

The supreme court went on to note that its decision could make it more difficult for juvenile courts to determine proper placement. However, the court suggested that the mother might submit to a voluntary examination by a court-appointed expert to evaluate the situation.

A concurring justice noted the anomaly that communications to psychiatrists have less statutory protection than those to psychologists. He concluded that "it would be arbitrary to believe that the Legislature intended the scope of a patient's privilege to depend on whether the attending therapist is a medical doctor or a psychologist" *(In re B.*, 1978, p. 428). In a subsequent case, in rejecting a defendant's claim under the privilege, the court lumped together the privilege possessed by both the psychologist and psychiatrist. However, the combination was not crucial for the case because the court determined that the communications in question were not covered by any privilege. Rather, "the testimony complained of concerned communications made by Miller [chief government witness] for the very purpose of future disclosure by these witnesses at Miller's own trial. The communications were not made in confidence" *(Commonwealth v. Goldblum*, 1982, p. 239).

In another criminal case, the defendant sought to cross-examine the key government witness concerning her confinement in a state mental health facility. A sharply split court concluded that there was no reversible error in limiting the cross-examination. Two justices concluded that a staff psychologist could not testify as to the witness' condition because of the psychologist–client privilege. There is some discussion that the cross-examination of the witness had been lengthy and that the fact that she had been in mental hospi-

tals for some period of time (as well as her treatment) had been brought to the jury's attention. However, there is no discussion of the constitutional right of confrontation that is often held to trump any privilege *(Commonwealth v. Garcia*, 1978). In a recent criminal case, an intermediate appellate court concluded that a defendant had placed his mental condition at issue by raising the insanity defense and thus could not prevent a psychiatrist from testifying. The court first rejected his attempt to bring psychiatrists within the more generous psychologist–client privilege. It then weighed the privacy interests of the defendant at issue and found that the need for the psychiatrist's testimony "clearly outweighs appellant's expectations of privacy when he has put the issue before the court" *(Commonwealth v. Petrino*, 1984, p. 1170).

PUERTO RICO

The "psychotherapist, whether a psychiatrist or a psychologist," is covered by the physician–patient privilege. There is a blanket exclusion for criminal proceedings, and there are multiple exceptions for many types of situations in civil proceedings (Puerto Rico Laws, 1983).

RHODE ISLAND

Like Illinois, Rhode Island has a comprehensive statute concerning release of health care information. The privilege includes doctors, psychiatric social workers, or psychologists, as well as a host of other health care professionals. The exceptions are of the standard variety, but are circumscribed to some extent. For example, "a claim for damages or other relief for 'pain and suffering' based solely on one's physical condition shall not be deemed to constitute the introduction of one's mental condition into issue" (Rhode Island General Laws, 1984). There are also exceptions for the *Tarasoff* situation as well as for a suspected child abuse. In addition, there is a section concerning treatment of information received by third parties.

In two cases, the Rhode Island Supreme Court was faced with the situation where a defendant had been limited in his cross-examination of a key prosecution witness because of the exercise of the privilege. The court indicated that the defendant's constitutional right of cross-examination had been denied. In one, the defendant had been charged with the murder of his daughter. In trying to establish that his wife had been responsible for the death, he subpoenaed certain records concerning child abuse investigations. The trial court quashed the subpoena, relying on the privilege. The supreme court reversed based on both the exception for child abuse reports and the defendant's constitutional rights. In a more recent case, the key prosecution witness had been a drug addict undergoing detoxification for drug addiction at the time of the offense. The trial court refused to admit the hospital records. Once again, the supreme court reversed:

> The defendant was denied any access to medical records that may have been relevant in impeaching the testimony of the only surviving eyewitness to the crimes for which he was convicted. This total denial we find constitutionally violative of his fundamental right of cross-examination. . . .
> Although the right of confrontation afforded a criminal defendant under the Sixth Amendment and art. I, Sec. 10 [of the Rhode Island Constitution], is not absolute, blanket denials of his access to "a certain class of evidence, even for the purpose of preventing a witness from suffering embarrassment on the stand, should not limit the Sixth Amendment right of a defendant to confront the witness against him." *(State v. Parillo,* 1984, p. 1355)

As part of its investigation of physician misconduct, the Board of Medical Review subpoenaed patient records from a physician alleged to have prescribed medication without examination. The Rhode Island Supreme Court upheld the subpoena against a claim of privilege:

> When a physician is under investigation for unprofessional conduct and the physician attempts to invoke the patient–physician privilege to prevent the investigatory committee from obtaining records necessary to its investigation, it seems apparent that the injury to society's interest in probity within the medical profession is much greater than the injury done to the patient's interest in the privacy of his medical records. A physician under investigation for professional misconduct subverts rather than supports the rights of the patient by distorting the patient's privilege to serve his own ends. *(In re Board of Medical Review Investigation,* 1983, p. 1376)

The court also noted that the board could protect the confidentiality of the records by keeping the patients' names confidential.

SOUTH CAROLINA

There appears to be no explicit statute providing for any psychotherapist, physician, or psychologist privilege. A few cases suggest that there is a generally accepted physician–patient privilege, and there are statutory exceptions for child abuse and workmen's compensation cases (South Carolina Code, 1983). One recent case explored an interesting aspect of use of psychiatrists by defendants in criminal cases. A defendant sought to call as a witness the psychiatrist who, at the direction of the co-defendant's lawyer, had examined the co-defendant. The trial court refused to allow the testimony based on the attorney–client privilege and the Supreme Court of South Carolina affirmed. The examination of the co-defendant had been at the attorney's behest and the psychiatrist in effect was an extension of the attorney. Because communications between attorney and client are privileged, so too are the communications between the client and the attorney's agent—the psychiatrist *(State v. Hitopoulus,* 1983).

SOUTH DAKOTA

Using the uniform rule as its guide, the South Dakota Supreme Court promulgated a physician and psychotherapist–patient privilege. The term "psychotherapists" includes doctors and psychologists (South Dakota Codified Laws, 1979, Sec. 19-13-6). In addition to the exceptions provided in the rule, communications in child abuse and neglect cases are not privileged (South Dakota Codified Laws, 1979, Sec. 26-10-15). A defendant in a criminal case involving a charge of sexual abuse of a minor attempted to use the exception to the privilege for court-ordered examinations to obtain a psychiatric evaluation of the state's chief witness. Although permissible in the appropriate case, the court held that the trial judge did not abuse his discretion in declining to order such an evaluation *(State v. McCafferty,* 1984).

TENNESSEE

One statute creates a psychiatrist–patient privilege that is only a qualified privilege because a court may determine "that the interests of justice require that the privilege be withheld." (Tennessee Code, 1980). Another provides for a psychologist–client privilege of the attorney–client variety (Tennessee Code, 1982). There are few cases construing either privilege. In a criminal appeal, the Tennessee Supreme Court held that the defendant had a right to have access to the key prosecution witness' psychiatric records in order to attack the credibility of his accuser. The court found that "the interests of justice" exception to the psychiatrist–patient privilege had been met and directed disclosure *(State v. Brown*, 1977). In a curious case, the husband and wife had been seeing a psychiatrist. In their divorce proceeding, the appellate court held that the communications to the psychiatrist were privileged but the privilege did not exclude either one of the parties from testifying as to statements made by the other spouse *(Ellis v. Ellis*, 1971). This conclusion seems to eviscerate the privilege.

TEXAS

Confusing statutes and rules make a definitive interpretation of the Texas psychotherapist–patient privilege speculative at best. Prior to 1979, there was no privilege. That year, the legislature adopted a broad statute concerning confidentiality of mental health information. A privilege was created for communications between a patient/client and a professional, broadly defined. The term encompassed doctors as well as others licensed or certified in Texas "in the diagnosis, evaluation, or treatment of any mental or emotional condition or disorder, or reasonably believed by the patient/client so to be" (Texas Revised Civil Statutes, Art. 5561h). This included psychologists, counsellors, and social workers. The exceptions were quite limited. There was no patient-litigant exception except for actions against a professional or by a professional involving a collection suit. Another exception concerned a court-ordered examination when the judge concludes that the patient was told that communications would not be privileged. One appellate court applied the privilege in a criminal case *(Tumlinson v. State*, 1983), but the legislature has now amended the statute to provide a general exception "in any criminal prosecution where the patient is a victim, witness, or defendant." There is a general *Tarasoff* exception for reporting information "to medical or law enforcement personnel where the professional determines that there is a probability of imminent physical injury by the patient/client to himself or to others, or where there is a probability of imminent mental or emotional injury to the patient/client" (Texas Revised Civil Statutes, 1984).

An appellate court applied the privilege to civil commitment proceedings and held that a psychiatrist may not testify as to communications by a patient unless part of a court-ordered examination with appropriate warnings *(Salas v. State*, 1979). Subsequently, the legislature enacted a medical practices act that provided for a physician–patient privilege for the first time in Texas and included a general civil commitment exception. The same appellate court concluded that as to doctors, there was no longer any privilege in commitment hearings *(Dial v. State*, 1983). The seemingly conflicting provisions of the two statutes were carried over into the new rules of evidence promulgated by the Texas Supreme Court for civil proceedings (Texas Rules of Evidence, 1984). Commentators have indicated that "the controlling provision . . . should be determined with reference to the purpose for which the patient/client consulted the professional: If for emotional concerns, the non-psychiatrist physician should be bound by Rule 510 [confidentiality of mental health information]. . ." (Goode & Sharlot, 1983, p. 373). The Texas Supreme Court sharply expanded the exceptions to the psychotherapist–patient privilege. There is now a general patient-litigant exception as well as "when the disclosure is relevant in any suit affecting the parent–child relationship."

Two former female patients sued a clinical psychologist alleging that during the course of their psychotherapy, he had had sexual intercourse with them *(Ex parte Abell*, 1981). Causes of action included "malpractice, assault and battery, fraud and deceit, and intentional infliction of emotional distress." The psychologist admitted the sexual intercourse but denied that it was part of his treatment. As part of pretrial discovery, the plaintiffs asked for a list of patients with whom the psychologist had had sexual contact; based on the privilege, he refused to answer. A sharply divided Texas Supreme Court upheld the nondisclosure based on the statutory privilege:

> It is apparent that a primary purpose of this statute is to protect the patient/client against an invasion of privacy. The need for such purpose is demonstrated by the facts in this case. . . . A "yes" answer thus would be required even if Abell merely touched other patients, but the inference drawn from a "yes" answer might be that Abell had sexual intercourse with other patients. This could prove highly embarrassing or perhaps even destructive of existing family relationships for women who were patients/clients of Abell. *(Ex parte Abell*, 1981, p. 263)

The four-person dissent concluded that the sexual contacts with female patients were "not a part of his treatment of them and were not encompassed within his professional relationship with them." The minority then went on to consider the constitutional privacy argument advanced by Abell:

> The question, therefore, resolves into whether Abell's former patients have a privacy right in the fact of psychological treatment which would spare Abell from disclosing their names. Even though sexual contact was not encompassed in this psychotherapist–patient relationship, the fact that these women were former patients indicates that they were in fact receiving some sort of treatment. Treatment for mental illness is not the bane it once was. The fact that the profession of psychotherapy has flourished indicates people's recognition and acceptance of psychotherapy. Many insurance policies now cover psychotherapy. In this enlightened age, the fact of treatment is not so fundamental to our concept of ordered liberty that disclosure of that fact in a civil proceeding constitutes an unconstitutional invasion of privacy. The U. S. Supreme Court in *Paul v. Davis* . . . intimated that a person's interest in his or her reputation is not a fundamental right. (p. 267)

There is some empirical support for the dissent's conclusion. A law professor and a psychiatrist discovered that most Texans were not aware of the existence of the Texas privilege and that the possibility of disclosure was not a significant factor in deciding whether or not to seek treatment (Shuman & Weiner, 1982). The rules promulgated by the supreme court apply only to civil cases. The statute on confidentiality of mental health information, with its now broad exception for criminal cases, applies to criminal matters.

UTAH

The general rule now states: "Privilege is governed by the common law, except as modified by statute or court rule" (Utah Code, 1983b). Previously enacted statutory privileges seem to still exist. "A psychologist licensed under the provisions of this act cannot, without the consent of his client or patient, be examined in a civil or criminal action as to any information acquired in the course of his professional services in behalf of the client" (Utah Code, 1983a). There are no statutory exceptions.

In construing the psychologist–client privilege, the Utah Supreme Court stated that its effect "is

to create another privilege and thus close another window to the light of truth. It is neither our duty nor prerogative to pass upon the wisdom of such a legislative enactment. But because it has the effect just stated, it should be strictly construed and applied" *(State v. Gotfrey,* pp. 1327–1328). The defendant in this case sought to prevent testimony concerning his communications during treatment with a psychologist at a state mental health clinic. Because the individual was not yet licensed, the Utah Supreme Court overruled the claim of privilege. Two justices dissented, noting the "effect of the interpretation of that privilege is to make an invidious discrimination in the quality of psychological services available to a person who can afford to consult a private practitioner and the quality of service that lesser advantaged persons may receive when seeking the same services from a government-sponsored institution" *(State v. Gotfrey,* 1979, p. 1329).

VERMONT

Using the proposed federal psychotherapist rule as well as the uniform rule, Vermont enacted a patient's privilege that is quite broad concerning psychotherapy. "A 'mental health professional' is a qualified person designated by the Commissioner of Mental Health or a physician, psychologist, social worker, or nurse with professional training, experience, and demonstrated competence in the treatment of mental illness, or a person reasonably believed by the patient to be a mental health professional." In addition to the standard exceptions, there are two special ones, "for information indicating that a patient who is under the age of sixteen years has been the victim of a crime," as well as an exception for "any report of a patient's medical condition required to be made by statute" (Vermont Statutes, 1983). In a recent case construing the previous statute, the Vermont Supreme Court applied the privilege narrowly *(In re T.L.S.,* 1984).

VIRGINIA

Very weak privileges exist in Virginia. There is one statute for physicians and licensed clinical psychologists (Virginia Code, 1977) and one for licensed professional counsellors, licensed clinical social workers, and again licensed psychologists (Virginia Code, 1983 Supp.). Each applies only in civil actions and provides an exception "when a court, in the exercise of sound discretion, deems such disclosure necessary to the proper administration of justice."

WASHINGTON

One statute provides for a physician–patient privilege (Washington Revised Code, 1983 Supp.) that is limited to civil actions and contains an exception for "any judicial proceeding regarding a child's injuries, neglect, or sexual abuse, or the cause thereof." There is a broader psychologist-client privilege of the attorney–client variety (Washington Revised Code, 1978). However, the courts have construed the two together. "Both statutes are procedural safeguards which derogate from common law and therefore are strictly construed. . . . The application of either privilege requires a balancing of the benefits of the privilege against the public interest of a full revelation of all the facts" (Petersen v. State, 1983).

The privileges have some applicability to criminal proceedings based on a statute that applies civil rules of evidence to criminal prosecutions "so far as practicable." A defendant sought the psychiatric treatment records of the key prosecution witness in a murder case. The trial judge reviewed the medical records in camera and decided that they were privileged and would not have assisted defense counsel (State v. Mines, 1983, p. 277).

> This sequestered observation protected the privacy between physician and patient and adhered to the legislative policy establishing the privilege. . . . Defense counsel have an obligation to ferret out all relevant evidence [that is] material and favorable to a defendant, but may not perform this duty by breaching the physician–patient privilege.

The appellate court also inspected the records and concurred with the trial judge's conclusions (State v. Mines, 1983). It was necessary to consider whether or not anything in the record would have assisted the defendant's counsel in cross-examination of the witness because of the defendant's rights under the federal constitution's confrontation clause.

The exception for child abuse cases has been given a broad reading by the Washington Supreme Court. There is no balancing; the privileges are abrogated:

> Thus, we cannot accept the appellant's theory that confidential communications between the perpetrator and a psychologist,

or a doctor, or a mental health center employee, are protected from disclosure and privileged in a judicial proceeding, according to the terms of the applicable statutes. Such protection might well be deemed to be in the public interest. But it is evident that, in its recent enactments, the legislature has attached greater importance to the reporting of incidents of child abuse and the prosecution of perpetrators than to counseling and treatment of persons whose mental or emotional problems cause them to inflict such abuse. (State v. Fagalde, 1975, p. 90)

This attitude is in contrast to those states that perform a balancing test in each individual situation or apply the exception only to the report of child abuse and not to all communications.

There was no legislative exception for civil commitment proceedings for other than the initial 14-day observation period. However, the supreme court had no difficulty creating the necessary waiver of the privilege. Deferring to the professional judgment of the state hospital's mental health professionals, the court indicated that the waiver was necessary to effectuate the commitment procedures:

> It is suggested that, unless the privilege is preserved for these patients, they will be reluctant to confide in the psychiatrists who treat them. But it is apparent from the very fact that these persons are hospitalized against their will, they are unable to recognize their need for help. Thus handicapped, they are apt to resist treatment and the confidences which it entails, in any event. (Matter of R., 1982, pp. 706–707)

In another context concerning civil commitment, the supreme court held that hospital personnel were prohibited from informing a trial judge of a probationer's involuntary commitment. This did not relieve the state from subsequent liability based on a failure to take "reasonable precautions to protect those who might foreseeably be endangered by [the probationer's] drug-related mental problems" (Petersen v. State, 1983).

WEST VIRGINIA

There is a statute related to confidential information concerning diagnosis and treatment (West Virginia Code, 1980), but West Virginia has not enacted an explicit privilege statute. The supreme court indicated that it did not view the statute as creating any sort of a general psychotherapist–patient privilege. . . . [It] does not define the relationship it is intended to protect, identifies only one party, i.e., the client or patient, and is written so broadly that the confidentiality is not limited to information essential to any confidential relationship. *(State v. Simmons,* 1983, p. 96)

There is a broad exception for any court proceeding in which there is a finding that the relevancy of the information outweighs the maintaining of confidentiality in addition to narrower exceptions for court-ordered examination, commitment, and dangerous situations.

WISCONSIN

Initially, psychologists were excluded from the rule of evidence creating the physician–patient privilege. However, over time, the rule was expanded to include a psychologist–patient privilege as well as a registered nurse–patient privilege. The definition is broad and includes those licensed as well as persons reasonably believed by the patients to be so licensed. The rule tracks the proposed federal provision but has a few more exceptions. For example, "there is no privilege in trials for homicide when the disclosure relates directly to the facts or immediate circumstances of the homicide," and the privilege is abrogated in cases of suspected child abuse (Wisconsin Statutes, 1984). The focus of the cases construing the privileges have been definitional in character. The state psychology board was investigating a psychologist who used a certain electrical device. The appellate court ruled that the subjects were not "patients" within the meaning of the statute, but were volunteers in a research experiment and thus the privilege did not apply *(State ex rel Pflaum v. Psychology Examining Board,* 1983). The commitment exception included petitions for continued confinement under the sex crimes act *(State v. Hungerford,* 1978).

WYOMING

Separate broad privileges exist for physicians (Wyoming Statutes, 1983, Sec. 1-12-101) and licensed psychologists (Wyoming Statutes, 1983, Sec. 33-27-103). There are few appellate cases construing the privileges; therefore, the extent of judicially created exceptions is not readily apparent. There is a statutory exception for proceedings growing out of child abuse reports, and the Wyoming Supreme Court has construed it broadly *(Matter of Parental Rights of PP,* 1982).

THE PRIVILEGE BEYOND THE UNITED STATES

The psychotherapist–patient privilege has not taken hold outside the United States. Weisstub's (1980) description remains apt: "The common law has declined to acknowledge a need for medical privilege. For the proper administration of justice, the view that the public need for full disclosure outweighs the individual need for private communication has maintained its stronghold" (p. 273). Civil law countries have been more generous in terms of a physician–patient privilege, but there is no special recognition for the psychotherapist.

England remains the bastion in refusing to recognize any testimonial privilege. Lord Denning, while master of Rolls, stated the law as it has been for hundreds of years:

> The judge will respect the confidences which each member of these honourable professions receives in the course of it, and will not direct him to answer unless not only it is relevant but also it is a proper and, indeed, necessary question in the course of justice to be put and answered. *(A.G. v. Mulholland,* 1962, p. 477)

Although there is some statutory protection for medical records, a subject beyond the scope of this chapter, there has been no movement to create a testimonial privilege. The British Medical Association has advised its members that "a decision to refuse [to disclose on order of a court], while illegal, is not necessarily unethical" (Finch, 1982).

Other commonwealth nations have been somewhat more receptive, especially Canada. Canadian appellate courts have returned to first principles in evaluating the claims of privilege. For example, the supreme court used the four-part analysis of Wigmore, quoted earlier in this chapter, to assist it in a decision concerning a question of privilege *(Slavutych v. Baker,* 1975). Justice Clement looked to Wigmore also:

> To me, the sanction given to these four conditions as the test for a claim of privilege provides a most useful and helpful rationale which should serve well the general public interest in determining such claims. Not

only does it provide a rationale: it also leaves room by the third and fourth conditions for adaptation of the principle to changing needs and conditions of society which is essential to the proper function of the common law. Former decisions on privileged documents must now derive their authority or guidance from their apparent conformity to the conditions, and on this view many must be passed over. *(Strass v. Goldsack,* 1975, p. 155)

Although this reliance on Wigmore might not have been necessary for the decision in either case (Laderman, 1976), these decisions reflect an openness about the question of privilege. Some courts have applied the method of analysis to cases involving psychotherapists. For example, in a divorce and custody suit, a wife sought to use a psychologist's report based on communications among the spouses and the doctor during mediation. The family court concluded that the communications met Wigmore's four tests of privileged information *(Porter v. Porter,* 1983). In another case, in a suit for custody of pet cats, the wife sought the testimony of the husband's "therapist," a family physician with no psychiatric training. Over objection, the court concluded that because the physician was not a psychiatrist and was not acting as a family or marriage counsellor, no privilege attached to the communications between the doctor and patient *(Torok v. Torok,* 1983). One court noted "the genius of the common law to move with the times to recognize existing realities," and urged recognition of the special role of psychiatrists *(Denbie v. Denbie,* 1976).

In addition, there is a qualified privilege under the Ontario Mental Health Act concerning "any knowledge or information in respect of a patient obtained in the course of assessing or treating or assisting . . . in a psychiatric facility." The qualification is broad and applies where a court determines "that the disclosure is essential in the interests of justice" (Ontario Revised Statutes, 1980). An Ontario court used Wigmore's four conditions in a criminal case to prevent the defendant from obtaining the testimony of three psychiatrists who treated the major witness *(R. v. Hawke,* 1974).

Although Ontario has taken the lead, other provinces have been active. In Newfoundland, a court quashed a search warrant for records made by a physician during a psychiatric assessment of a defendant in a murder case that allegedly contained admissions. The court concluded that to permit the warrant would compromise the necessary confidential atmosphere. The province also has a privilege created by statute *(R. v. Waterford Hospital,* 1983).

In Nova Scotia, a husband called a psychiatrist to testify about the wife's mental condition over the wife's objection in a custody suit. The court held the testimony inadmissible because it met Wigmore's conditions *(Mortlock v. Mortlock,* 1980). A proposed uniform evidence act included a privilege for psychiatric assessment; however, it was not enacted (Institute of Law Research and Reform, 1982).

Quebec, with its civil law tradition, has been the exception in Canada. Since 1909, there has been a specific provision of the province's medical act providing that "no physician may be compelled to declare what has been revealed to him in his professional character" (L.R.Q., 1977). However, the Quebec Court of Appeal undercut the statute in a 1968 decision and held that the law was not absolute *(Descarreaux v. Jacques,* 1969). The Charter of Human Rights and Freedoms contains a privilege that is only abrogated by an express provision of the law. It is unclear what effect this will have on the interpretation of the medical act (Knoppers, 1982).

Australia has seen no movement parallel to Canada. As one observer stated, "The cases are uniformly against the recognition of any privilege at common law arising from the doctor–patient relationship" (Cross, 1979). The only exceptions are Victoria (Evidence Act, 1958) and Tasmania (Evidence Act, 1959). Victoria includes an exception for sanity or testamentary capacity of the patient, whereas Tasmania also excludes all criminal cases.

New Zealand has a physician–patient privilege and recently extended it to criminal as well as civil proceedings. In addition, the definition of protected communication was broadened and now "means the communication made to a registered medical practitioner by a patient who believes that the communication is necessary to enable the registered medical practitioner to examine, treat, or act for the patient" (Evidence Amendment Act, 1980). The Law Revision Committee on Medical Privilege had considered a privilege for clinical psychologists but concluded "there is as yet an absence of statutory recognition and regulation of clinical psychologists." However, the committee felt that once recognized and licensed, the privilege should apply to psychologists.

Civil law countries recognize a physician–

patient privilege, although there is no special consideration given to psychotherapists, including psychologists. For example, France has a relatively absolute provision providing that physicians "and other persons who by means of their office or profession . . . are entrusted with secrets who reveal these secrets . . . will be punished" (France Code, 1980–81). There are exceptions for abortion and child abuse cases. Germany has a like provision (German Penal Code, 1961), as does Switzerland (Switzerland Penal Code, 1967) and most other European nations. For each penal provision, there is a comparative civil prohibition.

Israel has a physician–patient privilege, but it is qualified; disclosure is permissible when "the court has found that the necessity to disclose the evidence for the purpose of doing justice outweighs the interest in its nondisclosure" (Evidence Ordinance, 1972). All of Latin America follows the civil code nations. A typical example is Colombia, which has privileges for doctors noted in its civil procedure code and criminal procedure code; in addition, violation of the privilege is covered in the penal code (Colombia Código, 1978). There appears, however, to be a duty to report crimes to authorities. Whether the broad privileges applicable in civil law nations are followed in practice is unknown to this author.

REFERENCES

A.G. v. Mulholland, 2 Q.B. 477 (1962).
Alabama Code, Sec. 34-26-2 (1982 Supp).
Alaska Statutes, Sec. 47.17.060 (1983).
Allen v. Department for Human Resources, 540 S.W.2d 597 (1976).
Allred v. State, 554 P.2d 411 (1976).
Amburgey v. Central Kentucky Regional Mental Health Board, 663 S.W.2d 952 (1983).
Arizona Revised Statutes Annotated, Sec. 32-2085 (1983 Supp).
Arkansas Statutes Annotated, Uniform Rules of Evidence, Rule 503 (1979).
Atwood v. Atwood, 550 S.W.2d 465 (1976).
Barker v. Barker, 440 P.2d 137 (1968).
Bell v. State, 385 So. 2d 78 (1980).
Bentham, J. (1827). Draught for the organisation of judicial establishments. In The works of Jeremy Bentham (4th ed.) (Bowring ed., 1843). Published under the superintendance of his executor, John Bowring—New York: Russell and Russell, 1962.
Betty J. B. v. Division of Social Services, 450 A.2d 528 (1983).
Bond v. District Court, 682 P.2d 33 (1984).
Branch v. Wilkinson, 256 N.W.2d 307 (1977).
Caesar v. Mountanos, 542 F.2d 1064 (1976).
California Evidence Code, Sec. 1010 and 1024 (1966).
California Evidence Code, Sec. 1027 (1984 Supp).
California Law Revision Commission (1964). Art. V—Privileges.

California Penal Code, Sec. 1165 et seq. (1984 Supp).
Camperlengo v. Blum, 451 N.Y.S.2d 697 (1982).
Chidester v. Needles, 353 N.W.2d 849 (1984).
Clark v. District Court, 668 P.2d 3 (1983).
Code of Federal Regulations, Tit. 45, Sec. 1340 (1984).
Colombia Código Penal, Art. 307 (1978).
Colorado Revised Statutes, Sec. 12-63.5-115 (1978 Repl., Vol. 5).
Colorado Revised Statutes, Sec. 13-90-107d,g (1973).
Commonwealth v. Garcia, 387 A.2d 46 (1978).
Commonwealth v. Goldblum, 447 A.2d 234 (1982).
Commonwealth v. Mandeville, 436 N.E.2d 912 (1982).
Commonwealth v. Petrino, 480 A.2d 1160 (1984).
Congressional Record. (1974). Vol. 120, Part 30, page 40891.
Connecticut General Statutes Annotated, Secs. 52-146c-f (1984 Supp).
Cross, R. (1979). Cross on Evidence (p. 274). Wellington, New Zealand: Butterworths, 1979.
Davidge v. Davidge, 451 So.2d 1051 (1984).
Dawes v. Dawes, 454 So.2d 311 (1984).
Delaware Rule of Evidence 503 (1981).
Denbie v. Denbie, 21 R.F.L. 45 (1976), reporting a judgment from 1963.
Descarreaux v. Jacques, B.R. 1109 (1969).
Dial v. State, 658 S.W.2d 823 (1983).
District of Columbia Code, Secs. 2-1704.16, 14-307 (1981).
Doe II v. Roe II, 647 P.2d 305 (1982).
Doe v. Eli Lilly & Co., 99 F.R.D. 126 (1983).
Driskell v. State, 659 P.2d 343 (1983).
Duchess of Kingston's Trial, 20 How. St. Trials 355, 572–573 (1776).
E.H. v. State, 443 So.2d 1083 (1984).
Edney v. Smith, 425 F.Supp. 1038 (1976).
Ellis v. Ellis, 472 S.W.2d 741 (1971).
Esquivel v. State, 617 P.2d 587 (1980).
Evidence Act, Tasmania Statutes, Sec. 96 (1959).
Evidence Act, Victoria Statutes, Sec. 28 (1958).
Evidence Amendment Act No. 2, Statutes N.Z., Vol. 1, No. 27 (1980).
Evidence Ordinance, Laws of the State of Israel, Ch. 3, Sec. 49–50 (1972).
Ex parte Abell, 613 S.W.2d 255 (1981).
Ex parte Day, 378 So.2d 1159 (1979).
Federal Rules of Evidence, Rule 501 (1974).
Finch, J. (1982). Poly Law Review, 7, 46.
Florida Board of Bar Examiners re Applicant, 443 So.2d 77 (1983).
Florida Statutes Annotated, Sec. 827.07(8) (1984 Supp).
Florida Statutes Annotated, Sec. 90-503 (1979).
France Code Penal, Art. 378 (1980–81).
Georgia Code, Secs. 38-418, 84-3118 (1971).
German Penal Code, Sec. 300 (1961).
Gonzenbach v. Ruddy, 645 S.W.2d 27 (1982).
Goode, S., & Sharlot, M. (1983). Article V: Privileges. Houston Law Review, 20, 273.
Group for the Advancement of Psychiatry (1960). Report No. 45, quoted in Advisory Committee's Notes to Proposed Rules, 56 F.R.D. 183, 1972.
Hahman v. Hahman, 628 P.2d 985 (1981).
Hawaii Revised Statutes, 1980 Special Rules Pamphlet, Rules 504, 504.1 (1980).
Holloway v. Blue Cross of North Dakota, 294 N.W.2d 902 (1980).
Horne v. State, 677 S.W.2d 856 (1984).
Hunter v. State, 360 N.E.2d 588 (1977).

Husgen v. Stussie, 617 S.W.2d 414 (1981).
Idaho Code, Secs. 9-203.4, 9-203.6, 54-2314 (1979).
Illinois Annotated Statutes, Ch. 91 1/2, Sec. 801 et seq. (1984 Supp).
In re Albemarle Mental Health Center, 256 S.E.2d 818 (1979).
In re B., 394 A.2d 419 (1978).
In re Board of Medical Review Investigation, 463 A.2d 1373 (1983).
In re Brenda H., 402 A.2d 169 (1979).
In re Doe, 711 F.2d 1187 (1983).
In re Estate of Wilson, 416 A.2d 228 (1980).
In re Field, 412 A.2d 1032 (1980).
In re Interest of Spradlin, 317 N.W.2d 59 (1982).
In re J. P. B., 362 A.2d 1183 (1976).
In re Lifschutz, 467 P.2d 557 (1970).
In re Marriage of Ganmer, 303 N.W.2d 136 (1981).
In re Pebsworth, 705 F.2d 261 (1983).
In re Smith, 454 N.E.2d 171 (1982).
In re T.L.S., 481 A.2d 1037 (1984).
In re Winstead, 425 N.E.2d 943 (1980).
In re Zuniga, 714 F.2d 632 (1983).
In the Interest of M.R., 334 N.W.2d 848 (1983).
In the Interest of Zappa, 631 P.2d 1245 (1981).
In the Matter of Skarsten, 350 N.W.2d 455 (1984).
Indiana Code, Secs. 25-33-1-17, 34-1-14-5 (1976).
Institute of Law Research and Reform (1982). *Uniform evidence act, 1981.* Edmonton, Canada.
Interests of R.D.S., 259 N.W.2d 636 (1977).
Iowa Code Annotated, Sec. 622.10 (1983 Supp).
Jones v. Sayad, 654 S.W.2d 93 (1983).
Kansas Statutes Annotated, Secs. 60-1608, 60-1610, 74-5323 (1980).
Kentucky Revised Statutes Annotated, Secs. 319-111, 421.215 (1983).
Kimble v. Kimble, 239 S.E.2d 676 (1977).
Knoppers, B. (1982). Confidentiality and accessability of medical information: A comparative analysis. *Revue de Droit Universite de Sherbrooke, 12,* 396.
Krattenmaker, T. (1973). Testimonial privileges in federal courts: An alternative to the proposed federal rules of evidence. *Georgetown Law Journal, 62,* 61.
L.R.Q., Ch. M-9, Art. 42 (1977).
Laderman, S. (1976). Discovery. *Canadian Bar Review, 54,* 422.
Laurent v. Brelji, 392 N.E.2d 929 (1979).
Lora v. Board of Education, 74 F.R.D. 565 (1977).
Louisell, D. (1956). Confidentiality, conformity and confusion: Privileges in federal court today, *Tulane Law Review, 31,* 101.
Louisell, D. (1957). The psychologist in today's legal world: Part 2, *Minnesota Law Review, 41,* 731.
Louisiana Revised Statutes Annotated, Sec. 13:3734 (1983 Supp).
Loveless v. State, 592 P.2d 1206 (1979).
M. v. K., 452 A.2d 704 (1982).
MacDonald v. Clinger, 446 N.Y.S.2d 801 (1982).
Magwood v. State, 426 So.2d 918 (1982).
Maine Revised Statutes Annotated Rules of Evidence, Rule 503 (1978 Supp).
Manner of Adoption of H.Y.T., 436 So.2d 251 (1983).
Maryland Courts & Judiciary Process Code Annotated, Sec. 9-109 (1983 Supp).
Massachusetts Annotated Laws, Ch. 233, Sec. 20B (1983 Supp).
Matter of Doe, 649 P.2d 510 (1982).
Matter of Parental Rights of PP, 648 P.2d 512 (1982).

Matter of R., 641 P.2d 704 (1982).
Matter of Sonsteng, 573 P.2d 1149 (1977).
McGinnis v. McGinnis, 311 S.E.2d 669 (1984).
McKinney v. State, 466 A.2d 356 (1983).
Michigan Compiled Laws Annotated, Sec. 333.18237 (1980).
Michigan Compiled Laws Annotated, Sec. 600.2157, 722.574 (1968).
Minnesota Statutes Annotated, Sec. 595.02, 626.556 (1984 Supp).
Minnesota v. Murphy, 104 S.Ct. 1136 (1984).
Mississippi Code Annotated, Sec. 73-31-29 (1973).
Mississippi Code Annotated, Sec. 13-1-21 (1984 Supp).
Missouri Annotated Statutes, Secs. 210.140, 337.055, 491.060 (1983 Supp).
Montana Code Annotated, Secs. 26-1-805, 26-1-807, 41-3-404, 46-14-401, 50-16-314 (1983).
Mortlock v. Mortlock, 17 R.F.L.2d 253 (1980).
Nagle v. Hooks, 460 A.2d 49(1983).
Nebraska Revised Statutes, Sec. 27-504 (1979).
Nevada Revised Statutes, Sec. 49.225 (1981).
New Hampshire Revised Statutes Annotated, Secs. 329:26, 330-A.19 (1981 Supp).
New Jersey Statutes Annotated, Secs. 2A:84A–22.2 (1976).
New Jersey Statutes Annotated, Secs. 45:8B-29, 45:14B-28 (1983 Supp).
New Mexico Statutes Annotated Rules of Evidence, Rule 503 (1978).
New State Ice Co. v. Liebmann, 285 U.S. 262 (1932).
New York Civil Practice Law and Rules, Sec. 4507 (1983 Supp).
New York Civil Practice Law and Rules, Sec. 4504 (1963).
New York Revised Statutes, Vol. 2, Part 3, Ch. 7, Tit. 3, Art. 8, Sec. 73 (1829), quoted in *McCormick on Evidence* (Cleary ed., 1984).
North Carolina General Statutes, Sec. 8-53, 8-53.3 (1983 Supp).
North Dakota Rules of Evidence, Rule 503 (1983 Supp).
Note (1952). Confidential communications to a psychotherapist: A new testimonial privilege. *Northwestern University Law Review, 17,* 384.
Office of Mental Retardation v. Mastracci, 433 N.Y.S.2d 946 (1980).
Ohio Revised Code Annotated, Secs. 4732.19, 2317.02 (1981).
Oklahoma Statutes Annotated, Tit. 12, Sec. 2503 (1984 Supp).
Olander, A. (1978). Discovery of Psychotherapist–Patient Communications After Tarasoff. *San Diego Law Review, 15,* 265.
Ontario Revised Statutes, Ch. 262, Sec. 29-9 (1980).
Oregon Revised Statutes, Sec. 40.230 (1981).
Pennsylvania Consolidated Statutes Annotated, Secs. 5929, 5944 (1982).
People v. Boucher, 345 N.W.2d 670 (1983).
People v. Dace, 449 N.E.2d 1031 (1983).
People v. Lobaito, 351 N.W.2d 233 (1984).
People v. Phipps, 242 N.E.2d 727 (1981).
People v. Stritzinger, 194 *California Reporter* 431 (1983).
People v. Wilkins, 477 N.Y.S.2d 706 (1984).
Petersen v. State, 671 P.2d 230 (1983).
Petition of Catholic Charitable Bureau, 467 N.E.2d 866 (1984).
Porter v. Porter, 40 Ont.2d 417 (1983).

Post v. State, 580 P.2d 304 (1978).
Puerto Rico Laws Annotated, Tit. App. IV R. 26 (1983).
R. v. Hawke [1974], 16 *Can. Crim. Cases* 2d 438.
R. v. Waterford Hospital, 35 *Can. Crim. Cases* 3d 348 (1983).
Ramer v. United States, 411 F.2d 30 (1969).
Reese v. State, 458 A.2d 492 (1983).
Rhode Island General Laws, Sec. 5-37.3-1 et seq. (1984 Supp).
Roberts v. Superior Court, 107 *Cal. Rptr.* 309 (1973).
Rules of Evidence for United States Courts and Magistrates, 56 F.R.D. 183, 240 (1972).
Salas v. State, 592 S.W.2d 653 (1979).
Shaw v. Glickman, 415 A.2d 625 (1980).
Shuman, D., & Weiner, M. (1982). The privilege study: An empirical examination of the psychotherapist–patient privilege. *North Carolina Law Review, 60,* 893.
Simek v. Superior Court, 172 *California Reporter,* 564 (1981).
Sims v. State, 311 S.E.2d 161 (1984).
Slakan v. Porter, 737 F.2d 368 (1984).
Slavutych v. Baker, 1 S.C.R. 254 (1976).
Slovenko, R. (1960). Psychiatry and a second look at the medical privilege. *Wayne Law Review, 6,* 175.
Slovenko, R. (1966). *Psychotherapy, confidentiality, and privileged communication.* Springfield, Illinois: Charles C Thomas.
Smith v. Superior Court, 173 *Cal. Rptr.* 145 (1981).
Smith, S. (1980). Constitutional privacy and psychotherapy. *George Washington Law Review, 49,* 1.
Snethen v. State, 308 N.W.2d 11 (1981).
South Carolina Code, Sec. 20-9-40 (1983).
South Dakota Codified Laws Annotated, Sec. 19-13-6 et seq., 26-10-15 (1979).
Southern Bluegrass MHMR v. Angelucci, 609 S.W. 2d 931 (1980).
State Health and Social Services Department v. Smith, 600 P.2d 294 (1979).
State ex rel Pflaum v. Psychology Examining Board, 331 N.W.2d 614 (1983).
State in Interest of O'Neal, 303 N.W.2d 414 (1981).
State v. Andring, 342 N.W.2d 128 (1984).
State v. Aucoin, 362 So.2d 503 (1978).
State v. Brown, 552 S.W.2d 383 (1977).
State v. Brydon, 626 S.W.2d 443 (1981).
State v. Clark, 682 P.2d 1339 (1984).
State v. Corgain, 663 P.2d 773 (1983).
State v. Dress, 461 N.E.2d 1312 (1982).
State v. Eberwein, 655 S.W.2d 794 (1983).
State v. Elfird, 309 S.E.2d 228 (1983).
State v. Esposito, 471 A.2d 949 (1984).
State v. Fagalde, 539 P.2d 86 (1975).
State v. Farrow, 366 A.2d 1177 (1976).
State v. Felde, 422 So.2d 370 (1982).
State v. Gotfrey, 598 P.2d 1325 (1979).
State v. Hembd, 232 N.W.2d 872 (1975).
State v. Hitopoulus, 309 S.E.2d 747 (1983).
State v. Howland, 658 P.2d 195 (1982).
State v. Hungerford, 261 N.W.2d 258 (1978).
State v. Lewisohn, 379 A.2d 1192 (1977).

State v. Magnuson, 682 P.2d 1365 (1984).
State v. McCafferty, 356 N.W.2d 159 (1984).
State v. Miller, 680 P.2d 676 (1984).
State v. Milton, 526 P.2d 436 (1974).
State v. Mines, 671 P.2d 273 (1983).
State v. Odenbrett, 349 N.W.2d 265, 1984.
State v. Parillo, 480 A.2d 1349 (1984).
State v. Parson, 601 P.2d 680 (1979).
State v. R.H., 683 P.2d 269 (1984).
State v. Simmons, 309 S.E.2d 89 (1983).
State v. Storlazzi, 464 A.2d 829 (1983).
State v. Swier, 666 P.2d 169 (1983).
State v. Thresher, 442 A.2d 578 (1982).
State v. Toste, 424 A.2d 293 (1979).
Strass v. Goldsack, 6 W.W.R. 155 (1975).
Switzerland Penal Code, Art. 321 (1967).
Tarasoff v. Regents, 131 *California Reporter* 14 (1976).
Taylor v. United States, 222 F.2d 398 (1955), quoting M. Guttmacher and H. Weihofen (1952), *Psychiatry and the Law,* page 272.
Tennessee Code Annotated, Sec. 24-207 (1980).
Tennessee Code Annotated, Sec. 63-11-213 (1982).
Texas Rules of Evidence, Rules 509, 510 (1984).
Texas Revised Civil Statutes Annotated, Art. 5561h (1984 Supp).
Torok v. Torok, 44 Ont.2d 118 (1983).
Trammel v. United States, 445 U.S. 40 (1980).
Tumlinson v. State, 663 S.W.2d 539 (1983).
U.S. Code Annotated, Tit. 42, Sec. 5101 et seq. (1976).
U.S. Code Annotated, Tit. 42, Sec. 290dd-3 (1984 Supp).
U.S. Code Congressional and Administrative News, 7051 (1974).
United States v. Lindstrom, 698 F.2d 1154 (1983).
United States v. Meagher, 531 F.2d 752 (1976).
United States v. Nixon, 418 U.S. 683 (1974).
Utah Code Annotated, Sec. 58-25-8 (1983a Supp).
Utah Code Annotated, Rules of Evidence, Rule 501 (1983b Supp).
Van Goyt v. Alabama, 461 So.2d 821 (1984).
Vermont Statutes Annotated, Rules of Evidence, Rule 503 (1983).
Vincent v. LeMaire, 370 So.2d 190 (1979).
Virginia Code, Sec. 8.01-399 (1977).
Virginia Code, Sec. 8.01-400.2 (1983 Supp).
Washington Revised Code Annotated, Sec. 18.83.110 (1978).
Washington Revised Code Annotated, Sec. 5.60.060 (1983 Supp).
Weisstub, D. (1980). *Law and psychiatry in the Canadian context.* Toronto: Pergamon Press.
Wenninger v. Muesing, 240 N.W.2d 333 (1976).
West Virginia Code, Sec. 27-3-1 (1980).
White v. United States, 451 A.2d 848 (1980).
Wigmore, J. H. (1961). *Evidence,* 8, Sec. 2285 (McNaughton Rev.).
Wilson v. Bonner, 303 S.E.2d 134 (1983).
Wing v. Wing, 393 So.2d 285 (1980).
Wisconsin Statutes Annotated, Sec. 905.04 (1984 Supp).
Wyoming Statutes Annotated, Secs. 1-12-101, 33-27-103 (1983).

Author Index

Subject Index

About the Editor
and Contributors

The Editor

David N. Weisstub is Professor of Law at Osgoode Hall Law School of York University, Ontario, professeur titulaire de recherche at the Department of Psychiatry, Université de Montréal, and Senior Forensic Consultant to the Institut Philippe Pinel de Montréal, Québec. Dr. Weisstub has recently been appointed Policy Advisor to the Criminal Law Review Division of the Department of Justice of Canada, and serves as a consultant to the Federal Law Reform Commission. He has served in various government commissions and task forces in Canada and, as a member of the Ontario Advisory Review Board since 1974, has advised the Cabinet on the release of persons found not guilty by reason of insanity. Dr. Weisstub has been consulted by various governments in mental health law reform and has lectured extensively, in Canada and abroad, on the theoretical relationship between law and psychiatry. He is a member of many boards of editors and the author of numerous books and articles, including *Law and Psychiatry in the Canadian Context*, and *The Western Idea of Law*, co-authored with Joseph C. Smith. He is also the author of *Heaven, Take My Hand*, a volume of verse. Since 1977 he has been Editor-in-Chief of the *International Journal of Law and Psychiatry*. He is also the President-Elect of the International Academy of Law and Mental Health.

David N. Weisstub est professeur de droit à la faculté de droit Osgoode Hall à l'Université York (Ontario), professeur titulaire de recherche au département de psychiatrie de l'Université de Montréal, et conseiller principal en psychiatrie légale à l'Institut Philippe Pinel de Montréal (Québec). Le professeur Weisstub a récemment été nommé conseiller de la réforme du droit criminel au ministère de la Justice fédéral et expert auprés de la Commission de réforme du droit fédérale. Il a participé à plusieurs commissions et groupes de travail gouvernementaux au Canada et, en qualité de membre de l'Ontario Advisory Review Board depuis 1974, il a conseillé le Cabinet sur la libération des personnes acquittées pour aliénation mentale. Le professeur Weisstub a été consulté par différents gouvernements en matilére de réforme du droit de la santé mentale, et il a fait de très nombreuses conférences, tant au Canada qu'à l'étranger, sur les relations théoriques entre le droit et la psychiatrie. Membre de nombreaux comités de rédaction, il a publié plusieurs ouvrages et articles, notamment *Law and Psychiatry in the Canadian Context* ainsi que *The Western Idea of Law* écrit en collaboration avec Joseph C. Smith. Par ailleurs, il est l'auteur d'un recueil de poèmes intitulé *Heaven, Take My Hand*. Depuis 1977, il est rédacteur en chef de l'*International Journal of Law and Psychiatry*. Il est aussi le Président désigné de l'Académie internationale de droit et de santé mentale.

The Contributors

Michael J. Churgin is Professor of Law at The University of Texas at Austin. He has published widely, specializing in issues of mental health and sentencing. He has been a consultant to the National Academy of Sciences and has served on various community boards concerned with mental health and legal assistance to the poor. An initial recipient of the Kellogg National Fellowship, he investigated issues of emergency room service delivery to the mentally ill.

Michael J. Churgin est professeur de droit à l'Université du Texas à Austin. Il a publié de nombreux ouvrages et s'est spécialisé dans les questions de santé mentale et de sentences. Il a été consultant auprès de la National Academy of Sciences et a appartenu à différentes commissions communautaires qui traitaient de la santé mentale et de l'aide juridique aux personnes défavorisées. Titulaire du Kellogg National Fellowship, il a plus particulièrement étudié les questions de traitement des malades mentaux dans les services d'urgence.

Robert M. Gordon is a Killam Doctoral Fellow in the Department of Anthropology and Sociology, University of British Columbia (Vancouver, British Columbia, Canada). He is the coauthor of *Practising Poverty Law* (Melbourne, 1979), and has authored and coauthored several articles on the provision of legal services for mental health patients and various other aspects of Commonwealth mental health law. He is currently working on a social history of Canadian mental health legislation, a review of Canadian mental health law, and on a study of the relationship between law and the aging process in Canada.

Robert M. Gordon est un Killam Doctoral Fellow au Département d'anthropologie et de sociologie de l'Université de Colombie-Britannique (Vancouver, Colombie-Britannique, Canada). Co-auteur de l'ouvrage *Practising Poverty Law* (Melbourne, 1979), il a aussi publié seul ou en collaboration avec d'autres personnes plusieurs articles sur l'offre de services juridiques aux handicapés mentaux et différents autres aspects du droit de la santé mentale dans le Commonwealth. Tout en faisant actuellement l'histoire sociale de la législation canadienne en matière de santé mentale, il travaille aussi sur le droit canadien de la santé mentale et sur une étude de la relation entre le droit et la vieillesse au Canada.

Sarnoff A. Mednick is Professor of Psychology and Research Professor at the Social Science Research Institute, University of Southern California. He has completed major longitudinal projects in schizophrenia and criminality. One of his major areas of research concerns the biosocial bases of antisocial behavior. Dr. Mednick is Director of the Psykologisk Institut, in Copenhagen, where most of his research is conducted.

Sarnoff A. Mednick est professeur de psychologie et chercheur au Social Science Research Institute de l'Université de la Californie du Sud. Il est l'auteur de recherches importantes à long terme sur la schizophrénie et la criminalité. L'un des principaux domaines de recherche abordés touche les bases biosociales du comportement antisocial. M. Mednick est le directeur du Psykologisk Institut de Copenhague où il mène la plupart de ses travaux.

Terrie Moffitt completed her dissertation on mental illness, crime, and genetics at the University of Southern California. She is currently Principal Investigator of a longitudinal project being conducted in Dunedin, New Zealand, on the neuropsychological bases of a delinquency. She will assume the position of Assistant Professor of Psychology at the University of Wisconsin in September, 1986.

Terrie Moffitt a fait une thèse de doctorat à l'Université de la Californie du Sud sur la relation entre la maladie mentale, le crime et la génétique. Elle est actuellement le principal chercheur dans une étude á long terme sur les bases neuropsychologiques de la délinquance, étude faite à Dunedin (Nouvelle-Zélande). Elle assumera les fonctions de professeur adjoint de psychologie en septembre 1986 à l'Université de Wisconsin.

Vernon Lewis Quinsey is Director of Research at the maximum security division of the Mental Health Center of Penetanguishene, Ontario. He has published over 50 scientific papers in the areas of animal learning, prediction of dangerousness, assessment and treatment of sex offenders, institutional violence, behavior modification, and decision-making. Dr. Quinsey has served on the editorial board of several leading periodicals in his field and has acted as a consultant to various foundations and government ministries in Canada.

Vernon Lewis Quinsey est le directeur de la recherche á la division de sécurité maximale du Mental Health Center de Penetanguishene (Ontario). Il est l'auteur de plus d'une cinquantaine d'articles scientifiques sur des questions aussi diverses que l'apprentissage par les animaux, la prédiction de la dangerosité, l'évaluation et la traitement des délinquants sexuels, la violence institutionnelle, la modification du comportement et la prise de décision. Le professeur Quinsey a été membre de comités de rédaction dans des journaux de grande renommée dans son domaine, et il a été consulté comme expert par différentes fondations et de nombreux ministères gouvernementaux au Canada.

Laurence R. Tancredi, Kraft Eidman Professor of Medicine and the Law and Director of the Health Law Program at the University of Texas Health Science Center at Houston, is Editor of volume 7 of *Monographs in Psychosocial Epidemiology* on "Ethical Considerations in Epidemiologic Research." Dr. Tancredi has written numerous books and papers in ethics, law, and psychiatry. He received his medical degree from the University of Pennsylvania School of Medicine and his law degree from Yale. From 1972–1974, he was Senior Professional Associate at the Institute of Medicine of the National Academy of Sciences and served from 1979–1981 as Chairman of the Council on Governmental Policy and the Law of the American Psychiatric Association. He has served on the Steering Committee on Medical Injury Compensation of the National Academy of Sciences, was a member of the National Council for Health Care of the Department of Health and Human Services, and was a consultant to the American Bar Association's Commission on Medical Professional Liability. Dr. Tancredi was cochairperson of the Medical-Legal Research Committee of the Department of Health, Education and Welfare and is currently on the Editorial Advisory Board of the annual *Bibliography of Bioethics*, Kennedy Institute of Bioethics.

Laurence R. Tancredi, professeur Kraft Eidman de médecine et de droit et directeur du programme de droit médical au University of Texas Health Science Center de Houston, il est aussi le directeur de l'édition du volume 7 des *Monographs in Psychosocial Epidemiology on Ethical Considerations in Epidemiologic Research*. Il est l'auteur de nombreuses monographies et de différents articles sur l'éthique, le droit et la psychiatrie. Il a obtenu son diplôme de médecine à la faculté de médecine de l'Université de Pennsylvanie, et il est diplômé en droit de l'Université Yale. De 1972 à 1974, il a été Senior Professional

Associate à l'Institut de médecine de la National Academy of Sciences et a présidé le Council on Governmental Policy and the Law de l'American Psychiatric Association de 1979 à 1981. Il a été membre du comité directeur de l'indemnisation des dommages médicaux á la National Academy of Sciences, du National Council for Health Care au Department of Health and Human Services, et il a été consultant auprès de la commission de responsabilité professionnelle des médecins de l'American Bar Association. Le docteur Tancredi a aussi été le co-président du comité de recherche en médecine légale au Department of Health, Education and Welfare, et il fait actuellement partie du comité consultatif de rédaction de l'annual *Bibliography of Bioethics* au Kennedy Institute of Bioethics.

Simon N. Verdun-Jones is Chairman of the Department of Criminology at Simon Fraser University, Burnaby, British Columbia, Canada. He has written extensively in the areas of mental health law and criminal justice. He is currently engaged in writing a textbook on Canadian mental health law and is involved in a major research project concerning guardianship of the elderly in Canada. During the period October–December 1983, he was a Visiting Research Fellow at Macquarie University, Sydney, Australia, where he was able to gather much of the data necessary for the writing of the present chapter.

Simon N. Verdun-Jones est le président du Département de criminologie à l'Université Simon Fraser à Burnaby (Colombie-Britannique, Canada). Il a écrit de nombreux ouvrages dans les domaines du droit de la santé mentale et de la justice criminelle. Il rédige actuellement un manuel de droit canadien de la santé mentale et participe à un important projet de recherche sur le placement sous tutelle des personnes âgées au Canada. D'octobre à décembre 1983, il a été professeur de recherche invité à la Macquarie University de Sydney (Australie) où il a pu rassembler la plupart des données nécessaires à la rédaction du présent chapitre.

Jan Volavka is Professor of Psychiatry at New York University. He is Director of Research at Manhattan Psychiatric Center and Chief of the Clinical Research Division, Nathan S. Kline Institute for Psychiatric Research. His current research interests include patient violence, general psychopharmacology, and EEG.

Jan Volavka est professeur de psychiatrie à l'Université de New York. Il est directeur de la recherche au Manhattan Psychiatric Center et chef de la division de recherche clinique au Nathan S. Kline Institute for Psychiatric Research. Ses projets de recherche actuels portent notamment sur la violence du patient, la psychopharmacologie générale et l'EEG.